Communism and the Churches

A VOLUME IN THE SERIES

COMMUNISM IN AMERICAN LIFE
Clinton Rossiter, General Editor

BOOKS PUBLISHED TO DATE:

The Roots of American Communism by Theodore Draper

The Communists and the Schools by Robert W. Iversen

The Decline of American Communism by David A. Shannon

American Communism and Soviet Power by Theodore Draper

Marxism: The View from America by Clinton Rossiter

Communism and the Churches by Ralph Lord Roy

Ralph Lord Roy

COMMUNISM
& THE CHURCHES

Harcourt, Brace and Company · New York

To Margaret

". . . for her price is far above rubies"

ACKNOWLEDGMENTS

This study has depended upon the kind co-operation and assistance of hundreds of persons. It would be difficult to thank each of these individuals here—though several score are mentioned in the Bibliographical Essay. I do, however, wish to acknowledge the valuable aid rendered by a number of others who in one way or another made my investigations and writing possible.

Public and private libraries are essential to any major research effort. Among the many helpful librarians to whom I am indebted are Robert Beach and the Library staff at Union Theological Seminary; Miss Dorothy Woodruff and Mrs. Elsie Lund at the Library of Methodism's Board of Missions in New York City; Mrs. Mary Carey of the Swarthmore College Peace Collection; and Norman Jacobs of the Library of the Tamiment Institute.

While working on this study, I spent more than two and a half years as assistant minister at Metropolitan Community Methodist Church in Harlem. I want to express my gratitude to the staff and the congregation for their patience and add a special word of appreciation to William M. James, the senior minister, who gave me many of his insights and read part of the manuscript. I wish, too, to acknowledge the counsel of John C. Bennett and Reinhold Niebuhr, Dean of the Faculty and Vice-President respectively of Union Theological Seminary. Among more than thirty persons who read all or major portions of the study in manuscript or galley form, I am particularly indebted to Robert T. Handy, F. Ernest Johnson, John M. Swomley, Jr., A. J. Muste, Walter G. Muelder, Philip Adler, Charles C. Webber, Joseph N. Moody, and John La Farge, S.J.

Research assistants at various stages were Dmitry Grigorieff in the area of Russian Orthodoxy; Mrs. Karla Schriftgiesser Irvine, who studied the American Youth Congress and co-operated on the Armenian Apostolic Church; and Miss Robin Myers, who worked principally on Chapter 7 on Roman Catholicism. Colleagues in this series of volumes were informative and stimulating: Daniel Aaron, Moshe Decter, Theodore Draper, Nathan Glazer, William Goldsmith, Robert Iversen, and David Shannon.

The Fund for the Republic generously financed most of my research, and I am particularly grateful to Clinton Rossiter, editor of the series on Communism in American Life, for his patience, sound advice, and expert editing. Despite such generous assistance, however, I alone am responsible for the particular analyses of the issues treated and for any factual errors that may be in the text.

If any person helped me more than Professor Rossiter, it was my wife, Margaret, who patiently listened again and again as I read to her chapters under revision, who suffered with me the tortures of a study on such a delicate and perplexing subject, who typed the manuscript, and who gave up all semblances of domestic order so that this book finally could go to press.

RALPH LORD ROY

Swanton, Vermont
July 1, 1960

CONTENTS

xi

Contents

Communism and the Churches

INTRODUCTION

Communism and religion usually are viewed as bitter antagonists. Yet an official manual of the United States Air Force charged in 1960 that Communists and "fellow-travelers" had infiltrated the churches. Herbert Philbrick, for nine years an undercover agent for the F.B.I., has stated that "subversion in the sanctuary" is the most deadly and insidious menace facing America. A former Communist, Joseph Kornfeder, has estimated that 600 ministers joined the American Communist Party and that another 2,000 or 3,000 have been devout fellow travelers. And J. B. Matthews, widely regarded as an expert on Communism, has made the stunning assertion that "the largest single group supporting the Communist apparatus in the United States today is composed of Protestant clergymen."

Although the charges have been plentiful, the proved facts have been few. The purpose of this study is to discuss, as dispassionately as possible, on the basis of the information available, the questions about Communism and religion that have been frequently posed but never adequately answered. Did the Communist Party attempt to infiltrate American churches? If so, what were its methods of subversion? Were they successful? What organizations were special targets? What clergymen were involved? Is there cause for alarm today?

Many perils confront a study of this nature.

1) One problem is suggested by the ancient proverb "Let sleeping dogs lie." America has passed beyond the era when Communist infiltration absorbed the attention of many of our political leaders

and millions of our people. Is it wise, then, to raise the issue afresh? Would this not risk a new wave of accusations that could lead only to discord and injury? Is it not better to forget, and hope that others also will forget?

These doubts have considerable merit. Yet perhaps it is better that a study of this nature comes when it does, in a time when fewer Americans are stirred by political passion, and when it is possible to view the evidence without suspicion that everyone who explores the subject in print does so for untrustworthy purposes. Perhaps, too, it is important that such a record be produced for the sake of history, so that in some future generation the churches of our day will not be judged exclusively by well-publicized, sensational charges that never were confronted by the truth. Similar attacks on the churches may be made in another time; another time the churches may be better prepared to answer them.

2) There is also risk in searching for facts in an area where a certain amount of secrecy is implicit. Although the Communist Party in the United States has operated in the open, it has also operated underground. Some vital facts stored only in the minds of party members may be lost when these persons die. Even when such knowledge still exists, it may be deliberately concealed by some, misinterpreted, exploited, and warped by others.

In general, this study avoids reference to material that cannot be verified, and this presents a serious handicap. It means, for example, that when a distinguished minister has recalled how another clergyman (who denies the assertion) sought to enlist him in the Communist Party, this alleged episode has been omitted to avoid hazarding an injustice. It means that many fascinating personal sagas—in some instances bordering upon "reliable" gossip—are also omitted. So are unsubstantiated speculations about motivation: the story about a minister whose wealth burdens him with a feeling of guilt which leads him to espouse Marxism; the story of another, who is led into the Communist orbit by his wife; or of a third, whose pro-Soviet sympathies stem from rebelliousness against the stereotype of the pious preacher or from disgust with complacent congregations. Motives like these have been frequently suggested, usually by one clergyman in trying to explain the actions of another. They will not be cited here.

3) To piece together the complex and sometimes conflicting evidence of this study is a third precarious task. One honest eyewitness recalls an episode in a particular way. Another eyewitness, also trustworthy, offers a different version of the same event. Perhaps a printed story—appearing in a less reliable source but written nearer the event —contradicts both of the other accounts. Was the clergyman *definitely* present at a secret Communist meeting, as one ex-comrade testifies? Or was he *definitely* not there, as another former party member insists? Did a religious magazine receive funds from the Communist Party, as an "unimpeachable" source says? Or is this a "brazen lie" and an "absurd accusation," as the editor and several of his associates contend? In instances where such direct contradictions do exist, the episode is often relegated to the footnotes or omitted entirely.

This problem is most vexing when it involves testimony before Congressional committees. Should unsubstantiated charges, made under the protection of Congressional immunity—often by questionable witnesses—be repeated here when such charges cannot be either proved or disproved? The attempt has been made to exercise extreme caution in dealing with such testimonies.

4) Is it possible to discuss the subject of Communism and the churches without using "guilt by association"? Most critics of the clergy have made their serious indictments on the basis of association alone, a method as fallacious as it is simple. The pastor who "belonged" to ten "fronts" has been said to be roughly twice as much "involved" with the "Communists" as the pastor who "belonged" to only five "fronts."

The significant omissions of such an approach are obvious. *Which* fronts were they? *When* was the person affiliated? What was his *precise* relationship to each of them? *How* did the clergyman view this relationship? *When* did he resign? *Why?* What were the clergyman's over-all political attitudes and, especially, his views on Communism? If questions like these are unanswered, the citation of the number of "front affiliations" becomes meaningless.

On the other hand, there are observers who have made the error of discounting affiliations entirely. Some liberals have fallen into the habit of crying "guilt by association" whenever they hear a person criticized for support of a front; one's associations, however, are not totally irrelevant in life. These same liberals would look with alarm

upon membership in the Ku Klux Klan or the German-American
Bund or the America First Committee. Why, then, should they feel
so outraged when a clergyman is criticized for consistently supporting
dozens of front groups for several decades and for continuing to
support them today? Some of the loudest protests against "guilt by
association" come from the naïve; they have held fast to the conviction that the whole concept of "fronts" has been invented by reactionaries to intimidate progressives. Others view co-operation with
"fascists" as heinous, but they believe co-operation with Communists
is in the interests of world peace and a better society.

5) Another peril involves the matter of moral judgment. Implicit
in this study is the conviction that Communism is hostile to the ideals
of both religion and American democracy. Little attempt is made
here to justify this viewpoint. A vast body of literature that comments
in elaborate detail on the errors and evils of Communism, both in
theory and in practice, already exists. A few of its weaknesses may
be summed up briefly. Communism is illusory in its utopianism. It
fails to understand human nature. It presents the relative as absolute
and, as a result, crushes freedom and stifles creativity. It corrupts
truth whenever it thinks falsehood will advance its goals. It tailors
facts and history to fit its theories. It misunderstands the broad dimensions and legitimate claims of religion. Perhaps most serious of
all, especially with regard to the churches, it callously exploits the
finer instincts and ideals of mankind and then betrays them.

Many basic questions come to mind. How can a person of religious persuasion, and especially a clergyman, give aid again and
again to a professedly atheistic movement that does not even conceal
its desire to uproot religious faith? How can an honest minister deliberately lure unsuspecting colleagues into a questionable association
with such a movement? Yet, for years a small nucleus of clergymen
preyed upon the decency of other men of the cloth by soliciting their
endorsements, their support of public statements, their names on petitions, and their sponsorship of front organizations.

Moral indignation must be tempered by understanding. Communist sympathizers among the clergy are usually dedicated, intelligent,
and industrious men—more so than many of their fellow clergymen.
In some cases, they have placed the ideals of peace, brotherhood,
and abundance above what would appear to be their own personal

interests. They have followed their consciences to the best of their understanding and have refused to betray their particular set of religious principles, regardless of the pressure upon them. Probably their ideas and actions are rooted in their psychological history and they receive satisfaction from their unusual conduct, although it would be assuming broad prerogatives to charge them with a host of moral weaknesses that they do not have. One could, however, accuse them of moral blindness, of failing to see that, by implication, and often directly, they have condoned means which cannot lead to the utopian ends they envisage.

6) What criteria should be used in a study such as this? What, for example, justifies the harsh characterization of "pro-Communist"? The attention of this study is directed almost exclusively to the Communist movement which receives its inspiration and guidance from Moscow. It is not concerned with various communist traditions among ancient Jews or early Christians, within medieval monasteries, or in such Protestant sects as the Shakers. It does not attempt to deal with the small Marxist splinters in the United States—the Trotskyists, the Lovestoneites, and others—nor with the principal postwar cleavage centered in Tito's Yugoslavia.

Many loose indices have been used to "identify" the Communist sympathizer. Does he favor recognition of Red China? Does he favor a ban on nuclear tests? Does he belong to the National Association for the Advancement of Colored People? Does he subscribe to the *Nation* or the *New Republic?* These are typical of the absurd and false criteria used by some zealots as evidence of subversive intentions. Too often, well-meaning patriots have seen in divergence from their own views the seeds of treason. The damage that such irresponsible accusations has inflicted is incalculable.

There are, nevertheless, intelligent ways to approach this delicate problem. Many factors must be taken into account. Front affiliations, if carefully examined, may be considered. Opinions on Communism and the Soviet Union over the years may be noted. The Communist position on foreign policy has revealed so many twists and turns that no one but the hard-core Communist or Communist sympathizer could tag along without protest. The true believer did not deviate. Not until 1956, when Khrushchev denounced Stalin, was some free exchange of ideas allowed within the Communist orbit.

It is almost possible to provide a convenient check-list. Did the person considered support the Soviet purges of the thirties? Did he defend the Hitler-Stalin pact? Did he justify the Russo-Finnish War? Did he attack the Truman Doctrine and the Marshall Plan as "encirclement" of the Soviet Union? Did he uphold the blockade of West Berlin, denounce the North Atlantic Pact, oppose United Nations intervention in the Korean conflict, endorse the Stockholm Peace Appeal? If *all* of the answers are "yes," it seems fair to say that such a person has been in the Communist orbit.

Akin to this sixth peril is the problem of vocabulary. The principal descriptive terms are so well-worn that they are no longer adequate. Many of them were first employed by the Communists themselves—*e.g.,* "fronts" and "party line"—but now they engender such an emotional response that they interfere with objective discussion. An attempt to devise a new vocabulary, however, has been unproductive, and therefore, with reluctance, we use such unfortunate—but necessary—expressions as "pro-Communist," "Communist-inspired," "Communist-controlled," "Communist fronts," "Communist orbit," and even occasionally "party line" and "fellow traveler."

7) The question of context is central to the entire inquiry. It is natural to see things in clearer perspective when viewed with hindsight. Perhaps some of the groups supporting the Spanish Loyalists, unbeknown to most of their members, were controlled by the Communists. But would we not be appalled if many Protestant ministers had not responded to appeals against Franco, who was receiving generous assistance from Mussolini and Hitler? Today it is common knowledge that the Soviet Union has repressed Jewish culture and religion and has become openly hostile to the state of Israel. But is it so shocking that many American Jews were impressed during the thirties and forties by reliable reports that Russia was eradicating anti-Semitism, that it had transported millions of its Jewish citizens to safety far behind the lines during World War II, that it staunchly supported Israel in 1948 while Great Britain and the United States dallied? A number of important trade unions were dominated by Communists for many years. Are we therefore to heap abuse upon thousands of Roman Catholic workers who joined these unions and assisted the Communists in the field where they were most formidable and posed the greatest threat?

People naturally make choices on the basis of the facts as they understand them. They cannot be expected to do any more. In retrospect, certain choices may appear to have been unwise. This applies as well to the political world as elsewhere. Anyone who does not understand the spirit of the thirties and forties cannot hope to have an intelligent approach to the subject of Communism in American life. Whom should we castigate—the religious idealist who generously and sincerely gave of his time and talents in the hope of halting fascism, improving race relations, preserving civil liberties, and establishing peace? Should a veil of suspicion be thrown over his life of service because, in the course of his efforts, he supported a number of organizations later listed as Communist fronts? Or should criticism instead be directed at the proud and complacent critic who boasts that he "wasn't taken in once by the Commies"? In too many cases he saved himself from all association with Communists by indifference to social justice. This, of course, in no way excuses the perennial apologists for the U.S.S.R., especially among the clergy, who have used their prestige for years to propagandize on behalf of a ruthless regime and who knew precisely what they were doing.

8) There is a final peril to bear in mind as this study is read. Unless a reader understands the breadth of the vast church apparatus in America and the endless number of enterprises under its auspices, he might conclude that a disproportionately large number of clergymen have given considerable time and attention to Communist-inspired efforts. This is not true.

Thousands of Protestant ministers and Jewish rabbis, and some Roman Catholic priests, did sign petitions or sponsor meetings that have been called subversive. This fact must be measured against the broader church. We can illustrate what we mean in cold figures. Since 1930, there has been an estimated total of well over 500,000 ordained clergymen in the United States. Of these, approximately 85 per cent have been Protestants. The proportion who have been "affiliated" with Communist efforts in any way whatever has been exceedingly small—perhaps slightly over 1 per cent. Conversely, almost 99 per cent had no such "affiliation." The number who have been Communists, or persistent—and identifiable—fellow travelers, has been minute, in spite of continual efforts to involve clergymen in the Communist apparatus. Today, perhaps twenty-five of this number remain—or approximately seven one-thousandths of 1 per cent of American ministers, and most of these are not serving pulpits.

Another word should be added concerning the scope of this study—it is about Communism *and* the churches, *not* simply Communism *in* the churches. Consequently, an attempt is made to present the broader picture of church opinion on a number of critical issues: the Bolshevik revolution, the recognition of the U.S.S.R., the united front of the thirties, the Hitler-Stalin pact, and various controversial matters following World War II. Some of these details may prove tiresome to persons more interested in accounts of ecclesiastical intrigue. They are indispensable, however, to a fair presentation of the subject.

Most of the emphasis is upon the Protestants. Their clergymen, as a rule, can freely involve themselves in activities of a social and even political nature. Many of them already had been influenced by the social gospel, a religious movement totally independent of Marxism in its origins, which shared with it a utopian and, to some extent, an anticapitalist bias. The Protestants are also the ones who have been singled out for particular attack.

This study also reveals how the Communist Party wooed Roman Catholics and was successful to the extent of securing the support of thousands of Roman Catholic workers in labor unions. Sections also deal with interesting controversies that have raged within the Russian, Romanian, and Albanian Orthodox groups and among adherents of the Armenian Apostolic Church.

An effort is made to show the attitude of Jewish rabbis toward the Communist movement. However, no broad coverage of Communist influence among Jews is attempted, for two reasons—it was a phenomenon largely divorced from organized Judaism, and a separate volume on Communism and ethnic groups, including the Jews, is planned for this series on Communism in American Life.

The purpose of this study, then, is to bring to light the facts. Perhaps some readers will prefer to believe tales that better suit their prejudices. Some may still contend that the entire notion of Communist conspiracy is a myth manufactured by "reactionaries" to badger liberals and progressives. Others will hold fast to their hysterical view that the churches are infested with sinister agents of Moscow. We can only hope that this study will prove useful to those who are searching for the truth.

ONE • RED STAR IN THE EAST

Lhe grim cloud of war hung over the world in October 1917. The battlefields of France were red with the blood of many nations, but on the eastern front, the Russian Empire encountered another foe—its own people. The World War had led to one Russian defeat after another, and by 1917 the nation stood near bankruptcy and a total breakdown of law and order. Encouraged by the shrewd Germans, rebellion broke out, goaded by growing bitterness toward the arrogant czarist aristocracy and widespread poverty among the peasants and workers.

The Bolsheviks, led by Lenin, rose to power swiftly, and soon claimed all Russia. One of the first major acts of the new Communist regime was to sign the Brest-Litovsk Treaty with the Central Powers. Then, for two years, the Bolsheviks battled an array of rival armies, some from Russia, others from abroad, some democratic, others hoping to re-establish czarist rule. By 1921, the victory of the Red Army was complete and the new government girded itself against "capitalist encirclement."

How did Americans, and American churches and religious leaders in particular, view the emergence of the first state to claim allegiance to the doctrines of Karl Marx? Both the secular and religious press gave sparse coverage to the confused revolutionary period. American minds were centered elsewhere—on the battles in France, on the first casualty lists, on the debates over prohibition and the Eighteenth Amendment.

One stark reality did penetrate the fog, however. While there was

11

no particular fondness for the Czar, the Bolshevist triumph meant the collapse of the entire eastern front. Was it any wonder that Lenin and his followers were denounced as German agents?

The overwhelming majority of American churchmen had supported the request of President Woodrow Wilson for a declaration of war in April 1917. To make the world safe for democracy was to them a righteous cause. They were angered by Kaiser Wilhelm's crass imperialism, his lawless assault upon little Belgium, the ruthless attack of his submarines upon unarmed American ships, the stories of German atrocities like the oft-repeated charge that the Huns, satiated with pillage and rape, had cut off the legs of innocent Belgian children. Surely God was a God of justice and the church should support the war.

In 1933 Ray H. Abrams of the University of Pennsylvania published his famous volume *Preachers Present Arms,* on the support for World War I among the clergy. "The war is religious," said Joseph Fort Newton, pastor of the Church of the Divine Paternity in New York City, as he set sail for England with an American flag clutched in his hands.[1] James I. Vance, minister of the First Presbyterian Church in Nashville, Tennessee, urged Americans to "keep the flag and the Cross together, for they are both working for the same ends." [2] "The war for righteousness will be won!" exclaimed Frank Mason North, president of the interdenominational Federal Council of Churches and a founder of the Methodist Federation for Social Service.[3] Samuel McCrea Cavert, who was later to serve as general secretary of the Federal Council, described the contest as a "conflict between forces that make for the coming of the Kingdom of God and forces that oppose it." [4] A Y.M.C.A. booklet of the time, strangely entitled *The Practice of Friendship,* called it a "righteous war waged to save the very life of democracy." [5]

With the same sense of idealism, church leaders supported United States intervention against the Bolsheviks in 1918, when a token American force landed in Siberia. Its main mission was understood to be the bolstering of the eastern front against the Kaiser and his Bolshevik collaborators. Yet intervention seemed a moral responsibility for other reasons as well. "Pro-German" Reds were reported slaughtering thousands loyal to the Allied cause, including the leading intellectuals of the nation. The democratic government of Alexander Kerensky, which already had toppled the Czar a few months before the Bolshevik revolution, was being brutally crushed. Even the atrocity tales about the Germans did not compare to those depicting the Lenin mob. Churches were reported pillaged. Hundreds of priests were said to be massacred and nuns violated. The family was being replaced by free love and a community of women. Was it any wonder that devout churchmen were first shocked, then aroused, by such accounts?

The *Living Church,* an unofficial Episcopal weekly, echoed considerable church sentiment of the time. Even before the Bolsheviks took control, it had urged swift and firm American action. "The anxiety lest Russian chaos should continue to the end of the war, and so remove the benefit of Russian assistance to the allies, is a real one," said an editorial on June 16, 1917. The United States should "perform a greater service to Russia than any that thus far has been attempted." It should take over and administer the government of Russia for a period of, perhaps, five years. "Now, in Russia's greatest need, is the time for the United States to act as nearest friend." [6] When Lenin had triumphed and the new Soviet Union had pulled out of the war, the *Living Church* declared that the new regime had not alone betrayed Russia's allies, but had cruelly sacrificed Belgium, turned its back upon ravaged Armenia, and abandoned other innocent victims of the Central Powers and their Turkish partner.

As news of religious persecution spread, the *Living Church* found a new reason for assailing the Bolsheviks. "The awful sufferings of the Russian Christians and the Russian Church," said an editorial in December 1919, "must demand the constant prayers of the Christian people throughout the world." This was cited as proof that the Lenin regime was "a group of assassins recognized by civilized nations nowhere." [7] Earlier in the same year, the *Living Church* reported a revealing convention address of the Bishop of Harrisburg. The Bishop said:

As anarchism and Bolshevism thrive where the discontent and evil-minded throng the liquor saloon, this [prohibition] amendment has been passed just in time to protect the nation. . . . Had the Czar and his council removed the liquor saloons from Russia a year or two earlier, and had the titled classes observed the law themselves, the great peril which stalks Russia would never have gone to such maddened successes, and a constitutional democracy of sober men would be in control.[8]

The Federal Council of Churches, itself subjected to abuse from Right Wing extremists, soon made its disapproval of developments in Russia apparent. But its first concern was with the famine that swept the nation soon after the Bolsheviks seized power and most denominations set aside political considerations to respond generously to pleas for help. The Federal Council stated its position on Communism in its statement of May 1919 on "The Church and Social Reconstruction." Christianity calls for love and brotherhood, it said, but Communism teaches hate and class warfare. "The dictatorship of the proletariat in practice is a new absolutism in the hands of a few men, and is as abhorrent as any other dictatorship." [9] Later, the Federal Council pleaded with the Soviet Government to cease its persecution of religion.

Some religious leaders watched developments in Russia with mixed emotions. Among orthodox Jews this was widespread. The czars had been anti-Semitic, and many thousands of Jews in America had fled Russia and Poland to escape czarist tyranny. Jews made a significant contribution to various anticzarist movements. Yet, religious Jews in the United States knew from experience that socialism turned Jewish youth against religion. They feared that Bolshevism would not stop with the persecution of the Russian Orthodox Church, which had been so closely identified with the old regime. They sensed already that Judaism, too, would become a victim of the bold atheistic professions of the state.

The *Christian Century,* a weekly journal rapidly becoming a powerful Protestant voice, likewise took an ambiguous position. On the one hand, it condemned editorially the "repressive and unfriendly" acts of the Bolsheviks toward religion, which "have made sure that in the long run the people will turn against them," [10] and criticized certain journals for publishing "highly idealized accounts of conditions in Russia." [11] On the other hand, Americans were urged to maintain a balanced view. One of the editors, Alva W. Taylor, claimed that the Soviet Government "has as much right to its trial in the court of mankind as monarchy or Republicanism." The "radical and bloody reaction" of Bolshevism is not the civilized answer, Taylor wrote, "but why are we so much more agitated about it than we were over the bloody regime of generations under Czardom?" [12] He called upon the United States to withdraw all troops from Siberia. "Why should our lads die in a war that was never declared and for a purpose that is unsubstantiated?" [13]

FRIENDS OF THE REVOLUTION

Only a handful of American churchmen stood against American participation in World War I. Some of them belonged to traditional peace churches, such as the Society of Friends, the Mennonites, the Church of the Brethren, and small Protestant sects who viewed the commandment "Thou Shalt Not Kill" as meaning precisely what it said. Others included a scattering of Roman Catholic priests of Irish heritage who considered the defeat of England advantageous to the people of Ireland. There was considerable opposition to war among both Protestant and Roman Catholic clergy of German descent, though bitterness toward German-Americans was so widespread that these clerics generally kept their sentiments to themselves.

The most outspoken opposition to the war among religious circles came from a group of idealistic Protestant ministers, largely members of the Fellowship of Reconciliation, formed in 1915. Among this group some were initially to sympathize with the Bolshevik revolution. Theologically most of them were liberals. They were not pacifists in the precise sense that Quakers or Mennonites were. They had been influenced, to a greater or lesser degree, by the economic interpretation of history and were convinced that wars were rooted in economic competition camouflaged behind deceptive slogans. World War I, they contended, was a needless and ugly blood-bath to advance the imperialistic aims of the opposing powers. The blame for such criminal warfare rested with greedy business interests in their rivalry for raw materials and markets. This in turn could be traced to the very nature of the capitalist system.

It was a colorful assortment of Protestant ministers who espoused this view. Among them was a bishop, Paul Jones, president of the Church Socialist League, an Episcopal organization. Jones was a Pennsylvanian by birth and received an excellent academic background at Yale University and Episcopal Theological Seminary in Cambridge, Massachusetts. In 1914 he succeeded F. Spencer Spalding, also a Socialist, as bishop of Utah. When Jones opposed American entry into the war, he was denounced first for "pro-German Kaiserism," then for "red Bolshevism." In 1918 he was pressured into resigning his ecclesiastical post and later joined the staff of the pacifist Fellowship of Reconciliation. In 1934 Jones was restored to a seat (not a vote) in the House of Bishops, but he never again was in charge of a diocese. He died in September 1941 while serving as college pastor and as an associate professor at Antioch College.

Another pacifist Episcopalian was Irwin St. John Tucker, who had joined the Socialist Party the same week he was ordained in 1912. He was drawn to socialism by the conviction that it was a practical application of Christianity. During the war years, he was a member of the party's national executive committee and was among those sentenced to twenty years in Leavenworth for seditious activities. The principal evidence cited against him was his pamphlet *Internationalism, The Price We Pay,* which traced war to capitalism. Five million copies were distributed. The United States Supreme Court finally threw out the case on the grounds that the judge had been prejudiced. Later, Tucker quit the Socialist Party, helped institute "I Am an American Day" in 1937, and offered prayer at the Republican National Convention in 1944. In 1954 he joined the Roman Catholic faith, to which his wife belonged. Today he is an active Roman Catholic layman.

Others were destined to have more influence than Jones and Tucker. One of these was John Haynes Holmes, who condemned the war in his sermons at the Church of the Messiah, a fashionable Unitarian parish in New York City. Holmes kept his pulpit, but lost a large proportion of his congregation; they were replaced by an unusual assortment of religious liberals whom he later welded into the unique Community Church. Another was Harry F. Ward, professor at Boston University and the guiding personality in the Methodist Federation for Social Service. A. J. Muste was also a member of the pacifist-socialist group. Despite the widespread sympathy of his Congregational parishioners in Newtonville, Massachusetts, he felt obliged to resign and throw his efforts into the labor movement. John Nevin Sayre, an Episcopalian, maintained his pulpit at Suffern, New York, while actively promoting the work of the Fellowship of Reconciliation. There was a rabbi in their midst as well. The pacifism of Judah L. Magnes embarrassed many Jews who were afraid his stand would cast doubt upon Jewish loyalty. The best-known member of all the nonconformist clergy was Presbyterian Norman Thomas. Thomas resigned from his church work in East Harlem because its supporters were withdrawing their aid as a result of his antiwar activity.

It was among these clergymen that the revolutionary government of Russia received its most cordial reception. Their support aroused condemnation and their opponents argued in this manner: These ministers were theological liberals who had brazenly discarded the sacred doctrines of Christianity. They had joined the Socialists, a motley assemblage of radicals largely from abroad who were already demanding, in their broken English, the overthrow of a democratic government that had given them refuge. Then, during the war, these clergymen openly gave aid and comfort to the ruthless autocracy of the Kaiser. Now they were lauding saboteurs of Russian resistance and whitewashing Bolshevism's suppression of democracy, its slaughter of innocent thousands, and its persecution of religion. As Americans heard and read of these clergymen, they asked themselves quite naturally: What kind of ministers are they?

In January 1918, amid the war fever, a new publication was launched. Known as the *World Tomorrow,* it served as the unofficial organ of the Fellowship of Reconciliation. Norman Thomas was managing editor; Holmes and Ward were among the original members of its editorial committee. It was intensely religious in its idealism and continued to promote pacifism and democratic socialism until the thirties, when its financial failure forced it to merge with the *Christian Century.* The *World Tomorrow* viewed the Bolshevik revolution with sympathy. In April 1918, the editors observed: "Only those who have felt something of the passion for social justice and industrial democracy can realize how truly revolutionary Russia, with all its faults and excesses, is the promised land, the fatherland of the spirit to multitudes of radical workers throughout the world." [14] During the months that followed, the journal vacillated from ecstatic wonder to critical appreciation. In June 1918, it called for recognition of the new government as the "only sensible course." "As the Protestant Reformation brought religious freedom," wrote the editors, "as the French

Revolution brought political freedom, so this great upheaval of our own day may secure economic freedom for mankind." [15]

In February 1919, Norman Thomas, in an article entitled "What is Bolshevism?" made a careful attempt to weigh all available evidence. "Apparently we cannot get along without the devil," Thomas began. Now that Germany had been defeated, he suggested that the American press needed a new villain to replace the Kaiser. "They have set their vivid imaginations to work and have obligingly created for us a new and fearsome devil by the simple process of adding a Russian blouse, a ragged beard, and a few additional years to the figure who has served them so well during the period of the war. And so behold the Bolshevik stands forth!" [16]

Thomas expressed strong support of the U.S.S.R. but never was totally uncritical. "We again confess our own faith that the real victory of human freedom will be won at last by the group that is great enough to conquer wrong without the organized violence of war or terrorism . . . no nation or class is in a position to cast the first stone at the Russian revolutionaries who, for example, captured the city of Vladivostok without shedding a drop of blood." [17] We must leave the Russians alone, said Thomas, let them work out their own destiny, and learn from their successes and failures. "We must be patient with Russia—very patient, for it is a slow business leavening that old Czardom with the leaven of brotherhood and justice." [18] The Bolsheviks were to be judged more by their ideals than by the human excesses that unfortunately accompany any violent revolution.

The *World Tomorrow* castigated the American churches for their reluctance to support the Soviet Union. Labor demands friendship with the Russians, said one editorial. Even powerful manufacturing and commercial interests were eager to trade with the Bolsheviks. "But the churches are still silent, and by their silence they crucify Christ afresh." [19] Later, of course, Thomas and many of his colleagues on the *World Tomorrow* charged that Lenin and especially Stalin had betrayed socialism and abandoned the ideals of the revolution.

As America moved further into the twenties, more books and articles sympathetic to the Bolsheviks appeared in religious circles. Especially influential were accounts by churchmen who visited the U.S.S.R. Sherwood Eddy, a prolific writer and great missionary leader, launched his summer seminars on which he took leading clergymen to Europe, including Russia. They returned with impressive stories about the Russian Government's earnest program to better the lives of poor illiterate millions oppressed by the czars. In 1926 the members of the seminar, upon their return home, petitioned the President of the United States to recognize the Moscow regime. They did not argue the merits of the Communist system in practice, for they sharply disagreed on the matter. But they did urge recognition as a practical measure. Among those who signed the appeal were Eddy; Kirby Page, then editor of the *World Tomorrow;* G. Bromley Oxnam, then a young minister in Los Angeles; Charles Clayton Morrison, editor of the *Christian Century,* and Jerome Davis, professor at Yale University.

Of this group, Jerome Davis was especially active in interpreting the Soviet Union to America. While a student for the ministry, he went to Czarist Russia as a Y.M.C.A. worker. He was there when the revolution broke out and took advantage of his proximity to such swiftly moving history to investigate the situation at first hand. Davis became enamored with the Soviet experiment. While always professing specific criticisms of Communism, he has nevertheless been an outspoken champion of the U S S R since the days of the revolution. His efforts at independent analysis have been clouded by an emotional attachment to the Soviet regime that has colored nearly everything he has written on the subject. One of his major projects during the twenties was the editorship and publication of a series of pro-Soviet books.

Two of Davis' authors had interesting religious ties. One was Robert W. Dunn, who had been associated with Quaker relief work and then became active in the labor-union movement. For years he has served as executive secretary of the Labor Research Association, which supplies information to buttress Communist policies. Dunn was held in high regard by some religious leaders whom he knew personally, and his material was often used by Ward and other churchmen who sympathized with his political orientation. It was in part through his influence that two pacifist leaders, Anna Rochester and Grace Hutchins, moved into the Communist orbit. While Dunn has always denied any affiliation with the Communist Party, in recent years appeals from the *Daily Worker* for financial support have asked contributors to make checks and money orders payable to Robert W. Dunn.

A second author in the series edited by Jerome Davis was Julius F. Hecker. Hecker was born in Leningrad in 1881 but came to the United States for his higher education. He studied theology at Union Theological Seminary in New York City and Drew Theological Seminary in Madison, New Jersey, and from 1910 to 1916 he was in charge of the Russian section of New York's East Side Parish Settlement. Hecker returned to Russia in 1921 and became active in religious reform movements within Russian Orthodoxy. From his pen was to come a series of pro-Soviet books in English. The one in the Davis series was entitled *Religion Under the Soviets.* In 1932 he wrote *Moscow Dialogues,* dedicated to Harry F. Ward, and the following year his volume *Religion and Communism* appeared, dedicated to John Haynes Holmes. Later, word reached his American friends that Hecker had been arrested by the Russian Government and sent to Siberia.

Albert Rhys Williams was another who became absorbed in the Soviet Union. After training for the ministry and serving a Boston church, he became dissatisfied with organized religion. He left the East and went to California where, under the influence of Upton Sinclair and others, he became a Socialist. Like Davis, he was in Russia as a journalist in 1917. Williams was set afire by the revolutionary flame and enthusiastically waited for the entire world to embrace the new socialist order. His report on his experiences, *Through the Russian Revolution,* was a success at home and abroad, and his later books and articles in praise of the Bolsheviks had wide readership and influence. His precise relationship to the Communist movement has never been clear. Whether he has been a member of the Communist Party is still a matter for debate. He has remained loyal to his youthful dream that through the Russian revolution the social evils of the world can be swept away.

These, then, comprised the nucleus of idealistic men who showed special interest in the Soviet Union at its birth. Some changed their attitudes toward Russia in later years. Others have remained loyal to their initial commitment until today. Their influence far surpassed their numbers because they used their unusual talent to bring their vision of a new order to the attention of others.

BAD BISHOP BROWN

One of the most colorful ministers to be drawn into the Soviet orbit was "Bad Bishop Brown," as William Montgomery Brown liked to call himself. He became the only American bishop to hold membership in the Communist Party. He was born on an Ohio farm in 1855 of Scotch-Irish parents, and during the Civil War was left an orphan and "bound out" to a German family at seven. Nine years afterward county authorities placed him in the care of Jacob Gardner and his family. He came to them unlettered and uncouth.

At twenty-one, he set off for Omaha, and four years later met a distinguished philanthropist, Mrs. Mary Scranton Bradford of Cleveland, who took an interest in the education of worthy young men. "Comes now the Fairy Godmother into my life," he later wrote. "She was wealthy, cultured, and very religious." [20] Mrs. Bradford was William Brown's first love; his second and permanent love was her niece and adopted daughter, who became his wife. The Bradfords were devout members of the Episcopal Church and he soon joined, entered theological school, and began his ministry as a circuit missionary in Galion, Ohio. He was evangelical in his approach, warm in his personal manner, and enthusiastic about his calling. In eight years he was archdeacon of the Diocese of Ohio, and eight years later bishop of Arkansas, a post he held for fifteen years.

In 1911, on a leave for illness, he began casually to read Darwin's *Origin of Species.*

Suddenly a great light dawned. I was half through the book when it burst upon me. It was blinding. It was staggering. . . . The world that I had lived in up to that moment just disappeared. . . . Science did not speak to me as Jesus is said to have spoken to Paul, asking me why I persecuted it. Science simply left me floored to figure things out for myself as best I could.[21]

Brown read frantically—biology, astronomy, geology, philosophy, politics. One day, he ran across a newspaper letter signed "E.B." which spoke of the economic causes of the World War. He was an ardent pacifist and he wrote the editors, hoping to hear from the author. It turned out to be a woman. She suggested that he contact the

Socialist Party for additional material. He did and was deluged with literature. "Eventually," he wrote, "I read *Capital* by Karl Marx, a book and a writer of whom I had never heard before. This was another revelation. It was as important a revelation in its way as the revelation of Darwin. It gave me the first clear view of human society . . . it left my individualism about where Darwin had left my heaven and hell. Darwin was now my Old Testament, Marx my new." [22]

He began to revise his views on Jesus, and wrote:

Instead of Marx destroying my Christian faith, he illuminated it as it had never been illuminated before. I saw at once that I would have to re-write that book which I had started. For I saw now that the story of Jesus was humanely true, and that it was the most vital truth in all history. But Jesus, in this new interpretation of him, was not an historical character. He was neither a mere god, the creature of some theologian's imagination, nor a mere good man who lived in Galilee under the reign of the Caesars and who was executed by the bad people because he was so good. Jesus now became a symbol to me of all the liberators of humanity who had been persecuted and crucified since the dawn of time, by those who cared more for the preservation of institutions than for the liberation of humanity. He was a symbol, particularly of the working class, through whose agony and blood all humanity had been sustained and through whose sacrifice it could yet be redeemed.[23]

His philosophy became a peculiar blend of Marxism, Darwinism, and Christianity. It was naïve and crude in its attempts to be scientific. Brown embraced the latest scientific theories with enthusiasm and became vehement in his ridicule of traditional religious belief. Yet, he was psychologically unable to depart from the idiom and folklore of Christianity. Years after, he was able to write: "I did not then, and I do not now, reject the theology of the Christian Church. I am able to take everyone of the supernaturalistic fictions as a symbol of natural reality." [24]

In 1920 Brown and his wife published a bizarre paperback by the Bishop entitled *Communism and Christianity* under the aegis of the Bradford Brown Educational Company, Inc. The cover bore the striking motto: "Banish Gods from Skies and Capitalists from Earth." Inside, under a picture of Brown in his ecclesiastical robes, was the caption: "Rt. Rev. William Montgomery Brown, D.D., Fifth Bishop

of Arkansas Resigned; Member House of Bishops Protestant Episcopal Church; Sometime Archdeacon of Ohio and Special Lecturer at
Bexley Hall, the Theological Seminary of Kenyon College, Now
Episcopos impartibus Bolshevikium et Infidelium." (He had resigned
the bishopric because of ill health in 1912 but still retained his office
as a bishop of the church.)

"Both the Old and New Testaments are utterly worthless as history,"
he wrote.[25] Jehovah was the sun myth rewritten to fit the ideas and
aspirations of the ruling class among the early Hebrews, and the
Christian god, Jesus, was, he thought, an "improvement" over
Jehovah. At one point Jesus was compared to Eugene Debs and "if
he were here he would be in the penitentiary with the socialist, not
in the palace with the Christian." [26] Yet, later in the book, Jesus was
accused of being "what every capitalist is, an anarchist." Brown explained: "When a young capitalist asked Him, in effect, what he
should do in order to get to heaven in the sky, His reply as I interpret
it was, rob yourself by selling all that you have and give it to the
poor. This is anarchism. It is as far from being socialism as capitalism." [27] The booklet is filled with such exhortations as "Abandon
Christian Socialism for Marxian Communism," "Make the world safe
for Democracy by turning it upside down with the workers above and
the owners below," and "Revolutionize capitalism out of the state and
orthodoxy out of the Church." [28] Brown described the Bolshevik revolution as "the greatest event in the history of the world." [29]

The Bishop expected the world to respond to his new faith, and
the Communists to rejoice in his public endorsement of their position. Neither happened. Brown wrote pathetically: "One may imag-
ine that I was lonely. There was a flare of publicity, but even that
was hushed. The newspaper articles seemed to hint that I was a queer
case." [30] His religious friends avoided him. The few radical friends
he made patronized him. "Mrs. Brown and I felt very much alone,"
he wrote sadly. "All my adult life, while I was a mere cog in the ecclesiastical machine, gullibly swallowing the most fantastic notions of
life as sacred truth . . . I had been received everywhere with homage and respect; but now that I had done a little independent thinking I was generally shunned. . . ." [31]

Brown's fellow bishops felt compelled to take note of his writings
but preferred to avoid public display because heresy trials were un-

popular. Brown commented that the "reason for not trying me, as hinted by the papers, was that I was crazy." [32] In 1921 the House of Bishops decided not to press charges but to send a deputation to see Brown and secure his voluntary resignation. He refused to talk to the committee until the stigma of insanity was removed. The bishops still hoped to avoid a trial of a man whom they viewed, in the words of a colleague, Bishop Irving P. Johnson, as a "kindly old gentleman of venerable appearance . . . [and] an eccentric mind." [33] Johnson and many of his colleagues believed that Brown should resign because he had no moral right to attack and vilify the church and then use his association with it to promote his own views.

Events took a new turn when a copy of *Communism and Christianity* fell into the hands of the Bolshevik government and was translated into Russian and used as an instrument against the traditional Russian Orthodox faith. Several church leaders in the Soviet Union wrote the Protestant Episcopal Church in America to ask whether the book's author was actually a bishop of the church in good standing. Bishop Johnson said: "This Church would have been guilty of a brutal indifference to the misfortune of our persecuted brethren in Russia, if it had not taken immediate steps to repudiate the works of Bishop Brown in the only legal way in which it could be done. . . ." [34]

In 1923 the House of Bishops appointed a committee to frame charges against Brown, and in February 1924 a presentment was filed in the church commanding him to appear before the trial court. He was not going to surrender, and stated in his testimony: "My father was a Scotchman and my mother was an Irishwoman, and you know that they don't give in very easily." [35] His defense was confused. At times he argued that he should remain a bishop because his views were right and the traditional views wrong. Elsewhere, he emphasized that he accepted all the doctrines in symbolic terms. From time to time, he made the point that heresy trials were antiquated and that if heresy were really taken seriously by the church, many other clergymen, including some of his prosecutors, should be unfrocked as well.

The charges of heresy were based on quotations from *Communism and Christianity,* and Brown was found guilty. The case then went to an ecclesiastical court of review, which confirmed the judgment, and in 1925 William Montgomery Brown was deposed from the ministry. He sought relief in the civil courts to no avail, and eight annual appeals to the church for reinstatement were unsuccessful.

In June 1925, Brown was consecrated bishop in the Old Catholic Church of America, a tiny, schismatic offshoot from the Roman Catholic Church. Before this, he said, he had received an invitation from the so-called Living Church movement in the Soviet Union, a short-lived radical reformist faction in Russian Orthodoxy, but he refused the offer because it required a trip to Russia. Brown found some sympathy among the clergy. A few defended him on the basis of free speech. In April 1925, William Norman Guthrie, rector of St. Mark's in the Bowery in lower Manhattan, invited him to participate in a symposium on "Do Heresy Trials Serve Any Useful Purpose?" At the same time, Brown, a prolific letter writer, wrote Bishop William T. Manning and suggested that he, Brown, be asked to speak at the Cathedral of St. John the Divine while in New York. Manning was infuriated at the suggestion and sent out an episcopal communication expressly forbidding any parish of the diocese to have Brown as a speaker. John Haynes Holmes, minister of the Community Church, opened his pulpit to the deposed Bishop and a crowd of admirers and curious filled the edifice.

Brown was a devoted member of the Communist Party and contributed $12.50 per month to its coffers. He sent greetings and contributed articles occasionally to Communist publications. He advertised his books through their columns. His heresy trial was followed with great interest and amusement. In an editorial in January 1925, the *Daily Worker* commented upon it.

Bishop Brown wrote a little book entitled, "Communism and Christianism," which left the church as full of holes as a Swiss cheese and as smelly as Limburger. . . . It was a regular god-killer. What the bishop left of god intact even a self-respecting atheist could accept without losing his dignity.

In view of this it is not surprising that a collection of fossilized bishops should decide that Brown did not belong with them. He doesn't. A man with his views should feel just about as much at home with his formed [former] associates in the vineyard of superstition, as an ear of sweet corn in a barrel of dung.

William Montgomery Brown has our respect, but not our sympathy. We believe the punishment has added to his manhood. It is further testimony to his sterling character.[36]

It would probably have been more accurate had the *Daily Worker* said that Brown had their sympathy but not their respect. They were faced with a quandary. On one hand, they recognized that Brown's Communist partisanship might help break down the religious faith of others and lead them to support the Communist Party. They knew, too, that when he addressed Communist public gatherings, he attracted large numbers who were delighted by his bold antireligious statements. In December 1925, for example, a Boston audience went wild when he stated that "while Christ may have been great, Marx and Darwin were greater." [37] Brown journeyed across the country on speaking tours for the *Daily Worker,* for the International Labor Defense, and for other party causes.

Yet, the Communists knew that Brown was widely viewed as demented, and they feared that his opinions would reflect badly upon the party. They were also somewhat annoyed by his earnest desire to remain in the church. They had mixed feelings when Brown appeared at Communist meetings in ecclesiastical robes with a big cross dangling from his neck. His speeches were novel and colorful, but their content was as offensive to the hardened Marxist revolutionary as to the pious orthodox Christian.

At times the *Daily Worker* felt obliged to disapprove of the ex-Bishop's views. In 1931, for example, his booklet *The Bankruptcy of Christian Supernaturalism* came under attack in the *Daily Worker.* In it Brown contended that Communism and religion were comparable if the religion were not supernatural; even the "Soviet Russians" were religious in their devotion to the cause of a better society. The *Daily Worker* objected. "Devotion to a cause has nothing to do with religion," it replied. To talk about a "true" religion as opposed to a "false" religion is "merely getting lost in words and definitions. . . . This all does not deny that Bishop Brown has done—and is still doing—a great deal of good . . . [but] he makes mistakes and serious ones. . . ." [38] When Brown marked his eightieth birthday in September 1935, the *Daily Worker* paid special tribute to him. "We know that in these birthday greetings and our wishes to Bishop Brown," it wrote, "we are joined by the masses of his friends and comrades." [39] Yet, it was an especially lonely occasion for the old man. Not many weeks before, his devoted wife and partner had died.

Said the *Daily Worker:* "The revolutionary movement has lost a fine friend and willing supporter. . . . She has given unsparingly of her resources for the building up of the *Daily Worker* and the revolutionary workers' press in the United States." [40] For "Bad Bishop Brown" however, the loss was not to be weighed in such relative terms. During the years of controversy, when he was scorned and ridiculed, she had accepted his cause as her own. From then on, he lived in seclusion.

On October 7, 1937, Bishop Brown made his final and unsuccessful appeal for reinstatement as bishop to the General Convention of the Protestant Episcopal Church. On October 31, which is Reformation Day and All Souls' Day (Halloween), Bishop Brown died. The *Daily Worker* ran an obituary and a picture of him in his bishop's robes and printed a joint statement by Earl Browder, general secretary of the Communist Party, and William Z. Foster, chairman of the party:

The death of Bishop William Montgomery Brown has robbed the working-class movement of one of its noblest friends. A son of the people with a heritage of poverty and toil in his youth, Bishop Brown dedicated the last 20 years of his life to the cause of labor and oppressed humanity.

At an advanced age he was able to raise himself to the level of historical understanding, revaluing his entire intellectual outlook, relentlessly casting aside the illusions and prejudices of a lifetime, guided only by a profound desire for truth and his love of exploited and suffering humanity.

His honesty and clarity of mind led him to Marxism. It brought him youth in his old age and made him the champion of the great creative forces of our country and people, a fighter against all that is outworn and decayed and an obstacle to progress.

His vision and understanding were inspired by the courage of conviction, by the new socialist world built up in the Soviet Union and giving reality to the dreams and yearnings of mankind through the ages, by the irrepressible struggle of the American working class.

Bishop Brown understood the historical mission of the working class and the necessity of the Communist Party as the vanguard in the working-class struggle. A son of America, of its working people, he represented the noblest and best in our country. The spirit that lived in him was the spirit of the real America, the spirit of creative progress, democracy, and peace, the enemy of barbarous fascism. His death will be mourned by all lovers of liberty and progress. [41]

Bishop Brown would have been moved by such a tribute. He never forgot the oppressive days of his childhood; more than anything else, he wanted to be, in his own way, a champion of the "workers." He had suffered deeply because his marriage brought him considerable money. "I have not been a maker of wealth," he once wrote sadly. "I have simply been a receiver." [42] For more than twenty years he sought to make amends. His will left his entire estate to the Communist Party.

If Brown had been born twenty years later, he would have been more useful to the Communist Party. In the twenties, the party was hostile to religion and skeptical of all clergymen, whatever their professions of radicalism. At the time of his death, all this had changed. A bishop was a prize to be sought to adorn letterheads, to issue statements, to sign petitions, to make speeches. Brown missed all this. But he contributed to Americana a quaint personal saga that has been ignored by the party for which he sacrificed so much. "I have wondered why no mention is ever made of one Bishop Brown of Ohio," wrote a *Daily Worker* reader in 1944, "for although he has been dead for several years . . . it was one of his books that first influenced many of the working class toward Soviet Russia." [43]

Bishop Brown faced many disappointments and humiliations during his lifetime. None compared to the way in which he has been ignored since his death.

Obviously the Bishop did not typify the clergy who followed the Red star in the East. Indeed, he never became part of that closely knit nucleus within the churches that looked with special fondness upon the Soviet Union. Yet, in an extreme way, he demonstrates how some were led to embrace Communism as part of an intense rebellion against the orthodoxy of the church. He suggests, too, that there were instances in which a precarious emotional balance might predispose people to political aberrations, just as it has led them into bizarre religious cults or other forms of unconventional behavior.

TWO · RELIGION, AN "OPIUM OF THE PEOPLE"

The church, a *Daily Worker* columnist wrote in 1927, is a "gigantic fraud, manned by the greatest collection of specialized hypocrites that ever lied themselves out of working for a living." [1]

This summed up the attitude of the American Communist movement toward organized religion during the twenties—contempt liberally seasoned with ridicule. In party literature, religion was usually mentioned in small items without serious discussion. The more theoretical the publication, the less attention religion received. The antireligious writings of Marx and Lenin served as authoritative analyses of the problem, while the attitude of the new Soviet Government toward religion in the U.S.S.R. was accepted as the correct implementation of these analyses.

There was little debate within the Communist movement on the religious question, although an occasional reference might be made to those few who were either doubtful or squeamish about the party's bold antireligious pronouncements and activities. One writer in the *Worker* discussed these "muddle-headed radicals" who, he said, did not fully understand the role of the church as a prop of capitalist society. Hence, the church must be exposed to "rob it of a great deal of its ability to confuse and mislead the workers. . . ." [2]

The church was simply considered another façade for the ruling class, and one which, like the other instrumentalities of the capitalist state, might be counted upon to support the *status quo*. With the imminent destruction of the economic system, the church would collapse and the primitive phenomenon of religious belief and ritual would be wiped away by the truths of unshackled science.

Nonetheless, the Communist press, and particularly those organs that reached beyond the party faithful, gradually developed a number of tactics and themes directed against organized religion. Some of the best talents in the American Communist Party lent their efforts to the antireligious campaign. The most frequent writer on the subject was T. J. O'Flaherty, brother of the famous Irish writer Liam O'Flaherty. O'Flaherty had been reared a Roman Catholic. "Later on in life," he wrote on one occasion, "some of god's representatives did violence to my sense of justice and I became rather sympathetic to the devil." [3] O'Flaherty, who later left the party, treated religion with a wit and insight that was extremely rare among Communist writers. His biting sarcasm was supplemented by innumerable antireligious cartoons by Art Young, Robert Minor, William Gropper, Fred Ellis, William Siegel, and others.

PUPPET OF THE CAPITALISTS

The principal Communist argument against the churches was that they served only to buttress the exploiters, as in Czarist Russia and other countries. In America, the myth of church-state separation exists, Communists argued, and the working class may be easily misled into viewing religious institutions as independent. "To the revolutionist . . . " said a 1928 *Daily Worker* editorial, "all creeds, all churches, all temples of ignorance and superstition and fear, no matter what god or sets of gods they profess to worship, are useful to the capitalist class." [4]

The Communists produced considerable "evidence" to support their view.

For one thing, they laid great stress upon the wealth of the churches and the support received from vested interests. "Most Protestant churches are supported by millionaire capitalists," O'Flaherty contended.[5] So are Jewish synagogues, he said. Roman Catholicism was said to be somewhat more feudalistic in its operation, reaching through the medium of fear deep into the pockets of its laboring masses.

The old Trinity Church in New York City, an Episcopal parish in the Wall Street district, was one of the Communist symbols for the alliance between big money and religion. Its heavy endowment was condemned and it was accused of "swilling millions out of rent trough" through its wide property holdings.[6] In 1925, when a new campaign was launched for funds to complete the Cathedral of St. John the Divine in New York, the *Daily Worker* carried several articles that told how "toilers starve" while sums "stolen from workers" were being used for a mammoth and useless structure.[7]

Churches or clergymen with liberal reputations were not excepted from abuse. When it was announced that John D. Rockefeller, Jr., would be the principal financier of the new Riverside Church, where Harry Emerson Fosdick would serve as pastor, the *Daily Worker* commented:

Fosdick is a "modernist," but Rockefeller knows that he can be relied upon to philosophize about the bible and keep the minds of the workers from their troubles with the bosses, and the "silk stocking" crowd entertained.[8]

A second proof of the church's role in preserving capitalism was the alleged antagonism of religious forces toward the core of the revolutionary forces, the American proletariat. While some Americans viewed the churches, and especially the Federal Council of Churches, as too prolabor, Communist ideology taught that they could be counted upon to serve the bosses. "The true reason why the capitalists support the church," wrote a *Daily Worker* contributor, "is that they, more than any other means of propaganda, succeed in effectively doping the workers."[9]

The specific indictments were many. "Not one prominent minister in the steel region spoke out in favor of the strike," charged Bennett Stevens, author of the Communist pamphlet *The Church and the Workers*.[10] He was referring to the great steel strike of 1919. Of the Seattle general strike of the same year, Stevens charged: "Before and during the strike the churches did everything in their power to break the militant spirit of the workers by urging their members not to participate."[11] He accused the church "liberals," and particularly those of the Episcopal Church, of urging class collaboration in the

Communist-organized strike of 1926 in Passaic, New Jersey. The *Worker* sharply assailed the clergy of New Bedford, Massachusetts, for siding with the "textile barons" in 1928 by urging the acceptance of a "fake compromise offer." [12] Similar charges were pressed against the churches in strikes in the North Carolina cities of Gastonia (1929) and Marion (1930) and elsewhere.

Whenever and wherever the churches sought to play a constructive role in the field of labor, the Communists balked. At best the clergy were considered naïve, failing completely to understand the basic class cleavages that must inevitably end in conflict rather than accord. More likely, however, the clergy were linked in a sinister fashion to the bosses, who supplied their financial support. When the Brooklyn Federation of Churches announced in 1930 that it would hold factory meetings, the *Daily Worker* contributor "Red Sparks" suggested to workers that they query the visiting churchmen with such questions as these: "Does God approve of the speed-up? Why is it that when His Children were starving in the wilderness, it rained flapjacks, according to the Bible, while here and now it rains only blackjacks?" [13] When a group of rabbis announced themselves in favor of a five-day week, the *Daily Worker* was unable to view it as a humanitarian proposal. "It hurts the religious sensibilities of the whiskered divines to see the Lord's Saturday defiled on the Rialtos of America . . ." said O'Flaherty.[14]

The Communists also aimed their fire at those religious and charitable groups who offered competition for the allegiance of the workers, and particularly the unemployed.

Two key targets were the Young Men's Christian Association and the Salvation Army. The Y.M.C.A. was characterized as "notorious as a strike-breaking organization" led by a "craw-thumping, biblepounding, hypocritical crew. . . ." [15] The Young Workers League explained to its members that the Y.M.C.A. received financial support from American capitalists because it trained young workers and students for "participation in world wars for profit" and for the suppression of the proletariat revolt at home and abroad.[16] The Y.M.C.A. makes each victim "immune from unionism," "a better wage-slave," and "a more loyal son of Jesus." [17]

The attitude toward the Young Men's Hebrew Association was the same. A Jewish correspondent for the *Daily Worker,* reporting plans for a new Y.M.H.A. in Springfield, Massachusetts, compared the two associations in the following manner:

> The Y.M.H.A. differs from the Y.M.C.A. only in that one is Jewish and the other is not. The Talmud Torah is a free religious school where ancient rabbis are poisoning the minds of working-class children, as most of them are, with religious ceremonies and superstitions and the dead Hebrew language.
> Knowing the value of such organizations for keeping workers mentally enslaved, the rich Jews are donating freely. They have plenty of cold cash exploited from their workers, either in factories or in their stores and pawn shops.[18]

The attacks on the Salvation Army began in the early twenties and increased in frequency and virulence with the Depression. O'Flaherty set the tone for the criticisms in his column, "As We See It," in May 1925. "The salvation army," he wrote, "is of greater value to the capitalists than a fire-and-brimstone magician who can turn a chunk of clay into a democrat or republican politician." [19] The mission houses it maintained were assailed as filthy. Its food was depicted as stale and unhealthy. The organization itself was accused of squandering wealth on investments. The uniforms, music, sidewalk preaching, and general piety of the group left it open to sharp ridicule. A few instances of attempts by individual Communists to break up or otherwise interfere with street meetings were reported.

A third evidence of the subjection of the church to capitalist interests was the alleged support which religious forces give to policies of war and imperialism. The fact that pacifism was rampant in the churches during the twenties made no impression upon the Communists. They considered religious pacifism a façade designed to help the government "hide the preparations for war and military intervention." [20] It was also aimed at quelling the rumbling of class conflict among the masses. The principal figure of world pacifism, Mahatma Gandhi, became a target of the Communists. "No more humiliating figure crouches on the world stage," said a *Daily Worker* editorial, as it accused him of a "folded-arm policy" against British imperialism.[21]

Nor did the Communists accept the sincerity of the peace activities of the churches. "If any deluded christian was under the impression that followers of Jesus were enemies of war," O'Flaherty wrote, "they should read the history of the christian religion." He continued by crudely assailing the Roman Catholic interpretation of the Christian communion service. "It is no accident that a piece of biscuit and a glass of red eye are turned into the 'body and blood of Christ' at catholic services," he said.[22] By quoting individual clergymen now and then, Communist literature sought to prove that they could be counted upon to support wars regardless of their loud and pious protestations of pacifism during peacetime. Typical was this criticism which J. Louis Engdahl, coeditor of the *Daily Worker,* directed in 1924 at Frederick J. Libby, the guiding spirit of the National Council for Prevention of War:

> Libby may prate boldly in days of peace and he will win some applause from those who follow Christian hypocrites in subsidized pulpits. But we doubt not that Libby will be cheering for murder and Morgan when the next war breaks.
> It is so in all wars.[23]

Ironically, Libby did not endorse World War II but the Communists did.

The charge of supporting imperialism has been used consistently throughout the years in assailing the missionary outreach of the American churches. Such proselytizing activities, said the Communists, served as an entering wedge for political and economic penetration by capitalist interests. In some cases, the missionary was said to be a simple, naïve instrument of financial vultures; in other cases, a conniving partner in plunder, who welcomed government and big-business intervention. In reporting on missionary work, the *Daily Worker* wrote with relish: "Christian Filipino eaten for lunch by Negritoe cannibals." [24]

Particular attention was devoted to American religious work in China, where church investments of time and money were great and where an embryo Communist movement, then supporting Chiang Kai-shek, was emerging. The attitude of the Communists was well expressed in this "Imperialist Hymn" published in Eugene Lyons' *Daily Worker* column, "Footnotes to the News."

IMPERIALIST HYMN

Onward Christian nations
With guns and poison gas,
Forward Christian soldiers
For Mammon, God, and jazz.

Teach the yellow heathen
With Christian shot and shell
Respect for Christian Powers
And fear of Christian hell.

Don't they like old China
As it is run by us?
Then let them leave their country
And make no heathen fuss.

The stars and stripes forever,
Also the union jack,
Beneath their folds we'll plunder
And live on China's back.[25]

Perhaps the most extensive piece on religious activity appearing
in the American Communist press in the twenties discussed in unusual
detail Y.M.C.A. efforts around the world under the title "Political
Christianity Faces East." The author pictures the expansion of the
Y.M.C.A. on an international scale as a gigantic, well-planned conspiracy organized by capitalist interests. Experience taught American
business that a propaganda organization is necessary to pacify the
future victims of imperialism. Experience further taught them that
"religion is the best guise for this work of infiltration and penetration
of capitalist ideas so that exploitation could follow more swiftly and
surely." The author views Y.M.C.A. activity with great alarm. "The
whole orient is covered by the Y.M.C.A. as by a net," he wrote. It
even eyes Russia with "longing and flirtatious glances" but the Soviet
Government recalls that Y.M.C.A. work during the Bolshevik revolution was "mainly directed against the workers' government." [26]

POLITICS AND RELIGION

The Communist press of the twenties took a dim view of the well-publicized religiosity of rival political groups. Stories on the Teapot Dome scandals were laden with ridicule: *e.g.,* "Coolidge talks of J. Christ's Mount Sermon; but GOP prefers oil on the dome." [27] In like fashion, the Communists poked fun at the religious division among the Democrats, charging that both America's "papal representatives" and the competing anti-Catholic Klan gladly served the aims of Wall Street.

During the 1928 campaign, in which the Roman Catholicism of the Democratic candidate, Alfred E. Smith, played such an important role, the Communists were left unimpressed by accusations of religious prejudice. Jay Lovestone, national secretary of the Communist Party (who was expelled the following year), analyzed the issue as a smoke screen. Writing in the *Communist* immediately after the elections, he said:

> This year the contest for power in the camp of the bourgeoisie was so sharp, and their differences on issues so slight, that it became necessary to resort more than previously to the fake issue of bigotry vs. tolerance, bringing into play more than in any previous campaign those agencies of the capitalist state, the churches and religious societies.[28]

O'Flaherty used the controversy over Al Smith to announce that between the "two brands of religious opium peddled by the rival spiritual joss-houses there is no more choice than there is between two different kinds of poison, both equally deadly." [29] The 1928 Communist Party platform ignored religion completely, except to promise in a brief reference the "abolition of religious and Jingoist instruction." [30]

Socialist and labor-union leaders, here and abroad, were subjected to even sharper attack for their religious loyalties. The *Daily Worker* continuously accused the English Labour government headed by J. Ramsay MacDonald of betraying the working class. O'Flaherty wrote in 1924: "Mr. MacDonald is a Christian socialist, not exactly like Morris Hillquit, who is a Talmudic socialist, nor like LaFollette, who is reputed to be an agnostic socialist, but like Jesus of Nazareth, who was not a socialist at all." [31]

Norman Thomas was the most popular target of Communist scorn and ridicule during the twenties. Thomas was a graduate of Union Theological Seminary, a Presbyterian minister until he resigned his ministerial status in 1931, and Socialist candidate for President from 1928 to 1948. He was lampooned mercilessly through cartoons which customarily depicted him as a severely dressed pastor with a Bible tucked under his arm and a large cross hung from his neck. Thomas, the Communists contended, was wed to the religious notion of conversion and reconciliation, whatever his pretensions about championing the working class. "Thomas being a preacher wants to save the souls of all classes," O'Flaherty wrote, "and being a socialist preacher he believes that the capitalists, being the greater sinners, need salvation most." [32] A 1927 *Daily Worker* editorial suggested: "Had his former customers in the Brick Presbyterian Church on Fifth Avenue paid more lip service to pacifism and less to their poodle dogs, Thomas might not have quit. . . ." [33]

During the 1928 campaign, the intensity of the Communist attacks upon Thomas increased. The fact that he spoke before religious gatherings, and on at least one occasion closed a speech with prayer, was to them evidence that he was a fraud. The *Daily Worker* pointed to rural Protestant preachers, many of whom endorsed Thomas, as "key men" in the hold that reaction has among the backward section of the "petty capitalist class." The same editorial claimed that Thomas was having a "hell of a time with his flock" because they were all said to be flocking to Al Smith. Concluded the editorial: "There is no essential difference between what the Rev. Thomas's party offers and what the also-pious Al Smith offers except one will break strikes with protestant incantations, the other with catholic devotion." [34]

The miscellany column of the *Daily Worker* called "Handouts" continuously poked fun at Thomas. The following two items were typical:

> The socialist campaign-managers are laying great hope, it is reported, in the fact that Norman Thomas is a Presbyterian in good standing. What with Al Smith being a catholic, they say, Norman should have easy sledding in the solid south and other liberal neighborhoods.[35]

LOST—Presbyterian prayer book. Please return to Rev. Norman Thomas, Brickbat Presbyterian Church. Finder will receive reward of benediction worth seventy-five cents.[36]

When a reader suggested that antireligious diatribes were inadvisable, a 1924 *Daily Worker* editorial replied that while Communists wanted to unite all workers, including devout Protestants, Catholics, and Jews, they should fight "superstitions that help to keep these workers in slavery to the capitalists." [37]

Over the years nearly every denomination and sect came under Communist fire. The Roman Catholic Church was assailed regularly as "the bitter enemy of the emancipation of the workers of all lands from the robber rule of capitalism." [38] Judaism was ridiculed as primitive nonsense as relevant to modern life as the bow and arrow was to modern warfare. Ten years later, this 1927 O'Flaherty jibe at Rosh Hashana, a Jewish holy day, would have been denounced as anti-Semitic. O'Flaherty wrote:

A holiday is a holiday but why such a rebellious people as the Hebrews should tolerate the exorbitant admission fee of $10 to hear a cantor roar in a synagogue when they could have as much noise for nothing in our print shop when The DAILY WORKER is being gotten ready for the press, is beyond my understanding.[39]

As for Protestants, Luther was described as a "pampered son of an iron-foundry owner," a "pacifist-Fascist fraud." [40] John Wesley, the founder of Methodism, was dismissed as a "maniac." [41] Presbyterians and Episcopalians were attacked for their wealth. The Baptists and other denominations with a large fundamentalist membership were subjected to the sharpest ridicule. Discussing a forthcoming world Baptist convention, a *Daily Worker* article in 1928 outlined the "revolutionary program which is expected to be proposed to the Congress and which is expected to go a long way toward lightening the burdens of the working class." Five points were listed:

1) Perfume salts and warm water for baptism.
2) Prompter results from God following prayer.
3) More one-armed deacons for taking collections.
4) Solidarity between preachers and choir singers.
5) Defense fund for pastors jailed for murder, rape, and shop-lifting.[42]

ATTACKS UPON CLERGYMEN

The *Daily Worker* enthusiastically reported on scandals involving clergymen. In the years before the appearance of the *Worker,* the *Ohio Socialist* and the *Toiler* had adopted somewhat ambivalent positions on churchmen. On the one hand, they followed the Marxist line that the clergy were servants of the ruling class. Yet occasionally certain individual ministers were commended for their radicalism.

By January 1924, when the *Worker* became a daily newspaper, a portrait of a typical clergyman had emerged: a willing pawn of the capitalists in pacifying or battling the workers, a saboteur of the revolutionary impetus that would inevitably crush the system. His preoccupation with money molded his attitudes, as in the case of the minister of Lynn, Massachusetts, who opposed strikers because the fall-off in collections had "put Jesus back 19,000 bucks." There was always the hint that clergymen were engaged in their useless activities primarily to fatten their pocketbooks. Thus, a journey of a minister to Mount Ararat was headlined: "Seeking Noah's Ark Keeps Sky Pilot Employed." [43]

As time passed, chief emphasis was placed upon scandals involving individual clergymen. There appeared a sheaf of lurid stories of ministerial misbehavior under such headlines as: "Police Searching for Love Nest of Amorous Ku Klux Klan Preacher"; "Evangelist Arrested on Charge of Assault"; "Baptist Parson Cuts Wife's Head Off." Facetiously, certain crimes would be subjected to a special ideological interpretation. When a "rank and file" preacher in Georgia shot and seriously wounded a bishop, this was alleged to evidence "growth of the class struggle in the church with anarchistic tendencies. . . ." [44]

With unconcealed glee, O'Flaherty commented in July 1926: "We hate to appear supercritical of the church and its supporters, but we cannot help commenting on the almost daily reports of murders, rapes, burglaries, and other crimes committed by churchmen, particularly the type that seem to take religion most seriously." [45] This seeming breakdown of ethical standards among clergymen, while depicted largely in humorous terms, was welcomed as an important step in disillusioning the masses as to the basic value of the church. "At the rate contempt for religion is growing in the country," wrote one *Daily Worker* contributor, "another generation might see most of the clergy writing poetry for a living. The scandals of clergymen whose principal activity seems to be running away with their female choristers, the high death-rate among kitchen maids in the houses of priests, and the general moral decline among rabbis combined with the passing of hair as a desirable decoration for the human countenance, combine to make the life of the clergy anything but happy." [46]

The subsequent trials and occasional acquittals of accused clergymen enabled the Communists to press their contention that the churches were buttresses for the capitalist system. When, in 1924, a certain pastor was cleared of the charge of indiscretions with another man's wife, a *Daily Worker* editorial gave its readers this interpretation of the verdict.

> The reputation of the preacher could not survive an adverse decision and clergymen are too valuable to the capitalist system to allow half a dozen illicit love affairs to impair their usefulness. In this instance—and it is only one of many—the court and the church put up a united front against the common enemy. Capitalist courts and capitalist churches both live on the system. They must hang together or hang separately.[47]

In 1927 Sinclair Lewis' novel *Elmer Gantry* was greeted enthusiastically in most Left Wing circles, including the Communists. Its subject was a minister who lived a life of hypocrisy behind a façade of Protestant piety. O'Flaherty, who gave it a lengthy review, would only concede that perhaps not every clergyman's life "is one darn seduction after another." [48] By August 1927, the *Daily Worker* was offering *Elmer Gantry* free with each new subscription.

The Communists directed their contempt at the blue laws regarding Sunday activities and at moral censorship of books and movies. Prohibition was viewed with far greater seriousness. Alcoholism was a manifestation of capitalist oppression and would disappear when the United States was Communist. Meanwhile, however, prohibition must end. In 1926, for example, the central committee of the Workers Party gave the following interpretation:

The 18th Amendment and the Volstead Act were supported by the big capitalist interests as measures to help create a working class which would be more efficient and could produce great profits. . . .

The 18th Amendment and the Volstead Act have resulted in building up the highly profitable bootlegging industry and in the creation of a great government machine of spies, provocateurs, prosecutors, courts, etc., aiming at enforcing an unenforceable law. This government machinery is also becoming part of the strikebreaking apparatus.[49]

THEOLOGICAL RIDICULE

The decade of the twenties was characterized by a sharp theological cleavage within American Protestantism. The Communist press followed the "modernist-fundamentalist" controversy with some interest, showing no enthusiasm for either faction.

On the "modernist" side, liberal views of leading clergymen like Harry Emerson Fosdick had wide appeal. Thousands of clergy and laymen either rejected or reinterpreted orthodox affirmations about the nature of man, sin, history, and Jesus. To counter this "modernism," the self-described fundamentalist movement sprang up; its adherents accepted without dilution what they thought to be the fundamentals of the Christian faith. A well-known exponent was the popular evangelist Billy Sunday. Of the dispute O'Flaherty observed: "The liberal churches put . . . god through a fumigating process and serve him up to suit the tastes of their more advanced customers. . . ."[50]

In 1923 the *Worker* made its position clear in discussing the widely publicized theological quarrel between Percy Stickney Grant, liberal New York Episcopal minister, and his conservative Bishop, William T. Manning. Until the existence of God is proved, an editorial said, any discussion of religious doctrine based upon this presupposition is folly. Moreover, the principal dogmas of the church were part of "a mediocre compilation of obscene filth thrown together by sundry gangs of drunken ecclesiastics at the Council of Nicaea and further elaborated at a drunken brawl, known as the Council of Constantinople during the fourth century." Both Grant and Manning "seem to have taken an overdose of their own dope" and "have gone wild and are running amuck."[51]

Even Grant's charge that the church was controlled by big business did not impress the *Worker*. "If he does realize this," said another editorial, "then why doesn't he get out of it?" [52] The editors felt themselves vindicated a few weeks later when Grant said a kind word for Rockefeller. "So although he may be guilty of doubting the nursery tale of the divine origin of Jesus Christ, though he may doubt the virginity of Mary and the piety of St. Ann, the grandmother of Jehovah, he is still not an outcast." [53]

Fundamentalism served as a target for all leftists who sought to discredit religion. In 1927 Harry M. Wicks, member of the central executive committee of the American Communist Party, analyzed the emergence of fundamentalism as an instrument of a frightened bourgeoisie. When the social position of the middle class was more secure, Wicks reasoned, scientific ideas were viewed with tolerance and mild interest. As the middle class became increasingly threatened by progressive forces, the "religion of this declining class reflects its abhorrence of change." The bourgeoisie, he said, hoped to halt progress at a stage favorable to its own existence. "Thus it came to pass that the foremost political champion of the petty bourgeoisie, William Jennings Bryan, became the outstanding defender of its religious cloak, known as fundamentalism." [54]

The principal crusade of fundamentalist partisans in the twenties was to stop the spread of Darwin's theory of evolution. The issue was brought to world-wide attention in 1925 by the trial and conviction of a young Tennessee high-school teacher, John T. Scopes, for teaching evolution in the classroom in defiance of a state law. The trial was judged a farce by the Communists, and O'Flaherty wrote: "Capitalists would prefer that the workers still believed they owe their origin to a piece of dirt moulded by Jehovah's paws and set in motion by a whiff of his breath." [55]

The evolution controversy was welcomed as a further exposé of the intellectual bankruptcy of the churches. As usual, the chief weapon of the *Daily Worker* was ridicule. One Sunday, a Baptist minister in Butte, Montana, tied a monkey to his pulpit to illustrate his anti-evolution sentiments, and the Communist paper headed its story: "Congregation has hard time telling ape from skypilot." [56]

The mass revivals of Billy Sunday also occasioned caustic comment in the Communist press. Sunday was variously described as

director of a "three-ring religious circus in the interests of the Lord
and his own pocketbook," "campaign manager for Jesus and the
saints," and "the human windbag who has made . . . money [by]
making Christianity ridiculous." [57] He was accused of deliberately
scheduling revivals in strike areas where he preached "the necessity
of going back to work on the terms of the sweet-souled bosses who,
according to the Sunday doctrine, are the Lord's anointed." [58]

The evangelist's acrid attacks upon the Communists helped arouse
their ire. Once Billy was quoted as saying: "The next job of house-
cleaning will be to rid our country of this gang of good-for-nothing,
God-forsaken, weasel-eyed, hog-jowled, bull-necked, ragg-shagged,
bob-tailed, riff-raff bunch of radical, revolutionary, Red IWW Bolshevik imps who are a deadly poison to every element of American idealism." [59] The weekly *Toiler,* predecessor of the *Daily Worker,* retaliated
in equally crude language, describing Sunday as a "plain ordinary
skunk with the spirituality of a hyena, the sympathetics of a snake,
and the intelligence contained in 1000th of 1 percent of the brain of
an ass and fake besedi." [60]

Other fundamentalist spokesmen were lampooned mercilessly. The
Pentecostal leader Aimee Semple McPherson, controversial founder
of the International Church of the Four Square Gospel, frequently
was accused by the Communist press of operating a religious racket
as a façade for a debauched personal life. The Communist-oriented
New Masses, a monthly literary magazine launched in 1926, was impressed enough with her activities to carry a lengthy portrait.[61] Among
other popular targets of the Communists were revivalist Gypsy Pat
Smith, Uldine Utley, the girl evangelist, and J. Frank Norris, the
firebrand Texas parson who was indicted (later acquitted) for murder. In New York City, special attention was given John Roach
Straton of Calvary Baptist Church, noted for debating atheists on
the public platform. Straton was described as a "harrassed business agent of God," "staunch defender of amphibious Christianity,"
"assidious publicity seeker," and "chief medicine-man of New York's
tribal religionists." [62]

PROMOTING ATHEISM

In addition to its ridicule of religious doctrine, the American Communist Party actively encouraged militant atheism. The critique of atheism was characteristically Marxist. "It is a great mistake to think that God made the capitalists," said one *Daily Worker* editorial. "On the contrary, he is made in their image and he would not reign for twenty-four hours without their support. . . . He is worth every nickel that it costs to keep him in good condition. . . ." [63] Communist literature contained humorous jibes at popular concepts of God —a practice developed in the Soviet Union in the twenties after the earlier frontal assault upon the church had fomented popular resistance. When, for example, a manuscript of William Green's, President of the American Federation of Labor, was blown from his hand just as he was attacking the Communists, the *Daily Worker* headline said: "Pro-Communist God Bedevilled Green's Speech." The article suggested: "If there is a god he is a just god and a Communist god. The gentle south wind proved it." [64]

The Communist circle proudly claim to have first brought to the public the witty satires by Charles Erskine Scott Wood called *Heavenly Discourse*. They began to appear in the *Masses* in 1916, and for many years thereafter they were reprinted in the *New Masses*. They dealt humorously with theology, Puritanism, class war, and other aspects of American life and thought. The conversations were between God, Jesus, St. Peter, Billy Sunday, William Jennings Bryan, Voltaire, Rabelais, Tom Paine, Plato, Sacco and Vanzetti, and others. The orthodox were ridiculed, while rebels were treated sympathetically. God was depicted as an elderly man characterized by integrity, naïvety, and kindness who was sometimes "found standing on the upper back verandah of the universe—contemplating his finger nails." These satires received a warm welcome in both radical and intellectual circles. When they appeared in book form in 1927, O'Flaherty's review described them as "sound anticapitalist propaganda presented so entertainingly that the tired worker will unconsciously absorb it, amid chuckles and grins." [65] They appeared in *New Masses* as late as 1941.

Communists devoted considerable attention to saving their children from religious influences current in American society. This required, first, a thorough atheist and antichurch education in the homes and through party media. *Daily Worker* material for children, included under such headings as "Tiny Worker" and the "Young Comrade Section," frequently contained crude attacks upon religion. The result of this steady indoctrination was apparent in letters from child readers. One little boy wrote: "I wish the preachers would be chased out of here or go to work, so they would make a labor school instead of a church." [66] Another child was even more direct in her anticlerical remarks. "Our first teacher died and I was to her funeral. The priest is a great fool because he said such lies. I hate all priests." [67]

The party faithful also sought to shield their children from religious influences in public education. One spokesman challenged young Communists to lead the struggle on the issue of religion in the schools: "This fight will take us on to greater things. It is an effective means of agitation." [68] All Bible reading, prayer, and religious music were viewed as attempts of the capitalists to bury their "poison fangs still deeper into the hearts of the children." [69]

In 1925 a widespread counterattack was planned in New York by the Young Workers League and its Junior Section. The first two goals were the "enlightenment of our juniors on matters of religion" and the "training of picked juniors as propagandists and agitators." Leaflets were to be published, parents aroused, a united front with other Communist groups established, and protest meetings arranged. The *Daily Worker* announcement said: "When our juniors get real busy the howl of the bosses and their servants, the school authorities, will be heard all the way to Chicago." [70] There is no evidence that this strategy met with significant success.

Among the public at large, Communists employed other ways of promoting irreligion. They gave publicity to the debates that were held between atheists and believers, and for many years gave moral support to the American Association for the Advancement of Atheism, until the *Daily Worker* concluded, rather belatedly, that members of the group were "not atheists, but bourgeois; and they give us a pain in the neck." [71] Sometimes the party established organizations to rival religious institutions. In Chicago in 1924, several United Workers Sunday Schools were opened for the propagation of Marxism.[72] The following year, a mass demonstration against "Church Week" was announced in Cleveland.[73] There were occasional anti-religious meetings, plays, and dances—usually scheduled for the traditional Christian or Jewish holidays. In a few instances even more direct action was taken by individual Communists—the words "Vote Communist!" were painted on the wall of the fashionable Church of the Heavenly Rest on Fifth Avenue in New York. Others took delight in heckling street-corner evangelists. Perhaps the most dramatic device was a ceremony known as a "Red Baptism" performed in Brooklyn in 1931. It mocked the Christian sacrament to "expose the religious methods used to poison the minds of workers." [74]

The same year, 1931, witnessed an important event in organized antireligious activity. In September, the *Daily Worker* happily proclaimed the formation of the Workers' Anti-Religious League, the first of its kind in America. Two offices were opened, one in downtown Manhattan, the other in Harlem, with branches throughout the country an ultimate objective.[75] This followed the pattern of the League of the Godless in the U.S.S.R., which was spearheading the drive against religion in the Soviet Union.

The stated goals of the Workers' Anti-Religious League were to expose the reactionary role of the churches and such church-related groups as the Y.M.C.A., to spotlight the support given by the churches to American imperialism abroad, and to publicize the alliance of church and state in the repression of Negroes. The *New Masses* of October 1931 summarized the draft program of the organization, which stated its immediate plans. They would establish antireligious Sunday schools for children, sponsor Sunday-afternoon lectures for adults, supply trained speakers on antireligious topics, organize a research department, publish and circulate literature, carry on special work among the foreign-language groups, and inaugurate a massive campaign against "bible-teaching" in the public schools.

Another major goal was the "exposure of the aid that the churches were rendering to the white ruling-class in the legal lynching of the 9 Scottsboro boys." [76] Curiously, it was this same issue, the Scottsboro case, that was to bring about the quick demise of the Workers' Anti-Religious League. Through the case, the Communists were to find that their prejudice against the churches, based upon a mixture of Marxist dogma and general ignorance, had blinded them to a fact they were later to discover to their amazement—that it was to their advantage to use, and not abuse, churches and church people. The basic hostility of Communists toward religion persisted, but public antireligious activity increasingly diminished as the idea and structure of the united front took shape.

THREE · THE COMMUNISTS DISCOVER THE CHURCHES

The Communists stumbled across the churches in their efforts to infiltrate the Negro community. The Negro minister was viewed by the Communists of the twenties as one of the lowest forms of human life. "The duty of the preacher," a writer in the *Communist* charged, "is not alone to detract the mind of his congregation from their wretched conditions. It is also to serve the white plantation owners as their best agent in spying upon the activities of the rural populace. For so faithfully serving their masters, these lackeys often receive excellent wages." [1] Colored clergymen were depicted as ignorant and malicious traitors who eagerly collaborated with the enemies of their class and race.

According to party theoreticians, the emancipation of the Negroes after the Civil War simply changed their position from chattel to wage slave. The capitalists found in the uneducated Negro preacher "a potent instrument by which they could influence the Negro masses to their selfish interests." [2] They depended upon the clergy to keep the Negro workers waiting for their rewards in heaven while enduring poverty and oppression on earth. Yet this would soon change. A *Daily Worker* article observed in 1925: "Today increasing numbers of Negro workers, particularly in industry, are learning what their white brothers, thru bitter experience have learned—that the church is the handmaiden of capital." [3]

When this change did not come and Negroes did not flock to the Communist banner, party leadership was puzzled and disappointed.

In 1928 the Sixth World Congress of the Communist International
adopted a new line on the so-called Negro question in the United
States. The core of the new line was self-determination: the establishment of an independent Negro state out of the areas in the South
where colored Americans were the most numerous. The idea was
preposterous—a fact recognized by the Communists many years later
—but it seemed to implement the Leninist-Stalinist approach to the
national question. Moreover, the Communists thought they might be
able to exploit the black nationalist movement of Marcus Garvey,
which had reached its peak in 1925 and was now on the wane.

This new approach to the Negro question did not affect their attitude toward religion. The Sixth World Congress specifically resolved:

> In the work among the Negroes, special attention should be paid to
> the role played by the churches and preachers who are acting on behalf
> of American imperialism. The Party must conduct a continuous and care-
> fully worked out campaign among the Negro masses, sharpened primarily
> against the preachers and the churchmen, who are agents of the oppressors
> of the Negro race.[4]

Work with the Negro community made antireligion increasingly
hazardous. Some Communists were quick to realize that their appeal
was severely undermined when they attacked the churches. They discovered that many who might be receptive to their general program
were alienated when urged to sever their ties with religion. A few
comrades boldly asked that the churches be treated with less ridicule.
Occasionally a party member would even suggest that it was possible
to reach the masses through infiltration of the church; there were a
few attempts to achieve this goal. In 1929 this policy was specifically
condemned in the report on Negro work made to the Communist
Party convention:

> Some of our comrades in New York as well as elsewhere have had a
> wrong policy toward the church. Their conception of the extent to which
> we could utilize the Negro church is based on an underestimation of the
> role of the church as an instrument of imperialism. They thought that
> they could really make a dent in religion by boring from within. . . .
> Our recent experiences with meetings in the church ought to be adequate
> proof that we must intensify our agitation against the church, to break
> down the stranglehold it has on the Negro masses, and not to go to the
> churches to win these masses.[5]

The attacks upon the Negro churches and their clergy continued. When a number of ministers publicly endorsed Franklin D. Roosevelt for governor of New York State in 1930, the *Daily Worker* charged that the "pie-in-the-sky bunk dispensers" were again "playing their traditional role of treacherous betrayal of the Negro masses." [6] Later the same year, when another group of clergy gathered at the Lincoln Monument in Springfield, Illinois, the *Daily Worker* accused them of "maintaining the lying tradition of Abraham Lincoln as the emancipator and Christ as the redeemer." [7] Other articles in the Communist press accused ministers of fostering lynchings, robbing starving workers, and conspiring with racist overlords to preserve the patterns of white supremacy.

THE SCOTTSBORO CASE

In March 1931, nine Negro boys were arrested in Alabama and charged with the rape of two white girls of questionable reputation. The prospect of a fair trial in the Deep South was dim. The Communists were quick to see the possibilities in the case. Through it they could rally Negro support, unite and strengthen the party, expose the courts as instruments of capitalist oppression, and ridicule the pretensions of American democracy. The International Labor Defense, legal arm of the Communist Party, successfully pushed the National Association for the Advancement of Colored People to one side. Overnight, Communists around the globe turned the Scottsboro case into a world issue. Liberal groups were chagrined but helpless. The *World Tomorrow,* Protestant and socialist, predicted: "Communist doctrine makes it inevitable that the fate of the convicted boys will be made subservient to the cause of the dramatizing the class struggle in America." [8] This became increasingly obvious as the case proceeded.

Within a month after the Alabama episode, the *Daily Worker* was carrying reports of strong religious support for the Scottsboro defense. Crude militant assaults upon churches and ministers quickly yielded to stories which treated them with respect. Two of Chattanooga's large Negro churches opened their pulpits to spokesmen for the International Labor Defense. "Comrade Edwards" of the League of Struggle for Negro Rights, a Communist organization, was vigorously applauded by the congregation of the New Zion Baptist Church in Elizabeth, New Jersey. In Cleveland, the head of the Union Holiness Alliance pledged his organization's support of I.L.D.'s Scottsboro defense. In Detroit, a comrade obtained the co-operation of two churches: the United Church of America and the House of God, Which Is the Church of the Living God, Pillar, Ground of Truth. A Baltimore Negro preacher joined the I.L.D. Representatives of the I.L.D. invaded the countryside and, in town after town, spoke in churches and were received with enthusiasm. Religious organizations and leaders worked side by side with Communists in organizing parades, issuing protests, and circulating petitions.

The support received from the churches came as a surprise to the Communists. Comrade K.E. of Kansas City, Kansas, expressed his amazement in the *Party Organizer,* a publication for Communist organizers. Whenever he had suggested an approach to the Negro churches, his idea had been sharply rejected because the ministers were allegedly paid by "packing-house bosses." He established a Scottsboro Club. Non-Communists were drawn in. Soon the largest and most influential churches opened their doors to Communist speakers without hesitation. "Upon investigation," Comrade K.E. added with a note of recrimination, "we found that our comrades had never really tried to speak in the Negro churches before. They had simply built up the idea that it was impossible. . . ." [9] He warned party units elsewhere to avoid the error he had made in Kansas City.

The churches became an important source of funds for the party's work on the Scottsboro case. A member of the Young Communist League in Cleveland reported his experiences in the *Daily Worker* "for the benefit of other units." He organized a Scottsboro protest meeting in one of the two Negro churches in the neighborhood. More than 150 people attended. Before the comrade spoke, religious songs were sung and "the priest's assistant said some prayers." The request for funds was made by the chairman of the Communist unit. The "priest" reiterated the request. "He appealed to all the people that were present in the church to come up to the front and put their donations on the table. The people in the church came forth to the front and put nickels, dimes, and several quarters and one half dollar on the table. The collection brought in four dollars." [10]

There were still many opportunities for Communists to vent their antireligious wrath. Churches sympathetic to the N.A.A.C.P. often refused to open their doors to speakers of the International Labor Defense. When William L. Patterson, representing the League of Struggle for Negro Rights, urged the all-Negro Baptist Ministers Conference of New York to pledge their support to the I.L.D. and the clergy balked, the *Daily Worker* castigated them as "gowned tools of big business." It was only through the effort of "rank and file" members of the Conference, the *Daily Worker* added, that a mild telegram was sent in support of the Scottsboro boys.[11]

A party worker in Philadelphia wrote of the need of organizing the workers against the preachers to force the ministers into line.[12] The International Labor Defense in Norfolk, Virginia, held a sham public trial of a minister charged with "treason to his people." The clergyman failed to show up, proving that he was fearful of "the wrath of the workers and the ruthless exposure of the trial." A "jury" quickly found him guilty and the workers attending the proceedings "all arose in full support of the decision." [13] In New York City, a continual barrage was directed at several individual clergymen, such as L. H. King, the distinguished pastor of St. Mark's Methodist Church in Harlem.[14] The sharpest attacks were directed at George E. Haynes of the Federal Council of Churches. Writing in the *Communist* in 1935, James W. Ford, a Negro party leader, said of Haynes: "He should not be grouped indiscriminately with other types of Negro reformism. He represents the most reactionary and conservative type." [15]

There were cases in which the Communists used traditional religious forms—and particularly spirituals—to combat religious influence among the Negroes. In 1932 the popular Communist writer Michael Gold wrote a series on "The Negro Reds of Chicago" denouncing "the chains of slave religion" which "proved their worst handicap to freedom." However, he said, on Chicago's South Side "the old slavish spirituals are being written by a new race. . . . 'Gimme That Old Time Religion, it's good enough for me,' they used to sing at their prayer meetings. Now I heard them sing it fervently:

> Gimme that new Communist spirit
> Gimme that new Communist spirit,
> Gimme that new Communist spirit,
> It's good enough for me.

It was good for Comrade Lenin,
And it's good enough for me.

It's against the labor fakers,
    And it's good enough for me.
It has built the Soviet Union,
    And it's good enough for me.
It'll free the world of sorrow,
    And it's good enough for me."

Gold hailed many such "new songs and singers. At mass meetings their religious past becomes transmuted into a Communist present." [16]

Efforts to rally churches on the Scottsboro case proved so rewarding that the Communist Party was under strong pressure to abandon its antireligious agitation altogether. Some important changes developed without specific policy pronouncements. Comrades who were welcomed into churches did not exploit the opportunity to assail religious belief, but more and more they adopted the standard courtesies of speaking well of ministers. Distinctions gradually were drawn between friendly and hostile clergy. The stage was now set for another airing of the "religious question." Communist flirtation with Father Divine from 1934 to 1936 afforded an opportunity to examine the question in detail.

"PEACE" WITH FATHER DIVINE

Father Divine, the omnipotent ruler of "heavens" in many cities across the nation and even around the world, opened his Harlem headquarters in 1933. The "theology" of his followers has been crude. He has been accepted as God. Yet, there have been aspects of the movement that have won admiration and a devout following—particularly Father's ability and willingness to feed 2,500 free of charge daily during the height of the Depression. He also forbade all racism and attracted whites as well as Negroes into his cult without a trace of discrimination. True believers placed their worldly possessions in his care. They were to withhold only those funds needed to supply them with the barest necessities. Communal residencies were instituted and co-operative business enterprises were launched.

In June 1934, the Young Communist League, meeting in convention, included among its Harlem projects the thorough exposure of Father Divine. Within two weeks, however, this same cult leader and his flock were marching alongside Communists in a giant united-front parade. Father had little difficulty explaining the circumstances to his followers. "I am representing GOD on earth among men," he said, "and I will cooperate with ANY organization that will stand for the right and will deal justly." He expressed approval of the Communist position on social, political, and economic equality, but did not hesitate to condemn its materialistic philosophy. "God will use the good and discard the bad," said the *Spoken Word,* Father Divine's "positive magazine." [17]

The reaction in Left Wing circles was varied. Not a few Communists were uneasy about the co-operation, and radicals who opposed the Communist Party accused their adversaries of disgraceful compromise with superstition. Earl Browder, the party's leader, took a different view. He acknowledged that the "fantastic slogans" of Father's followers had "aroused very grave doubts in the minds of many comrades whether it wasn't a serious mistake to allow these religious fanatics to march in our parade. . . ." Browder defended the policy:

> This problem is perhaps an exaggerated example of the whole problem of reaching the backward masses and bringing them into participation with the most advanced section of the working class in revolutionary struggles.[18]

James W. Ford discussed the subject at greater length in an authoritative article in the *Communist* in February 1935. He assailed the Socialists and especially "the renegades from Communism" (Trotskyites) who had poked fun at the Communist Party's co-operation with Father Divine. These critics do not understand the importance of establishing contact with "backward undeveloped elements," Ford said. Through the churches, the party can reach the workers. It must recognize that the Negro people have pride in their churches and that in many ways the churches meet "their social and cultural desires." Communists should take a special interest in "the little preachers" because "they are close to the masses" and "they hate the domination of the big ministers" who speak for the ruling class.[19]

A few months later the controversy over Father Divine broke out again. Oakley Johnson contributed a *Daily Worker* series on conditions in Harlem and made a passing reference to Father Divine and his flock. "And like all racketeers," Johnson wrote, "he will sell them out when a crisis comes." [20] Ford again rushed to Divine's defense and received the red-faced support of the *Daily Worker*.[21] Within a few days Michael Gold joined the debate. "At first," he admitted, "such a united front seems grotesque." While no Communist can believe in this strange cult, every Communist believes in the Negro workers. Why, then, should it surprise anyone that a united front is formed? "For myself," Gold concluded, "I see as much sense in Father Divine's cult as in the elaborate and sometimes hypocritical twistings of logic of a John Haynes Holmes." [22] The controversy over Father Divine was considered sufficiently important to receive treatment in the *Communist International,* a theoretical journal of world Communism, which accused Oakley Johnson of committing an "inexcusable blunder." The drive against religion must go on, the magazine said, but through "organized educational scientific antireligious propaganda" and not by offensive and careless name-calling.[23]

Meanwhile, Father Divine continued to lend his prestige to Communist causes, endorse Communist candidates, sign Communist petitions, speak at united-front meetings, appear in Communist parades, reprint Communist articles and editorials, and laud the Soviet Union. At the same time, he was somehow above it all—unwilling to be disciplined and perhaps not enough in touch with reality to understand that he was being exploited. The strange alliance served both sides well—the Communists were provided a base of operation in the center of Harlem, many hundreds of new marchers for their parades, and new signatures for their petitions; Father Divine seemed flattered by the widespread publicity and the opportunity to gain a new spotlight at well-organized Communist functions.

A split was inevitable, however. Marxism made little impact upon either Father Divine or his followers and co-operation became increasingly embarrassing to the Communists. In parades, Father Divine would ride in a blue Rolls-Royce followed by a long line of cars and buses carrying his placard-toting flock. Some signs read "Free the Scottsboro Boys," but more proclaimed joyously, "Thank You, FATHER Dear." Even more humiliating to hard-core Marxists were

Father's comments. His typical opening greeting would be: "Peace Everyone! My original and usual salutation. Peace, good health, good will and a good appetite, with a heart full of merriness." Then after proclaiming the virtues of peace, Father would continue in this vein:

For this cause I Came, and I shall not be discouraged until we shall have contagionized [*sic*] the whole Universe with the SPIRIT of PEACE and UNITY, which I express. Oh, it is a privilege dear ones, to live in the Unity of the Spirit of Peace by bringing your bodies into subjection to the Fundamentals of Life according to the Constitution of our great Country.[24]

The stage was set for a break in January 1936, when Father Divine held an "International Righteous Government Convention" at St. Nicholas Arena in New York City. Several Communists were present to address the gathering. It was Father's speech, however, that won the acclaim of the devout and increased the skepticism in Communist ranks. He had been critical of labor unions in the past, but now, after two years of association with the Communists, he held more tenaciously than ever to his curious views. In his typical incoherent fashion, he warned: "Practically all of the different Unions, they think they have dominion over the people, and force them to work or force them not to work, and yet give them nothing. I have risen to PUT IT DOWN. . . . Why should the unions try to control the people and put them in slavery?" [25]

Some leading Communists still urged co-operation. Benjamin J. Davis, a Negro party leader, blamed such antiunion sentiments on racial discrimination within organized labor. "For the revolutionary movement to throw aside the Negro workers because they are religious-minded," Davis warned, "is to fall into a petty-bourgeois sectarianism and to condemn the people into continued slavery, terror, and misery." [26] Father Divine again was invited to participate in the 1936 May Day activities but only if he would correct his position on labor. He stubbornly refused. Relations grew worse each passing day. In September 1936, the *Daily Worker* noted, without comment, that charges of financial irregularity were being pressed against their former collaborator. When Father asked his followers to boycott the November election, the Communist press accused him of playing into the hands of reactionaries. To the Communists, Father Divine soon took his place again alongside the many other "vicious enemies" of the working class.

SHIFTING VIEWS OF RELIGION

The Communists accidentally were led into a new appraisal of the churches at the time of the Scottsboro case. In 1930 the clergy had been under sharp attack and religious belief was subjected to ridicule and mockery. Within a few years, the same clergy were being wooed and their faiths treated with respect and even apparent reverence.

The switch was vividly illustrated in the changing attitude toward Christmas in the columns of the *Daily Worker* between 1930 and 1936, shifting from crude hostility to indifference to vigorous exploitation. In a major statement of policy in 1925, the *Daily Worker* had summed up the earlier view in these words:

Christmas is a holiday with which the capitalist social structure absorbs some of the shocks incidental to the system of slavery, throws over the mind of the worker a haze of illusion of universal good will in a blood-thirsty social system, and absorbs a good business for its retail merchants on the margin of wages of the working class.[27]

In 1931 the first annual "Anti-Christmas Day" was held on December 25 in Cleveland, Ohio, sponsored by the Young Communist League and Young Pioneers. In a special "Anti-Christmas Circus" onlookers watched as Science knocked out Religion in what the *Daily Worker* described as "the most exciting boxing match of the year." They also saw Santa Claus bring presents to a worker's child: starvation, disease, war, ignorance, and "a few crumbs of charity." The Siamese Twins—John D. Rockefeller and the Pope—were on exhibit, while a "Talking Lamb" meekly repeated parts of the Twenty-third Psalm.[28] Other customary events scheduled for Christmas Eve were lectures exposing "the myth of religion" and a host of anti-religious skits, concerts, and dances.

Two years later, the policy had changed to indifference. Then in 1935, twenty-four Communist events were announced for Christmas Eve in New York City alone, and none of them was billed as anti-religious. The change of policy was completed in 1936 when, by early

December, the *Daily Worker* was suggesting Christmas parties as a means of raising money to support the paper. On Christmas Day 1936, the paper ran a banner headline bearing Christmas greetings to its readers. Front-page messages were published from several clergymen. A lengthy editorial contended that the Communist movement was a genuine friend of religion.

While the *Daily Worker* was re-evaluating Christmas, a serious discussion of religion was going on among Communists. No one played a more important role in the debate than Earl Browder, who served as executive secretary of the American party from 1930 until he was ousted in 1945. He was instrumental in halting the ridicule of religion that had characterized the twenties. Browder had an interesting religious background himself. A number of his ancestors were Methodist ministers who helped establish Methodism in the states of Virginia and Kentucky. His father became a Unitarian, and Earl, one of a large family, was reared in that denomination in Kansas, though he never himself was a member. Perhaps it was this liberal religious training that spared him from the feelings of rebellion and bitterness against political clericalism and religious dogmatism that many other Communists felt so intensely. Moreover, Browder had some understanding of the complexity of American religious life which many Communist leaders did not have. He was quicker to accept the idea that there were "progressive" as well as "reactionary" clergymen.

One of Browder's early statements on religion was made in 1935 when he was invited by a group of students at Union Theological Seminary in New York City to air his views. He restated the official Communist position against supernaturalism and acknowledged that within the party some religious discrimination would be practiced. "We would not, for example," Browder pointed out, "place in the most responsible leading positions of the movement people who had strong religious beliefs." But he made a bid for broader support among churchmen. "You may be interested in knowing that we have preachers, preachers active in the churches, who are members of the Communist Party," he said. "There are churches in the United States where the preachers preach Communism from the pulpits, in a very primitive form, of course." While "institutionalized religion is still used by the present rulers," he discerned encouraging "revolutionary trends" within the churches and urged Communists and Christians to unite against war and fascism.[29]

Browder's attempt to find a common ground between Communism and religion was greeted with skepticism by many party members. As late as 1935, the *Daily Worker* carried cartoons lampooning religious institutions and leadership. Several of the most effective were part of a series known as "The Ruling Clawss" by the ingenious *Daily Worker* cartoonist Redfield. Typical was one of two nuns on their knees before a large crucifix. One asks the other: "Shall we mention the unemployed again, Sister, or was yesterday enough?"[30] In another a fat capitalist, smiling smugly, says to a minister: "Your sermon was a pip, Reverend—next week tear into unions and tell them all about Heaven."[31] Such brazen satire drew approving guffaws from the party's faithful whose hatred of religion ran deep. Among some Jewish Communists, whose ancestors had often suffered through centuries of discrimination at the hands of fanatical European Christians, there was the added pleasure of hitting back at the despised symbols of this discrimination.

There was other evidence of open hostility toward religion as late as 1935. In January of that year, Michael Gold labeled God as "merely another puppet on the stage where capitalism lies to the masses."[32] In June 1935, the *Daily Worker* reminded its readers that "Communism is the irreconcilable foe of religion," which was described as "a spiritual dope" designed to drown the aspirations and just demands of the masses.[33] Two months later, Bennett Stevens' anticlerical pamphlet *The Church and the Workers,* published originally in 1932, was reissued and the price was reduced from ten to five cents to attract new readers.[34]

Such events as these, however, were running against the tide. Communist strategy was changing. The biting cartoons gradually ceased, to be replaced by new cartoons showing a swastika smashing the cross or quoting the Biblical message of "Peace on Earth." In earlier years, Communists had boasted that the church in Russia was being extinguished; now the same Communists stressed freedom of religion in the Soviet Union. In the twenties, there were instances in which Communists had been ousted from the party for attending church; now the party boasted that it had members of many faiths. There was praise for ministers who spoke out against fascism. Even the Pilgrim Fathers—once viewed as pious, bourgeois hypocrites—now received favorable attention in a Thanksgiving feature, "Pilgrims Fled European Tyranny to Sow Seeds of Mighty Democracy." [35] Browder liked to describe Communism as "Twentieth-Century Americanism" and he urged his comrades to join in the national reverence for the patriots and traditions of the past. By 1937, the *Daily Worker* even dealt courteously with the American Legion.

Sympathetic letters from churchmen were published more and more frequently in Communist periodicals. These letters served three purposes. They convinced some religiously inclined readers of the genuine tolerance of the Communist movement. They reassured the skeptical party member that not all churchmen automatically should be viewed as enemies of the working class. Finally, they conveyed the false impression, nurtured by the party, that there was considerable co-operation between the Communists and the clergy. A "Methodist Episcopal Layman" ended his letter with the words, "Defend the Soviet Union!" [36] An anonymous New York minister told of his enthusiasm for the *Daily Worker,* but asked the paper not to confuse religion in America with Roman Catholicism and Eastern Orthodoxy abroad. "No church in the world has taken such interest in the gospel of social action as has the church in the U.S.," he wrote.[37] A Congregational clergyman wrote that, after studying Communist theory and practice, he concluded that "Communists in Russia are practical Christians" and that the "principles of Communism are the outcome of the teachings of Jesus. . . ." [38] A letter from a "Christian Communist" in September 1936 said that Christianity and Communism were "inseparable." [39] The *Daily Worker* used the letter as a springboard to extend a "hearty welcome" to churchmen to join the party. At least one retired minister indicated that he intended to accept the invitation. He had visited the Soviet Union as a critic of Communism, he wrote, but he was delighted by what he saw there: "If this be Communism—mail me your application for membership!" [40]

INFILTRATION IN THE CHURCH

How successful were the Communists in wooing churchmen into the party in the thirties? Contrary to widespread opinion, there is no evidence that they ever embarked upon a careful, well-organized attempt to infiltrate the field of religion. Such a master plan was discussed from time to time, but the party gave priority to many other areas of concentration and particularly to organized labor. It was never equipped to launch a major effort to subvert the churches. Few members could qualify for such work and they were busy elsewhere. It was not difficult for a zealous Communist to work as a member of the C.I.O.; it took far more skill for a zealous Communist to work as a faithful believer. Moreover, it was soon discovered that clergymen did not make likely or reliable party members, but that some could be easily drawn into the rapidly growing front apparatus—discussed in Chapter 5. Why pressure them to join the party when they might serve Communism as effectively outside?

Probably the best source of information on Communist clergy is the 1939 testimony of Earl Browder before the House Committee on Un-American Activities, where he was quizzed by J. B. Matthews, who had become counsel to the committee. Two thoughts should be borne in mind as these excerpts from the testimony are read. First, Browder could have warped his testimony to protect party secrets. Second, Browder may not have been aware of the entire membership of his own party, as he himself admits. Against these considerations, however, is the fact that Browder has verified his 1939 testimony since he was ousted from the party in 1945 and that whatever outside evidence exists suggests that his testimony gave a generally accurate picture of the situation.

Mr. MATTHEWS. Did you say, Mr. Browder, to the students at Union Theological Seminary:

"You may be interested in knowing that we have preachers, preachers active in churches, who are members of the Communist Party."

Mr. BROWDER. I said that.

Mr. MATTHEWS. Do you think that a congregation of any church in the United States would knowingly retain a clergyman who had membership in the Communist Party?

Mr. BROWDER. I am quite certain of it.

Mr. MATTHEWS. Will you please give us the names, then, of the clergymen to whom you referred, or some of them, in this statement?

Mr. BROWDER. I will not.

Mr. MATTHEWS. It is important that they be kept secret, is it?

Mr. BROWDER. It is not.

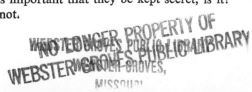

Mr. MATTHEWS. But there are clergymen active in churches—

Mr. BROWDER. (interposing) It is very important that they shall not have brought down upon them the spotlight of a national publicity campaign. That certainly would disrupt their congregation.

Mr. MATTHEWS. You know that there are cases where these clergymen are members of the Communist Party, and are known to be such?

Mr. BROWDER. To their own members.

The CHAIRMAN. Does that comprise all denominations?

Mr. BROWDER. No; I would not say all denominations.

The CHAIRMAN. Well, many denominations? It does not include the Catholics, does it?

Mr. BROWDER. At the present time we have not yet got the Catholic clergy in the party.

The CHAIRMAN. Do you have any Catholics in the Communist Party?

Mr. BROWDER. Oh, many Catholics.

The CHAIRMAN. You do?

Mr. BROWDER. Yes, sir.

The CHAIRMAN. And all other denominations?

Mr. BROWDER. I do not know that we have all denominations. We have Catholics; we have Methodists; we have Baptists; we have Unitarians; we have Mormons; we have Spiritualists. These are the ones that I have met and know about.

Mr. STARNES. Do you have any Holy Rollers?

Mr. BROWDER. I believe we have a Holy Roller in the South too.

Mr. MATTHEWS. Do you have members of the Communist Party who are clergymen or preachers in the Methodist Church?

Mr. BROWDER. No; not in the Methodist Church.

Mr. MATTHEWS. In the Baptist Church?

Mr. BROWDER. I believe there are Baptists, and Holy Rollers.

Mr. MATTHEWS. Baptists and Holy Rollers?

Mr. BROWDER. Yes, sir.

Mr. MATTHEWS. Not the Catholic Church?

Mr. BROWDER. Not the Catholic Church.

Mr. MATTHEWS. Presbyterians?

Mr. BROWDER. I am not certain about the Presbyterians.

Mr. MATTHEWS. Congregationalists?

Mr. BROWDER. Not the Congregationalists.

Mr. MATTHEWS. Quakers?

Mr. BROWDER. Not the Quakers.

Mr. CASEY. Unitarians?

Mr. BROWDER. No. That is my old church. I have done very little work there.

Mr. MATTHEWS. So far as you can remember, they are only in the Baptist Church and in the Holy Roller Church?

Mr. BROWDER. Those are the only ones that I am sure of.[41]

If Browder answered Matthews honestly, there were very few actual Communist Party members in American pulpits during the thirties. Browder said that there was not a single Methodist minister in the party out of the thousands of ordained clergymen of that denomination, scores of whom have been "suspected" of "Communist ties." There was no Congregationalist minister and no Unitarian minister. He made no reference to Episcopalians and Lutherans and Disciples of Christ and another dozen Protestant denominations. Nor did he mention rabbis. He was sure of Communist clergy among only the Baptists and the "Holy Rollers." [42]

The Browder testimony adds weight to a thesis suggested by other available material. While outright infiltration into the churches was seldom attempted, in instances where it occurred in the thirties the churches seem to have been Negro. Certainly, the Baptists and the "Holy Rollers" had particular strength among the Negroes. This infiltration was directed more at influencing the Negro community than at subverting the general field of religion. The Communists had learned through experience that social and civic life among the Negroes, especially in the South, revolved around the churches. They sought to reach colored Americans through their houses of worship.

James W. Ford analyzed the situation in his book of 1938, *The Negro and the Democratic Front*. "The Negro church has solid contacts with the Negro masses," he wrote.[43] There were innumerable churches attended by millions of colored working people who looked to their pastors for direction. A single sermon by a minister on the need for joining a labor union, for example, could result "in building almost overnight a Domestic Workers Union of five hundred members in Harlem alone." [44] The earlier Communist antagonism to the churches was wrong, Ford wrote, and a co-operative attitude must be shown. "Our Negro Communists are fraternizing with church people in order to organize them in the struggle for Negro liberation." [45]

Communist periodicals ran a number of accounts of how religious groups were successfully infiltrated. Almost invariably Negro organizations were the targets. The two following excerpts from party reports suggest the way in which the party operated.

From a report made at the New York District Convention of the Communist Party in June 1936:

I would like to emphasize the importance of our Negro and white comrades working within the churches. The churches offer us an opportunity to come into contact with every strata of the Negro people, to meet them and bring them into the various economic struggles with which we are not able to reach them otherwise. In New Rochelle, one of our comrades has a Sunday School class of 35 boys, where he has been able to build a forum and . . . bring some of them into the Y.C.L. [Young Communist League].[46]

From an article by J.S., "Negro Worker" in Florida, entitled "We Will Recruit the Negroes":

. . . we were able to bring into the Party five members from the Methodist and Baptist churches. They did not know anything about the Communist Party but they realized that anything the Party did was sort of a struggle to uplift the people. . . . We have several ministers in the town who do not want to come out in the open, but every time they meet someone whom they know to be a real Communist, they have a signed check for him, and consult him on what to do about it. They raise the money in their congregations.[47]

There were continual warnings from Communist organizers not to let the religious issue interfere with their work. A Negro longshoreman from Virginia wrote these words of advice to his comrades:

One bad approach that the average comrades have to the Negro is to argue with him about religion. Religious or not, if he is in the South he is Jim-Crowed just the same. Go to him, and if he begins to argue on the bible, just don't you argue with him. Say: "Sure! That's all right. The bible's all right. But what are we going to do about our conditions? What about jobs for our girls," and so on. This is the way to win him.[48]

From these accounts it is obvious that the Communists, whatever their weaknesses in strategy, met with at least some success in their efforts to infiltrate the Negro churches. Yet, even with this effort, the response among Negroes was disappointing to the party. The Communists had assumed from the twenties that Negroes would be their allies. Actually, the Negroes in the party never rose above 10 per cent of the total membership—which is approximately the Negro ratio to the national population—and usually it fell far below that proportion.

A number of factors contributed to this. Negroes usually read the same newspapers as other Americans, and they were not immune to the bias of the nation generally. The New Deal had emerged as a champion of the Negroes during the thirties, and the machinery of the Democratic Party in Northern cities was far more effective than that of the Communists, primarily because it could back up its promises with jobs and other benefits. Patterns of Negro life also hurt Communist recruiting efforts. Most Negroes had little in common with aggressive, sometimes frenzied, white comrades, as often as not foreign born, who tended to be either overbearing zealots or solicitous consorts. The Negro community, as a whole, did not respond to the kind of discipline and simplicity demanded by the Communist Party. Traditionally, the most successful organizations among Negroes, the churches and the lodges, were more flexible and more casual, satisfying needs for pageantry and status. Communists further tended to alienate the Negro through bitter criticism of middle-class or "bourgeois" society—the very goal toward which the majority of the Negroes were striving. The Communists had their greatest success among the Negro intelligentsia, but even here they found that these intellectuals were quick to deviate from party policies whenever their strong racial feelings ran counter to Communist dogma. In sum, most Communists were out of place among American Negroes. They were too doctrinaire, too disciplined, too zealous —and too white. Their efforts to achieve "Communist-Negro unity" were artificial, based on political logic rather than on sociological reality.

By the mid-thirties, the American Communist Party was not putting its principal emphasis upon recruiting members. Out of Moscow came a new set of instructions. Comrades around the world were to co-operate with all others—Socialists and New Dealers, believers and atheists, workers and bosses—who would help resist the rising tide of fascism that appeared to threaten the security of the Soviet Union.

This led to the emergence of a new strategy—that of the united front. It was an effective maneuver that was to change the course of the entire Communist movement in the United States.

FOUR · THE IMAGE OF RUSSIA
IN THE THIRTIES: PRO AND CON

America's Depression of 1929 and of the early thirties and the widespread belief that capitalism was doomed focused new and sympathetic attention upon the Russian experiment. Some of the severest critics of Bolshevism's political and religious suppression were now ready to re-examine at least the economic aspects of the Soviet system. The jargon of Marxism became increasingly fashionable among intellectuals, within segments of the labor movement, in some farm groups, and among social workers and the clergy.

A poll conducted by the *World Tomorrow* in early 1934 cast some light upon economic thinking among the Protestant ministers of the time. Of 20,870 participating, only 1,035, or less than 5 per cent, replied that capitalism was the system "less antagonistic to and more consistent with the ideals and methods of Jesus. . . ." Another 51 per cent chose "drastically reformed capitalism" and 28 per cent expressed their preference for socialism. Significantly, Communism received only 123 votes, only twelve more than fascism. It was obvious that Communism had little appeal, but it was also clear that the Depression had pushed the American clergy generally to the left.[1]

The first major test of American sentiment on the U.S.S.R. came in 1933. On November 16, the new President, Franklin Delano Roosevelt, abruptly extended recognition to the Soviet Government. In spite of the apparent suddenness of the move, the American people were prepared. The Soviet Union had been on its best behavior for many months. It had ostensibly abandoned the goal of immediate world revolution. It had signed the Kellogg Pact, negotiated agreements with its European neighbors, and expressed a willingness at world conferences to disarm completely if other nations would do likewise. The failure of other friendly nations to pay their war debts to the United States reduced the stigma that had been attached to Russia's repudiation of her prerevolutionary obligations. Besides, recognition did not mean approval—the United States had diplomatic relations with Fascist Italy, Nazi Germany, and militarist Japan.

Of special importance in church circles were reports that the ruthless persecution of religion had subsided and speculation that recognition might stop it altogether.

In the Protestant church press, the *Christian Century* and the *World Tomorrow* were among the most forthright in urging diplomatic ties with the Soviet Union. The majority of prominent Protestant religious leaders agreed. Harry Emerson Fosdick thought that "a frank recognition of the Soviet Union would do more good than harm." Episcopalian Henry Knox Sherrill felt that while there was "much to be said on both sides," recognition would be "wiser in the long run." Henry Sloane Coffin, President of Union Theological Seminary, inclined toward the same view, arguing that "we did not approve of the Czar's government but we recognized it and had diplomatic relations with it." [2]

In New York State in February 1933, 430 ministers signed a petition favoring recognition. For some, recognition was an open door for Christian missions. The conservative *Christian Standard* commented: "It is not at all impossible now, that the power of the gospel shall be felt again in Russia through the efforts of American missionaries." [3] The fundamentalist *Moody Monthly,* typically apocalyptic, thought the Second Coming might solve the prickly problems of diplomacy: "It may be, however, that our Lord shall come before such problems enter upon their serious solution, and thus many if not all of the readers of these words will be spared the trouble of grappling with them." [4]

A large number of Protestant clergymen, however, were opposed to ties with Russia primarily on the grounds of Soviet persecution of religion. The *Living Church* commented: ". . . this government that we are proposing to recognize is the same government that has carried on a consistent policy of persecution of religion, and an assault against the basic Christian philosophy of life unequalled since the Mohammedan menace of the seventh century." [5]

Jewish religious and secular leadership with its generally socialist-liberal orientation was more united in its endorsement of recognition. Most American Jews or their forebears had come from Russia or Poland and they welcomed the downfall of a czardom that had symbolized government-sponsored pogroms. The Communist-controlled government had officially outlawed anti-Semitism, and the discrimination which emerged to the surface under Stalin was not yet in evidence. Antagonism against the Soviet Union existed primarily among some of the Jewish labor groups who had battled Communists during the twenties, but even here the feeling prevailed that nonrecognition was unrealistic.

Some rabbis went on record as strong supporters of diplomatic ties with Russia. Stephen S. Wise of New York City's Free Synagogue, the leading figure in the Jewish community for many years, said it was "childish and, indeed, most unwise for us to withhold recognition from the Soviet Union"; De Sola Pool of the historic and wealthy Spanish and Portuguese Synagogue called it "indefensible" and " 'holier than thou.' " [6]

In sharp contrast to these Protestant and Jewish sentiments was Roman Catholic opinion. *America,* the Jesuit journal, objected on the grounds that Russia "stands for the destruction of religion, of natural and civic rights, and of all that is cherished by the Christian world. . . ." [7] Even the *Commonweal,* the liberal lay weekly, which frequently took an independent viewpoint, expressed fear that recognition would enhance the prestige of organized atheism.

INFLUENCE OF SHERWOOD EDDY

During the late twenties and throughout the thirties, few churchmen had more influence in molding informed Protestant opinion on the U.S.S.R. than Sherwood Eddy, a distinguished Y.M.C.A. leader. Eddy had visited Russia twice under the czars, in 1910 and 1912, and in 1926 had organized his first American seminar-tour of the Soviet Union with two dozen educators, social workers, editors, businessmen, and religious leaders. Eddy's seminar soon became an annual affair for many of the nation's key church leaders, who spoke and wrote widely on their experiences. Eddy himself was a prolific writer. From 1897 until 1955, when his autobiography, *Eighty Adventurous Years,* was published, he wrote thirty-six books, revealing a wide range of interest and concern: *India Awakening* (1911), *Suffering and the War* (1916), *The New World of Labor* (1923), *Sex and Youth* (1928), *Revolutionary Christianity* (1939), *A Portrait of Jesus* (1943), *I Have Seen God Work in China* (1944), *You Will Survive After Death* (1950).

Eddy was ambivalent toward the Soviet Union. In early 1924 he saw Russia as "a political, social and industrial challenge to the world, wherever nations, races, colonies, or classes are conquered or exploited." Still, he recognized her weaknesses:

Soviet Russia has not yet found the solution of its social problems in the frankly avowed materialism, atheism and anti-religious policy of the Communist Party, in their avowed disbelief in democracy, their dictatorship of the proletariat and their denial of liberty which dare not allow freedom of speech, of the press, or of action in opposition to the government.[8]

In 1931 his *The Challenge of Russia* was published, and three years later *Russia Today.* The U.S.S.R., he said, was a "land of limitless possibilities." "The communist philosophy seeks a new order, a classless society of unbroken brotherhood, what the Hebrew prophets would have called a reign of righteousness on earth. But these high humanitarian ends it seeks by means of class dictatorship and by all necessary use of force."[9]

There were bright sides to the Soviet experiment which Eddy and other visitors to Russia thought no honest observer could ignore. He pointed out that the Soviet Union guaranteed work for all, sought a minimum standard of living and an equitable distribution of the goods, provided housing and health programs and maternity and child care, including free public nurseries, abolished prostitution, and substituted a redemptive for a "vindictive" penal system. A mass campaign to end illiteracy had brought free learning to children of workers and peasants. Drama, music, and art were encouraged and underwritten by the Russian Government. Eddy contrasted the efforts of the Soviet Union to eradicate race prejudice with the persisting color problem in America and said in *Russia Today:* "There is probably less race and color prejudice in the Soviet Union today than in any country in the world that has a mixture of races." [10]

Many clergymen found the Soviet's strict social morality reassuring—the opposition to excessive use of alcohol; the emphasis on "clean" motion pictures, made neither for money nor for entertainment but for education; the new sex standards, which Eddy reported ambiguously as revealing "a stern almost Puritan element in Soviet morality though it is coupled with personal liberty and the absence of convention and external restraints." But the *Christian Century,* in its review of *Russia Today,* chided Eddy, "formerly a champion of personal morality in American colleges, now commending without a smile the new morality of communism, lauding the new sex standards of Russian youth, and admitting that 'in every age morality changes with experience.' " [11]

In neither *The Challenge of Russia* nor *Russia Today* was Eddy uncritical. He underscored four Soviet weaknesses again and again: "a paralyzing and ineffective bureaucracy," "the essential denial of liberty," "the danger of violence and compulsion," and "a narrow and exclusive dogmatic basis." His foreword to *Russia Today* said: "My latest visit to Russia confirmed and deepened my conviction regarding the four chief evils of the Soviet system . . . so enduring and so of the very essence of Communism itself that they would make it quite impossible for me to ever accept it." [12] In the realm of religion he had found that "every effective preacher or dynamic religious worker is either exiled, or banished, or placed under a ban of strict silence." [13]

Eddy's 1955 autobiography reminisces on these early trips to the Soviet Union "without any guide, spy, or official. . . ." "As I reflect on the visits of the American Seminar to Russia, I am amazed that we could go back regularly year after year and were allowed so much freedom." [14] Gradually, however, he saw "the whole Soviet Union sink to the level of a slave state, where all, consciously or unconsciously, were prisoners. . . ."

I saw the Soviet Union pass through three awful purges. Then I saw the chief purgers themselves eliminated. . . . I saw the official atheism of the Soviet system furnish the logical foundation for immorality and amorality. Then I saw in the distance some of the first of their slave labor camps, which I was never allowed to visit. . . . Finally, I saw this degraded slave state of Stalinism embark on its period of world conquest. . . .[15]

There were other writers whose views on Russia had particular influence upon the clergy—George Mecklenburg, a Methodist minister, who expressed views similar to Eddy's in a 1934 account entitled *Russia Challenges Religion;* E. Stanley Jones, noted liberal missionary-evangelist, whose widely read book *Christ's Alternative to Communism* (1935) was more anti-Communist; and Harry F. Ward, ecstatic in his praise of Russia in his 1933 book, *In Place of Profit*. But Eddy's writings, together with his seminars, had the broadest impact upon Protestant churchmen during the thirties. His views represented those of most well-informed American ministers, who sought, above all else, to approach the Russian experiment with an open mind. Like Eddy, they saw considerable good in the U.S.S.R. Like Eddy, they saw her seamy side. They looked to Russia to learn. Could she teach America any lessons? They hoped the Soviet Union might chart a new path to a better world, but they were aware that dictatorship, violence, and oppression could destroy its finest ideals.

THE MENACE OF FASCISM

Throughout the thirties, a string of international developments helped place the U.S.S.R. in a favorable light in the eyes of many Americans.

No other factor aided Communist propaganda in America more than the cult of Nazism in Germany. American Communists pointed to the oppression of their German comrades, among the first victims of Nazism. The principal foe of fascism was the U.S.S.R., the Communists said. Even among anti-Communists there was a growing conviction that Hitler was the real enemy to fear.

The Nazi attitude toward religion aroused clergy of all faiths. The wrecking of synagogues, the desecration of Jewish cemeteries, the blatant ridicule of rabbis—in addition to many other crude forms of persecution—were bitterly assailed in thousands of American pulpits. Jewish religious leaders naturally were outraged. Whatever criticisms could be directed at the Soviet Union, anti-Semitism was not then one of them. Christian clergymen were stirred also, and their ire continued to grow as Hitler turned upon Roman Catholic and Protestant clergy who refused to show sufficient enthusiasm for the new order. The Nazis set about to "de-Judaize" Christianity, and some zealots of the Third Reich even sought to replace Christianity altogether with the paganism of the early Nordic tribes.

American Communists quickly exploited the religious issue to help rally popular support. They played up all conflicts between Nazism and German churchmen; clergymen like the Lutheran Martin Niemöller, who resisted Hitler, became heroes in the Communist press. By 1933, the *Daily Worker* was carrying stories under such headlines as "Catholic Workers Clash with Nazis," and "Conflicts in German Church Show Protestants' Hatred of Nazi Rule." "Protest is not enough," a typical *Daily Worker* editorial said. "Action, united action of Jews, Catholics, Socialists, Communists, trade unionists, of people of all religious and political beliefs is necessary." [16] Communist units published literature designed to rally Roman Catholic support. In 1936, for example, the New York District of the Young Communist League called upon Roman Catholic youth to send telegrams to the German Consulate demanding the release of Ernst Thälmann, described as "leader of the struggle of the German people against Fascism!" [17] Thälmann was leader of the German Communist Party.

As it became apparent that Hitler intended to dominate Europe and probably the whole world, the weakness of the West seemed apparent before and especially after the Munich agreement in 1938. More and more people in the United States, both within and without the churches, looked to the Soviet Union as the only power with either the will or the strength to stand firm against fascism.

The Communists were also quick to exploit Fascist Italy's invasion of the ancient kingdom of Ethiopia in October 1935, an action met with widespread condemnation across the world. Fifty-two members of the League of Nations supported sanctions against the aggressor. Americans had been generally unconcerned about Italian Fascism but now they became aroused. The overwhelming majority were moved by pictures of native Ethiopian horsemen battling Fascist airplanes and tanks with only spears and courage.

The Ethiopian war brought the first major test of the pacifism that had flourished among religious leaders during the two decades following World War I. What should their position be on assistance to a victim of aggression? The pacifists' division was symbolized in a dramatic split between Eddy and Kirby Page, close personal friends and co-workers. Page, whose view won the support of many pacifist spokesmen, opposed any action against Italy on the grounds that coercion was morally wrong, might provoke a global war, and that the motives of the condemning nations (notably England, France, and Russia) were not above suspicion. One writer in the *Friends Intelligencer,* leading Quaker weekly, echoed this ambiguous moral situation: "Are the hands of those nations that are preparing to coerce Italy and save Ethiopia by economic and military force themselves clean of the spoils of empire in Africa?" [18]

Sherwood Eddy restated his refusal to sanction any future war in a letter to the *Christian Century.* "However," he continued, "Italy's aggression in Africa is forcing some of us to rethink our position. I favor effective economic sanctions imposed by the League of Nations." He suggested that maybe the Suez Canal should be closed and that, if necessary, Italy be blockaded. Should Mussolini retaliate by attacking Malta, Eddy thought the League should call upon the British and French fleets "to defend the point or points attacked." [19] As many ardent pacifists began to bend under the weight of world events, a number (but not Eddy) became willing to co-operate with Communists in organizations designed to combat fascism.

Events in Ethiopia had other consequences in the churches.

The Communists were able to obtain increased co-operation among Negroes. Some of Harlem's most prominent ministers joined with the Communists and others in making joint statements. In Los Angeles, a Communist-sponsored youth parade, adopting the slogan "March for Peace—Defend Ethiopia," included representatives from a number of Negro churches. A pro-Ethiopia meeting was held in the First African Baptist Church of New Orleans, sponsored by the American League Against War and Fascism. Three thousand Negroes and whites, led by Comrade Manning Johnson—and including several hundred followers of Father Divine—marched on May 11, 1936, in New York City to protest the announcement that Ethiopia had been incorporated into the Italian Empire.

The Ethiopian conflict also gave the Communists ammunition for their traditional contention (which was to be soft-pedaled soon after) that the Vatican was in league with fascists. The Pope, they charged, was quick to assail peace-loving Russia but did not utter a word against Italian aggression. As one bit of concrete evidence of alleged papal connivance with fascism, the Communists cited a Vatican reference to Queen Elena of Italy as the Empress of Ethiopia.

Finally, the Communists assumed an unusual pose when they became ardent champions of religious liberty. The Communist press made martyrs out of Ethiopian Coptic priests who died resisting the invaders. There were gruesome accounts of the deliberate bombing and strafing of peaceful Ethiopian Christian churches where women and children had gathered for prayer and refuge. The Pope was castigated when he encouraged missionaries from Italy to "Christianize" a nation which had embraced Christianity while the Romans were still worshiping their emperors.

The savage conflict between the Loyalists and Nationalists in Spain is discussed in greater detail in Chapter 8. Liberals in the United States overwhelmingly favored the Loyalists—an unwieldy coalition of Republicans, Socialists, Syndicalists, Anarchists, and (at the outset of the war) a small minority of Communists—against the Nationalists, led by Franco and supported by Germany and Italy. There were strong religious overtones to the Spanish Civil War. The Vatican openly supported Franco. Devout Protestants, most of whom feared both Communism and Roman Catholicism, were pulled in two directions. The net result in the United States was to improve the position of Russia and the Communists among pro-Loyalists, to hurt their position among pro-Nationalists. The first group was composed largely of Protestants and Jews, the second of Roman Catholics.

The Sino-Japanese War also provided effective material for Communist propagandists, especially among American churchmen. Before 1937, when war broke out between China and Japan, Chinese Communists had viewed the foreign missionaries as agents of capitalism and of cultural and economic aggression and imperialism. In those areas where Communists were in control, hundreds of missionaries left their posts. There were many stories of persecution. One of the sensational cases was the grisly public beheading in late 1934 of Mr. and Mrs. John C. Stam, conservative Protestant missionaries. Part of the American church press attributed the act to lawless bandits, others to Communists. An article in the *Presbyterian* declared: "They died against the outworks of Atheistic Communism, the scourge of this age, as Caesarism was the scourge of first century Christianity." [20]

Almost every missionary in China opposed Communism initially. In 1927, after Chiang Kai-shek split with his former Communist friends, missionaries rushed to his support. Their enthusiasm for Chiang was heightened in the thirties by his "New Life Movement" for social and moral reform, by the Christian faith of his wife, and by his own interest in Christianity, which led to his baptism.

Some of the bitterest comment on the Chinese Communists came from Sherwood Eddy, who had shown far more patience with the Russian Bolsheviks. "Whatever its theory," Eddy wrote in 1935, "communism *in China today* is not the pink romance of parlor bolsheviks but, all too often, grim slaughter." [21] Eddy was criticized by the *Christian Century,* which had taken a different view of the Chinese Communists: The mass of Communists were not Marxists at all, but "simply a horde of poor devils, who have been dispossessed of their land, forced into tenantry of a most degrading sort, delivered into slavery to money-lenders . . . and now strike out blindly, savagely, with the ferocity of the ignorant and the terrorized, in the chance of snatching some hope out of life." [22] It warned the Nationalists and the missionaries to recognize this economic problem and to deal with it before it was too late.

Moscow's call for a united front in the mid-thirties did not heal the breach between Chiang and his Communist adversaries, but an official policy of co-operation was hammered out in 1937, the year that Japan invaded China and precipitated a war that continued for eight years. This attack upon China had a great impact upon the missionaries, whose sympathies were wholly with China. Christians and Communists soon were fraternizing. Many visited Communist-governed territory and were impressed by the social and economic reforms, while Communists responded with appreciation for food and medical supplies sent by the churches. The Episcopal Bishop of Hankow had lunch with a Communist general and reported that the general had apologized for earlier persecution and asked for close co-operation in building a better world. "And is there not here," the

Bishop asked, "both solid ground and enduring inspiration for the United Front of all constructive forces which our day requires?" [23]

Treatment of Roman Catholic missionaries in the Communist areas of China was often different. Spanish, Italian, and German priests came from countries whose governments Communists despised; there was considerable resentment of the vast property holdings of Roman Catholic missions; and the continuous attacks of the Vatican upon Communism created ill feeling. In spite of this, the strongly anti-Communist Bishop of Nanking, Paul Yu Pin, was quoted in the pro-Communist press in an alleged appeal for closer relations between Russia and China "if the Western Democracies do not come to our help." [24] General Chu Teh, commander of the Communist forces, attended a Roman Catholic mass and afterward addressed a large audience on the need for Christian-Communist co-operation. [25]

In the United States, a mass "Stop Japan" rally was organized at Madison Square Garden in October 1937. Harry F. Ward of Union Theological Seminary was chairman, and several ministers and rabbis took part. A number of missionaries wrote articles for *China Today,* the periodical of American Friends of the Chinese People, the principal Communist-oriented group championing the cause of China during the thirties. It is amazing from today's vantage point that not a single important American church magazine and no important American religious spokesman saw any validity whatever in the Japanese claim that they were saving China from the Communists. Americans of all faiths overwhelmingly favored the Chinese. [26]

The promulgation of a new democratic constitution of the Soviet Union in 1936 was also a propaganda triumph for the U.S.S.R. "Liberalism, despised in the house of its friends," said a *Christian Century* editorial, "has won over an enemy." [27] Even the *Presbyterian,* an extremely conservative church journal, was impressed: "France emerged from her holocaust of revolution into ordered constitutional channels more than a century ago, and now Russia looks out over the way to establish something like a real human government." [28] From those already committed to the U.S.S.R. praise for the constitution came as no surprise. Harry F. Ward, for example, hailed it as proof that "the economic democracy" started in Russia "is the only sound base for democracy in the political field." [29]

The combined impact of all of these and additional events was great. The rise of Hitler, the Ethiopian War, the rebellion in Spain, the invasion of China, the 1936 constitution, Russian appeals for disarmament—these were some of the developments abroad that helped the Communist Party in America. As the Western world floundered in depression, fussed over colonies, and was partially swallowed up in fascism, to many the Soviet Union seemed honorable and content in contrast.

CRITICISMS OF RUSSIA AND COMMUNISM

Why, then, were the Soviet Union and the Communists not more successful in winning the confidence of American churchmen?

There were many reasons. The New Deal was meeting the crisis in the economic order in a manner that satisfied many. The memories of the bloody Bolshevik revolution and the continued persecution of the church were also vivid in many minds. Walter Van Kirk, a leader in the Federal Council of Churches, returned from a visit to Russia in 1935 to report that on every side "one sees unmistakable evidences of the liquidation of religion." [30]

The pacifist *Christian Century,* for all its optimistic assessment of the U.S.S.R. in the twenties, never lost its objectivity about Russia afterward. In 1934, when Russia and France reached a military agreement, it said: "By linking arms once more with France, soviet Russia finally abandons any international revolutionary significance." [31] Two years later, when the military bonds between Russia and France were tightened, Devere Allen echoed the disillusionment of many pacifist leaders: "Until recently, the international role of the soviet union has been admirable in Europe; its new 'line' places it in a diplomatic position scarcely distinguishable to the general public from that of the imperialist powers." [32]

Perhaps the most sophisticated and perceptive comments on the Soviet Union and the American Communist Party were made by Reinhold Niebuhr, who became professor of Christian Ethics at Union Theological Seminary in 1928 after thirteen years as pastor of a Detroit parish. Niebuhr was a fiery Socialist through most of the thirties and the principal figure in the Fellowship of Socialist Christians, organized in 1931. The Fellowship published the quarterly *Radical Religion,* and in its pages Niebuhr and others expressed their views.

Niebuhr was a sharp critic of American capitalism. He accepted the concept of the class struggle and ridiculed the popular pacifist idea that a better society could be achieved through a reconciliation between capitalists and the workers. Though twenty years later, in 1953, Niebuhr was to "confess" that he had been "too uncritical" of Marxism in the decade of the thirties,[33] he was never blind to the weaknesses of orthodox Marxist theory, the Soviet Union, and the American Communist Party. Communism he saw as a dogmatic religious faith that was essentially correct in its analysis of the capitalistic system but totally unrealistic in the program it offered to the Western world. Marxism's main error, he felt, was its utopianism. It did not understand the tendency of man's sinful, self-centered nature to bring corruption to any social order, however idealistic in theory. His book *Moral Man and Immoral Society,* published in 1932, protested against the optimistic view of human nature and society. The volume had a revolutionary effect on Protestant theology and its implications as criticism of both capitalist and Communist society were clear.

In 1935 Niebuhr summed up his major criticisms of American Communists in a significant article, "Our Romantic Radicals." Niebuhr wrote:

The communist party, having a great deal of realism to its credit in its analysis of the catastrophic character of modern capitalism, is nevertheless a hopelessly sectarian movement in American radicalism. It wins support from the most desperate sections of the American proletariat but seems unable to hold it. Its turnover is unusually large. Its dual union policy, temporarily held in abeyance, closes every real avenue into trade union territory. Its Negro policy is so unrealistic that it could have been fashioned only in Russia. Its dogmatism, involving not only politics but every question of culture, philosophy and art, would be acceptable to vast masses of our disinherited population only after decades of fascist decay and international conflict had reduced our still vital cultural traditions to complete decay. It carries too much excess baggage in terms of a complete world view, partly derived from Russia and partly from German rationalism, and this unnecessarily accentuates opposition to its politics.[34]

Through *Radical Religion,* Niebuhr expressed himself on many issues of international consequence. He crusaded against the rising fascist movement in Europe and against Japanese militarism. He ridiculed the "privileged classes" in England and France, whose fear of Bolshevism, he charged, made them vulnerable to appeasement of Hitler. He was a caustic critic of American isolationism, but never minimized the evils within the Soviet Union.

The purges caused Niebuhr the greatest concern. He watched the eerie Moscow trials of January 1937 in amazement as leading Communist zealots of twenty years before publicly exposed their conspiracies against the Soviet Union, confessed their secret ties with foreign fascists, and begged punishment for betrayal of the people. If these men were really guilty, Niebuhr's *Radical Religion* contended, it casts doubt upon the stability of a regime that "nourishes traitors for years in positions of highest responsibility. . . ." If, on the other hand, they were innocent and Stalin tortured confessions out of them, "we have an even sorrier picture of the Russian regime." *Radical Religion* went on to chide American apologists for the Soviet regime: "It must be rather uncomfortable to be under the necessity of finding Russia a kind of Kingdom of God, no matter what happens there." [35]

The purges continued into 1938; an editorial summed up the unhappy conclusions reached by Niebuhr and most of his close associates:

It is the business of Christian socialists to look at the facts honestly. Those facts point to a tragic deterioration of Russian politics. In some respects this turn of events in Russia is more disheartening than the slow suicide of Europe. We had reason to expect the gradual self-destruction of a capitalist society. The growth of political tyranny in a socialist society is really a more tragic fact. It is like the premature death of an infant rather than death which follows senescence.

We might as well make up our minds to the fact that a new society must be brought to birth in European civilization without too much help from the Russian experiment.[36]

The Soviet purges had their impact in many church circles. As early as 1935, the *Christian Century* found mass executions in the U.S.S.R. proof that there was no more liberty in Russia than in Germany or Italy. As more executions took place, the *Century* traced them either to "a pathological state of nerves in the central political authority" or to "great confusion" that was leading to a total disintegration of the Soviet officialdom.[37] *The Friend,* a Quaker journal, commented on the lesson of "how insecure is rule based on the suppression of opponents." [38] Methodism's *Christian Advocate* thought the purges would doom the Communist regime, that they were "as sure a sign of the beginning of the end as fever is of disease," [39] and a writer in the *Presbyterian* wondered "if anyone is safe in that strange land, so full of suspicion and hatred." [40]

Not all church leaders or religious periodicals attacked the purges, however. At least one conservative periodical, the *Christian Standard,* thought initially that they were a good sign, that they signified the final triumph of the Stalinist Right Wing over the followers of Trotsky, who demanded immediate world revolution.[41] *Zions Herald,* a New England Methodist weekly, always tried to find encouraging signs in Russia during the thirties and held to the possibility that reports of the purges might have "emanated from the propaganda factory of some power hostile to Russia. . . ." [42] Later, its editors joined the chorus that decried the slaughter of more and more top Soviet officials.

A few churchmen came publicly to the defense of the Soviet Union. One of them was William B. Spofford, Sr., editor of the *Witness,* an independent Episcopal weekly, who visited Russia in 1937 and accepted the government's justification for the Moscow trials. Even before, he had signed an open letter assailing the Trotskyites and defending the executions.[43] His trip only strengthened his conviction. While choosing his words with care, Spofford wrote that it was not difficult to believe "that men like Radek, Bukharin, and Yagoda, passionately holding opinions that were contrary to those held by the communists in Russia, were led into plots with foreign powers." [44] He felt at times, he added, that there was "greater concern for civil liberties in Russia" than in the United States.[45]

Another defender of the purges was Jerome Davis, who also signed an open letter supporting the trials.[46] Later, in his 1946 book, *Behind Soviet Power,* he described the trials as necessary, praised Stalin for acting wisely and patiently, and claimed that the executions probably saved Russia from a large fifth column when Hitler attacked. At the time of the purge trials, Davis told how it was only natural that some early revolutionaries would have turned against Stalin; how the Spanish Loyalists might have avoided civil war had they executed more fascists before hostilities broke out; and how reasonable it was to assume that agents of two hostile nations—Japan and Germany—should try to subvert the Soviet Government.[47]

The views of Spofford and Davis were rare, however. To all but a handful of clergymen, the purges were an outrage that no amount of careful "explaining" could justify. Scores of leading Russian intellectual and military leaders were being executed. These events left a scar that would not quickly disappear. There was something dreadfully wrong within the Soviet Union.

In spite of these internal developments, there were still many churchmen who looked to Russia for leadership against fascism. It was to be a traumatic experience when Moscow announced that the fascists and Communists had come to terms.

FIVE · THE STRATEGY OF THE UNITED FRONT

"**B**etween the clasped hands of the Soviet Union and the United States, there is a half-dug grave—the grave of American capitalism." The crowd at the Bronx Coliseum cheered as a slight bespectacled professor from Union Theological Seminary, Harry F. Ward, spoke these words.[1] They had gathered in November 1933 to celebrate American recognition of the Bolshevik regime a few days before. Now, he said, the working people of this nation, like those of Russia before them, would break the chains of exploitation and poverty and usher in an eternity of peace and plenty for all. Ward's participation in the emerging Communist front was to become more and more important a factor in the relationship of American churchmen to the Communist movement.

In the thirties the Soviet Union began to look for prominent clergymen such as Ward to serve as bridges between the churches and organized Communism. The government of Russia was hysterical in its fear of "capitalist encirclement." Marxist dogma had declared that decaying bourgeois society would resist defeat in a final, furious battle in which the exploited workers everywhere would overthrow the ruling classes. The Communists needed all the friends they could find.

The believing Communist saw what he thought were signs of an Armageddon. The capitalist depression had created a rebellious proletariat—hungry and embittered—who looked to Moscow for hope. The citadel of the working class was surrounded by threatening hostile powers. Japan had seized Manchuria, bordering on Siberia, in

1932. Fascism was rising in central Europe. Russia's western frontier was ringed by small feudal or military powers often counseled by czarist refugees. The English and French governments would support the anti-Bolshevik crusade. The Papacy already was sounding the trumpets for a "Holy War." In America, the bastion of "Yankee imperialism," the "fascist" New Deal had come to power through hypocritical promises to reform a dying social order. So went the Communist rationale. Was it not obvious, they argued, that the workers' frantic enemies would conspire to attack the motherland of socialism?

The Communist counterplan first called for a giant proletariat phalanx to protect the Soviet Union. Then democratic socialists, bourgeois liberals, and even Roman Catholic workers would be welded together for the impending class war. The idea of the European "popular front" and the American "united front" had been born.

The first halting steps toward the united front came in August 1932 when a World Congress Against War met in Amsterdam. Two popular intellectuals, Romain Rolland and Henri Barbusse, issued the call. The purpose of the meeting was "to arouse the peoples of the world against the bloody catastrophe threatening them as a result of imperialist rivalry, and specifically the danger of an attack on the Soviet Union." Of 2,196 delegates present, 830 were actual members of the Communist Party and most of the rest were enthusiastic sympathizers. Their resolutions assailed the League of Nations as "the immediate mouthpiece of the imperialist powers" and condemned pacifism as "foredoomed to failure." Delegates promised to struggle against capitalism, "that purveyor of the slaughterhouse," and to fight for the Soviet Union, "the country of Socialist construction which we will not allow to be touched." [2] Among thirty-one delegates from America, there was only one clergyman, Rabbi Israel Goldstein, now honorary president of the American Jewish Congress. He later severed his ties with the movement because he objected to Communist domination.

The American Committee for Struggle Against War was formed shortly after the Congress to promote the goals of the Amsterdam Congress in the United States. It had prominent backing. Theodore Dreiser was elected honorary chairman and the sponsors included Roger Baldwin, W. E. B. DuBois, John Dos Passos, Corliss Lamont,

Sidney Hook, Upton Sinclair, Thornton Wilder, and Scott Nearing. A Unitarian minister, W. Lester Mondale, and a Jewish rabbi, Henry M. Rosenthal, were the only two clergy sponsors. Like Goldstein, both withdrew when they became aware of the Communist control. Miss Winifred Chappell, who served with Ward as co-secretary of the Methodist Federation for Social Service, was also a sponsor; she continued to give her active support to innumerable Communist enterprises until her death in 1951.

On March 18, 1933, the executive committee of the Communist International, known as the Comintern, gave its official blessing to the united front. At first its aim was to wean laboring people away from "reformist" leadership, but when this met with little success and the specter of Hitlerism became more frightening, the Comintern in 1935 called for unity among all antifascist forces. The Communists in the United States embraced President Roosevelt and the New Deal, became loud champions of religious liberty, and sought friends within the churches. Their main goal was the creation of a network of front organizations through which they could win the sympathy and co-operation of millions of Americans.

AMERICAN LEAGUE AGAINST WAR AND FASCISM

The most important of these fronts stemmed directly from the 1932 Amsterdam Congress. In September of the following year, the First United States Congress Against War was held, with 2,600 delegates registering. They pledged to oppose "the extensive preparation for war being carried out under the guise of aiding National Recovery" and to resist "all attempts to weaken the Soviet Union." From this Congress came the American League Against War and Fascism.

For those who doubted the Communist origins of the American League Against War and Fascism, two episodes during the First Congress offered further proof. One was the dramatic entrance of the French Communist author Henri Barbusse. The orchestra struck up "The Internationale," the audience arose spontaneously, and hundreds of delegates raised their right arms, with fists clenched, in the Red salute. Barbusse responded with the same sign.

The other episode involved Jay Lovestone, former secretary of the

Communist Party, who was ousted in 1929 upon orders from Moscow. He had since organized the Communist Party Opposition. A delegate arose at the Congress to suggest that, since all antifascist support was needed, a Lovestoneite should be included in the executive body of the League. Rioting broke out in part of the hall. Earl Browder was asked to quell the disturbance, but his opening words only succeeded in encouraging further outbursts. "Comrades," he began, "this issue has no proper place at the Congress. We are not here to elevate into importance before the masses little groups of renegades whose purpose in coming here is part of their moral preparation for intervention against the Soviet Union." [3]

The formation of the American League Against War and Fascism led to sharp debate among churchmen about the Communists and the united front. Winifred Chappell reported that only fourteen delegates to this First Congress in 1933 had represented religious groups. Several of these, she added, were Negroes who were there "from class-conscious rather than 'religious' motives." [4] Actually, many religious pacifists were present and several addressed the delegates. Two others served as chairmen of sessions. One was Reinhold Niebuhr. The other was J. B. Matthews, a Methodist clergyman, who had become an embarrassment to many churchmen because of his extreme leftist views. He was selected the first national chairman of the American League Against War and Fascism.

Religious pacifists divided over co-operation with Communists through the League. They obviously disapproved of war between nations, but what did they think of revolutions and class struggle? One view was expressed by the pacifist Devere Allen, who attended the First Congress: "The presence of almost every important pacifist organization and every leader of pacifism who could get there, clearly shows that pacifists have decided that it is inconsistent to co-operate regularly with capitalists who believe in international war but disbelieve in class war, while refusing co-operation with workers who believe in class war though detesting international war." He was impressed, too, by Russia's fervent pleas for peace; yet, Allen was not naïve about the purpose and origin of the League: "The pacifists and other non-Communists who entered into this Congress did so with their eyes open, knowing well enough that the major interest of [the] Comintern was the prevention of a war against Soviet Russia, and knowing that in accord with Communist tactics, the Communists could be expected to conceive of a united front only as united primarily behind their own particular doctrines." [5]

Opposition to the united front came from many sources. An editorial in the *Christian Century* warned that "to commit America's peace effort to a blanket support of Soviet Russia is to commit—unless Stalin changes his tune—to war." [6] President Henry Sloane Coffin of Union Theological Seminary stated flatly that he would never join the American League Against War and Fascism until it became the American League Against War, Fascism, and Communism.[7] Allan A. Hunter, Los Angeles Congregational pastor, warned that Christians "must stop being gullible about the united front." [8] In the final analysis, he said, it is a commitment to the war method which means murder, lies, and hatred. John Sutherland Bonnell of the Fifth Avenue Presbyterian Church in New York City thought those who supported the American League "are entirely mistaken in their judgment of Communism, whether in Russia or in this nation." [9] G. Bromley Oxnam wrote that "Americans who are interested in maintaining the liberties of political democracy will repudiate the united front." [10]

The most persistent and articulate critic of co-operation between Communists and Christians was Kirby Page, pacifist Disciple minister and editor of the *World Tomorrow*. Again and again he sought to impress upon his readers the "shameless hypocrisy" of Communism, its essential rejection of peace, its suppression of civil liberties, its abhorrence of religion, and its deliberate fostering of enmity, dishonesty, and strife. Page had warned in 1932 that "a Communist revolution would instantly drive America into the hands of fascism." [11] He charged later that the united front was a Communist game aimed at destroying movements "that stand in the way of their winning the workers to violent revolution and civil war." [12]

It soon became clear that debate among churchmen was to center around one issue: the class struggle, or—as many pacifists interpreted it—class war. The principal battlefield was the Fellowship of Reconciliation, a pacifist organization of 10,000 members in 1933, which exercised an influence among the Protestant clergy far beyond its numbers. Pacifist sentiment was strongly evident from two polls among ministers in the early thirties. A partial table of the results follows.

	1931	1934
Number of questionnaires	53,000	100,000
Number of replies	19,372	20,870
Those who "believe that the church of America should go on record as refusing to sanction or support any future war."	12,075 (62%)	13,997 (67%)
Those who are "personally prepared to state that it is your present purpose not to sanction any future war or participate as an armed combatant."	10,427 (54%)	12,904 (62%)

Since fervent pacifists may have responded in larger proportion than others, the poll's precise accuracy may be questioned. Nevertheless, it gives a clear indication of the wide prevalence of pacificism among the clergy.[13]

The dispute over class conflict finally led to a serious schism within the Fellowship of Reconciliation. A tense session in October 1933 at Swarthmore College brought the underlying division into the open. The First Congress Against War and Fascism had been held only a few days before. John Haynes Holmes warned that pacifism was going through its second great trial. During World War I, he said, it "crumbled beneath our feet," and now it was losing ground rapidly in the face of class war. Professor Arthur L. Swift of Union Theological Seminary joined in warning that those favoring class war raise "the same old cry for 'a war to end war.' " Pitted against Holmes and Swift were Reinhold Niebuhr and Roger Baldwin. Niebuhr assailed as futile "continuing to be true to certain principles rather than to achieve social justice." The Christian must seek to reduce violence to the minimum, he said, but it is unrealistic to assume that a better society will be established without some forms of conflict and strife. Baldwin went even further. The struggle of the hour, he said, was between fascism and Communism, "between more violence and less violence." The neutral, he warned, was on the side of fascism.[14]

A carefully prepared questionnaire was sent to the members of the Fellowship of Reconciliation. The published tabulation of replies showed an overwhelming rejection of class war. The question was asked: "Should the F.O.R. hold to non-violence in the class war as well as in international war?" Yes, answered 877; 97 indicated no.[15]

One immediate result of the poll was the decision of the F.O.R. Council, by a vote of 18 to 12, not to re-employ J. B. Matthews, who was serving as one of the Fellowship's secretaries. Matthews had endorsed publicly, in a slightly modified form, participation in class war. He was bitter at the Council's action, charged it with undemocratic procedure, and chided the organization's majority for naïve reliance upon love and moral suasion in the face of the reality of mushrooming fascism.

Some distinguished members resigned. Their objections were stated most precisely by Niebuhr, who was fast becoming a powerful and caustic critic of the pacifists. In an article in the *Christian Century* entitled "Why I Leave the F.O.R.," he accused them of ethical perfectionism which revealed "the failure of liberal Protestantism to recognize the coercive character of political and economic life." He aligned himself with those who are pacifists "only in the sense that they refuse to participate in an international armed conflict. Perhaps it would clear the issue if we admitted that we were not pacifists at all."

In terminology characteristic of his writing at the time, Niebuhr set forth his position on the contemporary scene:

Recognizing, as liberal Christianity does not, that the world of politics is full of demonic forces we have chosen on the whole to support the devil of vengeance against the devil of hypocrisy. In the day in which we live a dying social system commits the hypocrisy of hiding its injustices behind the forms of justice and the victims of injustice express their politics in terms of resentment against this injustice. As Marxians we support this resentment against the hypocrisy. As Christians we know that there is a devil in the spirit of vengeance as well as in the spirit of hypocrisy. For that reason we respect those who try to have no traffic with devils at all. We cannot follow them because we believe that consistency would demand flight to the monastery if all the devils of man's collective life were to be avoided. But our traffic with devils may lead to corruption and the day may come when we will be grateful for those who try to restrain all demons rather than choose between them.[16]

The F.O.R. split was important to Protestantism in the thirties. It could be traced in some measure to the influence of Marxism upon the political and economic thinking of an increasing number of clergymen. Once the class struggle was accepted, a major obstacle to co-operation with the Communists had been overcome. There were other obstacles, however, which were eventually to injure the efforts of the united front to secure support within the churches.

WARD AND THE LEAGUE

In February of 1934, thousands crowded into Madison Square Garden to protest the suppression of Austrian Socialists by the government of Chancellor Engelbert Dollfuss. The mass meeting was called by the American Socialist Party in co-operation with various labor unions. Though uninvited, Communists were urged by the *Daily Worker* to attend. They deliberately threw the rally into bedlam. The scheduled appearance of Mayor Fiorello La Guardia and of Matthew Woll, an official of the American Federation of Labor, served as their excuse for disorderly conduct. La Guardia was viewed by Communists as a "tool of Wall Street" who concealed his reactionary ties behind a fake liberal façade. Woll was variously described in the *Daily Worker* as an "N.R.A. strikebreaker," a "trade union gangster and racketeer," and a "spokesman for fascism."

The impact of this Communist maneuver upon the united front was instantaneous. From Detroit, J. B. Matthews wired his resignation as chairman of the American League. Devere Allen was one of many pacifists who discontinued all ties with the League. In the opinion of the *World Tomorrow,* the event was additional proof of "the futility of all united front efforts as long as Communist tactics are what they are." [17] Edmund B. Chaffee, pastor of New York's famous Labor Temple, came to the same conclusion in an article in the *Christian Century:* "Seldom does contemporary life throw up a better example of the folly of trying to build a better world with no sounder ethic than that of expediency." [18]

Matthews' resignation may have been a boon for the League. His successor was Harry F. Ward, a person particularly well suited to assist the Communists in this capacity. Ward was a popular church-man, a prolific writer, and a fiery speaker. He was the key figure in the Methodist Federation for Social Service and chairman of the

American Civil Liberties Union. A professor for fifteen years at Union Theological Seminary, he already had considerable influence among some of the best-educated ministers in the nation who had sat in his classrooms. Each day he was in a position, through his lectures, to present his views to young and restless minds. Ward was not sympathetic with the pacifists, whom he accused of seeking "to divide the forces working for peace and freedom at this critical moment of history [and therefore] prevent the social movement in religion from making its contribution to the impending social revolution. It is an unpardonable sin. . . ." [19] To Communists, his most important qualification, of course, would have been his deep-rooted dedication to the Soviet Union.

Ward's chairmanship of the League was an important step in his controversial career. No clergyman has played a more important role in the saga of Communism and the American churches. In recent years, he has several times denied that he has ever been a member of the Communist Party. Yet, since the early thirties, he has devoted his academic prowess and his endless capacity for productive labor to a fervent crusade on behalf of the world Communist camp. It was through his influence that many churchmen first came into contact with the ideas and the apparatus of Communism.

Ward was born in London in 1873 and came to the United States at the age of eighteen. He was ordained a Methodist minister at the turn of the century, joined the faculty of Union Theological Seminary in New York City in 1918, and emerged in the twenties as one of the most articulate champions of radicalism in the churches. At first, he looked sympathetically upon a variety of reform movements that promised deliverance from American capitalism. He zealously urged upon others a "holy, impersonal hatred against an evil system that is wrecking human society." [20]

Ward's life reached a turning point in 1931. He went to Russia, spent almost a year there, and returned fired with ecstasy over what he had seen. The Soviet Union, he maintained, was bringing to the world a new concept that was in reality a fulfillment of the ethics of Jesus. Communism, he said, was systematically crushing the evil profit motive that spurred on the American economy and replacing it with incentives of service and sacrifice. The United States should set for itself the same goal.

When Ward became chairman of the League, four new members joined the League's national executive committee, three of them involved in church work, including Winifred Chappell. The call to the Second Anti-War Congress later in 1934 reflected increased clergy participation. Four Protestant ministers, three Jewish rabbis, and a scattering of active church laymen and women were among the call's forty-two signers.

Ward's keynote address at the Second Congress stressed the necessity of broadening the League to reach Americans of all political and religious persuasions. He summarized its progress during the first year: the acquiring of a full-time staff, an improved financial structure, the launching of a monthly magazine, *Fight,* and the establishment of active youth and women's departments. He sought to quell the fears of those who fretted about Communist domination. "It is quite illegitimate," he said, "for any political group to seek to dominate this organization for parties or purposes." [21] He assured his hearers that he had not seen a "single manifestation" of Communist control. Meanwhile, the *Party Organizer* and other Communist publications were instructing their readers to flock to the League. Party members, it said, must give "immediate effective assistance" and "draw the various organizations in which they are active into the campaigns of the American League." [22]

Religious participation increased in the Second Congress, in part because of Ward's position as chairman. Twenty-five delegates were listed as "officially representing the churches." This was still by far the smallest category of the 3,332 who registered. ("Youth" was the largest, with 749.) The Chicago Methodist minister W. M. Waltmire, chairman of the Socialist Ministers' Fellowship, spoke to the Congress on behalf of the religious participants. He listed four goals for progressive churchmen: 1) "unite our forces with the working class"; 2) "puncture sentimental pacifism"; 3) "show religious people fascism necessarily grows from decaying capitalism"; 4) "organize among religious people units of people who will stand shoulder to shoulder with the working class until victory is won." Waltmire concluded his remarks in heroic fashion: "I may be a preacher, but I am on the side of the workers from now until death." [23]

A major campaign to enlist churchmen in the American League was conducted between the Second Congress in September 1934 and the Third Congress in January 1936. A religious committee was established under the leadership of Herman F. Reissig, pastor of the King's Highway Congregational Church in Brooklyn. Reissig had become active in the League for a number of reasons that attracted other clergymen as well. His strong pacifist inclinations made its emphasis on peace appealing. As a pastor, he was disturbed by the unemployment and resulting deprivation evident among some of his parishioners. He was disillusioned with parish life, and particularly with the lack of social concern among his lay people. He detested the Hearst newspapers—which were a major issue of the thirties—and was delighted that the League so sharply attacked them. A final motivation, perhaps the most important, was his fear that Germany, Italy, and Japan could overrun the world if united action was not taken to halt them.[24]

Reporting to the Third Congress, Reissig stated boldly that churchmen in the League had the duty "neither to commend nor to vindicate religious beliefs or organization. Our function is to *use* religious forces in the defense of masses of people." [25] But Reissig was frustrated in his work. The religious committee helped the League to give an impression of broad representation, but it actually accomplished very little. In assessing the committee's work years later, Reissig recalled that most clergymen avoided any contact with the League, primarily because even at its peak it never quite achieved respectability. Too many lay people, in particular, were convinced that it was a Communist front. For their minister or rabbi to join in its activities could lead to parish difficulties.

Much of the actual planning for work among the churches was done by the executive committee of the American League, in 1935 known as the National Bureau. In a message of August 9, for example, the Bureau singled out trade unions and three religious groups for special attention. Roman Catholics were the first target. Specifically designated were the International Association of Catholic Alumni, League of Catholic Men, Knights of Columbus, Catholic Association for International Peace, and various sisterhood groups, "some of whom have signed our Women's Petitions for total disarmament." [26] The League seldom was able to enlist Roman Catholic support, but when it did attract an individual Roman Catholic, whatever his degree of contact with the church, it was an occasion for great rejoicing. Jewish religious, cultural, fraternal, and Zionist groups were also listed as targets. Among Protestants, increased attention was to be given to the Y's, ministerial associations, local parishes, and to adherents of the Lutheran and Reformed faiths "because of their German traditions and friendships." Such elaborate plans were impressive on paper, but the League differed little from many other organizations in failing to carry them out.

From 1935 to 1939, the League sought to broaden its base. In January 1936 it claimed to speak for 3,291,906 Americans; in 1937 for 4,025,920; by 1939 for 7,836,691. These figures are exaggerated, at least tenfold, possibly nearer one hundredfold. Actual dues-paying members never were more than 20,000 (which was below the membership of the Communist Party at the time). Circulation of *Fight* finally climbed to 28,000. In 1939 the League was claiming 241 affiliated groups, eighty of them in New York City alone. More important, it helped launch various other fronts to influence public opinion upon such diverse subjects as race relations, civil liberties, Italy's invasion of Ethiopia, the Sino-Japanese conflict, and the Spanish Civil War.

The Fourth National Congress of the American League, held in November 1937 in Pittsburgh, marked an important turning point. The name of the organization was changed from the American League Against War and Fascism to the American League for Peace and Democracy to free it from the stigma of Communist roots and for wider sales appeal. The second step was to adopt a rule that no political party could be affiliated. The Communist Party, the only party involved, withdrew. This was not only a tactical move to counter criticism of the League, but an apparent effort by the Communists to achieve a genuine united front in which they would play a less important role. They now planned to allow Ward and others whom they trusted to run the organization. They were willing to take this small risk with the hope of attracting more liberals.

THE LEAGUE AND THE CHURCHES

What was the success of the American League Against War and Fascism—and its successor—in their efforts to enlist American churchmen and influence American religious life? The impact was slight

The official number of "religious delegates" at the five congresses is evidence of this fact.

Congress	Year	Total Delegates	"Religious Delegates"
First	1933	2600	14
Second	1934	3332	25
Third	1936	2070	57
Fourth	1937	1416	26
Fifth	1939	1274	26

Any clergyman or church worker would have been given an enthusiastic welcome. Yet only a handful attended—usually the same persons year after year.[27]

Why was this true? The charge of Communism kept a large number away. Probably many more simply were not interested in—or could not find time for—social crusading. Some thought it unwise to mix religion and politics. Others simply rejected the program of the League. Many were pacifists whose energies went into genuine peace organizations.

The most important reason for this failure, however, may be traced to the League itself. It struggled to be a nationwide grass-roots movement, but fell far short of its goal. It was imported from abroad and always retained an "alien" flavor, no matter how Earl Browder and Harry F. Ward tried to Americanize it. The League never reached beyond a few large cities.

Yet the organization did achieve moderate success in involving religious figures in places of responsibility within its structure. A few of these individuals moved from the League into the Communist orbit and developed such intense loyalties and close ties that they never moved out again. Ward himself was among this number. He had shown considerable independence of the Communists throughout the twenties. After five years as chairman of the League, however, very little of this independence remained. Ward was the united front's principal recruiting agent among churchmen.

A survey of the League's leadership in 1935 illustrates how important a role was played by a small group of churchmen. Fourteen officers were listed in *Fight*. Ward was chairman. The executive secretary was Paul Reid, a Quaker and former student of Ward's at Union Theological Seminary. Herman F. Reissig was religious secretary. Charles C. Webber, then instructor at Union Theological Seminary, was secretary of affiliations. Women's work was headed by Miss Dorothy McConnell, church worker and daughter of Methodist Bishop Francis J. McConnell. A sixth officer was Waldo McNutt, affiliated with the Rocky Mountain Y.M.C.A. William B. Spofford, Sr., editor of the *Witness,* became vice-chairman of the League and served as acting chairman in the absence of Ward. The Negro community was represented on the National Bureau by Adam Clayton Powell, Jr., who joined the Bureau on July 1, 1935. Of this entire group, all but two, Ward and Spofford, turned emphatically against Communism in years to come.[28]

The League was also successful, in a less impressive fashion perhaps, in its ability to secure the co-operation of both clergy and churches in support of specific projects. There were peace rallies in cities across the country—Chicago, Boston, Pittsburgh, Baltimore, Denver, Detroit, Los Angeles, and elsewhere. Clergymen were always among the sponsors and usually among the speakers. Not infrequently they served as chairmen of the meetings, sometimes held in churches. There were also peace petitions, peace ballots, peace exhibits, peace concerts, peace prayers, peace festivals, peace bazaars, peace strikes, and peace parades. Clergymen participated in most of them.

The 1936 Second Annual Westchester County Peace Parade held in suburban New York serves to illustrate the role clergymen might play. The *Daily Worker* boasted that members of the Westchester County Junior League marched side by side with members of the Westchester County Communist Party. Clergymen were in the line of march as well. Six local churches and one synagogue were among the sponsors. An Episcopal rector and a Negro bishop spoke. Harold Paul Sloan, editor of Methodism's *Christian Advocate* was quoted in criticism of such co-operation: "How any Christian can march in a parade with communists is beyond my comprehension. I'd just as soon march in a parade of brewers. . . . Jesus Christ had no more contact with Karl Marx than heaven has with hell." [29]

Many churchmen also joined in American League protests against events in Germany. In 1936 a campaign was waged to have the Olympic Games transferred from Berlin. During the Ethiopian War *ad hoc* committees were established to rally support against Mussolini, especially among Negroes and Italian-Americans. It was not difficult to secure the support of Protestant and Jewish clergymen for a number of League functions related to the Spanish Civil War. When Japan invaded China in 1937 another door was opened through which the League could reach churchmen. Meanwhile, it took the lead in assailing the Hearst newspapers, supporting liberal social legislation, defending civil liberties (except for American "fascists"), and battling for racial justice.

One of the other main objectives of the League met with less success. It encouraged affiliation of various religious organizations, but the Fellowship of Reconciliation specifically voted not to affiliate and most other key social-action organizations either followed the F.O.R. example or simply took no action whatever. This apparently included the National Religion and Labor Foundation, the Unitarian Fellowship of Social Justice, the Rabbinical Assembly of America, the Council for Social Action of the Congregational Christian Churches, and other groups that at one time or another sent either delegates or observers to League congresses. Another of these was the Church League for Industrial Democracy, an independent Episcopal group, headed by William B. Spofford, Sr., vice-chairman of the American League. In 1935 the C.L.I.D. voted not to affiliate. Then, the following year, the *Witness* (edited by Spofford) reported somewhat ambiguously that the matter "was finally left in the hands of the executive committee, with the recommendation, however, that the Church League should join forces with the many organizations, both secular and religious, that are now part of this united front." [30] The *Churchman,* another independent Episcopal magazine, was apparently confused by the final resolution and reported that C.L.I.D. had become "a cooperating organization in the American League Against War and Fascism." [31] In February 1938, however, the issue was resolved. The proposal that C.L.I.D. become affiliated with the American League was overwhelmingly defeated.

The second organization in which affiliation with the American

League was a controversial issue was the Methodist Federation for Social Service. At the height of the League's activities, the three secretaries of the Federation were all leaders in its activities: Ward, Winifred Chappell, and Charles C. Webber.

In October 1934, the membership meeting of the Federation voted to affiliate with the American League. This was only the beginning of controversy, however. Sharp debate continued within the denomination and the Federation. The *Christian Advocate* criticized the affiliation and described the Federation as "once a valued agency for bringing before the church social questions that were in danger of being overlooked or underrated, now a professed propaganda society for the overthrow of the existing order." [32] The *Social Questions Bulletin,* the Federation's publication, hinted at the tension within the organization. The major opposition came from pacifists. Again and again Ward tried to explain through the *Bulletin* and at Federation meetings that the League was not Communist-dominated. The *Bulletin* gave no indication that the question of affiliation was ever voted upon by the membership again. There was considerable feeling that, were this opportunity offered, it would have been voted down. Ward apparently never allowed this to happen.

Hence, the impact of the American League Against War and Fascism upon the thousands of clergymen and churches was slight. Even the widespread respect for Ward was insufficient to banish the suspicion, disagreement, and antagonism that kept so many churchmen away. Had the League lived on, perhaps with time this all would have changed. But as the summer of 1939 drew to a close, events in Europe were digging it a grave.

AMERICAN YOUTH CONGRESS LAUNCHED

One of the groups wooed most assiduously by the Communists was youth. The generation of young people who came of age in the Depression decade was troubled; four million of them were unemployed. There was a strong undercurrent of anticapitalist opinion among them, especially college students, and many parents stood aghast at the radicalism that seemed to be running rampant across the nation's most fashionable campuses. The New Deal attempted to cope with the situation through the Civilian Conservation Corps and the National Youth Administration, and more than 400 other organizations were concerned primarily with the future of this "locked-out generation." It was not surprising that Henry A. Wallace should declare in 1933: "The depression of the past three years should create a genuine Youth Movement." [33]

The decade saw the rise of groups democratically controlled by young persons in their own interests. Characteristic of this trend was the emergence of the National Council of Methodist Youth in 1934, which grew out of a feeling of rebellion against a denominational youth program that had been largely planned and directed by adults. A historian of the N.C.M.Y. described the first gathering: "There were no decadent dilettanti twirling between listless fingers cigarets and the slender stems of cocktail glasses. Here was a flaming youth, to be sure, but a youth aflame with love for Christ, having caught the contagion of courage." [34]

The traditional Methodist abhorrence of smoking and drinking was not on the agenda. The delegates wasted no time before condemning American capitalism as "unethical, anti-social, and un-Christian" and declared boldly: "We endorse socialism, as being at present, the most workable political expression of Christian social ideals." They wore "decision cards," which bore this pledge: "I surrender my life to Christ. I renounce the Capitalistic system based on economic individualism and the profit motive and give myself to the building of an economic order based on co-operation and unselfishness. . . . I believe that the possession of wealth is unbecoming a Christian." [35]

To meet the demand for a national youth movement, the American Youth Congress arose. Critics and some former A.Y.C. participants have described it as the most successful Communist maneuver of the decade and perhaps the most effective of the many Communist fronts. Such characterizations tend to oversimplify a complex political picture; yet, they contain more than a germ of truth.

The secret of the success of the American Youth Congress rests in the façade of respectability it carefully exploited. It exuded an air of youthful excitement and idealism. At its 1939 peak it boasted 513 affiliated organizations with a combined membership of 4,697,915 —a deceptive claim, since only a small fraction of these millions ever took any interest in the A.Y.C. Sixty-three of the affiliated organizations were national, nineteen of them church groups, more than any other category. Religion was always kept in the forefront. The first chairman of the American Youth Congress was listed as a "YMCA representative" from Colorado, while its last chairman was a Georgia-bred leader in the student Christian movement. Its letterheads abounded with the names of religious groups and religious figures.

The stage for the emergence of the Congress had been set by the student antiwar strikes of the period. At first, the primary organizers of the strikes were members of the National Student League, controlled by Communists, and of the Student League for Industrial Democracy, a Socialist group. By April 1934, the Youth Section of the American League Against War and Fascism had taken over much of the initiative. An important focal point of the strikes was the Oxford Pledge, originating with Oxford University students in 1933, when they swore that "under no circumstances would they fight for King and country." Communists, of course, were never pacifists, but they eagerly promoted the Oxford Pledge in these early years believing that sooner or later the United States would become embroiled in another imperialistic war, probably directed against the Soviet Union.

These strikes provided an arena in which Communist youth could work with religious youth. As late as 1934, the Communist Party assailed "bourgeois controlled mass organizations" for "furthering class collaboration" and listed by name the Y.M.C.A., Y.W.C.A., and Christian Endeavor.[36] This overt antagonism was rapidly vanishing, however, as the united front took shape.

Peace was a popular issue among church youth, many of whom combined religious idealism with socialist theories about the cause and cure for war. Results of the *World Tomorrow* polls in 1931 and 1934 indicated the trend of thinking among students at the better-known Protestant seminaries. Four questions were of particular relevance. Responses to the 1934 poll of 1,436 students for the ministry are summarized below.

	Yes	No	In Doubt or No Answer
Do you believe that the churches of America should now go on record as refusing to sanction or support any future war?	78%	13%	9%
Are you personally prepared to state that it is your present purpose not to sanction any future war or participate as an armed combatant?	73%	15%	12%
Could you conscientiously serve as an official army chaplain on active duty in wartime?	30%	49%	21%
Do you regard the distinction between "defensive" and "aggressive" war as sufficiently valid to justify your sanctioning or participating in a future war of "defense"?	22%	60%	18%

The poll also attested to other forms of radicalism among these Protestant youth. Half of the students favored socialism and 36 per cent preferred "drastically reformed" capitalism. Thirty students chose Communism; only thirty-one, or 2 per cent, picked capitalism.[37]

The roots of the American Youth Congress were apparently apolitical. An energetic young woman named Viola Ilma, who had visited Europe and been impressed with the verve of the various continental youth movements, decided to do something constructive for American youth. Her enthusiasm was high, but her program was vague. She announced the First American Youth Congress, to be held at New York University in August 1934 and sent out invitations at random, naïvely believing she could bridge the ideological chasms that existed.

Shortly after the Congress convened, bedlam broke out. What took place then and later is instructive as to the means through which the Communists eventually gained control of an organization. A speaker from the floor suggested that a permanent chairman be elected. A spokesman for Miss Ilma replied that this was for the executive committee to consider and that, in any case, she should be chosen chairman because of her industry in organizing the Congress. A group labeling itself the "democratic control bloc" fought her leadership with support from the Y.M.C.A., the Y.W.C.A., the Young People's Socialist League, the Young Communist League, and other groups. The issue was resolved finally when Miss Ilma adjourned the meeting and left with her supporters. Most of the delegates remained, elected Waldo McNutt from the Rocky Mountain Y.M.C.A. as chairman, and chose a fifteen-member continuations committee including, largely, Communists and Socialists.

Thus the "democratic control bloc" had plotted its way into control of a national youth movement it had not created. Years later James Wechsler, then a member of the Young Communist League, now editor of the New York *Post,* reminisced that "we were persuaded that Miss Ilma was a potential tool of American reaction and the very vagueness of her thoughts was regarded as sufficient proof that she was dangerous. Our coup, we were certain, had halted fascism on its own five-yard line." According to Weschler, McNutt's election had been carefully planned. "It was not generally announced . . . that he had been present at the communist faction meeting the night before at which it was decided that he would be spontaneously chosen chairman the next day." [38]

In the months that followed, the complexion of the Congress began to change. It helped organize mass antiwar demonstrations drawing in more and more members of churches and synagogues. Youth Day was proclaimed for May 30, 1935, to coincide with Memorial Day. In New York City, thousands marched under the slogan "We Honor the Dead by Fighting for the Living." The march came to a climax with a speech by Angelo Herndon, Negro Communist hero, and by assembled thousands repeating a solemn pledge to wage an unrelenting struggle against war. Similar demonstrations were held in other cities. In Chicago, particular effort was made to involve theological students and Negro churches. In Pittsburgh, the daughter of a Methodist bishop was scheduled to be the main speaker.

In their efforts to co-operate with religious youth, the Communists proceeded cautiously. Gil Green of the Young Communist League recalls one of the stratagems.

Many religious youths were skeptical about uniting with the Communists, although they were against fascism, because they feared that this was a trap to force our atheist views upon them. This problem was solved by simply agreeing to permit all religious youth in the congress to hold church services Sunday morning. This did not compromise the Communist youth and yet showed the masses of religious youth that this was not a united front against religion, but against political reaction.[39]

The results delighted the party leadership. As early as July 1935, Earl Browder could write in the *Communist* that "a large part of the success of the Youth Congress Movement has been that it has gotten the religious organizations of youth." He continued boastfully:

> We have learned that the youth of America are organized, most of them in religious organizations, and we are getting them in the Youth Congress; it moves from success to success, and the bigger it gets the stronger becomes the position of the YCL in it. It is the broadest united front we have ever seen in America.[40]

One Communist technique was actual infiltration. In the fall of 1935, the *Daily Worker* stated: "The YCL in the US has gone directly into the Y's, settlements, churches, and there reached the masses of youth that are not yet organized into unions and sport organizations." [41] A writer in *Young Communist League Builder* explained the way in which a synagogue club was used as a façade to start a local committee of the American Youth Congress.

> We have two comrades in a synagogue club which is an affiliate of the AYC. The YCL approaches this club to join a local [AYC] committee which we are going to build. . . . At every meeting that was held there were only three organizations—the synagogue club, the IWO [International Workers Order] and the YCL. In examining our work we realized that by involving the synagogue club more in the building of such a committee much more could be accomplished. Through the work of our comrades the [synagogue] club decided it would take the initiative in calling as many organizations as possible to a meeting [to plan a delegation to the Third American Youth Congress in Detroit in July 1936]. Calls were sent in the name of the [synagogue] club to almost 50 neighborhood organizations. In order to guarantee the success of this conference a group of comrades visited the invited organizations. At the conference there were 35 delegates representing close to twenty organizations with a total membership of 900.[42]

In some instances Negro youth groups also were infiltrated. A member of the Young Communist League reported at length in the *Daily Worker* in 1935 on the success of his unit:

About four months ago the section assigned my unit to do work in a church. Our first task was to get into the church. Immediately we sent the Negro comrades to join one of the clubs. This was easy, but the problem of getting our white comrades into the church confronted us.

This did not prove difficult, the report continued. The minister's welcome "gave us the opportunity to send additional forces into the church."

They then set about to achieve two goals:

1) To raise the political consciousness of the club generally. This to be done by transforming the abstract religious discussions into political discussions of the every day problems of the youth, backed by action.

2) To build the club and affiliate it to the American Youth Congress. . . .

They met with immediate success on the first goal with discussions on Ethiopia and Angelo Herndon. "In both instances resolutions were adopted and telegrams sent." They were not as fortunate on the second objective; the Y.C.L. member sadly related the experience.

A comrade went to the pastor and asked him to send a delegate, instead of putting it before the club. The delegate was not sent and we learned a lesson, that is, the next time such a question arises, it is to be put before the club and not some "liberal" pastor.

There was some good news, however. A delegate from the church youth group had been elected to attend the next American Youth Congress meeting. A Negro girl had been recruited into the Y.C.L. and the Communists had "three other contacts that we expect to recruit soon." The principal problem to overcome seemed to be among the Communists themselves. The report complained that they did not work hard enough and that they alienated some church youth by their "inability to judge sentiment." It concluded hopefully: "We are taking steps to eradicate the unhealthy situation in the unit, and in overcoming these problems we will be able to build a mass unit in this church." [43]

The techniques described above proved effective for the Communists. In the case of the synagogue club, they deliberately exploited it as a façade. In the Negro churches, their principal aims were to indoctrinate the youth and pull them into the American Youth Congress. Religion served as a tool of its bitter foe.

CHURCH YOUTH GROUPS AFFILIATE

An important year in the development of the American Youth Congress, especially in its appeal to church groups, was 1936. In January, the A.Y.C. began to campaign for the American Youth Act, a moderate plan it had worked out to aid young people. This brought the A.Y.C. national publicity, forged its first major link with the New Deal, and led to a close relationship with Eleanor Roosevelt, who on several occasions was host to A.Y.C. leaders at the White House.

This new respectability had wide repercussions, especially among religious organizations. The first to act were the Industrial Assembly and the Business and Professional Assembly of the Young Women's Christian Association, which met in April 1936 in Colorado Springs. The Y's had a proud heritage of social concern rooted in Christian idealism. A number of Y.W.C.A. staff leaders of the thirties espoused a quasi-Marxist viewpoint, and their influence was evident in some of the movement's programs and literature. It was not Communism they embraced but a utopianism borrowed liberally from the prophets and the Sermon on the Mount and influenced by the strong anti-capitalist atmosphere of the times.

Affiliation with the American Youth Congress was hotly debated at Colorado Springs. Many of the adult advisers were highly skeptical but they did not want to act arbitrarily against the wishes of the young delegates. One proponent of affiliation contended that "we should add to other groups the benefit of our Christian idealism . . ." and insisted that they could later withdraw if the Youth Congress "did not go in the direction in which we desired. . . ." [44] Unfortunately, too few persons understood the subtlety with which the Communists operated.

In September of the same year, another Y group, the National Intercollegiate Christian Council, which included leaders of both the student Y.W.C.A. and Y.M.C.A., voted to affiliate. Additional religious groups were listed as affiliates, among them the Epworth League of the Methodist Episcopal Church, the Young People's Division of the American Baptist Publication Society, and Young Hadassah, a Jewish society. Affiliated local groups included the

Youth Council of Abyssinian Baptist Church of Harlem. The Christian Youth Conference of North America, representing seventy-one denominational organizations, decided against formal affiliation but voted to co-operate on special projects. As time went on, still more religious groups moved into the A.Y.C.—and sometimes out again. There remains considerable confusion about which organizations actually joined, since unauthorized "delegates" frequently showed up. In other instances, groups lent their names to the Congress but did not participate actively.

One of the most vigorous and alert organizations to join the American Youth Congress was the National Council of Methodist Youth. A key figure in the N.C.M.Y. was Franklin H. Littell, who quickly emerged as a leader in the anti-Communist faction within the A.Y.C. He and others allied with him hoped that by careful planning they could free the Congress from all threat of Communist domination. They were supported by the Socialists, the Fellowship of Reconciliation, a few labor unions, representatives from the Pilgrim Fellowship (Congregational), the Quakers, and usually the Trotskyists. Despite their efforts, they finally lost. The Communists were shrewd manipulators who carefully exploited the differences among their opponents. They loaded the meetings with delegates from "neutral" organizations, who inevitably ended up in their camp. The Communists could usually count upon the support of representatives of the Y.W.C.A., who too frequently reflected their own individual views and not those of the national organization.[45]

"We ask, O God, that this convention become a creative movement in human history dedicated to Thy name." With these words of prayer a minister opened the Fifth American Youth Congress. By this meeting in July 1939 at the apex of its short life, the Congress had lost almost all outward vestiges of radicalism. Like the Communist Party, it was swimming with the New Deal tide as part of its strategy to expand and consolidate the united front. Indicative of the prevailing sentiment was a Presidential straw vote among the delegates and observers. Roosevelt received 904 votes. His closest competitor was Mayor La Guardia, who received 58 votes.

An impressive list of adults lent their names to the call for the convention: four United States senators, six congressmen, Secretary of the Interior Harold Ickes, Postmaster General James A. Farley, several governors and leading officials of the New Deal, and many leaders in the world of religion. Mrs. Eleanor Roosevelt delivered the main address and closed with the words: "May God bless you all and bring you success in the coming years."

To further the image of respectability—and to allay the doubts of liberals—a resolution was passed expressing the opposition of the Congress "to all forms of dictatorship, regardless of whether they be Communist, Fascist, or Nazi, or any other type. . . ." [46] Significantly, the Communist leaders abstained on the resolution, while rank-and-file members of the Young Communist League and their hidden Communist allies supported it! This deception, they undoubtedly reasoned, was a small price to pay to keep the organization united, growing, and above suspicion.

Those who still harbored fears of "Communist domination" were comforted also by the election of Jack R. McMichael, head of the National Intercollegiate Christian Council, as chairman. At twenty-two, he had all the qualifications the Congress could ask. He was tall, blond, and good looking, with a thick Southern drawl. He had graduated from a Georgia church college and just returned from a year in China, where he did student Y.M.C.A. work. He was planning to enter a seminary the approaching fall to prepare for the Methodist ministry. He was widely viewed as a wholesome Christian youth—idealistic and intelligent, certainly untouched by the ideology of Karl Marx.

Within two months after the sessions adjourned, Hitler and Stalin had signed a pact and Europe was in the throes of another great war. The impact upon the A.Y.C. was immediate and severe. What the Communists had so carefully built up came tumbling down. They won undisputed control of the organization, but when the smoke of battle had cleared, they looked around to find that everybody else had left.

NATIONAL NEGRO CONGRESS

The united-front emphasis led to a new Communist strategy among Negroes. Unity, popular support, and respectability took priority over party sectarianism. By 1935, Communists no longer monopolized the Scottsboro case but they had acquiesced in the formation of a broad Scottsboro Defense Committee. A white Congregationalist minister of unimpeachable integrity, Allan Knight Chalmers, became chairman of the new organization, which received support from Reinhold Niebuhr, Harry Emerson Fosdick, John Haynes Holmes, William Lloyd Imes, Adam Clayton Powell, Jr., Bishop Francis J. McConnell, and a host of other key church figures.

The case of Angelo Herndon followed the same pattern. Herndon, a Negro Communist, was convicted in 1933 on the charge of violating an old Georgia anti-insurrection law enacted before the Civil War to deal with slave revolts. The specific indictment was that Herndon had led a relief march of Negro and white families on the capitol building in Atlanta. It was charged also that he was in possession of "insurrectionary literature," including the writings of Bishop William Montgomery Brown. Finally, after years of controversy in the courts, the United States Supreme Court set the conviction aside by a 5-4 decision in 1937.

The Herndon case gave the Communists another wedge into the churches. The International Labor Defense held rallies and collected funds in Negro churches. Like the Scottsboro case, at first it was a Communist monopoly, but by 1935 a united front called the Joint Committee to Aid the Herndon Case drew in many religious institutions and leaders. The Colored Methodist Episcopal Church, a powerful Negro denomination, demanded Herndon's freedom. Petitions supporting him were circulated in hundreds of churches, and individual parishes adopted strong resolutions. Persons of differing political and religious views joined in fighting for his release. Herndon himself spoke frequently before church groups.

The Communists made their major bid for Negro support in the thirties through the National Negro Congress. Prominent colored leaders for years had envisioned one organization that would unite all factions to advance the race. Recognizing this widespread desire, the Communists proceeded cautiously. They decided from the outset that the National Negro Congress would not be overrun with comrades, that white Communists would discreetly keep their distance and that acknowledged Negro leaders would be given the positions of prestige within the new front. They followed their customary practice of controlling the office of executive secretary, through which, if necessary, they could effectively manipulate the entire organization.

The first meeting of the National Negro Congress was held in Chicago in February 1936. Of the 585 delegates attending, 81 were listed as "religious." That Communists still did not understand how to appeal to churchmen was evident. Dissension soon broke out when inadequate homage was paid to clergymen accustomed to exerting great power in the Negro community. The ministers accused the leadership of slighting religion, of trying to undermine the churches, of challenging the influence of the clergy. To atone for their poor judgment, the Communists, tongues in cheek, supported a resolution which described the church as "the most potent agency to be used in the further progress and advancement of our people." [47] For their part, the church delegates pledged themselves to work with non-Christian groups, to encourage sermons on social and economic subjects, and to set aside one Sunday in every five to bring the work of the Congress to the attention of their congregations.

All major segments of Negro society participated in the founding of the National Negro Congress. Communists like James W. Ford, Angelo Herndon, James E. Jackson, Manning Johnson, and Abner W. Berry played vital roles in the new organization, but the party made certain that their members were heavily outnumbered among the officers, executive committee, and rank and file. One new personality on the scene was Edward Strong, chosen as chairman of youth work of the N.N.C. Strong, the son of a Baptist minister, had once been on the staff of a large Chicago Baptist church and later served as national vice-chairman of the American Youth Congress. At his death in 1957 at forty-two, he was head of the southern regional committee of the Communist Party. It is interesting to note that his funeral was held at a prominent Negro Baptist church in Brooklyn—a rare departure from the customary Communist practice of death vigils for comrades in secular halls or funeral homes. [48]

When the Second National Negro Congress met in Philadelphia in October 1937, there were tangible signs of its growing prestige. President Roosevelt sent his greetings and Mrs. Roosevelt was listed as a supporter. The Lieutenant Governor of Pennsylvania and the Mayor of Philadelphia were present to deliver speeches. The executive secretary of the N.A.A.C.P. addressed the Congress. Even the Association of Catholic Trade Unionists extended its best wishes.

Participation of church delegates, however, dropped from the previous year—from 14 per cent of the total in 1936 to just above 6 per cent in 1937. There were other signs that the churches were not playing a significant role—of twenty-six members chosen for the executive committee, only one was a minister. In contrast, there was far more concern about the mushrooming labor movement among Negro workers, and A. Philip Randolph, head of the Brotherhood of Sleeping Car Porters, was re-elected president.

The N.N.C. remained strong in some urban areas after the 1937 Congress even though it did not meet nationally again until 1940. In a few cities the Congress overshadowed the N.A.A.C.P. After 1937, the churches did not play an important role in the Congress; when they tried to co-operate there was friction between the clergy and the nonchurch forces. The *Communist* summed up the situation in these words: "Church participation failed to reflect the important role it plays in Negro life." [49]

The National Negro Congress—like the American League Against War and Fascism, the American Youth Congress, and a score of other lesser fronts—had a dim future awaiting it. Suddenly, they were to be set adrift on the rough waters of the Hitler-Stalin pact. They were to ride the waves for a time, hoping that some word from Moscow might rescue them. But instead they were allowed to drown.

SIX · THE CHURCHES AND THE SPANISH CIVIL WAR

"**Y**ou must hark back to the massacre of St. Bartholomew in the Dark Ages to find anything to compare with the massacres of Burgos. . . . Catholics are put to the sword for no other crime than refusing to join any army but the 'army of God.' " [1] These words of outrage did not come from a Roman Catholic diocesan paper but from the *Daily Worker*. The Communists had found another tool in their attempt to pry open the churches—a double-edged tool, for the Spanish Civil War aroused both Roman Catholics and Protestants in America.

Spain had been a stronghold of Roman Catholicism for centuries; it was here that the Inquisition flourished, here that the Jesuits were organized. With the coming of the twentieth century, free thought and anticlericalism spread rapidly and by the mid-thirties those hostile to the church had forced the separation of church and state, established public, nonsectarian education, nationalized considerable church property, and dissolved the Jesuit order—despite bitter protest from the Vatican. Progovernment mobs pillaged some sanctuaries, abusing priests and nuns. For many Roman Catholics, therefore, the Franco uprising against the government was a holy war. Most of the Roman Catholic press and clergy in the United States agreed.

Americans generally were less excited about events in Spain. A Gallup Poll in early 1938 revealed that a majority had "no opinion" or "no preference" on the war that already had raged two years between the government forces and the Nationalist rebels.[2] But to other millions, the conflict seemed like a rehearsal for an international battle yet to be fought. On one side stood an alliance led by Fascists, militarists, monarchists, and dispossessed landlords aided by Italy and Germany. Against them were the Loyalists, a Left Wing coalition, supported by democrats, Socialists, and Anarchists and by Russia and the Communists. The American Communist Party lost no time in directing its zeal and its organizational genius to the Loyalist cause. The Spanish Civil War became a major concern of the united front.

The Communists first were confronted by a serious dilemma: How should they approach Roman Catholics? At the outset, they thought they could turn the laity against the church. "Are Catholics to throw in their lot with the Nazis in Germany who arrested, tortured and reviled Catholics?" a *Daily Worker* editorial demanded in September 1936, two months after the civil war broke out.[3] But this tactic endangered the building of "progressive" labor unions among Roman Catholic workers, for the Communists soon discovered that attacks upon the Vatican alienated rather than persuaded most Roman Catholics.

The Communists then devised new ways to influence Roman Catholic opinion. Five main lines of argument and action gradually emerged.

First, they hotly denied the widespread charges that Loyalists indiscriminately burned and looted churches and committed atrocities against priests and nuns. A few churches had been destroyed and a few clergy killed, but they quoted one Spanish cleric as saying: "Their destruction was called for by the turning of convents into fortresses against the militias and making holy orders the uniform of the enemy of the people."[4] Land had been taken from the church, but only to meet the demands of the people and of the "democratic priests." The Communists pointed to alleged rebel abuses. Typical *Daily Worker* headlines charged that "Fascists Execute 30 Catholic Priests Loyal to Madrid" and "Fascists Slay Many Priests in Basque Area." By 1938, the Communist press was charging that Franco was indiscriminately killing Roman Catholics.

Secondly, the Communists frequently cited rebel use of Moorish soldiers against Spanish Catholics. Said one *Daily Worker* editorial:

The character of [Nationalist] arguments . . . is typified by the fact that while repeatedly affirming that Franco is defending Christianity in

Spain, not one word is mentioned about the employment of mercenary Moors not only against religious freedom but against the government chosen by the Spanish Catholics themselves.

Communists were urged to cover the neighborhood of every Roman Catholic church with leaflets "appealing to the Catholic population to help their brothers in Spain who were being slaughtered by hired Mohammedan Moors and Legionnaires." [5]

The Communists' third line of argument was that a host of Spain's most devout Roman Catholics were supporting the government—and there was considerable evidence for their claim. One of the centers of Loyalist strength was the Basque region of northern Spain, home of a pious Roman Catholic people whose long-sought autonomy had been granted by the Loyalist government in 1936. In late April 1937, the defenseless Basque holy city of Guernica was partly destroyed. Loyalists were accused of setting it afire; they in turn sought to prove that it was bombed by German planes. One Communist writer provided this vivid account: "A Catholic priest blessing the peasants in the market place was riddled with bullets, his battered body left lying in the gutter as a symbol of Franco's 'protection' of religious freedom against the 'reds.' " [6]

As a fourth strategy, statements by priests sympathetic to the Loyalists were especially highlighted. Arguments by the theological canon of Cordoba Cathedral for Roman Catholic opposition to the rebellion were widely quoted in the Communist press. He declared that a Fascist victory would mean renewed control of the church by the privileged; that the church opposed rebellion against a legitimate government; that Franco's Italian and German allies were hostile to true religion; and that Franco's insurgents were struggling to keep the masses in ignorance. He praised the "high moral tone" of the Loyalists, "even among those who call themselves Marxists." They may not be saints, he added, but "Christ did not come to save saints, but sinners." [7]

Less than four months after the rebellion broke out, supporters of the Loyalists in the United States—overwhelmingly non-Communist, it should be remembered—brought Luis Sarasola, a Spanish priest, to the United States. Sarasola traveled around the country addressing fund-raising rallies. Accused by Roman Catholic spokesmen of apostasy, he retorted: "I am not and never have been an apostate.

I am a Catholic, a Franciscan always ready to obey the orders of the church." [8] The Communists took full propaganda advantage of Sarasola's presence.

In a bold bid to influence Irish-Americans, Michael O'Flanagan, another priest, was brought from Ireland to speak on the Loyalists' behalf. O'Flanagan had been a leader in the Sinn Fein in early years and was widely known among Irish nationalists. Like Sarasola, he faced bitter criticism from the Roman Catholic press. Congressman Vito Marcantonio and several trade-union leaders with obviously Irish names—all speaking as "fellow Catholics"—rushed to O'Flanagan's defense.

Finally, Franco's ties with the Nazis were emphasized. "Stop murderous Hitler intervention in Spain. Stop Catholic persecution in Germany," said the *Daily Worker*.[9] An editorial sought to discourage financial aid to the Nationalists: "Every dollar given to fascist Franco, let American Catholics remember, is a dollar toward the suppression and murder of Catholics in Germany." [10]

AMERICAN CATHOLICS' VIEW OF SPAIN

Communist enthusiasm for the Loyalists tended only to confirm many Roman Catholics in their mistaken view that the Spanish Government was completely dominated by "Reds." The hierarchy remained a pro-Franco bulwark. Many diocesan weeklies bitterly denounced prominent public figures and daily newspapers which sided with the Loyalists; they helped inspire Roman Catholic laymen to send letters challenging any public expression of opposition to the Nationalists.

Some incidents suggested the exertion of strong religious pressure. One involved sixty members of Congress who sent a telegram addressed to the Loyalist Cortes (Congress) concluding: "Your struggle sets a stirring example to all democratic peoples. As members of one democratically elected parliament to another, we salute you." [11] The signers included such prominent conservative senators as Harry F. Byrd of Virginia and Kenneth McKellar of Tennessee. Immediately, a storm of protest arose from Roman Catholic clerics and laity. The National Catholic Welfare Conference canvassed the sixty signers and reported that only seventeen admitted they had intended to endorse the Loyalists. Perhaps there was much validity in the N.C.W.C. charge that "leftists" had tricked most of the congressmen, but Roman Catholic protests apparently sent some of those who signed scurrying for cover.

There were important exceptions to this pro-Nationalist sentiment among Roman Catholics. One unpublished poll taken during the war showed this surprising breakdown of opinion among Roman Catholics and Protestants: [12]

	Roman Catholics	Protestants
Pro-Franco	39%	9%
Pro-Loyalist	30%	48%
Neutral	31%	43%

No Roman Catholic publication championed the Loyalists, but a few sought to travel a middle course. In June 1938, the *Commonweal,* an influential liberal lay Catholic journal, swung from a position favorable to Franco to an attitude of neutrality. The switch was explained on the grounds that information about the war was so biased that not enough objective facts were available to make an intelligent judgment. What verifiable evidence existed did not reflect favorably either on the Loyalists, who permitted violence against churches and the clergy, or on the Nationalists, who had allied themselves with Hitler and Mussolini.

In December 1937, a "Mary M." wrote a pro-Loyalist article for the *Nation,* "A Catholic Speaks Her Mind," in which she said that non-Catholics should not assume that all of the laity followed the hierarchy on the Spanish issue.[13] The church, she said, had no authority in political matters. The Jesuit magazine *America* published a reply to her article in which it sought to explain why some Roman Catholics espoused the Loyalist cause.

Some Catholics are emotionally anti-Catholic and vocal. They are eager to air their grievances before non-Catholics, they are proud that they can look up to heaven and tell God that they are not like other Catholics. . . . These emancipated Catholics are nearly all corralled by the Spanish Red Loyalists. They are blushing pink with shame because their fellow Catholics of the United States cannot accept with joy the murder of some 14,000 priests and good Catholics in Spain, because we American Catholics cannot approve the closing of every Church in Loyalist territory and the ban on every public Catholic service. On the contrary, they grow red in the face inveighing against truths and calumnies that have been inextricably mixed up by Communist propagandists. . . . What a shameful affliction it is for some of our brethren to bear an Irish name and to have been born in a Catholic family. They feel it so keenly.[14]

In contrast to the Roman Catholics, American Jews—religious and secular both—overwhelmingly opposed Franco, the friend of Hitler. Jews were in the forefront of pro-Loyalist activities in the United States and innumerable rabbis spoke out against the Nationalists. The Christian Front, inspired by Detroit's Father Charles E. Coughlin, cited Jewish support for the Loyalists to stir up anti-Semitism.

PROTESTANT REACTION

Like their Roman Catholic compatriots, American Protestants overwhelmingly have always been hostile to Communism. Yet, during the Spanish Civil War the majority of Roman Catholics expressing a preference favored the Nationalists, while Protestants choosing sides were pro-Loyalist five to one.

What made the difference?

Those who supported the Republican government of Spain pointed out that it was not Communist. In the election of 1936, it was supported by liberal democrats as well as by Socialists, Anarchists, and Communists. At the outset of the war, the Communists were a small minority without significant influence. Franco represented forces widely viewed as reactionary: the church, the military, the Fascists, the monarchists, and the feudal landlords. The Nationalists were aided by Germany and Italy.

Another factor played a decisive role in influencing the attitude of many Protestants toward the civil war—anti-Catholicism. Among many liberals there has persisted a deeply ingrained fear of Roman Catholic authoritarianism and a persisting belief that fascism is its political manifestation. Had not fascism first come to power in Italy, the seat of the Papacy, and had not the Vatican quickly signed a concordat with Mussolini? Critics uncovered "evidence" of Roman Catholic collusion in Germany, including even Hitler's recollection in his autobiography that as a child he had sung in his Austrian church choir. The church's support of Franco was seen simply as another proof of the basic unity between Roman Catholicism and fascism.

But other reasons made many conservative Protestants equally suspicious of Roman Catholicism. It was viewed by them as essentially an alien force bringing into the United States traditions contrary to the best interests of the nation—"pagan" rituals in a foreign tongue, hooded nuns, unassimilable immigrants, "moral laxity" in such matters as alcoholic beverages, and political corruption in the urban areas of the Northeast. A shrewd, tightly knit hierarchy was seen as a powerful subversive force plotting the end of constitutional government. Such attitudes as these had contributed heavily to the defeat of Al Smith only a decade before.

This hostility toward Roman Catholicism, whether expressed in its refined or its cruder forms, helped create Protestant interest in the Spanish Civil War. At first, there was widespread anxiety in Protestant circles lest America, under pressure from Roman Catholics, support the insurgents. This was intensified when Cardinal Pacelli (later Pope Pius XII) visited the United States in the autumn of 1936. The *Christian Century* ran an editorial entitled "Cardinal Pacelli's Vacation" which warned against "joining hands with any ally who sees Communism as a peril but who is complacent toward fascism and cooperative with it." [15]

Many Protestant ministers co-operated with efforts to rally support for the Loyalists. The precise relationship of the Communists to the innumerable pro-Loyalist organizations, mass meetings, and public statements is not easy to ascertain. Certainly Communist dedication, industry, and "know-how" were important in the formation and work of various united fronts of the period. Yet, it would warp history to suggest that those who supported the Loyalists were "duped"—even in instances where they co-operated with Communists. Rival groups were willing to set aside many of their differences where the issue of the Spanish Republic was concerned. Perhaps no group made more concessions to achieve unity than the Communist Party itself.

Two important organizations were headed by clergymen. One was the American Friends of Spanish Democracy, led by Bishop Robert L. Paddock, a retired Episcopal bishop. Paddock was a life-long crusader for social justice. He first attracted public attention as a young man when he exposed vice on New York's lower East Side. In 1907 he went to frontier Oregon, where he scandalized the communities when he arrived in a flannel shirt and a dusty cowboy hat. His health broke in 1922 and he retired as a bishop. The following year he married the heiress to a large fortune, and until his death in 1939 he and his wife were generous benefactors of many charities and liberal causes. In his will, Paddock designated Bishop Paul Jones, Bishop Charles K. Gilbert, and William B. Spofford, Sr., as trustees of his large estate and directed them to distribute the net income to organizations whose activities "tend to the betterment or amelioration of the social order." [16] Income from his estate is still parceled out annually.

Paddock's enthusiasm for Loyalist Spain stemmed from his belief that a Franco victory would be a catastrophe for humanity. He had no affinity for the Communists but was willing to accept the co-operation of all who opposed Franco. Along with Harry F. Ward, Paddock served as cochairman of the first large Madison Square Garden rally to support the Spanish Republic, held on October 26, 1936. Luis Sarasola, the Spanish priest, was the principal speaker.

American Friends of Spanish Democracy rounded up signatures to a number of public statements. In November 1936, they sent a warm cablegram to the Spanish Prime Minister. Its signers included distinguished public figures like John Dewey, Roger Baldwin, Arthur Garfield Hayes, and Emanuel Celler, and clergymen like John Haynes Holmes, Walter Russell Bowie, John Paul Jones, and Rabbi Stephen S. Wise. Within a few days another statement released by Paddock carried the endorsement of fifty-six clergymen, many of them editors of religious periodicals. "No Christian who cherishes either religious liberty or the principles of democracy and liberty," it said, "can fail to support those who are sacrificing their lives in beating back this desperate attempt to return to feudalism and the rule of privilege in the hands of fascists." [17] Other statements of a similar nature were released throughout the Spanish war.

The second organization headed by a clergyman was the North

American Committee to Aid Spanish Democracy, perhaps the most influential united front formed to aid the Loyalists. Bishop Francis J. McConnell, a beloved symbol of liberalism within the Methodist Church, served as chairman. The executive secretary was Herman F. Reissig, a Congregational minister who had also been religious secretary for the American League Against War and Fascism. The North American Committee sought to co-ordinate the pro-Loyalist activities of such diverse organizations as the American League, the American Student Union, the League for Industrial Democracy, and both the Socialist and Communist parties. It claimed sixty units across the country co-operating to distribute literature and to collect money and clothing.

One of the North American Committee's most interesting pamphlets was "Catholics Speak for Spain." On its cover was a robed priest chatting amiably with Loyalist soldiers. Inside were excerpts from Roman Catholic clergy, politicians, and newspapermen expressing support for the Spanish Republicans. Among those quoted were Don José Antonio Aguirre, leader of the Basque Nationalist Catholic Party; Canon J. M. Gallegos Racaful of Cordoba Cathedral; Leocadio Lobo, a Madrid priest, who died in 1959 while serving a Puerto Rican parish in New York City; George N. Shuster, then managing editor of the *Commonweal;* and the noted French Catholics Jacques Maritain and Pierre Henri Simon.

The North American Committee to Aid Spanish Democracy was strongly under the influence of the Communist Party in spite of the efforts of McConnell, Reissig, and others to maintain the group's independence. In February 1938, it merged with the Medical Bureau to Aid Spanish Democracy, which maintained hospitals and ambulances in Spain and was even more closely identified with the Communists. In early 1940, during the time of the Hitler-Stalin pact, tensions within the organization erupted into the open. Reissig and his liberal supporters were bitterly castigated for refusing to follow the new Communist "peace" line, and the effectiveness of the Spanish relief movement was crippled when it split asunder.[18]

RELIGIOUS CROSS FIRE

Public controversy between Protestant and Roman Catholic spokesmen in the United States did much to injure relations between leaders of the two Christian groups. This was well illustrated when the Roman Catholic hierarchy of Spain published a lengthy open letter in 1937 justifying the Franco revolt against the Spanish Government. Among its points were these: 1) The church did not want war but was forced to resist unjust persecution. 2) The elections of 1936 were unjust. The Right and Center parties received more votes than the Left, but they elected 118 fewer deputies because of fraud at the polls. 3) The Communists had armed a revolutionary militia prior to the rebellion and in effect had renounced the national army of Spain. 4) The church could not remain neutral in a fight in which one combatant renounced God. 5) While the church recognized and regretted certain weaknesses in the Nationalist cause, only a Nationalist victory could bring justice and peace back to the country.

This pastoral letter provoked a swift and strong reaction in American Protestant circles. "Here is nothing but human arrogance and pride," said *Radical Religion,* edited by Reinhold Niebuhr. "It seems never to have occurred to these ignorant bishops to explain why the poor people of Spain hate the church so much." [19] A public reply was prepared by Guy Emery Shipler, editor of the *Churchman,* and signed by 150 Protestant clergymen, educators, and laymen. Shipler and his cosigners depicted the war as one between "the forces of democracy and social progress, on the one hand, and the forces of special privilege and their Fascist allies on the other." They accused the hierarchy of failure to utter a word of disapproval "of the systematic destruction of Protestant missions which have grown up in Spain since the Republic was established" and "of the execution of many Protestant ministers by the rebels." [20] This charge had been made first in November 1936 when the North American Committee to Aid Spanish Democracy published a list of alleged atrocities against Protestants and Jews.

A third party entered the controversy ten days later. A group of 175 American Roman Catholics claimed that the Protestant statement "misrepresented the facts and issues in Spain." Had not the rebellion erupted, a Soviet dictatorship would exist in Spain and the church would have been savagely oppressed. Already the Loyalists had "massacred virtually all priests in an attempt to destroy the Catholic religion." [21] Distinguished persons signed the protest: former governor Alfred E. Smith; Martin H. Carmody, Supreme Knight of the Knights of Columbus; John M. Dealy, National Commander of the Catholic War Veterans; and the editors of most well-known Roman Catholic periodicals and newspapers across the country.

Bishop Paddock proposed that three signers from each American statement proceed to Spain "with the shortest possible delay and there conduct a full investigation of the matters in dispute." [22] The Spanish Ambassador officially extended an invitation to such a fact-finding commission, but no official Roman Catholic reply was made. During the course of the conflict, a number of Protestants from both the United States and England visited Spain, but what they observed supported the views they held before they went.

For many Protestants, the war in Spain was a clear-cut contest between good and evil. William B. Spofford, Sr., saw it as "a struggle between reaction and progress; between human rights and property rights; between Democracy and Fascism." [23] Sherwood Eddy stated his views in even stronger language:

> The Spanish revolution is a struggle for independence like that of the American colonies. But it is a struggle against wrongs a hundred times as great as those our forefathers endured, wrongs suffered for two thousand years. It is a fight to halt the world advance of fascist dictatorships which mark the last stage of disintegrating capitalism.[24]

But there were some dissents among Protestant spokesmen. The *Presbyterian* continuously ridiculed "radicals" who were ready to fight in far-distant lands,[25] and the *Living Church,* an Episcopal weekly, pleaded with the bishops of the church to recognize the evils on both sides.

> The fact that the Roman Catholic hierarchy has chosen to take sides in the Spanish conflict is no reason for our own bishops to do so. . . . The cruelty is not all on one side in the Spanish conflict or in any other war. Spanish loyalists have shot down thousands of civilians in cold blood including priests, monks, and nuns.[26]

Even among Loyalist sympathizers, there was a sharp cleavage between those who wanted the United States to assist the Loyalists and those who advocated strict nonintervention. Many pacifists were faced with a crisis, and some were swept out of the pacifist movement altogether. Others supported the Loyalists on the grounds that they were involved in a "police action"—and that to supply them with arms was no different in principle from supplying policemen with billy clubs. The *Christian Century* bitterly assailed Franco, but at the same time stated the case for absolute neutrality. "Sympathies for one side or the other in that savage war are inevitable," it said, but "no group can do this country a greater disservice than to make it a partisan and a participant in that conflict." [27] On a later occasion it wrote: "The stark truth is that both sides—both Catholics and the shadowy liberal organizations trying to aid Madrid—are mixing in a terrifyingly dangerous business." [28]

The Spanish Civil War, to sum up, made a great impact upon America's religious circles—and the Communists were working assiduously right in the midst of it all.

Communist support of the Loyalists made the Roman Catholic hierarchy even more firm in its support of Franco. Among the laity, however—and especially among Roman Catholics in the labor unions—Communists doubtless exerted some influence, not as open party members espousing the Loyalist cause but as secret comrades speaking at union meetings and injecting their views into the multitude of official union publications that came regularly into millions of homes.

The success of the Communists within Protestant circles is equally difficult to assess. Perhaps if Communists had not been as active, even more Protestants would have supported the Loyalist cause. A few other conclusions seem justified.

First, Communist fronts and other organizations under heavy Communist influence were able to involve many leading churchmen. Some clergymen were officers. Of the twenty-nine national sponsors listed in the summer of 1938 by the Medical Bureau and North American Committee to Aid Spanish Democracy (the combined organization), twelve were in the religious field, including such distinguished bishops as Benjamin Brewster, Edward L. Parsons, and G. Bromley Oxnam and such well-known rabbis as Edward L. Israel and Abba Hillel Silver. None of these, of course, was sympathetic to Communism. They all hated fascism and believed that most Loyalists were democrats.

Second, the Spanish Civil War was another in a series of events in the thirties that put the Soviet Union in a favorable light. France, England, and the United States sympathized with the Spanish Republic but did nothing. Russia alone tried to help—another indication to some that she was the bulwark against fascism. There was also a growing feeling that Russia alone dared stand firm against the Vatican—a stance she was to demonstrate again after World War II.

The Spanish Civil War aided the Communists in a third way. It left behind a reservoir of fervent pro-Loyalist sentiment that could be tapped for other purposes in years to come. For another decade and longer, the Communists carried the torch for Spanish refugees. Their appeal was to touch many hearts and pocketbooks—and in doing so caused harm to the reputations of some outstanding church leaders.

The Communists were learning much about religion. The Spanish Civil War made them more aware than before of both the urgency and the possibility of appealing to churches of all faiths, including the Roman Catholic. In 1937 they were to launch a full-scale campaign—the "outstretched hand policy" to win the confidence of American Roman Catholics. It was far removed from the attacks upon Roman Catholicism of the two previous decades.

SEVEN · THE "OUTSTRETCHED HAND" TO ROMAN CATHOLICS

In October 1937, the French Communist leader Maurice Thorez proclaimed the policy of the "outstretched hand" to Roman Catholics. Jesus and Paul, he said, preached socialism. During the medieval period monasteries and nunneries, those "Communist groups in intention, deed, and action," fought against the feudal system. Gothic cathedrals are "pure jewels of people's art," and their builders can be compared with Russia's Stakhanovite heroes. Thorez now discovered in the encyclicals of the popes the same indictments of capitalism that the Communists had made.[1]

The "outstretched hand" policy led to an intense but brief one-sided love affair. The Communist propaganda apparatus in France and the United States set as its main goal co-operation with Roman Catholics. The Archbishop of Paris, after consultation with Pope Pius XI, quickly rejected the offer of co-operation. In doing so he concluded with a generalized statement to the effect that if Communists sincerely wished to be better acquainted with Roman Catholics "in order to give better respect to the religion which inspires them . . . the Church will not refuse to carry out this work of enlightenment."[2] A *Daily Worker* editorial promptly warped the Archbishop's words, which, it said, "declared in effect that it was the duty of the French Catholics to accept the 'outstretched hand' of the Communist Party for socially beneficial objectives."[3]

The American Communists parroted their French comrades with

enthusiasm. The party's national committee issued a statement lauding Roman Catholic laboring men who "have been among the staunchest fighters for the economic and civil rights of our people." [4] Statements by a cardinal, a bishop, two priests, and a nun were quoted and their "progressive Catholic sentiments" praised. The national committee expressed the certainty that "Catholics understand us and our aims. . . ." [5]

In early 1938, Earl Browder prepared "A Message to Catholics." "True," he said, "most Communists are not Catholics, although a growing number of the latter are joining our Party." [6] Yet, there is no need for friction between the two groups. "Only as a result of the rise of Soviet power," Browder continued, "were Roman Catholics given equality and freedom of worship in Moscow." [7] They are closer together than generally believed, he went on, in matters of ethics and family morality; both face bigotry in America; both are accused of owing allegiance to a foreign power; both are close to the problems and aspirations of the working class; both seek to make a better society based upon justice and equality for all; both face a deadly foe in fascism. "Surely in the face of this terrible menace, which hovers over America as well as Europe, we should all rise above differences to join hands for our common salvation, just as we would to meet some terrible natural calamity." [8]

The Communists went to great lengths to bring Browder's "message" to Roman Catholic attention. "In many branches," the *Party Organizer* reported, "copies of this brilliant pamphlet have been mailed to local priests and Catholic leaders." [9] In July 1938, a member of the staff of St. Patrick's Cathedral told the press that all the clergy there had received letters from the New York Committee of the Communist Party with Browder's remarks enclosed in pamphlet form. [10] The response of the church was predictable—a flat rejection. Undismayed, the Communists kept claiming that the Pope had accepted the outstretched hand and quoted statements by American Roman Catholic spokesmen, carefully lifted out of context, to convey the impression that these, too, had endorsed the united front. They distributed appeals to Roman Catholics in factories and at union meetings and outside the churches after mass Sunday mornings.

The Communist Party had come a long way from the antireligious period of the early revolutionary days to the "outstretched hand" of 1937.

What had happened during the intervening twenty years?

AMERICAN CATHOLICS AND THE EARLY BOLSHEVIKS

When the Bolsheviks seized control of Russia in 1917, American Roman Catholic spokesmen were more interested in American participation in World War I and crises in Ireland and Mexico than in the events of Eastern Europe. To be sure, there was distress at the breakdown of the Russian front and the rise of an atheist regime. Yet, some Roman Catholic observers predicted that good might result from the downfall of the Czar. Poland emerged as an independent nation devoted to the Papacy. The Bolsheviks had proclaimed equality for minority religious groups. And in October 1918, the Jesuit magazine *America* reported:

> The Holy Father has appointed bishops for six dioceses which the Czar had suppressed. The Titular of the new see of Minsk was recently consecrated at Warsaw, and another bishopric will be founded in Siberia. The Ruthenians are reported to be returning in throngs to the Church, and numberless Russians of all classes are becoming converts. So, notwithstanding the destitution brought upon them by the suppression of endowments, the Catholic clergy are full of confidence and enthusiasm. The Soviet's attitude toward the religious authorities is said to be "consistently and irreproachably correct," a slightly preferential treatment . . . indeed, being shown the Catholic Church perhaps because she was formerly oppressed by the Czar, and because the Orthodox clergy are suspected of holding reactionary opinions. Corpus Christi, it is reported, was publicly celebrated this year in Petrograd with great splendor.[11]

Optimism continued to characterize comments of a number of Roman Catholics for several years. A professor in Petrograd's Ecclesiastical Academy wrote in 1918 that "Catholicity is now flourishing where it barely breathed under the rule of the cowardly tyrant a couple of years ago." [12] A correspondent for the National Catholic Welfare Conference reported in 1921 that the Russian Bolsheviks— unlike those who appeared in Hungary, Bavaria, and elsewhere in Europe—were content to overthrow the despised Russian Orthodox

Church. "Thus, the Catholics, who labored under many restrictions and disabilities during the Czarist regime, found many new advantages in the new situation." [13] Stories poured out of Russia telling of religious processions through the streets, of the restoration of ikons in public and private places, of crowded churches and a revival of faith. Russia now appeared as a vast missionary field ripe for Roman Catholicism.

Trouble spots soon developed. Reports of the looting of churches, the murder of priests and nuns, atheist teachings in the schools, and widespread free love, divorces, and abortions caused growing uneasiness. In 1922 Pope Pius XI demanded of the U.S.S.R.: complete freedom of conscience for all, no interference in public and private exercise of religion, return of immovable property which was seized from religious bodies. The Communists claimed that the first two conditions were in force and that they had no intention of giving back vast estates. The most serious conflict between the Bolsheviks and the Church of Rome in these early years concerned the trial of Archbishop Zepliak and eighteen other priests charged with treasonable acts against the regime. Zepliak was sentenced to death, but the protests of the Papacy, supported by the United States and other countries, were so vigorous that the Soviet Union relented and spared his life. A monsignor, however, was executed.

In January 1924, Lenin died and some of the Roman Catholic press again sought to be optimistic. Said the distinguished London paper *The Tablet,* influential with the English-speaking intelligentsia of the church: "Not only Catholics, but decent people generally, await early news of the release of the imprisoned ecclesiastics in Russia." [14] With Stalin's ascent to power and his failure to relax the antireligious policy came the end of hope. The new Russia was accepted and regretted as a fact.

The whole Roman Catholic world prayed for Russia at the request of the Pope in September 1924 and plans were made for the conversion of Russian leaders and people. A seminary was opened for Russian boys in Vienna and young priests were trained for future missionary work in the U.S.S.R. The *Daily Worker*'s headlines proclaimed its response to the news: "Priests to Spy on Soviet Government" and "Roman Opium Joint to Train Dope Peddlers." A *Daily Worker* editorial in December 1924 even charged that "the so-called pontifical relief mission to Russia was an espionage and propaganda expedition, just like the American relief organization under Secretary [Herbert] Hoover." [15]

The Irishman T. J. O'Flaherty, himself a former Roman Catholic, summed up the Communists' general indictment of the Roman Catholic Church:

> The Roman Catholic Church is the bitter enemy of the emancipation of the workers of all lands from the robber rule of capitalism. It wants to keep them enslaved so that in their misery they will look to a world beyond the grave for consolation and a reward for the miseries they suffer in this world. While believing this humbug they are easy prey for the clergy of all denominations who in return for a fee, promise them access to the sanctum sanctorum of a deity who exists only in the imagination of the clergy who have commercialized religion and made it into the best paying business in the world today, outstripping even the oil business. [16]

Yet, beneath Communist malice, there was considerable fear and not a little respect, as Max Bedacht, one of the party leaders, indicated in the mid-twenties:

> The Catholic Church is and has been one of the strongest and most consistent counter-revolutionary forces in society. In [our] struggles we find this organization a formidable opponent. The reason for this is its ideological unity and its organizational centralization. If we revolutionists have not already learned these lessons in our experience, we could learn the value of ideological unity and organizational centralization from the Catholic Church. [17]

Papal pronouncements and appointments were viewed as part of the Vatican's sinister maneuvers. In 1924 several Americans were elevated by the Pope, an act scrutinized very carefully by a leading Communist writer, William F. Dunne. The Vatican, he wrote, now realized that the United States was the only remaining stable capitalist nation where Roman Catholicism was powerful. It would look increasingly to America for financial and political support. To prepare for this, the Pontiff was carefully consolidating his position among the various nationality groups in the country. Irish Catholics would be satisfied with the selection of Patrick Hayes as a cardinal; Roman Catholics of German descent would greet the elevation of George Mundelein to cardinal. A Lithuanian was made a monsignor and a Polish-American newspaper editor a knight of St. Gregory. Dunne saw it all as a plot hatched by the House of Morgan and carried out gladly by the Pope. The end result would be a bloody crusade to preserve and spread the power of finance capitalism. In exchange, the ruling class would allow the Vatican to "again make the catholic church the only religious power worth mentioning in Christendom." [18]

To document their case, the Communists pointed to Mexico. A revolutionary government had secured control of the country and in 1917 proclaimed a new constitution that sharply restricted the privileges of the church. Roman Catholic journals reported widespread atrocities against the clergy, the breakdown of law and order, and the oppression of the Mexican people by ruthless, atheistic forces. They warned that a beachhead for Bolshevism was being established on America's southern border. Some priests and laymen demanded action to insure justice and stability. The *Daily Worker,* on the other hand, saw American businessmen, regardless of creed, conspiring with the Pope. "There is no question," an editorial stated in August 1926, "but that Wall Street is seeking an excuse for intervention." [19] Without capitalist aid, the "black vultures of the papacy could not croak their propaganda against the welfare of the workers and peasants of Mexico." [20]

The Roman Catholic Church was savagely ridiculed in the Communist press. T. J. O'Flaherty analyzed its power in terms of its multifold organizations. "There are societies and sodalities for practically every one of the innumerable saints, virgins, ghosts and saviors dug out of the graveyard of mythology," he wrote.[21] Roman Catholicism thrives on ignorance, he continued, and the Papacy was afraid because the Mexican Government promised to abolish illiteracy. A *Daily Worker* editorial lampooned the church for invoking the "talismanic powers of sacred, saintly shinbones" on behalf of the Mexican hierarchy.[22] When the Knights of Columbus set a goal of one million dollars to assist the church in Mexico, the Communist paper reminded readers of the Inquisition: "How many thumb screws, racks and iron virgins one million dollars would buy." [23]

Communist headlines found many religious targets: "Priests enjoy luxury while miners starve; holy parasites give blessings for cash." "O, Be Jubilant! Pope Grants Wage Increase to Hard-up Cardinals."

Other articles told how St. Patrick's Cathedral "celebrated" the breaking of a gravediggers' strike, how the hierarchy took funds from poor boxes to propagandize against Russia, and how a working-class mother killed a priest who attacked her daughter. Roman Catholic charitable institutions were places "where the minds of the inmates are stunted with religious poison, where their labor power is exploited to the utmost to make profits for the catholic church, where sex is suppressed and terrorism reigns supreme." [24] Prelates were said to meet regularly with gangsters and Tammany Hall representatives behind St. Patrick's Cathedral to "divide boodle collected from the purveyors of the 101 varieties of crime in New York. Wherever exploitation exists, the church is not far away." [25]

THE VATICAN'S "HOLY WAR"

In 1930 the Soviet Government directed a new drive against religion. Pope Pius XI issued a statement which saluted imprisoned priests and nuns, deplored the atheistic indoctrination of youth, and called upon the whole world to unite in prayers for the faithful of Russia. Protestants, too, responded, among them the Archbishop of Canterbury and William T. Manning, Episcopal Bishop of New York, who set aside a special Sunday for prayer for the persecuted churchmen.

The American Communists were convinced that an attack upon the Soviet Union could be expected momentarily. An article in the *Communist* of March 1930 analyzed alleged papal strategy:

> The choice of issues and slogans (defense of religion, defense of the kulaks) has been calculated in the first place to mobilize the cannon-fodder which would be the first to be thrown into such a war, namely, the Catholic peasantry of Poland and Roumania. . . . From the Pope, the campaign has been extended to the Archbishop of Canterbury, to all the Protestant sects down to the Salvation Army, to the Jewish Rabbis. With one voice the "servants of God" call for blood, for the intervention of military power. The alliance of "cross and cannon" is open and brazen.[26]

From February through May 1930, the Communist press campaigned vigorously against the Vatican's "Holy War." Some traditional arguments were used, and new ones emerged with four major lines of debate.

1) Their attack upon religion generally was intensified; antireligious writings of Marx, Lenin, and Stalin were reprinted and clergymen were depicted as greedy puppets of the capitalists perpetuating fantasies of "heaven" to keep the workers from rebelling against conditions on earth. These same clergymen were said to fear Russia because the scientific emphasis in the Soviet educational system automatically doomed religious superstition. There would be no more jobs for "sky pilots."

2) The church was linked to other foes. A former pope was identified with a hated czar, while Pius XI was described as "the Vatican hireling of international imperialist banditry" [27] and accused of an alliance with Trotskyists and ties to Mussolini. Financial backing for the "Holy War" would come from Wall Street interests. One cartoon showed the Pope, heavily armed, praying to the dollar sign: "Give Rockefeller and Me Strength to Help the Poor Russians." [28]

3) Charges of religious persecution in the Soviet Union were denied and statements by leaders of the Orthodox Church praising the government were published. The Chief Rabbi of Minsk said Jews enjoyed religious liberty and warned fellow Jews throughout the world not to support Vatican policy.[29] The following day six other rabbis issued a similar appeal. Churches had been closed or religious observances restricted only to meet the "demands of the people," the Communists said. An instance was cited of a bishop of the Ukraine who left the priesthood and sought to dissolve his diocese because he had been awakened to the counterrevolutionary role of the church.[30]

4) The Communists assailed churches on the question of religious freedom, and recalled oppression of religious dissenters by the czars. A typical cartoon showed the ghosts of martyrs led by Galileo. Under it were the words: "The Pope Speaks for 'Freedom of Conscience.' " The Roman Catholic Church was described as "an institution whose record of torture, violence, and bloodshed fills pages of gory history over a period of a thousand years." [31]

American recognition of Soviet Russia in 1933 came over nearly solid Roman Catholic opposition. The National Council of Catholic Men had warned that the international obligations of any nation were meaningless if its leaders warred against God. Even the most liberal journals, such as *America* and *Commonweal,* attacked recognition. For the *Interracial Review,* Russia was outside the community of civilized nations.[32] The *Catholic Worker,* an independent radical critic of capitalism, declared in a page-one box: "The Catholic Worker believes that Soviet Russia, in view of its militant atheism, should not be recognized by the United States." [33]

ATTEMPTS AT A UNITED FRONT

Communist policy toward Roman Catholicism began to change slightly in 1933, the year the Comintern issued its first call for a united front, and by 1938 the American Communist Party placed fraternalism with the Roman Catholic Church among its principal objectives. Initially, an effort had been made to turn Roman Catholic workers against the hierarchy. Religious beliefs were not at issue; class unity was the goal. Communist propagandists said the enemy cut across religious lines: the Vatican was allied with the Protestant tories of England, the Shinto militarists of Japan, Jewish Wall Street financiers, and atheist Trotskyists. Workers of all creeds—and of no creed—were to achieve solidarity in the face of mounting capitalist oppression.

The attacks upon the hierarchy took many forms. Individual priests were held up to ridicule. The views of Charles E. Coughlin, the priest-demagogue of Detroit, were cited to prove the Papacy's alliance with fascism. "He takes his order from Rome, from the highest hierarchy of the Catholic Church," said Earl Browder in 1936.[34] The *Daily Worker* reported that in Detroit comrades joined "the Coughlin unit of the local church" to establish contact with its members.[35] Two months later the paper urged Communists on New York's West Side to reach workers by infiltrating various Irish organizations, including Coughlin clubs.[36]

There were many other avenues of attack. When the Legion of Decency was organized against immorality in the movies, one Communist writer claimed its real purpose was to secure firmer capitalist control over the propaganda media of the nation.[37] A statement of the Roman Catholic bishops in 1937 opposing the child-labor amendment to the Constitution was assailed in a *Daily Worker* editorial: "In defending the right of capital to suck profits from the undernourished bodies and growing minds of little children, the Catholic hierarchs are serving the brass god of Mammon!" [38] In international affairs, the Papacy was attacked continuously for its support of Italy's invasion of Ethiopia and its sympathy for the Spanish insurgents.

The Communists were optimistic about their chances of winning Roman Catholic workers. The party writer Michael Gold pointed to the unemployed councils organized during the height of the Depression. "It has been a common experience," he wrote, "that the Catholic workers in these Councils, working side by side with Communist workers in fighting against evictions and the mean, baby-starving chiselling of the relief bureaus, have shed most of their prejudice against Communists." [39] Gold noted that in at least one unemployed council Irish Catholics took the lead. He also saw signs of a growing number of "people's priests, close to the poor and their suffering, not moving in the upper-class world of the bishops and hierarchs." Louis F. Budenz, a former Roman Catholic who later returned to the church, wrote several articles analyzing alleged tension between working-class Roman Catholics and the hierarchy. The top ecclesiastical leaders, he said, are trying to deliver the masses "into the hands of Black Legionnaires and the Ku Klux Klan." [40]

In the publication *Party Organizer,* a Communist discussed his experiences with Roman Catholic workers at the Milwaukee Allis-Chalmers plant. The Communists nominated a slate of union officers who were subjected to "vicious Red-baiting" by the church hierarchy. The state committee of the Communist Party issued a leaflet addressed to Roman Catholics pleading for a united front. The Communists won the election easily, and, through the campaign they waged, recruited six Roman Catholics into the Young Communist League.

The same article also told how members of the Catholic Worker movement participated in a picket line against a pro-Nazi Volksbund meeting. Four pickets were arrested, two of them Roman Catholic.

At the trial the next morning, one of the four arrested, a member of the Allis-Chalmers local, stated openly in court that he was a Communist, and expressed his feelings of horror at the sight of children in Nazi uniforms, reminding the court of the Nazi bombs dropping on the children of Spain. The two Catholics, fellow-members of the union, followed immediately afterward with a statement to the Court that they had participated because they were Catholics and opposed the Nazi program of racial and religious persecution. These statements had wide publicity in the local press.

The effect of an active member of the union coming out openly as a Communist was healthy and positive. Since then this comrade recruited three more Catholics into the Party.[41]

The issue of fascism was always highlighted in appeals to Catholics. As early as the summer of 1935, a letter to *America* told how New York Communists had circulated pamphlets urging Catholics to join them against Hitler to "Save your churches, convents, and schools." [42] In October that year, the column "Party Life" reprinted a united-front appeal "To All Catholics" from the party unit of Springfield, Illinois. Other units were told to follow suit. Communist youth leader Gil Green pointed out that the controversy over holding the 1936 Olympic Games in Berlin was an excellent one around which to rally religious groups.[43] He ordered members of the Young Communist League to aid in distributing leaflets on the issue to all Roman Catholic churches.

Letters were published in the *Daily Worker* from "Catholic Communists." "J.D." of Chicago said he belonged to the Communist Party because "I believe it has the only real political program commensurate with the Christian concept of the equality of man." [44] Statements by priests sympathetic to labor were quoted, and the impression was sometimes left that they were also warm toward the Communists. Frequent references were made to Roman Catholics in Europe who had rallied to the Popular Front.

The extent to which the Communists would go to achieve the appearance of a united front with Roman Catholics was revealed in an incident related by Dorothy Day, leader of the Catholic Worker movement. She recalled how both Communists and representatives of the Catholic Worker organized anti-Nazi picket lines against the German ship *Bremen*. First the Communists urged the Roman Catholics to join their picket line. When this failed, they tried to join the Catholic Worker picket line—but that failed, too. When some of the Communists were arrested for pulling down a swastika, they told the police and newspapers that they were with the Catholic Worker pickets. Dorothy Day said later she regretted that a member of her group had not pulled the swastika down.[45]

THE LABOR MOVEMENT

In 1939 Earl Browder, speaking in Boston, said that there were more adherents of the Roman Catholic faith than any other religious group in the Communist Party.[46] By itself, this assertion may need clarification. Browder really meant that, while most Communists maintained no religious ties whatever, of those who did maintain such ties, the Roman Catholics outnumbered the others. Protestant Communists left their churches. Jewish party members repudiated the synagogues. A higher percentage of Roman Catholics continued at least nominal affiliation with their parishes, sometimes for family reasons, sometimes because the emotional or cultural bonds could not easily be broken. For others, particularly Communist labor leaders, their church ties were part of a strategy designed to deceive.

The Communist-front apparatus viewed individual Roman Catholics as choice sponsors and made a bid to obtain their support. They met with considerable resistance but enough success among laymen to feed their propaganda machinery. Very few clergymen became involved, but there were some exceptions. Priests frequently delivered invocations at union meetings secretly manipulated by Communists. The Brooklyn *Tablet,* weekly newspaper of the Brooklyn diocese, was always eager to expose leftists, and especially any within the Roman Catholic Church. Its targets included several priests who, it warned, were consorting with Communists and co-operating with Communist fronts. Even so distinguished an anti-Communist archbishop as Robert E. Lucey of Texas has been accused of supporting the Committee to Abolish the Poll Tax, listed in the *Guide to Subversive Organizations* of the Un-American Activities Committee.

Roman Catholics and Communists seemed to rub shoulders frequently in the political arena. The most persistent apologist for the Communists in the United States Congress was Vito Marcantonio, who served the upper East Side of Manhattan for several terms. He himself claimed to be a Roman Catholic, was elected in large part by Italian and Puerto Rican Roman Catholics, and was on hand to participate in his district's special holy-day festivities. When he died of a heart attack on a New York street on August 9, 1954, he was carrying a religious medal in his pocket. He was denied a Roman Catholic burial.

Congressman Jerry J. O'Connell of Montana was another Communist sympathizer who effectively exploited his religious ties in his campaign and while in office. In 1937, after crossing a Roman Catholic picket line to address a mass meeting of the American League Against War and Fascism, he declared: "I am a Catholic. I bow in no way in my Catholicism to any man or woman on that picket line, and I say to them that there is nothing in our religion which prohibits me from opposing Fascism and opposing war." [47] Before his death in 1956, O'Connell played a leading role in several Communist-front groups, especially those related to civil liberties.

There were many other instances in which individual Roman Catholics co-operated with the Communists—as suggested by these few random examples. Philip Marshall Connelly, who claimed to be a "liberal Catholic," was arrested as a Communist leader and convicted under the Smith Act in 1952. Californian Leo Gallagher, a frequent Communist candidate for public office, was accused of "hiding behind the Catholic Church." In 1936 the Roman Catholic educator William Martin Canning joined the Communist Party and left it two years later.[48] Helen Lynch, who died after a life of arduous work for the party, was honored by the party as an "Irish Catholic" Communist martyr. Candidates of the American Labor Party in New York State (after Communists became powerful in the A.L.P. during World War II) included many nominal Roman Catholics. Even Philip Murray, the top Roman Catholic labor leader in the country—who in later years vigorously fought Communist infiltration—allowed his name to be used by such organizations as the National Council of American-Soviet Friendship, the National Negro Congress, the Jewish Peoples Committee, and the International Workers Order.

The decade of the thirties witnessed a rapid development of trade unions. In addition to the American Federation of Labor, a new progressive association, the Committee for Industrial Organization (later called the Congress of Industrial Organizations), was established. In some areas, unionization was accompanied by strikes, mass picketing, and open violence. Most labor organizers were New Dealers; some were Socialists; an extremely effective minority were Communists. Through careful strategy, frequent deception, unrestrained name-calling, and militant leadership, Communists and their allies captured control of a dozen unions and wielded considerable influence in several more, some of them predominately Roman Catholic in membership.

One such union was the Transport Workers Union of New York City, representing most subway and bus workers. Its membership during the late thirties was overwhelmingly Irish and an estimated 95 per cent were Roman Catholic. Communists worked largely through self-described Irish Catholics who cleverly exploited their religion and national background. Some of them were actual party members; others were opportunists who used the well-disciplined Communists for their own advancement. The leader of the T.W.U. was Michael Quill, for fourteen years widely labeled "Red Mike," who was seldom mentioned in the *Daily Worker* without reference to his thick Irish brogue.

Maintaining control over the T.W.U. gave the Communists many headaches. One problem arose when union members joined the party and were urged to remain active Roman Catholics, whatever their private views toward religion might be. Such persons were under strict surveillance, since their continued church tie meant a risk that they might be influenced to turn against the party. Also the party's line on international affairs had little appeal to the Irish, whose internationalism frequently was limited to Ireland. The Communist attitudes toward Ireland flip-flopped. During World War II, that nation's neutrality and its bitter hostility toward England were assailed by the party as giving aid and comfort to Hitler. At other times the party championed the cause of Irish unity against "British imperialism."

Communist control was imperiled by the activities of the Association of Catholic Trade Unionists, formed in 1937 to aid in organizing unions and to emphasize the social teachings of the church. A.C.T.U. soon began to combat racketeers and Communists in the labor movement. By 1941, the *Labor Leader,* an A.C.T.U. publication, concluded that "Quill is a discredited Communist functionary who must be driven from the trade union movement." [49] The paper marveled at the success of the Communists. "How they became leaders in a union predominately Irish Catholic is a saga of communist technique and sabotage against the real founders of the T.W.U. who would not bow to the party's whip." [50] The *Crown Heights Comment,* another A.C.T.U. organ, stated the issue in 1946:

Michael Quill boasts of his Communist following and supporters. Whether New York's Catholic Irish know it or not that is a repudiation of all that they hold dear and sacred. To follow the leadership of one who has repudiated them in favor of the enemies of the Faith, is to choose Joseph Stalin in place of Jesus Christ. [51]

Quill replied by calling A.C.T.U. a "strike-breaking agency" allied with the enemies of the labor movement.

How did he and the Communists manage to maintain their hold over the T.W.U. in spite of these attacks from the church and a hostile metropolitan press? Quill's brogue, his maneuvering skill, his demagogic abilities, and his frequent protestations that he was "a good Catholic" played a vital role. At union meetings, Hogans and McMahons and Murphys, all swearing fidelity to the church, were on hand to lend him vigorous support. Typical perhaps was one Irish subway employee, who arose at one T.W.U. meeting to describe himself as a "damn good Catholic" and then to attack the A.C.T.U. as a union-busting crew of company stooges.

Another important reason why union members continued to support Quill was stated quite frankly in a letter to the Right Wing Brooklyn *Tablet* in 1947: Roman Catholics vote for Communists because they get things done! [52] They were said to be dedicated, efficient, and individually selfless. Once in power, their deftness in exploiting the organizational machinery to their advantage made them difficult to dislodge. When the issue of Communism was raised, they promptly diverted attention to real and imaginary enemies who sought to slice wages, cut benefits, lay off workers, and destroy the union.

Quill was never defeated. After World War II, however, he finally split with the party functionaries over the five-cent fare. The Communists opposed a raise; Quill knew that the increase would mean that the union's demand for higher wages could be met. In addition, he was under heavy pressure from the national C.I.O. to endorse the foreign policy of President Truman and, in 1948, he refused to support the Communist-favored Progressive Party. Without Quill, the Communists could not hope to retain control of the T.W.U. Almost overnight their influence was destroyed.

The Communist apparatus was also successful in gaining substantial support from Roman Catholics in the United Electrical, Radio, and Machine Workers of America. At its peak, U.E. had 600,000 members and enjoyed a wide reputation for effective progressive leadership. Its organization director, James J. Matles, wrote in 1947 that "both the president of the UE and a great majority of its Executive Board members, as well as great numbers of district and local officers are members of the Catholic faith." [53] But the power rested with Matles and Julius Emspak, the principal leaders of the pro-Communist faction.

James B. Carey, a young Roman Catholic, served as president of the union until 1941, when his split with the Communists over foreign policy led to his replacement by Albert J. Fitzgerald, who boasted of his membership in a Roman Catholic church in Lynn, Massachusetts. During World War II, the Communist leadership sought to strengthen its position among the rank and file by deploring anti-Catholicism, by praising progressive church leaders such as Bishop Bernard J. Sheil, and even by listing in the pages of the *UE News* novenas for members killed in action. Response among Roman Catholics was heartening. A U.E. strike of 1946 received some religious support, and in one New Jersey city money for the strikers was collected in nine Roman Catholic churches.[54]

After the war, James B. Carey led a fight against U.E. Communists with the support of most C.I.O. leaders and the active co-operation of the Association of Catholic Trade Unionists. Religion became an important issue. *UE News* hyphenated A.C.T.U. with the Ku Klux Klan—"ACTU-Ku-Kluxism." President Fitzgerald wrote to a dignitary of the church protesting that it would be unfortunate if "union members of other faiths were to gain the impression that unionists of the Roman Catholic faith cannot be assured of freedom from ecclesiastical interference and coercion. . . ." [55] Charles Owen Rice, a Pittsburgh priest, came in for particular abuse in U.E. literature, and when the Carey group was defeated at the U.E. convention in 1949, the *UE News* included a picture of Rice with opera glasses "shouting down orders" from the balcony.[56]

The C.I.O. took immediate steps to oust the U.E. and establish the International Union of Electrical, Radio and Machine Workers headed by Carey. A bitter fight began for control of locals throughout the country. Priests in many cities reminded Roman Catholic U.E. members of their responsibility to oppose Communism. Edmund F. Gibbons, Bishop of Albany, accused the U.E. of being an "adjunct of the Communist Party" and said "it becomes a matter of conscience not to support this organization in any endeavor whatsoever." [57] The U.E. fought back through appeals from Roman Catholic members—often in the form of throwaways distributed at factory gates or at union meetings—not to be intimidated by clergymen who meddled in union affairs. More and more locals joined Carey's I.U.E. until U.E. dwindled to a small fraction of its earlier strength.

Communists were important in numerous other labor unions with large Roman Catholic membership. They dominated the National Maritime Union of America through Joseph Curran, a Roman Catholic, until after World War II, when Curran broke with them and drove them out. Harry Bridges was described in the *Labor Leader* of A.C.T.U. as a "pseudo-Catholic" and his followers have included many Irish and Italian longshoremen, especially on the West Coast. Roman Catholics are numerous in the Mine, Mill and Smelter Workers, still effectively run by the Communists.

Upon first thought, this support given by thousands of Roman Catholic workers to Communist union leadership over the years seems incredible. There were a number of factors, however, that help to explain it. The Communists have always given their principal attention to the labor movement, and they were most adept in this area. Their strategy of using Roman Catholics to cloak their work was cleverly applied. Communists were disciplined, militant, industrious, and usually capable. In many instances, though a small minority, their supporters gave more serious attention to union matters and attended union meetings faithfully. Many devout Roman Catholics were accustomed to hearing the charge of "Red" directed at all unions; they were sometimes confused as to when the accusation was valid and when it was defamatory. Others felt that "my union affairs are not the business of my priest." Like workers of all faiths, Roman Catholics would tend to support shrewd, persuasive leaders who secured the most benefits for them, regardless of their ideology. At some times and in some places, the Communists appeared to meet this standard.

THE COMMUNISTS AND THE IRISH

American Communists have been active among nationality groups. Their main vehicle for reaching foreign-language groups was the International Workers Order, a fraternal organization chartered in 1930, which was firmly controlled by Communists; it was dissolved by New York State in 1954. The I.W.O. provided insurance at extremely reasonable rates and at its peak boasted 200,000 members and five million dollars in assets. In addition, under its broad umbrella was a host of foreign-language societies whose newspapers echoed Communist Party views. Among the most important newspapers circulated among Roman Catholic groups were *L'Unità del Populo* (Italian), *Glos Ludowy* (Polish), and *Narodni Glasnik* (Croat).

Efforts of the party to influence various nationality groups may be examined through their activities among the Irish-Americans, who were viewed as a special challenge. They were largely laborers; and yet, unlike many other nationalities, they spoke English, usually were not new arrivals in the United States, and held considerable political power in the large eastern cities. They were devoted to the Roman Catholic Church and largely devoid of the anticlericalism characteristic of many of their southern European coreligionists. They were usually strong nationalists, bitter foes of the British Empire, and proud of their own revolutionary heritage.

From the earliest years of the American Communist Party, considerable emphasis was placed upon the Irish struggle against the English. Marx was quoted on the importance of Ireland's freedom and unity, and James Connolly, a Socialist executed after the Easter Rebellion in 1916, was immortalized as a working-class martyr. The hunger strikes, sabotage, and guerrilla fighting of the Irish Republican Army were reported dramatically in the Communist press. There was always the implication that the mass of Irish laborers and peasants of Ireland would free themselves from the "superstitions" of the church, repudiate the hierarchy's "appeasement" policies, and flock to the Red banner. In America, T. J. O'Flaherty edited briefly a small party paper known as the *Irish People,* and attempts were made—never with much success—to promote an Irish Workers Club and an Irish Workers Republican Alliance. Communists were brought over from the old country to speak in major industrial cities in the hope that Irish-Americans could be drawn into the party orbit.

By 1937, the Communists had embarked upon a major but unfruitful effort to win sympathizers among Irish Catholics as part of their united-front strategy. The *Daily Worker* for St. Patrick's Day set the tone for the next four years. Louis F. Budenz, boasting of his Irish blood, wrote a lengthy article recounting the history of the Irish and the Irish-Americans. He told of their brave struggle against "the cruelest and crassest oppression" of the "British mailed fist"; how they came to the United States only to be "maltreated and exploited by the employing class"; how they were in the forefront of the labor battles of the nineteenth century; how the Molly Maguires pioneered in the fight against the bosses; and how Irishmen were playing a vital role in the building of the C.I.O. Budenz published an "Irish Roll of Honor" and included on it William Z. Foster, son of Irish revolutionaries, then national chairman of the Communist Party; Tom Mooney, "American son of Irish parentage, in his California prison on this St. Patrick's Day"; Elizabeth Gurley Flynn, American-born daughter of Irish nationalists and a party leader; and many more. Budenz concluded: "In the battle for democracy and Communism the aspirations for freedom of the Irish people are joined with the emancipation of all the working people." [58]

During the time of the Hitler-Stalin pact, Anglophobes were wooed zealously by Communist propaganda. Many Irish shared with the Communists the feeling that there was little choice between the English and the Nazis. In the first six months of 1941, the *Daily Worker* carried thirty-eight major articles on Ireland, seventeen editorials, various news stories, cables from "patriots" abroad, and comments by columnists. The Communists were also busy holding rallies. Typical was a memorial meeting to honor James Connolly in May 1940—the twenty-fourth anniversary of his "murder" by the British. Austin Hogan, president of the New York local of the T.W.U., told the audience in Transport Hall in New York City that "the most disastrous blow that we can give to the imperialist ruling class is to keep this country out of war." [59] Another meeting memorialized Helen

Lynch, "courageous Irish-American girl." The Brooklyn Young
Communist League distributed leaflets "For Irish Freedom" and had
an Irish Communist, Tom Dwyer, as a speaker. South Bronx was a
beehive of party work among the Irish. On one occasion, the Roman
Catholic priests of the area warned against an "Irish Republican
Organization" which was sponsoring dances to raise funds for "political prisoners in Ireland" and had passed out party leaflets after mass.

When the British hanged two Irishmen, Peter Barnes and James
Richards, in early 1940, the Moscow newspaper *Pravda* attacked
"the policy of persecutions and terror which the British ruling circles
are applying. . . ." [60] A protest meeting was held in the James
Connolly Hall in Manhattan, addressed by Elizabeth Gurley Flynn
and Pat Toohey, a Communist organizer among the miners. Toohey
said the executions proved England was "waging an imperialist war
and is conniving at the destruction of the independence and self-
determination of small nations." [61] In Boston, the Communist Party
of Massachusetts circulated 20,000 leaflets condemning the executions
and urging readers to protest directly to the British Consulate. A
Lincoln-Lenin Memorial Meeting in Philadelphia assailed the hang-
ings and passed resolutions supporting the struggle for Irish independence.

In her *Daily Worker* column, Elizabeth Gurley Flynn paid tribute
to the two "martyrs" and then urged upon her readers three emphases:
"Keep America out of war; help Ireland to be free and stop Great
Britain's war moves against the Soviet Union"—these, she said, "are
bound together in this historic hour, my fellow Irish." [62] Budenz
traced the executions to the "vultures" of the Bank of England. "My
own Irish blood boils at the continued persecution of the Gaelic
people—and I am as Irish as the present premier of Eire," he said.
President Roosevelt was plotting with Chamberlain to suppress Ireland and to "gang up . . . against the Land of Socialism." [63]

In February 1940, the national committee of the Communist Party
adopted a resolution entitled "Solidarity with the Irish People." It
blamed the Barnes and Richards executions on "British imperialists,"
demanded "civil and religious liberties" for the Irish, and stated that
the "liberation of the Irish people can best be advanced by Irish kins-
men in America actively participating in that growing movement of
the American masses against the present foreign policy by which our

country is being led, against the popular will, into a reactionary war in alliance with British and French imperialists." [64]

This anti-British line aimed at wooing Irish-American support was part and parcel of a broader Communist effort to keep America from aiding England as she stood alone against Hitler. Moscow dictated this new "peace" policy after the most startling diplomatic about-face in modern history. After a period of active support of collective security, party members in the United States were now to pose as pacifists and to shed bitter tears over the "plot" of Wall Street and the Roosevelt administration to drive the nation into war.

EIGHT · INTERVENTION TO ISOLATION—AND BACK AGAIN

In the early summer of 1939, the *Daily Worker* was echoing with cries of "Unite against Fascism!" By September, its slogan had changed to "Stay out of Imperialist War!" What had caused its abrupt retreat from intervention to isolation?

The united front suddenly collapsed with the shattering announcement that the governments of Hitler and Stalin had on August 23 signed a ten-year nonaggression pact. Poland soon stood in the path of a fearful blitzkrieg, and Great Britain and France declared war on the Nazi aggressor. What remained of the united front after the pact was battered further by subsequent events. Russia entered Poland on September 17 and occupied more than half of its territory in what appeared to be a deal with Germany. The Soviet Union attacked Finland during the winter of 1939-40. Then, in early 1941, Russia signed a neutrality pact with Japan and came to terms on the Soviet-Manchukuo border, which allowed Japan a free hand in China and helped pave the way for the attack upon Pearl Harbor.

The Soviet Union and the Communist parties around the world depicted the war as a battle between rival imperialisms, but to most Americans who had co-operated with the united front this view was unpalatable. They deserted the Communist orbit by the thousands. Even the hardened party faithful found it difficult to swallow. They were at first unbelieving, then humiliated, and finally some left the party, completely disillusioned.

DEMISE OF THE FRONTS

One of the first casualties of the Nazi-Soviet pact was the American League for Peace and Democracy. Its sixth annual parade fell only three days after the pact was signed. Forty thousand marchers were expected; less than 5,000 came.

Principal speakers at the rally were two Episcopal clergymen, William B. Spofford, Sr., acting national chairman of the League in the temporary absence of Harry F. Ward, and Thomas L. Harris, the League's executive secretary, who later left the ministry. Spofford admitted that he was "confused" by the international picture, but suggested that the pact was an ingenious master stroke to destroy the Nazi alliance with Italy and Japan: "There is no longer any Rome, Berlin, Tokyo axis." [1] Harris was even more ambiguous: "If the League stands for defense of the Soviet Union, it is because of the peace policies it represents and perhaps will continue to represent. If the League does not denounce the Soviet-German non-aggression pact, it is because the facts do not justify it." [2]

In early October, the American League came under sharp attack by the Un-American Activities Committee headed by Martin Dies of Texas. Ward was hailed before the committee, where he sparred with J. B. Matthews, the committee's expert on subversive activities. The League hoped to salvage support among liberals who detested Congressman Dies. Its religious secretary, a Methodist minister, Alson J. Smith, sparked a "mass" civil-liberties rally in Carnegie Hall and several weeks later released a statement from ninety-eight church leaders denouncing the Dies investigations. But it was too late. Few Americans were in a mood to worry about the "constitutional rights" of the League while Russian soldiers were crossing the frontier into Finland.

The precise circumstances surrounding the final disappearance of the League are in dispute. Its executive board released a statement to League members on September 23, 1939, that indicated the extent of the confusion. The League's first aim, it said, was to keep America out of war. It condemned Nazi aggression, but also spoke of British and French imperialism. It hinted of a division within the board on the question of the Soviet Union's occupation of eastern Poland. If it "later becomes clear" that the Soviet Union has committed aggression, then the League would favor an embargo on goods to Russia. "Meanwhile, the decision of the Board is that at this time, we neither condemn nor approve the actions of the Soviet Union." [3] The statement was signed by Ward.

A few days later, Roger Baldwin, one of the League's key figures, pulled out. "I do not for a moment suggest," he wrote, "that the policy of the American League is determined by the minority of Communists in its membership." He felt, however, that the pact proved that Communists were unreliable allies in the struggle against fascism; he did not want to co-operate with them any longer. [4] The crisis reached a peak when LeRoy E. Bowman, a member of the staff of the United States Office of Education and of the League's executive committee, confirmed a story in the press that he had offered a resolution in a closed session of the executive committee condemning both Germany and Russia for attacking Poland. According to Bowman, his resolution was rejected by a vote of 14-1. Bowman then offered a resolution that the League disband since it was apparently no longer a genuine united front. When this resolution was defeated, again 14-1, he left the League. [5]

By the end of 1939, Communists and their allies realized that the American League for Peace and Democracy could no longer serve a useful purpose as a peace front. It was showing a dangerous spirit of independence; its board even voted in favor of an embargo upon arms to the Soviet Union after the Russo-Finnish War erupted. On February 1, 1940, in a downtown cafeteria, a secret meeting of League officers adopted a resolution saying that the outbreak of war "has created a situation in which a different program and a different type of organization are needed to preserve democratic rights in war time and to help keep the United States out of war." [6] The League was thereupon dissolved.

As though to provide the League with a fitting burial, a testimonial was given to Ward the same evening. In his remarks, he denied again that Communists had controlled the League, defended Communist Party participation in its activities, denounced the Dies Committee for "creating the Communist myth" concerning the League, and assailed the press for its biased reporting of League activities. Ward also flayed efforts to aid Finland, and he blamed war hysteria on business interests and on the Roosevelt administration. The most promising sign in the situation, he said, was that "out of the labor movement there has come a slogan which is capturing the country— 'the Yanks are not coming.' " [7] Ward now threw his weight behind the Communist peace offensive.

Other fronts met the same fate as the American League for Peace and Democracy, but seldom as quickly.

The Dies Committee turned its attention in November 1939 to the American Youth Congress. The hearings produced little helpful information. The most sensational testimony was given by Kenneth Goff, once a member of the Young Communist League and the American Youth Congress, who eagerly identified a lengthy list of youths as secret comrades. Goff's testimony was worthless. He already had moved from Communism into the organized anti-Semitic movement, and his accusations were based more on malice than fact. His false charges are still circulated by the Un-American Activities Committee more than two decades later.

Mrs. Eleanor Roosevelt came to the defense of the American Youth Congress in its bout with Congressman Dies and J. B. Matthews. She was confident that all the charges against the Congress were untrue. She had become closely acquainted with most of its leaders and tells in her book *This I Remember* how on one occasion while entertaining a group of them in the White House she quizzed them about their political ties. "In each case they said they had no connection with the communists," she recalls, "had never belonged to any communist organizations and had no interest in communist ideas." [8]

In February 1940, when the American Youth Congress staged a pilgrimage to Washington, Mrs. Roosevelt housed some of the officers in the White House. By August 1940, however, she had surrendered all hope for the A.Y.C. and disassociated herself from them. President Roosevelt was in a different mood as the delegates stood on the White House lawn in a pouring rain. He bitterly assailed a resolution of the New York American Youth Congress which echoed Communist attacks on United States foreign policy—attacks, he said sharply, that were "twaddle, based perhaps on sincerity, but at the same time ninety percent ignorance. . . . " [9] There were boos as he spoke. After he finished, he abruptly advised the rain-soaked youths to go home and change clothes before they caught pneumonia.

Even before the announcement of the Hitler-Stalin pact, the American Youth Congress had started to disintegrate. The majority of the pacifists—including the National Council of Methodist Youth—had withdrawn. The departure of astute anti-Communists, who might have been able to save the organization from complete Communist domination, left little hope for the Congress's independence. The Christian Youth Council of North America stopped co-operating. Jewish groups, including Young Judea, pulled out. The only major religious organizations to remain were the Young Women's Christian Association and the National Intercollegiate Christian Council.

The rest of the story involves many conflicting reports and testimony. The individual delegates from the Y.W.C.A. and the N.I.C.C. split among themselves at the Sixth American Youth Congress at Geneva, Wisconsin, in July 1940. Harriet Pickens, representing the Business and Professional Council of the Y.W.C.A., was one of the leaders in the final efforts to save the organization from the Communists. The anti-Communists were successfully outmaneuvered and badly beaten. Some of the other religious youth, and especially Jack R. McMichael, gave valuable support to the Communists. The American Youth Congress was securely in Communist hands after the summer of 1940; when America entered World War II, it disappeared.

The fate of the National Negro Congress has no special significance for the churches since they were not deeply involved in the Congress after 1936. But the Congress's final chapter did lead to the emergence of an articulate and influential anti-Communist bloc within the Negro community which was to play an important role in years ahead.

The president of the N.N.C. since its inception had been A. Philip Randolph, pioneer labor leader and principal organizer of the Brotherhood of Sleeping Car Porters. Randolph had served notice prior to the Third National Negro Congress, scheduled for Washington in April 1940, that he would not be a rubber stamp for the new party line, and with this advance warning the Communists began to organize large delegations from Communist-controlled labor unions and fraternal groups. To their distress, they found too few Communist and fellow-traveling Negroes to assure victory in the anticipated show-down, so they assigned nearly 400 white supporters to the meeting. Resolutions were passed assailing Roosevelt's "war-mongering" and British and French imperialism. The Communists were in control.

Randolph was not intimidated, however, and rose to inform the conference that he was not a candidate for re-election, that he objected to the Congress's ties with the Communists, and that he opposed "any co-operation with the Soviet Union." Many delegates were deliberately rude. Some left the hall. Ralph J. Bunche, then professor at Howard University, has described the response to Randolph's remarks: "There was an embarrassing silence and no applause when Randolph concluded. It was apparent that the whole thing was cut and dried, for while Randolph was speaking Max Yergan moved up to the front row." [10]

Yergan, a former Y.M.C.A. leader in Africa, was quickly elected president in Randolph's place. The Communists had "saved" and destroyed the National Negro Congress all in the same day. Even more important, Randolph and his labor allies learned a lesson about Communist deception that they never forgot.

THE RELIGIOUS WORLD REACTS

The national chorus of disapproval of the Nazi-Soviet pact and the events that followed resounded all through the church press, from the Methodist *Christian Advocate* to *Advance,* the level-headed Congregational organ, to *Zions Herald,* whose faith in Russia was "fatally shaken," to the conservative *Christian Standard,* which predicted that Stalin "is planning for a slice of Poland"—a prediction soon to be proved accurate.[11] A few dared hope that the pact, while sinister in intent, might have some beneficial by-products. Articles in the *Presbyterian* and the Baptist *Watchman-Examiner* suggested that the pact had cooled the friendship between the Axis powers.[12] The *Christian Century* asked: "Does the pact contain the usual provision making it void if either party attacks a third? If so, it may check Hitler rather than encourage his aggression." [13]

Others, like A. J. Muste, who expressed his views regularly through the *Presbyterian Tribune,* found a certain satisfaction because partisans of both Hitler and Stalin were embarrassed by the pact:

Perhaps the immediate lesson for Americans and all Christians to take to heart is that democracy cannot work in harness with either Fascism or Communism, that we had better shut our ears to the clamor of Coughlinites, Bundists, Kluxers, et al, who seek to pin the label of Communism on anything or anybody they don't like, and also to the clamor of Communists and others who fling the epithet Fascist or Nazi at anyone who dares differ with them.[14]

Reinhold Niebuhr used the pact to lash out at those who still showed blind faith in the Soviet Union:

How wrong all the more naïve marxists have been about their interpretation of history! Russia was for them the Kingdom of God. The Russian trials did not disturb their faith and I suppose this new Russian line won't disturb it either. But it's a rather ridiculous faith. What Russia has done as a great power is understandable enough; but what it has done as the fatherland of socialism, to which millions of united fronters in every nation have given their devotion, is despicable. Even more despicable is the frantic effort of the Daily Worker to make the worse appear the better reason. The logic of these communist journalists is almost as far-fetched as nazi logic.[15]

The Soviet attack upon Finland caused even more revulsion in religious circles than the pact. "Finlandia" was sung in many churches, special offerings were taken, and clergymen of all faiths used their pulpits to condemn unequivocally the Soviet Union and to praise the valor of the Finns. The *Messenger* of the Evangelical and Reformed Church assailed it as a "brutal attack on a small peace-loving nation of Protestant people!" [16] *Fellowship,* the magazine of the Fellowship of Reconciliation, called Communist claims that Finland attacked Russia "ridiculous and nauseating." [17] Niebuhr's *Radical Religion* specifically replied to the Communist charge that Finland was fascist: "Let it be recorded, even though it is on Finland's grave, that the significance of her history lies in her rejecting Mannerheim's fascism, and building a very solid democracy, one third of the economic life of which rests upon cooperatives. If this is not a democratic civilization there is none." [18] Lutherans showed a special interest in the conflict. The *Lutheran,* organ of the United Lutheran Church, said in an editorial: "If ever a nation assumed the part of a bully and pushed its way by sheer weight of numbers and extent of resources upon an unoffending neighboring people, Russia is that bully. . . . For us who are Lutherans, there is the additional grief because the Finnish folk are almost entirely Lutheran." [19]

A number of leading clergymen publicly revised their earlier high estimate of the Soviet Union. John Haynes Holmes expressed the sentiments of many in his sermon of January 21, 1940, "Why We Liberals Went Wrong on the Russian Revolution." [20] "I must confess that this Russian experience has been the supreme disillusionment of my life," Holmes said. "I have been deceived, deluded and disgraced—sold out by those I trusted most; and I am as deeply afflicted as I am utterly disgusted by what has happened." [21] Liberals failed in not anticipating this Russian disaster, he continued, when many signs should have given them warning. Liberals were right in hailing the overthrow of the Czar, Holmes said; they were right to welcome Lenin's control of a state engulfed by anarchy and starvation; they were right to acclaim efforts to develop a unique economic system based on equality; they were right to support the peace efforts of Maxim Litvinov, commissar for foreign affairs "and the leading peace minister of his day," though Litvinov's fall in 1939 marked the shift of Russian policy to imperialism. "Stalin has come upon the scene, unrecognized and unknown, as the new Napoleon of our day." [22]

Where, then, did liberals err? Holmes answered that in their enthusiasm for economic and social justice, liberals were ready to condone evils that "in our own hearts we knew to be wrong." They ignored cruelties in Russia they would have condemned elsewhere. "Worst of all, many of us accepted tacitly, if not openly . . . that most dangerous and ultimately disastrous idea that can lodge within the human mind—namely, that the end justifies the means." [23] The sermon listed many specific situations in which liberals failed to raise their voices in protest against Soviet tyranny: the dissolution of the Constituent Assembly at the very outset of the Bolshevik regime; the imprisonment and execution of political opponents; the brutal expropriation of the kulaks; the purging of Lenin's comrades by Stalinist tyranny.

It remained for the Hitler-Stalin pact to "strip away the last veils of self-deception from the eyes of liberals, and to set them steadfastly against the cruel and bloody regime which they should have uncovered years before." [24] Finland, for many, was the final revelation. "We are through," said Holmes. "Russia is forever spewed out of our mouths." The Russian people are back in a captivity "worse than any ever known in the darkest days of the Tsar." [25] Even so, the 1917 revolution might not have been in vain. The French revolution produced a Napoleon, but brought to mankind a new impulse to political democracy. The Russian revolution "conceivably" might contribute to the furtherance of economic democracy.

AMERICAN PEACE MOBILIZATION

Those Communists and fellow travelers whose faith remained unshaken continued in the service of the Soviet policy. The switch from savage denunciations of Hitler to similar attacks on England and France was made rapidly. By October 1939—less than six weeks after the pact—the antiwar speeches of Eugene V. Debs were revived and the isolationist speeches of Charles A. Lindbergh were printed. In November, Armistice Day was exploited to remind people of the horrors of World War I, a pamphlet, "Yanks Are Not Coming," reached a reported 50,000 persons, and the twenty-second anniversary of the Bolshevik revolution was celebrated with demands for peace and friendship with the U.S.S.R. By 1940, the direction of the Communist movement was established. Front groups were rescinding their earlier endorsements of Roosevelt for a third term; he had now become in their eyes a notorious warmonger. Their new heroes were pacifists and isolationists. Church statements condemning war were seized upon and publicized. Yanks-Are-Not-Coming Committees were formed. Efforts were made to exploit antagonism toward England, especially among Irish-Americans. Gory battle pictures were displayed. The mothers-want-peace theme was pressed, and dramatic appeals were made to save the "flower of our youth."

A national Communist-inspired peace movement gradually developed. An Emergency Peace Mobilization in Chicago was announced for Labor Day weekend 1940. Two United States senators, Gerald P. Nye and D. Worth Clark, agreed to speak, but withdrew when they became aware of the conference's orientation. Among the meeting's original seventy-one sponsors were Congressman Vito Marcantonio, Professor Dirk J. Struik of Massachusetts Institute of Technology, Max Yergan of the National Negro Congress, and Julius Emspak of the United Electrical, Radio and Machine Workers of America, all faithful spokesmen for the Communist viewpoint. More than one-third of the names on the official call were clergymen or religious workers. Yet, of the 5,653 delegates and visitors who attended, only 67 were listed under the "church" category—or little more than one-tenth of 1 per cent. The main support came from Communist-controlled labor unions, fraternal groups, and youth organizations. The churchmen were being used as camouflage.

One episode at the Chicago meeting illustrates its political bias. A delegation of auto workers from Flint, Michigan, offered a resolution condemning aggression of all kinds, specifically naming both Germany and Russia. Those managing the conference found an easy way out: they announced that resolutions submitted by individual groups could not be considered, that only one general declaration of policy would be adopted. When that declaration was finally made, it contained no condemnation of wars of aggression and no mention of either Germany or Russia—but it did attack the "war policies" of President Roosevelt.[26]

On the last day of the conference, at which the American Peace Mobilization was organized, the *Daily Worker* reported that delegates "leaped cheering to their feet and voted unanimously to have a people's delegation from 40 states in Washington at the doorsteps of Congress tomorrow morning to notify the Roosevelt administration that the nation flatly opposes conscription." [27] In the November campaign, A.P.M. assailed both Roosevelt and Willkie. Local peace committees were organized in various cities and A.P.M. threw itself into the defense of conscientious objectors. It protested Lend-Lease, loans to Britain, and convoys to protect American shipping. It focused attention on high "war" taxes and rising prices, supported strikes in basic industries affecting preparedness, exposed "Yankee imperialism" in Latin America and the Far East, and endorsed Ireland's running quarrel with England. In the name of "twelve million Americans," it sent greetings in January 1941 to a Communist-sponsored English People's Convention which was demanding a "people's peace" and "friendship with the Soviet Union." In April, it sponsored an American People's Meeting in New York. In May, A.P.M. threw a picket line in front of the White House with signs denouncing war profiteering, conscription, aid to England, and Roosevelt dictatorship. To the query Isn't an English victory preferable to a Hitler victory?, an A.P.M. leaflet gave this blunt reply: "No. An English victory will result in the same sort of imperialist, anti-democratic peace as will a Nazi victory." [28]

On June 22, 1941, when the German army invaded Russia, the party and its allies had to reverse themselves again. They feared that the Soviet Government might collapse and they demanded unlimited aid to Russia and, now, "democratic" England. The attack upon Russia, they said, should be regarded as an attack upon America itself. Roosevelt was again enshrined as a world statesman. The pacifists, the isolationists, and others who continued to oppose intervention were transformed into "fascist" appeasers, callous about the fate of the Jews and the oppressed nations of Europe. Meetings were quickly organized, including a mass rally at Madison Square Garden addressed by Thomas L. Harris and others. Telegrams flooded Washington demanding immediate action. Special appeals were made to Americans of Slav background to join the crusade to save their big Russian brother.

Within the American Peace Mobilization, the confusion of the Communist leadership was evident. On June 21, the day before the Nazi attack, the A.P.M.'s national board publicly hailed the 1,000-hour anti-intervention vigil at the White House. The picketing was ordered stopped, but Americans were urged to redouble their efforts for peace in a declaration that ended: "Don't let that first shot be fired. Get out and stay out of World War II." The A.P.M. newsletter, *Facts for Peace,* dated June 24, 1941, was caught between a lead story announcing A.P.M.'s new attitude toward the war and the rest of the newsletter with its regular diatribes against British imperialism and American warmongering. For the next few days A.P.M. statements urging immediate united action against fascism went out on old letterheads marked "NEWS from the Peace Front." On June 27, 1941, F. Hastings Smyth, on behalf of A.P.M.'s national religious committee, wrote a letter to Roosevelt demanding "genuine assistance to the Soviet Union and United China." Within a month, the national board voted unanimously to change the name from American Peace Mobilization to the American People's Mobilization. On August 1, the remodeled A.P.M. opened "Smash Hitler Week" and shortly after adopted the official slogan "For Victory Over Fascism." Finally, the organization was allowed to collapse altogether. Peace was no longer the Communist Party's goal.[29]

THE CLERGY AND A.P.M.

The American Peace Mobilization quoted Protestant ministers, Roman Catholic priests, and Jewish rabbis against intervention and made a special effort to rally church youth. In September 1940, A.P.M. delegates held a religious service on the steps of the Capitol, and at the American People's Meeting the following April a Sunday-morning church service was included in the official program. There were hymns, an invocation by a rabbi, a responsive reading led by a Negro pastor, and a sermon delivered by Ward.

In general, there was very little response from the churches. Of the 5,038 persons attending the American People's Meeting in April 1941, only forty-eight were listed as workers in the field of religion and several of these were affiliated with the Y's. Most clergymen who favored peace were expressing their sentiments instead through legitimate pacifist organizations, especially the Fellowship of Reconciliation, whose executive committee issued a warning in 1940 against co-operation with "political and propagandist organizations which openly welcomed Communists into membership."[30] Altogether the A.P.M. claimed that about one hundred different clergymen in one way or another sponsored its meetings or its statements or its other activities. With all the effort exerted, this was poor response.

A detailed study of thirty-five of these clergymen suggests that most of them were totally unaware that they were assisting a Communist front, if they did in fact lend it their names.[31]

About half of the thirty-five—contacted more than fifteen years later—denied any affiliation with the American Peace Mobilization. A Midwest Congregational minister wrote: "I never saw or communicated with anyone who, to my knowledge, was connected with any subversive organization . . . and I have no use for Communism whatever." A Lutheran clergyman in Pennsylvania did not recall any A.P.M. association. "I certainly would not support any movement or organization which had Communistic leanings," he said. An Episcopal minister in Indiana answered simply: "Did not support this organization at any time." When a copy of the call to the American People's Meeting was sent him, listing his name as a sponsor, he replied: "It amazes me to find my name listed. . . . I am not a little resentful as I take a dim view of this type of operation." Loyd F. Worley, Methodist leader in the field of social action, specifically stated that he had never supported A.P.M. "in any way, shape or form. As far as my influence went, I discouraged any participation because I readily recognized its associations."

A second group recalled their endorsement but regretted it. A Universalist minister, who attended the Chicago meeting that launched A.P.M., confessed "I didn't know the Commies were organizing it— which they undoubtedly did." A Congregationalist said that he supported A.P.M. because of his "early and naïve belief that a Christian pacifist could co-operate with Communists," and an eastern Episcopal clergyman wrote: "As I remember, my signature got on the sponsor's list due to a 'form letter' asking for it for a great cause for peace. I never went near the meeting or group. . . . I will have to watch my signatures in the future."

A leading Congregationalist, who could not remember any specific tie with A.P.M., recalled that "once in about 1940 or 1941 I inadvertently permitted my name to be used by what I thought was a peace organization—only to catch it within two days and write asking my name be withdrawn." A few became involved through local peace groups. A pastor of the Evangelical and Reformed Church reported that the affiliate of A.P.M. had been "at that time the principal 'peace' organization in the town, and, while I do not recall actually joining it, I worked with it." He resigned in sharp protest after it changed its objective in June 1941. A distinguished rabbi resigned for the same reason: "Having been, for many years, a pacifist, I accepted, in 1940, every invitation to join any movement which protested against war. The only time in my life I ever sent an angry letter was in June or July 1941 when Peace Mobilization abandoned peace and agitated for our entrance into war. I withdrew in a rage." A Negro pastor traced his involvement to the influence of Harry F. Ward, who was his professor at Union Theological Seminary.

Several ministers said that the names on the letterhead had encouraged them to lend A.P.M. their support. From a Pennsylvania Methodist came this explanation: "Eight or nine names on the list I saw were personal friends of mine, men who could be depended on. . . . I sent them a token check for $3.00 on February 28, 1941 and if that meant I was a sponsor, it was inexpensive. This was my last contribution to A.P.M., and it has no significance other than as an expression of my interest in peace."

Some who showed no sympathy for Communism also showed no regret at having co-operated with the American Peace Mobilization. A Baptist minister in New York State recalled that there was no hint of Communism in literature he received: "Quite naturally I co-operated, and would do so again—if I thought there was a possibility of keeping this country out of war." An Episcopal bishop said that the charge that A.P.M. was Communist-dominated "came out later" and that "there was then and is now no way of telling to what extent that was true." A Methodist district superintendent, who could not remember any association with the organization, noted that he had supported many peace movements "and am glad that I have had the opportunity. . . . This must have been one of those many projects which I endorsed with the hope of keeping America out of war."

Most of these men only lent their names. Fewer than a dozen clergymen took an active role either in the American Peace Mobilization or the Communist peace movement generally. Several had been important in the League for Peace and Democracy, men like Harry F. Ward and William B. Spofford, Sr. A.P.M.'s national chairman, John B. Thompson, was a relatively new minister on the scene. One of the vice-presidents was Jack R. McMichael, who simultaneously was serving as chairman of the American Youth Congress; another was Katherine Terrill, a key figure in the Council for Social Action of the Congregational Christian Churches. Among the ministers were Donald L. West, Owen H. Whitfield, Malcolm Cotton Dobbs, F. Hastings Smyth, and Owen A. Knox.

The role of John B. Thompson in the American Peace Mobilization remains an enigma. He has publicly announced his opposition to Communism.[32] He was serving as a Presbyterian pastor and as a professor at the University of Oklahoma when, in 1940, he emerged as a leader in the Committee to Defend America by Keeping Out of War, a short-lived group which launched A.P.M. At about the same time he was elected president of the Southern Conference for Human Welfare and subsequently sought to bring Conference members into his peace activities.[33]

Thompson was an ideal choice to head A.P.M. He was a new and attractive personality who had not been labeled because of prior political activities. He was a capable speaker who did not mouth the clichés of the Communists. His speeches were moderate in tone and filled with Biblical allusions; yet, he was critical of "the great nobles of power and privilege" who, he said, were fostering the war scare for profit.[34] The fact that Thompson was a young minister from Oklahoma provided needed camouflage for the A.P.M.

Donald L. West is best known as a poet whose verse reflects his political views.[35] He was born in 1903 on a little mountain farm in Georgia amid hunger and deprivation, worked for an education, and received his Bachelor of Divinity degree from Vanderbilt University, where he came under the influence of Alva Taylor, a dynamic professor who instilled social idealism in many of his students. He was ordained by the Congregational Church but has not served a parish during most of his life. West first joined the Socialist Party, then in 1934 drove an old motorcycle to New York City, where he joined the Communist Party.[36] He became an active Communist functionary in various parts of the South.

His role in the American Peace Mobilization was not central. At the time, he was serving a Congregational parish in Meansville, Georgia. He published a little paper, *The Country Parson,* which warned against American involvement in the war [37] and spoke at meetings where he denounced "imperialists" and castigated church leaders who favored intervention. When the A.P.M. announced its revised program after Hitler's attack upon Russia, West had no difficulty following along. He wrote the A.P.M. office that its new view of world affairs "should clarify much of the confused thinking among those genuine anti-fascists who have been groping around ineffectively. . . ." [38] West remained in the Communist orbit during and after World War II.[39]

Perhaps the most unusual clergyman in the American Peace Mobilization was F. Hastings Smyth, superior of the Oratory of Saint Mary and Saint Michael House, then in Cambridge, Massachusetts. The Oratory was sponsored by the Society of the Catholic Commonwealth, and an A.P.M. memo referred to him as a "Boston Catholic leader." He was in fact an ordained clergyman of the Church of England who never affiliated with the Protestant Episcopal Church in this country. His special interest was in experimental liturgical forms, but earlier he taught chemistry for three years at Massachusetts Institute of Technology, from which he had received a Ph.D.

Smyth had been attracted by the Marxist analysis of society and in 1940 discussed the relationship of Christianity to Marxism in his book *Manhood into God*. He rejected the Marxist utopianism, but declared that there is "an extensive common ground upon which both Catholics and Marxists might meet and work together." [40] He looked on Russia benignly: "We may entertain a good hope that undemocratic faults, if they exist in Russia, are there as accidents, rather than as properties of Communism. . . . There is nothing in the nature of a Communist economic system itself which necessarily makes for either violence or dictatorship." [41]

Smyth later explained his association with the American Peace Mobilization in these words: "I was not convinced that the English were whole-hearted in their opposition to Nazism." [42] He feared that the Conservative government of Neville Chamberlain would come to terms with Hitler if Germany launched an attack upon Russia. In later years he continued to defend the progress and potential of the Soviet Union, but by 1957 he was depicting modern Russia as "one of the most powerful, one of the most ruthless imperialisms of history." [43] Smyth died in April 1960 at the age of seventy-one.

Owen A. Knox is a Methodist minister reared in the American West, where he observed at close hand the exploitation of miners by the mine owners. After his ordination, he became involved in a C.I.O. strike in Camden, New Jersey, then went to Detroit in 1936 so that he might serve among industrial workers. Knox remained there for more than twenty years and was active in the unionization of the automobile plants.

Knox, now in Massachusetts, has always been a critic of Communism. Yet, during the time of the Hitler-Stalin pact, he innocently supported in one fashion or another such front groups as the International Labor Defense, the American Committee for Protection of Foreign Born, the Citizens Committee to Free Earl Browder, and the National Committee for People's Rights. In 1940 he became chairman of the National Federation for Constitutional Liberties, which later merged into the Civil Rights Congress. On one occasion he lost three teeth in a scuffle at a tumultuous civil-rights rally, and on another he was handled roughly by Washington police when he sought to lead an all-night prayer meeting on the steps of the national Capitol sponsored by the American Peace Mobilization. He was a member of A.P.M.'s national board and of its religious committee, and spoke at some of its meetings.

Knox was a sincere dedicated pacifist at the time. When Germany invaded Russia in 1941, the National Federation for Constitutional Liberties sent out, over his signature and without his permission, a letter urging a favorable attitude toward the war now that the Soviet Union had been attacked. Upon learning of this deliberate deception, he resigned immediately with a stern protest. "War is the antithesis of everything for which I stand," he told the press. He accused the national office of "strong Russian sympathies." [44]

In retrospect, Knox traces his involvement in Communist fronts to his assumption that other people who shared his ideals worked as openly and honestly as he did. His experience with the Communists was disillusioning, and he never lent his support to their efforts again.[45]

THE DEAN OF CANTERBURY AND *The Soviet Power*

Among the world's English-speaking clergy, the best-known champion of the Soviet Union has not been an American, but Hewlett Johnson, Dean of Canterbury, whose book *The Soviet Power* received great attention from the American Communists during the time of the Hitler-Stalin pact. In September 1942, Earl Browder recalled: "The biggest single job carried out by the Communist Party in this period was the distribution and sale throughout the country of two million copies of . . . *Soviet Power*." [46] It was published by International Publishers, a Communist press, and was translated into twenty-two languages and into Braille.

Johnson has been a curious ecclesiastical figure. In his enthusiasm, his naïveté, and especially in his appearance, he resembles the former Bishop of the Protestant Episcopal Church, William Montgomery Brown. He was born in 1874 near Manchester, England, the son of a prosperous manufacturer and one of nine children. After ordination, he spent many years in parish work, became Dean of Manchester in 1924, Dean of Canterbury in 1931.

When he came to Canada in 1935 to observe a successful Social Credit Party in action, his visit was ridiculed by some churchmen, among them William B. Spofford, Sr., editor of the *Witness,* who later lauded Johnson's political views. "The venerable and gaitered Dean of Canterbury, England," Spofford wrote, "came to America this fall to sell us on Social Credit, but instead he sold himself on our radio chin-wagger, Father Coughlin of Detroit. He spent twelve hours with the Detroiter and was so impressed that he told reporters that Coughlin was 95% right." [47] Though the Dean never discarded his Social Credit bias entirely, he gradually became convinced that the movement in Alberta had become corrupted, but that "the most important elements of Social Credit are incorporated in the Soviet financial system—the control of money by the state so that it cannot be a commodity, subject to private manipulation and speculation and the pricing of goods." [48] "One country where they dare let the industrial machine go is Russia," the Dean said in the thirties. "One country where there are no unemployed is Russia. One country where the standard of living—though far below that in America and England—is yet rising is Russia." [49]

In the epilogue to *The Soviet Power,* Johnson presented his views on the contemporary world scene. The Soviet entered into a pact with Hitler not only to "lessen the danger of war" but to guarantee "Russian safety in view of repeated efforts of Britain to appease and win Germany." [50] His defense of later Soviet moves illustrates the proficiency of Communist sympathizers in the art of rationalization. Russian occupation of eastern Poland was "urgent and vitally necessary if further minorities were to escape Nazi tyranny." [51] The absorption of Estonia, Latvia, and Lithuania "was necessary if Hitler was not to complete his control over the Baltic and the Baltic States." [52] France fell because of "a corrupt governing class, sympathetic to Fascism" and England was isolated because of the desire of "the ruling class . . . to insult and injure the Soviet Union." [53] The Dean defended Russia's invasion of Finland as vital to the protection of Leningrad and the narrow ice-free channel leading to Murmansk.

The Dean of Canterbury and *The Soviet Power* proved to be extremely useful instruments in Communist efforts to influence public opinion. Soon after the war broke out in 1939, Johnson wrote a series of articles, published in the *Witness,* and reprinted for widespread distribution, which assailed Britain's economy and "ruling circles" and glorified the Soviet Union. The A.P.M. invited him to speak at the American People's Meeting scheduled for April 5-6, 1941. "We cannot give too much emphasis to the inspiring effect your presence at the American People's Meeting would have," said the invitation sent by John B. Thompson. "Your name is known to millions here through your magnificent work for peace and democracy throughout the world [and] through your courageous stand on behalf of an end to the European war on people's terms." [54] Johnson replied that he would come if possible, but shipping facilities were unavailable.

There is irony in the fact that while Nazi bombers were blitzing the British countryside, the Dean of Canterbury, which is an ancient see of the Established Church, was actively co-operating with an American organization which demanded that the United States refuse all aid to England. Perhaps in the sweep of history the most significant aspect of the Hewlett Johnson story is the freedom he exercised while his nation stood alone against Hitler and Mussolini. But the Dean was to be recast in another role as soon as the German army crossed the border into the Soviet Union. The "imperialist war" was a thing of the past. The socialist motherland now was endangered, and Communists and their allies—both in England and the United States— became the most zealous of patriots.

NINE · THE ERA OF GOOD WILL

Lhe attack on Pearl Harbor came as a relief to anxious American Communists, frenzied over reports of swift German advances into Russia. The wartime alliance between the United States and the Soviet Union blossomed into an era of good will between the two countries. Leaders in American government, business, labor, education, and the arts—with only rare exceptions—used lavish terms to express their admiration for Russian courage and sympathy for the heavy Russian sacrifices. The resistance of Leningrad, the defense of Moscow, and the victory at Stalingrad led millions of Americans to forget the shock of the Hitler-Stalin pact.

There were significant pockets of skepticism left. Some Eastern Europeans in the United States had hoped that somehow—perhaps by a stalemate on the eastern front—both Nazism and Communism could be blotted out. Among a few ardent Irish-Americans, intense loyalty to America was mixed with reluctance to fight for either the British or the Soviet Union. The same was true of a sprinkling of German-Americans and Italian-Americans who suffered in silence as they read how United States military might was ripping their birthplaces to pieces. Those who clung to isolationism continued to resent what they viewed as President Roosevelt's prewar belligerency, which, they said, deliberately blocked all avenues to peace.

Perhaps the core of antiwar sentiment was found among Protestant clergymen. The majority of ministers went along with American participation—some enthusiastically, some more reluctantly—but many thousands never abandoned their pacifist position. The membership of the Fellowship of Reconciliation actually doubled during the 1942-45 period. The major denominations did not rush to endorse the conflict as they had in World War I. Even among those who believed the war was just, there were those who felt it was a regrettable compromise with their religious faith. The rights of conscientious objectors were defended and pulpit pacifists were not ousted or abused as had been true twenty-five years before.

Ironically, in recent years some of the ministers who refused to endorse World War II—Russia's great "War of National Liberation"—have been subjected to absurd charges of Communist sympathies. Among those falsely accused have been Kirby Page, George A. Buttrick, John Haynes Holmes, A. J. Muste, Henry Hitt Crane, and many more. Not only did these men oppose the war, but most of them worked toward its early end through a negotiated peace. They publicly condemned the obliteration bombings in both Germany and Japan.[1]

Had the Communists had their way, the plight of these pacifists would have been a serious one. The *Daily Worker,* which had wooed pacifists only three years before, warned in early 1944: "Any honest, win-the-war liberal who continues to blink at the menacing, disruptive nature of these so-called 'pacifist' groups in this country is doing a disservice to real liberalism and contributing to sabotage of the war effort." [2] A. J. Muste had followed a colorful political path in the preceding two decades, moving from religious pacifism to Trotskyism, and then back again to religious pacifism in 1936, when he became pastor of New York City's Labor Temple. Nevertheless, Communists sought to discredit him as a "Trotskyite traitor" throughout the course of the war.[3] John Haynes Holmes was depicted as "a notorious example of a fake 'liberal' who had constantly tried to stir opposition to the Allied war effort." [4] Quakers came under indictment also. Various pacifist groups specifically accused by the Communists of disloyalty were the Fellowship of Reconciliation, War Resisters League, National Council for Prevention of War, and the Women's International League for Peace and Freedom—described by the *Daily Worker* as "the fountainheads for the widespread pro-fascist campaign for a negotiated peace with Hitler and Hirohito." [5]

In general, however, the Communists were filled with good will for the churches, whether Protestant, Roman Catholic, or Jewish.

They wept over Nazism's attack on religion, hailed the news that Russian Orthodoxy was enjoying a renaissance, and praised the American churches, in particular the Episcopalians, for their contributions to Russian war relief. They found new meaning in religious holidays when, as in 1944, Abraham Chapman, leading Jewish Communist, wrote that "the road to freedom this Passover is the road to collaboration with the Soviet Union. . . ." [6] They took an ambiguous position toward the Vatican, yet always deploring "Catholic-baiting" and applauding "progressive Catholics." Perhaps indicative of the *rapprochement* were the large ads in the Communist press urging readers to see the movie "Going My Way," in which Bing Crosby played "the singing padre of the roughest parish in New York!" [7] In theaters nearby, the popular feature was "Song of Russia."

American Communists were at the height of their prestige. The interests of the United States and the Soviet Union were so intertwined that it was patriotic for senators, congressmen, governors, judges, generals, and captains of business and industry to support Communist fronts, not out of sympathy for Communism but out of dedication to wartime unity. Therefore, it confuses rather than clarifies the facts when extremists in more recent times scour the wartime years to find evidence of subversion among the clergy. The most obvious "super-patriots" from 1942 to 1945 were the Communists themselves!

ELIOT WHITE JOINS THE PARTY

On August 19, 1943, the *Daily Worker* trumpeted for the first time the news that a minister had openly joined the Communist Party. Eliot White proudly announced that he and his wife had found in Communism "the teachings of the Bible, which I promised my Bishop, when I was ordained to the Ministry of the Episcopal Church nearly fifty years ago, to follow in my life and preaching." [8]

White rocketed to a position of honor within the party apparatus. He began a weekly column, "Toward the New Day," for the Sunday edition of the *Worker,* which was accompanied by a picture of him in his clerical garb. In 1944 he delivered the opening address at the convention of the Communist Political Association and was elected its vice-president. In the postwar period he became an organizer of the

Publishers New Press, sponsor of the *Daily Worker*. Today, at ninety years of age, he is still a Communist and continues to profess his belief that Communism is bringing to the world the social order that Jesus envisioned.

The Whites were proud of their proper Boston background. It was his great-great-uncle, he boasted, who hung out the light in the old North Church steeple to warn Paul Revere. Mrs. White traced her lineage to Elder Brewster and two later governors of the Commonwealth of Massachusetts. Both had been educated at the finest schools —he at Harvard, class of 1892; she at Smith, class of 1894. Their membership in the Communist Party, White said, was in keeping with the deeds of their revolutionary ancestors, who would applaud their stand "on the side of conserving the rights and hopes of the people as a democratic unity against every effort to deprive them of their blood-bought heritage." [9]

The parish ministry of White was neither long nor distinguished— though at times newsworthy. He was rector for a decade at St. John's Episcopal Church in Worcester, Massachusetts, and spent the next fourteen years as assistant minister at famous Grace Church at Broadway and Tenth Street in New York City. His ties with Grace Church were severed in 1931, when he publicly defended Judge Ben Lindsey, a proponent of companionate or trial marriages. White dramatically protested his dismissal by picketing the Cathedral of St. John the Divine, diocesan headquarters of Bishop William T. Manning, carrying a placard reading: "Bishop, I ask you for Justice." [10] Later he designated himself as "Pastor of Greater New York." In 1943, when he announced his membership in the Communist Party, he had not served in a parish for twelve years, nor has he served one since.

Those who had followed White's career were not surprised at his announcement. He was a member of the Socialist Party for many years. Gradually, he moved into the Communist orbit and faithfully followed the zigzags of the party line. White attributes the development of his socialist views to books like *Looking Backward* by Edward Bellamy, William Stead's *If Christ Came to Chicago,* and the writings of Henry George and Robert Blatchford, an English Socialist, but attributes to the books of Hewlett Johnson, Dean of Canterbury, part of the impetus which prompted his decision to join the Communist Party.

During his ministry in Worcester, he became actively involved in the social crusades of the day, particularly in the struggle for shorter working hours in New England's textile mills. In Worcester also he enraged many citizens by battling for the right of Communists to hold a public forum. Later, during the Depression, he walked on many picket lines in his clerical garb. On one occasion, shortly after he was dismissed from Grace Church, he led a group of clergy and theological students in a picket line on behalf of striking employees of the Brooklyn Edison Company. Louis F. Budenz, editor of the *Daily Worker* when White became a party member, reported that "the goon squad of the Brooklyn Edison Company cruelly assaulted him, knocking out several of his front teeth." [11]

White cannot be viewed in the same light as hardened Communists. He was, and continues to be, essentially a religious romantic who considers the Communist Party an earthly instrument "for bringing in the Kingdom of God." Some party members have eyed his naïveté and religiosity with disgust; others see him as a half-humorous, half-pathetic figure; still others like his simplicity, dedication, and personal charm. In 1955 he described his reception into the party in these words: "We were received at once most cordially as 'comrades' and *never*, then or now, has the Party in any way whatever shown anything but the warmest fellowship and good will." [12]

On August 29, 1943, White and his wife contributed two articles to the *Daily Worker* under the headline "A Minister and His Wife Tell: 'Why We Joined the Communist Party!'" White recalled that he was first attracted to the party by denunciations of desirable social measures as "communistic." America, he said, should adopt the economic system of the Soviet Union, "by far the best hope of recovering the democratic values the Republic of the United States was founded to safeguard. . . ." As for atheism, he had found that the Communist movement "maintains the teachings of the Bible." [13] On another occasion he wrote regarding his membership:

. . . I am conscientiously glad to feel myself more than formerly in harmony with the Gospel declarations concerning the Christian Church of the First Century, when the Apostles wrote and acted fresh from the most intimate fellowship with our Savior, Jesus Christ, Himself, (Acts II:44, 45 and IV:32).[14]

These passages from Acts refer to communal life among early Christians. White has always made liberal use of Biblical texts to justify his political views.

The Whites spoke widely on their decision to become party members. Through his column in the *Worker,* he sought to recruit other clergymen. In February 1944, he asked with his characteristic flair: "Will you not now come in and help us hasten this beautiful though so ravaged and suffering world nearer to the righteousness and joy of God's eternal plan?" [15] He assured them that their religious convictions would receive "respect and honor" from fellow comrades. White sought to encourage others by stating that not a single Episcopalian had, to his knowledge, criticized his membership. Church members should remain in the church when they join, he said. "And let no one think this incurs the outworn accusations of 'boring from within,' as if some kind of hidden human termites were seeking to weaken the supports of true religion and ethics." [16]

Most of White's columns had no political significance. On one occasion, he contributed a piece entitled "Nature Notes for February." In another, "Column for Children," he included a number of verses for youngsters. Sometimes he would relate simple human-interest stories. Typical of White's extravagant and poetic language was this tribute to the *Daily Worker* on its twentieth anniversary:

O Daily and Sunday Worker, live and win yet more victories for the people and their all-important unity of action until the New Day, dreamed by all the prophets, martyrs, and forerunners, shall have dawned! [17]

White now lives with his daughter in Arlington, Massachusetts, close to his ancestral Boston. Two tragic events have left their mark: his wife died; he has become blind. Yet, his faith in both Christianity and Communism continue. "Jesus Christ, the Son of God, will prevail everywhere," he said in 1956.[18] He found the Khrushchev revelations of that year "very disappointing" but "such weaknesses are not inherent in Communism." Russia is still the greatest force for peace and progress in the world today. When the classless society is obtained, the Kingdom of God will have come. "A victory for the people's world will be a victory for Jesus."

Eliot White is today continually cited as evidence that the Communists have deeply penetrated the churches. But he is essentially a naïve romanticist who has embraced Communism without any understanding of its meaning in the world of reality, nor has he had an influence upon the clergy or organized religion. He is a lonely dreamer.

THE PARTY RECRUITS NEGRO MINISTERS

The effort of Eliot White to interest fellow Episcopal clergymen in joining the Communist Party met with no response. About the same time, however, the Communists were stepping up their activities among Negroes. The party had discovered in the early thirties the great influence ministers had among Negroes, and during World War II they wooed them assiduously through flattery, through appeals to racial pride and racial outrage, and even through membership in, and financial support of, some "progressive" churches. By 1944, they were able to report some success.

Shortly before World War II erupted, the Communists began to crowd around Adam Clayton Powell, Jr., a dynamic and influential Harlem Baptist minister. In 1941 he had swung with the Communists from isolation to intervention. In April, he was heaping abuse upon those favoring aid to "British imperialism"; by October, after the Nazi invasion of Russia, he was "fully aware of the necessity of uniting all democratic forces, both Negro and white, for a people's crusade to smash Hitlerism, both domestic and foreign." [19]

With Communist help, Powell first went to the New York City Council and later became the first Negro to represent Harlem as a United States congressman. During the war, he campaigned for Benjamin J. Davis, successful Communist candidate for the City Council; he plugged Communist causes through *People's Voice*, a newspaper he founded and once proudly described as the "Lenox Avenue edition of the *Daily Worker*"; [20] he addressed and sponsored many Communist fronts, some of which viewed his parish, the huge Abyssinian Baptist Church, as a base from which they could operate in the Harlem community.

Precisely what motivated Powell in his alliance with the Communists is difficult to say. He himself claims that in view of the circumstances of the time, he could best advance the welfare of the Negro people through co-operation with the well-organized Communist and American Labor Party machinery. His critics have characterized him as an opportunist, who makes political pacts with any group or individual able to further his own personal ambitions. He broke with the Communists after the war, when their assistance was no longer helpful and could prove detrimental. Powell seems to be one of the few who was more successful in exploiting the Communists than they were in exploiting him.

Powell's 1945 book, *Marching Blacks,* lauded the Communist Party. "Today," he wrote, "there is no group in America including the Christian church that practices racial brotherhood one tenth as much as the Communist Party." He discussed the attitude of Negroes toward Communism:

> The Negro has always had a peculiar viewpoint toward communism. For one, he does not fear it as do some white Americans in high places. He appreciates the communists for their unceasing efforts on his behalf. He will support common causes, join willingly in the united fronts, and fight side by side in every crusade, but he does not join the Party.[21]

Powell was generally right. The Communist Party never had much success in recruiting Negroes—and even less success in holding them once they joined. During World War II, however, it seems to have penetrated more deeply than ever before into the churches and to have enrolled a number of the less-educated clergy. This was particularly true after the Communist Party dissolved in May 1944 and the broader Communist Political Association took its place. A few items from the *Daily Worker* illustrate the trend.

March 13, 1944. The Rev. Solomon Freeman, pastor of an African Methodist Episcopal Church in Rockaway Beach, Long Island, is "one of the newest and proudest recruits to the Communist Party there."

April 25, 1944. Two pastors and eight parishioners of a small Baptist Church in Harlem joined the Communist Party following an address by Benjamin J. Davis, at the church. Davis administered the oath of membership.

May 7, 1944. The Rev. Samuel J. Comfort of Philadelphia tells why he became a Communist. "As a minister of the Gospel of Jesus Christ for many years," he writes, "I feel to be in good company and very much at home among the Communist people. . . . To unite our efforts with a people who strive to put an end to disfranchisement, Jim Crowism, segregation and all manner of economic injustice, is to join with a people who are striving to make visible the Kingdom of God upon the earth."

July 12, 1944. The energetic thirty-three-year-old organist of the New Redeemed Baptist Church in Harlem will be honored by her congregation at a special testimonial at the Progressive Methodist Church with Benjamin J. Davis as main speaker. She has recruited more than 120 into the Communist Political Association during the recent membership drive, which set a record. She is described as a "dignified, good-looking" woman who married at the age of thirteen and has two sons in the service. "I am furthering my Christian work," she told the *Daily Worker*. "Joining a political group makes my work so much broader. I come in contact with so many good and important people."

A closer look at the case of Solomon Freeman suggests some interesting answers to a number of questions. Why did he join the Communist Party? Who contacted him? What did he do as a member?

Freeman, who died in 1958, was an unsophisticated minister who first came into contact with the Communist Party while a pastor in Harlem. He became a member after he became pastor of an A.M.E. Church in Rockaway Beach, Long Island, where he was recruited by a determined woman who, together with her husband and four other white Communists, attended his church services occasionally. Their friendliness played an important role in influencing him to join.

As a Communist, Freeman's main responsibility was to recruit Negroes, and especially fellow ministers. Some whom he approached, such as Powell, flatly turned him down. Other clergymen showed interest, and several of his prospects even promised to join, but twelve years later he could not recall that any of them did.[22] He did, however, recruit thirty members of his congregation and others in the neighborhood. A Communist nucleus was formed around him and his white comrades. Their Thursday-evening meetings, usually held in the sanctuary of the church, opened and closed with prayers. The Communist group sang many hymns and spirituals. They were part of a larger party club of about one thousand members, approximately three-fourths of them Negro. Sunday mornings in the pulpit Freeman plugged the *Daily Worker,* which was on sale in the church.

Freeman left the party after eighteen months. He moved from Rockaway Beach to Brooklyn and simply let his membership lapse. When he was approached for his dues of one dollar per month some weeks later, he refused to pay them on the grounds that he "didn't want to bother with it any more." Ideology neither brought him into the party, nor did it play a role when he dropped out. His membership had no more significance to him than joining a local Democratic club or perhaps a Masonic lodge. In 1956 he reminisced about his former comrades: "They were nice people who treated me fine."

Freeman's experiences were not typical but neither were they unique—especially during World War II. The Communist Political Association in many areas was run like a social club emphasizing patriotism and national unity. Ironically, while the party was meeting with these successes in recruiting Negroes, it decided that the struggle against racial discrimination was "disruptive" of the war effort and should be postponed.

ORLEMANSKI FLIES TO MOSCOW

No clergyman stirred more enthusiasm among the Communists during World War II than the Roman Catholic priest Stanislaus S. Orlemanski. Victory in Europe seemed assured by 1943, and controversy began to rage over the future of Poland. In London, the Polish government-in-exile was planning for its return to Warsaw. Under its aegis, free Polish troops were fighting alongside the Western allies on the battlefronts in North Africa, Italy, and, later, France. In Moscow, another group of Poles, largely Communists, prepared to follow behind the Red Army and establish a government closely allied with the Soviet Union.

Most Poles had distrusted their Russian neighbor to the east even before it had conspired with Hitler to divide their nation in 1939. Polish-Americans strongly favored the return of the government-in-exile in London, strengthened in their conviction by the united opposition of the Roman Catholic hierarchy in America to the Moscow faction. Nonetheless, such Communist-oriented, Polish-language newspapers as *Glos Ludowy* and such Communist fronts as the American Slav Congress zealously worked to convince Americans of Polish background that a Kremlin-supported regime would be preferable.

Orlemanski came into public prominence in 1943. He had been born in the United States of devout immigrant parents, one of four sons who entered the priesthood. Before he was ordained, he had distinguished himself as a baseball player and as a journalist. In 1917 he was assigned to Our Lady of the Rosary Church in Springfield, Massachusetts, where he served until his death on March 16, 1960, at the age of seventy.

His political views made him controversial among his fellow Roman Catholic clergy. He disliked the Polish "ruling class" and during World War II began to reveal an admiration for the Soviet Union. He helped establish the Kosciuszko League in Detroit to fight "pro-Nazi" elements among Polish-Americans. In December 1943, he spoke at a Polish-Soviet amity rally in New York City sponsored by the National Council of American-Soviet Friendship, and his speech was printed in full in the *Daily Worker*. He denounced the American bishops as "nothing but a clique of politicians . . ." for their anti-Russian statements and assailed "some great philosopher, Rev. Fulton Sheen [who] is chasing up and down the land talking about Poland . . . when it comes to politics and diplomacy, he is as ignorant as the oak tree in the weeds. I would advise this gentleman to preach more about Ireland and forget Poland." Orlemanski called on fellow Poles to "join hands with Russia to completely destroy Hitlerism and to bring peace and prosperity to the Polish nation for centuries to come." [23]

Four months later Orlemanski startled the world by abruptly leaving his Massachusetts parish to fly to Moscow to confer for two hours with Stalin and Molotov. He issued a statement describing them as "great men" and referring to Stalin as "a friend of the Polish people" eager to work in close harmony with the Vatican. Roman Catholics need not fear, he said, because Stalin is fully aware that Poland is devoutly Roman Catholic and "will not tolerate any transgression in that regard." All Stalin wants is "a free, independent and democratic Poland" friendly to the U.S.S.R.[24]

Orlemanski was acclaimed by many, denounced by more. The State Department was criticized for allowing the trip. The attitude of his parish was variously reported—some said his parishioners gave him united support; others said that they were surprised and disapproved. Orlemanski did not retreat. "If I am a Communist," he said, "then so is the entire Roman Catholic hierarchy of Belgium, which announced that it would not admit to the church or bury in consecrated ground anyone who will fight on the side of Hitler against Soviet Russia." [25] He claimed to belong to "no clique, no faction, nor party." [26] From Moscow he brought back with him written assurances from Stalin that the Soviet Union wanted to co-operate with the Vatican against Nazi persecution of the church. At the same time Orlemanski was being given these assurances, however, Russian newspapers were pointing to him as evidence that "working class priests" were rebelling against Vatican policy.

The public waited to see what would happen to Orlemanski when he returned to Springfield. His bishop suspended him immediately on the technical grounds that he had not obtained permission to leave his parish over a Sunday. Orlemanski replied that he would take his case to the Pope himself: "You are hereby notified that I am no longer under your jurisdiction but under the jurisdiction of the Apostolic Delegate [papal representative] in Washington." For the *Daily Worker,* the episode was a test case: Was the Roman Catholic Church genuinely antifascist, or, rather, an enemy of the people?

The storm over Orlemanski came to a sudden end a few days later when he apologized to his bishop and promised to drop his extra-parish political activities. "I regret my seeming disregard for the legislation and directives of my church," he wrote his superior. "It is now my fixed purpose and promise to cease and separate myself from all activities which are not in accordance with the rule and mind of the Catholic Church." [27]

With this statement of contrition, Orlemanski was reinstated and disappeared from public view.

The fear of Soviet influence and expansion which lay behind the Roman Catholic Church's disciplining of Orlemanski was an indication that the Vatican's quarter-century duel with the Soviet Union was to enter a new phase. So were relations between Russia and the United States. The era of good will was nearly over and soon these allies would be engaged in the cold war.

TEN · THE CHURCHES AND THE COLD WAR

The cold war dominated the postwar decade. As Communist influence spread, America tried to contain Soviet power through economic assistance, defensive alliances, and—in the case of Korea—through armed resistance to military aggression. A new threat loomed in Asia, where Communists won control in China. Meanwhile, this East-West power struggle was reflected on the domestic scene in stern measures taken against the American Communist movement.

The response of the United States Government to the course of world events met with sharp criticism from many of its citizens. On one extreme, there were those who condemned American policy-makers for "softness" toward the Soviet Union and Communist China abroad and for blindness toward the threat of subversion at home. By 1950, they had found a symbol in Senator Joseph R. McCarthy.

Other Americans hoped that somehow a *rapprochement* might be possible between East and West so that the world might be spared another war. They believed the government too unimaginative and rigid in its attitude toward Russia and the new Chinese Government and too severe in its repression of the Communists. But they were not all of one mind nor can they be fairly described as one group. A few were Communists and Communist sympathizers—a number that continuously dwindled during the 1945-55 decade. Many millions more, however, were men and women of decent, humanitarian impulses who emerged from World War II with strong faith that the

175

wartime unity between Russia and America could be maintained during times of peace.

There was widespread affection and admiration for the Soviet Union in the United States following the victory of the United Nations over the Axis. And why not? For almost four years the agencies of government, the press, the theater, and the world of literature had been striving to create good will toward the Soviet Union. The Roosevelts and the Willkies and the Eisenhowers and men of prestige and position everywhere in the allied West toasted the might of the Red Army, the bravery of the Russian people, and the leadership of Marshal Stalin. It was difficult to accept immediately a new set of facts: that the same Red Army was a threat to United States security; that these same brave Russian people were really enslaved; that the same Marshal Stalin was a sinister evil man.

CHURCHMEN VIEW THE SOVIET WORLD

Four early postwar incidents that stirred debate reflect the attitude among many churchmen of the time. The first involved a prominent Southern Baptist clergyman who has been berated for his observations on religion in the Soviet Union. Another shows how some Methodist leaders were led by their Christian idealism into sending to 22,000 ministers a book lauding Stalin. The third concerns the reception given a report by seven Protestant clergymen of their 1947 visit to Yugoslavia. Finally, a comparison of the reaction to the 1945 and 1948 visits by the Dean of Canterbury suggests the rapid change of American attitudes from good will to disillusionment.

The Newton Report. A controversy raged in 1947 over the booklet *An American Churchman in the Soviet Union,* written by Louie D. Newton, then president of the Southern Baptist Convention. He and six other Americans had visited the U.S.S.R. in the summer of 1946 for the American Society for Russian Relief. Newton was impressed by the religious freedom he observed, especially among Baptist churches, though he carefully noted that the extent of his travels was limited and that his judgment might be based on inadequate investigation. He concluded: "I shall ever be grateful for the experience which deepened my admiration for the 200,000,000 people of the U.S.S.R. and calls me anew to prayer that our leaders may find the way to lasting peace." [1]

For his honest observations, Newton was subjected to widespread abuse. Such perennial critics of Protestant leadership as J. Frank Norris of Fort Worth, Texas, rose on the floor of the Southern Baptist Convention to assail him. But the critics were far more formidable than Norris. When *Life* magazine accused him of fellow-traveling, Newton objected sharply. *Life* revised its opinion and stated that "after studying Dr. Newton's more recent speeches in which he discusses ways of combating Communism through positive Christianity, *Life* now believes that the doctor is neither Communist nor fellow traveler." [2] Unfortunately, *Life*'s revised statement did not atone for damage inflicted by the original erroneous charge.

The Writings of Jerome Davis. Davis was continuously in the middle of controversy. In 1936 he was dropped as professor from the faculty of the Yale Divinity School on the grounds that he was deficient as a scholar. He claimed it really was a punishment for his attacks upon capitalism and he was able to arouse a national storm over his dismissal. He then became the president of the American Federation of Teachers until the anti-Communist faction, led by George S. Counts, rallied to defeat him by a narrow vote (344-320) the day the Nazi-Soviet pact was signed. [3] Then, in 1943, his $250,000 libel suit against the *Saturday Evening Post* reached the courts. In 1939 the *Post* had carried an article by labor writer Benjamin Stolberg describing him as a "communist" and "Stalinist." [4] After a hung jury, Davis received $11,000 in an out-of-court settlement.

Davis published the book *Behind Soviet Power,* focusing principally on Stalin, in 1946. "It would be an error to consider the Soviet leader a willful man who believes in forcing his ideas upon others," Davis wrote. "Everything he does reflects the desires and hopes of the masses to a large degree." [5] It was Stalin who was largely responsible for the democratic constitution in 1936, who led the peace forces during the thirties, who stamped out all remnants of racial and religious prejudice, who "was patient and acted slowly" in eliminating "traitors in high places" in the purges, who prepared the Red Army against Hitler and directed its main thrusts during World War II, who became the liberator of the peoples of Eastern Europe and the great champion of peace. *Behind Soviet Power* also spoke well of Molotov,

Mikoyan, Kalinin, Kaganovich, and Beria, and even defended the G.P.U. and the N.K.V.D., Russia's secret police.

Davis met with considerable success in his search for endorsements from influential political and religious figures. Joseph E. Davies, former American ambassador to Russia, wrote the introduction. Daniel A. Poling, the conservative editor of the *Christian Herald,* devoted his syndicated column to a discussion of the book, describing it as "the most challenging and at the same time objective study on Russia that has yet appeared." [6] Several years later, Poling confessed that he had not read the book before writing his strong endorsement.[7]

In May 1947, the administrative committee of the Board of Missions and Church Extension of The Methodist Church mailed 22,000 copies of *Behind Soviet Power* to Methodist ministers. An accompanying letter depicted the book as an important source of information since "the rapid spread of Russian influence throughout the world today is the most significant challenge to the World Mission of Christ." Ministers were also asked to read along with Davis's book a recent statement of the Federal Council of Churches on "Soviet-American Relations," written by John Foster Dulles.[8]

Jerome Davis was writing for *Classmate,* a Methodist youth publication, about the same time. One article, called "Joseph Stalin," repeated many of the statements from *Behind Soviet Power* and concluded: "No doubt he has serious faults. He loves power; he may be ruthless in getting it. But can we go out to serve God and the common people of America as sincerely and courageously as Stalin did for what he believed was best for his people?" [9] In another *Classmate* article on "The Youth of Russia" Davis praised the guerrilla activities of Soviet youth against the Germans—an unusual subject for a man of peace—and offered the dubious assertion that "the boys and girls in Russia, for the most part, go to church on Sunday. . . ." [10]

This widespread publication of Davis's views is another indication that many distinguished clergymen in the United States sought to preserve American-Soviet good will in the postwar era. From today's vantage point it is easy to see that the Methodists were ill advised to believe that these writings could contribute toward that goal; but to find in this episode any evidence of a "Communist conspiracy" would seem to display an ignorance of both the era and of the church leaders involved.

Seven Ministers in Yugoslavia. A number of Communist fronts were propagandizing on behalf of Tito when the postwar decade began. They aimed their appeal primarily at Americans of Serbian, Croatian, and Slovene ancestry. The center for their activity was Pittsburgh and their principal vehicle was the American Slav Congress, founded in 1942. The Congress involved a number of clergymen, including several Serbian Orthodox priests who returned to Yugoslavia under shadowy circumstances.[11]

In October 1946, Sava Kosanovich, Yugoslav Ambassador, discussed religious freedom in his homeland at a dinner for Yugoslav relief held in New York City. It was a timely topic because of the recent imprisonment of Louis Stepinac, a Roman Catholic archbishop convicted for collaboration with the Nazis. Many Roman Catholic spokesmen had asked America to intervene on his behalf. Protestants were divided but many were convinced that Stepinac was guilty as charged. The Ministers' Union of Philadelphia warned:

If the United States, which is the government of all the people, should accede to the request of the Roman Catholic Church and interfere in the internal affairs of Jugoslavia, it will establish a precedent that will undermine the historical American position of separation of church and state.[12]

Among those hearing Kosanovich was Guy Emery Shipler, editor of the *Churchman,* which had already taken a vigorous stand against Stepinac. As a result of the dinner, Shipler and six other ministers left in 1947 for Yugoslavia, as guests of the government. Two of them were well-known Soviet sympathizers, Claude C. Williams and William Howard Melish, and four others were politically independent: Emory Stevens Bucke, editor of *Zions Herald;* George Walker Buckner, Jr., editor of the *World Call;* Phillips Packer Elliott of the First Presbyterian Church in Brooklyn; and Samuel Trexler, former president of the Lutheran Synod of New York.

The ministers reported churches of all faiths open and free of government interference. They found Stepinac healthy in an "immaculate whitewashed room . . . flooded with sunlight from two windows," and concluded, on the basis of evidence they were shown, that the charge of collaboration with the Nazis was justified. Bucke did not sign the part of the report dealing with Stepinac since he did not interview the Archbishop. "We did not hear anything but the government's side of the case," he added.[13]

The clergy were sharply criticized when they returned to the United States. To the Scripps-Howard newspapers the trip was "a hoax from the start." [14] Everett R. Clinchy, president of the National Conference of Christians and Jews, said the ministers had failed to see that "fundamentally the philosophy of a police dictatorship is as diametrically opposed to Protestant Christianity as to Roman Catholocism." [15] William T. Manning, retired Episcopal bishop of the Diocese of New York, charged that "no man who loves right and freedom, unless he has been most strangely deceived, can approve or commend the Tito government." [16] Roman Catholic groups and publications were particularly severe. Led by the Knights of Columbus, they asked "our separated Christian brethren" to repudiate the report. Two Illinois congressmen, Fred R. Busbey, a Republican, and Martin Gorski, a Democrat, suggested that Congress investigate the whole episode. As the debate progressed, more than 2,600 Protestant ministers signed a statement endorsing the publication and distribution of the prepared report in the interest of free speech and a free press.

Perhaps many of the findings of the ministers, especially regarding Stepinac, were justified. But too many of the visitors had gone with strong prior prejudices. An objective team certainly would have included Roman Catholics and Eastern Orthodox. The seven clergymen should not have been surprised to have their report greeted with considerable skepticism.[17]

Dean of Canterbury in America. Hewlett Johnson came to the United States in November 1945 as a guest of the National Council of American-Soviet Friendship. At Grand Central Station he was met by the city's Police Commissioner, representing the Mayor, and rushed with screaming sirens to a press conference. From there he went to Washington as a guest of Joseph E. Davies, former ambassador to Moscow, and at Davies' home discussed world affairs with the Speaker of the House of Representatives, a number of senators, the Secretary of Commerce, five justices of the Supreme Court, and a score of other dignitaries. Later he conferred with President Truman.

The highpoint of the Dean's 1945 visit was his appearance at Madison Square Garden. Eighteen thousand rose to cheer the prelate of England's established church, dressed in his apron and gaiters, a huge cross suspended from his neck, and he responded by paying glowing tribute to the U.S.S.R., bastion of state-sponsored atheism. With him on the platform were Davies, Paul Robeson, Nikolai V. Novikov of the Soviet Embassy, and Dean Acheson, then undersecretary of state and son of a former Episcopal bishop of Connecticut. Before leaving New York, Johnson addressed 400 clergymen on religious freedom in the Soviet Union.

William Howard Melish, who accompanied the Dean on his American tour, recorded many of his comments, including his views on Stalin. "Stalin was less impressive than I expected him to be—in appearance, in dress, and in manner of speech," Johnson said. "He did not seem to have the powerful incisive mind that Lenin possessed, but I had the feeling constantly that there was a power behind Stalin which gave him greatness." Johnson was particularly impressed by "how little of a personal dictator he seemed to be, so contrary to the accepted view. How much less than Mr. Churchill!" [18]

Johnson visited America again in 1948. When he first applied for a visa, he was refused because the National Council of American-Soviet Friendship, again his sponsor, was on the Attorney General's subversive list, published shortly before. An "Ad Hoc Committee of Welcome to Dean Johnson" was formed with the support of many prominent churchmen who were annoyed by the government action. The Dean received a visa and started his tour with John Whittier Darr, Jr., a young Congregational minister, as his public-relations representative.

The Dean's views had not changed. On the question of Berlin, a source of East-West tension at the time, he embraced the Russian position entirely. The Marshall Plan, he said, was "going from worse to worse . . . and will soon be discredited." He praised the "new democracies" of Eastern Europe. "I was in Hungary during the recent election," he reported. "The government chosen, though friendly to the Soviet Union, was most emphatically the government of the people's choice." [19] He described it as "the fairest election I have ever seen." [20]

Much of the press was antagonistic to Johnson in 1948 and helped inspire a flurry of protests, cancellations of meetings, and withdrawals. Many church leaders would have preferred to ignore the visiting dignitary altogether, but were pressured into public disapproval of his ideas. In Canada he encountered especially sharp hostility from recent east European refugees.

Yet, the Communist press and two Protestant magazines, the *Churchman* and the *Witness,* depicted the response as overwhelming. His first appearance was before an overflow congregation at the Church of the Holy Trinity in Brooklyn, where William Howard Melish was assistant rector. In Boston, Johnson addressed a noon audience at St. Paul's Cathedral. In Detroit, a Roman Catholic judge introduced him at the crowded music hall. He was greeted by the president of the Catholic Knights of Wisconsin in Milwaukee. Hundreds were reported turned away in Chicago. In New York City, he joined Wallace in addressing 20,000 at a postelection Progressive Party meeting in Madison Square Garden. One of the Dean's final acts was to visit the office of the *Daily Worker.* He himself was a member of the Board of Editors of London's *Daily Worker.*

The contrast between Johnson's reception in 1945 and in 1948 indicates how rapidly the reservoir of good will toward the Soviet Union was running out. But there were still many among the churched and the unchurched who were ready to give serious attention to the words of the Dean of Canterbury. His opinions, however warped, had a far greater impact upon the clergy than anything Earl Browder, William Z. Foster, or the *Daily Worker* might have said. Herein rested the Dean's major contribution to the Communist cause.

SPOTLIGHT ON CHINA

Both American Communists and American churchmen watched with interest and concern events in postwar China—the savage civil war between Chiang Kai-shek's Nationalists and the Communist armies, resulting in the flight of the Kuomintang government to Formosa.

A heated debate developed among China missionaries, many of whom felt that a Communist victory would crush missionary activity and bring persecution to Chinese Christians. Others looked forward to peace, convinced that Chiang had lost popular support, and that emergence of a third democratic force was no longer possible. They reassured themselves that for many centuries the Chinese had swallowed up their conquerors and that the Communists would be no exception. They remembered, too, that in the period of the twenties, when the Kuomintang had been hostile to missionaries, their work had survived and even grown stronger. Behind this optimism was, of course, hope; most missionaries desperately wanted to stay in the land to which they had given their lives. Here was the yield of their dedicated labor: large churches, universities, hospitals, orphanages, and other institutions. Surely, if all else failed, God would intervene to save China from atheism.

The Communist occupation brought quick disillusionment. Some missionaries were imprisoned on vague charges of espionage. Some were denounced by the persons they had aided most. Most of those who did not flee were at first detained, then ordered to leave—even those who wanted to co-operate fully with the new government or who sought to avoid political issues altogether. Many have kept alive the hope of a postrevolutionary period when the doors of China will again swing open. A number contend that negotiation with the new regime might be the quickest way to reopen these doors.[21]

Only a few Americans, like the authors Edgar Snow and Anna Louise Strong, were enthusiastic about the Communist regime. Their opinions were promoted by such groups as the Committee for a Democratic Far Eastern Policy (dissolved in 1952) headed by Maud Russell, who had been a Y.W.C.A. worker in China from 1917 to 1943. Among publications giving unqualified praise to the Chinese Communist government have been the *Far Eastern Spotlight,* organ of the Committee for a Democratic Far Eastern Policy; the *China Monthly Review,* which was edited by John W. Powell in Shanghai; and the *New World Review* (until 1951 *Soviet Russia Today*). Over the years relief was sent to Communist-controlled areas through the China Aid Council and the China Welfare Fund.

Within the Protestant churches, clergymen who have been generally uncritical of the Soviet Union have been equally uncritical of Communist China. Such ministers as Stephen H. Fritchman, John W. Darr, Jr., Jack R. McMichael, William Howard Melish, Richard Morford, and William B. Spofford, Sr., discussed in greater detail later, gave their support to the Committee for a Democratic Far Eastern Policy. The *Witness,* the *Protestant,* and the *Social Questions Bulletin* lent their influence to the Chinese Communist government.

Material published in the *Churchman* bristled with condemnation of fellow Protestants who did not agree. Typical were these comments reprinted from a 1948 issue of the New York Chinese-language newspaper, the *China Daily News:*

In American churches there are many who still use Christianity as a means to promote the evil cause of Chiang Kai-shek. Included in this group are Walter Judd, a representative in Congress and ex-missionary doctor in China; Henry P. Van Dusen, the "Christian theoretician" for reaction, President of Union Theological Seminary, Chairman of the Associated Board of the Thirteen Christian Universities in China and the back-stage director of reactionary missionary policies; Henry Luce, publisher of *Life, Time* and *Fortune* and the proclaimer of the "American Century," and Frank Price . . . who carries on anti-communist secret service tasks under cover of being a missionary. If these people are allowed to continue these activities, the Christian Church will soon become an enemy of the entire Chinese people. They are actually pushing the church to its deathbed.[22]

Not even John R. Mott, noted Y.M.C.A. officer and Nobel Peace Prize winner in 1946, escaped sharp censure. An article in the *China Monthly Review* described him as "a leading agent of American Imperialists who helped to organize many international Christian organizations through which the American Century planners were able to carry on their work." [23]

Less than a half-dozen Protestant missionaries from North America have been loud in their praise of the new Chinese regime. Two are of special interest.

Dryden L. Phelps, a beloved northern Baptist missionary, served for thirty years in West China and for many years on the faculty of West China Union University at Chengtu. William Lyon Phelps, famous Yale University professor of English, was his uncle. He became convinced that the Communist cause in China was just, had the support of the people, and would triumph. "People like Van Dusen, Bullitt, Luce, Wedemeyer are blind guides," he warned in 1947.[24] He accused Roman Catholic priests in North China of inventing false anti-Communist propaganda and implored the board of the American Baptist Foreign Mission Society to meet the challenge of the crisis by sending to the field men with progressive ideas.

In 1950 Phelps wrote a personal letter to William Howard Melish.

Melish made a few changes to make it appear to be a letter to the editor and sent it on to several journals for publication. Appearing in *Soviet Russia Today,* it read in part:

I am a missionary of the American Baptist Foreign Mission Society, at this University since 1921, with the exception of furloughs. Now we are having a thrilling experience of reorganizing every phase of our University life, and of Chinese society. It is the most profoundly religious Christian experience I have ever been through. I absolutely believe this to be the most comprehensive renaissance the human spirit has ever experienced; and the most dynamic change in human history. God is working alongside of these Communists. . . .

Ninety-five percent of the U.S. Press on the Far East is absolutely false. Believe the opposite, and you will be close to the facts.[25]

Baptist headquarters, bombarded by protests, asked Phelps to return to America for a conference, and on January 22, 1952, he appeared before the Board of Managers of the American Baptist Foreign Mission Society. Phelps assured the officials that he and his wife "have never been and are not now, Communists. . . . When, a year and a half ago, in August of 1950, I wrote that God was working along side the Communists, I did not mean—and I did not say— that Communists are religious or that they are Christians, though some of them are; nor did I mean to say that God is working only with the Communists, or with all Communists, or with all that the Communists do." Phelps said his opinions were based upon his observations that the new government was carrying out "Christian" activities and that significant things were happening "expressive of the Christian spirit and for which Christian teaching may be in part responsible."

The board asked for his resignation on the grounds that he had unwisely identified himself publicly with one political faction, contrary to the board's policy. It specifically stated, however, that they believed Phelps' actions and opinions were promoted by "his supreme and dominating purpose—to preach and teach the Christian faith." [26] Despite his unpopular political views, Phelps is highly regarded by those who have known him.

J. Spencer Kennard, Jr., another northern Baptist, has held far more extreme views than Phelps. Kennard spent many years in Japan but was expelled in 1935 for his protests against the militarist government. He taught at West China Union University at Chengtu, with Phelps, until he returned to the United States in 1944. When he asked to go back to China, the Mission Board refused his request on the grounds that his political partisanship was opposed to the best interests of their work. Kennard was convinced that Chiang's Kuomintang government had intimidated the board.

The fiery Baptist has made no attempt to hide his enthusiasm for the Chinese Communists. In early 1945, several months before Japan surrendered, he wrote a series of articles in the *Protestant* lauding the "Partisans" (Communists). Later he embraced the entire Communist version of the Korean conflict, including the assertion that South Korea attacked North Korea. Such facts were not known to the American people, he said, mainly because "Jesuit agents" had infiltrated into the State Department.[27] Kennard has supported a large number of organizations within the Communist orbit in the postwar period, among them the American Committee for Protection of Foreign Born, American Peace Crusade, Civil Rights Congress, Committee for a Democratic Far Eastern Policy, Council of Greek Americans, and the National Committee to Secure Justice in the Rosenberg Case. In recent years he has been a college teacher.

One of the curious sidelights of the Chinese civil war involved the Chinese Students' Christian Association in North America. The C.S.C.A. was founded in 1909 primarily to work among the two to three thousand Chinese studying in American colleges. It was sponsored by the Committee on Friendly Relations Among Foreign Students, which also had organized similar groups among Japanese, Filipinos, and others.

The Chinese students carefully followed events in their homeland. While many came from wealthy, pro-Kuomintang families, some of the most promising students disapproved of what they considered the decadent Chiang regime and sympathized with the Communist revolution. By 1948, national C.S.C.A. leadership had passed into their hands and there was the strange spectacle of a Christian group zealously propagating Marxism. Idealism, patriotism, and the desire to return home and participate in the new life of their country led more and more students to romanticize the revolution in China and become hostile toward the United States Government. This political orientation, incidentally, never influenced the C.S.C.A. in the western states, notably California, where most of its members were American-born and did not watch developments in China closely.

The C.S.C.A. dissolved soon after war in Korea broke out in 1950. Some of its leaders returned to China to assume responsible positions in the new government. The last executive secretary of the group was Siu May Ting, whose husband, K. H. Ting, was active as a student Christian leader. After their return, he was named president of Nanking Union Theological Seminary and, in 1955, was consecrated Anglican bishop of Chekiang. Ting attended a meeting of the central committee of the World Council of Churches in Budapest, Hungary, in August 1956, where he described the Chinese revolution as "an act of God." In 1958 he characterized the World Council of Churches as "nothing but window dressing for western imperialism." [28] He obviously has come to terms with the Communist regime —apparently out of sympathy, but possibly in an effort to salvage the work of the church. The future of this work remains in doubt.

THE PARTY REASSESSES CHRISTENDOM

While the debate over the Soviet Union and China continued, American Communists were re-evaluating religion and the church in terms of the cold war. Their wartime plea for Protestant-Catholic-Jewish unity had come to an abrupt end in 1944 as tension mounted between Russia and the Papacy over the fate of Poland, Hungary, and other Roman Catholic areas into which the Red Army was advancing. The party ridicule of religion, like that of the twenties, did not return, nor was there much concern over church activities confined within the United States. There were, instead, serious discussions of the role of world Christendom as a "conspirator" with Wall Street against the onward march of international Communism.

V. J. Jerome, a leading Communist theoretician, interpreted the postwar line on Roman Catholicism in the April 1946 *Political Affairs,* a Communist monthly.[29] The Papacy, he said, was frantic in the face of the rising tide of democratic forces who reject superstition, resent the church's gross wealth, and are aware of the Vatican's alliance with decaying capitalism. Jerome cited the 1946 appointment of thirty-two cardinals as evidence that the Vatican was "stretch-

ing out its tentacles to every continent. . . ." The assignment of
three additional cardinals to Germany was depicted as "a move to
reinforce the pro-fascist Catholic groups in their attempt to hold together and reorganize the remnants of defeated Nazism on a new
demagogic basis." The assignment of a cardinal to Armenia was a
maneuver "directed at Soviet Armenia." Three of the four new
American cardinals—John J. Glennon of St. Louis, Samuel A. Stritch
of Chicago, and Edward A. Mooney of Detroit—were from the Mid-
west, "the terrain of the clerico-fascist offensive. . . ." The selection
of Francis J. Spellman was the "most outstanding and spectacular
elevation of all, in America or elsewhere" because of Spellman's
"friendship for fascism." Jerome pointed with pride to the vote of the
two Communist members of the New York City Council, Benjamin J.
Davis and Peter Cacchione, against a Council resolution expressing
"a great deal of satisfaction and pride" in Spellman's elevation.

Jerome's article explicitly repudiated the "outstretched hand" policy
of Earl Browder. Browder was ousted from the party in 1946, and
his disapproval of the new anti-Catholic emphasis had played some
small role in his removal. The policy, Jerome said, had been based
upon the illusion that there was a progressive wing within the Roman
Catholic hierarchy—part of the "Browderite roseate prospect of the
progressive post-war role of 'enlightened imperialism.' " [30] Jerome
called instead for a struggle "to drive a wedge between the reactionary
Hierarchy and the masses of the Church." He was optimistic: "The
masses of Catholic workers in the C.I.O. are supporting the general
line of this great progressive trade union center," and in the struggle
against fascism "Catholic workers will take their place in the forefront."

In November 1946, Jerome wrote another major piece, on "A
World 'Christian Front.' " [31] The article reiterated charges against the
Vatican, but this time opened fire upon its "Protestant collaborationists." The principal villain was John Foster Dulles. "This powerful
Protestant layman represents in himself the transmission belt between
finance capitalism and Protestant clerical reaction," Jerome charged.
Dulles, he said, seeks to make Protestantism a "Vatican-tied instrument of imperialism's anti-Soviet drive." His influence within both
the Federal Council of Churches and the World Council of Churches
was seen as propelling those two groups into the reactionary camp. As

a sign of Dulles' growing power, the article cited his new position as a director of Union Theological Seminary in New York, whose president, Henry P. Van Dusen, Jerome accused of urging aid to Chiang Kai-shek "in the name of an anti-Soviet-US foreign policy."

Simultaneously the Communists were perfecting their technique of exploiting the opinions of clergy who had no sympathy with Communist goals and methods. When the bishops of the Protestant Episcopal Church protested some of the procedures of the Un-American Activities Committee, the *Daily Worker* gave a full report.[32] Similarly, publicity was given to scores of other items of church news: Rabbi Abba Hillel Silver criticizes the Marshall Plan;[33] a post of the Catholic War Veterans attacks the Mundt Bill;[34] a pastor in Connecticut opposes United States interference in the Mindszenty case;[35] twenty-two ministers assail the North Atlantic Pact in a Good Friday plea;[36] Negro Baptists urge ban on the A-bomb;[37] Methodist Bishop Oxnam warns against an alliance with Franco;[38] Bishop Sheil of the Roman Catholic Church denounces witch-hunters.[39]

Citing with approval such comments of church groups and leaders did not mean that the Communist Party had abandoned its basic antagonism toward religion and supernaturalism. This was indicated by the 1949 volume *The Twilight of World Capitalism,* by William Z. Foster, Browder's successor, which included a chapter on "The Decline of Religion." Foster was born of Irish Catholic parents and had been urged by his mother to become a Roman Catholic priest. He wrote: "My first long step towards a rational working class view of life and politics came through the liquidation of the boyhood beliefs that I had been so carefully taught during my boyhood."[40]

Foster restated the basic Communist tenet that religion and socialism were contradictory and irreconcilable—an emphasis that had been soft-pedaled during the Browder era. Religion was needed by primitive man to explain the mysterious, but now science is freeing man from such quasi-mythological religious forms as Christianity, whose gods are becoming vaguer and indistinct. "Eventually man, in his intellectual advance, will arrive at a fully scientific socialist world . . . and then, accordingly, he will finally altogether dispense with his gods and their imaginary eternal rewards and punishments."[41]

This process has already gone a long way under capitalism, which itself "is basically destructive of religion."[42] Foster cited many evi

dences of this. Fifty years ago there were sharp nationwide controversies over minor theological differences that divided the Protestant
sects; today, he wrote, many sects are coming together in a church
unity movement to save what is left of their declining strength. Among
Roman Catholics, he found an increasing reluctance to accept the
myths, the miracles, and the morals traditional to that faith. In countries like Poland, Hungary, Czechoslovakia, Italy, and France, the
Communists have a large Roman Catholic following. With the international triumph of socialist society, any supernaturalism that managed to survive would, he predicted, die a natural death.

Foster sought to analyze the apparent religious revival of the postwar period. "Undoubtedly," he wrote, "large numbers of people,
especially of the bourgeoisie and petty-bourgeoisie, are frightened and
confused at the wholesale mass slaughter, oppression, and impoverish-
ment, at the economic crises, fascist tyranny, wars, and revolutions at-
tendant upon the decline of world capitalism, and they look to religion
in their despair." [43] For the overwhelming majority of workers, however, fear is being replaced, he continued, by new courage, by the certainty of a people's world, and by a new and wholesome materialistic
outlook on life.

Spurred on by this faith, the Communists and their supporters
labored earnestly to reach the "masses" of America with a message of
hope and an assurance of ultimate victory. The postwar period was
still to provide many more opportunities to exploit those who professed this very supernaturalism the Communists abhorred.

ELEVEN · COMMUNIST FRONTS AND THE CLERGY

The principal channel through which Communists pursued their goal in postwar America, as in the thirties, was the front group. Fronts using misleading names and impressive letterheads existed for nearly every conceivable purpose. Some, such as the American Committee for Protection of Foreign Born, traced their history back many years. Others, notably the Civil Rights Congress, were amalgams of two or more from the past. Still others were established to do battle only on one issue or to engage in only one brief encounter and then to die.

During critical periods, new fronts sprang up almost daily. There were fronts for young and old; for mothers, wives, and daughters; for veterans and the jobless; for Jews, Negroes, Poles, Italians; for American-born and foreign-born. They were never called fronts, as was occasionally true when the concept was originally put into practice. Now they were councils, committees, conferences, congresses, clubs, forums, foundations, federations, societies, and associations. There were also schools, dramatic groups, information centers, even summer camps for "democratic living." These fronts were established to defend, to free, to uphold, to win, to secure, to aid, to battle, to resist, to fight, to struggle. They wanted peace, justice, democracy, the Bill of Rights. They did not want war, injustice, white supremacy, unemployment, higher rents, rising food costs, police brutality, inadequate housing, censorship, militarism, monopolies.

The Communists might have been expected to organize a "Ministers' Conference to Preserve the Constitution" or a "Democratic Union of Clergymen" or a "National Committee of Protestants, Catholics and Jews for World Peace." But this was not the case. Perhaps such plans were discussed from time to time within the secrecy of party councils but discarded as unwise and unnecessary. Clergymen were already proving much too useful in a wide variety of fronts, lending an air of dignity, strength, and innocence to scores of letterheads.

THE SIGNIFICANCE OF FRONT AFFILIATIONS

It is at this point that the facts need to be clarified so that there will be no misunderstanding. Many eminent clergymen who are alleged to have supported these fronts have been subjected to heavy abuse in recent years. There has been a deliberate and malicious campaign to associate them—through their "front affiliations"—with the Communist Party. Not only have the individual ministers been slandered, but, through an indiscriminate manipulation of words, such interchurch agencies as the National Council of Churches and the World Council of Churches have come under heavy fire.

This wanton misuse of guilt-by-association is unfair, unethical, and often purposely exploited to mislead and arouse the gullible.

There was a pattern by which a typical Communist front operated in the postwar period. First, it focused attention upon a humanitarian goal—perhaps putting a Negro news commentator on a radio station or giving Communists in prison a Christmas amnesty or asking for a ban on atomic and hydrogen bombs. It adopted a name which gave no hint to the average person that it was Communist-controlled —like the Committee to Uphold the Bill of Rights or the American Committee for Yugoslav Relief or the Idaho Pension Union. Then it began to canvass for sponsors to give it additional respectability. Quite naturally a few "Reverends" on a letterhead would help.

The strategy from this point on varied, but willful deception usually played a role. A letter, or in some cases a telephone call or a telegram, would be sent to a number of leaders in the religious world. An appeal might read like this: Within a few days, the state of Mississippi will execute Willie McGee, a thirty-four-year-old father of four young children, unless this legal lynching is stopped. He was convicted of the "rape" of a white woman by an all-white jury after a two-minute trial in a courtroom crowded by a mob of white supremacists. His "confession" was signed only after continual beatings by the police. Will you, as a distinguished clergyman, join other religious and civic leaders to save Willie McGee's life?

Such a marshaling of the arguments would be impressive. It was easy to believe that a Negro in Mississippi would not receive a fair trial. It was also widely known that Negroes had been railroaded to their death on other occasions for the false charge of rape. Most significant, many ministers were opposed to capital punishment on principle. Was it any wonder that some clergymen would respond?

Once this first step was successful, the others followed quickly. With several "big names" on a letterhead, a larger mailing could be sent out. Now the appeal would be altered slightly to begin: "Won't you join Bishop . . . , the Rev. Dr. . . . , and other distinguished clergymen of all faiths who are appealing to the Governor of Mississippi to spare the life of Willie McGee?" This would be followed by a repetition of the facts of the case as interpreted by the Communists.

Over the years hundreds, indeed thousands, of ministers responded to such heart-rending appeals. Should they, as a result, be listed as "Communist fronters," "Communist sympathizers," or even "Communist dupes"? They had no intention of supporting Communists; they wanted simply to keep McGee from being executed. If the only appeal to reach them on McGee's behalf was sent out by a Communist front, it was unknown to them. The very compassion that marks the superior pastor has ironically led many of them into the Communist trap.

An analogy may make the matter even clearer. Is a person a racketeer—or sympathetic to racketeers—because from time to time in the course of his life his generous nature leads him to contribute innocently to a fake charity? Or, to focus upon the issue somewhat differently, is it best to stop giving to charities altogether because there are fraudulent ones in the field? Unfortunately, this latter course has been followed by more and more ministers in the realm of social action.

They lent their names to a number of "worthy causes" later revealed to be Communist fronts. Subsequently, they have been "listed" by the Committee on Un-American Activities and subjected to suspicion among their parishioners and friends. To avoid further difficulty, they now refuse to lend their names to any cause, however deserving it may be.

There is bitter irony in the fact that Communists and the noisiest anti-Communists have together robbed so many clergymen first of their unblemished reputations and then of their legitimate concern for social justice and world peace. To avoid perpetuating this kind of injury, the ministers who innocently lent their names to various Communist fronts are generally not mentioned here at all so that persons who carelessly (or "carefully") misread the references will not find further opportunity to cause them undeserved harm.

The situation is complicated, however, by the fact that not all ministers who supported Communist fronts have been tricked. A small group of clergymen—as the following pages will show—have knowingly and consistently supported the Communist-front apparatus. In many cases, they have held important positions in various front groups and have enticed fellow clergymen into them. The most important of this "progressive" nucleus of clergymen can be identified quite easily. There is evidence that a number of them are idealistic and self-sacrificing; but the evidence is also overwhelming that during the first postwar decade they believed that the world Communist camp was essentially correct in all of its major areas of disagreement with the United States.

Who are these ministers? Altogether they would not total more than twenty-five. A few, such as Harry F. Ward and William B. Spofford, Sr., first accepted the Communist viewpoint during the Depression period. Jack R. McMichael entered the Communist periphery in the days immediately prior to the war. During the conflict, they were joined by William Howard Melish, Stephen H. Fritchman, Richard Morford, J. Spencer Kennard, Jr., and a handful more. John W. Darr, Jr., became an active member of the nucleus for a while following the war. Later, Kenneth R. Forbes joined the group. Many of them, it should be emphasized, have spent little or no time as parish pastors.

EXAMPLES OF FRONT ACTIVITY

A quick survey of five Communist-inspired efforts during the postwar decade will serve to illustrate the various ways in which the Communists and the "progressive" ministers co-operated and in many cases sought to lure unsuspecting clergy.

1) Many Americans—ranging all the way from the Communists to Senator John W. Bricker—disagreed with the Truman Doctrine of 1947, which proposed that military aid should be given to Greece and Turkey. One front group combating the Truman Doctrine was the American Council for a Democratic Greece. John W. Darr, Jr., a vigorous social-actionist, emerged as its secretary.[1] Darr released statements to the press, organized rallies, sent telegrams of protest, and arranged demonstrations before the Greek Consulate— all opposing American policy and supporting the "democratic partisans" who were conducting guerrilla warfare against the government. Darr was aided by William Howard Melish, Richard Morford, Harry F. Ward, William B. Spofford, Sr., and Kenneth Leslie, lay editor of the *Protestant,* who also accepted the Communist view of world affairs. The curious result was that this small group of Anglo-Saxon Protestants became key activists in a front group whose letterhead carried only Greek names. Greek Orthodox priests, incidentally, were conspicuous by their absence.

The National Council of American-Soviet Friendship received broader support in its efforts against the Truman Doctrine. One of its moves was to round up the signatures of 175 ministers, among them several distinguished bishops, to a statement condemning the Truman Doctrine for abandoning "true moral leadership in favor of reliance on naked military and economic power." At the time, the N.C.A.S.F. was headed by William Howard Melish. Richard Morford, a Presbyterian minister, was executive secretary. In 1946 Morford refused to turn over the files and records of the organization to the Committee on Un-American Activities, was charged with contempt of Congress, and was imprisoned for three months in 1950.[2]

2) The Civil Rights Congress was founded in 1946 at Detroit through a merger of the International Labor Defense and the National

Federation for Constitutional Liberties. The C.R.C. was to serve as the legal arm of the American Communist movement, but this was not clear in 1946. Nearly a score of Protestant and Jewish clergymen signed the call to its founding convention. Among them were prominent pacifists like the Quaker scholar Rufus M. Jones, W. Russell Bowie, then of Union Theological Seminary, and the Harlem minister Shelton Hale Bishop—all of whom deplored Communist emphasis on violence and class war and withdrew when Communist control became evident.

Also issuing the call were members of the same group of "progressive" churchmen, among them Stephen H. Fritchman, Jack R. McMichael, Claude C. Williams, and Ward. Ward and Benjamin E. Mays, a Baptist minister and president of Morehouse College, were named honorary chairmen. Mays withdrew soon; Ward continued to serve for many years. William Howard Melish was chosen one of the five vice-presidents; Richard Morford participated in the program.

3) The principal instrument of the Department of Justice in its efforts to destroy the effectiveness of the Communist apparatus was the repressive Smith Act, passed by Congress in 1940. It was first used against a group of Trotskyists during World War II, when the Communists had urged its rigid enforcement. When indicted under the same act, the Communists sounded a different note: suddenly it became "unconstitutional" and a tool of a growing fascist state. Many Americans were skeptical of any attempt to curtail civil liberties, including freedom for Communists. Their support was avidly solicited by the Communists through a number of front organizations.[3]

One of these fronts was the Non-Partisan Committee to Defend the Rights of the 12 Communist Leaders. On its letterhead were the names of John W. Darr, Jr., William Howard Melish, seven other Protestant ministers, and two Jewish rabbis. To entice additional clergymen, the Committee circulated among them an editorial by Jack R. McMichael reprinted from the *Social Questions Bulletin* of the Methodist Federation for Social Action. Another two dozen clergymen signed an *amicus* brief prepared by the Lawyer Defense Committee, a Communist front established on behalf of several attorneys for the party leaders sentenced for contempt.

On one occasion, five little-known ministers from Chicago attended the Smith Act trials at Foley Square. They attacked Harold R. Medina, the presiding judge and a favorite target of Communist propaganda, and labeled the whole case a "frame-up." The group said they had been invited to New York by fellow ministers in the East and named John W. Darr, Jr., and J. Spencer Kennard, Jr., as two of their hosts.

4) The sometimes subtle role of "progressive" clergy in securing names of other ministers for statements, appeals, and petitions was illustrated by an amnesty appeal for imprisoned Communists in late 1952. A plea, addressed to President Truman, asked that "these political prisoners return to their wives and children in time for Christmas" and characterized their only crime as "a lively conscience in the face of what they consider the inequities of society and the advocacy of social change which they believe will result in a larger benefit for all. . . ." [4]

Only clergymen were requested to sign, and 161 responded. The names of Fritchman, McMichael, Melish, Spofford, and others of like mind were there. But among those signing were also nine bishops (seven of them Protestant Episcopal), twelve seminary professors, and an array of church journal editors and denominational leaders. One reason why the appeal was so successful was that the ten listed as initiators included a distinguished Massachusetts bishop and not a single prominent Soviet apologist. Two of the ten—Charles A. Hill and Edward D. McGowan—had co-operated frequently with the Communists, but neither of their names was recognized by most signers. Significantly, it was McGowan who released the statement and the list of its signers to the press.

Many anti-Communists were also interested in offsetting the bad effects of the Smith Act, and many statements assailing it originated in anti-Communist circles. In 1955, for example, another petition requesting a Christmas amnesty was initiated by A. J. Muste and a group of his associates. Unlike the 1952 appeal, which left the impression that the prisoners were innocent social zealots, the new request for amnesty specifically took issue with the philosophy and program of the Communist Party. Among distinguished signers were Mrs. Eleanor Roosevelt, Norman Thomas, historian Henry Steele Commager, and playwright Elmer Rice. [5]

5) The most important postwar effort of the Communists to arouse mass support in the United States and around the world centered upon Ethel and Julius Rosenberg, executed in June 1953 for spying

during World War II on behalf of the Soviet Union. The case had many dramatic aspects: the fatal testimony of a brother, David Greenglass, against his sister, Ethel Rosenberg; the plight of the two young Rosenberg sons; the charges of anti-Semitism; continuous appeals to the President and the Supreme Court; picket lines, motorcades, rallies, petitions, "death watches," and prayer meetings; the publication of tender letters between Ethel and Julius as they awaited death; their quiet composure as they departed for the electric chair just before the Jewish Sabbath began, still protesting their innocence; thousands of sympathizers parading through downtown New York singing "Go Down Moses" amid cries of "Long Live the Rosenbergs!"; a funeral service conducted by a distinguished rabbi with the Twenty-third Psalm read by W. E. B. DuBois alongside their grave. The Communists had added two more names to a long list of martyrs.

It was inevitable that the Rosenberg case should arouse considerable interest in religious circles, in spite of pleas from leading Protestant, Roman Catholic, and Jewish clergy not to support the clemency efforts. An appeal for clemency came from twenty rabbis in Jerusalem. A leaflet by an Orthodox rabbi in New York—printed in both Hebrew and English—was widely distributed in Jewish neighborhoods. There was a mass prayer vigil in front of the White House. Altogether 2,800 ministers and rabbis signed petitions—some Communist petitions but more non-Communist—requesting the commutation of the death sentence.[6] Delegations of clergymen called upon the President, senators and congressmen, and members of the Supreme Court.

The Communists viewed as their greatest strategic victory the action taken by Pope Pius XII. He directed the Apostolic Delegation in Washington to inform the American Government that the Vatican had received many communications asking him to intercede on behalf of the Rosenbergs. Was this papal move a cautious gesture to intervene on behalf of clemency? It was widely interpreted in this way throughout Europe and by many in America, and the Communists used the Pope's action for effective propaganda. A throwaway circulated by the National Committee to Secure Justice in the Rosenberg Case bore this headline "His Holiness, the Pope says: 'Spare the Rosenbergs.'" One Roman Catholic group that lent its full support to the clemency campaign was the Catholic Worker movement.

What was the influence of the Communists among those church-men who involved themselves in the Rosenberg case? Communists obviously directed the international publicity to stir up bitterness against the United States, and their few clergy friends quickly fell into step. In addition, a small number of innocent ministers co-operated unwittingly or perhaps foolishly with the party apparatus. The overwhelming majority, however, protested the death penalty independently and had their own good reasons for wanting clemency · —reasons that had no relevance to Communist goals: they did not believe in capital punishment; they thought the penalty too severe for the crime; they were afraid that such executions at a time of national hysteria and war in Korea might be regretted later; they found no modern American precedent for such extreme measures; they believed the death of the Rosenbergs would assist, and not hurt, the world Communist movement.

THE NEGRO AND THE COMMUNISTS

America's Communists entered the postwar decade eager to make amends for their neglect of civil rights for Negroes. They blamed Earl Browder, now a convenient scapegoat, for soft-pedaling the race issue during the war. Browder denied the accusation and replied that the party had compromised its race policy immediately after Hitler's attack upon the Soviet Union while he was in a federal prison. In any case, the Negro question rose to new importance when victory had been achieved. The aim of the Communists was to weld the Negroes, together with the Left Wing of the labor movement and other progressive elements, into a strong resistance force against what was seen as growing American fascism at home and imperialism abroad.

The support of the Negro was solicited on many levels and in many fields: housing, employment, consumer activities, and so on. The Communists renewed a practice—abandoned during the war—of ex-ploiting every incident involving a Negro. If a Negro were accused of murder or rape or burglary—whether in Alabama or New York or California, whether innocent or guilty—his case was blown up in America and especially in other parts of the world as further evidence that imperialism goes hand in hand with racist terror. The individual

Negro himself became primarily a cog in Communism's international propaganda machine.

The most important and elaborate piece of propaganda was a petition called *We Charge Genocide,* presented to the United Nations by the Civil Rights Congress in 1951.[7] It was introduced by a startling photograph of two Negroes hanging by their necks from a tree—a picture which the *Daily Worker* had been reprinting for many years. The petition accused the United States Government of deliberately practicing "institutionalized oppression and persistent slaughter of the Negro people." "It is genocide for profit," charged the report.[8] More than 200 pages of specific cases named Negroes who had been killed, beaten, or maltreated.

To America's shame, many of the indictments were true. Yet, the petition was intended as propaganda and read as such. Action against Negro Communists or their colleagues was cited as evidence of genocide. The "venerable Dr. W. E. B. DuBois, elder statesman of the Negro people," was indicted "for his advocacy of peace." Paul Robeson, "a spokesman for the American Negro people," was denied a passport because he "endangers the profits of war." [9] Benjamin J. Davis, Pettis Perry, and Claudia Jones, imprisoned Communist Party officials, were described as "working class leaders" whose only offense was fighting for the Negro people. The petition charged with complicity a lengthy list of persons, agencies of government, and organizations, beginning with the President, Congress, and the Supreme Court, and proceeding through various Ku Klux Klan groups. The impression is deliberately created that they all co-operated in a massive conspiracy. As "patriotic Americans," the petitioners asked the United Nations to condemn the United States for genocide and take steps to prevent its continuance.

We Charge Genocide was translated into many languages and spread throughout the world and especially in Africa and Asia. The fact that it was endorsed by ninety-four "patriotic Americans" increased its effectiveness. Most of the Negro Communist Party leaders signed, as well as perennial Negro fellow travelers. White signers included Howard Fast. The three ministers endorsing the petition were Eliot White, open member of the Communist Party since 1943, and Negro clergymen Charles A. Hill of Detroit and Obadiah Jones of St. Louis. Hill and Jones played significant roles in postwar Communist efforts among the clergy.

Hill, who is pastor of Hartford Avenue Baptist Church, has been accused of party membership because he took refuge in the Fifth Amendment before the House Committee on Un-American Activities in 1952. He did so, he stated, on the advice of George W. Crockett, Jr., who served both as one of the defense attorneys for the Communist leaders in the Smith Act trials of 1949 and as counsel for Hill's church, of which Crockett is a member. In January 1956, Hill again refused to answer questions regarding Communist affiliation when he appeared voluntarily before the Subversive Activities Control Board to contend that the American Committee for Protection of Foreign Born—in which he had served as a leader—should not be listed as subversive. "Well, personally from my religious standpoint, I do not intend to tell anybody my political beliefs," Hill said. "I think if we follow the scriptures, Jesus said by their fruits you should know them. My fruits for thirty-five years in Detroit and longer than that have been to advance the kingdom of Jesus Christ. . . ." [10]

Despite Hill's adamancy before governmental bodies, other information suggests that he has not been a Communist. In 1941 he resigned as vice-chairman of the Michigan Civil Rights Federation because he refused to belong to any organization "that is controlled or dominated by Communist influence." [11] He announced his withdrawal from the National Negro Congress at the same time and for the same reason. While his ties with the Communists tightened during the war, in private conversation he says that he has never been a Communist and does not agree with various party positions. He asserted before the Un-American Activities Committee that the "Communist Party has had nothing to do with any of my activities." [12]

In 1952 Horace White, Negro pastor of the Plymouth Congregational Church in Detroit, wrote of Hill in the *Michigan Chronicle,* a Negro weekly:

The Rev. Mr. Charles Hill has been used by the Communist forces for a number of years. He himself is not a Communist in any sense of the word. He is just thoughtless in attempting to meet the many problems which confront the Negro population in America. . . .

The Communists know that he has a lot of energy for right which is not matched with an intelligent analysis of the evil against which he fights. Therefore the Communists have wrapped him up without actually letting him in on the know.

Hill actually thinks that so long as he is fighting discrimination nothing else matters. So the Communists take his hand and feed him the Communist line mixed in with his personal fight against race discrimination in America. Hill actually is none the wiser.[13]

The motivation of Obadiah Jones, another Baptist minister, was very different from Hill's. Jones was a member of the Communist Party from 1947 to 1954, but as an agent of the F.B.I. He was chairman of the Civil Rights Congress in St. Louis for three years and in 1954 surprised his comrades by appearing as the key government witness in the case against five Communist leaders in a Smith Act trial in that city.

Hill and Jones represent two extremes: Hill, a frequent ally of the Communists; Jones, an undercover agent for the government. What has been the stand on the Communist issue of the other 40,000 Negro clergymen in the postwar decade? Three conclusions seem justified.

1) There was little overt and organized anti-Communism among them, largely because of the race issue. For some Negroes, a person's political affiliation is secondary to his position on race. Communists took the lead in battling dramatically against discrimination in employment, housing, and education. This explains why even among many conservative Negroes there has persisted a strong undercurrent of admiration for such Communist sympathizers as Paul Robeson and W. E. B. DuBois. They are viewed as "good race men."

2) There has been even less pro-Communism among Negro clergymen. Communist leaders like William L. Patterson visited a number of prominent clergymen in an attempt to enlist their support, but with no discernible success. There are indications that a handful of less-educated ministers enrolled in the party without really understanding its ideology and program. The vast majority, however, had no significant contact with Communism or Communists.

The most reliable testimony on the question of Negro clergymen who became Communists has been given by Mrs. Barbara Hartle, a former party organizer. She was imprisoned under the Smith Act, but in April 1954 appeared at her own request before the Committee on Un-American Activities. Mrs. Hartle named two Negro ministers who had been Communists in the State of Washington, neither of them pastors of a congregation.[14] One of those identified, Clinton Redwell of the Colored Methodist Episcopal Church, asked for the opportunity to testify the following day. He had been recruited by the Communists in 1948, he said, but "at that particular time I didn't know it, because I thought it was the Progressive Party." He told how, as a party member, he had given prayers at various Communist meetings. He left in late 1949 "after I found that it wasn't any good and it was advocated to overthrow the Government of the United States."[15]

3) Most Negro clergymen who were drawn into front groups were attracted by the issue of civil rights. Many organizations sprang up around specific episodes, like the Communist-backed Citizens Memorial Committee for the Martinsville Seven—seven Negroes who had been executed for rape in Virginia in 1951. Of the eighteen original sponsors, ten were ministers or church workers. The fact that the Communists were taking the leadership of such groups kept many away. Others did not know the sponsorship. Some did not care.

A number of Negro pastors were active in the fight against the Smith Act. Again the party cleverly exploited the race issue by charging that the Communists were being persecuted because they threatened white supremacy. The trials were said to be engineered by Dixiecrats whose next move would be to imprison the N.A.A.C.P. leaders. Twenty-seven Negro clergymen, including four bishops, signed a full-page statement carried in the *Daily Worker* in mid-1948 decrying the "Gestapo-like arrests of Communist leaders" and calling on the government to "halt its fascist-like attacks upon opposition minorities."[16] Thomas S. Harten of Brooklyn's Holy Trinity Baptist Church, as reported in the *Daily Worker*, voiced similar sentiment. At a meeting of Baptist pastors in Harlem he said that he would pray for the exoneration of the Communist leaders. Why? Because the "northern Republicans joined with the lynching southern Dixiecrats to defeat the Civil Rights Bill."[17] Later the same year Harten urged Negroes to vote for Benjamin J. Davis, Negro Communist leader, then in prison, for the New York City Council.[18]

Edward D. McGowan was another Negro minister who played a role in defending top Communists. McGowan, an able Methodist pastor in the Bronx, later in Maryland, was involved in several postwar front activities, including the National Committee to Defend

Negro Leadership, an organization established to defend Negro Communist leadership. On April 30, 1953, before the National Fraternal Council of Negro Churches in America (representing twelve denominations and seven million members), McGowan gave an effective address defending Paul Robeson, the "greatest artist of this century," W. E. B. DuBois, the "greatest scholar of this century," and Benjamin J. Davis, who, he said, has been "fighting for a better way of life for the Negro people." Men of color, he said, must stand by all Negro leaders under attack from the forces of reaction.[19] When McGowan moved from the New York City area, he left behind close friends who were inclined toward the Communist position—and he himself edged farther and farther away from the periphery of the Communist movement. Today he is a pastor in Washington, D.C.

Several events forced some ministers into choosing between a pro-Communist position and an anti-Communist position. Perhaps the most important was the struggle for control of the Council on African Affairs. The C.A.A. focused its attention upon developments in Africa and concerned itself primarily with the end of colonialism and the emergence of independent nations. Some of its projects received support from churches, as when in 1946 it sent food to South African famine victims.

The C.A.A. had among its officers and council members many prominent Negro leaders holding various political views, but it was firmly under the control of Communists and their allies. Paul Robeson was chairman. Among council members were Herbert Aptheker, Charles Collins, W. E. B. DuBois, W. Alphaeus Hunton, Vito Marcantonio, Ferdinand C. Smith, and Doxey Wilkerson—all apologists for the Soviet Union.

The key position of executive director was held by Max Yergan, an important figure in the Communist camp. Gradually, Yergan's political orientation changed. In late 1947 he was successful in freeing the Harlem weekly *People's Voice* from Communist control. Then he began to charge that the Communists cared nothing about the genuine welfare of the African people, but sought only to exploit them for political purposes. The *Daily Worker* in turn began to pound Yergan mercilessly. He was an "Uncle Tom," a "traitor," a "race hater," and "a master of slick double-talk, weasel words and pompous empty verbiage." [20]

The first open split came in February 1948 over a debate about the United States Attorney General's listing of the Council as a Communist front. Yergan had prepared a statement saying that the Council was "neither Communist, Fascist nor subversive in any respect." Robeson scoffed at the statement as "red-baiting." Two factions emerged and began to hold separate meetings. A court battle was averted only when Yergan resigned and the disarrayed remains of the organization fell completely into Communist hands.

This story has significance for the churches in two important ways. Yergan had been viewed as a leading religious figure when he served in Africa with the Y.M.C.A. from 1920 to 1937. He returned convinced that the white man in Africa, including his missionary enterprise, was erecting an imperialistic apparatus to oppress the natives. For twelve years he was an able, willing, and effective front man for the Communists. Shortly after he left the Council on African Affairs, he returned briefly to the Y.M.C.A. when he flew to Paris in 1948 to help establish a group to improve race relations in Africa. Then his thinking swung rapidly to the far right. By May 1952, Yergan voluntarily appeared before the Senate Internal Security Subcommittee (headed by Senator James O. Eastland of Mississippi) investigating the Institute of Pacific Relations and testified that he had never been a member of the Communist Party, but had been drawn deeply into the Communist network.[21]

Nearly all the churchmen affiliated with C.A.A. sided with Yergan. Robeson was supported by his brother, B. C. Robeson, pastor of Mother A.M.E. Zion Church in Harlem, whose fraternal loyalty never wavered even though he himself is a Republican. Among Yergan's backers were Bishops W. Y. Bell and R. R. Wright, Jr., and clergymen Adam Clayton Powell, Jr., David N. Licorish, Shelton Hale Bishop, and W. H. Jernagin. Their position demonstrated that Communist prestige had fallen rapidly among Negroes since the war and that, faced with a clearcut pro- and anti-Communist alignment, liberal Negro clergymen were ready to throw their weight against the Communists.

THE WALLACE CAMPAIGN

Henry A. Wallace, American Vice-President from 1941 to 1945, announced his candidacy for President in December 1947. Wallace became a symbol to whom many thousands flocked during early 1948. The Communists represented only a small fraction of these original Wallace enthusiasts, most of whom were liberals or idealists or pacifists or malcontents who feared that neither the Democrats under President Truman nor the Republicans were interested in extending the reforms of the New Deal at home or reaching a *rapprochement* with the Soviet Union abroad. In July 1948, the movement met in Philadelphia and organized the Progressive Party, "Gideon's Army" to be led against the foe in a crusade of righteousness. The Communists became increasingly influential in the new party as the election drew near.

The new party was not oblivious of the role of religion in American life. In contrast to the confusion of the Democratic and G.O.P. conventions, the assembled Progressives bowed in reverent silence as the blessing of the Almighty was invoked upon each session. A memorial service for the war dead—conducted above a loud din at the other two conventions—was as solemn as a church service. The platform concluded: "Under the guidance of Divine Providence, the Progressive Party, with strong and active faith, moves forward to peace, freedom and abundance."

There was a religious flavor in the personality of Wallace himself. He appeared as an indignant modern-day messiah who borrowed liberally from the Old Testament prophets when he spoke of the day when men shall "beat their swords into plowshares, and their spears into pruning hooks." In a convention press conference, columnist Westbrook Pegler arose to question Wallace about alleged correspondence with a Russian-born artist and mystic or guru. Pegler's apparent intent was to depict Wallace as some kind of religious crackpot. Wallace replied sharply: "I never engage in any discussion whatsoever with Westbrook Pegler." [22] Progressive Party publicists countered with frequent reference to Wallace's ties with the Protestant Episcopal Church.

The Progressive Party's bid for support of various cultural and nationality groups had religious overtones. No group was more courted than American Jews, religious and secular alike, and the final vote indicated that Wallace met with his greatest success in heavily Jewish wards. A proclamation of the Irish-American Committee for Wallace and for Peace, addressed "To All Irish Americans," stated: "We stand with all peace loving Americans, including leading churchmen like Cardinal Dougherty of Philadelphia and student organizations like the National Federation of Catholic College Students in opposing [the] attempt to militarize our country." Attempts to discredit Al Smith in 1928 were compared with the smears against Wallace in 1948. Similar appeals were published in German, Polish, Spanish, Greek, Italian, Czech, Lithuanian, Hungarian, and other languages.

Much of the cultural tone of Progressive Party rallies was reminiscent of the evangelical traditions of rural, Protestant America. The role of music was especially important. For many years, protest movements in America, and especially those of the Left Wing, had written new words to fit the familiar melodies of gospel songs and Negro spirituals. The International Workers of the World pioneered in this effort at the beginning of the twentieth century. "Onward, Christian Soldiers" became "Onward, One Big Union." "There is Power in the Blood of the Lamb" became "There is Power in a Band of Workingmen." "Take it to the Lord in Prayer" was radically revised to read "Then dump the bosses off your back." Perhaps the best-known parody used the melody of the gospel hymn "In the Sweet Bye and Bye":

> Long-haired preachers come out every night;
> Try to tell you what's wrong and what's right.
> But when asked about something to eat,
> They will answer in voices so sweet.

> CHORUS

> You will eat bye and bye,
> In that glorious land above the sky.
> Work and pray, live on hay;
> You'll get pie in the sky when you die.

In the period after World War II, a Communist-oriented group known as People's Songs (later called People's Artists) made a significant contribution in this field. They preserved many of these early I.W.W. songs, added new verses, and then seized upon other religious melodies. Some new lyrics were written specifically for the Wallace campaign. The spiritual "Joshua Fit the Battle of Jericho" became "Wallace Come to Battle for 'Merica." The verses to the melody of "Jacob's Ladder" contained such lines as "We are building a people's party" and "Henry Wallace is our leader." Paul Robeson, who sang from coast to coast in Wallace's behalf, wrote new words for the two traditional tunes "Get on Board" and "Old Time Religion."

The Progressives had very little impact upon religious life in America. In spite of the widespread idealism among the clergy in 1948, there is no evidence that they responded to the Wallace movement. Nevertheless, the clergy were represented in positions within the Progressive Party structure. At the convention itself, Charles A. Hill was named to the nominations committee. Four Protestant clergymen were assigned to the platform committee, among them Don West of Georgia, who was listed without his ministerial title. The biographical notes on "convention personalities" listed thirty-four "religious leaders" including Archbishop Adam Phillipovsky of the Russian Orthodox Church and a number of Negro pastors attracted by the strong stand of the Progressives on civil rights. There were two rabbis. Among familiar names were those of the four Protestant ministers John W. Darr, Jr., Edward D. McGowan, William Howard Melish, and Richard Morford. Not all "religious leaders" who attended were listed, nor did all those listed attend. There were a few isolated instances in which support of Wallace caused difficulties between ministers and their congregations.

Progressive Party strategists sought to make the new party a grassroots movement with wide appeal to millions of middle-class Americans. Many of the big names in the party—Wallace, Glenn Taylor, Elmer Benson, Rexford G. Tugwell, C. B. Baldwin, Clark Foreman, and others—had an old American flavor about them. They tried desperately to follow the tradition of the earlier third-party movements: the Republicans of 1856, the Populists of 1892, the Bull Moose Progressives of 1912, and the La Follette Progressives of 1924. But they failed. The campaign never caught fire outside a few large cities, and Wallace received 1,157,172 votes, even less than the States Rights ticket of Dixiecrat J. Strom Thurmond. Almost half of this Progessive tally was from New York City alone. It is reasonable to assume, of course, that well over 90 per cent of the clergymen, like Americans generally, voted for either the Democrats or Republicans. Indeed, if a careful check were possible, perhaps it would show that many more ministers cast their ballots for Thurmond than for Wallace—though this would hardly be a fact of which the churches could be proud.

The lack of support which clergymen gave to the 1948 Progressive movement is additional evidence that there was very little sympathy for Communism among the clergy. Thousands of them might endorse statements demanding peace or sign petitions for a condemned Negro convict or even be tricked into involvement with a Communist front. Yet, when given an opportunity to come to the aid of the major post-war organizational efforts of the Communist Party and its friends, they showed decisively that they were not interested.

The Communists were disappointed with the failure of the Wallace third party. For the next four years they clung to its structure, still hopeful that the anticipated economic collapse would swell its ranks. Most Progressive Party leaders, including Wallace himself, soon abandoned the movement. By 1952, the Progressives polled only 140,023 votes. The Communists decided to "go to the masses" through other means. Already they had launched a nationwide "peace" offensive to try to crush America's will to resist aggression in Korea, and to discredit the United States in the eyes of the world.

TWELVE · THE COMMUNIST PEACE CAMPAIGN

"**P**eace" to the Communists has never meant the absence of war. It does not exclude revolutions grounded in the class struggle, warfare conducted against colonialism, or bitter civil strife like that in China or Korea. In short, peace does not rule out war that the Communists themselves might initiate or support—and the strategy of such "peace" became a powerful weapon of international Communism in the years 1946-56.

There were a number of Communist-inspired "peace" efforts soon after World War II came to a close.

In 1946 "Win the Peace" conferences were held in Washington and New York City. Resolutions castigated "fascist bands . . . striking against the Polish people," requested forced repatriation of refugees from Communism described as "Fascist elements," and demanded an end to a campaign of "vilification and smear against the Soviet Union." Many clergymen supported the conferences. William Howard Melish was elected vice-chairman of the New York Committee to Win the Peace. Among the twenty ministers and eight rabbis named to its various committees were Jack R. McMichael, Richard Morford, Edward D. McGowan, and Harry F. Ward. Delegates attended the conference from the Methodist Federation for Social Service, the Abyssinian Baptist Church in Harlem, the National Federation of Temple Youth, and a group calling itself the National Council of Non-Church People in America.

A second example of the party's early postwar "peace" activities was its campaign against universal military training. This represented a sharp reversal of previous Communist policy: in 1945 *Political Affairs,* a party monthly, had attacked the Federal Council of Churches for opposing U.M.T.[1] One facet of the new drive was led by John W. Darr, Jr. Darr took the initiative in calling a National Youth Assembly Against Universal Military Training in February 1948 and many church youth responded. The Darr group soon collapsed, especially after John M. Swomley, Jr., a former Methodist youth leader and director of the National Council Against Conscription, warned legitimate pacifist groups that it was for all practical purposes a Communist front.[2]

In March 1949, the Cultural and Scientific Conference for World Peace was held in New York City at the Waldorf-Astoria Hotel, sponsored by the National Council of the Arts, Sciences, and Professions. The Conference had a special panel on religion and ethics addressed by six speakers—four prominent Episcopal clergymen, a rabbi, and a British philosopher. The Waldorf Conference launched a series of similar meetings that were held across the globe during the next few years. It marked the beginning of the postwar Communist "peace" campaign.

LAUNCHING THE STOCKHOLM PEACE APPEAL

The next major move came a year later in Stockholm, Sweden, when a committee calling itself the Partisans of Peace began the circulation of what became known as the Stockholm Peace Appeal. The Appeal was to serve as the most important Communist propaganda device in the postwar period and eventually boasted 500,000,000 signatures. It was brief, carefully phrased, and free from the usual anti-American slogans that typified most Communist literature. The entire appeal, in one of its English-language versions, read as follows:

We demand the outlawing of atomic weapons as instruments of intimidation and mass murder of people.

We demand strict international control to enforce this measure.

We believe that any government which first uses atomic weapons against any other country whatsoever will be committing a crime against humanity and should be dealt with as a war criminal.

We call on all men and women of good will throughout the world to sign this appeal.

Whether accidentally or deliberately, the Appeal was well timed. Three months later, in June 1950, the troops of North Korea launched their attack upon South Korea. The Communists hailed the "liberating" armies in one breath, demanded "peace" and the end of American "aggression" in the next breath.

Religion was exploited by the Communists around the world. Patriarch Alexis in Moscow, in the name of the Russian Orthodox Church, endorsed the Stockholm Peace Appeal soon after it was launched and urged "our independent Orthodox brethren churches" to support it "so that efforts for peace may be aided by all believers." [3] One hundred and twenty Romanian clergy announced they had signed it.[4] The chief rabbi of Poland said it must be signed by "men of good will everywhere . . . and, above all, by every Jew." [5] Lutheran bishops in Latvia unanimously supported the Appeal,[6] as did "patriotic priests" in Poland, Hungary, and Czechoslovakia.[7]

Outside the Soviet bloc, Dean Hewlett Johnson stated: "A million signatures will annoy the warmonger. One hundred million signatures will wreck their plans and save the world." [8] The Communists claimed that in France three Roman Catholic clergymen in the National Assembly, a number of priests, and Roman Catholic "youth leaders and intellectuals" signed the Appeal and that the Archbishop of Trieste endorsed it in Italy. Roman Catholic writers and professors throughout Latin America were quoted as lauding it. When Pope Pius XII made a statement warning against the gross destructive powers of modern weapons, his words were seized upon as evidence that even the Vatican looked with favor on the Stockholm Appeal.

The reaction of the World Council of Churches, representing the majority of Protestants, was immediate. Its central committee, meeting in Toronto in July 1950, stressed the importance of peace through negotiation, but gave its support to collective United Nations resistance to the attack upon South Korea. It criticized the Stockholm Peace Appeal for demanding that atomic weapons be outlawed "without effective international inspection and control" and warned that the Appeal "must be regarded as a strategy of propaganda rather than a genuine peace proposal." [9] A few days later, representatives of the

Federal Council of Churches, the National Catholic Welfare Conference, and the Synagogue Council of America issued a strong statement charging:

This spurious peace petition which has already deceived many well-meaning people here and abroad, is a camouflage designed to confuse the free societies and to conceal the aggressive policies revealed in the invasion of Korea.[10]

Church leadership came under sharp fire. Harry F. Ward charged the World Council with capitulating to "American imperialism." The Toronto resolution, he warned, means that it "now has no moral authority for most of the people of Asia and Africa who see the mass killing in Korea as another example of the white man's attitude to other races." [11] Kenneth Leslie, editor of the *Protestant,* accused the churchmen of conspiring to "help prepare the people of the West and put them in the proper frame of mind for war." "We do not believe in the good faith of the World Council of Churches," he wrote. He lauded "democratic church leaders in Eastern Europe," then added: "The question that keeps recurring to us is: how can the Hungarians (and we shall let them symbolize all Eastern churches) sit down and hold communion with a group of men who serve not the God of peace but the God of war?" [12]

The independent Episcopal weekly, the *Witness,* edited by William B. Spofford, Sr., minimized the official Protestant statements [13] and then embarked upon a curious maneuver. Spofford excerpted a phrase from the Toronto statement calling for "a just settlement by negotiation and conciliation," appended a demand for the seating of Communist China in the United Nations, and then asked churchmen to "support the World Council of Churches" by signing this *Witness* appeal.

Spofford claimed that more than 700 signed, but admitted that other Protestant leaders—among them Charles P. Taft, Douglas Horton, and G. Bromley Oxnam—had protested. Oxnam wrote:

It seems to me hardly fair to quote the World Council of Churches in connection with the Korean situation without quoting the entire document. It is true that the phrase you quote appears in the resolution adopted by the World Council. It is also true that the World Council endorsed the action taken by the United Nations in seeking to end the aggression by the North Koreans. The World Council did not link the proposal to seat the representatives of the Communist government in China with this resolution at all. It seems to me that this communication . . . is likely to mislead our people as far as the World Council is concerned.[14]

Two other independent Episcopal publications, the *Living Church* and the *Southern Churchman,* also criticized Spofford's tactics.

Spofford was supported by Guy Emery Shipler, editor of the *Churchman,* who himself signed the *Witness* appeal. During the war in Korea, Shipler's editorials were critical of both the Soviet Union and the United States but an amazing amount of slanted material found its way into his magazine's news sections, especially whenever Roman Catholicism was involved. The *Churchman* carried one report that North Korea was the stronghold of Protestantism, while the south was the center of Roman Catholicism. On the same page another story noted that the South Korean Ambassador to Washington, John Myan Chang, was a Roman Catholic whose sister served as a mother superior in a church convent.[15]

These attempts to turn Protestants against the United Nations police action conveyed a totally false impression. Missionary officials estimate that from 50 to 80 per cent of all Protestants in North Korea fled to the south either before or during the fighting. By the end of the war, there were approximately 1,250,000 Protestants in South Korea—as compared with 250,000 Roman Catholics. It is true that Chang is a well-known Roman Catholic. What the *Churchman* failed to note was that President Syngman Rhee, then the main target of Communist attack, is a Methodist and that Chang has been Rhee's major political opponent.

ORGANIZING THE PEACE FRONTS

The Communist Party and its allied organizations promptly began to circulate the Stockholm Peace Appeal. A U.S. Sponsoring Committee for the World Peace Appeal (the official name for the Stockholm statement) was formed, with an Episcopal minister in Massachusetts serving as cochairman. Hundreds of peace groups began to mushroom across the country, many little more than names. Their members went from door to door asking people to "sign for peace."

The Communists sought to disguise their effort in many different ways. One of their strategies was to quote the attacks of ultraconservative newspapers upon "Mr. Truman's war." Many of these same newspapers accused Truman of "softness" toward Communism, lauded General Douglas MacArthur, and praised Senator Joseph R. McCarthy. The Communists carefully excerpted only lines that could be cited to prove that "Americans want peace."

Before their peace campaign ended, the Communists claimed that several hundred clergymen had signed the Appeal. Some persons who have been listed denied receiving it, among them Donald P. Redfield, a Methodist minister in Montana. "I was never approached with the Stockholm Peace Appeal," he wrote. "The Stockholm Peace Appeal is utterly foreign to my philosophy of life. If my name appears on such a petition, it is either a forgery or a case of some other person having the same name." [10] Others recalled that they had not signed. Bernard A. Kassilke, a Wisconsin Methodist explained: "I received such a petition in the mail, but I *never* signed. . . ."

Many were unaware of its Communist origins. Kenneth R. Tweed, a Connecticut Congregationalist, confessed that he had been "taken in and wish utter disassociation from any Communist attachment whatever." Chester E. Hodgson of New York still agreed with the Appeal, "but that those who sponsored it were not honest and used clergy of good will for their ends infuriates me." Those who defended their action offered a variety of reasons. Perhaps typical was that given by George L. Paine, a retired Episcopal minister in Boston. "I have been a pacifist many years and believe in favoring every proposal or action that tends to promote peace rather than against peace. . . . Treat your 'enemy' as a friend and in time you win him."

The principal front group to emerge in the United States was the American Peace Crusade, headed jointly by Willard Uphaus, a Methodist layman, and Thomas Richardson, a Negro union leader. The A.P.C. was organized in early 1951 when, according to the *Daily Worker,* "a few persons interested in blocking the course toward war met in a restaurant in New York." [17] Its first major activity was a peace crusade to Washington in March 1951. A "religious committee" asked clergymen across the nation to pray for peace and for the success of the pilgrimage. Twenty-four ministers and rabbis signed the request—some perennial fronters, others tricked into giving their support. Dudley H. Burr, a Connecticut Congregational minister, led a delegation to the Department of Justice to protest the "persecution" of peace advocates, while another group, which visited the Department of Defense, was headed by Charles A. Hill of Detroit and Maud Russell of the Committee for a Democratic Far Eastern Policy. An outdoor prayer meeting was held.

A bolder effort to exploit religion came later that year. Three separate "peace prayer vigils" were held simultaneously in New York City on October 7, 1951, sponsored by the Interfaith Committee for Peace Action. Thirty ministers and rabbis were listed as signers of the call, including among them Hill, Spofford, and Kenneth R. Forbes. At least one of their number, Presbyterian John Paul Jones, in a letter to the New York *Herald Tribune,* publicly disavowed his support. Others said they had not authorized the use of their names.

Protestant clergymen chaired each of the three gatherings. Seven thousand New Yorkers "braved torrents of rain" to attend, the *Witness* said.[18] Each half-hour of fiery political speeches was followed by a series of prayers and a hymn (obviously unfamiliar to most of those attending). A movie-newsreel man from Tass, official Soviet news agency, took pictures of the event to show Russians that the American people did not support the official position of their government. The *Daily Worker* waxed eloquent about the prayer meeting:

> Workers, housewives, students, professionals, merchants, Negro and white, of all political opinion and denominations joined in united prayer for immediate cessation of war in Korea. They cheered clergymen, labor leaders and Negro spokesmen who challenged the bipartisan warmakers and pleaded for a great people's peace coalition.[19]

One incident at the prayer vigils caused concern within the Society of Friends, which Communists were assiduously courting and whose traditional pacifism they unscrupulously exploited. Clarence Pickett, a Quaker leader, had contributed a prayer to be read. Instead of using it as an aid in meditation, as Pickett had intended, it was coupled with a message from the Dean of Canterbury as proof that the vigils were "non-Communist." A leader of the American Friends Service Committee objected in a letter to Uphaus: "This is a perversion of our intent in participating which we must protest." He stated the Quaker policy on co-operating with other organizations:

The use of other people's names as fronts or the active participation with groups whose ultimate objectives are short of the universal and religious ones which are ours cannot be permitted. Our own concern for peace stems out of our deepest religious convictions and our 300 year testimony along this line, and has no temporal relationship to the political platform of any one country or party which currently happens to use the same words.[20]

This technique of exploiting all religious peace sentiment was well exemplified in a 1955 pamphlet, *The American People Want Peace,* written by Jessica Smith, editor of *New World Review.* "Among Protestant churches practically every major denomination has expanded or set up a department devoted to peace education and action," she wrote.[21] Jewish rabbis and organizations were demanding peace. Roman Catholic priests and laymen, despite pressure from the hierarchy, were found "in increasing numbers" among the supporters of peace and the "Christmas message of Pope Pius XII and his powerful Easter message against the horrors of nuclear weapons undoubtedly served as a stimulus for greater peace activity among Catholics." [22]

A maze of fronts and other activities continued to promote the Communist peace campaign among churchmen and Americans generally. A New York Peace Institute was headed by the Methodist minister Edward D. McGowan. The Lobby for Peace enrolled a score of ministers and rabbis. Charles A. Hill was chairman of the Michigan Peace Council, and John W. Darr, Jr., served as acting secretary of an Ad Hoc Committee to Re-Establish the Right of Public Platform for Peace Groups. A "Methodist lay woman" in Illinois, Mrs. Mary Phillips Buckner, widely circulated the Stockholm Peace Appeal among ministers of her denomination and later helped establish Save Our Sons (SOS), a group which threw its weight behind the Communist peace campaign.[23] The American-Russian Institute in San Francisco in 1953 published a book of greetings to the Russian people, *We Pledge Peace—A Friendship Book.* It included many references to religion and carried messages from Harry F. Ward, Kenneth Leslie, Eliot White, Jerome Davis, and other churchmen.

Propaganda among Negroes was tailored to the race issue. The fighting in Korea was depicted as a war of white Americans against "the colored people of Asia." Any friction between individual Negro and white soldiers (so carefully censored by the Communists during World War II) was now a matter for indignation. Reports were published that Negro troops were forced to kill Koreans against their will.

The Peace Information Center was headed by the Negro scholar, W. E. B. DuBois, a man with a distinguished record of earlier accomplishment who did not enter the Communist periphery until after World War II. By 1952, he was important enough to the Kremlin to receive the International Stalin Prize for his peace work. On one occasion, the Center released a list of seventy-six Negroes who had signed the Stockholm Peace Appeal, more than half of them clergymen. DuBois helped inspire the Negro People's Committee for Peace and Freedom, with headquarters in Harlem, which sponsored an all-night prayer vigil "to implore the power of God to move in the United Nations" so that a cease-fire might be achieved.[24]

The Communists took advantage of political ignorance. A typical case involved Bishop Mother Love Deborah, a leader in a small Negro sect. Bishop Deborah served as chairman of the Woman's Peace Committee in the Bedford-Stuyvesant section of Brooklyn and was a sponsor of American Women for Peace. The *Daily Worker* was ecstatic in its praise of this "black-hooded figure . . . praying to her God with deep earnestness to touch the Nation's leaders and 'turn their hearts toward peace and security.' " All of the members of her congregation signed the Stockholm Appeal and she circulated five petitions outside the church. "It is a command of God that we should get that petition signed," Bishop Deborah told a reporter from the *Daily Worker,* adding: "and signing it is a prayer." She could not understand "why there are so many religious leaders who don't like the word peace. . . ."[25]

CHURCH "PEACE" LEADERS

Most clergymen who were "involved" in the peace campaign came no closer to the actual Communist apparatus than their own desks. Their participation was limited to signing the Stockholm Appeal or lending their names to an innocent-sounding front group. Only a score of churchmen gave time to the Communist peace movement.

Willard Uphaus of New Haven, Connecticut, emerged as the leading religious figure in the peace campaign. Uphaus, an active Methodist layman, a pacifist, and former college teacher, was from 1934 to 1951 executive secretary of the National Religion and Labor Foundation, an interfaith group of clergymen and trade-union leaders. His genuine radicalism and deep-rooted but ingenuous idealism made him vulnerable to postwar Communist propaganda.

In May 1950, Uphaus served as director of the Mid-Century Conference for Peace convened in Chicago by the Committee for Peaceful Alternatives to the Atlantic Pact. The Fellowship of Reconciliation charged that both the Conference and its sponsoring Committee had been launched to provide fronts "through which Communists could work without being easily detected and labeled." [26] Nevertheless, the support was broad and resembled some of the united fronts of the thirties in which Communists and known sympathizers played a very small public role.

Uphaus went to Warsaw in 1950 to attend the Second World Peace Congress, which created the Communist-dominated World Peace Council (also called the World Council of Peace). He spoke on behalf of the sixty-six American delegates, including ten Protestant ministers and a Jewish rabbi. "What sort of America did we leave to come to Warsaw?" Uphaus asked. Those who "speak out for peace" are jailed; "our labor leaders" in parts of the country "are branded as subversive and are beaten and imprisoned illegally"; a controlled radio "slants the news, omits accurate information, and distorts the truth"; the American people "are being told frankly that they must accept 'guns instead of butter' for the defense of the country." The United States was suffering from "the overweaning arrogance growing out of wealth and power, our isolation and the white man's condescending attitude toward peoples of other colors and cultures." One bright sign was the demand of the "workers" for peace; already three million had signed the Stockholm Peace Appeal. [27]

Uphaus' Warsaw speech made him popular among those pushing the "hate-America" line, but cost him respect in religious and labor circles. In April 1951, the board of the National Religion and Labor Foundation asked for his resignation as executive secretary on the grounds that his speech had made his continued association detrimental to the Foundation's work. Now Uphaus turned his full attention to the Communist peace campaign. In June 1951, he was elected codirector of the American Peace Crusade and served until 1955, when the Crusade dissolved. In 1952 he assumed the task of organizing American participation in the Congress of the Peoples for Peace held in Vienna that year.

He spoke and wrote widely on the Korean conflict. A typical comment comes from an article in the *Witness* of January 1953:

> "Stalemate hostility" is a neat phrase for what is going on in Korea. While it lasts we can extract more precious tungsten from the hills of Korea. We will go on with the British and French imperialists, expending blood and treasure, in a futile effort to stop the onward march of the colored peoples to freedom and independence.[28]

In February 1953, Uphaus became executive director of World Fellowship, Inc. Under his leadership, World Fellowship provided a forum on its 300-acre New Hampshire estate for many persons, a number of whom agreed with his views. When the overzealous New Hampshire Attorney General, Louis C. Wyman, demanded a list of 1954-55 guests—raising a serious civil-liberties question—Uphaus refused to comply. He was found guilty of contempt and fought the case to the United States Supreme Court, which upheld Wyman in a 5-4 decision. In December 1959, Uphaus, then sixty-nine, went to jail amid widespread protest. Before he was led away, a prayer meeting conducted by Loyd F. Worley, Methodist minister from Hartford, Connecticut, was held in front of the state capitol at Concord.[29]

Another important personality in the Communist peace campaign was Joseph F. Fletcher, professor of practical theology at Episcopal Theological Seminary in Cambridge, Massachusetts. Fletcher, who was born in New Jersey in 1905, received a broad education at the University of West Virginia, Kenyon College, Yale, the School of Economics of the University of London, and Berkeley Divinity School. Like some other Episcopalians, he has been influenced by Christian sociologists in England as well as by the American social-gospel tradition. His writings have demonstrated this social concern; among his books are *The Church and Industry, Christianity and Property,* and *Morals and Medicine*. He combined the qualities of a widely respected scholar with the earnest activity of a crusader and the unorthodox views of a rebel.

Fletcher's co-operation with innumerable front groups began in the early forties, but perhaps most significant was his affiliation with three Communist Party schools. At various times he served as a guest lecturer at the School for Democracy in New York City (later merged with the Workers School to form the Jefferson School of Social Science), as a member of the board of directors of the Abraham Lincoln School in Chicago, and as a member of the board of trustees of the Samuel Adams School in Boston. He threw himself into the postwar peace movement and in 1949 was a sponsor of the Cultural and Scientific Conference for World Peace and the American Continental Congress for World Peace. The following year he tried to stir American interest in the Warsaw Peace Congress and was elected a vice-president of the World Peace Council, which he later called "the only genuinely international, interideological, unofficial peacemaking activity that goes on in the world today." [30] Fletcher declined the election on the grounds that he did not want to be tied down to any organization. In 1951 he gave his support to the American Peace Crusade and the People's Peace Congress in Chicago. In 1952 he was a sponsor of the American Continental Peace Congress, an initiator of the National Peace Referendum, and a member of the U.S. Sponsoring Committee for Representation at the Congress of the Peoples for Peace.

Fletcher always showed signs of independent thinking. "Working with Communists is not a very popular thing, and my friends get very nervous about it," he said. "I am a democratic fellow who doesn't go in for any 'ism' at all." [31] He also sensed some of the complexities of international politics: "In human affairs, in every conflict or contest, there is never a case of all good on one side and all evil on the other." [32] But he saw disaster in American policy: "The unholy trinity of landlords, the ecclesiastics, and the generals does the same reactionary work wherever it exists." [33]

The direction of Fletcher's thinking was evident in a 1950 sermon at the Church of the Holy Trinity, where he filled the pulpit at the invitation of William Howard Melish:

You people in Korea!—both in the North and in the South. You in the North have been misled somehow into trying by force what you have not won by negotiation, and the resulting war was your own reward. "Repent you of the evil." And you Koreans in the South—I know that you had no real government and no true freedom to vote and earn your livelihood from the land, free of landlords. That is why your resistance to your brothers from the North ceased almost at once, making it a war between Americans versus Koreans. . . .

You people everywhere, who listen to the Voice of America! Did you hear our radio report that an American workingman lost his job last week and was thrown out of the factory with a broken back because he circulated a petition to ban the use of atom bombs? I signed that petition too, my friends in Nagasaki, and that worker's back is my broken back, too. Did you hear how "free Americans" in New York last Wednesday were denied permission to speak freely and publicly on questions of foreign policy and how policemen brutally beat up those who protested while photographers snapped them grinding men's heads under their boots.[34]

Two young Episcopal clergymen in the Boston area were closely associated with Fletcher's peace activities. One was Robert Muir, secretary of the American delegation to the Warsaw Peace Congress; the other, Warren H. McKenna. They first came to public attention when in June 1950 the Massachusetts Action Committee for Peace, headed by Muir, staged a picket parade while Secretary of State Dean Acheson was receiving an honorary degree at the Harvard commencement. McKenna and his wife paraded with their ten-month-old baby and their five-year-old son, who had a picket sign in his hand. Muir was arrested that same day for obstructing foot traffic as he delivered a peace speech to students. He later left the ministry. McKenna went to England convinced that the United States had become fascist, but in 1957 reappeared as spokesman for the American delegation that went from the Moscow Youth Festival to China in defiance of State Department regulations. He now serves a parish in Massachusetts.

The American most active in the World Peace Council was John W. Darr, Jr., who served in Prague as the American secretary of the Council from his election to that post in 1950 until he returned to the United States in 1953. In his capacity as American secretary, Darr traveled widely, including a trip to Communist China in 1952. Darr has never served as a parish pastor, and, after returning from abroad in 1953, he left the ministry to go into teaching; his name was removed from the roll of Congregational ministers.

A Jewish rabbi prominent in the Communist peace campaign was Abraham J. Bick, Ukrainian-born immigrant who led an Orthodox congregation at a Jewish home for the aged in Manhattan from 1943 to 1950. During the forties he became active in several fronts, like the American Birobidjan Committee, promoting interest in Russian Jewry. He emerged as a frequent contributor to such party publications as the Yiddish-language daily, the *Morning Freiheit,* and the English-language monthly *Jewish Life.*

Bick was a sponsor of the American Peace Crusade and attended both the 1950 Warsaw Peace Congress and the 1952 Vienna Peace Congress. In February 1953, he was scheduled to speak at a peace rally in Toronto, but was stopped by police at the airport and sent back to the United States. In 1956 he appeared before the Committee on Un-American Activities under subpoena and invoked the Fifth Amendment on all questions dealing with his peace-campaign affiliations.[35] By 1960, he had drifted out of the Orthodox Jewish community entirely and no longer used the title of rabbi.

One Canadian clergyman, James G. Endicott, received the International Stalin Prize in 1953 for "outstanding services in the struggle to preserve and consolidate peace." Endicott came from a pioneer missionary family, and like Dryden L. Phelps and J. Spencer Kennard, Jr., he taught for a time at the West China Union University at Chengtu. He traveled around the world on behalf of the World Peace Council, which he described as "the greatest, most universal, most effective movement of the people of the world that has so far appeared in all history." [36] The World Council of Churches seemed to him aligned with "American imperialism." He said in 1952:

> The only thing left for the World Council of Churches to discredit itself completely in the eyes of Asia and give final proof to the rightness of the exposure of Imperialism under the cloak of religion, is for it to deny or keep silent about the present large scale American germ warfare against the Chinese people.[37]

This charge of germ warfare was raised by another Canadian, Kenneth Leslie, who had returned to his native Nova Scotia from New York in 1949. When the World Peace Council appealed "to the conscience of mankind" against "American atrocities," he wrote that "The *Protestant* associates itself with this appeal and calls upon all those who preach religion to denounce the use of germs as allies in war." [38]

The germ-warfare accusation was handled cautiously by Americans who echoed it, since they knew that their fellow citizens would be enraged by such an unproved charge. The *Witness,* for example, rushed to the defense of "distinguished' persons from the West who pressed the accusations. "The best known of these are Dean Hewlett Johnson of Canterbury, and the Rev. James G. Endicott, a former missionary of the United Church of Canada, who was born in China and worked there as a missionary for 22 years." The *Witness* added: "Suspicion is mounting throughout the world that the American authorities have no better defense than to abuse the opponent's attorney." [39]

The Communist peace campaign publicly received support from one Irish Roman Catholic priest. Clarence Duffy was a native of the United States but returned with his family to Ireland, where he became a parish priest, absorbed with Christian socialism and with rehabilitation of the mentally ill. He came again to America. Always critical of Communist ideology, he nevertheless co-operated with Communists, signed the Stockholm Peace Appeal, and denounced "U.S. military and civilian warmongers" in speeches and in literature. He declared that "Western Europe is being organized by the United States under the Marshall Plan and the Atlantic Pact for another and more devastating war to bolster laissez-faire capitalism founded in and promoting un-Christian selfishness, greed, and exploitation." [40]

In 1949 Duffy, who never served an American parish, went to Lawrence, Massachusetts, to aid the Progressive Party candidate for mayor, Amos Murphy, minister of the First Unitarian Society. Duffy's clerical collar and his stout Irish nationalism apparently did not win the sympathy of all hearers for he charged that a "plain clothes policeman" sent an egg sailing in his direction. The New York Diocese quickly repudiated Duffy's political activities.

The story of Arthur W. Moulton, retired Episcopal Bishop of Utah, shows how people can become deeply involved in Communist-inspired activities without any awareness of their involvement. Moulton signed the Stockholm Peace Appeal, addressed the 1949 Waldorf Conference, sponsored the American Peace Crusade and other peace fronts, and in 1951 was awarded the International Stalin Prize for his peace work. These affiliations might suggest to many that Moulton was sympathetic with Communism. Actually, he is simply another example of the exploitation of a good will and a good name.

Moulton's principal role within the Communist-front apparatus was as honorary chairman of the American Committee for Protection of Foreign Born. In 1956, a few weeks before his eighty-third birthday, he appeared before the Subversive Activities Control Board as a witness for the A.C.P.F.B. During the testimony, Moulton's naïveté became clear. He had been notified of his election as honorary chairman without previous consultation. He had never contributed to the organization. He did not know the position of the Committee on any of the key issues of the day. He had never attended an annual convention or any of its conferences or banquets. He had never even visited its offices. His innocence was evident in his verbatim comment about the reasons for his own involvement:

A little bit afield but it would seem to me that the very name American Committee for Protection of the Foreign Born, I don't know, there is something about that name that I would think would bring people. Why (indicating) well, well, I think it would bring people to create tremendous interest in it and support and so on. Again I say that if you could see this impressive sponsors, that is the thing that attracted me to it. I believe it, its integrity. I believe that it is an honest and true Christian undertaking to protect the people that come to our shores.[41]

Asked his opinion on the charge of Communist control of the group, he protested: "It is false. It is not true. It is false. It is defamatory. Of course that is wrong. Of course it is." [42]

His questioners raised the issue of the Stalin peace prize of 100,000 rubles and Moulton replied that he had turned it down because "I am an American. . . . I can't take Russian money." [43] Why did he think he had been chosen to receive it? "They sent me that because, I expect, I belong to the Fellowship of Reconciliation. That is an international peace group. I think that, I don't think that Mr. Joe Stalin was at all interested, but I, well, I don't know. . . ." [44]

What Moulton—and other clergymen—did not know, of course, was that the Communists considered them valuable weapons in their front apparatus. As Americans read that bishops and other clergymen had been lured into the Kremlin-directed peace campaign, public concern and resentment grew. This concern and resentment soon spilled over into a raging controversy that reached the halls of the United States Congress.

THIRTEEN · PATRIOTS, EX-COMMUNISTS, AND CONGRESSMEN

While Marxist Communism has been an outspoken foe of religion, ironically, more damage has perhaps been done to America's churches by the noisiest antagonists of Communism. In their efforts to protect religion from "Red atheism," too often they have directed their fire instead at the legitimate social concern of both Christianity and Judaism. Some of these efforts have been motivated by sincere conviction; others unfortunately by opportunism; some even by vindictiveness or demagoguery.

This campaign reached its peak during the McCarthy era. Joseph R. McCarthy, junior Senator from Wisconsin, took advantage of the stalemate in Korea and of frustrations in domestic and international affairs to project an image of a State Department riddled with agents of Moscow. Some private patriot groups heard his accusations as a call to action. In Congress, hearings held in public and in private focused a grim spotlight upon trade unions, the movie industry, colleges, and other major elements in American society.

Yet the anti-Communist crusade of the early fifties, however irresponsible in many of its methods, was based on more than myth. There was a genuine need to awaken millions of Americans to the actual nature of the Communist movement. Naïveté about Communism was prevalent; anti-Communism frequently was effectively discredited as "Red baiting" and "fascist." Efforts to depict the Communist Party as it was—a puppet of the Kremlin committed ultimately to the overthrow (violent if necessary) of the traditional United States

226

form of government—were dismissed by many as hysterical. It was still fashionable in some circles to co-operate with Communists, who were thought to be "extreme liberals," perhaps too zealous and too leftist, but essentially "right" on the issues that counted—world peace, racial equality, rent control, low-cost housing and medical service, and adequate schools.

Such an attitude as this, especially when voiced by the intellectual elite, caused resentment among many Americans. How did such an opinion differ from treason when the United States was then waging a life-and-death cold war with the Soviet Union? A whole series of developments aggravated the situation. The Yalta agreements allegedly yielded to Soviet demands in Eastern Europe—was America deliberately betrayed at Yalta? Russia blasted an atomic bomb—had spies stolen America's atomic secrets? China fell to the Communists— why had so many foreign-policy experts insisted that they were only agrarian reformers? Alger Hiss was convicted of perjury—how many more trusted State Department officials were involved in similar plots?

Attacks upon the churches for alleged radicalism had been widespread for many years. Some accusations in the McCarthy era were rehashes of charges made after World War I. In the thirties, attacks had become more frequent, many stemming from nationalist groups that also dealt in anti-Semitism and white supremacy. In 1931, for example, E. N. Sanctuary, an "intellectual" leader among the nationalists, charged in his book *Tainted Contacts* that the Federal Council of Churches was guilty of four cardinal evils: "socialism, communism, internationalism, and pacifism." Sanctuary, better known for his diatribes against the Jews, operated through front organizations of his own—the American Christian Defenders, the World Alliance Against Jewish Aggressiveness, and the Tocsin Publishers.

Three years later, in 1934, Elizabeth Dilling's *The Red Network* was published. Mrs. Dilling, herself an Episcopalian, named 460 organizations allegedly assisting "the Communist-Socialist world conspiracy with its four horsemen, Atheism, Immorality, Class Hatred, and Pacifism-for-the-Sake-of-Red-Revolution." *The Red Network* became a "handbook for patriots" and even today her descriptions are quoted verbatim to discredit liberal groups. She relied heavily upon Sanctuary's *Tainted Contacts,* Harry Jung, head of the American Vigilante Intelligence Federation, Nesta Webster, author of anti-

Semitic tracts, General Amos Fries, head of the so-called Friends of the Public Schools, and reports of the Lusk Committee, which conducted sensational investigations into radicalism in New York State.

In the years that followed, more joined the chorus against "Red influences" in the churches. Some have been effective principally among members of the racist fringe, such as Gerald Winrod of Wichita, Kansas, editor of the *Defender Magazine,* and Gerald L. K. Smith, who made a career out of crude denunciations of Jews, Negroes, and Protestant leadership. Other extremist groups aimed their appeal at more reputable and affluent segments of American society. The Constitutional Educational League, headed by Joseph Kamp, circulated its literature widely, including its 1948 pamphlet *Behind the Lace Curtains of the YWCA.* Kamp accused the Y.W.C.A. of "helping to promote the atheistic philosophy of Karl Marx" and of extolling "the alleged virtues of Godless Russia." Merwin K. Hart, head of the National Economic Council and an active Episcopal layman, has assailed "communistic trends" in religious circles and especially within his own denomination. The Church League of America, operating out of the Chicago area, and now headed by Edgar C. Bundy, pressed similar charges. On a more theoretical and less abusive level, "collectivist" thought among the clergy has been challenged by two well-financed national groups, Spiritual Mobilization, publisher of *Faith and Freedom,* and the Christian Freedom Foundation, publisher of *Christian Economics.*

One organization devotes most of its time to attacks upon the churches and thus merits special attention. It is called the International Council of Christian Churches, whose United States affiliate is known as the American Council of Christian Churches. These carefully chosen names have misled some people into believing that the I.C.C.C. and the A.C.C.C. are major church groups. Both are tiny splinter factions tightly controlled by Carl McIntire of Collingswood, New Jersey, who was ousted from the ministry of the Presbyterian Church in the U.S.A. in 1936, charged with "disapproval, defiance, and acts in contravention of [its] government and discipline. . . ." He created the two groups, has held their important offices, uses his personal periodical, the *Christian Beacon,* as their mouthpiece, coins their catch phrases, and writes most of their resolutions. As a consequence, the I.C.C.C. and A.C.C.C. have been known collectively as the McIntire group. His methods have led to many schisms among his followers, so that most persons initially attracted to his movement have withdrawn in protest.

McIntire's dislikes are manifold—he denounces the Southern Baptist Convention, the American Bible Society, the National Association of Evangelicals, the Inter-Varsity Christian Fellowship, Youth for Christ, the Moody Bible Institute, and all of the other important religious groups, without regard to theology or political orientation. He attacks Billy Graham as a compromiser. He has described Brotherhood Week, sponsored by the National Conference of Christians and Jews, as a "gross perversion of scriptural teachings." He has depicted Eastern Orthodoxy as "idolatrous" and "pagan." Many of his sharpest words have been directed at Roman Catholicism. In 1945 McIntire wrote:

> As we enter the post-war world, without any doubt the greatest enemy of freedom and liberty that the world has to face today is the Roman Catholic system. Yes, we have Communism in Russia and all that is involved there, but if one had to choose between the two . . . one would be much better off in a communistic society than in a Roman Catholic Fascist set-up. One wonders sometimes if all the antagonism of the Roman Catholic Church to Communism . . . is not being played up especially in the United States at the present time for the purpose of gaining advantage for the Roman Catholics. . . . America has to face the Roman Catholic terror. The sooner the Christian people of America wake up to this danger the safer will be our land.[1]

McIntire's main preoccupation in recent years has been to press the Communist charge against Protestant leadership in America and around the world, and especially against the World Council of Churches, the National Council of Churches, and their member denominations. He accuses them of promoting Communism in their resolutions, in their Sunday-school literature, and even in their relief work. The hand of Moscow was discerned in the publication of the Revised Standard Version of the Bible in 1952 when McIntire charged the committee of distinguished scholars with trying to "destroy the historic faith." When the National Council pleaded for better race relations, McIntire said it was fostering racial strife "in which the Communists delight." When John Foster Dulles was appointed Secretary of State, McIntire objected that his associations with "radical" church leaders made him politically suspect. Any major action or statement of the National Council has been attributed by McIntire to "Communist influence" among the clergy.

The influence of McIntire in the United States is slight and his following is miniscule. He has been able, however, to stir up controversy in certain missionary areas where his inflammatory charges of "modernism" and "Communism" have had a greater impact. Many Protestant churchmen have become particularly incensed at the manner in which he has gone into Roman Catholic countries in Latin America and elsewhere, has promptly called a press conference, and then has made sensational accusations against Protestant leaders—accusations which are carried in the newspapers and tend to create suspicion of all Protestant evangelistic work. In 1959 McIntire played a role in the split within the Presbyterian Church in South Korea, which had been viewed as a model accomplishment of the missionary enterprise. Distressed by this development, the distinguished fundamentalist scholar Donald Grey Barnhouse, editor of *Eternity* and pastor of the Tenth United Presbyterian Church in Philadelphia, made this comment: "One of two things must be true. Either Carl McIntire is an honest man dedicated to a false cause . . . or, he must be branded as a man who is utterly and thoroughly dishonest. . . ." [2]

But perhaps the most serious single attack upon the churches prior to the McCarthy era was contained in a chapter in the 1949 book *The Road Ahead,* written by John T. Flynn, once a New Deal liberal, later a passionate spokesman for the extreme Right Wing. He accused the leadership of the Federal Council of Churches of promoting a socialist revolution from behind a pious façade of religion. Flynn pinpointed a half-dozen responsible church leaders, among them Bishop G. Bromley Oxnam, E. Stanley Jones, Reinhold Niebuhr, and John C. Bennett. Almost one million copies of *The Road Ahead* were distributed, 725,000 of them circulated in an inexpensive edition by the ultraconservative Committee for Constitutional Government.

Ministers across the nation preached sermons in reply to Flynn's accusations and groups passed resolutions condemning *The Road Ahead* as a slur against the churches. The Federal Council of Churches challenged many of the charges and wondered aloud about the im-

partiality of Flynn, a Roman Catholic, in his treatment of Protestantism. Why, they asked, had Flynn only directed his attacks at Protestants when the National Catholic Welfare Conference had endorsed
most of the "socialist" policies approved by the Federal Council.
To add to the confusion, *The Road Ahead* endorsed the rabidly
anti-Catholic American Council of Christian Churches. Some observers saw Flynn as an embittered man, still smarting from unfair
attempts to label him a "Nazi sympathizer" during World War II
because of his prewar isolationism.

ATTENTION FROM THE HOUSE COMMITTEE

The Committee on Un-American Activities of the House of Representatives began to dabble directly in the religious realm in 1948
when it issued the pamphlet *100 Things You Should Know About
Communism and Religion.* It was written in the question-and-answer
style of a catechism and many of the answers were so simplified as
to render them distortions: "4. *Would the Communists destroy the
Bible?* Every copy they could find. And they would jail anybody
trying to print new copies . . . 27. *Was Marx crazy?* Perhaps. But
Marx was not the first evil and crazy man to start a terrible world
upheaval. . . . "

The questions then turn to Communist efforts to infiltrate the
churches.

72. *Are there Communist clergymen?*
    Unfortunately, yes.
73. *Do they admit they are Communists?*
    Some do, but except in special cases, the Party requires Commu-
    nists to keep their membership secret.
74. *Will you give an example of the "open" type of membership?*
    The Rev. Claude C. Williams, a Presbyterian minister, whose con-
    gregation expelled him for Party activity. . . .
81. *Is Communist propaganda ever sneaked into church publications?*
    Yes. For instance, the Christian Register, official Unitarian pub-
    lication, has carried Earl Browder's eyewash that a good Chris-
    tian can be a Communist. It is significant that the minister re-
    sponsible for doing this has since been removed from his editor-
    ship by the church.

There are various mistakes in these answers. Claude C. Williams, for example, was never an open member of the party. Earl Browder had already been ousted by the Communists when he contributed in October 1947 one article in a five-article symposium in the *Christian Register*. The symposium considered, pro and con, the question "Can a Real Unitarian Be a Real Communist?" The editor at the time was a staunch anti-Communist; Stephen H. Fritchman, the former editor, whom the committee researchers must have had in mind, had been ousted several months before.[3]

Blanket assertions created suspicion without offering any evidence. One question read: *"Is the YMCA a Communist target?* Yes. So is the YWCA. Also, church groups such as the Epworth League." The Y's, of course, are valuable organizations and by no means pro-Communist. Even more inaccurate was the reference to the Epworth League, which was dissolved in 1939 when three branches of Methodism united—nine years before the committee report was issued.[4]

In March 1953, Chairman Harold H. Velde, Illinois Republican, made a chance remark in an interview that his Un-American Activities Committee might investigate several church groups and individual clergymen. Some Protestant leaders took the news calmly and even welcomed an opportunity to disprove publicly the charge that the churches were honeycombed with Communists. For a larger number, however, Velde's suggestion seemed like a violation of the principle of separation of church and state. And even if such an investigation were constitutional, they believed that the Un-American Activities Committee was not competent to undertake it.

Coincidentally, within a few hours after Velde's statement, the general board of the National Council of Churches met and promptly adopted a statement criticizing the procedures of Congressional committees and warning against "national regimentation." The board authorized the president of the Council to appoint a Committee on the Maintenance of American Freedom to guard against developments that endanger liberty. The fifteen persons named included Henry Knox Sherrill, presiding bishop of the Protestant Episcopal Church, chairman; Mrs. Mildred McAfee Horton, former head of the WAVES; Mrs. Norman Vincent Peale; Charles E. Wilson of the General Electric Corporation; and G. Bromley Oxnam, Methodist bishop in Washington, D. C.

It was Oxnam who stated in precise language the view of many. "I believe the Communist party is a conspiracy," he said, "and that conspirators should be discovered, tried, and, if guilty, punished. I believe that the Federal Bureau of Investigation is far better qualified for that duty than Mr. Velde's committee." [5]

Within a week, Representative Donald L. Jackson of California, member of the committee, arose on the floor of the House to defend it against growing attacks. Departing from his script, he charged that "Bishop Oxnam has been to the Communist front what Man O'War was to thoroughbred horse racing, and no one except the good bishop pays much attention to his fulminations these days." Jackson continued:

Having served God on Sunday and the Communist front for the balance of the week, over such a long period of time, it is no great wonder that the bishop sees an investigating committee in every vestry. If reprinting Bishop Oxnam's record of aid and comfort to the Communist front would serve any useful purpose, I would ask permission to insert it here, but suffice it to say that the record is available to any Member who cares to request it from the committee. [6]

The Bishop swiftly took up the challenge.

First, with the co operation of the *Washington Post* he dissected his "record," which had been distributed by the House committee and to which Jackson had made reference. There were twenty-three citations alleging Oxnam's association with one or another Communist front. He took each of the assertions of the report, analyzed them one by one, and then produced a table of statistics.

The committee report on me consists of 305 typewritten lines. Of these:
Two are introduction;
Sixteen are a summary of the organizations mentioned in the report;
One hundred twenty-eight concern organizations never listed as subversive, or quotations from journals that are not related to subversive organizations or activities;
Seventy-two are from an obscure newspaper in Princeton, Ill., the utter falsity of which might have been disclosed in half an hour's conversation had a committee investigator bothered to walk the 300 yards from the Capitol to my office;
Sixty-four are devoted to organizations which I never belonged to;
Twenty-three refer to organizations listed as Communist fronts to which I once belonged but from which I had resigned prior to the pub-

lication of Attorney General's list of subversive organizations and concerning which I have made full explanation above.[7]

Oxnam debated Jackson on the "American Forum of the Air" on April 26, 1953. He emphasized two objections. 1) The files of the committee are based on the "scissors and paste" technique which brings together only evidence casting suspicion upon the individual concerned, without any attempt to present a balanced picture. 2) The committee's research staff had demonstrated gross incompetence as proved by the many errors in the committee files. Then Oxnam requested the right to appear before the committee to set his record straight. The committee reluctantly agreed and the hearing was set for July 21, 1953.

Preparation began in earnest. Oxnam and his staff began to dig through his correspondence and speeches dating back as far as thirty years; they were to prove exceedingly useful. On May 1, the Methodist Council of Bishops expressed regret that he had been "subjected to accusations that were untrue by methods that were manifestly unjust" and declared that "Bishop Oxnam needs no defense at our hands." [8]

The Bishop's enemies were busy, too. Carl McIntire began circulation of a pamphlet, *Bishop Oxnam, Prophet of Marx,* in which he charged that "as perhaps no other man, Oxnam represents the popular, radical, pro-Communistic element in religious circles in America." [9] The American Council also sought to funnel new "evidence" against Oxnam into the committee files. The lead in this was taken by Edgar C. Bundy, a free-lancing "expert" on Communism who roams around the nation attacking the National Council of Churches. Typifying his approach was this announcement of a forthcoming appearance, which appeared in the Wichita Falls (Texas) *Record* on January 12, 1953:

How are the Communists Invading the Churches? Congress says they are! Mr. J. Edgar Hoover says they are! Captain Bundy will tell how they are, with explosive documentation which will make some people sore and others shocked! *Russia's Religious Fifth Column Within the U.S.A.* Moscow's dearest friends discovered in pulpits and seminaries in the USA. Captain Bundy exposes a man honored by the largest Protestant group in the USA and identifies him with numerous communistic organizations. *The Master Stroke of the Communists—the Perversion of the Bible.* Who was behind the new Standard Version of the Bible? Captain Bundy reveals the subversive activities of so-called "scholars" who worked on the unauthorized changes made in the RSV and explains why no American Christian should own one.

Later, in 1958, Bundy published *Collectivism and the Churches.* The accusations in the book are profuse and aimed in all directions. The National Council of Churches and the World Council of Churches are depicted as mammoth ogres headed by "leftists" and "pacifists" and "collaborators with communism." An entire chapter, entitled "Mr. Dulles and Some Collectivistic Churchmen," seeks to cast doubt upon the loyalty of John Foster Dulles, whom Bundy tries to link with Alger Hiss.

EXECUTIVE HEARINGS IN NEW YORK

The Un-American Activities Committee held a series of executive hearings in New York City in early July 1953, hopeful of obtaining evidence that would incriminate Oxnam and other clergymen. The secret testimony was not published until several months later and then came out under the misleading title "Investigation of Communist Activities in the New York Area." Among the witnesses who appeared were four ex-Communists: Joseph Kornfeder, Leonard Patterson, Manning Johnson, and Benjamin Gitlow. The testimony of these four has been relied upon heavily by the committee and therefore must be examined carefully.

Joseph Kornfeder, a native of Slovakia, had come to the United States as an immigrant tailor in 1917 and had joined the American Communist Party when it was formed in 1919. He rose to become a member of the party's central executive committee (later known as the national committee) and did work for the Communists in Moscow and in Colombia and Venezuela. Kornfeder, known as Joseph Zack to the Communists, quit the party in 1934 because of disagreement over the arrest of Trotskyists and over the police-state atmosphere he had found in the Soviet Union. The *Daily Worker* reported his expulsion on December 15, 1934, and accused him of Left Wing deviationism and of "spreading slanders of a counter-revolutionary Trotskyite nature."

Kornfeder's testimony to the committee was not very useful. He cited the People's Institute of Applied Religion, directed by Claude C. Williams, as an example of a Communist maneuver within the churches; yet, he did not know Williams' denomination, whether he was a minister in good standing, or where the headquarters of the People's Institute was. He had no first-hand knowledge about whether Williams was a party member, though he added: "Well, I am myself certain that he was a member of the party by the nature of his activities." [10] When he made reference to the 2,300 "preachers" who signed a petition asking that Julius and Ethel Rosenberg be spared the death penalty, Gordon H. Scherer, Republican of Ohio, asked if some of these were not "just idealists and pacifists." Kornfeder answered: "I do not think so. I think that those 2000 were pretty close to the machine." [11]

Kornfeder estimated the number of "secret party members" among the clergy. "Those, I believe, will not exceed 600," he stated. "It may be an underestimation, but I am convinced that their party base is rather narrow in this operation." [12] When asked at the hearing to identify any Communists "associated with any religious denomination," Kornfeder replied: "Well, there were some preachers in Ohio who were involved in the movement, but I just do not recall the names." [13] Finally, he mentioned Bishop William Montgomery Brown of Ohio, dead since 1937, who was unfrocked for heresy by the Protestant Episcopal Church in 1925.

Why the committee regarded Kornfeder as an expert on religion and Communism in 1953 is difficult to understand. He had not been a Communist for nearly two decades and during the time he was in the party it had made no serious attempt to reach the clergy. His work as a member had been confined principally to the trade-union field. After his testimony, he traversed the country repeating his estimate of Communist infiltration in the church, though by 1955 he was suggesting that the number of Communist clergymen had dropped to "only 400." [14]

Leonard Patterson had joined the Communist Party in 1930. He had been brought up on his parents' farm in the South, received little formal education, and came to New York, as many young Negroes did, in search of a better future. Five years later he joined the Young Communist League, and two years later, the party. He left the party in 1937. Patterson testified at the hearings that he was an officer and ordained deacon of Mount Calvary United American Free Will Baptist Church in Brooklyn. He discussed primarily two Methodists, Harry F. Ward and Jack R. McMichael, both of whom he "identified" as Communist Party members. The evidence offered in the case of both men is sparse and open to serious question. He claimed, for example, that McMichael helped map out the capture of the American Youth Congress in 1934, but McMichael was only eighteen years old at the time and a college sophomore in Georgia.

Perhaps Patterson's unreliability as a witness is best attested by his testimony at Baton Rouge, Louisiana, in 1957, before that state's Joint Legislative Committee, which was looking into alleged subversive influences in "racial unrest." Patterson co-operated with the committee's leadership in its attempt to undermine the effectiveness of the National Association for the Advancement of Colored People by falsely labeling it "Red." In the course of the hearing, he was asked if he knew any Negro Communist ministers. "Well," he replied, "I knew some in New York, but I lost their names. . . ." [15]

Manning Johnson had joined the party in 1930, rose to membership on its national committee, and severed his Communist ties in 1940. (On July 2, 1959, he died at the age of fifty-one of a heart ailment.) Indicative of Johnson's approach were his statements about the 2,300 ministers who signed the Rosenberg clemency appeals. The Communist Party had made "deeper and deeper inroads in the religious field," he said, and "I am reluctant to discount the possibility of them actually having 2300 clergymen." [16] He was asked to evaluate the United Christian Council for Democracy on the basis of its program in 1939. "Speaking as an expert," Johnson replied, "[the Council's program] indicates that the policy of the organization is based upon the program of the Communist Party." [17] In 1939 this was not true. It was not until World War II and particularly the postwar period that the United Christian Council for Democracy, abandoned by the liberals and headed by Richard Morford, and later by John W. Darr, Jr., began to work closely with American Communists.

Johnson's testimony described Communist strategy in the field of religion as a broad conspiracy. Communist professors led by Harry F. Ward, he said, were planted in seminaries, where they organized cell groups. Church publications were even easier to infiltrate. Johnson suggested that there had been hundreds, perhaps thousands, of ministers in the party. The result was that the Communists "managed to pervert and weaken entire strata of religious life in the United States." [18]

Like both Kornfeder and Patterson, Johnson appeared before Louisiana's Joint Legislative Committee investigating racial unrest in 1957. He characterized the N.A.A.C.P. as a "vehicle of the Communist Party" and Martin Luther King as "a dastardly misleader." [19] In commenting on Mrs. Eleanor Roosevelt, he suggested that "somebody should muzzle her and put her in a cage." [20] When Johnson left the impression in his Louisiana testimony that he was somehow connected with the United States Department of Justice, a department spokesman disclaimed any such association whatsoever. Apparently he had been promptly dropped in 1954 as a paid consultant after charging that Ralph J. Bunche was a Communist sympathizer.

Benjamin Gitlow had first been a Socialist, joining that party at sixteen and winning election to the New York State Legislature as a Socialist in 1918, at twenty-seven. He was instrumental in the organization of the American Communist Party in 1919, and served three years in prison, until Governor Alfred E. Smith pardoned him—the first man to be convicted as a Communist in the United States. In 1924 and 1928 he ran as the Communist nominee for Vice-President, and by 1929 he was general secretary of the party. He was ousted the same year, however, when he refused to follow the Moscow directive that control of the party be handed over to William Z. Foster.

Gitlow's principal remarks at the 1953 hearings concerned various ministers and rabbis who, he said, were willing instruments of the Communists in the twenties. He first gave a list of five names: Albert Rhys Williams, Kirby Page, Sherwood Eddy, Jerome Davis, and Harry F. Ward. Of this group, he testified that he knew only Albert Rhys Williams to have been a Communist—an assertion denied by Williams. A few minutes later he revised his list, dropping Page and Eddy, and adding Bishop William Montgomery Brown and William B. Spofford, Sr. Then, on the following page of testimony, he introduced a third list of ministers, "who carried out the instructions of the Communist Party or collaborated with it" before the creation of the front apparatus in 1935. Page and Eddy were still missing. Bishop Brown was now omitted as well. A few more were included, among them Tucker P. Smith, Irwin St. John Tucker, John Haynes Holmes, Judah L. Magnes, and Stephen S. Wise. Gitlow finally maintained that four ministers met in the twenties with Robert W. Dunn, head of the Labor Research Association, who acted as liaison man between the party and the clergy. These four were identified as Williams, Davis, Ward, and Spofford.

Gitlow's testimony did a serious injustice to many of the clergymen he named. Kirby Page and John Haynes Holmes were fervent Socialists and pacifists who, whatever their hopes for Russia after 1917, always spoke out vigorously against the Communist doctrine of class war. Sherwood Eddy saw evils in the Soviet system, even though he was genuinely impressed by some advances wrought by the Bolshevik revolution. Irwin St. John Tucker had vigorously fought Communist attempts to dominate the Socialists and by the mid-thirties he was a Republican. Tucker Smith, also a Socialist, was known in Left Wing circles as particularly anti-Communist. Despite his admiration for Russia, Davis had always made his disagreements with Communism known, and neither Ward nor Spofford became uncritical of the Soviet Union until later.

A storm broke over the two rabbis named. Gitlow's accusations against Protestant clergymen were nothing new, but the rabbinate had come under less attack. Gitlow, himself of Jewish background, listed two of the most prominent rabbis in American Jewish history— Judah L. Magnes, a pioneering Zionist leader who had, in fact, left America by 1922 to settle permanently in Palestine, and Stephen S. Wise, founder of the American Jewish Congress.[21] Both had died before 1953 and could not reply to the Gitlow charge.

Others rushed to their defense. Israel Goldstein, president of the American Jewish Congress, and Maurice N. Eisendrath, president of the Union of American Hebrew Congregations, issued a joint statement describing the committee's release of the Gitlow testimony as "a shocking and frightening betrayal of elementary public responsibility and decency." [22] The Synagogue Council of America, representing the major congregational and rabbinical groups in the United States, condemned the committee for its "cowardly attack." Rabbi Irving Miller, president of the Zionist Organization of America, accused the committee of almost "unbelievable irresponsibility." Among the few who supported Gitlow were Rabbi Benjamin Schultz, director of the American Jewish League Against Communism, and the *Tablet,* official organ of the Roman Catholic diocese of Brooklyn.

Under fire, Gitlow staged a strategic retreat. On September 24, 1953, the Peekskill (N. Y.) *Evening Star* published a letter of defense from Gitlow, who was a resident of nearby Crompond:

> It was the purpose of this testimony to show how the communist movement, from its very inception—though anti-religious and in principal [*sic*] atheistic—was able to attract a number of well-meaning, liberal and social-minded religious leaders such as Rabbis Magnes and Wise. The charge was not made that they were ever communists or members of the Communist Party.

While it is true that Gitlow had not accused the two rabbis of joining the party, was it less damaging to assert that they had "carried out the instructions of the Communist Party or collaborated with it. . . ."?

Gitlow also testified at length regarding the Methodist Federation for Social Action. His remarks, however, showed that he had no first-hand information on the Federation. Instead, he sought to analyze various articles from the *Social Questions Bulletin* and in this manner create the impression that the Federation was spearheading the "infiltration" into the churches. In his confusion, Gitlow listed as suspect such leading Methodist clergymen as Franklin H. Littell, Walter G. Muelder, Charles C. Webber, and Ernest Fremont Tittle—all articulate critics of Communism.

TESTIMONY OF HERBERT PHILBRICK

Testimony on Communist influence in the churches was also given by Herbert Philbrick, who for nine years had served as an undercover agent for the Federal Bureau of Investigation, emerging into public view when he testified in the first Smith Act trial of Communist leaders in 1949. Philbrick had written *I Led Three Lives,* recounting his life as a "communist, citizen and counterspy," and from this book came a television series of the same name.

Philbrick was a twenty-five-year-old Boston advertising man when he innocently joined a Communist youth front in 1940. After discovering its true purpose, he contacted the F.B.I. and, at their request, he moved deeper and deeper into the Communist orbit until he joined the Young Communist League in 1942 and the Communist Party in 1944. He served on the advertising staff of the New York *Herald Tribune* after leaving the party, wrote and spoke widely on the threat of Communist subversion, and testified before various investigatory committees. In general, he has been more moderate than others who had been members of the Communist Party. In *I Led Three Lives,* for example, he paid tribute to the contribution of the American Civil Liberties Union, a group which is eyed with grave suspicion by Right Wing extremists.[23] Philbrick also made remarks critical of Senator Joseph R. McCarthy.[24]

In his testimony on the churches before the Un-American Activities Committee in July 1953, Philbrick spoke of a special "ministers' cell" in Boston, claimed that the Communist Party assigned young men to the ministry, and named clergymen in the Boston area whom he thought were secret members of the Communist Party. He had been assured that his testimony would not be made public and he had been carefully smuggled past the press into the hearing room so that reporters would not know of his presence there. When the testimony was released in September, Philbrick protested furiously. He had only given leads, he pleaded, not verified facts. His 1953 testimony must be examined, therefore, with his own attitude toward it in mind.

Two years earlier, in 1951, Philbrick had testified before the same committee, then investigating Communist activities in Massachusetts, concerning such a ministers' cell. He claimed that he might have become "well acquainted with that group" if he had stayed in the party two months longer. "I would say these people were at least posing as ministers of the gospel and playing the part of ministers and religious leaders while in fact they were Communist Party members using the cloak as a cover-up for their true motives and intents." [25] Philbrick said he could not identify any of the individuals "by direct legal evidence."

His contention that a ministers' cell existed in Boston may be accurate, but some factors tend to weaken his testimony. Philbrick never had any communication with the cell, and whatever information he had came to him second-hand. He offered no specific details as to its function and he has produced no corroborating evidence since the testimony to strengthen his case. In addition, there has never been any other public suggestion by Communists or ex-Communists that the party actually organized cells for ministers.[26]

Philbrick also claims that "so far as I can determine" cell members were Communists before they became ministers. He recounts the following from the time he was a student in a party school:

One of the students in this special course was a young theological student who was already a member of the Communist Party, but was being assigned by the Communist Party to move into the religious field, and that meant that he would have to go through his preliminary training at college and then go into a religious seminary and then be ordained as a minister in one of the major denominations.[27]

Philbrick did not learn the person's name.

This assertion, too, raises more questions than it answers. Such a student would face tremendous difficulties. He would be forced to conceal his atheism throughout the three years of seminary; he would have to go into the ministry and serve as a pastor while disbelieving the faith and profession he publicly espoused; and he would be subjected to continuous religious and other influences that could wean him away from the party.

In the most sensational part of Philbrick's testimony, he listed specific ministers who he said were Communists or operating under party discipline. He offered their names only after the persistent urging of Counsel Robert L. Kunzig, who reiterated that "we are in here in executive session, and this testimony [is] confidential. . . ." [28] The witness stressed, as he had earlier, that he had no legal evidence, that he was giving only his personal opinion, and that his identifications were based largely upon hearsay or upon a clergyman's Communist-front affiliations. He could point to only one Communist clergyman with any degree of certainty. This was Eliot White, who, as Philbrick acknowledged, had publicly announced his party affiliation.

The clergymen Philbrick accused of Communist ties were Stephen H. Fritchman, a Unitarian editor and youth leader who became pastor of the First Unitarian Church in Los Angeles in 1948; Donald Lothrop, pastor of Boston's Community Church; Joseph F. Fletcher, professor at Episcopal Theological Seminary in nearby Cambridge;

Kenneth DePew Hughes, the rector of St. Bartholomew's Episcopal Church in Cambridge; and Anthony de Lucca, described by Philbrick as "formerly a minister in Wakefield, Massachusetts." Fritchman is discussed in greater detail in Chapter 19 and Fletcher in Chapter 12. Lothrop and Hughes are discussed briefly below. It has not been possible to make contact with an Anthony de Lucca.[29]

Philbrick testified regarding Lothrop:

> One of the most active centers of Communist Party activities then and now in Boston is the Community Church of Boston. The Community Church is headed by Rev. Donald Lothrop, L-o-t-h-r-o-p. He is one of the individuals who, I am sure in my own mind, is operating under Communist Party discipline. I have no doubt about it at all, and I would not make the statement if I had the faintest doubt as to where that man's loyalty lies.[30]

Lothrop, a Universalist minister, is a tenth-generation descendant of the Rev. John Lothrop, who settled in America in 1634. He was educated at Tufts College and at Crane Theological Seminary, served a parish in Iowa, then in Wakefield, Massachusetts, and since 1936 at Community Church, a unique nonsectarian organization that seeks "to apply ethical ideals to all forms of social and economic life." [31] Although Lothrop is minister of Community Church, most of the sermons and lectures are given by invited guests. Some of these guests had embraced a viewpoint extremely sympathetic to Soviet policy, but the pulpit of the church also had been open to vigorous critics of Communism.

Lothrop has freely discussed his unorthodox politics. He acknowledges that during the thirties he enthusiastically endorsed the general position of the American League Against War and Fascism; that in the forties he favored the approach to world affairs taken by Henry Wallace; that in the fifties he still believed that Americans must exert pressure upon their government to obtain a less hostile attitude toward Russia. He has implemented his opinions by supporting a dozen front organizations—associations he defends. In 1949, for example, he was a sponsor of the Cultural and Scientific Conference for World Peace. In justifying such activities he has written: "In general let me say that I have and would support any effort at peace, and the creation of international understanding." [32]

Lothrop has found himself in agreement with the Communists on most political issues. Yet, he has pointed to distinct differences in three significant areas. First, he has consistently supported Zionism, while the Communist position has vacillated over the years. Secondly, he supported President Roosevelt's foreign policy during the period of the Hitler-Stalin pact. Thirdly, when the Communists were favoring the prosecution of Trotskyists under the Smith Act during World War II, he states that the Community Church was raising money for their legal defense.

After Philbrick's testimony was released, Lothrop gave an unequivocal reply. "I am not now and never have been at any time a member of the Communist Party," he said. He continued: "This is the weasel trick of a coward who will not state that I am a Communist. He has hidden behind this trick phrase so that he cannot be libeled. If he should state that I was a Communist, then he is a liar." Lothrop added: "It is a curious thing that government bodies and the public are supposed to give greater credence to a man who is willing to give his soul to the Communist Party than those men who at no time were Communists." [33] This reflected the view he holds that Philbrick may have been, in fact, a genuine Communist who only later worked with the F.B.I.

Philbrick felt obligated to give further evidence to support his testimony on Lothrop, now that it had been challenged. Specifically, he claimed that he had appeared many times on the platform of the Community Church while a Communist Party member. Lothrop asked him to produce proof that he had ever been on the church's platform; Philbrick did not respond to the challenge. Lothrop wrote: "The truth of the matter is that I don't know Mr. Philbrick, that he never spoke from the platform of the Community Church at any time, and that I had never heard of him until he first became a government witness in New York." [34]

Though urged to seek a hearing, Lothrop refused on the grounds that such a request would give "honor to that which is dishonorable. . . ." [35] He did agree to respect a subpoena, but the committee let the issue die. "I feel that the failure to issue a subpoena was an admission of guilt on the part of the Committee for having overstepped the bounds of decency," he said.[36] Meanwhile, the Boston Association of Ministers backed Lothrop in a resolution regretting that he "had been attacked in this fashion, and that his independent, courageous liberalism has been misrepresented to the community." [37]

Of Kenneth DePew Hughes, Philbrick said:

> MR. PHILBRICK. Another minister—and I almost feel like saying—quote— "minister" in each of these cases because they are something entirely different from what I comprehend to be a true minister of the Gospel—
>
> MR. CLARDY. You would say they were a disgrace to the ministry?
>
> MR. PHILBRICK. I certainly would, sir. Rev. Kenneth DePew Hughes of St. Bartholomew's Church in Cambridge, Mass., is another one of those who worked with the Communist Party over the period of years, and so far as I know, is still working with the party today. [38]

Philbrick does not here specifically accuse Hughes, a Negro rector, of belonging to the party, nor has he ever made that charge. Yet, in the context of the hearing, the reader naturally would assume that Philbrick thought Hughes was not a worthy minister and that he might well be a member of the ministers' cell group. To this Hughes replied: "If Mr. Philbrick is implying that I have been associated with any secret cell organization, he is an infernal liar. . . . The only secret organization to which I belong is the Masons and the only secret meetings I have ever attended are Masonic meetings." Hughes has co-operated with Communists and stated after the Philbrick testimony was released that he would "work with anyone, whether they be Communist, Republican, or Democrat, who is for peace, low-cost housing, lower prices and such other laudable objectives which will benefit America." [39]

The ministerial association in Cambridge came to Hughes' defense, expressed its disapproval of Philbrick's vague and unsubstantiated testimony, criticized the committee for not giving Hughes an opportunity to speak for himself, and exhorted "members of our churches to remain firm in the freedom of the Christian faith against every force that would threaten our liberties or our confidence in each other as Christians, and in the work of the church." [40] The Episcopal Bishop of Massachusetts, Norman B. Nash, undertook an investigation of the Philbrick charges against both Hughes and Fletcher. Nash issued a statement which noted that they had denied—orally and in writing —that they were ever members of the Communist Party or under its discipline. "I believe them," said the Bishop. He added that they both recognized that the Christian faith "is inconsistent with an atheistic Marxist philosophy. They both reaffirm their loyalty as citizens of our country." Nash was publicly critical of some of their activities, however, and cited specifically Hughes' work with the Progressive Party and Fletcher's involvement in the Communist peace campaign. "They justify their membership and activities of this sort as motivated by their obligations as Christian ministers to work for social justice and for international friendship and peace. I believe them to be sincere, though I consider that they have not always been wise in espousing their activities." [41]

Prior to his appearance before the Committee on Un-American Activities, Philbrick had written an article for the *Christian Herald* of April 1953 called "The Communists Are After *Your* Church!" In it he made some sweeping generalizations. "I know that the Communist threat to your church is greater now than at any time in twenty years," Philbrick wrote. "This is the story of what I know—as much of it as may be revealed—told so that you will realize that subversion in the sanctuary is the most deadly and insidious menace facing America today. . . ." Despite Philbrick's alarming allegations, the evidence is overwhelming that by 1953 the influence of the Communists in the churches was at a low ebb.

Philbrick's syndicated column appearing in the New York *Herald Tribune* and other newspapers made similarly broad charges. Published under the title "The Red Underground," the articles had a sense of urgency. The Communists were tightening their grip on California or stepping up their infiltration in the folklore field or plotting a comeback in the labor unions. Sometimes the column would warn groups like the Fellowship of Reconciliation. The F.O.R. had scheduled a dinner in Cambridge in November 1954, and Philbrick wrote in a column that "communist agents" had received orders to "move in" on the meeting. F.O.R. included "many loyal and sincere individuals," he said, but he admonished that the organization was in grave danger of being sold the "co-existence theme" manufactured in Moscow. It might also pass resolutions favoring the recognition of Red China or promoting "fear of the possibility of atomic warfare." Philbrick told F.O.R. members to examine carefully the background of all new members and all guests to find out if they had pro-Communist records.[42]

Such an article is not likely to help an organization. To many of the public, the Fellowship of Reconciliation would become suspect. Distrust would be spread within the group itself, with an immediate stigma upon all new faces that might turn up for the dinner and all new applicants for membership. If Philbrick actually had valuable information on Communist infiltration efforts, he could instead have cautioned its leaders personally or by letter and not through the medium of a newspaper.

Philbrick's warning about resolutions might tend to influence policy decisions by cultivation of fear that the adoption of certain resolutions (actually supported by many anti-Communists) would indicate that Communist influence had been important at the dinner. He implied that the organization could be easily infiltrated and manipulated even though few groups have been more alert to the Communists than the F.O.R. Its executive secretary, John M. Swomley, Jr., has strenuously and intelligently fought Communist influence for many years. Indeed, few persons in the United States have shown more competence and discernment in this regard. *Zions Herald*, Massachusetts Methodist paper, attacked this Philbrick column in an editorial, "Recipe for a Smear": "The beautiful thing about this kind of cooking is that you do not have to vouch for the authenticity of the ingredients. . . . If you have a reputation as a former F.B.I. agent, so much the better." [43]

Philbrick sought to discredit a number of religious journals and especially the *Churchman,* discussed in greater detail in Chapter 17. Again and again he described it in such terms as "a foremost transmission belt of propaganda favorable to the Communists." [44] Editor Guy Emery Shipler challenged Philbrick's assertions and in April 1959, when the New York *Herald Tribune* was no longer carrying the Philbrick column, it published an apology. Following an "independent investigation" of the facts, the newspaper wanted "to correct any unfavorable misunderstanding which may have arisen from these articles regarding 'The Churchman,' Dr. Shipler and Miss [Edna Ruth] Johnson [the managing editor]."

While the Herald Tribune has occasionally disagreed with opinions expressed by "The Churchman" this newspaper desires to emphasize that nothing contained in the articles was intended to reflect upon the integrity of "The Churchman," Dr. Shipler or Miss Johnson, or their adherence to religious principles.[45]

In summary, Philbrick has demonstrated little knowledge and even less understanding of the specific subject of Communism and the churches. It is unfortunate that he has made so many careless and sensational statements on the issue, especially in the light of the fact that his opinions carry so much weight.

THE SAGA OF J.B.

While ex-Communists were testifying before the Un-American Activities Committee, the nation was in an uproar over the charges of J. B. Matthews. On June 22, Matthews had been appointed executive director of the Senate Permanent Subcommittee on Investigations headed by Senator McCarthy. Within a few days the July 1953 issue of *American Mercury* appeared with Matthews' article "Reds and Our Churches." It began with the alarming words: "The largest single group supporting the Communist apparatus in the United States today is composed of Protestant clergymen."

Thousands of Americans, ministers and laymen alike, raised a storm of protest. Three distinguished clergymen—a Protestant, John Sutherland Bonnell, a Roman Catholic, John A. O'Brien, and a Jew, Maurice H. Eisendrath—telegraphed President Eisenhower to denounce the statement as "unjustified and deplorable." Eisenhower replied that "I fully share the conviction you state" and praised the churches as "citadels of our faith in individual freedom and human dignity." [46] Matthews resigned, stating that he refused "to permit the question of religion to be used in an attack on Senator McCarthy." McCarthy "very reluctantly" accepted his resignation.

Behind this bare recital of the facts lay two interesting and important stories. First, the emergence of J. B. Matthews in this episode brought again into focus an almost legendary figure who had retired from the public eye after an earlier life steeped in controversy. Second, the allegations of the article itself must be weighed. Were they true?

Joseph Brown Matthews, known simply as J.B., was born in Hopkinsville, in the heart of the Kentucky Bible belt, in 1894, the third of seven children in a family that was Methodist in religion and Republican in politics. He went to Asbury College in Wilmore, Kentucky, where his facility for linguistics and his fascination with the ancient classics led him to major in Latin and Greek. Later he received an M.A. degree from Columbia University, a bachelor of divinity degree from Drew University, a master of sacred theology degree from Union Theological Seminary; then he studied at the University of Vienna. He was a scholar of considerable vigor and accomplishment.

Matthews served as a missionary in Java, where he taught native Methodist preachers and produced a score of books in the Malay language. His growing enthusiasm for the cause of Indonesian nationalism did not endear him to Dutch authorities there, and after seven years he left the islands under pressure from mission executives. Back in America, he taught at such schools as Fisk and Howard universities and at Scarritt College in Nashville, Tennessee, where he became a fiery advocate of racial integration. Influential Nashville citizens protested, and Matthews found it wise to resign.

Over the years, Matthews had developed into an ardent pacifist, and in 1929 he accepted an offer to become one of the secretaries of the Fellowship of Reconciliation. He began to swing farther and farther to the left, became the first chairman of the new American League Against War and Fascism, joined with a minority in the Socialist Party to urge a more revolutionary program, and finally was ousted as a secretary of F.O.R. when he announced his essential agreement with the Marxist doctrine of class war. At a Madison Square Garden rally in 1935 Matthews told a cheering crowd: "We must unite to defend the Soviet Union without any 'ifs,' 'ands' or 'buts.'" [47] Later he was to look back on this period and say that probably he had been more closely associated with the Communist Party's front apparatus than any other non-Communist in America.

Matthews expressed his hostility toward organized religion in *Partners in Plunder,* a book he coauthored in 1935. One of these "partners" was the church. The Federal Council of Churches was seen as a tool of the capitalists, and missionary officials were said to be "bound and gagged" by the owners of industry. The Protestant Episcopal Church was dominated by J. P. Morgan and the Presbyterians by Andrew W. Mellon, while the views of such Methodists as Francis J. McConnell were weighted "in favor of the ruling business class." Of the Rockefeller family he wrote:

Rockefeller money made possible the noble edifice on Riverside Drive, New York City, where the Reverend Harry Emerson Fosdick comforts the Rockefeller dynasty with this declaration: "Personally, I dread the thought of collectivism which Russia represents as I would dread the devil." So does John D. Rockefeller, Jr., dread it! [48]

Events of 1935 changed the course of Matthews' life. He became head of Consumers' Research, an organization that evaluated retail products and reported objectively to the public on its findings. When the employees struck, Matthews quickly traded his "working class" slogans for the attitudes of a typical employer faced by what he viewed as excessive demands. The *Daily Worker* announced a "mass trial" of Matthews in October 1935 in which the "vicious opportunism of J. B. Matthews, his betrayal of labor, union-smashing, red-baiting and armed attacks on peaceful pickets and their sympathizers will be brought out fully. . . ." [49] He reacted slowly at first, as evident in his resignation from the National Bureau of the American League Against War and Fascism, addressed to Harry F. Ward:

Being fully aware of the embarrassment which my membership on the League's Bureau must be occasioning you and the League, I hereby tender my resignation to take effect immediately. I cannot tell you how much I regret the necessity of this step and the incidents which make it necessary. It is especially painful to me to be under this necessity at precisely the time when I hoped to become more active in the work of the League. In taking leave, may I express my deepest hope that the work of the League may grow in effectiveness day by day as it confronts the deepening crisis of the world situation. Nothing can ever cause me to forget or to cease to appreciate the part which I had in the formation of the League or the value of the personal associations with its loyal workers both in the central offices and in the field. [50]

These attacks upon him, coupled with general disillusionment and difficulties in his domestic life, pushed Matthews toward the opposite pole. When he tried to warn people, including the churches, that groups like the American League had Communist origins, he met with considerable abuse. He began to regard himself as an innocent victim of a Communist plot. In 1938 he left Consumers' Research, which had been virtually destroyed by the strike, and within a few months appeared as a star witness before the Un-American Activities Committee, then headed by Martin Dies. His analysis of the use of fronts, of their interlocking relationships, and of their exploitation of prominent individuals was largely accurate. The Dies Committee added Matthews to its staff as chief investigator until 1945. He then became a consultant to the Hearst newspapers, where he gathered around himself a flock of former Communists.

Matthews initiated the massive filing system of the committee, which contains reference to the front affiliations of millions of Americans. He and his staff scavenged for letterheads, printed programs, public statements, and petitions, but regarded the *Daily Worker* as their most valuable source of new listings. Matthews has followed this pattern in most of his articles and speeches in recent years: he presents a target's name and then lists his "communist front record." There is little effort to interpret the record. The dates of the affiliation, the precise nature of the fronts, and the degree of association are ignored. The reader is left to assume that the larger the number of organizations, the more notorious the individual in question. While this weakness was less apparent in "Reds and Our Churches" than in later articles, its effect was seen there, too. "Reds and Our Churches," however, directed its principal criticism at five churchmen who, in fact, were leaders in the front apparatus: Harry F. Ward, Kenneth Ripley Forbes, Jack R. McMichael, Willard Uphaus, and Joseph F. Fletcher.

James A. Pike, then dean at the Cathedral of St. John the Divine in New York City, was quick to accuse Matthews of carelessness: "I am not acquainted with the full record of every minister named by Mr. Matthews," Pike said. "But I do know something about my own Church." Matthews had headed the list of prominent Communist collaborationists with the names of eight Episcopal bishops. Of these "top leaders," Pike pointed out, three had been retired for years; one was not only dead but his successor was also dead; one was not the bishop of the diocese named—and was retired; one did not exist at all—nor was there or had there been a bishop of that name in the history of the Episcopal Church. The two left were bishops of small dioceses and neither could remotely be called Communist. Pike continued: "My secretary, who draws much less salary than Mr. Matthews has been getting, saves me from 'bulls' like this by a simple check with an inexpensive volume called the Episcopal Church Annual. I am sending one to Mr. Matthews as a gift." [51]

Matthews ignored dates. In 1935 Earl Browder spoke to a group of students at Union Theological Seminary, boasting that the Communist Party had some ministers in its membership. The Matthews article quoted Browder, but omitted reference to the year of his statement. Matthews described the People's Institute of Applied Religion as a "Communist school which is run, sponsored and subsidized by Protestant clergymen" and he made reference to an Institute conference held in a cathedral. He did not point out that the People's Institute had disappeared by 1953, that its leader, Claude C. Williams, was running a one-man operation from Helena, Alabama, and that the conference in a cathedral was held during World War II.

The article's opening statement that ministers comprised the "largest single group supporting the Communist apparatus in the United States" constituted a semantic abuse. The word "supporting" conveys to the average person the impression that the clergy were deliberately co-operating with the Communists. In 1953 only about twenty-five Protestant clergymen, less than a dozen of them parish ministers, were publicly and knowingly working with the Communists—far fewer than the number of labor leaders and less than the number of lawyers, members of a profession renowned for its conservatism. Most of these few ministers were given prominent positions in the Communist orbit where they could serve most effectively as camouflage.

The basic weakness of the Matthews article, then, was that it painted in bold, broad strokes a portrait of a massive conspiracy within the churches that did not exist. "Reds and Our Churches" also indicated a deeply rooted bitterness toward the ministry. Why should "cowardly politicians," Matthews asked, shield the clergy from the spotlight of truth? Why should they be immune to investigation while other citizens were forced to account for their traitorous acts? This antipathy toward Protestant church leaders had continued for more than twenty years. In the early thirties Matthews was labeling them "tools of capitalism." In the early fifties he was accusing them of "supporting the Communist apparatus." He was wrong in both instances. [52]

These attacks upon the churches were arousing more and more

clergymen, who believed that their profession was being maligned and that a veil of suspicion was being cast over the Protestant pulpit. There were signs of a mounting conflict as major denominations and their leaders began to stiffen in their resistance and then take the offensive. They anxiously awaited the Oxnam hearing—confident that the Bishop would win the encounter, but aware that anything less than victory could lead to even greater harassment of the churches.

"**M**r. Counsel, will you please
call the witness."

"Will Bishop Oxnam please step forward."

It was July 21, 1953, and a sturdy, vigorous clergyman of sixty-two made his way forward. Television lights bore upon him as he took the oath and sat down before a barrage of microphones. One of the most controversial leaders of American Protestantism was pitting himself voluntarily against the heavy artillery of the Committee on Un-American Activities. A curious nation watched the strange spectacle of congressmen engaged in a grueling ten-hour duel with a bishop.

A distinguished audience, including many members of Congress and prominent clergymen, crowded in to witness the battle, some standing for hours in the rear of the room. Most spectators sympathized with the Bishop, but there were antagonists, too. Just before the proceedings began, five guests of Representative Jackson were ushered to a front seat reserved for their arrival. They were leaders in the American Council of Christian Churches, led by Edgar C. Bundy.

In his brief opening remarks, Chairman Velde emphasized that the encounter should not be viewed as an investigation into religion. The sentiments of individual committee members, he said, were not necessarily the opinions of the whole committee—an apparent reference to Jackson's remarks on the floor of the House. The committee was not concerned with "factional disputes between various church groups or personalities." [1] Because of the "unusual circumstances attending the hearing," Velde said that Oxnam would be allowed to make a prepared statement, but that "it should be understood that this does not establish a precedent." [2] Oxnam stated his life-long opposition to Communism, suggested an end to the whole "public file" system, asked Jackson to apologize for his derogatory remarks, and told the committee that "the churches have done and are doing far more to destroy the Communist threat to faith and to freedom than all investigating committees put together." [3]

He was handicapped by the attitude of the tribunal. Only one committee member, Clyde Doyle of California, openly came to his support. Two other Democrats, Morgan M. Moulder of Missouri and James B. Frazier, Jr., of Tennessee, and Republican Bernard W. Kearney of New York—the only Roman Catholic on the committee— sat mute during most of the hearing. Kearney failed to appear during the evening session. Four Republicans dueled with the Bishop. Velde sought to be fair but he went on the defensive whenever Oxnam accused the committee of negligence. The antagonism of Kit Clardy of Michigan was evident in his tone—his smile and grandfatherly appearance turned out to be misleading. The few words which Gordon H. Scherer of Ohio directed at the Bishop were strong with contempt. Oxnam's most vigorous foe was Jackson, later described by the Bishop as "a smooth talking, superficial opportunist." [4] This quartet was joined by Francis E. Walter, Pennsylvania Democrat, bitter over Oxnam's attacks upon the McCarran-Walter immigration act, who suggested that maybe Oxnam was "not concerned with the number of Communists coming into this country." [5] The Bishop also faced the hostility of Robert L. Kunzig, the committee counsel, while his own attorney, Charles C. Parlin, was not permitted by committee rules to speak.

Much of the evidence cited against Oxnam came from highly unreliable sources and especially the *Daily Worker*. "Personally," Oxnam protested, "I do not think the *Daily Worker* is good authority for anything." [6] The committee also depended upon individuals and newspapers at the other end of the political spectrum, and a great deal of biased material was introduced into the record from the Right Wing *Bureau County Republican* of Illinois, a weekly newspaper in Chairman Velde's district. Counsel Kunzig even quoted a thirty-year-old criticism of Oxnam by "Bob" Shuler, a Methodist minister in Los Angeles. Shuler's objectivity as a witness could be judged by his proud statement in 1950 that he hoped to "live to see in the White House a man who has the strength, the power, the virility, the courage, the ability, the Christianity, the conviction, the personality, and the love of country which I believe Gerald L. K. Smith has." [7]

Oxnam had already demonstrated the inaccuracy of the committee's information in his analysis of his "public file" in the Washington *Post*. Now the counsel produced a throwaway publicizing a 1923 mass meeting of the International Workers of the World with Oxnam as an announced speaker. "I did not speak at that meeting," Oxnam stated categorically. "I never worked with the IWW." [8] He went on to offer proof of his denial. Representative Doyle objected: "I don't like the idea of us producing for this witness documents way back in the year 1923 for the first time." [9]

The committee tried to discredit the Bishop by linking him with churchmen whose sympathies with Communism were well known. Oxnam was apparently expected to bear responsibility for the political views of all Methodists. At one point, the counsel introduced an article by Winifred Chappell, written in 1934, which urged American youth, in the case of war, to sabotage military preparations (see Chapter 16). Jackson insisted upon reading the entire article into the record, perhaps hoping that her extreme views might be confused in the public mind with Oxnam's. Her statements, Oxnam said, were "deplorable," but what could he have done about them?

At another point, Counsel Kunzig brought up "a certain Harry P. Ward" whom he identified as "head" of Union Theological Seminary in New York. Oxnam was quick to point out the correct middle initial—"F."—and to note that he had been a professor—not president. The counsel continued: "You *know* he is a good friend of yours! Is that right?" [10] He had known Ward well in the twenties, Oxnam said, but they had split over the issue of Communism and had seen each other only once since 1936. Despite this reply, Kunzig read into the record the testimonies of Manning Johnson and Leonard Patterson, who "identified" Ward as a member of the Communist Party—an accusation Ward promptly denied. [11]

One of the most revealing encounters of the hearing occurred when

Kunzig accused the Bishop of having supported the *Protestant*. Oxnam had allowed his name to be used as an editorial adviser from May 1940 to February 1942—at a time, incidently, when the *Protestant* was bucking the Communist position during the period of the Nazi-Soviet pact by favoring aid to England against Hitler. Oxnam said he had resigned after Roger Baldwin of the American Civil Liberties Union told him that the magazine had Communist support. He had also been uneasy about serving as an editorial adviser when he had absolutely no voice in the magazine's policies. But Kunzig insisted upon putting into the record the testimony of Louis F. Budenz, which charged that the *Protestant* had been directed by the Communists to promote anti-Catholicism. Kunzig then pulled out a trump card: a copy of the *Protestant* in which Oxnam had written an article entitled "Monsignor Sheen and Clerical-Fascism." [12] Oxnam asked that the whole article be inserted in the record to show that it did not link Sheen with fascism, but, rather, urged Roman Catholics, Protestants, and Jews to work together for a just and durable peace. The *Protestant*'s editor had given it a misleading title.

Oxnam's activities in one other area called for a special word of explanation. During World War II, and for a very brief period after, he had taken a friendly view of the U.S.S.R. His affiliation with the National Council of American-Soviet Friendship while a bishop in Boston was the first charge brought up during the hearing. He had participated in a Boston "Salute to Our Russian Ally" meeting in 1942, sponsored by the National Council of American-Soviet Friendship. Why? Oxnam replied by reading names on the rally's letterhead: Lord and Lady Halifax, Secretary of State and Mrs. Cordell Hull and other members of the cabinet, five United States senators, Governor and Mrs. Leverett Saltonsall, Mayor and Mrs. Maurice J. Tobin, such labor leaders as William Green and Philip Murray, such editors as William Allen White, and such authors as Dorothy Thompson. America and Russia, he reminded the committee, were wartime allies.

Oxnam had an opportunity to offer a dramatic illustration of his point. Kunzig carefully built up a case around the fact that for five months in 1943 he had been chairman of the Massachusetts Council of American-Soviet Friendship. Who had asked him to serve? Oxnam replied that he had been contacted by Dirk J. Struik, a professor at

Massachusetts Institute of Technology. Didn't the witness know that
Struik was an active Communist? No, he did not. Testimonies by
Herbert Philbrick and others were introduced as evidence against
Struik. Kunzig then cited the Attorney General and several investigatory committees which had described the National Council of
American-Soviet Friendship as a Communist front. Oxnam's critics
on the committee seemed pleased and relieved that so early in the
hearing they had been able to trap the Bishop. But their pleasure was
short-lived.

> Bishop Oxnam. I am just wondering—I realize the impression that is
> being created here, Mr. Chairman, by this kind of procedure. I could
> read at this moment into the record, if you will allow me, a statement
> by Gen. Dwight D. Eisenhower to the national council of this organiza-
> tion dated November 1945, which reads:
> American-Soviet friendship is one of the cornerstones—
> Mr. Velde. Just a minute, Bishop. I think we have been overly fair in
> granting you the privilege of making a statement.

Velde's effort to stop Oxnam met with an angry outburst from the
audience. Doyle objected to the chairman's ruling and Velde acquiesced. This was Eisenhower's message:

> American-Soviet friendship is one of the cornerstones on which the
> edifice of peace should be built. To achieve this friendship nothing is
> more important than mutual understanding on the part of each of the
> institutions, traditions, and customs of the other. As an American soldier
> and lover of peace I wish your council the utmost success in the worthy
> work it has undertaken.

Oxnam had turned what had seemed like a crippling blow into an
important psychological victory. The immensely popular President
had himself given "support" to the National Council of American-
Soviet Friendship.[13]

When the hearing came to a close, the committee members present
unanimously adopted a motion saying it had "no record of any Communist Party affiliation or membership by Bishop Oxnam." [14] They
refused to go any farther, however, and agree to correct his file.

There was unusual newspaper and television coverage of the hearing and the overwhelming majority of editorials felt the Bishop had
won. The New York *Times* said that "in its clash with Bishop Oxnam

the un-American Activities Committee clearly came off second best." [15] The Minneapolis *Morning Tribune* believed that Oxnam had "struck a powerful blow for true Americanism. . . ." The Baltimore *Sun* felt the hearing had dealt successfully with the "unwarranted slurs on Bishop Oxnam's patriotism . . . and the current move in Congress to do something about cleaning up congressional investigatory methods is strengthened by this episode." The Philadelphia *Bulletin* was gratified that the Bishop "proved resolute and strong enough to defeat his detractors, but it should never have been necessary to put him through such an ordeal." [16]

Nevertheless, Oxnam was criticized also. The Omaha *World-Herald* accused him of carelessness—"a commentary on the caliber of his leadership in intellectual, if not religious affairs." [17] The *Tablet,* organ of the Roman Catholic Diocese of Brooklyn, wrote that an "objective reading of the testimony can result only in the conclusion that Bishop Oxnam is either stupidly gullible or a master of deviousness. It is hard to believe that a stupid person could rise to the eminent post of bishop of the Methodist Church." [18] The *Protestant* (whose name had been changed to *One*) reported that Oxnam had "scraped and bowed" before "an agent of fascism." [19] Others attacked the Bishop for dissociating himself from Ward. Milton Mayer, free-swinging columnist for the *Progressive,* wrote angrily: "To get the pack's fangs out of his neck, he threw Harry F. Ward to them— Harry Ward, that fighting old fool for Christ, who would have gone Communist or anywhere else his good heart led him. . . ." [20]

Oxnam was sensitive to this latter criticism—he was not interested in badgering Ward, who he acknowledged had contributed heavily to the social concern of the church in earlier years. Yet, his admiration for Ward as a person could not bridge the deep chasm between them on Communism and the Soviet Union. Oxnam had read a letter at the hearing, written in 1936, in which he had criticized Ward for embracing "the Communist position as to objective, if not as to method." The letter added: "Too often they—his associates—prefer a fight to an advance. They would rather throw bricks than build with them." [21]

The long-term results of the Oxnam hearing are not easy to assess. There are observers, especially among the clergy, who view July 21, 1953, as the day McCarthy suffered his greatest blow—even though he was not directly involved. Some say that this one episode, more than any other, united liberal and conservative churchmen, aroused by the methods of the Un-American Activities Committee. Perhaps these contentions exaggerate the truth; many events were helping to cause public opinion to revolt against the loose accusations of the time. But Oxnam's counteroffensive certainly was one of them.

MATTHEWS AND MACKAY

Controversy also raged in 1953 over the scheduled appearance of J. B. Matthews before the same committee. On July 20, the day before the Oxnam hearing, the committee voted to invite him to document his statement that Protestant clergymen comprised "the largest single group supporting the Communist apparatus" in the United States. All five Republicans and Moulder favored his appearance; three Democrats voted against it. Moulder told reporters that the hearing would clear the air. "Such shot-gun charges as Matthews made," he said, "should be subjected to cross examination." Doyle protested that Matthews would use the "committee as a forum to air his charges further and get more publicity to increase the sales of a magazine." [22]

Months slipped by and Matthews continued to air his views in speeches and in articles but the promised hearing did not come. Then, in February 1954, Velde again announced that Matthews would be a witness, though he would appear in executive session. "Unless the vote is changed," Velde said with a touch of reluctance, "I suppose we are duty-bound to hear him." [23]

Enthusiasm was ebbing. McCarthy was on the wane. The entire subject of Communist infiltration was losing its appeal. The committee had been subjected to a heavy avalanche of criticism because of the Oxnam hearing. Many feared that once Matthews testified the subject would explode again—and in a Congressional election year. Behind the scenes the committee and its staff were involved in considerable bickering. In the spring of 1954, the Congressmen reversed themselves by a 5-4 vote and decided not to call Matthews. Velde "regretted" the decision; some saw in it the heavy hand of "ecclesiastical pressure"; but others heaved a sigh of relief now that another troubling spectacle had been averted.

One of the churchmen Matthews termed a "top collaborator" with the Communists was John A. Mackay, in 1953 president of Princeton Theological Seminary and moderator of the General Assembly of the Presbyterian Church in the U.S.A.[24] Mackay had come from Scotland to the United States as a youth and had risen swiftly to positions of leadership within the church. He had been under attack during the postwar years for alleged "Communist ties," but his strong evangelical views made most informed observers discount such charges immediately. While Oxnam's emphasis had always been upon an improved social order, Mackay had concentrated more on religious education and the church's missionary activities, especially in Latin America. He had become convinced, through his missionary work, that both Protestantism and American democracy were faced with a formidable foe in Roman Catholicism.

This view of Roman Catholicism goes far in explaining his alleged "Communist-front record" as Matthews and the Committee on Un-American Activities compiled it. Writing in 1950, for example, Mackay defended his support of the American Friends of Spanish Democracy, listed by the committee as a front organization (though not listed by the Attorney General). He had rejoiced when Spain became a republic, he said, and he was ashamed when the United States and Great Britain "betrayed" the new government in fear of Hitler and Mussolini "and because of Roman Catholic pressure." Mackay added: "I gave my name in good faith to an organization whose objective was to promote a cause in which I was passionately interested and in which I am passionately interested today." To be labeled a Communist sympathizer for this, he wrote, is "the kind of malicious innuendo which violates the American, and still more, the Biblical tradition of reverence for truth." [25]

Mackay discussed the Matthews attack in a letter to the New York *Times*. He had "never supported any cause which, on its own merits, was unworthy of support by an independent Christian citizen of this country who is sensitive to human situations." If Communists, "unknown to me and for their own reasons," were interested in the same cause, that did not invalidate the cause nor make him in any way responsible for Communist policy. "I have been consistently concerned with human freedom," Mackay stated. "I am not ashamed of any document I ever signed or of any cause I ever sponsored, whether it was in the interests of Republican Spain, or in favor of Spanish refugees from Fascist tyranny, or to advocate the repeal of the McCarran Act." [26]

Mackay continued his battle against what he described as a "Twentieth Century American version of a Sixteenth Century Spanish Inquisition." His next move was to urge the twenty-six-member General Council of the Presbyterian Church (U.S.A.) to take a stand against the "stifling anti-communism" of the time. A statement he prepared was debated and amended by the General Council and, in October 1953, adopted unanimously. It acknowledged that Congressional committees had "rendered some valuable services" in their exposure of "the insidious intervention of a foreign power in the internal affairs of our country," predicted that Communism was "foredoomed to failure" because it "leaves God out of account" and "enslaves in the name of freedom," but went on to warn that "dangerous developments are taking place in our national life." The churches were urged to stand fast against those who would meet Communist tyranny with another tyranny equally as antagonistic toward freedom.[27]

This "Letter to Presbyterians," as it was known, was released to the press in early November. Before the week was out, a long list of newspapers had commented on it. The New York *Times* called it a "profoundly anti-Communist document" which warned Americans of the dangers in the current campaign against subversion.[28] The Pittsburgh *Post-Gazette* described it as one of the most "soundly conceived and beautifully worded" documents that had come to its attention.[29]

Others denounced it bitterly. No one spoke out more sharply than Daniel A. Poling, editor of the *Christian Herald,* who charged that the Letter expressed the "exact sentiment" and, in several instances, used the "exact language" that had appeared in the *Cominform Journal,* an international Communist publication.[30] Herbert Philbrick wrote that the "Letter to Presbyterians" supported "not only the complete foreign policy program of the Soviet Union, but also contained all the fundamental premises of Marxism, Leninism and Stalinism concerning class struggle, imperialism, force and violence, and revolution." [31] These Poling and Philbrick charges were, in a word, ludicrous.

In May 1954, the Presbyterian General Assembly, representing the entire denomination, adopted the "Letter to Presbyterians" by a unanimous vote. It was only one of many church pronouncements deploring the hysteria of the times. A pastoral letter issued by the House of Bishops of the Protestant Episcopal Church in November 1953 acknowledged Communism as Christianity's greatest avowed enemy, but condemned "trial by uninformed public opinions . . . accusations by hearsay." Americans must beware of "creeping fascism," it said.[32] The Council of Bishops of the Methodist Church protested against "those who in the name of Americanism employ the methods of repression, who speak with the voice of democracy but whose hands are the hands of tyranny," [33] and the American Baptist Convention warned against those "so intent upon combatting the menace of communism that they adopt the very principles and methods which makes communism itself frightening." [34] Other Protestant denominations and thousands of ministers echoed these sentiments and were joined by Jewish rabbis and Jewish religious groups. Although Senator McCarthy had strong clerical and lay support among Roman Catholics, one leading bishop, Bernard J. Sheil of Chicago, assailed McCarthyism as "phony anti-communism that mocks our way of life, flouts our traditions and democratic procedures and our sense of fair play." [35]

VISITORS FROM ABROAD

In 1954 a new controversy arose over the Second General Assembly of the World Council of Churches. The World Council represents nearly 200,000,000 Christians—largely Protestants, but including Eastern Orthodox, Old Catholics, and the ancient churches of Ethiopia and India. It had been under fire from both the Communist Left and the extreme Right since its birth at Amsterdam in 1948.

The Communist attitude was reflected in the 1948 statement of the Clergymen's Union of Bulgaria, which claimed to represent 2,000 Orthodox priests. They charged that Protestantism was "under the influence of imperialism" and trying to lure to its side "the Holy

Orthodox Church, employing mainly traps of the ecumenical movement embedded in the plan of work of the World Council." [36] In the trial and conviction of fifteen Bulgarian Protestant leaders in 1949, one of the "proofs" offered against them was that they had ties with the representatives of the World Council, "an agency of American imperialism." [37] The central committee of the World Council in 1950 condemned the North Korean attack upon South Korea and assailed the Stockholm Peace Appeal, causing the resignation of T. C. Chao of China—one of the vice-presidents of the Council—who heard in the voice of the World Council "the voice of Wall Street." [38]

The seeds of the controversy of 1954 were planted when delegates from Czechoslovakia and Hungary decided to attend the Evanston Assembly in August and international conferences of Presbyterians and Lutherans the same summer. The problem first came to the fore in late 1953 when some leaders of the World Council had expressed fear that the United States Government might keep delegates from the Soviet orbit out and discussed the possibility of moving the assembly to another country to avoid this risk. Right Wing extremists then opened fire, including Carl McIntire, to whom the issue was a handy weapon to use against his perennial enemies. McIntire accused John Foster Dulles of serving as the World Council's "agent" in its effort to bring in "Communists." Then in the spring of 1954 the Cook County (Chicago) Council of the American Legion adopted a resolution protesting the entry of Eastern European delegates. The powerful and conservative Chicago *Tribune,* however, cautioned that the resolution was "well intentioned" but contrary to the best interests of the nation.[39]

In mid-July 1954, the State Department announced that eleven Czech and Hungarian delegates had been granted permission to attend. The experiences of these visitors in the United States, the State Department announcement said, might lead to "a spiritual strengthening of the churches of Czechoslovakia and Hungary in the face of constant and ruthless pressure to which they are subjected." Some may "have found it possible to reconcile their faith with public support of communism," yet Americans should not be alarmed—the "spiritual foundation on which this nation rests is too strong to be adversely affected by any pro-Communist activities in which this small group of delegates from Communist-dominated areas might attempt to engage." [40]

Most Protestant churchmen greeted the State Department decision warmly, but many Eastern European refugees chorused in protest. One of their most articulate spokesmen was Bela Fabian, former leader of the Hungarian Democratic Party. To him the delegates from his native land were "minions of the Communist regime in Budapest, men who are willingly furthering the Kremlin's overall design for subjugating the churches of Eastern Europe." To allow these "Communist Quislings" in the United States, he declared, was for the World Council of Churches to strike "yet another blow at the spirit of resistance of the enslaved peoples of Eastern Europe." [41]

On July 22, 1954, Representative Alvin M. Bentley, Republican of Michigan, took the issue to the floor of Congress. Though he did not fear subversion, he said, "we sully the memory of those brave individuals who have suffered in defending the cause of religious freedom behind the iron curtain." The subcommittee he headed, Bentley announced, would conduct public hearings simultaneously with the Evanston Assembly to expose the Communist ties of the Czech and Hungarian delegates. [42]

A Czech theologian and a Hungarian bishop drew most of the fire. Joseph Hromadka, who taught at Princeton Theological Seminary during World War II, had returned to Prague to become dean of the Jan Hus Theological Faculty. After the 1948 Communist coup in Czechoslovakia, he became the foremost spokesman for Christian coexistence with Communism. He believed Communism exemplified in practice many of the social principles of the Christian faith. He had attended several Communist peace congresses, and in July 1952 accused the United States of using bacteriological warfare in Korea. A year later, when Hromadka received the first Czechoslovak Peace Award, his puzzled American friends sought to explain his conduct. Some said that he was maneuvering to continue the work of the church in a hostile environment; others thought his intense patriotism and his desire to remain in Czechoslovakia left him little alternative but to support its government, even though he might harbor grave reservations about many of its policies; still others assumed that he had fallen victim to effective Communist propaganda.

Hromadka's most forthright remarks were contained in an interview with his personal friend Donald Grey Barnhouse of Philadelphia. "I come to the United States as a Christian," Hromadka said. "I could not come as a Communist, as these accusers have said, for I am not a Communist." He revealed a Calvinistic approach to his own role in history. "We must live where our Lord has placed us," he said. "Christ demands of me that I live among Communists. . . . When people ask me if I can be critical of the Communists of my country, I say, 'Every sermon that I preach is a criticism of Communist ideology. In standing for Christian ideology against Communist ideology I am performing my most loyal service to my country.' " [43]

Janos Peter, the controversial bishop of the large Hungarian Reformed Church, aroused far less sympathy and defense. His visa was sharply restricted and a confidential "State Department source" referred to reliable information that Peter was a member of the secret police.[44] Peter was a stranger to America and remained aloof during his visit, perhaps because of the widespread suspicion. On one occasion, however, he gave abrupt answers to a list of questions submitted in advance by reporters. Was he a Communist? "It would be impossible." Can Christianity and Communism coexist? "Yes." Are Hungarian Protestants satisfied under the Communist government? "Yes." In prewar Hungary, Peter said, the Roman Catholic Church was in a favored position and "the greatest land owner in my country"; Protestant churches were "second-rate." Now the two were treated as equals.[45]

As the Evanston Assembly met, a string of refugee witnesses appeared in New York City before the Bentley subcommittee and recounted Communist persecution of churches and the clergy. Bentley invited Bishop Albert Bereczky of the Reformed Church of Hungary or "any member of your delegation" to testify. Franklin Clark Fry, president of the United Lutheran Church of America, wired a stern rebuke: "As you know these men are here exclusively for church conferences and this fact heightens the clear impropriety of your proposal." [46] A number of refugees picketed at Evanston, quietly reminding passers-by that the real voice of the Czech and Hungarian churches was stilled.

Significantly, four of the Hungarian delegates, once they returned home, joined in castigating their hosts. They spoke of the "horrors of American life" and the "savagery of the American press." Peter told

hair-raising stories about the "secret police" and the manner in which
the State Department sought to arouse hostility against him. Bishop
Laszlo Dezsery of the Lutheran Church said that John Foster Dulles
had "tried to exclude the Eastern churches from the assembly" and
reported that ministers' sermons were "censored" by the F.B.I. Bishop
Bereczky expressed concern about the "ill treatment" of American
babies who were forced to compete in a crawling contest.[47] With the
coming of the Hungarian revolution in October 1956, in which many
ministers died fighting against the Communist regime, Hungarian
Protestants ousted Peter and Bereczky—until Russian tanks suppressed the uprising. Other members of the Evanston delegation,
however, suffered because they supported the revolt.

The cold war thawed a bit in the next two years. The Korean conflict came to an uneasy end, McCarthy's influence declined, and, in
Russia, after Stalin's death and Beria's execution, the stern policies of
the Politburo were somewhat eased. In November 1954, Khrushchev
deplored the persecution of the churches under the former regime and
promised that priests and believers would no longer be subject to
severe disabilities.

As the thaw continued, the way was open to more exchange between East and West. Delegations, cultural troupes, and tourists
journeyed between the United States and the Soviet Union. It was
natural that churchmen should join the procession. America's spiritual leaders had wearied both of accounts of how free and flourishing
religion was in Russia and of contrary reports that all faithful Christian clergy were dead or in prison. Now they could study the situation first-hand. In 1955 groups of Baptists and Quakers visited the
Soviet Union.[48]

The next year a two-way exchange was organized. In March 1956,
nine American church leaders arrived in Moscow with Eugene Carson
Blake, president of the National Council of Churches, as chairman.
Blake was accompanied by Franklin Clark Fry; Henry Knox Sherrill,
presiding bishop of the Protestant Episcopal Church; Roswell P.
Barnes, associate secretary of the National Council of Churches;
Walter Van Kirk, executive director of the National Council's depart-
ment of international affairs; Herbert Gezork, president of Andover-
Newton Theological Seminary; D. Ward Nichols, a bishop of the
African Methodist Episcopal Church; Charles C. Parlin, Methodist

Wall Street lawyer, who had served as counsel to Oxnam at his 1953 hearing; and Paul B. Anderson, prominent Y.M.C.A. leader and expert on the Soviet Union and the Russian language.

In Russia the group witnessed some encouraging signs and reported that churches were crowded, seminaries were full, and religion was hampered by fewer restrictions than in the past. Yet, freedom of religion, as the United States knew it, did not exist. "It's pathetic," said Van Kirk, "that the only role religion can play here is to help relieve the drudgery of life for the people from day to day." [49] The church had no right to carry on effective educational work and had little contact with youth. Services were attended largely by older women. Most churches had been closed after the revolution and were now reopened as museums or cultural centers. The clergy could not comment freely on political, economic, or social matters, but they were expected to serve as propagandists for Soviet policies. Metropolitan Nikolai, the second-ranking prelate of the Russian Orthodox Church, listened while Americans challenged his support of the World Peace Council and criticized some bitterly anti-American statements he had made during the Korean conflict. A sharp interchange followed and the Metropolitan advised his guests that the past should be forgotten.

The American delegation was aware that the Soviet propaganda machine would exploit the visit and openly expressed resentment of the grinding cameras and blinding klieg lights. Blake pointed out that:

The real issue with regard to the risk of conversations, delegations and common work toward peace with the Soviet churches is the same issue faced by President Eisenhower at the summit conference in Geneva.

It was clear at Geneva that the Russians would use the meeting for their own propaganda purposes. I have no doubt that our visit to Russia and the Russian churchmen's return visit and our co-operation will be used for Soviet purposes in the satellite countries and elsewhere.

But we believe there is no reason to suppose that their propaganda will be more effective than ours. If we behave cynically and without hope in this situation, we will be rightly charged with being faithless and hopeless. There is no position worse in which a Christian church can find itself.[50]

Their trip aroused some criticism despite its obviously good intentions. The recording secretary of the National Council of Churches,

Ralph M. Arkush, himself Russian Orthodox, had abstained when the original vote to send a delegation had been taken. Forty-six clergymen in the United States who had fled Croatia, Estonia, Latvia, Lithuania, Slovakia, and the Ukraine circulated a declaration describing the trip as a gain for the Soviet Union. Meanwhile, malicious critics busily dug up what they claimed were "Communist-front records" of several of the nine delegates and offered them as evidence that the trip was part of a Communist conspiracy.

But a deluge of dissent, far more vociferous, was to come when eight churchmen from the Soviet Union paid a return visit three months later. At its head was Metropolitan Nikolai who, like Bishop Peter in 1954, had been accused of being a "Soviet agent." He was dressed in the flowing garb of the church, adorned with his white *klobuk,* the miter of his archepiscopal office. He and the rest of the delegation—three other Russian Orthodox clerics, a Latvian Lutheran bishop, an Armenian bishop, and two Baptists—were met by boos and shouts of "Soviet spies, go home!" when they landed at New York. At Yale University, pickets carried placards, "Go Home, Agents of Bulganin and Khrushchev" and "What Happened to Thirty-Four Ukrainian Bishops and Churches?" At Independence Hall, there was a noisy demonstration. Ironically, the Soviet delegation's warmest reception came on Wall Street, where it attended a dinner at the First National City Bank building and heard a capsule lecture on the capitalist system.

Some of the hecklers on the trip were professional antagonists of the World Council of Churches who seized upon every opportunity to vent their hatred against Protestant leadership. "We are naturally embarrassed at discourtesy shown to our guests," Eugene Carson Blake said, "but we have explained to them that American liberty allows such activities even when in grossly bad taste." [51] Even some of the Soviet delegates seemed moved by the *émigrés* who had fled from Communist persecution and who met them in anger and tears. Archbishop Gustav Turs of the Latvian Evangelical Church spoke warmly of American hospitality to refugees from his land despite an effort by Metropolitan Nikolai to divert him: "I want to express thanks for the help which American churches have given my fellow Lutheran Latvians," he said in Toledo, Ohio. [52]

Nikolai himself tried to be conciliatory. He expressed his regret for a statement he made in 1949 calling Pope Pius XII an "agent of American imperialism." It was made, he said, in "a period of high tensions and misunderstanding." [53] In Philadelphia, he remarked as he stood before the Liberty Bell that "although it no longer rings it continues to speak as a symbol of human liberty." [54] But, most important, at Greenwich, Connecticut, he condemned the Communist Party's materialism, which, he said, denies "all that we regard as holy." [55]

A few months later a similar interchange of delegates between East and West would have been impossible. In October 1956 came the Hungarian revolution. As president of the National Council of Churches, Blake cabled the Russian Orthodox Church, urging its officials to oppose violence, to support the Hungarian people in their desire for freedom, and to "join in our prayers" for peace and just settlement in the Middle East. Nikolai replied that the Russian Orthodox Church was opposed to "aggression" in the Middle East. As for Hungary, he was carefully vague: "Our Government is giving material aid to those who suffer in Hungary. In this our churches are participating. We shall devotedly and unceasingly labor for peace as the final goal of the Kingdom of God." [56] In his 1957 New Year's message, Patriarch Alexis chided "certain highly-placed foreign ecclesiastics" for holding Russia responsible for a revolution caused by "those who spread discord." [57]

Blake's plea, however ineffective, represented the first official exchange of messages between the main body of churches of the United States and the Soviet Union since the Bolshevik seizure of power. This was a long way from the Oxnam hearing three years before, when the churches were on the defensive. Now it was clear that Protestant leadership could be astutely anti-Communist and still keep the channels of communication open. When Russia failed to heed the pleas of many nations for Hungary, the churches stepped in to save as many of the refugees from Communism as they could. Thousands were brought to America by Church World Service, relief arm of the National Council, during the next few years. Many of the National Council's critics were loud and abusive in their words; the National Council was courageous and compassionate in its deeds.[58]

FIFTEEN · IN THE NAME OF RELIGION

The Committee on Un-American Activities has singled out several religious groups for attack. The People's Institute of Applied Religion also listed by the United States Attorney General as "subversive"—has been called by the committee "one of the most vicious Communist organizations ever set up in this country."[1] Another committee target has been the *Protestant,* described as "a magazine which fanatically spreads Communist propaganda under the guise of being a religious journal."[2]

Were the People's Institute of Applied Religion and the *Protestant* guilty as charged? What influence have they had in the churches? What has been their role in recent years?

Each story centers around a colorful and complex individual. The People's Institute was launched by a minister from the western Tennessee hill country who boasted of Cherokee blood. Claude C. Williams has devoted a lifetime to an attempt to revolutionize Christian teaching and practice; in 1954 he was ousted from the Presbyterian ministry for heresy. The *Protestant,* which once claimed to speak for 5,000 clergymen, was edited by Kenneth Leslie, a Canadian Baptist layman, and it reflected his vivacity, impulsiveness, and romanticism.

Williams was born in 1896 and was raised in a two-room shack and in the rigid traditions of the Cumberland Presbyterian Church. He rebelled against his fundamentalist background, left his family's denomination, and decided to become a minister in the Presbyterian Church in the U.S.A. He studied at Vanderbilt University, where he met two young clergymen with a similar Southern background and a similar enthusiasm for the social gospel. One was Donald L. West, later a member of the Communist Party and a "people's poet." The other was Howard Kester, who founded the liberal Fellowship of Southern Churchmen, upon which Williams was to pour forth his bitter ire.

From Vanderbilt, Williams was sent to the mining area of Paris, Arkansas, to pump new life into its dying parishes. His unorthodox views on the Bible, his close relations with labor unions, his attacks upon segregation, and his smoking, drinking, and swearing aroused his congregation. Once he placed a nudist magazine in the church's reading room and, when criticized, defended nudism as a sincere revolt against the hypocrisy of "middle class society." The pictures of three of his heroes hung on his parsonage walls: Jesus, Debs, and Lenin.

In 1934 some of his parishioners asked the Presbytery to remove him for being derelict in his church duties, for preaching beliefs contrary to Presbyterian doctrine, and for espousing the "cause of communism." [3] When he was directed to leave, he appealed. Willard Uphaus of the National Religion and Labor Foundation, investigating the case, declared that Williams owed his ouster to bigotry. The *World Tomorrow* urged its readers to contribute to an appeal fund; Reinhold Niebuhr took up Williams' cause; and many liberal religious journals editorialized on his behalf. But Williams lost his appeal. To the Communist Party of Arkansas the incident was justification for its antagonism toward the church: "We see in this the distinct class character of the Church which is merely a tool in the hands of the ruling class, the capitalists." [4]

Williams found his Arkansas experience disillusioning. He wrote in *Radical Religion* that after five years in the South he no longer had faith in "the effectiveness of old line political parties, of the schools, churches, and of the State Federation of Labor under present leadership, as instruments of social change." [5]

He moved away from these institutions in his search for social justice, and in the spring of 1935 was instrumental in organizing a hunger strike in Fort Smith, Arkansas. For this he was sentenced to three months in jail and fined $100 for "inciting dissension" among relief workers. Next he founded the New Era Schools of Social Action and Prophetic Religion in Little Rock and began to lay the foundation for what he envisioned as a mass "people's movement." He worked organizing sharecroppers; one day in 1936 he was seized by six hoodlums and brutally flogged alongside a highway in Crittenden County, Arkansas.[6]

Williams found time to read extensively, particularly in the Communist classics. Many years later a sympathetic biographer was to trace this leftward swing:

> The sweetness and light of Christian Socialism began to give him a pain. After reading Lenin's *State and Revolution* and *Imperialism* he found his views taking even firmer and clearer shape. He was inspired by Lenin, by his parallel greatness as theoretical and active revolutionary, by his incisiveness and surefootedness, by his quick analysis of a situation, and by his faith, which under the most terrible buffetings was a rock, like the faith of Jesus.[7]

By 1938, Williams was serving as director of Commonwealth College in Mena, Arkansas, and serving on the executive council of the Southern Tenant Farmers Union. After one council meeting, he left his coat at the home of J. R. Butler, union president, and Butler discovered in its pockets a secret report to Communist headquarters. It included this sentence: "Since the reorganization of the school in August, 1937, when a Party member became director of the school (Claude Williams), there has been on the campus complete political unity. . . ."[8] The document referred also to Williams' association with the Southern Tenant Farmers Union. If the proper moves were made, it said, it would be possible "to capture the union for our line at the next convention." Butler immediately announced that Williams would be tried and, if found guilty, ousted from the union's council. Williams denied that he was a Communist—though admitting that he had been one earlier—and traced the document to an ill-informed member of the party who had just returned to the college after eighteen months in Spain. The union leaders were not convinced. They voted his expulsion unanimously.

PEOPLE'S INSTITUTE ESTABLISHED

Williams' second ouster did not discourage him in his plan for a "people's movement." With funds provided by Northern friends, he established the People's Institute of Applied Religion; it boasted thirty national sponsors by the end of 1940. Official endorsement of the People's Institute came from the Methodist Federation for Social Service, the Church League for Industrial Democracy (Episcopal), and the National Religion and Labor Foundation.

Detroit, during the war, presented a unique opportunity for a socially conscious religious movement. The city was crowded with Southerners, both white and Negro, not yet assimilated into well-established congregations. Store-front churches mushroomed, and there unlettered preachers gathered little groups seeking to perpetuate the religious traditions of the South. Another result was the emergence of powerful, persuasive demagogues who attracted thousands of followers through direct appeals to their prejudices and frustrations. To meet this situation, the Presbytery of Detroit decided to invite Claude C. Williams and his People's Institute to the city to develop and direct a program for these newcomers.

The People's Institute sought to reach the hundreds of preachers, largely Negroes, who held jobs during the week and led small congregations Sundays and evenings. Williams conducted classes for them, using colorful and simple charts to prove that the Bible had come out for higher wages, vacation with pay, and the closed shop. Occasionally, the group would break into song to the tune of familiar gospel hymns or spirituals, but with new words. "When the Saints Go Marching In" became "When the Union Marches In." He issued elaborate certificates to those who attended.

The theology was new, too. Over the years Williams worked out an interpretation of Christianity that supported the main tenets of Marxism. He said his sourcebook was the Bible, "the people's book . . . an account in religious prose, parable, and legend of the struggle of the Ancient Lowly for the Reign of the People." [9] The product of Williams' theological efforts was not profound, nor even original, but many found his unusual approach intriguing.

Williams contended, as classical Marxism did, that "church religion" was controlled by the dominant economic system. Roman Catholicism came into existence to buttress medieval feudalism, he said. He offered this explanation for Protestantism:

> Protestant church religion came into being to enhance the rise of capitalism. It proclaimed the divine right of property. It deified the kings

of finance, the lords of commerce and the captains of industry. Today this church religion is directed by remote control from the Chamber of Commerce, the National Association of Manufacturers and the offices of cartel imperialists.[10]

He attributed Protestantism's failure to the "Christ-centered theology of Paul," who was charged with corrupting the original "people's movement" launched by Jesus.

He hatched out a "gospel" all his own (Rom. 2:16), through which he destroyed labor unions (Acts 19:24-41) and dished out the opiate of contentment (I Tim. 6:6-15); returned slaves to their masters (Philemon) commanding them to obey (Eph. 6:5; Titus 2:9, 10); said the fascist powers of Rome were ordained of God, demanding that the people be subjected unto them (Rom. 13:1-5); preached male chauvinism (Eph. 5:22, 23), permitting women neither to teach nor even to speak in public (I Tim. 2:11-12; I Cor. 14:34-35).[11]

All of Protestantism was bogged down by Pauline doctrine, he said, except for "a sprinkling of Unitarian liberalism and ethical culture."

Williams claimed that common sense denied the supernatural—"an unscriptural invention of theology." [12] God he defined as "a Symbol of Struggle for Freedom, Security, Brotherhood." [13] Sin was equated with ultraindividualism; salvation with "a collective effort of the workers and other victims of this world system to save themselves from the oppressors." [14]

Jesus emerged as the hero of Williams' theology, "a class-conscious leader" who headed a revolutionary movement aimed at "fascist Rome." Williams gave this account of final events in the life of Jesus:

The Galilean began to organize the oppressed of the whole world against Rome (Matt. 11:28-30). He was shadowed and framed by the stooges of the Roman Empire (Luke 20:20). On the night before he was lynched, he called his disciples together in an underground meeting (Luke 22:1-12). Here he expounded the nature of the people's movement (Luke 22:25-27), the danger of traitors (John 13:38), the nature of the opposition (John 15:18-20). . . . He warned against individualism or shooting forth as a branch lest they be plucked off. He stressed the power of unity (John 15:4-7). Early the next morning he was condemned by religious Quislings and crucified by a Gentile Gestapo (Matt. 20:18, 19).[15]

Williams had little contact with the Presbytery that sponsored his work. He did establish close relations with Charles A. Hill of the

Hartford Avenue Baptist Church, and with a friend from earlier years, John Miles, Negro minister who openly professed his admiration for the Communists but denied membership in the party. Miles had studied at Yale and Harvard and had served both Baptist and Congregational parishes. In Detroit, Williams helped him open the People's Church, which was to dissolve in 1950. When Miles died in 1959 at the age of seventy-one, the *Worker* extolled him as "a champion in the fight for civil rights." It reported that "many notables from labor, community, and political life, including leaders of the Communist Party, attended the funeral. Rev. Miles was a subscriber to the Worker for the last 10 years and spoke last May Day on a trip he had just made through the deep south. His passing is mourned by the volunteers and the editorial and circulation staff of the Worker." [16]

Nineteen forty-four marked a high point for Williams and his People's Institute. A popular biography of Williams was republished, under the title *A Faith to Free the People*. Its author was Cedric Belfrage, who eleven years later would be deported to his native England after his refusal to tell a Senate subcommittee whether he was a Communist. Also in 1944 the People's Institute held a successful "People's Congress" with 200 registered delegates at Detroit's St. Paul's Episcopal Cathedral.

The political slant of the gathering was evident: Harry F. Ward was the main speaker. Three representatives of the *Protestant,* including editor Kenneth Leslie, attended. A discussion on the Tehran Conference was led by George F. Addes, Communist-supported secretary of the United Automobile Workers; Howard Selsam, director of the Jefferson School of Social Science, a Communist Party institution; and Richard Morford, then vice-chairman of New York State's American Labor Party.

Despite these successes and new financial backing from the Unitarian Service Committee, it was obvious by the end of the war that Williams had been a failure in Detroit. His hostility toward the church was annoying his sponsors. He seemed to enjoy shocking audiences by telling them that ministers should read less Shakespeare and more Marx. His dress was unkempt and so, often, was his language. To his admirers, his boldness was an attribute of a modern-day prophet. To a growing number of critics, however, it was evidence of instability and irresponsibility. The Presbyterians quietly stopped their sponsorship, and Williams and his People's Institute moved to Birmingham, Alabama. He continued his affiliation with the Detroit Presbytery, receiving church disability payments because of ill-health.

The character of the support for the People's Institute was changing also. When America entered the war in 1941, the Institute's sponsors had included such prominent Protestant leaders as Bishop Francis J. McConnell, Liston Pope of Yale Divinity School, and Edwin McNeil Poteat of the Colgate-Rochester Divinity School. By 1946, these names had disappeared from the letterhead. Many of the remaining ministerial sponsors shared Williams' general political orientation: Stephen H. Fritchman, William B. Spofford, Sr., Joseph F. Fletcher, Jack R. McMichael, Richard Morford, John W. Darr, Jr., and Donald L. West. Edna Joyce King (Mrs. Claude Williams) served as executive secretary. The two associate directors were Winifred Chappell and Owen H. Whitfield. Whitfield, the prototype of the folk hero, was an uneducated Negro sharecropper, a part-time preacher, and organizer for the United Cannery, Agricultural, Packing and Allied Workers, a C.I.O. union ousted in 1950 because of Communist domination. Cedric Belfrage was research director and Lynn Ward, talented son of Harry F. Ward, was the organization's artist.

WILLIAMS UNDER FIRE

In 1948 the People's Institute was placed on the Attorney General's list of subversive activities. The same year, it was attacked by the Committee on Un-American Activities; Williams issued a reply. "If Wall Street is the government," he wrote, "then I am disloyal to it. . . . If government by the *people,* including the Negro people and all other minorities, is communism, then I am a communist, for I believe in just that!" [17] In 1950 Williams sent an open letter to President Truman to register as an agent of a foreign power: a "colonist of the Kingdom of Heaven" and a member of the "Way of Righteousness . . . the oldest underground movement of history and the most effective. . . ." [18]

On May 12, 1953, the Presbytery of Detroit voted to set up a special committee to examine all documents relating to Williams' status in the church. In January 1954, he appeared before a judicial commission to be tried on four charges:

1) The accused holds doctrinal views which are contrary to the Holy Scriptures and to the creed confessed in this church.

2) The accused is charged with a studied and determined effort to subvert and corrupt the Christian faith of this church, by preaching and promulgating the heretical doctrine which he preaches and by falsely representing the Protestant Christian movement.

3) The accused has been publicly charged with following the Communist Party line and with holding a Communist Party membership.

4) The accused has absented himself from the sessions of the Presbytery for a period of upwards of three years and has labored outside the bounds of the Presbytery without permission. . . .[19]

Williams argued that the charges "arise out of pressure of the political views and criticisms instead of out of the ordination vows." [20] There may have been some truth in his contention, but plans to drop him from the Presbytery rolls had been discussed off and on for several years because he had not attended any meeting since 1946, had failed to notify the Presbytery of his change of address, and because mail sent to him had been returned "address unknown." Meanwhile, his nominal affiliation with the Presbytery was proving an embarrassment to the denomination and provided a handy weapon for those irresponsible critics who wanted to charge it with harboring heretics and Communists.

He defended himself by claiming that his views were scriptural and by attributing his failure to fulfill his responsibilities to the Presbytery to a misunderstanding rather than to deliberate negligence. The charge of Communism, Williams said, was false and, if pressed, would set a dangerous precedent that could stifle freedom of the pulpit. The commission agreed to drop the charge of Communism on "technical grounds" but voted "a censure of admonition" on that count. He was found guilty of the other three charges.

Williams immediately announced that he would appeal to the higher courts of the denomination. The *National Guardian* established a defense fund to help defray his expenses. Ex-Congressman Vito Marcantonio expressed confidence that "this case will finally be resolved on the side of intellectual, spiritual and economic freedom, despite the darkness in which our nation seems to be enshrouded." [21]

Royal Wilbur France, attorney of a newly organized Religious Freedom Committee, prepared a brief on behalf of Williams stating that modern scholarship supported many of Williams' religious views and that if judged by Calvinism, hundreds of other Presbyterian ministers were also heretics.

The appeal to the Synod, and later to the entire church, was turned down. Williams, at fifty-eight, had been unfrocked. "I hold no ill will against any of my brethren in Michigan," he commented, "but I am disappointed that they upheld irresponsible charges as being equivalent to guilt." [22]

What truth is there in the charges of Communism against Williams and the People's Institute? The available evidence points in two directions.

First, Claude C. Williams willingly co-operated with the Communist Party and its members. He sympathized with Communist goals and supported Communist policies. He solicited their financial support and received the enthusiastic plaudits of the Communist press—and made no effort to dissociate himself from them. He has admitted that he was a member of the party for a few months in 1937. He praised the Soviet Union for rendering more service than the churches did to religion. When an attempt was made just prior to World War II to oust him from the board of the National Religion and Labor Foundation unless he indicated some criticism of Russia, he asked: "Who am I to question the integrity of 190,000,000 people from whom I am removed?" [23]

Williams' attacks upon the Socialists and liberals also indicated his sympathy for the Communists. He wrote in 1947:

Religious "liberalism" with an apparent partisanship for labor is manifested in such groups and movements as Dr. John Haynes Holmes' Community Church in New York, Henry Hitt Crane's Central Methodist Church of Detroit, Fred Shorter's People's Church of Seattle, the Religion and Labor Foundation, Reinhold Niebuhr's Union for Democratic Action and the Conference of Southern Churchmen. But we shall merely delude ourselves if we look for true religion in these climates.

Instead of using religion to unite labor and the progressive forces, and for all the good first intentions of many of them, these groups have fallen into the fascist-inspired, Vatican-directed "anti-Communist" trap. Together with their smart boy Reuther, with the Social Democrats, Ethical

Socialists, Thomasites and Trotskyites, they can be expected to support
the biggest union-busting program the Master Capitalists of America have
ever inaugurated. . . .[24]

But other evidence suggests that perhaps Williams remained, in a
sense, independent of the Communists. A few persons who have
known him have reported that in private conversation he displayed
bitterness toward what he viewed as the sectarianism of Communists.
At his heresy trial in 1954, Williams gave this account of his relations with the Communists:

I have continually been one of the most severe critics of Communist
tactics and approach, and especially in the South. There is no group in
America who knows I am not a Communist as well as the Communists
themselves. . . . Don West, Whitfield and myself in the South, persons
who have been born and reared in the South and stayed down there, are
questioned by these groups and called individualists. Recently I was so
dubbed in a speech at New York and criticized that I would not co-
operate with them. People who have been born in the South and left the
South and carried east, have been the oracles on the South and know
nothing about the South at all. . . . I have never been recognized as a
trustworthy person by Communist people officially.[25]

At the same trial he discussed why he had worked with Communists:

We were almost obliged to work with people whom we assumed were
Communist people, if we did anything in the South during the early time
of the New Deal; but I have differed vigorously with them on many
fundamental things and especially the viewpoint of atheism. . . . I will
venture to say this and I think it will be understood here, we follow the
error, many times, and we may repent, publicly or otherwise. I would
not join the Communist Party today at all.[26]

Whatever the facts, Williams has continued his activities from his
Helena, Alabama, headquarters. Since 1954 he has tried to move
around the South despite poor health and has been visiting Negro
community leaders, holding conferences, and distributing literature.
There are those who believe that he continues to be subservient to
the Communist Party. Certainly he is still ready to co-operate with
Communists. Others see him as the same undisciplined and undiplo-
matic rebel that he was thirty years ago. In 1957 he broke into the
news again briefly when a cross was burned in front of his house.

THE *Protestant* LAUNCHED

The first issue of the *Protestant* appeared in December 1938 as the *Protestant Digest,* and, as suggested by its title, most of its articles were excerpted from other religious journals. It was greeted by many clergymen as a boon to Protestantism—something that might serve Protestants as the *Catholic Digest* served Roman Catholics. It demonstrated strong political biases, to be sure, but the early issues gave little indication of pro-Communist sympathy. The main foe was fascism: in Germany, in Italy, in Spain.

Important changes were soon made. The *Protestant Digest* ceased being a digest and in the fall of 1941 became known as the *Protestant.* The name of editor Kenneth Leslie had appeared alone on the masthead during its first half-year of publication; gradually a long list of distinguished contributing editors and editorial advisers appeared. The *Protestant* adopted a militant anti-Catholic attitude and increasingly appealed to Jews for support on the grounds that it was fighting Christian anti-Semitism. Meanwhile, in 1939 its editorial office had been moved from 14 Beacon Street in Boston to 521 Fifth Avenue in New York City.

Leslie's enthusiasm for the Soviet Union also came to the fore. When the Hitler-Stalin pact was signed in August 1939, the magazine moved to Russia's defense. "Through Litvinoff Russia tried honestly and patiently to cooperate in building a world system of collective security," an editorial stated. "She was snubbed at every turn. Should she be blamed then for turning to bi-lateral action at the last moment?" [27]

When hostilities broke out in Europe a month later, however, Leslie did not follow the Communist cries of "imperialist war." After France fell in June 1940, he called for all-out aid to "save Protestant England" from fascism and its "Vatican supporters." His faith in Russia remained unimpaired. "A fully accredited ambassador should fly to Moscow today," Leslie wrote in October 1940, to seek an understanding over a common course of action against Hitler. America was urged to remove its "anti-Godless crusaders" from leadership positions to prove to Russia that she was truly antifascist.

When Germany invaded the Soviet Union, Leslie was torn between fear that Russia might collapse and delight that the Hitler-Stalin pact was a thing of the past. "He is human, this Russian," he wrote. "He will not forget it if we put out our hand to him in this hour of his need." [28] He accused the Roman Catholic hierarchy of heading an "anti-Soviet drive against Roosevelt's efforts to save American democracy" and attacked pacifists for mistaking compromise with Hitler for the peace of God. Within a few weeks, the *Protestant* claimed it had the signatures of 1,200 ministers on a letter to the President demanding aid to Russia and pledging that "whatever sacrifices you may lay upon us we shall more than gladly accept." [29]

The *Protestant* set the pace for pro-Soviet sentiment after Pearl Harbor. In the first issue of 1942, the lead editorial was entitled "God's Red Army." "It is not because Russia has saved us that we thank God for the Red Army," Leslie began. "It is simply because of what Russia is and because of the quality of the Red Army itself, the spiritual quality of the soldiers. . . ." [30] In April 1942, the *Protestant* sponsored a "Te Deum" meeting in Carnegie Hall to honor the Russian troops. Leslie presided and his poem "Ivan and John" was sung by three choral groups, including one from Adam Clayton Powell's Abyssinian Baptist Church. The Dean of Canterbury, Hewlett Johnson, spoke from London to the 2,000 persons attending and urged "a western offensive now."

This demand for a second front in Western Europe was, of course, the Communists' main theme during the first months of the war when American forces were still retreating before the Japanese in the Pacific. "The people are watching very carefully the materialization of the promised second front," Leslie wrote in June 1942, but "big business is as yet not quite willing to gear its effort wholeheartedly with Russia, and therefore the gears of the global war are with monotonous repetition being stripped to the bone-crushing tune of *too little, too late*." [31] To hasten the second front, he urged that the Russian General Semyon Timoshenko be named commander of all allied forces.

In October 1942, the *Protestant* announced that 1,000 ministers had signed its petition for a declaration of war on Franco Spain and Vichy France. Later it charged that "Nazi sympathizers" were in control of Finland—"what the Russians have contended from the beginning." [32] Leslie revived the issue of Russia's seizure in 1940 of Estonia, Latvia, and Lithuania, which, he said, had been justified "to insure the economic and military bases of her country." [33] Even Stalin's expulsion of Trotsky was re-examined. "It is plain now that if the Soviet Union had followed Trotsky instead of Stalin," he wrote, "the Germans and the Japanese would long since have met in Delhi. . . ." [34]

The animosity of Soviet Communism toward religion never raised a doubt in Leslie's mind. While the West "praised the Nazarene Carpenter with its words," the Soviet Union "based its civilization upon the simple principles of this carpenter. . . ." [35] He referred to the Bolsheviks as "new Protestants." In 1943 he wrote dramatically: "If there is a heart of justice in the universe it is beating now in the Red Army. I believe in that heart. I call it God." [36] Yet Leslie predicted the eventual return of "true Christianity" to Russia. The equivocal attitude of the capitalist nations toward Jesus had "prevented the Union of Soviet Socialist Republics from acknowledging the place he should have in their hearts, the place he will ultimately have in their hearts." [37]

The *Protestant* maintained that Russia defeated Hitler while the fighting of the Western powers was "in the nature of major holding operations." [38] With the end of the war, Leslie gave full endorsement to Soviet foreign policy. "The Soviet Union makes mistakes, but moves in one direction," Leslie wrote. "The Anglo-Americans make mistakes, and move in the *opposite direction.*" [39] When Britain and Russia quarreled over Iran in 1946, Britain was guilty of "provocation." When the United States came to the aid of the Greek Government against Communist guerrillas, Leslie called it "American pro-fascist aggression." [40] He said the Marshall Plan was "approved by the Papacy," and thereby part of "Fascist strategy." [41]

Meanwhile, the *Protestant* watched developments in China closely. In 1945 it described the Communists there as "the world's heroes today." [42] The same month Leslie sent a telegram to President Truman demanding a "hands off" policy in the name of "5000 clergy of the Action Committee of the *Protestant.*" Who all these clergymen were and how they happened to be on "the Action Committee of the *Protestant*" was never explained. Leslie had claimed that 5,000 had signed a wartime statement circulated by the *Protestant* protesting anti-Semitism, and apparently Leslie had begun to assume that he could invoke their support on any issue he wished to raise.

A crisis hit the *Protestant* in 1948. In January, Leslie released a telegram to Wallace pledging support of his candidacy against "the business and church cartels which lead us to war and want." "We believe that Harry Truman and his Democratic Party have delivered the United States straight into the hands of the bankers, bishops, and soldiers," he wrote in the *Protestant*.[43] He noted with satisfaction that Communists had supported Wallace: "It happens that Communists have made a splendid reputation for themselves among the common people of Europe in the resistance movement. In this country they have organized much if not most of whatever resistance has developed against our imperialistic foreign policy." [44]

Most of the *Protestant*'s prominent "editorial advisers" already had abandoned it because of its pro-Communist views. In 1946 a group of its most active supporters resigned over the issue of Leslie's "one-man rule." [45] Now with the endorsement of Wallace many more pulled away and the magazine was forced to suspend publication from June 1948 to January 1949. Leslie made a painful admission after the *Protestant* reappeared. "We promised we would publish and here we are!" he wrote. "We sent a postcard appeal to over 10,000 of our subscribers. 200 answered and this magazine literally is theirs." [46]

The *Protestant* never regained its former prestige. It shrank to a small publication edited in Nova Scotia and renamed *One,* later called the *New Christian*. To replace those who resigned, Leslie invited various Hungarian church leaders to become editorial advisers, among them the bishops Albert Bereczky and Janos Peter. Also listed was the Dean of Canterbury. American clergymen whose names continued to appear as editorial advisers included Stephen H. Fritchman, J. Spencer Kennard, Jr., Edward D. McGowan, and Claude C. Williams.

Leslie became increasingly bitter against church leaders. He charged that "the whole Protestant apparatus (bar the fundamentalist fringe) fell head over heels into the clero-fascist net and became a powerful aid to its job of preparing the USA to take on the role of the Hammer of 'God.'" [47] He blamed the collapse of the *Protestant* on "an embarrassed Protestant leadership which let us down."

He singled out the World Council of Churches for sharp attack and wrote in 1955:

This particular Ecumenical Movement is vitiated at its root where it draws sustenance from the beneficiaries of the *status quo*. At the centre of the movement stands The Union Theological Seminary, whose president Van Dusen openly venerates the middle classes, whose Dulles has led the churches astray so often, whose Luce openly hails the American Century of world domination, whose Niebuhr smokescreens the whole imperialist operation with pious double-talk.

Those who would oppose this aggregation must stay no longer in their midst. . . .[48]

United States "imperialism" threatens the peace of the world, Leslie charged, while "the churches who claim to speak out for God are silent."

At Toronto in 1950 they were vocal enough in support of the U.S.-"U.N." attack on Korea. Today when their erstwhile spiritual adviser Dulles moves over the world scene triggering war as he goes these men of the Church sit silently and bow their heads and "pray for peace." They pray to Satan and they really *pray for war*.[49]

Year after year he continued to echo bitter pro-Communist views. When South Korea attacked North Korea—Leslie's interpretation of what happened—the United States "acted in the Ku Klux Klan tradition of the lynch mob." [50] When a revolution overthrew the government in Guatemala, the country had been "murdered by order of the US Secretary of State." [51] The United States, he concluded, "has been harnessed to the ultramontane faction of the Vatican" and "through Dulles the US big business octopus wraps its tentacles around the dying empires and their colonies." [52]

THE APPEAL OF THE *Protestant*

During World War II the influence of the *Protestant* was at its peak. It was a lively aggressive publication filled with bold assertions and novel ideas that inevitably stirred thought and controversy. Leslie's petitions, telegrams, and public statements brought him and his magazine constantly into the public eye. Occasionally, the *Protestant* would purchase space in metropolitan dailies and publish acrid denunciations of anti-Semitism or of the Vatican or of Franco Spain. Along with the denunciations were the names of hundreds of ministers who endorsed them.

The relative success of the *Protestant* from 1938 to 1948 was due in large measure to its impressive sponsorship. Its masthead at one time or another listed as "editorial advisers" such prominent church leaders as Reinhold Niebuhr, Paul Tillich, Charles S. Braden, George A. Buttrick, Sherwood Eddy, John A. Mackay, Wilhelm Pauck, Edwin McNeil Poteat, and many more. Editorial advisers had no role whatsoever in determining the *Protestant*'s policies, and all of these men named withdrew their support when they found that Leslie's views diverged sharply from their own.

But why did they consent to be editorial advisers in the first place? And why did they withdraw their support? A 1955 study asked these questions of more than ninety clergymen.[53]

The replies indicate that Leslie took unusual liberties in adding editorial advisers to his list. C. Harrison Becker, a Presbyterian minister, complained that "on the basis of one article published by 'The Protestant' I wrote them a letter giving my reaction and the next issue came out with my name as one of the advisers of the editorial board." Archbishop Adam of the Russian Orthodox Church stated that he had "never been connected with that . . . magazine in any capacity," that he had never subscribed to it, and that he had only seen a copy on one occasion.

This carefree use of names sometimes got Leslie into difficulty. Once, the *Protestant* purchased a full page in the New York *Herald Tribune* in which to urge a second front. The names of hundreds of ministers were listed as endorsees. A few days later the *Protestant* admitted that many of the names had been erroneously included in the advertisement. Leslie explained away the confusion as "a clerical error." [54]

Some editorial advisers agreed with Sherwood Eddy that a "uniting Protestant journal was needed by divided Protestantism." Eddy later withdrew when rumors reached him that Leslie was pro-Communist. Tracy M. Pullman, Detroit Unitarian minister, supported the *Protestant* at first because he wanted "a united Protestant voice speaking for freedom and dignity of the individual." Pullman resigned because of the "increasingly anti-Catholic emphasis of the magazine and my unwillingness to be associated with a definitely anti-Catholic movement as such."

Reinhold Niebuhr was listed as an editorial adviser from May 1939 to May 1940. Like others, Niebuhr was attracted by the hostility of the *Protestant* toward fascism. "I joined the advisory board . . . on invitation without knowing its general orientation except that the editor was anti-Nazi," he wrote. He resigned and tried to persuade others to resign "when it became apparent that the magazine was pro-communist and violently anti-Catholic."

The editor's colorful personality and contagious idealism attracted many. One theologian recalled that he had "some earlier personal acquaintance with Kenneth Leslie as a mid-West poet . . . and was willing to give him a hand to start a magazine in the east interpreting Protestantism." Others heard him speak at luncheons and meetings sponsored by the *Protestant* and were impressed. Still others received letters from him. One former editorial adviser admitted: "Having been sent a request to act in an advisory capacity, and being entirely unaware of any other than traditional influences at work, I, as a young man, considered the invitation flattering."

Endorsements by prominent public figures influenced some. Walter M. Horton, a professor of theology at Oberlin College, remembers that, enclosed with an appeal for his support, was a statement from Mrs. Eleanor Roosevelt, who later withdrew her endorsement. She had said: "The *Protestant* awakens those of us who happen to be Protestants to a realization of our responsibilities and interests in the world." [55] Horton grew disturbed by the virulent anti-Catholic articles and then by Leslie's pro-Soviet views. "I remember submitting an article on some aspect of the problem of 'just and durable peace' and getting the article back so blue-penciled that I did not recognize my own views. That finished me. I withdrew at that point. . . ."

Another theological school professor, Wilhelm Pauck, wrote that he had joined the editorial advisers upon the invitation of "my friend Paul Tillich, because, like him, I was greatly interested in furthering a discussion of war aims." Pauck withdrew because the editor never asked his advice and ignored his protests against false propaganda. "He finally took my name off the masthead of his magazine only after *several* demands on my part." Tillich's name was dropped a few months before, when he became convinced that the magazine was completely uncritical of Russia and that religion had become a matter of secondary importance.

While the anti-Catholicism of the *Protestant* proved repulsive to some, it pleased others. Methodist minister Otto Brand regarded Leslie "as a sincere and militant opponent of a Catholicism which in publications systematically abused the Protestant faith," but he left the magazine when he became suspicious "of certain added followers." An editorial adviser in England approved of its criticism of the efforts of the Roman Catholic hierarchy "to dominate U.S.A. policies." The pastor of an American French-speaking congregation gave his support to the *Protestant* because it was supporting the Free French and "was clearly hostile to the Vatican, then an ally of the Axis—and now its heir."

Many clergy were drawn to the *Protestant* because of its concern with anti-Semitism. Chester E. Hodgson, a Methodist, traced his support to "my desire to combat anti-Semitism and this *The Protestant* seemed to be doing at the time." He withdrew in 1950 when dissension on the magazine was rife and when it was obvious that it had swung from battling anti-Semitism to "an espousal of the cause of Communism." Hodgson said that he "allowed his name to remain on the magazine long after I disagreed with it but finally I could not stomach it any longer. . . ."

Karl M. Chworowsky, a Unitarian minister, was also influenced to become an editorial adviser partly because of its "fight against every form of Anti-Semitism here and abroad." He resigned eighteen months later, however, when "it had become increasingly clear that its editorial policy was becoming steadily more pro-Communist and un-American." Chworowsky added this interesting comment: "However, I still maintain that its editor, Kenneth Leslie, is a poet of real ability and an editorial writer of no mean caliber. I consider him 'a good man gone wrong.' "

Alson J. Smith made the sharpest comments on the *Protestant*'s special interest in the Jews. He was dropped by Leslie, he said, for allegedly "sabotaging" him and "trying to steal my magazine . . . I would have quit if Leslie hadn't fired me first because his methods were repugnant to me, particularly his cynical use of professional money-raisers to get money out of Jews by threatening them. . . ."

The *Protestant* was financed largely by Jews. Fund-raisers would visit wealthy summer and winter resorts and speak to Jewish groups on the work of the magazine and its sponsors. They would discuss the activities of the National Committee to Combat Anti-Semitism and the Commission to Eliminate Anti-Semitic Statements in American Textbooks—two committees organized by Leslie. They would say that the *Protestant* was extremely influential among the clergy and that it was in a good position to battle against "hate for the Jews" within the churches. To encourage more liberal contributions, America was depicted as on the verge of a nationwide pogrom. Typical was this 1945 appraisal by Ben Richardson, a Negro minister and then associate editor of the *Protestant:*

An unparalleled wave of anti-Semitism is sweeping across America, leaving in its wake the battered and disfigured faces of Jewish children, pillaged synagogues and terrified communities of Jewish people. The victims of this Gentile violence are without sanctuary. They despair of turning to the police for help. Too often they have found evidence of police consent and even complicity in the outrages. But neither do they turn to Jewish defense agencies. They know that these agencies invariably deny the obvious anti-Semitism in the incidents and decry the complaining victims as alarmists.

These anti-Semitic outbursts are not isolated sporadic happenings. They are all part of a blueprint fascism has drawn for the post-war world.[56]

It was inevitable that leading Jewish agencies should take notice. The American Jewish Committee advised against contributing to the *Protestant:*

Backed by no official Protestant organization, *The Protestant* . . . belies its name by circulating largely among Jews and by seeking a major part of its financial support from Jewish organizations and individuals. This, we believe, is inherently wrong, the more so when a careful study of the files of *The Protestant* reveals that the periodical tends to arouse animosity and distrust among people of different creeds.[57]

The Anti-Defamation League of B'nai B'rith expressed a similar opinion.[58]

These repudiations, combined with the development of the cold war, led to the magazine's quick collapse after World War II. The *Protestant* had played a more important role than the People's Institute of Applied Religion, but neither Claude C. Williams nor Kenneth Leslie ever carried much weight in church circles. To offer them up, as some have done, as evidence of serious "Communist infiltration" in the churches is to attach undue importance to two sideshows that never advanced beyond the fringes of Protestantism.

I n 1948 a publication of the Un-American Activities Committee called the Methodist Federation for Social Action "a tool of the Communist Party denounced by numerous loyal American Methodists." [1] Four years later the same House committee produced an 88-page "review" of the Federation's history to prove that it had followed the Communist Party line over the years.[2] Then, in 1956, the Senate Subcommittee on Internal Security, under Chairman James O. Eastland of Mississippi, released a *Handbook for Americans* which stated that "the Communists have formed religious fronts such as the Methodist Federation for Social Action. . . ." [3]

The Methodist Federation was founded in 1907; the Bolshevik revolution occurred in 1917; and the Communist Party in the United States was formed in 1919. So the Eastland Committee's charge is disproved by a glance at history. The Federation has never been an official denominational agency, but for almost forty years, most prominent leaders of American Methodism were among its members and it received the support of the General Conference, the church's quadrennial national sessions. In 1952, however, the Methodist Church repudiated the Federation. The rise and fall of this organization's prestige is central to the question of Communism and American religion.

From the outset, a guiding figure in the Methodist Federation for Social Service (its name prior to 1947) was Harry F. Ward, one of the five churchmen who met to organize the Federation.[4] Like thou-

sands of Methodists, Ward was swept into the social-gospel movement that had fired Protestantism in the early twentieth century.
One of the principal ambitions of his life was to make the Federation's
influence powerful within the church. To a large degree, as Federation secretary he was successful, only to see it rapidly lose ground
as he reached his old age.

Almost immediately after it was founded, the Federation made an
impact upon Methodism and upon Protestantism generally. In 1908
the Methodists adopted their farsighted Social Creed, in large measure inspired by the new Federation. The same year, the Federal
Council of Churches, at its first meeting, approved the Creed with
only minor changes. This was one of many notable contributions of
the Federation during its long history—and these contributions must
not be overlooked even though attention here is necessarily focused
upon the more controversial political activities carried on in its name.

By 1914, the Federation reported a thousand members, largely
ministers, with an influence far exceeding their number. American
entry into World War I caused them considerable consternation. Was
it "a war to end wars" or, as men like Ward saw it, a conflict rooted
in the despised capitalist system? The *Social Service Bulletin,* official
organ of the Federation, discovered a silver lining—the Bolshevik
revolution, which it greeted as "a genuine economic and industrial upheaval" placing "one of the world's great states in the hands of the
working class." [5]

Throughout the twenties, Ward and the *Bulletin* displayed sympathy
for the new Communist government, but there was little distinguishing
their views from those of non-Communist liberals who felt that the
"Russian experiment" should be watched with understanding, patience, and hope. The Federation concentrated chiefly upon the
growing labor movement and the protection of civil liberties. Nevertheless, by the early thirties, Ward had veered sharply toward the
Communist Left. The Depression only confirmed his gravest fears
about capitalism. For nearly a year, in 1931-32, he traveled through
Russia, and returned enthusiastic about what he had seen. [6] About
the same time, the American Communist Party was beginning to
emerge from its self-imposed chrysallis of isolation. Looking among
nonparty radicals for friends, it found one in Ward.

Winifred Chappell, who together with Ward ran the Federation office, was even more ecstatic over Communism. In 1932 she announced publicly her support of Earl Browder and waited expectantly for the approaching revolution.[7] "We stand on the brink of a world war," she wrote in the *Bulletin* in May 1932. "Here is something to test ourselves by: Will we be for or against the downtrodden ones—the workers, the farmers, the colonial peoples—when their exploiters come to judgment . . . ?"[8] In the *Epworth Herald,* a Methodist youth publication, her startling advice to young men looked forward to the day of revolution:

Accept the draft, take the drill, go into the camps and onto the battlefield, or into the munitions factories and transportation work—but sabotage war preparations and war. Be agitators for sabotage. Down tools when the order is to make and load munitions. Spoil war materials and machinery.[9]

Ward and Miss Chappell, a Methodist deaconess whose radical views were rooted in deep religious idealism, determined the content of the *Social Service Bulletin* (which was renamed the *Social Questions Bulletin* in 1933). From the New York City headquarters they sent out Communist books and free back issues of the *Moscow News* and depended heavily upon information supplied by the Labor Research Association, the principal Communist "fact-finding" agency in the United States. They gave generous aid to the emerging network of Communist fronts.

The New Deal failed to impress the two. The *Bulletin* "exposed" the "fascist propensities" of Roosevelt's administration, relying upon material from the Labor Research Association and from the *Daily Worker* and *New Masses.* The National Recovery Administration used "military phraseology." The Federal Communications Commission was established to place all public media under one dictatorial head to insure successful war propaganda. The Civilian Conservation Corps was designed to give "300,000 youth out-of-door training and military discipline."[10] The Public Works Administration (P.W.A.) would be involved primarily in army and naval construction. "While the welfare activities of the New Deal keep some of the victims of the profit system from actually starving," the *Bulletin* said, "the repression carried on under its aegis prevents the sufferers from using democratic forms to change the system."[11]

In the autumn of 1934, the Federation officially took a position against the profit system, and the November 1934 issue of the *Social Questions Bulletin* carried a descriptive statement, still printed on each issue. It read in part:

The Federation rejects the method of the struggle for profit as the economic base for society and seeks to replace it with social-economic planning to develop a society without class or group discriminations and privileges. In seeking these objectives the Federation does not commit its members to any specific program, but remains an inspirational and educational agency, proposing social changes by democratic decision, not by violence.

Ward and Miss Chappell called for the destruction of capitalism with growing frenzy. "It is increasingly clear that there is no middle ground between accepting the system and abolishing it," said the *Bulletin* in March 1935. To hasten the abolition of capitalism, the Federation published a series of eighteen "Crisis Leaflets" for widespread distribution. Six dealt with the breakdown of the profit system; six outlined the way out, holding the U.S.S.R. up as a model; six suggested strategy and tactics.

The policies of Ward and Miss Chappell and the *Bulletin* did not go unchallenged by many Federation members who themselves rejected capitalism. Some were disturbed at the "secular" rather than "spiritual" emphasis of the organization. Others were aghast at the manner in which Ward and Miss Chappell seemed to condone the antireligious Bolshevik regime and their apparent approval of violence. But there was no serious effort to oust them from within, because Ward was highly regarded as a man of industry, dedication, and intelligence, and he was deeply entrenched in the Federation's chair of leadership.

Moreover, to most of its members, the Federation was not to be judged by Ward's ideology anyway. Hundreds of Methodist ministers and laymen gave their support to the Federation in the thirties despite Ward because they were seeking to implement the denomination's Social Creed, with its emphasis on a just economic order, full equality for all citizens, and an enduring peace. When Federation members met in groups across the nation, they did not focus their attention upon Ward or upon the *Bulletin*. Their concern, instead, was with their particular role as Christians in striving toward a better society both in America and around the world. Many viewpoints were always expressed.

Meanwhile, controversy grew outside the Federation. A Hearst series appeared: "Rid the M.E. Church of 'Red' Incubus." A Methodist clergyman from Oklahoma, Rembert Gilman Smith, began the circulation of a pamphlet called *Methodist Reds*. It offered a new name for the Federation—the "Marxist Federation for Social Strife." Methodists from several states met in Chicago in July 1935 and organized a laymen's group which announced: "We are going to demand a settlement of the status of the Communist-influenced Methodist Federation for Social Service, and of clergymen and church officials who use their positions to preach Socialism and Communism. . . ." [12] These critics were mainly ultraconservatives whose real target was not Communism, but all forms of prophetic social thinking within the church.

Federation opponents failed to sway the quadrennial General Conference of 1936. They had tried to deprive the organization of the title "Methodist," but the General Conference decided that the word "Methodist" could not be denied to any group tracing its lineage back to the social concern of John Wesley, the founder of Methodism. All unofficial organizations were requested to make their independent status clear at all times, however, and thereafter the Federation began to carry the designation "Unofficial" on its letterhead—a policy persisting until the present time. A commission was appointed by the General Conference to investigate all unofficial agencies, but the entire matter was dropped when Ward insisted that the Federation be spared such scrutiny until a similar study was instituted of other groups, particularly on the extreme right. [13]

When the Communists stopped attacking the New Deal and sought a united front, the *Social Questions Bulletin* quickly fell in step. It now focused upon the American League Against War and Fascism and tried to stir enthusiasm for collective security and for aid to the Spanish Loyalists and China. A widening schism resulted in the organization, where pacifist sentiment was strong. In early 1939, the membership was polled on the executive committee's statements favoring the sale of defense weapons to "victim nations"—the major goal of the united front at that period. Only 161 voted on the issue, a poor sampling of the membership. Of these, 110 supported the executive committee, but 51 did not.

When the Hitler-Stalin pact led the Communists to switch overnight from collective security to ardent isolationism, Ward and the *Social Questions Bulletin* again adjusted rapidly. They no longer asked aid for growing lists of "victims of fascist aggression" but criticized all military preparedness and attacked "war-mongering" of the Roosevelt administration. The *Bulletin* frequently attributed poverty, labor trouble, and racial tension to the "pro-war" policies of the American Government and its big-business bosses.

To Ward the war was a war between rival capitalist powers. The Soviet Union's position was essentially the only correct one. He supported the Russian occupation of the eastern half of Poland on several grounds: that it was a legitimate defensive act, that it could not be considered aggression because the legitimate Polish Government had collapsed before the Soviet Union moved in, and that this Polish territory belonged to the U.S.S.R. anyway—it had been "taken by force from the Soviet contrary to the Versailles decision." [14]

Ward did, however, diverge from the Communist Party position on the Russo-Finnish War. He joined with another Federation leader, Charles C. Webber, in introducing a resolution to the executive committee in support of an embargo on war supplies to Japan and a "similar embargo upon the Soviet Union." [15] Ward warned in the *Bulletin* that the resolution must not be used to incite emotions against the U.S.S.R. He obviously preferred to ignore the Finnish war as much as possible; in his book *Democracy and Social Change,* published in 1940, he referred to it only to complain that the press had deliberately given false reports to arouse anti-Communism.[16]

When Nazi troops suddenly pushed across the Russo-German border in June 1941, Ward went along with the Communists again, but only after obvious soul-searching. In the *Bulletin* of October 1941, he was still accusing the "capitalist elements" in Great Britain, France, and the United States of responsibility for Hitler. But, while not calling for immediate American participation in the war—as many Communists did—he urged in the *New Masses* of November 11, 1941, that the United States and Russia "now cooperate effectively in overcoming the enemies of freedom and equality both without and within." [17]

Ward did not try to obtain Federation support for his own attitude toward the war, even after Pearl Harbor. The organization had decided earlier it would be wise to avoid the war question altogether in view of the sharp differences within its membership. In the *Bulletin* of October 1941, Ward said that "the new relations of Great Britain and the United States with the Soviet Union in no way touch the grounds on which we reached the decision to put the war question outside the scope of our program." [18] Throughout World War II, he was faithful to this policy and many Federation members remained firm pacifists. He busied himself in various united-front activities, nonetheless, and occasionally wrote in the *Bulletin* of the "struggle between democratic and reactionary forces within the United Nations" or warned against "attempted Anglo-American domination of the world after the war." In 1944 Ward's book *The Soviet Spirit* glorified the Soviet resistance to the Germans.[19]

A crisis was precipitated in the Federation in October 1943 with the announcement that Ward and Bishop Francis J. McConnell, who had served as president since 1912, planned to retire the following May. It was also apparent that interest in the Federation was falling off rapidly. The report of 1942-43 showed that 1,800 members during that year alone had withdrawn or failed to renew their memberships. Many factors were responsible. Pacifists were disappointed because the Federation was not opposing the war; others withdrew because the Federation was not supporting the war. In a poll on the Federation's future, only 331 of the 2,135 members responded, two-thirds voting that the Federation should continue. Hundreds were obviously dissatisfied. "The present organization, rightly or wrongly, is considered too pro-Russia, and not distinctly religious centered," a Michigan member complained in the *Bulletin,* probably reflecting the views of many.[20]

The Federation weathered the crisis. Within four years its membership had quadrupled, and there were sixty-five chapters across the country. The war was over, and the country settled down to peace and co-operation through the United Nations. In such an atmosphere ideological differences, for the most part, were temporarily submerged.

LEADERSHIP OF JACK R. MC MICHAEL

Aggressive and youthful leadership also helped. In late 1944, Jack R. McMichael was chosen as the new executive secretary. McMichael, only twenty-seven, brought to the Federation an agile mind, dedicated social concern, and unusually broad experience. Born and reared in Quitman, Georgia, he had gone to Emory University, served as cochairman of the National Intercollegiate Christian Council, and entered Union Theological Seminary in 1939. While in the seminary, he was chairman of the American Youth Congress. Union gave him a fellowship, and McMichael moved to California, where he continued his studies at the Pacific School of Religion, served a pastorate in Alameda, and then became a chaplain in the United States Maritime Service.

When McMichael first was considered for the position of executive secretary, several persons objected because he had sided with the Communists in the American Youth Congress. The criticisms came from a group of young pacifists who had themselves been in the American Youth Congress, where they had fought Communist domination and lost. John M. Swomley, Jr., associate secretary of the Fellowship of Reconciliation, wrote directly to McMichael and challenged him to disavow completely the Communist line. McMichael wrote back that he had never been a Communist, had never been controlled by Communists, and had "disagreed with Communists at times on matters of program." [21]

The skeptics were assured that McMichael had changed since the days of the American Youth Congress. But they soon were again accusing McMichael of following the Communist Party line, especially on major international issues. His report to the executive committee in 1946 warned of "an alarming unfolding of the anti-Soviet bias tendencies of American foreign policy," attacked the United States position in Greece as reactionary, and scored the "continued and perhaps deepening American policy of grabbing military bases across the face of the earth" and America's "criminal misuse of atomic energy." [22] McMichael's 1947 report warned against a Vatican-instigated holy war, praised the "democratic" government

of Poland, and blamed the United States for provoking Soviet vetoes
in the U.N. No Soviet policies appeared to need challenging.

Federation material, including the *Bulletin,* reflected McMichael's
views. Typical was the *Social Action Handbook,* published in 1945
and designed to guide Federation chapters and members. Much of
the *Handbook* information was unbiased and useful; other sections,
however, were slanted. In a recommended reading list of seven books
on "Foreign Affairs" none was critical of Russian policy and four
were openly pro-Communist: *Religion in the U.S.S.R.,* by William
Howard Melish, published by the National Council of American-
Soviet Friendship; *Soviet Women,* by Rose Maurer, also published
by the N.C.A.S.F.; *The Challenge of Red China,* by Gunther Stein;
and *The Soviet Spirit,* by Ward. The *Handbook* also recommended
organizations from which to obtain "valuable publications and materials." Nearly half operated within the Communist orbit—National
Negro Congress, International Labor Defense, American Committee
for Protection of Foreign Born, National Federation for Constitutional
Liberties, American Youth for a Free World, Committee for a Democratic Far Eastern Policy, Council on African Affairs, National Council of American-Soviet Friendship, and others. The only political
party mentioned was the American Labor Party, a New York State
political organization supported by the Communists in the postwar
decade.

The programs of the Federation followed a similar pattern. At the
national membership meeting in 1946, there were three main topics
—Russia, colonialism, and China. Jerome Davis spoke on Russia
and Richard Morford acted as resource leader. Mrs. Eslanda Robeson, wife of Paul Robeson, spoke on colonialism, part of her expenses
to the meeting being paid by Max Yergan. The resource leader on
China was Maud Russell of the Committee for a Democratic Far
Eastern Policy.

One of the earliest Federation leaders to withdraw was Bishop
Oxnam, who resigned in June 1947. He was convinced that Mc-
Michael was too closely identified with the Communists, but the
specific events that led to his resignation were the *Bulletin* attacks
on John Foster Dulles, Martin Niemöller of Germany, and Toyohiko
Kagawa of Japan. To the *Bulletin,* Dulles was a malicious partisan
of Wall Street–Nazi cartels, "not fit" to be chairman of the Com-

mission on the Basis of a Just and Durable Peace of the Federal
Council of Churches.[23] Niemöller and Kagawa, the *Bulletin* said,
"are considerably tarnished, if not with fascism, at least with the
type of nationalism that is inconsistent with the evangelical Christian
ideal." [24]

In October 1947, Rabbi Benjamin Schultz, leader of a congregation in Westchester County, New York, wrote a series of articles for
the Scripps-Howard chain of newspapers on Communist influences
among Protestants, Catholics, and Jews. The Methodist Federation
was one of his targets. Within a few weeks, the same newspapers
assigned feature writer Frederick Woltman to attend the Federation's
membership meeting in Kansas City, Missouri.

Woltman's point of view was well known. Immediately before the
meeting, his article headlined, "Methodist Minority Group Gives
Reds Sounding Board for their Party Line," charged that the Federation had "for years . . . closely followed the Communist Party line
on many issues." "If the Federation and its scheduled speakers run
true to form in Kansas City," he wrote, "the Soviet dictatorship will
be extolled, America's entire foreign policy will be castigated, Yugoslavia's Communist dictator Tito will be gently whitewashed, and
Chiang Kai-Shek will be denounced." [25]

The advance program was indeed cause for considerable appre-
hension. McMichael had worked closely with the Civil Rights Congress in securing resource leaders in the area of civil liberties, and the
guide selected was Carl Marzani, formerly employed by the Office
of Strategic Services, who had been convicted for making a false
statement regarding Communist Party membership. Another guest
speaker, Feng Yu-hsiang, known as the "Christian General" of China,
was a bitter critic of Chiang Kai-shek and sided with the Chinese
Communists. Jerome Davis was again chosen as the expert on American-Soviet relations and Ward as the authority on minority rights.

The Woltman articles drew immediate response from the Federation and the Methodist Church generally. Privately, some leaders
were indignant that McMichael had allowed his own bias to dominate
the program. General Feng's presence drew particularly heavy criticism among churchmen, including many liberals who continued to
have high regard for Chiang, a fellow Methodist. When some contended that a pro-Chiang speaker should have been invited, Mc-

Michael replied that Representative Walter H. Judd, former medical missionary in China, had been asked to speak; but Judd denied receiving an invitation. In any event, it was clear that any invitation to Judd would have been an afterthought, designed to deter criticism. Nevertheless, a large and distinguished group of Methodist leaders signed a statement protesting Woltman's sensationalism and challenging some of his facts.

Reading over the various charges and countercharges confuses rather than clarifies the picture. Perhaps the most controversial of Woltman's assertions was that McMichael had been a leader in the Young Communist League. The United Press picked up the charge, and in some papers McMichael was described as "former chairman" of the Young Communist League. McMichael threatened to sue and warned in the *Social Questions Bulletin:* "So brother Woltman, Scripps-Howard, the New York Times, and the United Press are in for a bad time." [26] The *Times* published a retraction under the heading: "McMichael Tie in Error." The *Times* said: "The Rev. Jack R. McMichael has never been chairman of the Young Communist League nor is he connected with any other Communist organization." [27] Woltman stood firm. The *World-Telegram* replied: "To give him his say, Mr. Woltman's Dec. 30 article carried Mr. McMichael's denial. At the same time, the *World-Telegram* knows individuals who were members of the American Youth Congress and the Young Communist League when Mr. McMichael was a member of both and are willing to say so." [28]

As a result of the Woltman series, the Federation anticipated difficulties at Methodism's General Conference in late April 1948. Delegates were sent anti-Federation material. Requests from local churches —known as memorials—asked that the Federation be reprimanded, curbed, disavowed, or repudiated. The Federation circulated its own materials, including a letter from Clyde R. Miller, head of the organization's Commission for Propaganda Analysis, who traced the attacks to the American Government and to the Roman Catholic Church. "This policy is obviously related to the world political policy of the Vatican State," Miller wrote. "It is no secret that a virtual alliance now exists between top American and Vatican politicians." [29] The General Conference avoided a showdown on the issue, in part because of the desire of many delegates to escape a public and divisive debate, but also because of the threat of a nationwide railway strike that hastened adjournment.

The attacks did not influence the manner in which McMichael continued to run the Federation's headquarters in New York City. McMichael plugged material published by Communist fronts and distributed some of it through the office. Occasionally a front organization would reprint *Bulletin* articles with his consent, and circulate them to further their cause. He mailed out dozens of letters that protested, demanded, and condemned in the name of the Federation. He worked closely with key persons in the Communist-front apparatus and was quick to respond to their request for help.

An incident in 1950 was typical. The Board of Education in New York City was seeking to weed out alleged Communists in the public-school system, and the United Public Workers—a Communist-controlled union expelled from the C.I.O. later the same year—was seeking to arouse opposition to the Board's efforts. Edwin S. Smith, director of the Teacher's Division of the U.P.W., asked the Federation to contact the president of the Board of Education immediately. Smith wrote: "Urge that the Board of Education recognize the right of teachers to belong to organizations of their own choosing; that the Board refrain from withdrawing from the Teacher's Union any privileges which it now enjoys . . . ; that the Board refuse to be a sounding board for organizations or officials who wish to destroy the Teacher's Union. . . ." The next day, McMichael dutifully sent off a letter to the president of the Board of Education, beginning "we urge" and listing *verbatim* the demands stated in Smith's letter.[30]

Some of McMichael's actions drew particular fire. On February 8, 1949, a letter of his appeared in the New York *Times*—written in his capacity as executive secretary of the Federation—which interpreted widespread Roman Catholic protests against the imprisonment of Cardinal Mindszenty of Hungary as part of an effort to promote a holy war. McMichael implied that Cardinal Spellman of New York was implicated "morally and financially in efforts to restore the hated, reactionary Hapsburg monarchy."

McMichael sent copies of his letter to Federation members across the country with an appended note urging them to write newspapers, radio stations, President Truman, Secretary of State Acheson, and senators and congressmen to challenge the assumption that "laws to which ordinary mortals are subject fail to apply to members of a church hierarchy." [31] Some Federationists responded favorably; others felt uncomfortable. Wade Crawford Barclay, former editor of the *Social Questions Bulletin* and a member of the executive committee, objected because McMichael's letter had not been cleared through the administrative committee. Barclay claimed that there was much to be said on both sides, but that certainly Hungary was not a "free, democratic state," as McMichael seemed to assume. Another Methodist clergyman, Owen M. Geer, also challenged McMichael's action:

> My chief objection to the position that the Federation seems to be taking is that where we do not follow the party line completely, we at least seem to be always uncritical regarding the actions of Soviet Russia or communist controlled satellites of Russia. We are not necessarily quieting war hysteria by statements which can be interpreted only as being pro-communist, rather than being an objective analysis of the situation.[32]

The year 1950 was decisive in the history of the Methodist Federation for Social Action. A severe blow was struck in February when the *Reader's Digest* published the article "Methodism's Pink Fringe" by Stanley High, one of its editors. It pulled together a collection of facts and quotations to produce an alarming picture. A number of High's assertions were misleading; he said, for example, that the Federation was growing rapidly when, in fact, membership had fallen off sharply. A more serious weakness was his failure to indicate the divergent points of view within the organization. He tossed men like Walter G. Muelder, Dean of Boston University's School of Theology, into the same political caldron as McMichael and Ward.

There was irony in the fact that High should have written this article, for, in his own youth, he had been viewed as a "radical" himself. He had accompanied Frank Mason North, one of the founders of the Federation, throughout Europe and Asia and had dedicated his early book, *The Revolt of Youth,* to North. While never embracing Communism, he had deplored the "greed of American capitalism" and had singled out for particular criticism United States policy in the Philippines. From active youth work, High became a speech writer for President Roosevelt, and then a free-lance writer, finally an editor of *Reader's Digest*. High was a Methodist minister's son, a graduate of Boston University's School of Theology and once a candidate for the ministry of the Methodist Church. In 1950 he was an elder in his local Presbyterian church and a member of the Commission on International Relations of the Federal Council of Churches.

Hundreds of sermons were preached about the High article, many in defense of the Federation. Some resented such an attack from outside the Methodist Church. John E. Marvin, editor of the *Michigan Christian Advocate,* ran an answer entitled "A Presbyterian Tells Us Methodists, But Not Much." Oxnam also wrote an effective reply and submitted it to the *Reader's Digest.* In it, the Bishop defended "the right of Mr. High to attack the present leadership of the Methodist Federation for Social Action or the policies of the organization," but protested that it was written "in such fashion that the uninformed reader gains the impression that bishops and prominent officials are in effect in a conspiracy to 'promote conclusions which give aid and comfort to the communists.' " [33] *Reader's Digest* never published the Oxnam article.

The editor of the Methodist *Pastor's Journal,* W. W. Reid, wrote an open letter to High. "I remember," said Reid, "you were 'of us' in those days when we aspired to climb the mountain and see the gold of the sunrise—contemptible of the clinking gold at the base. . . . But after a while you left us for 'wider' fields of journalism, for ghost writing at the White House, for sallies into more 'popular' and 'current' journalistic endeavors, perhaps even finding the gold at the base of the mountain. . . ." [34]

The High article aroused immediate response within the denomination. On April 20, 1950, the Methodist Council of Bishops adopted a resolution noting that the Federation "does not speak for the Church, and over it neither the General Conference nor the Council of Bishops has jurisdiction." It deplored "certain positions taken and statements published . . . in the Federation's official Bulletin." [35] In August, the Bishops of Methodism's Southeastern Jurisdiction adopted an even sharper anti-Federation resolution. The following month the Board of Publication voted to oust the Federation from the Board-owned Methodist Building in New York City in which the organization had rented space for more than thirty years. McMichael accused the Board of Publication of "unbrotherly landlord coercion," implying that its action could be traced to Federation criticism of certain of its labor policies. [36]

Meanwhile, on the extreme right, there was considerable agitation as various groups organized to save the Methodist Church from radicalism in general and from the Federation in particular. A Committee for the Preservation of Methodism, formed in Houston, Texas, distributed thousands of copies of a 35-page booklet that inquired in its title "Is There a Pink Fringe in the Methodist Church?" Other groups that sprang up included the Volunteer Committee of Methodist Laymen in Jackson, Mississippi, the Committee of Loyal American Methodists in Manning, South Carolina, and the Protest Committee of Lay Methodists in Baltimore, Maryland. In October 1951, a national coalition, the Circuit Riders, Inc., was founded "to oppose all efforts to propagate Socialism and Communism and all other anti-American teachings in the Methodist Church." [87]

The Circuit Riders has continued to function from its Cincinnati headquarters, distributing quantities of material exposing alleged subversive influence within the churches. Under M. G. Lowman, it has circulated indiscriminate charges of Communist "affiliations" against leaders of Methodism and of other major Protestant denominations. Later, in 1960, the Methodist General Conference adopted by an overwhelming vote a resolution specifically condemning the activities of the Circuit Riders.

FEDERATION FACTIONALISM

Ironically, the High article and subsequent attacks from the Right Wing temporarily strengthened McMichael within the Federation by making him appear to be a symbol of resistance to the McCarthyism of the times. Yet, his liberal opponents were busy.

The attempt to replace him became well organized under the leadership of John M. Mecartney, a divinity student at Garrett Biblical Institute, a Methodist seminary in Evanston, Illinois, and an active member of the Socialist Party. Mecartney had protested the policies of the *Social Questions Bulletin:*

Every writer on foreign policy whom I have read in the *Bulletin* has been a Soviet apologist. Sure, they might admit that Russia did some things wrong. "But there were reasons to explain them. And look how much worse the US was." Where has there been a writer selected who would call a spade a spade in regard to Russian imperialism as well as American militarism? Where has there been a writer who presented the socialist "third force" position that peace comes neither through US get-tough militarism nor through the appeasement of Russian imperialism? Why has peace been associated with excusing Russia when peace did not come by appeasing Hitler? Why have there been no articles supporting the Marshall Plan which every Christian denomination and every demo-cratic socialist movement endorses? [38]

In the summer of 1949, Mecartney launched a drive against Mc-Michael. He worked openly and tirelessly, with a spirit of concilia-tion, but also with a firm conviction that the Federation must have a new executive secretary. In his research he sought to confirm all his findings with McMichael himself, and whenever there was a conflict of evidence, he was quick to accept the word of McMichael as con-clusive. In 1950 Mecartney's finished document, signed by ten other leading Federation members and marked "Confidential," was released to the executive committee.[39] Its main contention was that "A person might make a few mistakes over the years in signing wrong state-ments," but that "no one repeatedly makes so many mistakes as our executive secretary unless he is either naïve or purposely inclined to support groups with a pro-Communist bias." Either case, said the document, is sufficient reason to replace McMichael. Mecartney at-tached a long list of Communist-controlled organizations and confer-ences which McMichael had backed.[40]

A militant defense of McMichael was offered by Albert E. Barnett, Southerner, noted New Testament scholar, and at the time a pro-fessor at Garrett Biblical Institute. In a reply of greater length and sharper language than Mecartney's, Barnett charged that the "docu-ment under examination is a socialist line document . . . a 'flank movement' in a campaign to make the Methodist Federation a Socialist sect." [41] Barnett borrowed nearly all of his rebuttal material from a memo prepared by McMichael in his own behalf.

The Mecartney document was debated at the 1950 membership meeting held at Wilberforce University in Ohio. When a resolution was offered supporting McMichael, it won by a vote of 58-2, with ten abstentions—Mecartney and a representative from the Federa-tion's Pacific Northwest Chapter alone opposed it. Many factors had worked in McMichael's favor. Most of his critics did not attend. Of the eleven who released and publicly subscribed to the Mecartney document, Mecartney was the only one there. The registration was seventy—approximately 2 per cent of the total membership. Some had already given up hope of ousting McMichael; others preferred to avoid the spotlight of national publicity. The High article, as noted already, strengthened McMichael's hand within the Federation. The feeling of group loyalty was strong. Mecartney's case, however valid, was labeled "guilt by association," a technique that was infuriating liberals in 1950 because of its indiscriminate use by the Committee on Un-American Activities and other governmental agencies and private groups.

The battle against McMichael continued in various Federation affiliates across the country. This was especially true at the School of Theology of Boston University, a Methodist seminary. Under the guidance of several faculty members, the Boston Chapter conducted a thorough investigation of the national body. In the spring of 1951, it sent a letter "To Our Brethren of the Federation" contending that McMichael exercised "excessive control" and had been able to insure his continuance in office through "determining the time, date, and place of committee meetings; cancelling or postponing them when he thinks it is to his advantage; editing *SQB* in such a way as to give an impression of support for himself and his views; personal propagandizing he is able to do as a by-product of his trips across the country at MFSA expense on MFSA business; and the utilization of the national office machinery for the furtherance of his own views and tenure." [42] The letter also accused McMichael of deliberate distortions. It cited an article on "The United Nations Commission Reports on Korea" compiled by McMichael in the December 1950 *Bulletin.* In it McMichael posed questions and then, in reply, gave alleged excerpts from the reports of the United Nations Commission on Korea to create the impression that the claims of North Korea were upheld by the Commission. Dean Muelder examined the Commission reports and charged that McMichael had lifted material out of context and had even presented as fact propaganda from the North Korean radio—propaganda which the Commission had carefully described as "rumor and unverified report." McMichael had also placed quotation marks around materials that he had paraphrased.[43]

Other criticisms of McMichael from among Federation members were related only indirectly to his political views. Some characterized him as a poor administrator because he was too busy supporting secular causes. On a personal level, he was reprimanded for lack of tact, for intolerance of diverse viewpoints, for picking his friends within the Federation on the basis of their political beliefs, and for encouraging persons with no religious interest or affiliation to join the Federation.

In September 1951, the Federation met at the First Methodist Church of Evanston, which was made available to it through the efforts of its pastor, Harold O. Bosley, who had withdrawn from the Federation several years before when he lost confidence in its leadership. An avalanche of criticism descended upon Bosley and the church, and the Chicago *Tribune* suggested in an editorial that permission to use its facilities implied that the pastor and congregation were "indorsing the organization." [44] The Cook County Council and the Evanston posts of the American Legion asked the church to close its doors to the meeting. Bosley refused solely because he believed in the right of free speech for all groups, including the Federation. He was away from Evanston during the conference, and upon his return found that some members of his congregation had left the church or were attending services elsewhere. In a stern letter to McMichael, Bosley accused the Federation of callously disregarding the welfare of the parish by baiting the Chicago press and by other indiscreet behavior.

At the meeting, McMichael won a new two-year term by a vote of 50-6. Significantly, however, the membership present refused to go along with some of his major recommendations; many who wanted to retain him as executive secretary obviously did not share his political bias. A resolution favoring the immediate recognition of Communist China was defeated. The meeting voted 22-15 in favor of seating Communist China in the United Nations, but only on the condition that a truce in Korea was negotiated first.

McMichael's re-election resulted in further attrition within the Federation. The Boston Chapter pulled out. The entire West Coast area, where support had been strong in earlier years, likewise withdrew its support. In Detroit, another former stronghold, enthusiasm faded. Already the National Council of Methodist Youth, a sparkplug of idealism within the denomination, had declared that "until the Methodist Federation for Social Action makes some changes in its present administration, we can no longer suggest that youth leaders support it." [45]

Several prominent Boston clergymen, including Emory Stevens Bucke, editor of *Zions Herald,* and Edgar S. Brightman and L. Harold DeWolf of the School of Theology, resigned. Clarence T. Craig, Dean of Drew Theological Seminary in Madison, New Jersey, regretfully withdrew because he felt the organization no longer served a useful purpose. The Federation treasurer, Gilbert Hugh LeSourd, resigned both as an officer and as a member. Bishop James C. Baker of Southern California, whose membership in the Federation went back many years to his early ministry, first pleaded with McMichael to step aside and then, when he refused, left himself. An Illinois pastor wrote McMichael: "Won't you please either stop embarrassing the Methodist Church or get out?" Two elderly bishops, Francis J. McConnell and Lewis O. Hartman, struggled to hold the organization together. In their personal correspondence, they expressed grave doubts about McMichael's leadership, but recalled the Federation's years of valuable service and decided not to leave it.

1952 GENERAL CONFERENCE

The widespread public criticisms, and especially the Stanley High article, had created a strong demand for firm action by the 1952 General Conference. Memorials poured in from churches and individuals across the country asking for repudiation of the Federation. Its sympathizers were numerous, but persons willing to defend its leadership were very few.

In February 1952, the Circuit Riders, Inc., and other Right Wing groups won an important victory when—in part due to their urging—the Committee on Un-American Activities published the 88-page *Review of the Methodist Federation for Social Action.* This self-described "careful and studied review" was largely a collection of newspaper and magazine articles haphazardly thrown together and published at government expense under the committee's imprimatur. A sprinkling of quotations from random issues of the *Social Service Bulletin* of twenty years earlier were included. The committee relied heavily upon the articles of Woltman and High, the Chicago *Tribune,* the Hearst newspapers, the *Bureau County Republican,* and the *National Republic,* a radical Right Wing magazine published in Washington, D. C. The review was poorly organized at many points and ignored entirely the period from 1938 to 1947, which included the decisive years of the Hitler-Stalin pact. Despite these and other deficiencies, however, it had a heavy impact upon General Conference delegates.

In May, the General Conference convened in San Francisco. New York attorney Charles C. Parlin led a fight for a resolution which expressed disapproval of "many of the statements and policies" of the Federation, requested it to "remove the word 'Methodist' from its name," and endorsed the action of the Board of Publication in ordering the Federation to leave the Methodist Building. A few rose before the delegates to speak against the resolution. Henry Hitt Crane of Detroit requested a commission to investigate all unofficial groups using the word "Methodist." [46] To Raoul C. Calkins, pastor from Des Moines, Iowa, the resolution was the result of the pressures of the times and would be regretted later.[47] Emory Stevens Bucke, who had already resigned from the Federation, opposed any statement against the organization on the grounds that "the General Conference of the Methodist Church may not legislate on a matter which is not its own creation." [48] Bishop Edgar A. Love, a Negro Methodist leader, who was unable to get the floor, had intended to urge the delegates to "think twice before they single out the Federation or any one body of Methodists for adverse action. . . . The Federation, whatever its faults, has not failed to seek to break down the barriers which deny the brotherhood for which the Gospel of Jesus calls." [49]

When the vote was taken by a show of hands, the resolution was adopted by a margin of more than ten to one. The General Conference then authorized the establishment of an official Board of Social and Economic Relations to carry on education within the church and to fill the vacuum. Efforts to have the anti-Federation action rescinded at the 1956 General Conference were unsuccessful.

The General Conference had robbed the Federation of its claims of denominational support; it now stood as a repudiated organization. McMichael charged in the *Bulletin* that the delegates had been swayed by hysteria, had failed to mention unofficial groups promoting reaction and even racism, and had enacted "thought control which would make our freedom-loving founder John Wesley turn over in his grave." McMichael raised the race issue. Eight of the ten Federation critics, he said, had been Southern whites, while debate was cut off "before a single Negro speaker had been heard." [50]

After the General Conference, other prominent churchmen resigned and an antagonism of considerable significance developed between McMichael and Barnett, his former champion. He wrote McMichael that "when we lose men like these, we must find the answer in ourselves, not them!" [51] An open break between the two came after McMichael's "World Economic Report" in the *Bulletin* of June 1952. Contrasting "Private Enterprise Countries" with "Centrally Planned Economies," he concluded that, except for Yugoslavia (Tito was opposing Stalin's leadership at the time), the Communist nations were making progress while the rest of the world was in serious economic difficulty. McMichael said that his conclusions were based upon a United Nations report but Barnett responded by accusing him of "pro-Communist motives." [52] "In the name of Jesus Christ," Barnett was willing to attack weaknesses in American society but in the "name of Joe Stalin, I will make no attack on anything." [53]

Bishop Love finally agreed to accept the Federation presidency after the 1952 General Conference with the understanding that McMichael would resign in June 1953. As that date approached, a new compromise was worked out: The Federation would vacate its New York office and McMichael would take a parish in California, but serve as a secretary responsible for the *Social Questions Bulletin*. Three more co-secretaries would work with him, among them Willard Uphaus, then cochairman of the Communist-inspired American Peace Crusade. Barnett quickly attacked this arrangement as a trick to keep the Federation "in the pro-Communist category." [54] On April 7, 1953, Barnett resigned, and a month later Bishop Love followed suit. Among other members who withdrew were Bishop W. Earl Ledden of Syracuse, Bishop Matthew W. Clair, Jr., of St. Louis, and Georgia Harkness of the Pacific School of Religion. Dr. Harkness wrote McMichael that "it sounds the death knell of the MFSA to have your name and that of Willard Uphaus as the secretaries." [55]

When Bishop Oxnam appeared before the Un-American Activities Committee in July 1953, he was asked if he had ever voted for McMichael as executive secretary of the Federation. "I do not believe I ever did," he replied. "I felt it was a mistake to have him there." Oxnam said he thought McMichael was "so tied up with the Communist group whether or not he were a Communist . . . that that organization ought not to be under that leadership. . . ." [56] However, Oxnam was angered when the secret testimonies of Manning Johnson and Leonard Patterson were introduced into the public record "identifying" McMichael as a Communist.

Bishop Oxnam. Mr. Chairman, was Jack McMichael called before the committee? Did he have any opportunity to answer that? I am not pleading for him, but did he have a chance to answer what was alleged?

Mr. Velde. As far as I am concerned, Mr. Jack McMichael has never been called before the committee.

Bishop Oxnam. Then this is given to the public all over the nation before the man accused has had so much as an opportunity to answer.

Mr. Scherer. Do you concur that Reverend McMichael is a member of the Communist Party today? You said so yourself.

Bishop Oxnam. That isn't correct at all. I am dealing with procedures and I was dealing with the procedures when I made the statement.

Mr. Scherer. On the basis of the testimony we had in New York, sworn testimony of any number of witnesses, and on that basis how could any reasonable person come to any other conclusion than that Dr. Ward and Reverend McMichael are dangerous Communists?

Bishop Oxnam. That isn't it.

Mr. Scherer. What is it?

Bishop Oxnam. That a man is accused before a decision is reached, and I do not believe this is a court.[57]

McMichael was subpoenaed two days after the Oxnam hearing. The press reported that at a meeting in his little church in Upper Lake, California, members of the congregation—largely farmers and dairymen—stood up one by one to express confidence in their pastor. McMichael's bishop, Donald H. Tippett, a critic of McMichael's leadership in the Federation, announced that "until civil charges are brought against him—and proved—we will support him." [58] The

Federation sent out an urgent appeal for funds and declared that "the fact that the MFSA is the first religious organization to be attacked by the Velde Committee is something of a tribute to the effectiveness of our witness. . . . May God grant . . . that the MFSA will prove one more stumbling-block to this creeping fascism." [59]

The hearing itself was held July 30-31 in Washington, D. C. The autocratic, accusatory, badgering manner of the committee's counsel, Robert L. Kunzig, and such committee members as Kit Clardy, Donald L. Jackson, and Gordon H. Scherer was continuously thwarted by McMichael's voluble, evasive, and defiant testimony. McMichael sought to represent himself as a "poor Methodist preacher" who didn't know much about Communism but did know his Bible, which was on the table before him. He resented his enforced absence from his church work and particularly objected to the public release of testimony that he was a Communist which, he said, "my 6-year-old girl and my 8- and 10-year-old boys heard over the radio." [60]

McMichael tried to harass a committee that was seeking to harass him. He was twenty minutes late for the opening session, continuously insisted upon consulting old diaries to check dates "because I want to be as helpful as I can," and constantly interrupted committee members and strayed from the subject. Whenever any committee member made a critical comment, McMichael would demand an opportunity to reply because—in words he repeated facetiously—"I know you want to be fair."

McMichael enraged the committee members, provided a spectacle for those in attendance, gave reporters color for their stories, and delighted his supporters, who were convinced that he had outfoxed his inquisitors. Clardy described him as "the most obtuse witness we have had willingly." [61] "I practiced law for pretty nearly 30 years," he said. "If this witness had appeared in any court in which I had practiced during all that time he would have been in jail." [62] Scherer said McMichael used the "typical tactics that have been followed by the Communists who have appeared before us." [63] Walter added: "They haven't been so clever." [64] To which Scherer replied: "No; they haven't been so contemptuous either." [65] Chairman Velde at one point threatened to order him removed forcibly from the room.[66] William Howard Melish, however, wrote McMichael to express admiration for his "quick-wittedness in refusing to give simple yes or no answers to trap questions—and your courage in resisting the attempt to browbeat you which are constantly apparent in the transcript." [67]

McMichael compared his association with Communists with the association of Jesus with sinners. Early in the hearing, in discussing the American Youth Congress, he admonished Kunzig: "Remember about Jesus and the publicans and the sinners, and I considered the Communists sinners and I followed the practice of Jesus." [68] Later, when McMichael acknowledged that he had spoken at the Columbia University chapter of the American Student Union, this exchange followed:

Reverend MC MICHAEL. In the same way Jesus spoke at meetings of Pharisees and publicans and sinners.
Mr. SCHERER. Can't we leave Jesus out—
Reverend MC MICHAEL. It's a little hard for me to leave Jesus out. You may be able to do it—
Mr. SCHERER. In a situation like this? [69]

He had a similar run-in with Clardy on the question of his association with Cedric Belfrage, later deported to England, charged with membership in the Communist Party in the thirties.

Mr. CLARDY. I asked if you had been associated with him in any organization.
Reverend MC MICHAEL. No.
Mr. CLARDY. Now, were you or not?
Reverend MC MICHAEL. No; what I'm thinking about is the fifth chapter of Luke, when Jesus, associating with publicans and sinners—
Mr. CLARDY. That is not an answer to the question, and will you please quit likening yourself to Christ?
Reverend MC MICHAEL. I am not likening myself to Him, but I assure you He associated with publicans and sinners—
Mr. CLARDY. Will you answer my question—
Reverend MC MICHAEL. And if He were alive today—
Mr. CLARDY. Yes or no?
Reverend MC MICHAEL. He would have been called before this committee a long time ago because of guilt by association.[70]

McMichael's conduct alienated many. Murray Kempton, liberal columnist for the New York *Post,* usually quick to defend unpopular causes, described "The Reverend" as a "folksy, weedy, balding

Georgia boy . . . the soul of irreverence, sniggling, and weasling and larding his auditors with every Pecksniffism of the lower Protestantism. . . ." He charged that McMichael followed "the Communist line for 14 years, that he knew exactly what he was doing and that he used every trick in the book (ad nauseam) yesterday to avoid admitting it." Kempton concluded his column: "We'd all be better off if the Un-American Affairs Committee would go home. A fellow-traveler's opinions are his own business, but there is such a thing as service to the truth and this McMichael is a bum; and he is no less a bum for being in trouble with Harold Velde." [71]

The principal goal of the House committee was to prove that McMichael was, or had been, either a member of the Communist Party or of the Young Communist League—or both. This would lend credence to their assertions—weakened by Oxnam's testimony—that there were many Communists among the clergy. McMichael flatly denied under oath that he was ever affiliated with either the party or the League.[72] When the testimonies of Leonard Patterson and Manning Johnson were read to McMichael, he called them "liars and perjurers" who ought "to be so tried and charged." Johnson presented himself for identification before McMichael but McMichael stated emphatically three times: "I don't know him!" [73] He was refused the right of questioning Johnson. Representative Jackson hinted that the Justice Department might start perjury proceedings against McMichael—but no such action was taken.

The testimony of Martha N. Edmiston and John J. Edmiston, two former undercover F.B.I. agents, seems more credible. The Edmistons did not know whether McMichael had been a Communist and confessed that they had been unsuccessful when they tried to find out. The most they could say was that during the time of the Hitler-Stalin pact the Communists viewed McMichael as one who "could be trusted on the peace groups." [74] This was not very conclusive.

There were some contradictions between the McMichael and the Edmiston testimony, but they were not very significant. The Edmistons had said, for example, that McMichael had spoken at a meeting of the Ohio Youth Congress in Columbus, Ohio, in May or June 1940. McMichael, with the assistance of his diary, replied that he was "confident I did not attend any such meeting in Ohio in May or June of 1940." [75] McMichael failed to recognize the Edmistons when they were presented to him at the hearing; but they had said that they talked with McMichael only once—at the same Columbus meeting which he did not recall attending. Perhaps the most important item in the testimony of the Edmistons was a quotation which she had jotted down while listening to McMichael speak at the national conference of the American Youth Congress in Philadelphia held July 4, 1941, eleven days after Germany invaded the Soviet Union. "We'll take up arms in defense of Russia, who is now our ally," she had quoted him as saying, "and lay down our lives if need be." [76] During the period of the Hitler-Stalin pact, McMichael, in line with Communist policy, had fought all aid to England and had opposed all efforts to build up America's defense. He consistently has claimed, however, that he did not follow the switch with the Communists after the invasion of the U.S.S.R., that he did not favor immediate American participation in the war.

THE FEDERATION REGROUPS

After 1953, the year the Federation closed its New York office, the organization's prestige continued to decline. Membership dropped to a new low, and there were voices pleading that it be allowed to die by dissolution rather than to suffer the agony of further disintegration. One of the severest blows of 1953 was the resignation of Henry Hitt Crane, who had been named a leader in the new Board of Social and Economic Relations. Typically, he showed no signs of bitterness or reproach. The immediate cause was an executive committee meeting of the Federation, attended by only four members, which adopted resolutions on complicated issues of public policy. Crane decided that the Federation had "ceased to have the power effectively to make any significant, constructive, social contribution to our contemporary world." He suggested that it dissolve since it deserves the "dignity of an honorable 'Finis.' " [77]

About the same time, Charles C. Webber, another influential figure within the Federation, submitted his resignation. He had joined in 1915 while a student for the ministry at Boston University's School of Theology and he served as executive secretary of the Federation from 1936 to 1943. Like others, Webber came to his decision to withdraw with a deep sense of sadness since he had always shared the belief of many Methodists that the denomination desperately needed an unofficial, independent organization that could pioneer in the realm of social concern. After Webber left the employ of the Federation in 1943, he became active in labor-union work as an organizer for the Amalgamated Clothing Workers of America and then as president of the Virginia C.I.O. Council from 1946 to 1953. Today he is the A.F.L.-C.I.O. representative for Religious Relations.

Despite these setbacks, the Federation secured as its president Loyd F. Worley of Hartford, Connecticut, a minister who commands enormous respect. Worley is a soft-spoken man of unusual charity and integrity, akin in his views and temperament to Bishop Francis J. McConnell, one of the great figures of modern American Methodism. He is a pacifist who publicly opposes the principles of Communism but earnestly holds to the belief that the charges against the Federation, Ward, and McMichael are false. "The MFSA may doubtless have erred in judgment at times, but it has never been subversive or unAmerican to my knowledge," says Worley.[78] Worley attributes the antagonism to McMichael largely to the fact that "as a Georgia-born boy he has maintained a New Testament attitude on the race issue." [79]

The principal focus of the *Social Questions Bulletin* in the fifties continued to be upon foreign policy, and particularly upon the issue of peace. The most pressing matter from 1950 to 1953 was the war in Korea. McMichael compared it with America's own Civil War in such a manner as to suggest that the North Koreans came as liberators.

Did we have a Civil War or a War Between Two States, the Confederacy and the Union? When Northern armies crossed the Mason-Dixon Line and marched into the South, were they unifying one country, or committing aggression? The Editor's grandfather, a Methodist Georgian, enlisted with the Confederate Army; was captured by Northern soldiers in *South Carolina*. He and other Confederates had little doubt who the aggressor was. But "aggression" to some Southerners was "liberation" to others; Negro slaves for whom Lincoln wrote an Emancipation Proclamation, counterparts perhaps of South Korean peasants today who conduct guerilla warfare, hate landlordism, and want land.[80]

The *Bulletin* stressed high business profits resulting from the war, noted ominously how rumors of peace brought a slump on Wall Street, vividly depicted alleged American atrocities, and focused attention upon racial angles that were exploited by Communists around the world. "Widely used by white GI's against Koreans and other colored people," wrote McMichael, "is the derogatory and bigoted racist term 'gook.' " [81] On the prisoner repatriation issue, he implied support of the Communist position through his frequent practice of asking carefully phrased rhetorical questions. While the United States insisted that, for humanitarian reasons, North Korean and Chinese prisoners should not be forced to return to their respective countries against their will, McMichael countered: "As for strictly humanitarian concern for prisoners, has it been practiced in the camps where our troops admittedly have shot and slain unarmed prisoners? And is humanitarian concern, either for prisoners or non-prisoners, shown in our insistence that the murderous fighting go on until the prisoner issue is settled our way?" [82]

Ward's monthly column, "Behind the Headlines," echoed the position of the Soviet Union with greater forthrightness. "Asia and Africa will not forget," Ward said in reference to Hiroshima and Nagasaki, "that it was upon people of color that we first dropped the A bomb and then the fire bombs." [83] This theme became an important Communist propaganda weapon during the war in Korea, though there had been no such moral outcry by the Soviet Union or Ward in August 1945 when the civilian populations of these two ancient and beautiful Japanese cities were decimated. Ward gave credence to the charges of germ warfare as well. As his authority, he cited the report of the International Commission of Scientists, a group organized by the Communist-led World Peace Council. "The scope of this investigation, the scientific temper of the report, the restraint of its findings, the qualifications of its authors, require rebuttal by facts if they can be produced," wrote Ward.[84]

The *Bulletin* contributed in a variety of ways to the Soviet-inspired peace crusade. Willard Uphaus described his experiences at the Warsaw Peace Congress on the front page of one issue. When Arthur D. Kahn offered McMichael 250 free copies of *Speak Out! America Wants Peace,* McMichael accepted the offer with gratitude. The book told of Kahn's travels from coast to coast under the sponsorship of the American Peace Crusade.[85] There were some revealing reversals in attitude. In 1947 the *Bulletin* had accused Martin Niemöller of Nazi sympathies; now his firm opposition to German rearmament made him a great peacemaker. The same year the *Bulletin* had also accused Toyohiko Kagawa of supporting the militarists of Japan; in 1954 the *Bulletin* was "greatly impressed" when he protested hydrogen bomb tests.[86]

The annual membership meetings held each summer became the focal point of much Federation activity. The programs reflected the bias of McMichael and his supporters—in 1952, for example, the speakers included Stephen H. Fritchman, Martin Hall, Dryden L. Phelps, and Willard Uphaus. There were subtler influences in the resolutions. In 1954, to cite one year, the Federation's demand for armament control endorsed, in effect, the Soviet position by making no mention of enforcement or inspection demanded by the United States. A resolution expressing gratitude to organized labor for opposing restrictive legislation singled out only the United Electrical Workers—a union expelled from the C.I.O. in 1949 because of Communist domination. In still another resolution, one assailing the Mc-Carran-Walter Act (a legitimate target, to be sure), the Federation "heartily" recommended the work of the American Committee for Protection of Foreign Born, one of the oldest front groups in the United States. Many Federationists who supported these resolutions were totally unaware of the implications of these skillful insertions.

A crisis for the Soviet Union—and for those who sympathized with her around the world—began in 1956 with the publication of Khrushchev's secret February speech denouncing Stalin before the Twentieth Congress of the Communist Party of the Soviet Union. In April, came a wave of remorse about Soviet anti-Semitism. By the autumn, Poland had experienced workers' riots and Hungarians were revolting against their "people's government."

For years, Stalin had been unassailable among American Communists and their allies. They viewed each move he made as the work of a genius. They had claimed that his bloody purges between 1935 and 1938 were a necessary and astute move against fascist plots. Now Khrushchev said that "honest Communists" had been victims in the purges; "no longer able to bear the barbaric tortures, they charged themselves (at the order of the investigative judges—falsifiers) with all kinds of grave and unlikely crimes." In the same manner, Stalin's admirers had always insisted that the Soviet Union was a model of the harmony in which diverse nationalities could live. All these national groups were said to be enthusiastic in their support of the government. Now Khrushchev recounted that during World War II Stalin had ordered "mass deportations from their native places" of entire minority groups—the Chechen, Ingush, Balkar, Kalmuck, and other peoples—each accused by Stalin of wartime treason. "The Ukrainians avoided meeting this fate," Khrushchev continued, "only because there were too many of them and there was no place to which to deport them." [87]

On April 4, 1956, another development jolted the Communist camp. As late as 1953, the *Churchman* had played up an offer of $1,000 by the Chicago Council of American-Soviet Friendship for any evidence of anti-Semitism in the U.S.S.R.—an offer designed to counter the damaging stories alleging Russian repression of Jews and Jewish culture.[88] Now a Communist newspaper in Warsaw, the Yiddish *Folks-Shtimme,* pointed an accusing finger at the Soviet Union. Overnight the American Communist press, which for years had hailed Russia as the only nation free of anti-Semitism, began to decry the liquidation of Soviet Jewish life and the killing of well-known Jewish community and cultural leaders.

The third major crisis in the world Communist movement in 1956 began with the workers' riots in Poznan, Poland, and deepened with the Hungarian revolution, which was soon suppressed by Russian tanks. Dissension among American Communists grew so widespread that even the *Daily Worker* opposed Soviet intervention.

McMichael and Ward avoided any discussion in the *Bulletin* of the Khrushchev revelations. Ironically, just as these revelations were coming to light, Ward's monthly column hailed the "internal strength" of Russia's East European satellites, "testified to by capable neutral observers and capitalist press correspondents. . . ." Ward castigated Eisenhower for asking for the peaceful "liberation" of these countries from Soviet domination. "Considering the rate of emancipation of those peoples and the several bondages of the past does he really think that the clock can be peacefully turned back?" [89]

When the Hungarian crisis burst forth into street fighting in Budapest, McMichael and Ward reacted in different ways. McMichael criticized the Soviet Union; Ward carefully avoided any published judgment. Wrote McMichael: "The Soviet Union sent its generally unwanted troops and tanks to Hungary, resorted to violence and repression against Hungarians, and imposed on that nation a government without popular support." He was obviously deeply impressed by the fact that "virtually all the younger generation and working class and citizenry of Hungary" opposed the government, and roundly condemned the Soviet Union for refusing admittance to the United Nations Secretary-General and a neutral fact-finding committee.[90]

Beclouding the international scene at the time, however, was the joint Anglo-French-Israeli attack upon Egypt, to which the *Bulletin* devoted even more attention. McMichael wrote that he approved of official American policy in the United Nations on the issue of Hungary and of Egypt, but he took the opportunity to review "our own past misdeeds." Soviet troops should leave Hungary; and "we should remove our troops from Iceland as requested by that land's people and parliament." If the Warsaw Pact furnished a legal justification for Soviet tanks in Hungary, that pact was "stimulated by the anti-Soviet North Atlantic Pact. . . ."[91] Other United States sins were noted: American intervention in China and Formosa, in Guatemala, in Korea.

In the same issue of the *Bulletin,* Ward pleaded that the swift movement of events made it impossible to write more than "some general remarks" about the responsibilities of the "religious conscience" in the situation. He needed more facts before he could assess guilt, he said. "What was the part played by fascist, clerical reaction in the Hungarian revolution?" Ward asked. "Did our liberation policy, and the activities of our Central Intelligence Agency . . . involve us in any responsibility?" He was heartened by developments in the Soviet Union following the Twentieth Congress. "In Russia there are signs of an uneasy conscience and a change of policies." In America, he added sadly, "the prevailing mood is to thank God we are not sinners like the British colonialists and the godless communist 'imperialists.' "[92] In the *New World Review* of November 1956 Ward wrote: "Those of us who want to see the democratic forces in the Soviet Union overcome the anti-democratic tendencies recently revealed, will do well to spend our energies in stopping our Congress from appropriating millions to support those trying to overthrow it, and in changing our foreign policy so that it will cease bringing the world to the brink of war."[93]

The 1957 membership meeting of the Federation adopted a noncommittal resolution on Hungary, attaching to it support for the Soviet proposal that all foreign troops be withdrawn between the Atlantic Ocean and Russia's western border.

We deplore the tragic events in Hungary of late 1956. We wish to prevent any future Hungaries.

Therefore, we call upon the government of the United States to make every effort to negotiate an agreement with the government of the U.S.S.R. regarding the withdrawal of Soviet troops from eastern Europe and the corresponding withdrawal of U.S. Troops from Western Europe.[94]

In 1957 the Federation also celebrated its fiftieth anniversary. That same year the *Handbook for Americans,* describing the Federation as a "religious front formed by the Communists," was published by the Senate Subcommittee on Internal Security. With the backing of the Emergency Civil Liberties Committee and the Religious Freedom Committee, the Federation secured a temporary injunction against further distribution of the handbook until the United States Circuit Court of Appeals ruled that it had no jurisdiction over a document of Congress. Further attempts to stop the distribution of the handbook failed.

The future of the Methodist Federation for Social Action is uncertain. Some believe it will wither away; others see evidence that it will persist as a small group of Soviet sympathizers, more undenominational and interfaith than Methodist; still others think that it will regain some of its former status. Much depends upon the orientation of Federation leadership, upon international and domestic developments, and upon the degree of effectiveness of the denomination's official Board of Social and Economic Relations (which merged in 1960 with the Board of Temperance and Board of World Peace into the Board of Social Concern). At the moment, the Federation stands weak and discredited.

What may be said fairly in summary about the Federation and the Communist movement?

First, the Federation is not, nor has it ever been, a Communist front. It was not founded by Communists, but, rather, by leaders of the Methodist Church. Its members have not been Communists; indeed, the overwhelming majority of Federationists through the years would condemn the hatred, the dishonesty, and the violence that has characterized Soviet Communism. Federation leaders have not been

Communists either—certainly not the scores of bishops and educators and pastors who held high office. There is no conclusive evidence that either Ward or McMichael was ever a member of the Communist Party or actually under its discipline. The organization's policies conflicted with Communist policies on essential matters—none more striking than the fact that the Federation weathered World War II without supporting it.

A second conclusion, however, concerns the two leaders whose influence outweighed that of all others. Ward and McMichael proved to be consistent, determined apologists for the Soviet Union and the world Communist movement. There may have been a few exceptions, such as Ward's support of an embargo on Russia during the Russo-Finnish War, and McMichael's distress over Soviet intervention in the Hungarian revolt. Nevertheless, both have been convinced that in the international arena the Communists stand for freedom, justice, equality, and abundance, while America's capitalistic profit system inevitably means war, poverty, discrimination, and oppression. Their belief had been reinforced in the postwar world by what they viewed as United States alignment with the "forces of reaction"—the colonialists in Africa, Rhee and Chiang in Asia, monarchs of the Middle East, and Franco in Spain.

The history of the Federation is incomplete, however, unless there is an understanding about its total impact over the years. Because of the Federation and its work, hundreds of clergymen have opposed injustice and exploitation and have preached thousands of sermons on economic justice, racial brotherhood, and world peace. The Federation made a significant contribution to the labor movement, and long before integration became a national objective, it was pointing out the cruelties and contradictions of second-class citizenship. The Federation's interest in peace—while at times appearing unrealistic to many—was in keeping with the eternal plea of all true religion that "nation shall not rise against nation neither shall they learn war anymore."

These facts compound the tragedy of its decline. Unfortunately, Ward and, particularly, McMichael were not willing to step aside at crucial times and give the Federation an opportunity to be effective.

In eighteenth-century England, a brilliant and dedicated student planted the seeds of revivalism that swept across the British Isles and then America. The movement of John Wesley was in large measure a protest against the social evils of his day. The early Methodists were perfectionists and asked those who joined with them to abide by a rigid moral code. People could be better than they were, they said, and in time the idea spread that society, too, could be transformed. Methodists in the United States became active in reform movements like the antislavery crusade, the battle against "demon rum," and the efforts of labor to secure recognition of its rights. Methodists were leaders in the Protestant social-gospel movement, and the Methodist Federation for Social Action grew out of genuine social concern. Those who have helped to destroy the Federation's effectiveness by the manipulation of its program in service of pro-Communism have not served their religion well.

SEVENTEEN · THE *WITNESS* AND THE *CHURCHMAN*

The Protestant Episcopal Church has been described facetiously as "the Republican Party at prayer." The truth is that few religious groups in the United States can boast of a richer diversity in membership, whether gauged by politics, geography, race, theology, or ritual. One of the curious effects of this diversity has been the debate among Episcopalians over alleged Communist influences in their midst. The controversy has focused mainly upon one social-action organization, two religious journals, and a Brooklyn parish.

There has been a long history of reform among the Episcopal clergy. One rallying point early in the twentieth century was the Church Socialist League, founded in 1911 to combat the capitalist system. Among its members were two bishops, both of Utah, F. Spencer Spalding and Paul Jones. The League was scarcely on its feet when World War I erupted and the organization was split over the position it should take on the conflict. The small remnant of the Church Socialist League finally merged with a newer group, the Church League for Industrial Democracy, which gradually gained considerable prestige within the denomination.

The story of C.L.I.D. revolves around the personality and opinions of William B. Spofford, Sr., a conscientious rebel who has enjoyed pouring forth anathemas upon the wealthy and proper elements of the church and society in general. Spofford has played the role of the gadfly who has sought to arouse the complacent by disputing popular, unimaginative ideas. In spite of the acidity of his pen, he has kept the high regard of many who admire his sincerity, his idealism, and his selfless dedication.

Spofford, born in 1892 in Claremont, New Hampshire, was ordained an Episcopal minister during World War I, and went to St. George's Church in Chicago, where he served without pay. To support himself and his wife, he worked for five years as labor manager of a clothing firm and became acquainted with the embryonic trade-union movement. By the mid-twenties, he was executive secretary of the Church League for Industrial Democracy—which he served for a quarter-century—and managing editor of the *Witness,* a distinguished independent Episcopal weekly which in the fifties claimed the largest circulation of any Episcopal weekly. The prestige of the *Witness* is still high today.

The Depression pushed the Church League for Industrial Democracy farther left. As in other church groups of the time, there was considerable difference of opinion on political and economic questions among its members, though there was unity in their rejection of unfettered capitalism. The pacifists saw the war issue as paramount. Others embraced the program of the New Deal. A third group were democratic socialists. A small but vocal minority looked to the Soviet Union for solutions to America's economic problems and were ready to work with Communists in attaining common objectives.

Spofford was in this last group. In 1933, when the matter of Russian recognition was being debated, he wrote in the *Witness:* "Russia, the avowed enemy of God, has, in my opinion, done more to advance the purpose of God to establish here upon earth His kingdom than any nation on the face of the world, during the last decade and a half." The antireligious campaign of the U.S.S.R. failed to dampen his enthusiasm. "I don't like the way she denies God," he said, "but I honestly think we worry about it a great deal more than God does." [1] Yet his was not a blind faith in Russia, and he expressed concern over Siberian exiles and other victims of the police state. This criticism seemed to subside, however, after Spofford visited the Soviet Union in 1937 and returned to write that the people were "literally singing in the streets" [2] and that fully 98 per cent of the population revered Stalin.[3]

Meanwhile, Spofford and the Church League for Industrial Democracy were subjected to increasing criticism within the denomination. In the fall of 1937, William T. Manning, the conservative Bishop of New York, joined in the attack. The dispute became focused upon the Church League forums which had been incorporated into the official program at the triennial General Convention of the Protestant Episcopal Church. Manning charged that the meetings were "purely propagandist with more than a tinge of Communism." If political and economic issues were to be discussed at them, "in simple fairness" all sides should be represented.[4] Spofford replied that the speakers did, in fact, present different views and that "there is not a Communist in the lot." [5]

The issue continued to stir controversy in the immediately following years. The *Living Church,* another independent Episcopal weekly, directed its fire at Spofford and, especially, his ties with the American League for Peace and Democracy. In one editorial entitled "Fr. Spofford and the Communists," the *Living Church* stated:

No, we do not honestly believe that Fr. [Father] Spofford is a Communist. He is honestly trying to apply revolutionary Christianity to modern society. In this we agree with him. But we feel that he is singularly blind to the fact that Communism is quite as much a denial of Christianity and a menace to the Church as fascism. . . . It is not because we are opposed to the Church League for Industrial Democracy but because we are in favor of it that we deplore the association, through the executive secretary and his chairmanship of the League for Peace and Democracy, with the destructive forces of Communism. . . . When the Church League for Industrial Democracy abandons its complacent attitude toward Communism and bases its program squarely on the platform of Christian radicalism our enthusiasm will increase a hundred fold.[6]

Spofford gave an earnest reply. "I am not a member of the communist or any other party," he wrote. He had voted for Republicans, Democrats, and Socialists but never for a Communist. There were "reasonable" Christian objections to Communism in theory and practice, he thought, but he was happy to be co-operating with the American League for Peace and Democracy.[7] On this point Spofford never changed his mind. Sixteen years later, in 1954, when he testified before the Subversive Activities Control Board, he reiterated his opinion that the American League "was right." At the same hearing, he described himself as a Democrat, again denied that he was ever a Communist, and volunteered the information that Earl Browder had asked him to serve as secretary of the American League, but that he had refused because "my job definitely was in the Episcopalian Church." [8]

FOR PEACE, FOR WAR

The Hitler-Stalin pact in 1939 presented Spofford with an opportunity to demonstrate his political independence. But his attachment to the Soviet Union proved stronger than many of his friends had realized, and with only slight difficulty he swallowed the new Communist line. The *Witness* immediately ran an article warning that it was "vile and unjust" to blame Russia. "If there is any condemnation, much greater condemnation must be levelled at Britain." [9]

When the *Living Church* criticized Spofford for defending the pact, he answered sharply: "What these people fail to understand is that Russia is a functioning socialist state and as such is a congenital foe of fascism, whether the out-and-out variety found in Germany and Italy or the more subtle kind to be found among the ruling cliques of England, France, and the United States." [10] After Hitler attacked Poland, Spofford cautioned his readers that it may only be a "phoney war." By mid-1940 he was using virulent language in denouncing England, American preparedness, and "Roosevelt war-mongering."

Other views did find their way into the pages of the *Witness,* as when Bishop Frank E. Wilson, an associate editor, praised Finland's valor in resisting Russia. But Spofford's attitude dominated. He soon published and reprinted for distribution a series of articles by Hewlett Johnson, which emphasized Britain's poor living standards, traced the war to England's "plutocracy," and offered Soviet Communism as the desired alternative.

Spofford did not have as much influence with the members of the Church League for Industrial Democracy. C.L.I.D. pacifists—among them Bishop W. Appleton Lawrence, John Nevin Sayre, and Shelton Hale Bishop—were not fooled by the Communists' new peace line. A second group consistently favored aid "short of war" to England, among them four prominent bishops—Edward L. Parsons, Beverly D. Tucker, William Scarlett, and Henry Knox Sherrill. Those few who supported the Communist position were led by Spofford and Miss Mary Van Kleeck, daughter of an Episcopal clergyman and for years associated with the Russell Sage Foundation. Joseph F. Fletcher, another key figure in C.L.I.D. and then dean of the Graduate School of Applied Religion in Cincinnati, championed a fourth position. He favored aid to England on the condition that England first pledge to end colonialism. This sharp cleavage within C.L.I.D. meant that it could adopt no specific statement on foreign policy.

As executive secretary, Spofford took advantage of his opportunities to promote his own political views. The key speaker for the C.L.I.D. General Convention forums in October 1940 was to be John L. Lewis, head of the United Mine Workers. Lewis was not sympathetic to the Communists and their friends, but they were pleased with him because of his firm stand against interventionism. He canceled his address after he decided to make a nationwide radio speech the same evening in support of Wendell Willkie's presidential candidacy. His prepared remarks were read at the gathering.

Miss Josephine Roche, president of a fuel company, and one of Lewis's many non-Communist admirers, spoke for management. The Chinese situation was discussed by John B. Foster, an Episcopal missionary, who already had expressed his sympathy for China's Communist "Partisans" in *Witness* articles. Other scheduled speakers included Max Yergan of the National Negro Congress and Jack R. McMichael of the American Youth Congress. Roger Baldwin was the only champion of United States foreign policy to speak.

The Nazi attack on Russia in June 1941 caught Spofford off guard. Mary Van Kleeck had just contributed a series of articles which, among other subjects, dealt with the cruelty of the British blockade of the European continent. Now all criticism of England ceased. New statements by Hewlett Johnson, enthusiastically prowar, were played up in the *Witness*. Spofford sought to camouflage his flip-flop by charging that indeed it was the anti-Communists who about-faced— now that Russia was in the war they no longer wanted to stop Hitler! "Highly respectable ladies and gentlemen have changed their line," he said unabashedly.[11]

There was a new sense of unity in the Church League for Industrial Democracy and in the Protestant Episcopal Church generally. Pacifists alone stood aloof. Both conservative Anglophiles and liberal interventionists suddenly found the zigzagging fellow travelers in their corner. The new climate was demonstrated in October 1941, when Bishop Manning joined with Fletcher in signing a public appeal for all-out aid to the Soviet Union. Soon after the attack upon Pearl Harbor, Fletcher told an annual meeting of the Church League that the war was "the violent phase of a world revolution—the first war of a new collectivist order. . . . Our choice for the future . . . is between good and bad planning, between democratic and fascist collectivism." [12]

During the war the *Witness* was satiated with material praising the Soviet Union. Spofford was instrumental in establishing the religious committee of Russian War Relief. By the summer of 1942, he warned: "Instead of glibly talking about 'the godless Russians,' we had better be at the more important business of urging that second front." [13] He exploited the wartime atmosphere to scold "red baiters," especially within the churches, and "pro-fascist reactionaries, Soviet-hating social democrats, pacifists, and Vatican-liners" who "always join forces whenever there is the slightest opportunity to poke at the one nation that is successfully fighting our enemy, Nazi Germany." [14]

In 1945, as the war neared an end, Spofford stepped up his attacks. He described the *Christian Century* as "that anti-administration, anti-Soviet journal of undenominationalism, that is weeping crocodile tears over the fate of Estonia, Latvia, Lithuania, and Poland and tearing its hair because the [Yalta] meeting was held in Russia. . . ." [15] Spofford attended the San Francisco Conference in 1945 and concluded: "As for moral leadership, I do not think anyone can deny that the Soviets took it in the opening days of the conference and held it throughout. . . ." [16] As Christmas approached, he became ecstatic. "There is a star in the east," he wrote. "Wise men will follow it as far as its beams cast light and do so without fear merely because its color happens to be red." [17]

THE POSTWAR DECADE

Spofford's emotional attachment to the Soviet Union continued into the postwar era. Whenever Russia and America clashed, Russia was right, America wrong. Suspicion of the U.S.S.R., he said, was manufactured by two different friends of fascism: "There is the propaganda which originates in the Vatican and is forcefully promulgated all over the world, and particularly in America, by Roman publicity agents. Then there are those so strongly wedded to the status quo that they would rather see an atomic war than to have their investments threatened by new ideas." [18]

An examination of the *Witness* during the postwar decade reveals that the magazine, but particularly Spofford, took positions that paralleled in a very precise fashion the positions of the Communist Party. This can be illustrated by focusing upon four areas: American foreign policy, events in Eastern Europe, discussion of Communism by churchmen, and the question of civil liberties.

1) Spofford traced all East-West tension to the West. An editorial in the *Witness* on the Truman Doctrine accused the United States Government of "waging an undeclared war . . . allegedly against Communism and the Soviet Union but actually against the development of economic democracy." [19] In opposing the Marshall Plan, which had broad support in the churches, Spofford described it as the "economic implement" of the Truman Doctrine and said it was "simply absurd" for Christians to feel as though they had no choice but to support it.[20] The North Atlantic Pact was seen as a maneuver "to isolate Russia and ignore her vital interests in the post-war world." [21]

The *Witness* boosted the Communist peace campaign—peace pilgrimages, peace ballots, peace slogans, etc. Spofford lauded the World Peace Council as "a people's movement" which was "forcing the western warmakers to reconsider their aggressive intentions." [22] Only "our deeply ingrained 'guilt by association' hokum" brought about American distrust of the Council, he said.[23] A new axis, he warned in 1955, was replacing the old German-Italian-Japanese entente. "Here is the present one—Chiang Kai-Shek, the Roman Church, and the U.S. State Department." [24]

2) The "people's democracies" of Eastern Europe were lauded and news of religious persecution there was dismissed. The *Witness* had harsh words for Cardinal Mindszenty of Hungary, a front for that "whole crowd of 'world-war-three-now' people which includes, Vatican, State Department, and other spokesmen for powerful forces." [25] Even the imprisonment of Protestant leaders left him unmoved. When

fifteen ministers were convicted of espionage in Bulgaria, the *Witness* gave a brief account, taken from an unidentified source, which emphasized how other Bulgarian Protestants had "denounced" the accused clergymen. When Lutheran leaders were purged in Hungary, Spofford headlined the story: "Lutherans Weed Out Reactionaries." [26]

In sharp contrast, when Czech Protestants issued a peace appeal, the *Witness* made it the "Story of the Week." [27] Careful coverage was given to "patriotic" movements among Roman Catholic priests in Czechoslovakia, Poland, Hungary, and elsewhere. Spofford devoted an entire column to assessing a new Hungarian textbook which said that Christianity was originally a working-class movement, later taken over by capitalists. He suggested that the textbook be examined by Western churchmen, not for Marxist tendencies, but for its truth, and "if they discover what I suspect they will, permission might be obtained to translate these books for use in our church schools." [28]

3) The *Witness* rushed to the defense of Stephen H. Fritchman, William Howard Melish, Jack R. McMichael, and other ministers who came under fire for Communist sympathies. But there was no such toleration for those who criticized the Soviet Union. When Otto A. Piper, a professor at Princeton Theological Seminary, spoke out against Russia in 1946, Spofford suggested that all "perpetrators" of this "poisonous stuff" ought to be "tried as enemies of humanity, along with Piper. . . ." [29] After Martin Niemöller voiced some anti-Soviet sentiments in 1947, the *Witness* ran an article, "Niemoller Supported Hitler." [30] Three years later, Niemöller charged that West Germany was "begotten in the Vatican and born in Washington," [31] and suddenly the *Witness* forgot his "Nazi" past and his words were accepted as authoritative.[32] When Eugene Carson Blake, leading Presbyterian spokesman, contrasted Russian totalitarianism with the "free society of the West," Spofford charged him with "using the techniques of the propagandists." [33]

Even the news columns of the *Witness* revealed the bias of its managing editor. In 1949 Bishop Otto Dibelius of Berlin raised the war-prisoner issue at a meeting of the World Council of Churches. "Forgive me if I speak as a German," he said, "but how long shall we have to wait for our prisoners of war to be returned from Russia?" The *Witness* appended this comment: "However, the millions of dead in Kiev, Karkov, Stalingrad, and the Russian countryside, killed by the invading German armies, were not present to give the Bishop an answer." In the same item, Joseph Hromadka of Czechoslovakia, a Protestant apologist for Communism, was described as leader of "the more moderate delegates." [34]

4) Spofford emerged from World War II with a different view of civil liberties from that which he held in the thirties. In March 1939, he discussed whether the German-American Bund should be allowed full freedom of expression. "The answer to this in my judgment," he wrote, "is that if we really believe in democracy and freedom we are not justified in abandoning them even in the face of real danger from anti-democratic forces." [35] But by the war's end, he contended that civil liberties should be denied to "undesirable" elements. He resigned as a director of the American Civil Liberties Union in protest against its policy of defending the right of Gerald L. K. Smith, the anti-Semitic agitator, to free speech, and charged that the A.C.L.U. was assisting fascist-minded groups. "In any case," he concluded, "for me the struggle of the people throughout the world for freedom and justice is far more important than defending the 'rights' of people who are obviously the enemy of the people in this struggle." [36]

Spofford naturally demanded full freedom for the political Left. By 1952, he was convinced that "we are fast approaching fascism of the German variety." The only forces fighting for the preservation of the Bill of Rights, he said, were the Communists—"certainly not organized Christianity." Rome was enthusiastic about fascism; Protestantism was following Rome's lead. "If [saying] this makes me a fellow-traveler," Spofford added, "then I will have to take it and grin, with a hearty cheerio." [37]

Theoretically, Spofford did not control the editorial content of the *Witness;* a board of editors met occasionally in New York City to discuss forthcoming issues. The magazine concentrates on church news. Spofford usually was given a free hand in the political realm because most of the other editors were specialists in other fields. His impressive array of facts, combined with his zeal and persuasiveness, tended to overwhelm his colleagues. Time and again they went along with him rather than create friction. In addition, Spofford chose and edited the news items.

There were occasions when Spofford found himself unable to win majority support. There were also times when articles reflecting an

anti-Communist position would appear in the *Witness.* Those who
worked with Spofford have pointed out that he never insisted upon
complete conformity. They suggest, too, that he has not been influenced as much by the Communist line as by "an arrested case of the
united front mentality" stemming from the thirties. There were occasional schisms within the staff. In 1953, its editor, Roscoe Foust, then
pastor of the Church of the Ascension in New York City, resigned,
partly because of political differences. Spofford now is a part-time
farmer in Tunkhannock, Pennsylvania, where the *Witness* is published. The magazine still is widely read and in some communities it
is the principal Episcopal weekly.

Meanwhile, in 1947 the Church League for Industrial Democracy
had changed its name to the Episcopal League for Social Action. It
emerged from World War II without the influence or enthusiasm of
former years; many of its earlier supporters had allowed their affiliations to lapse. Spofford and those who shared his views gained greater
control until by 1950 the group could claim only two hundred dues-
paying members and was generally ignored by the Protestant Episcopal Church.

Some members were encouraged soon after the war by the resignation of Spofford as executive secretary. But by 1951, Kenneth
Ripley Forbes, a seventy-three-year-old retired minister, had taken
over the post. Forbes had served churches in New England and Pennsylvania. He had been state chairman of the Pennsylvania Civil Rights
Congress, signed the Stockholm Peace Appeal, sponsored the American Continental Congress for Peace in 1949, co-operated closely with
the American Peace Crusade and its many projects, and served as
a member of the United States sponsoring committees of both the
Peace Conference of the Asian and Pacific Regions and the Congress
of the Peoples for Peace.

Forbes also became a member of the editorial board of the *Witness,* and his articles were as inflammatory as those of Spofford. The
American Government, he believed, was "fascist in principle" [38] and
was "planning for aggression," but there was "no real danger of
military aggression from Soviet Russia." [39] The Korean conflict, he
said in 1951, is "unsanctioned by Congress and regretted now by
probably a large majority of Americans." [40]

In 1953 a meeting of the Episcopal League for Social Action was held at the Church of the Holy Trinity, where William Howard Melish was acting rector. Resolutions were passed opposing the American position on prisoner exchange in Korea and asking clemency for the Rosenbergs. Among the officers elected were Fletcher, Mary Van Kleeck, and Elizabeth Frazier—each a supporter of the Spofford-Forbes position. One of the vice-presidents chosen was Bishop Stephen F. Bayne, Jr., of Olympia, Washington, who had not been consulted in advance. As soon as he read of his election, Bayne submitted his resignation, in part because he supported U.N. action in Korea, which the League had attacked. Special guests included Harry F. Ward, Claude C. Williams, Richard Morford, and John W. Darr, Jr. On the program were Dorothy Haven of Connecticut, who reported on her trip to the Communist-inspired Vienna Peace Congress, and Paul Robeson's wife, Eslanda Robeson, who shares her husband's political views.

The liberal *Episcopal Churchnews* commented upon the meeting:

> Had the Episcopal League for Social Action deliberately set out to lose friends and alienate Churchmen who fear Communism, its leaders could hardly have chosen more effective means of doing so. Social action is one thing, and coddling communist sympathizers is quite another. To the distinguished list of reputable and respected Churchmen who are associated with ELSA we say "Clean house!" Perhaps ELSA might then emerge as a positive and constructive force for social action, redeemed from the stigma of communist sympathy, and an organization whose resolutions might not so easily be dismissed as possibly, and even probably, tainted by Communism.
>
> The Episcopal Church needs a purified ELSA. But it can get along without the ELSA it has.[41]

The opinion expressed by the *Episcopal Churchnews* was widespread within the denomination. However, the days of controversy over the Church League for Industrial Democracy were gone. There was not enough interest in E.L.S.A. to stir debate. The group had become an isolated clique, not directed by Communists, to be sure, but led mainly by men and women who were ready to follow where the Communists wished to lead.

THE *Churchman*

Although the political orientation of the *Witness* may be traced to Spofford's contempt for American capitalism and his undisguised reverence for the Soviet Union, the case of the semimonthly magazine the *Churchman* is not as simple. Yet in the public press generally, the *Churchman* has been under sharper attack. The *New Leader* has called its editor, Guy Emery Shipler, "America's Red Dean." [42] There is no evidence to warrant such a description for, unlike Spofford, Shipler has hewn his own distinctive path through the political jungle.

The *Churchman,* an independent journal launched in 1804, claims to be the oldest religious magazine in the English-speaking world and has been a champion of liberal theology in the Protestant Episcopal Church. Shipler joined the staff in 1917 and since 1924 has been editor. He had been ordained in 1910 after graduating from General Theological Seminary in New York. Under his influence the magazine has undergone many changes. Its Episcopal bent has not disappeared entirely but has been superseded by an interdenominational flavor. Gradually it has turned more and more to political matters. Its fresh, stimulating character has won and held the interest and respect of many Protestant leaders. Despite the controversy that has whirled around it, the *Churchman* has made a major contribution to social awareness in the churches.

Shipler was strongly influenced by such leaders in the Protestant social-gospel movement as Walter Rauschenbusch, Josiah Strong, and Washington Gladden. "I must admit," he wrote on one occasion, "that I am such a moth-eaten traditionalist as to be able to state my Christian social creed in one sentence by Rauschenbusch, as follows: 'The essential purpose of Christianity was to transform human society into the Kingdom of God by regenerating all human relations and reconstituting them in accordance with the will of God.' . . . I have never consciously deviated in my parish ministry or as editor of The Churchman, however inadequately I may have fulfilled its high ideal." [43]

During the thirties, the *Churchman* was an independent progressive organ that frequently criticized Communism and the Soviet Union. An editorial in 1939 warned that "when a Liberal attempts to co-operate with the Communist for some worthy cause, the latter often tries to steal the show in the interests of the party." [44] Shortly there-after, the *Churchman* sharply condemned the Hitler-Stalin pact, which "made it possible for the Germans to overrun Poland and Den-mark and Norway and Holland and Belgium and France." [45] Shipler was numbered among those churchmen who spoke out vigorously for aid to England—a move which Communists bitterly opposed.

Since World War II, the *Churchman* has also shown signs of con-siderable independence. In 1949 it editorialized on Tito's rift with Moscow:

> Russia has followed its usual technique, like that of the Roman hier-archy, of calling names. Yugoslavia has answered with reasoned argu-ment and factual statements. The Yugoslav press has printed the com-munications from Russia; Joe Stalin's press has obviously not dared to print the communications from Yugoslavia.[46]

Yet, the *Churchman* was also hospitable to material championing Communism or the Soviet Union during the first postwar decade. It ran articles by Harry F. Ward, William Howard Melish, Stephen H. Fritchman, J. Spencer Kennard, Jr., Joseph F. Fletcher, Willard Up-haus, and James G. Endicott. The managing editor, Miss Edna Ruth Johnson, wrote glowing profiles of such apologists for Russia as Eliot White, Hewlett Johnson, Ida Pruitt, formerly with the Y.W.C.A. in China, and Cedric Belfrage, editor of the *National Guardian*. The magazine reported sympathetically on the activities of the Committee for a Democratic Far Eastern Policy, the Civil Rights Congress, the American Committee for Protection of Foreign Born, the National Council of American-Soviet Friendship, the World Federation of Democratic Youth, and other organizations allied with the Commu-nists. The *Churchman* gave considerable publicity to the Stockholm Peace Appeal, the Mid-Century Conference for Peace, and the War-saw and Vienna peace congresses. It displayed particular interest in the Communist-controlled countries of Eastern Europe and published, without change, propaganda taken directly from the *Hungarian Bul-letin, Polish Newsletter, Yugoslav Information Bulletin,* and other government handouts.

Critics of the *Churchman* worked diligently and with considerable success to cripple its prestige in the late forties. One indication of this was the controversy stirred over the Churchman Award, which the magazine presented annually to an American who made a noteworthy contribution "to goodwill and better understanding among all peoples." Franklin D. Roosevelt, William Allen White, Wendell Willkie, Bernard Baruch, and Dwight D. Eisenhower had received the award in the past.

In 1948 it was to be given to Secretary of State George C. Marshall —another indication of the *Churchman*'s political independence, for the Marshall Plan was under sharp attack in Communist circles as "imperialistic." Marshall at first accepted, was flooded with protests, then withdrew with the explanation that he had been under the impression that the magazine was solely religious. The *Churchman* tried to give a "special citation" to Israel, but Israel's United Nations spokesman, Abba Eban, also turned it down.[47]

The position of the *Churchman* on world affairs can be understood only against the backdrop of its antipathy toward Roman Catholicism. It sees the American Government today as the puppet of the Vatican. "We know that the Vatican is the main driving force behind our warmongers," the *Churchman* said in 1947.[48] Shipler, of course, is voicing the sentiment of a minority of Protestant clergymen, among whom there persists a feeling that Rome is an equal—and possibly greater—threat to peace and progress than Moscow. Some see the Vatican and the Soviet Union locked in a death struggle, especially in Eastern Europe, and between the two competing forces they see little choice.

This crusade against Rome picked up enormous momentum in the *Churchman* during and after World War II. In 1945 Shipler urged an alliance between Russian Orthodoxy and Protestantism against the Vatican. Later, the magazine devoted considerable space to reporting the lavish expressions of loyalty which churches in Russia and Eastern Europe gave to their Communist regimes, and quoted Patriarch Alexis' praise of Stalin as "a great and wise leader" and his description of Moscow as "the reliable supporter of all peace-loving peoples."[49] The appeal of Archbishop Luka of the Crimea to Christians in the "Anglo-Saxon countries" to "thwart the bloody plans of the militarists" was reported.[50] The *Churchman* even printed the text from the Bulgarian Orthodox Church lauding Stalin on his seventieth birthday for "statesmanlike vision and encouragement." [51] There were accounts of the endorsement of the Stockholm Peace Appeal by leaders of Russian Orthodoxy, the Lutheran bishops of Latvia, and spokesmen for Hungarian Protestantism. The assumption seemed to be that these statements and appeals were made by legitimate church leaders who were free to follow other courses of action had they wished.

Conversely, the *Churchman* showed little sympathy for clergy arrested and imprisoned by Communist governments. Even when they were Protestants—as in Hungary and Bulgaria—Shipler chose not to comment. A story in 1953 on the flight of refugees from East Germany was headed: "Mostly Roman Catholics Pour Into West Zone." [52] Actually, East Germany was 90 per cent Lutheran and the overwhelming majority of refugees from there were Lutherans.

In 1955 a series of *Churchman* articles sought to expose the role of the Vatican in world affairs. They took the form of a "Report to F.D.R." on the decade since his death. The articles were reprinted as a pamphlet and described in the *Churchman* as "useful for private and public talks for informing editors, and letting people in general know what actually transpired." [53] The author was an anonymous "Washington Observer."

"Unbiased historians," the articles said, "are able today to trace the role of the Vatican as the powerful instigator of the cold war." [54] They charged that during the struggle against the Axis, the Papacy had been secretly allied with Mussolini and Hitler. After the war an "insidious campaign" was carried on by a group of "Vatican operatives" to poison Americans against their Russian allies. Chief among these agents was said to be the Jesuit Edmund A. Walsh, then Dean of the Foreign Service School of Georgetown University, where many diplomats are trained. President Truman was described as having been brought into line by the hierarchy, the Knights of Columbus, and the influential Roman Catholic politicians in the Democratic Party. "Quickly, our foreign policy became a carbon sheet of the Vatican Master Plan," and the policy of containment "destroyed all opportunity for an American-Russian understanding." [55] Meanwhile, said the *Churchman,* Senator Joseph R. McCarthy of Wisconsin was being groomed to spearhead the drive for "a Vatican-sponsored fascism" in the United States. [56]

Russia did not emerge from the articles as an unblemished hero. The "Washington Observer" warned that a Vatican-Moscow agreement reminiscent of the Hitler-Stalin pact might be pending:

The tragedy is that the American people again will have to suffer for the mistake of falling into the Vatican trap. After we had served the world-wide interest of the papacy, after having "turned Axis defeat into victory," after having squandered, directly and indirectly, hundred billions of dollars for the reconstructing and strengthening of the Vatican "Lebensraum" in Europe and Asia, the pope is ready to shift its front again and make a deal with Moscow. European press reports have stated that the Vatican has revised its world position and is ready for a large scale settlement with the Soviets on East European problems.[57]

Anti-Catholicism, and not pro-Communism, then, seems to be the guiding bias of the *Churchman*. Whatever sympathy the *Churchman* demonstrates for Soviet policies appears to be mainly a by-product.

Obviously, neither Spofford's admiration for Russia nor Shipler's anti-Catholicism, making him vulnerable to Communist propaganda, reflects the opinions of three million members of the Protestant Episcopal Church in the United States. Both sympathy for Communism and bitter anti-Catholicism are rare among Episcopalians. Perhaps, indeed, it is a tribute to their tradition of freedom and tolerance that the *Witness* and the *Churchman* have escaped repudiation by the whole denomination.

A venerable Episcopal church in Brooklyn Heights served as the setting for acrimonious controversy for ten years from 1947 to 1957. The Church of the Holy Trinity provided a lavish stage for this bitter struggle that at one point found two rival ministers attempting to lead the same Sunday worship service at the same time. Behind the tug-of-war for possession of the premises were deep political and religious issues.

In 1904 Holy Trinity's vestry called John Howard Melish, who accepted the invitation on condition that the old pew-rental system be abandoned—a system which tended to limit the congregation to the wealthier class. The new rector's influence was quickly felt in Brooklyn. He developed a strong parish program that included particular emphasis on amateur athletic clubs. He took a forthright liberal position in the theological debate raging within the Episcopal Church and within Protestantism generally. He welcomed to his pulpit fellow churchmen who espoused the unpopular political and social causes of the day. Sometimes his views stirred dissension within his congregation, especially when he refused to sanction American participation in World War I. Yet John Howard Melish endeared himself to his parishioners. The central role he was to play in the controversy of later years was thrust upon him because he was the parish rector and the father of his son.

William Howard Melish was born in the rectory in 1910. After Harvard, Union Theological Seminary, Cambridge University in England (where he rowed at Henley), and Episcopal Theological Seminary, the younger Melish joined the staff of Christ Church in Cincinnati, where his father had served a generation before. In 1939 he came to Holy Trinity. He was tall, impeccably dressed; the New York *Times* said later that he had the appearance of "a Wall Street customers man."

William Howard Melish traces his interest in the Soviet Union to 1941, when Russia and the United States found themselves allies against Germany. The following year he joined the New York Council of American-Soviet Friendship at the invitation of another Episcopal clergyman, Thomas L. Harris. In 1944 three articles by Melish appeared in the *Worker,* the weekend edition of the *Daily Worker.*[1] The most significant of the pieces, "Where Are the Communists Going?," noted that clergymen had been sent a book by Earl Browder. They should read it carefully, he urged, keeping an open mind on the matter of Communism.[2] The same year, he dispatched congratulations to the *Daily Worker* on its twentieth anniversary. "I realize that many of the causes in which I have taken an interest are deeply indebted to your paper's continued interests and its readers' support," he said.[3] He was listed as a member of the sponsoring committee of the 1945 Fund Campaign for the *Daily Worker*'s support.[4]

There were other indications of his direction. Soon after the American Labor Party's 1944 split with the anti-Communist wing, which left to form the Liberal Party, Melish became a vice-chairman of the A.L.P. executive committee.[5] In June 1944, he contributed an article to *Soviet Russia Today* on "Russia and the Four Freedoms," praising Soviet emphasis on freedom from fear and want, and defending the suppression of freedom of religion and speech—such freedom "could be misused to prevent or hinder the successful outcome of the revolutionary process."[6] In early 1945, the Communist literary magazine, *New Masses,* began a monthly column, "Ringing the Changes," signed by Melish.[7]

Melish's enthusiasm for Russia continued after the war and he became increasingly involved in the elaborate and thriving Communist-front network. In 1947 he was chairman of the Joint Conference Against Intervention in Greece and Turkey, which protested the Truman Doctrine as "fascism." He was active in the Win the Peace Conference in New York. He served as escort to the Dean of Canterbury on his tour of the United States and marched in two annual

May Day parades. He also was vice-president of New York Civil Rights Congress and was a member of the Board of Trustees of the Jefferson School of Social Science.

CONTROVERSY OVER MELISH BEGINS

The principal beneficiary of William Howard Melish's attention in his nonpastoral activities was the National Council of American-Soviet Friendship. In February 1943, he was one of its five original incorporators and head of its religious committee. He was vice-chairman in 1945 and chairman from June 1946 to March 1949. His association led to unrest among Holy Trinity's parishioners, especially when in December 1947 the United States Attorney General placed the organization on the list of subversive activities. Shortly after, Melish appeared on "Town Hall of the Air" to discuss anti-American propaganda in Europe and was accused publicly of Communist sympathies by Major General William ("Wild Bill") Donovan, head of the wartime Office of Strategic Services.

At the next meeting of the church's vestry, the elder Melish was challenged about his son's affiliations but flatly refused to try to curb his activities. A growing chorus demanded that his son be dismissed. Criticism mounted when *Time, Life, Newsweek,* and other influential periodicals pointed an accusing finger at the younger Melish after the National Council of American-Soviet Friendship picketed an anti-Communist movie. In 1948 he was a delegate to the Wallace Progressive Party; amid the accompanying hubbub, Dean Hewlett Johnson was invited to preach from the pulpit of Holy Trinity.

Holy Trinity's vestrymen finally took matters into their own hands and asked the Bishop of Long Island, James Pernette DeWolfe, to investigate the case. The Bishop sided with the unhappy vestrymen, and the standing committee of the diocese adopted a recommendation that both ministers resign. A few days later, the vestry by a 9-2 vote officially petitioned the Bishop to dissolve the relationship between John Howard Melish and the parish. DeWolfe hoped for a compromise that would oust the son and leave the father. This proved impossible, and the Bishop thereupon ordered the father to retire on a pension.

He obeyed the Bishop's order, but did not surrender. He and his son and their supporters appealed the Bishop's decision in the courts, asking reinstatement. Then they organized the Committee to Retain the Rector. An eloquent pamphlet, *The Melish Case: Challenge to the Church,* was mailed to all Episcopal clergymen and also to deputies planning to attend the denomination's 1949 General Convention. Young Melish went to the convention with Lewis G. Reynolds, senior warden of Holy Trinity and one of his father's strongest backers. They tried to secure the adoption of a resolution stating, in effect, that a minister could not be removed against his will when the clear majority of parishioners favored his retention. The resolution was defeated without debate. Three other resolutions also died quietly: one lauding DeWolfe for his decision; a second forbidding Episcopal clergymen to belong to subversive organizations; a third condemning the editorial policies of the *Witness.* The General Convention was obviously in no mood to be trapped in the complex political issues involved.

Some church journals came to the Melishes' defense, convinced that freedom of the pulpit was at stake. In April 1949, at a critical point in the court contest, many of Brooklyn's prominent clergymen sponsored a reception to honor John Howard Melish for his forty-five years of service to Holy Trinity and the borough. Within a year, eight bishops and 1,123 ministers of the Protestant Episcopal Church asked permission to file a brief in his favor. In late 1950, when the state courts had ruled against him, the case advanced to the United States Supreme Court, where 2,576 clergymen prepared to submit another brief in his support.

Besides the civil-liberties issue, there was another important facet of the controversy, symbolized by the striking contrast between the Melishes and DeWolfe. Both father and son were proudly "low church" in their attitude toward ritual and "broad church" in their theology. DeWolfe was Anglo-Catholic in both. "Low" churchmen attributed to the "high church" Bishop everything they feared in the Anglo-Catholic movement: a return to "medieval pomp and ceremony," iron-clad rule by ecclesiastical superiors, and a closer relationship to Roman Catholicism. In the midst of the dispute, DeWolfe asked all parishes in his diocese to offer prayers for Cardinal Mindszenty of Hungary, prisoner of the Communist government but no favorite of many liberals. To his opponents, this was further evidence that he was both reactionary and unduly disposed toward the Vatican.

The Supreme Court refused to hear the case, and the original vestry had won its battle in the courts. Meanwhile, events moved swiftly within Holy Trinity. The congregation replaced several anti-Melish vestrymen with others more favorable. They then seized upon a canon-law provision that another rector could be dispatched to Holy Trinity only at the request of the vestry. They promptly decided not to ask for a new rector but to invite the younger Melish to remain as acting rector.

There was a curious irony about this turn of events. By 1951, the beloved seventy-six-year-old rector was out. But so were the vestrymen who had fought against him. The church had come under the control of the son, the real target of the vestrymen in the first place.

A relative calm settled over the parish from 1951 to 1955. Many of Melish's opponents stayed away, accusing him of using the pulpit for partisan political purposes. Melish published some of his sermons in a 1953 book, *Strength for Struggle,* in which he defended his role in the church and expressed particular fear of Roman Catholicism. He had said in his 1952 Reformation Sunday message:

It is not an accident that the last two Attorney-Generals have been Roman Catholic, or that the head of the Central Intelligence Agency is Roman Catholic, or that the F.B.I. is staffed with many Roman Catholics, or that the largest number of department heads of Roman Catholic allegiance in our history sit in President Truman's cabinet, that the State Department is the particular honeycomb of Roman Catholic activity.[8]

He warned that Protestant Americans were being pushed gradually into a "new Bonn-Rome-Madrid-Lisbon axis."[9]

THE DISPUTE ERUPTS AGAIN

A series of events in 1955 lit fires of controversy once more. Several pro-Melish vestrymen, led by Reynolds, experienced a change of heart. By December, the vestry was split again: three for, six against Melish. Suddenly the majority sent out a notice that at their January 1956 meeting the election of a new rector would be considered.

Melish's supporters launched a counteroffensive. "We are perfectly sure," they said in a letter to parishioners, "that the people of Holy Trinity parish do not want a rector chosen for them without having any say in the matter or even knowing his name." [10] They accused the vestry of planning to bring an Anglo-Catholic to Holy Trinity. Reynolds termed this charge a typical smokescreen and named as the choice of the vestry Irving S. Pollard, assistant at St. Bartholomew's Church in Manhattan, a "low church" parish. The January meeting was boycotted by Melish's three supporters, but the other six met and officially nominated Pollard. They declared that "the employment of the Rev. William Howard Melish by the vestry will cease and he will be required to vacate the premises now occupied . . . within thirty days after notice that the Bishop's approval had been received." [11] They asked the Bishop to send a supply minister to take charge of the services the following Sunday.

While the vestrymen were in session, nearby in the church about one hundred Melish supporters held a prayer meeting and hymn sing. When the six emerged from their meeting, they were greeted with sharp words and hostile stares. The deliberate absence of the other three posed a thorny question: Was a quorum present? Melish's supporters contended that in the particular case of Holy Trinity, with only an acting rector, a quorum required the presence of the two church wardens and five vestrymen—a total of seven. However, the Bishop ruled that canon law described a quorum, in the absence of a rector, as the church wardens and "one less than a majority of the vestrymen"—a total of six.

The dramatic swing of the six, especially of Reynolds, away from allegiance to Melish to a demand for his removal was based on a series of complex factors.

The political climate of the times cast a cloud over the scene. Between 1947 and 1955, millions of Americans re-evaluated their approach to Communism. It was a time of the gross injustice of McCarthyism, but also a time of a wider recognition that Communism was a brutal, aggressive totalitarian force, not an ultraliberal and idealistic philosophy. Reynolds began to wonder if Melish, after all, were a Communist sympathizer. He accused him of bringing to Holy Trinity speakers known for pro-Communist bias without the vestry's prior knowledge.

Less concrete evidence—perhaps significant, perhaps irrelevant—ruffled Reynolds. He told how when he dropped by the church early in the morning, he would find Melish in conference with strangers who were never introduced to him, strangers who left the impression that they were not there on spiritual missions. Reynolds was also annoyed by what he described as Melish's fear that he might see the mail first. "It was as though he was afraid I'd find out something." [12]

The influx of new people into the church, and especially into places of leadership, worried old-time members. For years men like Reynolds had sacrificed time and money to assist Holy Trinity and to aid the Melishes. The father had maintained strong personal ties with these members, but they felt that the son was no longer interested in them once they had served as instruments for gaining control of the parish. They sensed that he felt a closer kinship with those newer members who shared his own interests and political orientation, and who gradually began to dominate more and more areas of church life. Older Melish supporters felt betrayed.

Inevitably, several vestrymen began to see the character and personality of Melish in a different light. He was no longer a brilliant crusader who stood boldly for righteousness. Now they described him as "dictatorial" and "unctuous." He was accused of incompetence as an administrator and of ineffectiveness and indifference as a pastor. He was charged with an attitude of condescension toward parishioners who did not respond to his political views. Perhaps Melish's personality did undergo a major change after the trying events of earlier years. But perhaps the change was more in the minds of his critics. What had once been viewed as strong leadership now seemed to them dictatorial. What was formerly interpreted as dignity now appeared as pomposity.

Reynolds and his colleagues were also concerned about the welfare of the parish. They contended that membership and attendance had fallen off sharply—a contention disputed by the Melish camp. They charged that Holy Trinity was becoming a tightly knit political clique drawing from far and wide rather than a religious center for the community. It was isolated from the neighborhood, for the impression was widespread that it was a "Red church." Its relations with the diocese were poor. Reynolds warned: "In order to survive as a

Protestant Episcopal Church, we must re-establish complete and nor-
mal relations with the diocese and community at large." [13]

Sunday, January 15, 1956, brought one of the most dramatic episodes in American church history.[14] The Bishop had acceded to—
indeed, welcomed—the action of the vestry in calling Pollard. He
asked Robert Thomas to conduct services at Holy Trinity until the
new rector assumed his duties. All forty locks of the church were
changed to keep Melish out. Early Sunday morning a group of Melish
supporters broke open the door of the sacristy and pried open the
lock on the outside bulletin board. On Saturday night the sign had
announced that Thomas would preach; by Sunday morning Melish's
name was there instead.

At 8:30 A.M. Thomas arrived, only to find Melish administering
communion to a group of thirty loyal supporters at a side altar.
Melish's lawyer handed him a protest signed by Melish: "I order
you to refrain from holding services in this church." Thomas began
to read the communion ritual from the main altar for a group of
nine worshipers. The voices of the two ministers mingled with one
another. At one point, the Melish group almost shouted the Lord's
Prayer in an obvious effort to drown out their antagonist.

Tension grew in the sanctuary as people arrived for the regular
morning service. Outside, an elderly Episcopal minister walked to and
fro before the red stone English-Gothic structure carrying a sign which
admonished: "Honor, Follow, Obey the Bishop." Eighteen police
were there to preserve the peace, and more than fifteen detectives
moved among the crowd. A battery of pressmen sought to interview
the principal contestants. In the balcony, cameras focused upon the
chancel. Thomas had left the sanctuary for breakfast. As Melish sat
quietly in the front, his eighty-one-year-old father was pushed in a
wheel chair to sit beside the altar.

At 10:45 A.M., fifteen minutes before the customary hour, Melish
began the morning ritual at the main altar. Thomas came back from
breakfast to find his path blocked by an angry church member. With
detectives on each side of the aisle, and escorted by Reynolds, Thomas
finally reached the altar. "Mr. Melish!" Reynolds called. "You are
out of order." Melish paid no attention and aided by the organist led
the congregation in singing "Onward Christian Soldiers." Thomas
walked into the pulpit, but the microphone was dead. He turned to

the altar and tried to speak to Melish, but Melish was leading a prayer.

Melish announced Psalm 28; Thomas countered with Psalm 118. The overwhelming majority followed Melish. "Mr. Melish," Thomas said, barely loud enough to be heard above the responses of the people, "I refuse to make a mockery of this church and this religion." With this he walked out, with forty incensed men and women behind him. In the vestibule Thomas told reporters: "The rest is up to the Bishop."

As Melish stood in the vestibule after the benediction, one lady admonished him: "You are a disgrace to the Episcopal Church and the most brazen sap I have ever seen." Melish replied calmly: "I am glad you told me to my face." [15]

The next day the press in many parts of the country—and even abroad—headlined the story. Within the Protestant Episcopal Church there was growing sentiment, even among Melish sympathizers, that the conflict had assumed scandalous proportions and that some kind of immediate and decisive ecclesiastical action was necessary. Foes of Melish followed various paths. The six vestrymen asked the courts to keep Melish from the church. Bishop DeWolfe announced a full investigation of Melish's conduct to see if it should incur episcopal censure, suspension, or unfrocking. A bill was introduced in the New York Legislature which would change the Religious Incorporations Law so that there would be no doubt that the six anti-Melish members of the eleven-member vestry constituted a quorum. This bill aroused sharp criticism as governmental interference in church affairs, and was quietly shelved.

The Melish camp sought to hold out until the congregation met on April 2, when the composition of the vestry could be changed. The locks were replaced again. Melish had the keys this time. A letter to four hundred Episcopal ministers in the New York area recounted the events of the fateful Sunday morning and restated the case against the Bishop. A number of ministers of different denominations came to Melish's defense.

Meanwhile, Irving S. Pollard, rector-elect, decided against accepting the call to Holy Trinity. The vestry met and nominated a new man, George W. Barnes of Hollywood, California, who also turned down the bid, on grounds of health. A third minister, Herman S.

Sidener, chaplain of the Cathedral School of St. Paul in Garden City, L. I., agreed to come, and the Bishop made plans to hold an installation service at Holy Trinity on Monday, March 5.

DISSOLUTION OF HOLY TRINITY

The installation service was impressive and colorful.[16] More than one hundred Episcopal clergymen had come to the crowded church. Melish did not attend, but his position had been plainly put in his morning sermon the previous day:

> We are not overwhelmed nor misled by a display of ecclesiastical pomp and circumstance devised by some press-agent mind that may take place tomorrow afternoon. Many a clergyman, especially a mission priest, will be doing what he is asked to do, without his participation reflecting his true, innermost feelings. No matter how many may be there, clergy or laity, this service of institution will be illegal; and, if it is illegal, as we are certain that it is, we can leave its occurrence safely in the hands of God. God is never mocked.[17]

Prior to the act of installation, DeWolfe read part of the liturgy from the Book of Common Prayer: "But if any of you can show just cause why he may not be instituted, we proceed no further, because we would not that an unworthy person should minister among you." The first objector to present himself at the chancel was Phillips Brooks, a Negro vestryman at Holy Trinity, who contended that it was improper to install Sidener while court action was still pending. The Bishop replied that he was acting in accordance with canon law, not civil law. Two other objectors came forward—E. DeWitt Ramel, another pro-Melish vestryman, and Hubert T. Delany, attorney for Melish and former justice of the Domestic Relations Court in New York City. Delany's father had been the first Negro bishop in the Protestant Episcopal Church.

The installation proceeded despite the interruptions. Five days later, however, Justice Edward Baker of the New York State Supreme Court ruled that no quorum had been present at the disputed vestry meeting. The ruling was appealed and upheld and from February 1956 to June 1957 Melish continued in the pulpit of Holy Trinity with the backing of the courts.

These were sixteen tumultuous months.

On April 2, 1956, when the congregation held its annual meeting, Melish supporters planned to fill the six vestry seats up for election. Reynolds charged that Melish had packed the church membership list, and said he had drawn up his own list of eligible voters. New York laws provided that only members could vote "who have been regular attendants at its worship and contributed to its support for at least twelve months prior to such election." The same statute makes the presiding officer—in this case Reynolds—judge of the qualifications of voters, receiver of the votes cast, and declarer of the result of the votes cast.

Reynolds disqualified some persons present, and bedlam broke loose. Another anti-Melish vestryman moved that the meeting adjourn. Reynolds ruled that the majority of those eligible to vote favored adjournment. He walked off with the ballot box, accompanied by about forty supporters. Approximately two hundred stayed and unanimously elected six pro-Melish vestrymen. Two foes of Melish, Reynolds and J. Royal Rutledge, were not up for election. Later that year, however, at a special parish meeting, Reynolds was ousted on the grounds of conspiring to undermine the authority of the vestry, disregarding the desires of the congregation, and disturbing Sunday-morning service (on January 15, 1956) "and causing a public scandal." Rutledge was ousted for co-operating with Reynolds. Rutledge, who is a Negro, had accused Melish of deliberately seeking to paint his opponents as racists—this, said Rutledge, was "a great injustice." [18]

The Diocese of Long Island gave what support it could to Melish's opponents. The administrator of the diocese ruled that the old vestry continued in office because the "rump session" following adjournment had been illegal. In May 1956, two rival delegations from Holy Trinity went to the annual diocesan convention and by an overwhelming vote the anti-Melish group was seated. The delegates also voted the Bishop the power to appoint a rector to any parish where the pulpit has been vacant for a year. The debate indicated that the resolution was aimed specifically at Melish.

In April 1956, the Communist-dominated World Peace Council awarded Melish the International Peace Prize (which had been known as the Stalin peace prize). He said the award came as a surprise because he had not participated in the Council's work, but he accepted it on behalf of himself and his congregation. Reynolds was quick to point to this as "leaving no doubt as to . . . [Melish's] political affiliations." He felt it ironic that Melish should be a leader for international peace—on Russian terms—while serving as a symbol of strife in his parish, his diocese, and in the Protestant Episcopal Church generally.[19]

During the Hungarian revolution, in November 1956, Melish again came under a spotlight when the National Council of American-Soviet Friendship held its annual rally. Hundreds of shouting, angry anti-Communist pickets stood outside Pythian Hall in Manhattan, throwing eggs, tomatoes, and sticks. A bottle of ammonia, aimed at Paul Robeson, splattered the coat of a nearby policeman. Three clergymen spoke to the gathering: Richard Morford, executive director of the National Council of American-Soviet Friendship, Harry F. Ward, and Melish.

It was a time for Communists and their sympathizers to admit their errors. It began with the Twentieth Congress of the Communist Party of the Soviet Union when Stalin was roundly denounced by Khrushchev. The American Communist Party was wracked with remorse and dissension and it became fashionable to bemoan Stalin's betrayal of socialism and to confess overzealousness in lauding the U.S.S.R.

Melish followed this pattern with his speech at the New York rally. As part of his own confession, he quoted Stanley Evans of England, an Anglican minister who had apologized for the Soviet cause for many years. Melish applied the words to himself:

Most of us who have written and spoken about Russia and Eastern Europe, while we have reported truthfully and gauged accurately some aspects of Soviet Life and the life of the new Democracies, have been grievously wrong about others. Our appreciation of the good and of the forward strides led us to reject uncritically much of the evidence which did not suit our particular interpretations. There is probably nobody who writes in support of the U.S.S.R. of whom this is not true—and it certainly includes the present writer.[20]

Melish chose his words carefully in commenting on Hungary. "We are all guilty of talking ideals and acting in contradiction to them," he said. He attributed the overthrow of the Guatemalan Government in

1954 to the United States and then balanced it against the Hungarian revolution. "All of us are compromised," he continued. "The Soviet Union is now plagued with a Hungary and will pay a heavy price before this involvement, however needful it may have seemed to them, is finished." [21] How much independent thinking this statement represents is difficult to judge, since the editorials of the *Daily Worker* viewed events in Hungary in a similar manner.

Melish's participation in the rally—more than what he said—caused widespread resentment. Bishop DeWolfe immediately charged that "this one supply priest has brought scandal and disgrace to this diocese and serious unrest among Christian people everywhere." "I am shocked beyond words," DeWolfe continued, "at the presence of ministers of Christian churches at the rally to celebrate what has aptly been called the 'bloody founding, the bloody past and the bloody present of the godless Soviet Union.' " [22] Melish wrote to his Bishop to express the vestry's "joint indignation" at DeWolfe's criticism without first finding out what he had "actually said." [23]

In June 1957, the Appellate Division in Brooklyn ruled, in a 4-1 decision, that Herman S. Sidener, not Melish, was the rightful rector. It found that, according to the ecclesiastical law, there was a quorum of the vestry present when Sidener was called, and that the civil courts were obligated in this case to follow the laws of the church. Melish appealed, but the decision against him was upheld.

On the first Sunday of July, Sidener conducted his first services at Holy Trinity. Melish attended and received communion. Beneath an outward calm, there was considerable tension and bitterness. A letter to Sidener was circulated urging him to leave the parish "that did not choose you and does not want you," [24] and several members walked out when they saw that Melish was not in the chancel. When Sidener asked Reynolds "and any one he wants" to receive the collection, eight pro-Melish vestrymen were immediately on their feet, marched forward and passed the collection plates. The situation worsened a week later when the new rector was floored and injured slightly in a scuffle with a Melish supporter during the social hour following the morning service.

DeWolfe decided to take firm action. On Sidener's third Sunday, a letter from the Bishop to Sidener was read to the congregation. It said in part:

My solemn judgment therefore to you, as the rector, is that the church and all the parish buildings be closed until the litigation is settled in the courts. I am moved to this conclusion because it is my responsibility as bishop to see that nothing disturbs the peace of the church and I cannot tolerate the church edifice being used as a battleground. All the church buildings should be closed, and by this I mean all, except the rectory which temporarily, by stipulation of the court may be used solely for living quarters for the Rev. William H. Melish and his family.[25]

Church services stopped immediately. Later Melish left the rectory, his father remained upstairs, and the courts declared that the 1956 vestry headed by Reynolds was legally in control of the church's property, including $400,000 in church funds. Sunday worship was not attempted, for fear of provoking new scenes of disorder, though the facilities of the church were used for a variety of parish and civic activities. Sidener sought to minister to the members of the congregation, but by 1960 it had become uncertain as to who the members were. Meanwhile, Melish took a position with the Southern Conference Educational Fund, Inc. He also had become the principal spokesman for the Religious Freedom Committee, formed in 1954.

Suddenly, on May 17, 1960, the 600 delegates to the ninety-third convention of the Diocese of Long Island were asked by DeWolfe to declare the Church of the Holy Trinity extinct. According to Sidener, the parish no longer had twenty-five attending or contributing members nor a sufficient number of male persons qualified to serve as wardens and vestrymen. When the motion was put before the convention, it received the loud applause of the delegates and not a voice was heard against. Melish was present at the session, but neither he nor any of his supporters protested. Apparently there had been no hint of the proposed action prior to the moment it was brought to the convention.

The future of the church structure remains in doubt. Diocesan authorities denied that there is any plan to reactivate the parish under a different name. Rumors were heard that the structure might be sold, especially since two other Protestant Episcopal churches—St. Ann's and Grace—amply serve the neighborhood. From more reliable sources came reports that Holy Trinity would be used for some diocesan project or institution. The possibility still remained that Melish supporters would resist any attempt by diocesan officials to occupy the premises. Meanwhile, John Howard Melish, the eighty-five-year-old rector emeritus, ill with Parkinson's disease, continued to reside in the nearby rectory and receive an annual pension of $7,694.

THE MELISH TESTIMONY IN 1954

In June 1954, the Subversive Activities Control Board held hearings on the National Council of American-Soviet Friendship, which was contesting an Attorney General's order that it register as a Communist organization. The principal government witness was Louis F. Budenz, former editor of the *Daily Worker,* who had returned to the Roman Catholic Church and joined the faculty of Fordham University. Budenz's integrity was a matter of public debate. Senator Dennis Chavez of New Mexico, himself a Roman Catholic, arose on the Senate floor in 1950 to denounce him.

As a private citizen and a public witness, this man has impeached and exposed himself as a devious, conspiratorial, warped personality who uses words and information as instruments of propaganda and not for their intrinsic truth. Budenz is constitutionally unable to give a straight answer, justifying his foul means by the perverted ends he seeks. I do not think he knows truth from falsehood any more.[26]

Budenz readily "identified" a long list of "Communist Party members" for the Subversive Activities Control Board—among them, William Howard Melish, William B. Spofford, Sr., Richard Morford, Joseph F. Fletcher, and several other clergy. The evidence he produced was at best scanty. Under cross-examination, he would give some unverifiable account of meeting the accused at "an enlarged National Committee meeting" of the Communist Party or of hearing from some party leader "officially" that the person in question was a party member.

There were innumerable contradictions between the Budenz charges and the testimony of others. One interesting case involved William B. Spofford, Sr., whom Budenz said he met in the forties, "sometimes for lunch, sometimes on the street, sometimes at small meetings held in mid-Manhattan" to "discuss Communist Party matters." Spofford, he said, had been especially interested in Communist penetration of certain educational institutions, such as Columbia University and Union Theological Seminary.[27]

A month later Spofford gave his side of the story. He had, he said, met Budenz in 1934 under curious circumstances. In the early thirties, A. J. Muste had led an independent political group known as the Conference for Progressive Labor Action in which Budenz had been a leader. Budenz had a frontal-sinus condition that necessitated a serious operation in 1934. Bishop Robert L. Paddock paid for the operation, and Spofford, on a mission of mercy, brought the money to Budenz' home in Brooklyn. "Did you ever meet Mr. Budenz socially after 1934, on the street, for lunch, or at meetings?" Spofford was asked. "No. No. I am sure not," he replied.[28]

Neither Spofford nor Budenz, upon whom the burden of proof rested, offered any concrete evidence to prove their contentions. Among those who knew Spofford personally, including those who emphatically disagreed with him, there was general agreement that his word should be accepted. He had always been forthright in espousing his unorthodox political associations and views and it would have been totally out of character, they felt, for him to conceal his past under fire.

Budenz had much more to say about Melish. In "late 1944 or early 1945" he claimed that he visited him at the Holy Trinity rectory to find out more about Melish's attitude toward the Communist Party before his selection as chairman of the National Council of American-Soviet Friendship. Budenz recalled the conversation.

In substance, I said that I was aware that Mr. Melish was a member of the Communist Party and that our discussion would be on that level. I discussed the question of his attitude toward Communist Party leadership and the matter of Communist Party discipline. Mr. Melish declared that he understood these matters thoroughly; that he had the highest regard for the leadership of the Communist Party and its integrity; that he thought the leadership of the Communist Party was in [*sic*] inspiration for all those who were interested in progress; and that his attitude was in becoming a Communist, to become one who understood fully the obligations which rested upon a member of the vanguard of the proletariat. There was more discussion to the same effect, but that is the substance of it.[29]

Melish gave an entirely different account. Checking his memorandum book, he said that Budenz had come to see him on May 5, 1944, at 10 A.M. The reason for his visit was to ask Melish to write an article for the *Daily Worker,* which he agreed to do. Melish then responded to this series of questions.

Q. Did you have any discussion with Mr. Budenz about the Communist Party discipline?

A. I did not, sir.

Q. Did you tell Mr. Budenz in that conversation that you fully understood the obligations which rested upon a member of the vanguard of the proletariat?

A. No.

Q. Aside from this one conversation which you had with Mr. Budenz or on the preceding telephone conversation, have you ever had any other conversation with Mr. Budenz on any occasion whatsoever?

A. To the best of my knowledge on no other occasion.

Q. Reverend Melish, are you a member of the Communist Party?

A. I am not.

Q. Have you ever been a member of the Communist Party?

A. I never have been.[30]

The testimony of Melish brought out a number of other interesting points. He testified that "to my knowledge" no members of the board of directors of the National Council of American-Soviet Friendship were Communists.[31] He had joined the May Day parades because "I was interested in the identification of . . . the clergy with the masses of the people here in the city. . . ." [32] He recalled that he had first become interested in Russian War Relief as the representative of Bishop James P. DeWolfe. DeWolfe, he said, telephoned him when Melish was on vacation in Lake George and asked him to return to New York to attend an organizational meeting of Russian War Relief.[33] Melish at first denied that he was ever a sponsor of the Daily Worker Fund Campaign of 1945, and when confronted by a photostatic copy of the newspaper listing his name, testified that he could not remember being a sponsor. One of the most surprising interchanges also involved the *Daily Worker.*

Q. Reverend, do you know as a matter of fact, that the Daily Worker is the official organ of the Communist Party in the United States, or at least the official news organ?

A. That is hearsay. I don't know that, sir, of my own knowledge.[34]

Melish was asked a number of questions regarding his views on Communist theory and practice. While his interrogators proved themselves incompetent in the field and while Melish seemed at many points either hesitant or evasive, he did make a number of significant observations. "I do not describe myself as a Marxist," he said.[35] He saw Marxism as containing "an element of truth" and "an element of falsehood." He chose "at random" two points at which he disagreed with the Marxists: their "doctrine of man" and their "general optimism as to social organization and the ease with which the human problem can be solved by social organization." [36] He also denied the Marxist doctrine that religion is a temporary state that will ultimately pass away in a Communist society.[37] "I disagree with that point of view," Melish said, "but I am not afraid of that point of view." [38]

Did he believe that a person could be both a Communist and a Christian? At first Melish responded: "I would not advise any individual that they can be both, but I do know there are Christians in the world today who do believe that they can be both living in other countries." He then confessed, "I don't know the answer, sir." [39] A few minutes later he said: ". . . a Christian may be a Communist in terms of his view of society from a Christian premise but he may not in my opinion be a Communist in terms of the Marxist philosophy." [40]

Perhaps in these words Melish was summarizing his own view. He may, as he suggests, reject such facets of Marxist philosophy as its utopianism, its view of the nature of man, and its atheism. But Melish was an ally of the Communists before and during the postwar decade. As a person of considerable intellect and perception, he was hardly as naïve about time-honored party organs as the *Daily Worker* as his 1954 testimony indicated. He earnestly believed that the Soviet Union, whatever mistakes in judgment it might make, was the vanguard of a better and socialist world. The ten-year controversy that focused upon him only made him hold on to this view with greater resolve.

There are several ways of assessing the Melish case. It had a dramatic quality that, in the eyes of many churchmen, reached humiliating proportions. The legal issues it raised were complex and the decisions of the courts will prove to be historically significant. The religious undercurrents and the clash of strong personalities added other dimensions to the controversy. Most of those outside of Holy Trinity who came to Melish's support saw freedom of the pulpit at stake. His opponents believed as sincerely that they were protecting the church from usurpation and subversion.

After more than twelve years of rancor, costly court battles, and scandalous public exhibitions, the strife succeeded only in the dissolution of a historic congregation and perhaps the permanent closing of a beautiful old church.[41]

American Unitarianism takes pride in its tradition of freedom. It has no official creeds and no required liturgies. The independence of each of its 110,000 members, like that of each congregation, is zealously preserved and nourished. Unitarians run the theological gamut from theism to agnosticism and naturalism. There are those who call themselves Protestants and those who prefer to avoid any identification with Christianity whatsoever. It is not surprising, therefore, that some persons with unorthodox views either in theology or politics—or in both—should be attracted to Unitarianism rather than to more traditional sects.

American Unitarianism arose in the late eighteenth century, principally in Massachusetts, still the church's stronghold. By 1805, it had won control of the theological faculty of Harvard University, and twenty years later a missionary and publication society was established. It was known as the American Unitarian Association, until its 1960 vote to merge with the Universalist Church of America to form the Unitarian Universalist Association. In the offices of the A.U.A. on Beacon Hill, across from the Boston Common and next door to the gold-domed State House, a fierce controversy broke into the open in 1947. The issue was alleged pro-Communism in the *Christian Register,* the denominational magazine founded in 1821.

In 1943 Stephen H. Fritchman, a minister and journalist, became editor of the *Register.* Fritchman, then forty-one, was born in Cleveland, educated at Union Theological Seminary, and ordained first as a Methodist minister. After joining the Unitarians, he served parishes in Massachusetts and Maine. In his varied career, he had been religious editor of the New York *Herald Tribune* for three years, had taught English literature at New York and Boston Universities, and had written several books. In 1938 he became director of American Unitarian Youth and remained in that post until 1947, combining his work with the *Register* editorship after 1942. In whatever responsibilities he undertook, Fritchman displayed unusual vigor and ability, intellectual brilliance and eloquence, and personal magnetism.

By late 1945, charges were already being raised that the *Christian Register,* under Fritchman's direction, was serving as a medium of Communist propaganda. The accusations multiplied until Unitarians were divided into two camps—pro- and anti-Fritchman. Fritchman's defenders said his critics were trying to muzzle free speech and were throwing an ideological smokescreen around what was essentially a power struggle within the denomination. They argued, too, that the American Unitarian Association should have no authority to act as a censor over a magazine with a long record of independence. Fritchman's opponents replied that the *Register* under his editorship was no longer a free voice, because, they said, pro-Communist views were solicited eagerly while anti-Communist views were systematically excluded. When the battle was over, Fritchman was out.

There were many early signs of Fritchman's general political orientation. In 1940, for example, he was a sponsor of the Committee to Defend America by Keeping Out of War and of other groups that were part of the Communist "peace" apparatus during the time of the Hitler-Stalin pact. The impact of his views upon the choice of articles in the *Register* became obvious in the special United Nations issue of the magazine in February of 1944. It included part of Paul Robeson's speech before the Massachusetts Council of American-Soviet Friendship; articles favoring the Communists in China and in the Baltic countries; a glorification of the Soviet Union by Albert Rhys Williams, called "Russia's Contribution to the United Nations"; and a review of Hewlett Johnson's *The Secret of Soviet Strength* describing it as a "must book" for 1944 and adding that "the millenial hope of the ages is now in process of realization on a grand scale— in Soviet Russia." [1]

In the World Order issue of November 1944, the same bias was apparent. Louis Adamic contributed a pro-Tito article on Yugoslavia.

Another piece, "The New Poland," praised Communist plans for that country. A Canadian missionary in China, Earl Willmott, discussed "China Youth Today" from a viewpoint sympathetic to the Communists there. Ilya Ehrenburg, leading Soviet writer, contributed an article and Dirk J. Struik reviewed Earl Browder's *Teheran, Our Path in War and Peace.* Struik wrote: "We believe that the study of this book can help every serious citizen to straighten out his ideas on war and peace." [2]

Early in 1945, a highly significant article appeared in the *Register,* by Howard Selsam, discussing the establishment of new schools "of the people": Jefferson School of Social Science, Samuel Adams School for Social Studies, George Washington Carver School, and others founded by the Communist Party. Selsam himself had been a leading party theoretician, and several of his books, including *What Is Philosophy?,*[3] have presented in academic terms the Communist view of religion. Fritchman served as a member of the board of trustees of the Samuel Adams School. Throughout 1945 the *Register* carried articles by Howard Fast, Paul Robeson, Harry F. Ward, and others who accepted the Soviet view of world affairs. During the same year, the *Register* started its campaign against Germany's Martin Niemöller—a campaign that continued into 1947. An editorial accusing Niemöller of pro-Nazi sympathies ended with these significant words: "If any doubt this, let them read the Religious News Service interview with Niemoller in which he blatantly preached Hitler's great sermon: distrust of the Soviet Union." [4]

Neither Fritchman nor the *Register* seemed to indicate any change of attitude with the rise of the cold war. He continued to give considerable time to a lengthy list of Communist-oriented activities, among them the American Slav Congress, National Federation for Constitutional Liberties, National Negro Congress, the *Protestant,* American Youth for Democracy, Joint Anti-Fascist Refugee Committee, National Committee to Win the Peace, Civil Rights Congress, People's Institute of Applied Religion, and the National Council of American-Soviet Friendship. He took a special interest in developments in China and sponsored the Committee for a Democratic Far Eastern Policy.

Fritchman's activities were carefully reflected in the content of the *Register.* Among the many articles on Oriental questions was an editorial attack upon Toyohiko Kagawa for his alleged co-operation with Japanese militarists; [5] similar stories on Kagawa were appearing in other pro-Soviet journals. An article in April 1946 attempted to sell *Register* readers the Women's International Democratic Federation, a worldwide Communist organization. In another piece, W. E. B. DuBois expressed his view that "it was Russia and Russia alone, under a communist regime, that saved the British Empire and the American Commonwealth from the domination of Germany, Italy, and Japan." [6] The 1946 World Order issue suggested that local churches might want to arrange special programs on international affairs on topics like "Georgia—U.S.A. and U.S.S.R." For materials on the American Georgia, readers were referred to the National Association for the Advancement of Colored People; for materials on the Soviet Georgia, the National Council of American-Soviet Friendship was recommended. [7]

THE BEGINNING OF THE CONTROVERSY

Fritchman's policy did not go undisputed. As early as December 1945, a letter from a leader among Unitarian youth, Charles M. Sherover, protested "the apparent political line of the *Register* editors who insist on consistently identifying the various communist groups in foreign countries as *the* democratic forces, and who see in the foreign policy of the Soviet Union the one and only hope and guiding star of democratic freedom and progress." [8] The following issue carried an interview with Hewlett Johnson which Donald Harrington, pacifist minister at the Community Church in New York City, denounced as "as brazen a bit of straight Communist propaganda as you have yet injected into the *Register*. Its obvious purpose is to lead uninformed people to believe that there is no difference between Soviet purposes, methods and practices and those of liberal, American democracy." [9] In reply to such criticism, Fritchman said the *Register* did not intend to "lend its pages to Mr. Hearst's and Mr. Howard's campaigns of hate against a great and honorable people." No "accurate" facts, however critical, that would help readers clarify their thinking about Russia would be refused space. But, he added: "Criticism, like charity, begins at home." [10]

The position of Fritchman that stirred most protests, however, was his attitude on civil liberties. The *Register* of January 1946, which included the interview with the Dean of Canterbury, also carried a Fritchman editorial attacking the American Civil Liberties Union for defending the right of free speech for Gerald L. K. Smith. "Can any Unitarian read the words of our American fascists and feel these things must be given free expression until they reach the stage that Europeans know too well, of cutting tongues and gassing ministers in Dachau?" [11]

First to defend the American Civil Liberties Union in the letter column of the *Register* was John Haynes Holmes, New York minister and president of the A.C.L.U. William B. Spofford, Sr., rushed to applaud Fritchman's position as "sound." [12] Later the same year, Fritchman, in an attempt to clarify his position, said he supported free speech—but only so far. "We believe Americans or Britons or Russians or anyone else has a right to decide that men are *not* free to preach race hatred, appeals to violence or incitement to aggression against peaceful neighbors." [13] This Fritchman stand on civil liberties alienated many ministers and made them more receptive to the charge that the *Register* under his editorship was not, in fact, open to diverse viewpoints on the critical issues of the day, especially in the field of foreign policy.

Controversy began to mount. A few local parishes canceled all their *Register* subscriptions. In September 1946, the first written protest from within Unitarian headquarters was prepared by Melvin Arnold, who had recently been chosen director of the new division of publications. Arnold accused Fritchman of allowing "free criticism of every national and international policy which is also criticized by the U.S.S.R., but never the reverse." [14]

Meanwhile, conservatives within the denomination were being aroused. Larry S. Davidow, a Detroit lawyer, demanded immediate action. Davidow accused Fritchman of "a studied and deliberate campaign" of proselytizing on behalf of "the Communist Party cause." The board of directors of the American Unitarian Association refused by a 25-6 vote to remove Fritchman, but appointed a committee of four, including Arnold, to "advise" Fritchman in publishing the *Register*.

Through the winter of 1946-47, the climate of conflict grew more and more heated. Under pressure from both conservatives and liberals, Fritchman resigned as director of the American Unitarian Youth in January, after nine years in that position. The reason officially given was that he needed more time to devote to the *Register*. The content of the *Register* changed considerably under the careful scrutiny of the advisory committee of four. But Fritchman had not surrendered, and many ministers rallied to his support because they were convinced that the very essence of Unitarianism—its freedom—was in danger of being stifled.

Fritchman's opponents were organizing for battle. Among conservatives, a little booklet entitled *The Strange Case of Mr. Fritchman* had considerable influence. It was written by Edward Wilcox, a minister in Lynn, Massachusetts, who accused Fritchman of affiliation with twenty-four Communist fronts. Another Massachusetts minister, Wilton E. Cross of Taunton, urged individual churches to withhold all contributions to the United Unitarian Appeal until Fritchman was replaced. Anti-Fritchman liberals led by Harrington, Holmes, and Arnold were aided considerably by Homer A. Jack of Chicago, who circulated his pamphlet *The Threat of American Communists to the Liberal Church and Other Institutions*. A. Powell Davies, fighting pastor of All Souls Unitarian Church in Washington, D. C., added his eloquent and influential voice against Fritchman's retention.

Fritchman and his chief antagonist, Melvin Arnold, conflicted sharply in personality as well as ideology. Arnold became convinced that the pro-Soviet bias of the *Register* was not accidental or the result of naïveté, but reflected its editor's loyalty to the Communist program. Why else, he asked, would Fritchman go outside the denomination to solicit articles by many contributors who "are either part of what might be termed the *New Masses–Daily Worker* coterie, or are leaders in organizations in which there admittedly is a considerable communist participation." [15] Later Arnold issued a directive as director of the division of publications, which included this statement of policy:

The Division of Publications, in selecting authors and editorial contributions, is not engaged in "selling" month in and month out either the status quo or any closed system of ideas, or values, or "isms"—social, economic, political, theological—whether advocated by high, low, middle, left, or right. As an example, we are not in the business of press-agenting capitalism, socialism, communism, Marxism, Single Taxism, and so forth —or of the status quo. As a corollary to this, we in our selection of authors and articles do not have any "sacred cows"—we do not recognize any ideas, system, or countries as either above criticism or as subject only to kid-glove handling.[16]

A crisis came in April 1947, when the May issue of the *Register* was in preparation. Fritchman had written an editorial, "Americans Bearing Gifts," in which he berated the "irresponsible" Truman Doctrine as well as most other major aspects of United States foreign policy. "The forces for evil and those for good have never represented such vast combinations as at this hour in history." On the evil side he placed American policymakers under the influence of "a few Americans desiring investments and foreign markets." He denounced the substitution of "Truman's two worlds for Franklin Roosevelt's and Wendell Willkie's one world."

Contrary to the procedure outlined by the board of directors of the American Unitarian Association, Fritchman failed, before he left on a nation-wide speaking tour, to submit page proofs of his editorial to the committee assigned to work with him. Arnold spotted the editorial, telegraphed Fritchman in Oklahoma that the committee would not accept it, and urged his immediate return to Boston if he objected to its deletion. Fritchman did not return. The statement of the Unitarian Commission on World Order on "The Greek Crisis" was put in its place. The statement opposed both the Communists and "the present government" of Greece, asked for economic assistance, but urged "extreme caution in proceeding with financial and military aid to Greece." [17]

Fritchman was infuriated. He denounced it as outright censorship and on May 8 sent a letter to all ministers announcing his plan to resign as editor and then to appeal his case to the entire denomination. Meanwhile, the executive committee of the board of directors suspended him from his editorship. The move was supported by Frederick May Eliot, the distinguished president of the American Unitarian Association. At the annual May Meetings of the denomination, held in Boston a few days later, Fritchman's supporters insisted upon his reinstatement. Most of them did not share his political views but believed that freedom of the press was at stake. Others pointed to faulty organization, to giving Arnold authority over the publications of the church that seemed to overrule the powers of the *Register* editor. "A paper cannot be edited by two individuals unless they are heavenly twins!" one group wrote. They asked that Arnold's apparent right of veto be rescinded.

Fritchman and his opponents both raised the political issue. In his remarks to the May Meetings, he traced his difficulties to his refusal to utter "a few vitriolic words on the Soviet Union" and to give "a friendly salute to the irresponsibles who are determined to have profits even if it means atomic desolation." [18] At the same session, Davidow dramatically pointed to Fritchman and shouted: "I insist he is a communist and I invite him to start action on libel!" Davidow described the *Register* as "a Beacon St. edition of the Daily Worker." [19] Most of the discussion, however, focused upon freedom of the press—one group insisting that Fritchman had destroyed it, another saying that he was trying to save it.

After a tense debate, the delegates to the May Meetings voted overwhelmingly to uphold Fritchman's expulsion. Soon thereafter, Arnold became managing editor of the magazine, while the American Unitarian Association appointed a rotating board of editors to write the editorials; Arnold continued until 1956 in his post as director of the publication division and of its book-publishing arm, the Beacon Press.

The dismissal of Fritchman was rigorously denounced in various Protestant journals. Guy Emery Shipler, editor of the *Churchman,* wrote an article on "The Unitarian Gestapo" which began: "Up at the charming Unitarian vatican. . . ." [20] The *Witness* accused the Unitarians of "tossing principles out the window." [21] Fritchman was "too liberal to satisfy the reactionary members of the church," *Zions Herald* said, and complained: "We can no longer look to the Unitarians for liberal leadership. . . ." [22] The Universalist *Christian Leader* commented that "no editor worth his salt could work long under the conditions laid down for Fritchman." [23]

The battle was not quite over. Fritchman's supporters organized a Committee of 100, including thirty-seven ministers, which distributed a twenty-page *Letter to Unitarians*. They accused Fritchman's critics of using "disreputable methods . . . such as wire tapping, efforts to search Mr. Fritchman's apartments and files, trailing his movements, opening his office safe, furnishing the House Un-

American Activities Committee with so-called 'evidence' against him, then turning to this committee (which Unitarians twice denounced, in May Meetings, 1946 and 1947) for material to use in discrediting him." [24] Fritchman's liberal critics denied that they were involved in such abuses and blamed them on some overzealous laymen.

Meanwhile, Friends of Democracy, an independent research and educational organization in New York City, prepared a special report analyzing the contents of the *Christian Register* for 1945 and 1946. It charged that under Fritchman's editorship the magazine had been "one-sided . . . almost invariably supporting a pro-Communist line," and assailed this "consistent pro-Communism" as "incompatible with liberalism." [25] The report dealt a severe blow to the Committee of 100 and other Fritchman partisans. Friends of Democracy had a strong New Deal–Fair Deal bias and commanded considerable respect among liberals. It was headed by a fellow Unitarian minister, Leon M. Birkhead, a colorful crusader who had devoted many years of his life to fighting anti-Semitism, white supremacy, and "native fascism."

The controversy began to subside, and the whole issue lost its impetus when Fritchman accepted a call to the First Unitarian Church of Los Angeles in 1948.

AMERICAN UNITARIAN YOUTH AND UNITARIAN SERVICE COMMITTEE

While the *Christian Register* was the focal point of attention, other controversies embroiled two other Unitarian agencies—one within American Unitarian Youth, which also concerned Fritchman; the second in the Unitarian Service Committee, through which the denomination had been conducting extensive relief work in Europe since the close of World War II.

In 1938 Fritchman had assumed the leadership of the Young People's Religious Union, later known as American Unitarian Youth, now merged with the Universalists into Liberal Religious Youth. Resolutions passed by the youth group (A.U.Y.) in 1945 gave rise to the question of Communist influence. They censured United States foreign policy on many counts, including the refusal to support "independence to colonial people as proposed by the USSR," the "allied intervention against democratic forces in Belgium, Italy, Greece and

Trieste, the bolstering of the reactionary Kuomintang government faction in China with no aid to the anti-Fascist 'Communist' Chinese armies, and the repeated acts of our military government in Germany, discouraging democratic movements and perpetuating Nazism." On the domestic scene, they expressed abhorrence of "red-baiting" and demanded "the outlawing of the Fascist forces that spread these poisons." [26]

One former A.U.Y. leader became involved with those who supported the postwar effort to develop a world-wide pro-Soviet youth movement. Mrs. Martha Fletcher, an energetic and charming young woman who had assisted Fritchman in his youth work from 1943 to 1945, served for three months in 1945—immediately after she had left the A.U.Y. staff—as chairman of the U.S. Arrangements Committee for the World Youth Conference held later that year in London (though she did not attend). The same Mrs. Fletcher was later accused by Herbert Philbrick of heading his Communist cell, a charge which she denied.[27] In 1949 she went to France, later returned, and is today with her husband, who teaches at a Midwest college.

Out of this World Youth Conference in 1945 developed the World Federation of Democratic Youth, an international Communist front. Its chairman was a Communist deputy in the French Assembly; its two secretaries were Communists from Great Britain and Australia; three of its four vice-chairmen were either Communists or within the Communist orbit at the time. Yet, stirred by postwar feelings of international good will and urged on by Fritchman, the A.U.Y. conference decided in 1946, by a 46-0 vote (one abstention), to affiliate with the World Federation of Democratic Youth.

The same summer in which Fritchman resigned from his A.U.Y. work, the youth organization voted to have a committee conduct a full study of the World Federation of Democratic Youth to decide whether affiliation should be continued. Charles W. Eddis of Toronto, now a Unitarian minister, directed the investigation. In a lengthy report submitted by the committee, the World Federation was described as "predominantly a communist-run organization" in which liberals had little possibility of influence. The report warned that most liberal groups had either withdrawn or been suspended and that A.U.Y. soon may be "the only non-communist youth organization in the sea of communists and communist supporters in the WFDY."

Yet, in an effort to give the full picture, the Eddis study acknowledged certain benefits in continued affiliation—an "opportunity to meet, work, play and exchange ideas with the youth of the world" and to portray "to the world, America and the West as it really is, not as the Soviet Union would like to see it portrayed. . . ." [28]

The A.U.Y. report was circulated widely, not alone among Unitarians, but among other youth leaders as well. Its impact was felt immediately. In 1948 the A.U.Y. voted to sever all connections with the World Federation of Democratic Youth, charging that it was an "instrument of communist policies."

Controversy raged also over the relief work of the Unitarian Service Committee in Europe and, especially, among the refugees of the Spanish Civil War. Foes of the Franco regime—democrats, Socialists, Communists, and others—had poured into southern France after the final defeat of the Loyalists. Reports began to come from the Mediterranean city of Toulouse that the workers were aiding Communist refugees but refusing help to Socialists and others. Members of Solidaridad Democratica Espanola, Spanish Socialist organization, filled out affidavits making even more serious charges that the flag of the French Communist Party waved over the Unitarian headquarters, that pictures of Marx and Stalin were hung on the walls of the hospital maintained by the U.S.C. and that 90 per cent of the Toulouse staff were Communists. Norman Thomas and other American Socialists began to protest to the Boston headquarters of U.S.C.

In 1946 the executive committee of the Unitarian Service Committee was shown a copy of a letter to Reinhold Niebuhr written from Paris by Francis A. Henson, who had served briefly in the early thirties as executive secretary of the National Religion and Labor Foundation and as cosecretary of the American League Against War and Fascism. The letter charged that Madame Herta Tempi, director of U.S.C. work in France, was a secret member of the German Communist Party, and that Noel H. Field, U.S.C. European director, was a member of the American Communist Party at least and probably was an N.K.V.D. agent.[29] A committee of three was named to investigate: William Emerson, chairman of the Unitarian Service Committee; Edward A. Cahill, minister and associate director of U.S.C.; and John Howland Lathrop, minister of the Church of Our Saviour in Brooklyn. The three went to Europe, investigated, and returned with the verdict that the charges were false.

Despite this report, uneasiness about the situation continued.

During the war the Joint Anti-Fascist Refugee Committee designated the Unitarian Service Committee as "its sole agent for relief in France." From January 1, 1943, to September 20, 1946, it gave the U.S.C. a total of $270,000.[30] The Joint Anti-Fascist Refugee Committee was Communist-controlled and the question in many minds was: Would a Communist front entrust such a responsibility to an organization whose program was not "reliable"?

The role of Madame Tempi and particularly of Noel Field was even greater cause for concern. Field had been one of the mysterious figures of international intrigue. He was a tall, handsome intellectual who had worked in the thirties with the Department of State, then with the League of Nations. After the League's dissolution in 1940, Field became U.S.C. director for all European relief activities in the spring of 1941. In November 1938, J. B. Matthews had testified before the Dies Committee that Field was a Communist.[31] In later years Hede Massing, former wife of Gerhart Eisler, told how Field had worked with the espionage apparatus she headed in the thirties.[32] Both Mrs. Massing and Whittaker Chambers testified during the trial of Alger Hiss in 1948 about Field's Communist undercover work.

By the fifties, Field had become even more of an enigma. In 1949 he disappeared into eastern Europe, followed by his wife, his brother Hermann, and his foster daughter, Erica Wallach. Several times during the next few years his name cropped up in the various "treason" trials in eastern Europe. The Communists charged that the convicted "traitors" had collaborated with Field, described as an American intelligence agent. Suddenly, in 1954, Field and his German-born wife were released after five years in Communist jails. The Hungarian Government announced that they had been imprisoned on false charges, and immediately they sought and received asylum in Hungary. Hermann Field, freed a few weeks later by the Polish Government with similar official apologies, returned to the United States. At the time of the Hungarian revolution, Field issued a statement saying life was too "exciting" there for him to return to America.[33] In June 1957, he defended the suppression of the revolt and hailed "the onward march of Hungary and other countries of the Socialist camp along the highroad toward communism, which all other nations will ultimately follow in their own manner and their own good time." [34] Some observers have suggested that Field may have been a double agent.[35]

The Unitarians, of course, had no way of knowing all these things about Noel Field when they were evaluating the Unitarian Service Committee's European relief work in 1946. Had these facts been before them at the time, the committee who went abroad to investigate the charges doubtless would have gone with a clearer understanding and with a more skeptical attitude toward the sweeping denials of the U.S.C. workers in Toulouse. Most informed observers suspect that, unknown to its American sponsors, several persons—including Noel Field and Madame Tempi—were exploiting the Unitarian Service Committee in behalf of their own clandestine political activities.

Discussion of the overseas activities of the U.S.C. continued in 1947. Reports from other European countries also told of Communist infiltration. That year, Raymond B. Bragg, a Minneapolis minister, went to Boston to head the Committee. He visited Europe to make a first-hand study and also asked a fellow Unitarian clergyman, Jack Mendelsohn, to check on the political orientation of the work there. Mendelsohn's report confirmed in large measure the charges of serious Communist influence. In Vienna, he found that the U.S.C. office was staffed by Austrians who openly professed their loyalty to the Soviet Union. He discovered that Socialists and anti-Communist intellectuals in Vienna viewed the U.S.C. there as an appendage of the Austrian Communist Party. In Czechoslovakia, he also found the U.S.C. personnel overwhelmingly pro-Communist.

Obviously, Field had to go. Bragg had already dismissed Madame Tempi, who had taken all of the U.S.C. files with her when she left the Paris office. In September 1947, a unanimous decision was made to oust Field. Bragg's action was swift and thorough—which was not as easy only two years after the war as it would have been later.

If there had been just cause to mistrust the European relief work of the Unitarian Service Committee—which some still do not believe—that cause had now been removed. The U.S.C. program has come increasingly to merit the highest respect. The organization has become particularly noted for its excellent teams of doctors, teachers, social workers, and other professionals who have performed in educational and humanitarian projects in all parts of the world.

FRITCHMAN IN LOS ANGELES

After the critical year of 1947, controversy over alleged Communist influence within Unitarianism moved from the denominational offices on Beacon Hill to southern California.

Fritchman was invited to the First Unitarian Church over some opposition within the congregation as a result of the *Christian Register* dispute. The church already had established a radical tradition under Ernest Caldecott, who had served as pastor since 1933. But Caldecott's roots were deep in Los Angeles and he had a wide personal following there, even among conservatives who were not as favorably disposed toward Fritchman. Within a few months, there was a large turnover in the composition of the typical morning congregation; many familiar faces were missing, while many new ones were there. Aside from all political considerations, Fritchman's admirers considered his sermons timely and practical, his administrative abilities unusual, his personality an asset to the church in the community, and the program he directed as varied and always stimulating. His critics accused him of turning the church into a social club and of casting aside many old-timers, including faithful staff members.

Much that he has done in Los Angeles is praiseworthy. He played a central role, for example, in the battle against the loyalty-oath fever of the early fifties. As a result of a popular referendum and legislative action, California decided that all tax-exempt organizations would be required to declare annually that they do not advocate the overthrow of the national or state government. Fritchman immediately protested, and on February 21, 1954, a special membership meeting of the church adopted by a 206-31 vote a resolution instructing the Board of Trustees to refuse to make such a declaration. Many clergymen of other denominations felt similarly, and a few other churches were equally defiant. During the course of the controversy the Bill of Rights Fund, established in 1954 under the chairmanship of Corliss Lamont, awarded the First Unitarian Church $1,000 "to assist in that institution's court battle" against the California oath. The issue was finally settled when the United States Supreme Court ruled that the law was unconstitutional.

But a number of events tended to alienate the liberal support that may have otherwise coalesced around Fritchman.

First, the church's Unitarian Public Forum brought to the city a large number of prominent pro-Soviet speakers: Dirk J. Struik, Harry Bridges, Anna Louise Strong, Paul Robeson, Victor Perlo, Maud Russell, Leo Huberman, Harry F. Ward, and many more. But other views were represented, too, as in April 1952, when Bishop G. Bromley Oxnam participated. Oxnam was questioned about this during his public hearing in 1953. His reply jolted Fritchman.

> I received an invitation to lecture at a forum which was held at the First Unitarian Church. I also lectured at the Santa Monica forum and at the Westwood Hills Methodist Church. I had no knowledge whatsoever that Mr. Fritchman was in any way related to the Communist Party.
>
> May I say this, that since that time and I will not name the men, but two prominent officials of the Unitarian Church have conferred with me and gave me information that gave me grave doubts concerning Dr. Fritchman, and had I known what they informed me I would, of course, not have lectured at his church.[36]

Soon after the Oxnam hearing, the Un-American Activities Committee released the text of Fritchman's testimony at an executive session given two years before, in 1951. Fritchman had pleaded the Fifth Amendment to all queries regarding his affiliations, including the question: "Are you a member of the Communist Party, Reverend Fritchman?" However, Fritchman told the committee—and reiterated in a letter to Oxnam—that he had denied membership in the Communist Party under oath on an earlier occasion.[37]

Working closely with Fritchman in the Los Angeles church have been a number of persistent Soviet apologists, among them Hugh Hardyman, a leader in the Communist peace campaign, Earl Robinson, a favorite folk-artist in popular demand at Communist gatherings, and Martin Hall, a free-lance lecturer and writer specializing in foreign affairs. Hall claims to have been an active member of the anti-Nazi underground in Germany from 1933-36.[38]

Fritchman became a severe critic of American Unitarian Association leadership and of the general direction of denominational policy.

"I tremble at times when I see how respectable we Unitarians are becoming," he said in 1954. "If we are not careful we will be invited into the National Council of Churches." [39] In the early fifties, Fritchman's influence was strong in several Unitarian churches in the southern California area, though this influence seems to have lessened by 1958. Three congregations experienced splits during that period: the Unitarian Community Church in Santa Monica, the People's Church of San Fernando Valley in Van Nuys, and the First Unitarian Church of San Diego. These splits had many facets in addition to the political one and few persons involved were Communists or Communist sympathizers. However, in each case there was a small but vocal minority pushing hard for a program of social action reflecting the then current Communist Party position.

A brief recapitulation of events in San Diego is illustrative. The conflict focused particularly upon speakers who were invited to the church by a lay group headed by Harry C. Steinmetz, a member of the faculty at California State College.[40] Peter H. Samsom, the minister, felt that Steinmetz and his political compatriots were trying to turn the church into a platform for fellow travelers and, as a result, were bringing the church into disrepute in the city. To counter this, the Board of Trustees adopted a series of regulations restricting the freedom of the Steinmetz faction— regulations which led to outcries against "repression" and "dictatorship."

One of the incidents which forced the issue to a climax involved Jerome Davis, who came to speak in November 1952. The Board of Trustees had specifically ruled that publicity for speakers must be restricted to the use of the church's mailing list and its weekly bulletin. Davis, however, appeared on a telecast, during which the name of the church was mentioned. In his address on November 18 he placed the blame for the continued fighting in Korea on American war-profiteers. Conflict reached a new peak, and within a few months Steinmetz and his followers had been renounced by the church and had organized a small, separate group later known as the Community Unitarian Fellowship.

Some observers saw the struggle primarily in terms of the clash between Samsom (who went to Cleveland in 1956) and Steinmetz, both strong personalities. This was certainly an important part of the total picture. But political differences played a key role as well.

The splinter Community Unitarian Fellowship brought together Communist sympathizers, independent-minded radicals, and even a few old-time Socialists.[41] The Fellowship looked to Fritchman for inspiration and guidance.

Fritchman, meanwhile, was experiencing problems of his own. The 1956 crisis in the Communist world, beginning with Khrushchev's Twentieth Congress address and ending with the Hungarian revolution, caused him distress and concern. "Colossal errors were made in the Soviet Union which almost led to the destruction of the new revolutionary regime," Fritchman admitted in 1958. It was Fritchman's view that the "worst crimes of Stalinism" were chiefly the result of two factors: "the isolation of Russian Bolshevism in a threatening capitalist world, and the assimilation of the isolated revolution with the Russian tradition." The victory of the Chinese Communists "has finally marked the end of that isolation." The United States must bear much of the blame, Fritchman said, for contributing "to the making of a devil theory of Russia originated in New York and Washington. . . ." But he was heartened by reports of reform from within the Soviet Union which indicated "something fundamentally sound in the teachings of Lenin and of the socialist leaders, which few Americans in positions of prestige and power will yet admit." [42]

When the revolution erupted in Hungary, Fritchman expressed strong disapproval of Soviet repression. In a sermon of November 25, 1956, on the need for self-examination, he said of the Hungarian "rebellion": "I find individuals unwilling or unable to make a moral judgment on evidence coming to them not only from admittedly anti-Soviet sources, but also from on the scene British Daily Worker reporters who have sent eye witness statements of Soviet brutality against unarmed Hungarian Communists and Socialists on the streets of Budapest. Whether one's politics are left or right, one who lives a life of the mind and conscience and is no robot of current social forces should be able to make a moral judgment. Twenty-three London staff workers of the Communist Daily Worker did protest white washing of such brutality—four resigned." [43]

Nevertheless, Fritchman's identification with Communist causes continued. Soon after the Twentieth Congress, he contributed an article on "The Pulpit Perilous" to *Mainstream,* the Communist literary journal, in which he lauded Harry F. Ward, a former professor of his, as the "greatest" religious prophet of the present time.[44] In 1958 he wrote a chapter in the book *Toward a Socialist America,* a symposium including essays by such leaders within the pro-Soviet orbit as John Howard Lawson, Herbert Aptheker, Victor Perlo, W. E. B. DuBois, and Philip S. Foner. "Socialism of a modern, workable, scientific form," Fritchman wrote, "is sweeping the earth because there is no comradeship possible, no self-respect or fraternity possible, in the chaos of capitalist organization." [45]

Fritchman had co-operated with the Communist peace campaign at the height of its activity during the war in Korea. In May 1959, he attended and addressed the tenth anniversary meeting of the Communist-dominated World Peace Council in Stockholm, Sweden. "No five days of my life up to now," Fritchman stated in an ecstatic sermon upon his return, "can equal in importance these days from May 8 to 13. . . ." He hailed the Council's "truly great accomplishments during the past decade" which, he said, "have been suppressed or distorted beyond recognition in our press." Fritchman cited as its most impressive accomplishment the first Stockholm Peace Appeal.[46]

Then, in August 1960, the fifteenth anniversary of the bombing of Hiroshima, Fritchman traveled to Tokyo where he attended and addressed the sixth World Conference Against Atomic and Hydrogen Bombs. The host organization, the Japan Council Against Atomic and Hydrogen Bombs, was described by the New York *Times* as "a Communist-dominated group." [47] Non-Communists simultaneously sponsored a memorial meeting in Hiroshima.

Fritchman continues to be a subject for heated discussion when Unitarians of different views gather together to converse about denominational matters. His defenders still insist that he has been unjustly criticized, that he has suffered considerable discrimination both within and outside Unitarianism because of his honest convictions, and that he is a courageous, independent-minded radical rather than a devotee of the Soviet Union. His critics have been worried lest he become—and some see signs of this—a greater influence within the denomination. They remain convinced that his main loyalty is not to liberal religion nor to free inquiry, but that he has been and still is emotionally and intellectually committed to the aims and program of the world Communist movement.

TWENTY · CONFLICT WITHIN EASTERN ORTHODOXY

Moscow has not only been the focal point of the world Communist movement. It is the seat of the Russian Patriarch, who claims spiritual authority over Russian Orthodox churches throughout the world. Many Americans who profess that faith, however, refuse to recognize his authority, charging that he is a puppet of the Soviet Government. For more than forty years controversy has raged within the Russian Orthodox Church in America, and today three separate factions vie for support and for control of the church's vast properties.

Russian Orthodoxy was first planted upon the soil of the New World in the eighteenth century after the discovery of Alaska and the Aleutians by two captains of the Russian Imperial Navy. The Russian Orthodox Church was established in North America upon the arrival of eight monks at Kodiak Island in 1794. Many natives were converted, a bishop was appointed, and a cathedral was erected. When the United States purchased Alaska in 1867, the American Government promised to recognize the property and rights of the Russian Orthodox there. In 1872 the episcopal see was moved to San Francisco, and in 1905 to New York City.

Russian Orthodoxy in the United States received its principal impetus, however, with the return of large numbers of Roman Catholic Uniates to that fold. Toward the end of the nineteenth century many Carpatho-Russian and Galician Slavs from the Austro-Hungarian Empire emigrated to America. They settled in various industrial centers, especially in the Pennsylvania mining areas. Their forefathers had been Orthodox and had acknowledged the authority of the pope only under pressure from the governments of Hungary and Poland. They had been allowed to retain their eastern liturgy and such customs as the married priesthood.

A sizable colony of Uniates settled in Minneapolis. When the Roman Catholic bishop of the diocese refused to recognize their priest, Alexis Toth, because he was married, Toth and his 360 parishioners asked the Russian Orthodox bishop in San Francisco to receive them back into the Eastern Orthodox confession. Permission was granted in 1891—paving the way for the return to Orthodoxy of an estimated 225,000 Carpatho-Russians and Galicians.

Friction over the married clergy was the immediate but not the basic issue that caused the mass Uniate secession. Many came to America with a deeply rooted loyalty to Russia that had served as a symbol of animosity toward Polish and Austrian rule. Their ethnic bonds as Slavs superseded ecclesiastical ties forced upon them as a result of political fortunes. Meanwhile, the Russian Orthodox Church was also nourished by newer immigrants: peasants from the poorer western regions of Russia, who came for economic reasons and planned to return to their homeland; young men who left to escape conscription; political dissidents who fled rather than face forced exile to Siberia. This third group increased rapidly after the turn of the century, but most of them did not join the church, which they viewed as a tool of the Czar.

The Bolshevik revolution in 1917 abruptly cut the American church off from the mother church and ended all financial support from Russia. Many local parishes were thrown into confusion as a result of financial difficulties, personal ambitions, class differences, conflicts over church organization, and political issues. Some of these tensions had already found expression in hostility toward individual priests, many of whom were ill-equipped to cope with the situation. Priest-monk Gregory, rector of a church in Hartshorne, Indian Territory (Oklahoma), wrote "I consider my presence here among rude and insensitive former uniates meaningless. . . . Lately they have shown insincerity, hypocrisy, lack of confidence, and animosity toward the priest." [1] There were threats of major schisms. On February 7, 1917, *Russky Golos,* a revolutionary Russian-language newspaper published in New York City, carried an article about the "growth of independent Orthodox Russian churches in America." According to a statement signed by three priests, churches with a combined constituency of more than 5,000 had banded together to form a new ecclesiastical organization based on democratic principles.

Radicalism played a leading role in the disturbances. The Socialist Party, which had polled nearly a million votes in the 1912 Presidential election, had a strong Russian wing, which in 1919 was to become a dominant force in the new American Communist Party. Its members in some instances organized antireligious meetings. Comrade S. Zorin of New York traveled from city to city addressing Russian Socialist meetings on "The Truth about God" and "Religion and the State." When, in March 1917, he spoke in Ansonia, Connecticut, he invited the local Russian priest to debate him. The Russian-language Communist paper, *Novy Mir,* reported that he had "tremendous success. . . . There were 300 people. The priest did not come. He is jumping around in his church like a devil gone berserk, cursing socialists and all who follow them." [2]

Within the church there were those who interpreted the revolutionary situation in Russia as a signal to launch a fight against traditionalists among the clergy, institute broad ecclesiastical reforms, and unite the church with secular progressive forces. In September 1917, a priest in Philadelphia, Vasily Kurdiumov, urged the Russians there to seize church properties from the bishops. "Be brave, loyal to each other and strong!" he counseled. Remember that "we all came from the people. We are all children of the laboring family. . . ." [3] On October 31 of the same year, the "progressive party" within the Russian Orthodox clergy met in New York City under the leadership of the priest John Kedrovsky. The meeting endorsed such reforms as the marriage of bishops—which was forbidden. Some of the most violent reactions were among Russian Orthodox parishioners in Canada. In 1919 members of a parish in Toronto actually sold their church because the Bolshevik revolution had made God unnecessary. These developments, however, did not reflect most Russian sentiment in America, and certainly not among the clergy, even though many favored political changes in Russia, including the modification or complete abolition of the czarist system.

In the confusion following the establishment of the new Union of

Soviet Socialist Republics, three developments played an important role in determining the direction in which the church was to move: the Living Church movement was launched in the Soviet Union and secured a beachhead in America; the bulk of the Russian Orthodox parishes in the United States declared their autonomy from the church in the U.S.S.R.; a legal battle began for control of extensive church holdings.

KEDROVSKY, KARLOWITZ, AND BENJAMIN

To undermine the strength of traditional Orthodoxy, still a vigorous force among the masses of the people, the Bolshevik government was sympathetic to a short-lived reform effort in Russia popularly known as the Living Church. This abortive movement brought together a diverse group of churchmen: progressives, idealists, reformists, malcontents, and opportunists. At a *sobor* (conference) in the spring of 1923, they adopted many radical innovations in canon law, proclaimed themselves the proper authorities of the Russian Orthodox Church, and deposed the Patriarch and his Synod. In praise of the Lenin regime, one resolution read:

> The Sobor declares capitalism to be a mortal sin, and the fight against it to be sacred for Christians. The Sobor sees in the Soviet Government the world leader toward fraternity, equality and international peace. The Sobor denounces the international and domestic counter-revolution, and condemns it with all its religious and moral authority.[4]

The Living Church appointed Kedrovsky, a married man, Archbishop of America. Kedrovsky returned to the United States, walked into St. Nicholas Cathedral in Manhattan, and announced: "I am the Metropolitan of the Soviet All-Living Church and I am here to take control of all Russian Church property."[5] His claim was immediately challenged by Archbishop Platon, head of the American diocese. Kedrovsky was a suspended priest, Platon said, and a married man could not be archbishop anyway. He was an instrument of the Soviet Government, and the *sobor* that appointed him was illegal, uncanonical, and political in its origin. Kedrovsky carried his fight to secure church properties to the courts in 1924. As though in support of his action, a document appeared, allegedly issued by Patriarch Tikhon, head of the whole Russian Orthodox Church, accusing Platon of "public acts of counter-revolution" and dismissing him from his office. The authenticity and authority of the document, as of many other documents during this chaotic period, were in doubt.

An American *sobor* was called at Detroit for April 1924 to clarify the status of the church and to resist Kedrovsky. The *sobor* proclaimed the Russian Orthodox diocese in the United States temporarily a "self-ruling church" until the meeting of an all-Russian *sobor* "which will be legally convoked, legally elected, [and] will sit with participation of representatives under conditions of political freedom. . . ." Resolutions termed the Living Church movement "a dissenting and separate sect" and attacked Kedrovsky as "a usurper and imposter from an inimical religious sect without any authority to speak for our church. . . ." Platon was unanimously elected "archshepherd and ruling bishop." [6]

Kedrovsky pushed his case in the courts. He had some appeal among the "white clergy"—a term referring to married priests. He attracted much more sympathy, however, among some American Protestants who interpreted the Living Church as a new Reformation. Two leaders of the Methodist Episcopal Church brought greetings from the United States to the 1923 Living Church *sobor* in Moscow. One was Methodist Bishop Edgar Blake, named as an honorary member of the *sobor*. The other was Lewis O. Hartman, later a bishop, then editor of *Zions Herald*. They promised the delegates $50,000 to assist the Living Church educational program. The promise created a severe controversy within Methodism, and the bishops of the denomination finally made an equivocal statement which expressed appreciation to Blake and Hartman while in effect repudiating the offer. Nevertheless, some funds were raised among American Protestants. Later, when Kedrovsky's suit reached trial, Hartman gladly testified about his observations in Moscow. The Living Church, he assured the court, was certainly the legal supreme church administration in the Soviet Union.

The Protestant denomination with the closest affinity to Eastern Orthodoxy, the Protestant Episcopal Church, took a strong position against Kedrovsky and, led by Bishop William T. Manning, issued statements and rallied its clergy in Platon's support. Indeed, such a close identification developed in the public eye that Platon's opponents imputed to him a plan to subordinate his diocese to the Episcopalians. George Craig Stewart, rector in Evanston (later Bishop of the Diocese of Chicago), summed up the reaction of many Protestant observers in the *Witness,* of which he was associate editor:

We hold no brief for reactionaries, but we submit that any ecclesiastical group of orthodox churchmen in Russia which at one meeting deposes its saintly patriarch, resolves to support and further an atheistic government, palliates the spoliation of its own shrines and holds out its hands of welcome to Protestantism, to Methodist theological courses and to Methodist money, is on the face of it disloyal to the foundation principles of the Holy Orthodox Church. It is not a reforming council, but a revolutionary rump parliament. We hope that American Methodists will carefully investigate the facts and repudiate the pact. America is careful not to recognize the Soviet government. Surely American Methodism will refuse to underwrite its ecclesiastical henchmen.[7]

The legal battle over St. Nicholas Cathedral, known as the First Cathedral Case, had a long, seesaw history. On December 24, 1924, the New York Supreme Court handed down a decision favoring Metropolitan Platon, basing its view upon three findings—that the 1923 Living Church *sobor* was invalid; that Kedrovsky was a married man and therefore not eligible for the episcopate; that Kedrovsky's control of the cathedral could have serious political effects. The court said:

There is a graver consideration in the attempt of this new Church, a product of the Russian dictatorship, to obtain control of a country-wide religious organization in America with hundreds of clergymen and branches scattered all over nearly all the states and having upwards of a quarter of a million members. The property used by the Russian Church totals in value an immense sum. If the Soviet authorities can gain control of all these, what a base for their revolutionary propaganda they will have secured.[8]

The Appellate Division of the court reversed the judgment in October 1925. Relying heavily upon the testimony of Hartman, it decided that the 1923 Living Church *sobor* was sanctioned by Patriarch Tikhon (deposed by this same *sobor*), that the Living Church's "Holy Synod" was continuing the prerevolution Holy

Synod, and that Kedrovsky had been duly appointed to head the Russian Orthodox Church in America. Curiously, a judge appointed Julius Hecker as commissioner of deeds to certify Kedrovsky's appointment. Hecker was a Russian-born American Methodist minister who had returned to the Soviet Union and became an enthusiastic and prolific writer in praise of the Bolshevik regime.

After April 1926, when he gained possession of the cathedral, Kedrovsky embarked upon a campaign to secure other Orthodox properties. His legal attempts failed, and less than half a dozen parishes voluntarily accepted his authority. Meanwhile, Trinity Church (Episcopal) in New York City invited Metropolitan Platon to hold services in the vestibule of its Chapel of St. Augustine. The sanctuary was converted into two chapels and the larger was consecrated in 1926 as St. Mary's Cathedral of the Russian Orthodox Greek Catholic Church of America. In 1943, the same group—which henceforth shall be described as the American Metropolia—dedicated the Protection of the Holy Virgin Procathedral on Manhattan's lower East Side.

Kedrovsky and Platon were not the only contenders for control of American Russian Orthodoxy. After the Bolshevik revolution, some areas in the south of Russia remained anti-Communist for many months. Isolated from Moscow, the bishops there organized a temporary synod. Eventually they gathered in Karlowitz in Yugoslavia and proclaimed themselves the legitimate ecclesiastical authority among Russian Orthodox throughout the world. The group has been variously called the Russian Orthodox Church in Exile, the Russian Orthodox Church Abroad, the Russian Orthodox Church Outside Russia, the Karlowitz Synod, and the Bishops Synod Abroad. From the outset, this group of *émigré* bishops and their followers—among them many of the elite under the czarist state—set as their goal the liberation of Russia. The first Karlowitz convention in 1921 passed this resolution: "And may (the Lord God) return to the all-Russian throne His Anointed, strong in the love of the nation, the lawful Orthodox czar of the House of Romanov." [9]

In 1923, the Bishops Synod Abroad recognized Metropolitan Platon as the rightful head of the churches of North America, but Platon refused to place himself under its authority. The bishops angrily withdrew their support, and this provoked the American Metropolia into a severe indictment of the Synod. "We have scandal and fighting enough from those who are our enemies," said a 1926 resolution. "For the sake of the welfare and dignity of the Church, and for the love we all bear to Christ and duty we owe to His Church, may we not be spared the destructive interference of those we call our brothers, but who are unable or unwilling to assist us? [Since] they are unable to build the Church in America, will they not please cease tearing it down and breaking it in pieces?" [10]

The Bishops Synod Abroad retaliated by appointing Bishop Appolinarius, Platon's own vicar for the State of California, as the only lawful archbishop of the Russian Church in North America. Two churches in New York City—the Holy Cross Cathedral of the Bronx and the Church of the Holy Fathers in Manhattan—joined with him, as did a small number of other parishes. This group was to be augmented after World War II when thousands of Russian *émigrés* fled to America from nations where the Communists seized control. In 1930 they were incorporated as the Ruling Bishop and Diocesan Council of the Russian Orthodox Catholic Church of the Eastern Confession.

By the thirties, therefore, the Russian Orthodox in the United States were faced with three alternatives: to affiliate with Platon's autonomous American Metropolia, Kedrovsky's Living Church, or Karlowitz's Bishops Synod Abroad. In 1933 still another contender was to enter the field.

This was a decisive year in Russian-American circles. The new Roosevelt administration established diplomatic relations with the U.S.S.R., a step sharply debated within the American Russian Orthodox churches. Many laymen strongly favored recognition, and the *Daily Worker* happily reported an episode in Cleveland where parishioners booed their priest when he spoke against it.[11] Perhaps more typical of devout Russian Orthodox sentiment in America, however, was a resolution unanimously adopted at the annual convention of the Federated Russian Orthodox Clubs at Detroit, Michigan, in September 1933. It accused the Communist Party in the Soviet Union of "viciously and inhumanly" attempting to eradicate religion and demanded that the United States refuse recognition until specific conditions were met: acknowledgment by the Soviet Union of the complete independence of the Russian Orthodox Church in the United

States; free and unmolested access by American citizens of the Russian Orthodox faith to churches and shrines in Russia; and the right of the church to carry on missionary activities in the U.S.S.R.[12]

The same year, Archbishop Benjamin Fedchenkoff, a former military ordinary of the White Russian Army—and ironically one of the founders of the Bishops Synod Abroad—arrived in New York from Paris for what was billed as a lecture tour. It was soon revealed that he was acting as representative of the Holy Synod in Moscow, then under Metropolitan Sergius. Benjamin brought with him a "pledge of loyalty" for Platon and clergy in America to sign. Its most important sentence read: "I will abstain from participating in political life in general and particularly in relation to the Soviet Union."

Platon refused to sign and reaffirmed the decisions reached at the 1924 Detroit *sobor* rejecting the authority of Moscow over the American church. Benjamin quickly proclaimed himself the new head of the Russian diocese in America, and on July 9 received the support of Metropolitan Sergius, who warned all Russian Orthodox to avoid communion with the "schismatics" following Platon's "rebellious" leadership. In August 1933, the Holy Synod in Moscow condemned Platon and suspended him and his followers from the church. Platon was specifically censured for following a course "directed to the benefit of party and class, and not faith and church, designed to satisfy an irreligious crowd blinded by political fanaticism and also conditioned by a shameful desire to take into account the wishes of non-Orthodox circles. . . ."[13]

Benjamin attracted only a meager following, known in conversation as the Patriarchal group. His headquarters and small chapel were in a Brooklyn apartment. By 1945, only thirteen parishes had recognized his authority, but he won enthusiastic support from pro-Soviet elements within the Russian-American press never before concerned with the welfare of the church. Chief among these was *Russky Golos,* which acclaimed Benjamin because "as a pro-Soviet newspaper [we are] solely interested in the question of loyalty to the Soviet Union."[14] Benjamin's presence in the United States was significant primarily because the Moscow Patriarchate now had a beachhead on American soil.

The period between Benjamin's arrival and World War II was a time of consolidation among Russian Orthodox in America. Two key personalities left the scene in early 1934. In March, fifty-four-year-old Kedrovsky collapsed while directing a rehearsal of his choir and died of a cerebral hemorrhage before medical aid could be summoned. The St. Nicholas Cathedral passed under the control of his son, Nicholas Kedroff. One month later, Metropolitan Platon died and was succeeded by Feodor Pashkovsky, who became known as Metropolitan Theophilus. Theophilus sought to unify warring Russian Orthodox factions and in 1935 was successful in achieving a *rapprochement* which continued for a decade with the Bishops Synod Abroad. He reached an accord also with an independent Carpatho-Russian diocese of about forty parishes. By 1940, Theophilus claimed jurisdiction over 400,000 faithful, divided into 330 parishes and eight dioceses.

INFLUENCES OF THE WAR PERIOD

When Nazi Germany attacked the Soviet Union in June of 1941, Russian-Americans took three distinctly different approaches to the crisis.

One small group had longed so fiercely for the destruction of Communism in the U.S.S.R. that they wished, though often secretly, that Hitler would crush the Soviet Government and prepare the way for the Czar's restoration. Many partisans of the Bishops Synod Abroad shared this viewpoint. After Germany's attack, Archbishop Vitaly, one of the Synod's prominent leaders in America, signed a petition to President Roosevelt imploring him not to assist the Soviet Union. "All Russians passionately wait for the coming of the blessed hour of their liberation," said the petition. "Russians will not voluntarily fight for Stalin, even if we send them our best military experts and give them the best American equipment. Every American dollar sent to the treasury of the Comintern would be considered by the Russians as an attempt by this country to prolong the agony of their miserable existence under the red yoke. . . ." [15]

A somewhat larger number not only supported Russia against Hitler's attack but were, or became, apologists for the Soviet regime. They were rarely Communists. Archbishop Benjamin typified this group and led the attack upon all who voiced disapproval of the

Soviet Government. He participated in the activities of a number of Communist fronts, although there is no indication that he was ideologically a Marxist. He traveled tirelessly across the country, visiting Russian Orthodox churches outside of his own jurisdiction. His fiery speeches blended the images of Holy Russia and the Soviet state into one. For the sake of God and country, he pleaded, all Russian Orthodox must return to the leadership of the Moscow Patriarchate. Later reports of Soviet victories deepened the conviction and increased the number of Soviet sympathizers. In a few Russian Orthodox parishes, the red flag was flown at services.

Most Americans of the Russian Orthodox faith stood between the two extremes. They continued to distrust the Stalin regime; yet news of the German destruction of cities and villages and the resistance of the population stirred them deeply. Their feelings were well expressed in the words of an Epistle issued by the bishops of the American Metropolia on October 9, 1941, two months before Pearl Harbor.

Having been separated from our motherland by a great distance, but spiritually being close to her always, we cannot be silent witnesses and passive spectators of the bloody Golgotha of our much suffering people. As our flesh and blood, we have to carry them in our hearts, suffer with their sufferings, weep with their bloody tears, and use all our efforts and means to save them. . . .

Other important developments during the war had great influence. The Orthodox Church in Russia, in a burst of patriotism, called upon all believers to join in resisting the Nazis in the name of their faith. Responding to this pledge of loyalty, Stalin loosened the restrictions on religious life. On September 4, 1943, high church dignitaries were received by Stalin and Molotov, who said they had no objection to the election of a patriarch—an office vacant since 1925. Four days later, eighteen bishops convened in Moscow and chose Sergius, who worked closely with the war effort until he died in May 1944. His last official act before his death was to send a message of gratitude to Bishop Manning, chairman of the Russian War Relief Clothing Drive in the United States. When Metropolitan Alexis was elected to succeed Sergius, he dispatched a letter immediately to Stalin, "the God-appointed leader of the peoples of our great union," which pledged loyalty "to the motherland and the government headed by you." [16]

The re-establishment of the Patriarchate was interpreted widely in the United States as evidence that the Soviet Union had abandoned its antireligious policies in favor of full religious freedom. Metropolitan Benjamin was unreserved in his enthusiasm. "It should be made clear that this does not place any degree of control or restraint upon the Church such as was exercised by the Czar," he said. "On the contrary, it guarantees the complete independence of the Church in that separation of Church and State is established by the Soviet Constitution." [17] Metropolitan Theophilus more cautiously called the patriarchal election "beneficial for the welfare of the Russian Church and people, provided the election was free and canonically correct." [18] The bishops of the Metropolia voted in October 1943 to elevate in prayer the name of the Patriarch of Moscow and All Russia at divine services, even though they publicly expressed doubts about his freedom. Meanwhile, the Bishops Synod Abroad, meeting in October 1943, in Vienna, deep in Nazi territory, condemned the patriarchal election as illegal and farcical.

The largest group of churches, affiliated with the American Metropolia, began to debate anew its attitude toward the Moscow Patriarchate. The pressures for affiliation were heavy. In addition to pro-Sovietism, pan-Slavism, and Russian patriotism, there was a growing sentiment that only spiritual ties with the mother church would keep Russian Orthodoxy in America alive. Many clergy also realized that if no attempt was made to reach some accord with the Moscow Patriarchate, churches might be forced by their parishioners to renounce the American Metropolia and join the Patriarchal group under Benjamin. Against all these factors was the continuing fear that the Moscow Patriarchate was not free, that the Soviet Government was using it as a political tool, and that relations with it would mean subjection of the American churches to Communist influences.

On January 31, 1945, a local *sobor* of the Russian Orthodox Church was held in Moscow. The American Metropolia sent two delegates, though they arrived in Moscow after the *sobor* had adjourned because of transportation difficulties. The new Patriarch Alexis presented to his United States guests a decree calling for an All-American *sobor* to elect a Metropolitan, subject to confirmation by the Moscow Patriarchate; he would bear the title of Patriarchal Exarch of All America (including South America) and Canada. The decree also warned as a condition of recognition by Moscow that the American Orthodox church must pledge to abstain from any political activities opposed to the interests of the U.S.S.R. and must give similar instructions to all churches. The council of bishops of the Metropolia formally rejected Alexis's proposals, expressing particular dissatisfaction over his endeavor to restrict their political freedom.

Nevertheless, in September 1945, Patriarch Alexis dispatched Archbishop Alexis of Yaroslav and Rostov to the United States to continue negotiations. At the airport he was met by representatives of the American Metropolia, by Benjamin and some of his followers, by a group from the Protestant Episcopal Church, by the Soviet Vice-Consul, and by members of the Civic Committee, an independent group of Russian laymen interested in establishing ties with the Moscow Patriarchate. The secretary of this Civic Committee was Alexander L. Kazem-Bek, a curious political figure in Russian *émigré* circles. Kazem-Bek was leader of an organization known as Young Russians which sought to arrive at some synthesis between monarchy and the Soviet state. Later he became a professor of Russian language and literature at Connecticut College in New London. In the fall of 1957 he left the United States for Europe under the pretext of getting medical treatment in Switzerland, but suddenly appeared in the Soviet Union, sharply castigated the United States as a land without culture, and announced his intention to remain in the U.S.S.R.

The visit of Archbishop Alexis did not clear away the roadblocks to reconciliation. He submitted three principal prerequisites—the Americans must recognize the authority of Patriarch Alexis; all ties must be broken with the Bishops Synod Abroad, which had fled Yugoslavia to Munich, Germany; an All-American *sobor* must be held under the Archbishop's chairmanship. If these conditions were met, again the Patriarch promised that his interdict against the American Metropolia would be lifted. In December 1945, the bishops of the Metropolia sent a firm reply: "Not having recognized the interdict laid on the North American Church, the Council does not deem it necessary to discuss the conditions for its removal." [19]

These ecclesiastical maneuvers could not fail to win attention within American Communist circles, especially among Communists of Russian origin. Their early postwar ambivalence toward the Russian Orthodox Church was evident from the discussion of religion at the

October 1945 session of the plenum of the American Russian Fraternal Society, most of whose leaders were Communists.[20] The speakers addressed one another as "Comrade," referred to the U.S.S.R. as "our Fatherland," and depicted the United States as fast becoming a "nest of fascism." The discussion of the church was raised by "Comrade K" of Hartford, Connecticut: ". . . some comrades believe that . . . since in the U.S.S.R. they allegedly observe religious rites, this is reason to do the same thing here. . . . It is necessary to correctly inform the Executive Committee [of the branches] about this issue." "Comrade R" noted that in "Bayonne [New Jersey] they are asking how they should behave toward the Church, and from other districts, too. This issue will become paramount. How should we behave?"

Considerable feeling that the traditional antagonism toward the church should be re-examined was expressed at the plenum. "Our relationship with the Church, under these conditions, cannot be what it had been before," one comrade said, and pointed out that the religious issue was closely related to the question of support of the Soviet Union within the Russian American community. Another speaker cautioned that the church should not be viewed as homogeneous; there were some progressive elements even if "the real estate is in Theophilus' hands." Still another observed that the church's aid to the Stalin government during the war "must be taken into account when we consider our relationship here. I think that it must be the task of our organization to do everything in order that these [church] people can unite with us." "My personal opinion," he added, "is that a religious man is a thousand times better than a nonreligious person who has anti-Soviet policies."

The discussion revealed considerable skepticism about *rapprochement* with the church. "Comrade B" reported on his experiences while touring the branches of the Society:

Some comrades sharply complain as though somebody ordered them to go to church. Nobody orders us to do that. But to go to the churchgoing masses—this we have to do. Indeed, the people in the churchgoing circles are no different in their character than we are. Their religion should be left alone, until they change their minds themselves. . . . For this there is the press and the literature. . . . To come to them directly, and to abuse them, would be incorrect. They should not question us about our views on religion, on belief, and neither should we question them, or criticize their spiritual conduct.[21]

There was danger also that some members of the American Russian Fraternal Society would go too far in displaying public enthusiasm for the church, especially in preparation for the arrival of Archbishop Alexis, anticipated at the time. One reported:

> In Bayonne, they want to become parishioners and in this way seize the church premises. . . . There is in some branches a wish not to wait until the priests organize the reception [for Archbishop Alexis] but to do it themselves first. This would suit Theophilus, so that he could say that the Archbishop had been sent by the "Bolsheviks" and that "Bolsheviks" turn out to greet him. . . . We must be very cautious on the religious issue. . . . There are members who are church members and members of the Society at the same time. We must give such members definite instructions.[22]

POSTWAR FRICTIONS INCREASE

The failure of Archbishop Alexis's mission to the United States was a severe blow to the cause of unity. Yet, the majority still wanted to strengthen ties with the mother church. Two bishops, several clergymen, and a number of leading laymen lost patience with the negotiations and left the jurisdiction of the American Metropolia to join Metropolitan Benjamin. These actions did not necessarily indicate pro-Soviet political views; more often they reflected the belief that separation from Moscow made the Metropolia schismatic. This sentiment might be better understood by hypothesizing a somewhat analogous situation within the Roman Catholic Church. If a Communist revolution in Italy somehow were to take away the freedom of the pope—possibly even forcing him to voice pro-Communist political views—many Roman Catholics in the world might still contend that on matters of faith and morals he would remain the supreme authority. In a similar manner, numerous Russian Orthodox in the United States have felt a keen desire to be under the spiritual authority of the Moscow Patriarchate.

In 1946 another attempt at reconciliation was made. The Metropolia officially requested a formal, though loose, affiliation with the

Patriarchate. When Alexis sent Metropolitan Gregory in the summer of 1947 to work out an agreement, however, Metropolitan Theophilus refused to meet with him, and in his discussions with other ecclesiastical officials, the obstacles proved insurmountable. The American Metropolia was unwilling to sacrifice some of the prerogatives of its autonomy. Rebuffed, Gregory issued a Pastoral Epistle before leaving the United States, calling upon all "wishing to seek their spiritual salvation in the one Holy Orthodox Church under the aegis of the Most Holy Patriarch of Moscow and All-Russia, Alexis, to unite until the time of complete general unity, around his legal representative in North America, the Most Reverend Macarius." [23] In 1947 Macarius had succeeded Metropolitan Benjamin when Benjamin received a new appointment in the Soviet Union at his own request.

With the breakdown in negotiations, the bishops of the Metropolia decided to postpone indefinitely any future consideration of ties with the Moscow Patriarchate. In a Pastoral Epistle, the bishops declared: "The only possibility at present, both for the Russian Church itself and for us, is the strengthening of one another in prayer upon the paths given us by God." [24] No serious attempt to bridge this chasm has been made since 1947. A Patriarchal Decree from Moscow, dated December 26 of that year, widened the gap even farther by declaring that Theophilus and his bishops were subject to an ecclesiastical trial for causing division within the church.

The political role of the Moscow Patriarchate helped consolidate the split. In March 1949, Alexis appealed to all independent Orthodox churches to stand against "warmongers"—an apparent effort to enlist world Orthodoxy, including its American wing, in the Communist "peace" campaign. [25] A year later, the bishops of the Soviet Union sent a message to Stalin, hailing him as "the teacher and friend of the workers." [26] Alexis gave full support to the Communist-inspired Stockholm Peace Appeal "in the name of the episcopacy, the clergy and faithful of all dioceses of the Russian Orthodox Church throughout our great fatherland." [27] Shortly after the outbreak of war in Korea, Alexis and the Holy Synod sent a message to the United Nations protesting "the inhuman extermination of the peaceful population of Korea taking place by the American air force." [28] The *Journal of the Moscow Patriarchate* was filled with distorted accounts of the Korean conflict, many of them excerpted from "peace addresses" of prominent Orthodox clergy. Metropolitan Nikolai assailed "the Anglo-American heads of imperialistic reaction," [29] who instituted "the bestial, bloody aggression of the U.S.A. in Korea" [30] and gave detailed descriptions of alleged American crimes. In a speech before a "peace" meeting in February 1951, Nikolai charged:

These civilized savages arranged shooting matches with living targets, binding peasants to posts with barbed wire and shooting each of them over the heart as the target. Reviving the customs of the young fascists, young yankees photographed these scenes for their family albums and sent them home to their fiances and wives. . . . Cases are known when children, born in prison, were trampled by the soldiers' boots in front of the mother, and then the mother was killed.[31]

During the postwar period, control of Russian Orthodox property, and especially possession of St. Nicholas Cathedral, again became a source of friction. The Living Church movement in Russia had collapsed quickly in the twenties, and after Kedrovsky's death the cathedral became, in effect, a family institution with a miniscule congregation and insufficient funds to keep the building in good repair. In 1945 the New York State Legislature passed a statute which recognized the administrative autonomy of the American Metropolia and required all properties in the state originally part of the pre-1917 North American diocese to be administered under its jurisdiction. An action began in the New York courts to recover St. Nicholas Cathedral from the Kedroff family. In an effort to ward off likely defeat in the courts, John Kedroff turned the cathedral over to Benjamin, who claimed it in behalf of the Moscow Patriarchate. A long litigation began. By 1952, the case had reached the United States Supreme Court, and in an 8-1 decision, it struck down the New York statute as an interference in "the free exercise of religion." The case was remanded to the lower courts for decision. As the appeals continued, the Patriarchal group maintained possession of the cathedral, and in 1956 Metropolitan Nikolai celebrated a three-hour pontifical liturgy there. In December 1959, the New York Court of Appeals decided, in a 4-3 decision, in favor of the Metropolia and the case was appealed to the United States Supreme Court. Then, in June 1960, the Supreme Court unanimously reversed the decision of the Court of Appeals, and the cathedral today seems to be firmly in the hands of the Patriarch group.

Those judges who have supported the claims of the American Metropolia have generally based their opinions upon the Communist issue. In 1949, for example, Justice John Van Voorhis of the Appellate Division of the New York Supreme Court summed up some of these arguments in a very pointed fashion. Instead of being schismatics, he said, the Metropolia is adhering to tradition "from which the Russian high church authorities departed when, yielding to force, they accepted what might be termed the Russian Orthodox Church of the Communist Obedience." [32] Since the Moscow Patriarchate has become a tool of the Soviet Government, it has in effect forfeited its rights as an ecclesiastical tribunal. To grant the representative of this Patriarchate the power to control American church property is similar to surrendering it to the Soviet Government. What, Van Voorhis asked, if the Nazis had taken Moscow and become masters of the Russian Orthodox Church? Would the American courts be obliged to turn the cathedral over to a Nazi-approved Patriarchal representative? "It is sound legal doctrine," he concluded, "to treat as null and void the words and acts of persons or officials who have been deprived of their freedom of action." [33]

Justice Joseph M. Callahan, on the other hand, pointed out that the freedom of the Russian Orthodox Church in the U.S.S.R. was not at issue. While it obviously was not free (nor had it been free under the czars, when the cathedral was built), it did exist and was conducting its affairs according to the canons of the church. Callahan summarized his view: "The law requires us to hold that the decision of the church judicatories on the question of whether bishops must be appointed or may be elected must be controlling on us, and the right to use the cathedral would rest in the archbishop selected by those judicatories." [34] Callahan's opinion on the case, like others before and after, tried to preserve the principle established in the famous case of *Watson* vs. *Jones* (1871), that the state must not pass judgment in disputes over dogma, discipline, or other internal affairs of a religious body.

While the case was in the courts, the Moscow Patriarchate appointed Archbishop Boris as the Exarch for North America in the spring of 1953. The State Department permitted the Archbishop to come to the United States on a sixty-day visitor's visa but would not extend his stay. In apparent retaliation, the Soviet Union ousted the

Roman Catholic priest Georges Bissonnette, who was serving American Roman Catholics in Moscow, and refused to allow Bissonnette's successor, Louis Dion, to take up his duties in the Russian capital.

To some observers, the solution seemed obvious. The United States should admit Boris in return for the Soviet Union's admission of Dion. Actually, the two cases differed radically. Russia's actions broke the Roosevelt-Litvinoff agreement of November 1933, recognizing the Soviet Government, in which the U.S.S.R. expressly agreed to allow clergy to serve in Moscow. The agreement was not reciprocal, probably because in 1933 the Stalin regime would have scoffed at the notion that, at any future time, the Soviet Union might be interested in sending clergy to the United States. Even had the agreement been reciprocal, however, it would not have applied to the Boris case. The clergymen provided for by the Roosevelt-Litvinoff agreement were expected to serve non-Russians. Boris would come to the United States to work almost exclusively with United States citizens. In the eyes of the State Department, Soviet church leaders had identified themselves with Soviet foreign policy to such a degree that it was awkward to have a Russian prelate guiding an American church.

Boris reacted sharply, publicly questioned the "Christianity" of the American Government, and hinted that the State Department decision was made under the influence of "renegade" Russian Orthodox. When asked if he approved of the atheistic, Communist regime, he evaded the question except to reply that at least the Communists did not interfere in church affairs, as the American Government did. Leaders of the Patriarchal group in America wrote an open letter to President Eisenhower, protesting the State Department decision, which, they said, "involves the deprivation by the Government of the rights of thousands of American citizens to exercise their religion in a manner they see fit." "Mr. President," the letter asked, "what possible harm can come of allowing Archbishop Boris to reside here in the United States? Will anyone seriously contend that he would constitute a threat to our 'internal security'? Whatever his political views may be, surely it may be assumed that out of consideration for his American flock, he will not express those views publicly." [35]

George Kennan, former ambassador to the U.S.S.R., came to the defense of Boris, and several Protestant journals also denounced the State Department action. The *Churchman* published a harshly worded article, reproving the American Metropolia and the Bishops Synod Abroad as well as the State Department.[36] The *Living Church* also opposed the State Department action, and the *Christian Century* observed: "The whole episode of Archbishop Boris' visa puts the United States in a petty light, as though seeking chances to indulge in pin-pricking with no better purpose than to annoy the Russians." [37] The New York *Times* warned editorially that the State Department was "venturing into dubious ground, both diplomatically and ecclesiastically." [38]

In January 1959, without explanation, the Soviet Union reversed its decision and Dion went to Moscow. The American Government, however, still refused to grant Boris the right to stay in the United States—but Boris has been visiting the churches under his jurisdiction from time to time on temporary visas.

The situation among Russian Orthodox believers in the United States remains uneasy. Each of the three factions continues to believe that it has adopted the correct position. The American Metropolia, officially known as the Russian Orthodox Greek Catholic Church of America, has by far the largest following—more than 350 parishes (about fifty of them in Canada) and perhaps more than a half-million adherents. Its ruling bishop is Metropolitan Leonty, and most of its younger priests are prepared at St. Tikhon's Seminary in South Canaan, Pennsylvania, and St. Vladimir's Orthodox Theological Seminary in New York City. The bulk of its membership are of Carpatho-Russian and Galician descent and of Roman Catholic (Uniate) background.

The Bishops Synod Abroad, now generally called the Russian Orthodox Church Outside Russia, claims a constituency of approximately 75,000 in the United States. In November 1950, it moved its international headquarters from Munich to New York City, and in 1958 it secured the famous George F. Baker mansion on Park Avenue for its church offices. The ruling prelate is Metropolitan Anastassy, and a seminary is maintained at the Holy Trinity Monastery at Jordanville, New York. The membership of the Russian Orthodox Church Outside Russia largely emigrated to America after World War II from Eastern Europe or from China, to which they had fled after the Bolshevik revolution. Many of them are nostalgically pro-czarist and descend from the Russian elite. The Synod also has dioceses in Latin America, Western Europe, and Australia and New Zealand.

The Patriarchal group, with an estimated 25,000 followers, is still known under the name of the Archdiocese of the Aleutian Islands and North America of the Russian Orthodox Church. Its parishes have varied in number from twenty to forty (a dozen of them in Canada). It maintains no seminary; one of its principal assets is its well-edited, bilingual publication, *One Church*.

How does this conflict among the three Russian Orthodox groups relate to the problem of Communism and the churches today? The threat of actual Bolshevik control of vast religious property in the United States has diminished considerably over the years. Opponents of the Patriarchal Exarchate have suggested that churches affiliated with Moscow could be serving as centers for Soviet undercover work, even espionage—but evidence has never been produced to justify such an assertion. Perhaps the most serious danger is that those who maintain ties with the Moscow Patriarchate will feel compelled to defend not only the acts of the church in Russia, but of the Soviet Government as well. They are also exposed to such Communist-influenced propaganda as that which the Moscow Patriarchate spread during the war in Korea. In short, they inevitably face the possibility of a serious conflict between their loyalty to the United States and to their mother church.

Balanced against this, however, is the sincere and understandable desire of the Patriarchal group to maintain the bonds with their co-believers abroad. They are motivated by religious considerations as far as can be discerned. Perhaps they are in serious error to continue ties with a Patriarchate exploited so obviously by the Soviet Government. But it would be less than fair to ascribe Communist political views to the Patriarchal Exarchate on the basis of the evidence available.

By 1960, there was some reason to hope that the Moscow Patriarchate might be taking a more outspoken stand against at least one of the government's policies: its active promotion of atheism. The *Journal of the Moscow Patriarchate* carried the terse announcement in June 1960 that the Holy Synod had excommunicated several priests, including a prominent professor of theology in Leningrad, for writing articles or pamphlets against the church that were published by the "atheist press" of the Soviet Union.

ROMANIANS AND ALBANIANS

The charge of Communist influence within a number of the Eastern Orthodox churches in the United States—Serbian, Bulgarian, Ukrainian, and others—has not been seriously pressed.[39] Two other nationalities, however, the Romanians and the Albanians, have been torn with political controversy instigated by the existence of Communist governments in their native lands. The facts are muddled by a vast complex of unsubstantiated charges and countercharges.

From 1900 to 1914, an estimated 100,000 Romanians emigrated to the United States, largely for economic reasons, many planning to return eventually to their homeland. About 75 per cent were Orthodox, and by the thirties, fifty parishes had organized a diocese which, though autonomous, requested the Holy Synod in Bucharest to send a bishop. In 1939, their bishop went to visit Romania, and never returned.

After the Communists came to power in postwar Romania, the Holy Synod under Patriarch Justinian, who had been enthroned in 1948, collaborated either willingly or through coercion with the new government. Justinian sent a telegram in the name of the Orthodox population to the United Nations protesting "against the savageries and against the atrocities committed by the American Army in Korea." [40] At the 1952 Conference in Defense of Peace, in Moscow, attended by representatives from most churches in the Soviet orbit, Metropolitan Sebastian brought the greetings of Justinian and the Holy Synod "to the entire Soviet people, and to its leader, Joseph Vissarionovich Stalin, the banner-bearer of the world peace front." [41] Sebastian boasted of the Romanian Orthodox Church's denouncement of "the iniquities perpetrated, in whatever part of the globe, by American imperialists. . . . " [42]

Meanwhile, among the Romanian Orthodox in the United States, two rival factions were engaged in a barrage of abusive name-calling that obscured the real issues. They described one another as "murderers," "liars," and "racketeers." [43] The initial division between them apparently stems from World War II, when the church in America disagreed over King Carol, who had fled Romania when the pro-Nazi Iron Guard took control. The pro-Carol faction was led by Glicherie Moraru, who claims to have served as Carol's chaplain. He was arrested, tried, and sentenced to five years in an American prison during the war as a "non-registered foreign agent"—but later received a Presidential pardon. Leading the opposing faction were two priests, Simeon Mihaltian and, later, John Trutza.

The Moraru–Trutza antagonism intensified in the struggle for control of the diocese and its property. In 1950 Moraru and his supporters decided suddenly to renew ties with the Holy Synod, and convinced Andrei Moldovan, a priest in Akron, Ohio, to go to Romania for ordination as a bishop. Moldovan announced from his pulpit that he was going to Hot Springs, Arkansas, for medical treatment; his parishioners received post cards from Hot Springs—but it turned out that he had arranged for a friend to send them in his name. He was on his way instead to Bucharest. He returned as His Grace Bishop Andrei, and one of his first acts was to excommunicate Trutza for eighteen "serious offenses and sacrileges." With the backing of the Patriarchate, Moldovan went into the courts to secure control of all property of the episcopate.

Trutza and his allies charged that the Communists were plotting to infiltrate the American Romanian church through Moraru and Moldovan. In July 1951, they met and reaffirmed the complete autonomy of the Romanian Orthodox Episcopate of America, electing as their bishop, Viorel D. Trifa, a postwar refugee from Romania. Trifa's ordination by Ukrainian Orthodox prelates in the United States was followed by the charge from the Moraru–Moldovan group that the ordination was uncanonical. They accused him also of participating as a youth in a "protestant" reform movement; of fleeing trial in Romania for Germany, where he was imprisoned; and of escaping to Italy, where he joined the Roman Catholic Church. The most serious indictment involved his political activities as a young man. He was said to have issued an anti-Semitic manifesto in January 1941 urging support for the Iron Guard and the Nazis. Trifa gave a totally different account. He said that he had opposed the Iron Guard regime of Ion Antonescu, that he had never participated in any "protestant" reform movement, that he was imprisoned for four years at Buchenwald and Dachau by the Nazis, and that he taught ancient history in an Italian Roman Catholic missionary college— "but I never became a Roman Catholic." [44]

The charges from the opposition Trifa group (Trutza died in 1955) against Moraru and Moldovan are almost as harsh. Moraru is described as "the instigator and the boss of the ring"; "unfortunately, he wears a priest's collar, but he has never assumed the responsibility which goes with this distinction." [45] Moldovan is said to be "dominated by ambitions far greater than his capabilities." [46] While they "may not be Communist," they "receive their orders and they have pledged their loyalty to Patriarch Justinian and to an organization which condemns America and American ways and lauds the Communism of Soviet Russia." [47] Moraru has replied that their diocese is autonomous and that his faction is not required to follow the Patriarch and Holy Synod in political matters.

There is little evidence to suggest that Communism plays an important role in the controversy—except as a propaganda weapon. The political background of several leaders on both sides is unsavory. Some were sympathetic to fascism, others were monarchists favoring a quasi-feudalism. The Moraru faction seems to have established ties with Bucharest neither for religious nor political reasons, but as a calculated move to strengthen its position in the United States— a move that has proved to be a boomerang. Subservience to Bucharest, even if only spiritual, naturally leads to the same risks as subservience to Moscow; the church in Romania, like the church in Russia, is exploited by the Communist state.

Meanwhile, the Trifa group has gained legal control of church property; it has gradually become dominant among Romanian Americans, and today claims fifty-one parishes and 50,000 communicants. In 1960 it became a diocese under the jurisdiction of Metropolitan Leonty of the American Metropolia, and Trifa's ordination was confirmed by Russian Orthodox hierarchs.

The Albanian story focuses upon a versatile individual, Bishop Fan S. Noli, who has been accused of sympathy for the Communist government of Albania.[48]

Approximately 60,000 Albanians had come to America before World War I, but a third of these returned home in the twenties. Boston is today the center of Albanian activities in the United States, and a number of active political groups and several Albanian-language newspapers have their headquarters there. The population of Albania, under Turkish rule for four centuries, has been 70 per cent Moslem, but in America the majority of Albanians are Orthodox. Noli, their spiritual leader, migrated to America in 1906 and formed Vatra, or the Pan-Albanian Federation of America, which had eighty-seven chapters by 1920. Vatra's *Dielli,* which Noli established in 1909, claims to be the oldest Albanian newspaper in continuous publication in the world. Noli is a man of considerable culture and education who translated the church liturgy into Albanian, served for a time as Albania's representative to the League of Nations, and then for seven months as Albania's premier. He was ordained a bishop in 1923, one year after the Albanian Church declared its independence from the Patriarch of Constantinople, under whose jurisdiction it had been since the eighth century.

Noli, now an American citizen, says that the charges against him of pro-Communism go back nearly forty years to his support of a broad land-reform program for Albania and to his later opposition to the dictatorial monarchy of King Zog. He has not, he has declared, participated actively in politics or political controversy since his return to America in the thirties.

The attacks against him have continued, however, in part because Noli is honorary president of Vatra, whose paper *Dielli* has been accused of sympathies for the Communist government of Albania. Noli denies any control over the paper's political opinions. *Dielli's* editor, G. M. Panarity, a Moslem, once did look with some favor upon many of the reforms of the postwar Albanian Communist regime of Enver Hoxha. Channels of communication, he believed, should be kept open to Albania, where many Americans still have relatives. Most important, he reasoned that under the Moscow-protected Communists, Albania might have a chance to preserve her national identity against her traditional foes, the Italians, Greeks, and Yugoslavs. His attitude was best summed up in the old expression, "Let's not rock the boat."

The total picture, however, was even more complex. While Noli and Panarity and *Dielli* were demonstrating considerable tolerance toward Hoxha's Communist regime, they sided with the United States on other issues on which American and Soviet policy clashed. Nor were they ever uncritical of the Albanian Government, and their criticism intensified with the increased weight of evidence that Hoxha was a tool of Moscow. During the fifties, *Dielli* clearly moved into the anti-Communist camp.

Attempts to undermine the spiritual authority of Bishop Noli have failed. He is still leader of the Albanian Orthodox Church in America, an autonomous body unaffiliated with the Holy Synod in Albania. Fourteen of the seventeen parishes in the United States are under his jurisdiction, and he estimates his total constituency at 20,000. Those who still continue to raise the cry of "pro-Communist" against him—or against Panarity and *Dielli*—are committing an injustice.

There is a lesson in this brief review of the Russians, Romanians, and Albanians, and it is this: When a charge of Communism is directed against any Eastern Orthodox group in the United States, it must be examined with special care. The existence of ties with mother churches abroad is not itself enough to justify such an accusation. Nor is the accusation warranted by the fact that some Americans of Eastern European background may approve of certain developments within their native lands. There were, as an illustration, anti-Communist Russians who felt considerable pride when the first sputnik sped into orbit. Observers must also bear in mind that many *émigrés* hold extreme conservative political and social views and are quick to label as "Communistic" any opinions more liberal than their own.

Nevertheless, these ecclesiastical and other bonds with their native lands can lead to exploitation by the Communists. During World War II, for example, the nationalistic sentiments of many Russians and other Slavs in America were channeled into support of a variety of front groups. Among Orthodox Americans of Eastern European origin it is the prudent person who can see behind the seductive Communist propaganda on the one hand, and on the other keep from falling victim to the political accusations so freely and abusively employed.

TWENTY-ONE · THE ARMENIAN SCHISM

Noah's ark is said to have rested on Mount Ararat after the whole world was inundated by the Flood. A tradition claims that the Kingdom of Armenia was founded by Haig, a descendant of Noah, on the shores of nearby Lake Van. In the centuries that followed, this ancient mountainous nation was the setting for continual warfare between great empires, and the country and its people were divided again and again among the major powers. Today, in the United States, Armenians are still divided—but this time against one another. The Armenian Church is the principal field of battle.

The Armenians, proud of their long and unique religious history, claim that their kingdom was the first state to establish Christianity as its official faith. In 301 A.D., Gregory the Parthian, known as St. Gregory the Illuminator, succeeded in converting the royal family, and the king's subjects followed his example. From the Holy See in the city of Echmiadzin (also, Etchmiadzin), the nation's spiritual life was nourished under the leadership of the principal hierarch, known as the Catholicos. Through centuries of subjugation, the church became the reservoir of Armenian culture and the symbol of the Armenian yearning for independence. No ties with Eastern Orthodoxy or with Roman Catholicism existed after the fifth century, when it identified itself with the monophysite "heresy." [1]

Armenia witnessed a new awakening of national consciousness in the nineteenth century after three centuries of Turkish rule. A number of brilliant Armenian writers, influenced by the philosophies of the

American and French revolutions, stimulated the revival of patriotism. An insight into the direction of two of the political parties that disagreed on the course of their nation's future is fundamental to an understanding of the bitter factionalism existent among Armenians in America today.

The Ramgavar ("of the people") Party was founded as a liberal, constitutional faction, placing emphasis upon the maintenance of order and consequently appealing to most business and middle-class elements. The Ramgavars believed that national independence should be sought through means that would avoid leading the country into chaos. They gave strong support to the church. Their main rival, which had been organized earlier, in 1890, was the Armenian Revolutionary Federation, whose members are still called Dashnags (also written as Tashnags, Dashnaks, and Tashnaks). Many Dashnag leaders were socialists, favored revolutionary tactics against the Turks, and were critical of religion though some acknowledged that the Armenian Church was an instrument for national unity.

In 1878 Turkey lost a war with Russia and was forced to grant independence to Bulgaria. The rulers were frantic with fear that other Christian minorities, aided by the Czar, would rebel. In 1896, following Turkish massacres of the preceding year, Dashnags attacked a Constantinople bank in a desperate effort to bring the plight of Armenians to the attention of the world. Again Armenians were slaughtered by the thousands. In 1905 many more were slain in retaliation for an unsuccessful revolutionary attempt to kill Sultan Abdul-Hamid. There were even more grotesque massacres during World War I; in the struggle between Turks and the Allies, the Armenians were stigmatized as disloyal. One million were killed, and the plight of the "starving Armenians" aroused sympathy around the world.

The Allied defeat of Turkey and the successful Bolshevik revolution permitted Armenia's emergence in 1918 as an independent nation. With one-third of its citizens dead, and its territory in ruins, the Armenian Revolutionary Federation took charge of the government. The leadership caliber of the Dashnag rule from 1918 to 1920 is still a matter of heated debate. By 1921, with the acquiescence of the new Soviet Union, Turkey had increased its holdings over Armenian territory; two other areas, claimed by Armenia, were ceded to Azerbaijan; the remainder, in the province of Erevan (Yerevan), was occupied by the Red Army and became Soviet Armenia. Some decried Communist aggression; others felt that Erevan had been saved from the Turks.

ARMENIAN FACTIONALISM IN AMERICA

During these years of persecution, thousands of Armenians sought refuge elsewhere. Almost 250,000 live today in the United States, many concentrated in Massachusetts—in Boston, Worcester, and Watertown; in New York City, Philadelphia, Chicago, Detroit, and Union City, New Jersey; and in Los Angeles and Fresno, California. Most Armenian Americans are constituents of the Armenian Church, though an estimated 15,000 are Protestants and perhaps 3,000 are Roman Catholics. Armenian Church leadership is fearful that many of its youth are being swallowed up in the American melting pot.

The national church, however, is split asunder by bitter strife between two hostile camps for influence in the Armenian community. There is little intercommunication between the rival groups, and even marriage between partisans of the two factions is discouraged. While time has served to heal, especially among those born in the United States, it has only acerbated the wounds of others.

Stated in its simplest form, the religious issue has become this: Should exiled Armenians in the "Diaspora" continue to give allegiance to the Catholicos at the Holy See in Echmiadzin in Soviet Armenia? Standing against Echmiadzin are the Dashnags, a well-organized, disciplined group led by intelligent, dedicated—but often fanatic and romantic—nationalists who have become bitter foes of the Communist regime of Armenia and also of its sympathizers. Support of Echmiadzin is found among Ramgavars and two minor political groups: a handful of Hunchags (Social Democrats) who trace their history from 1877, and several hundred unabashed Soviet apologists who promote their views under auspices of the Armenian Progressive League. All political parties together do not directly involve more than 20 per cent of Armenian Americans, but the principal newspapers circulating among Armenian Americans are published by these political groups.

The schism within the Armenian Church in the United States goes back to 1933. That was the year of the public debate over recognition of Russia by the United States, but Armenians were agitated by their own controversies: the proper date to mark as Armenian Independence Day and the proper flag to be flown. The Dashnags insisted that May 28, the anniversary of the founding of their republic, was Independence Day; their opponents in general celebrated November 29, the day when Armenia became part of the Union of Soviet Socialist Republics. The Dashnags continued to use the tricolor of the independent state as their flag; the others favored using either the flag of Soviet Armenia, the American flag, or no flag at all.

On July 2, 1933, at the Century of Progress Exposition in Chicago, Archbishop Leon Tourain, head of the Armenian Apostolic Church in America, was scheduled to speak. Though the facts are disputed, apparently it had been decided to fly no flag to avoid controversy. When a number of Dashnag women appeared with the tricolor and tried to place it on the platform, Tourain enraged the Dashnags by refusing to speak until it was removed. He argued that the church should remain aloof from politics. The Dashnags, however, had suspected earlier that Tourain was sympathetic to Communist rule in Armenia; now they were convinced. A month later, at a church outing in Massachusetts, the controversial Archbishop received a blow on the head.

The atmosphere became increasingly tense as preparations got underway for the annual conference of the church. In August 1933, the Philadelphia police were summoned when rival factions came to blows over the choice of delegates. The conference opened in New York City in September and reports told of delegates coming armed to the sessions. Tourain stayed away to encourage unity, but the assembly was soon at variance over procedure. Tourain's supporters requested closed sessions; the Dashnags wanted them open. The trustees of the host parish, the Church of St. Gregory the Illuminator, sympathized with the Dashnags and ruled that the doors could not be shut. When Tourain's partisans decided to move the conference to a hotel, the Dashnags refused to go with them. Each group, claiming to represent the majority of church members, then met separately and elected its own slates of officers. This marked the beginning of the American schism.

Antagonism toward Tourain mounted as events strengthened his opponents' belief that he was sympathetic to Soviet Armenia. He denied this, but argued that Armenia was being aided materially by the Soviet Government, without interference in the church's freedom. Messages from Echmiadzin that implied endorsement of Tourain's position on the flag and urged support of Soviet Armenia contributed to the tension. So did the statement of a member of the Supreme Council at Echmiadzin castigating Dashnags for "interfering with church affairs among the Armenians in the colonies"; he warned that any hostile acts against the Communist regime would be "unacceptable and fateful to the true Armenian." [2] In November, Tourain attended a dinner given by Maxim Litvinoff, Soviet Commissar of Foreign Affairs, to celebrate America's recognition of the Soviet Union.

Christmas Sunday of that year Tourain was preparing to celebrate mass in the Holy Cross Church at 578 West 187th Street in Manhattan. In the glow of candles, the bearded prelate, garbed in the ecclesiastical robes of the ancient East, made his way through the incense-filled church down the aisle toward the altar, blessing the congregation as he moved. When he reached the chancel, he was suddenly surrounded by a band of assailants; one thrust a six-inch butcher knife four times into his body. The worshipers stood unbelieving as the Archbishop fell dying to the sanctuary floor.

The murder had been deliberately staged in public by men who knew they would pay dearly for their crime. Nine were eventually convicted, all of them affiliated with the Dashnag Armenian Revolutionary Federation. Despite the weight of the evidence, the Dashnags have persistently denied any role in the murder, suggesting even that the Communists may have been responsible. The principal Dashnag newspapers, the Armenian language *Hairenik* and the English-language *Hairenik Weekly,* both condemned the trial as unfair and the verdict as unjust.

The murder brought chaos to the Armenian community. Several priests with Dashnag affiliations were unfrocked by Echmiadzin. Some churches took steps to oust their Dashnag members. In Boston, Chicago, and elsewhere rioting occurred. The Armenian community was torn asunder. Friend turned against friend. One would not buy in another's store. Even husbands and wives, parents and children became bitter foes. To the Dashnags, the Communists were to blame for the tragic cleavage. The *Hairenik Weekly* commented:

The social and economic boycott launched by one part of the Armenian community in this country against the other, the disruption of the unity of our people, the split in our church, the hectic efforts on the part of certain Armenian organizations to convict the nine innocent Armenians who were recently sentenced by the New York court, all constitute a part of the same communist scheme to destroy the institutions of this country, making certain gullible Armenians their instruments.[2]

Some Communists had been active among the Armenians, but their influence was slight and, at that time, they had little interest in the church. The *Daily Worker,* in a lengthy account of the Tourain murder, described it as "the culmination of a fierce struggle between two American bourgeois parties for control of the Armenian Church and mass organizations in North and South America." It expressed no special affection for Tourain:

The Armenian masses who have long suffered the pogroms instigated by the Turkish bourgeoisie are throughout the world hailing Soviet Armenia. Archbishop Tourain, himself a member of the same Turkish class that brought about the pogroms, was finally forced by the pressure of the Armenian masses to accept Soviet Armenia as the free homeland of the Armenian people.[4]

Communists now, however, stepped up their efforts to win support among American Armenians. On January 5, 1934, the *Daily Worker* reported that 1,500 persons attended a New York City rally protesting the assassination of Tourain, which was sponsored by the Friends of the Soviet Union and the American Committee to Aid Soviet Armenia, two groups controlled by Communists and their sympathizers. Party members worked closely with the Armenian Progressive League and the remnant of the Hunchags who, in 1935, signed a formal treaty of alliance with the American Communists.[5] The League's activities concentrated increasingly upon the church, where it tried to develop some pockets of influence. Its youth organization, Armenian Youth of America, attempted to win a foothold in a number of parishes—with only little success. The League's main impact came through its several branches and its two newspapers, the Armenian-language *Lraper* and the English-language *Armenian Tribune*. It centered attention annually on the November 29th anniversary of the establishment of Soviet Armenia and at times attempted to tie its activities into the broader pro-Soviet movement of the country. In 1939, for example, the principal speaker at the League's annual New York anniversary celebration was Methodist Harry F. Ward, chairman of the American League for Peace and Democracy.

POSTWAR DEVELOPMENTS

The Dashnags hunted for ways to discredit their critics as "Communists" or Communist dupes, while they themselves were not allowed to forget the Tourain assassination. It became the "bloody shirt" of the controversy, waved even when Dashnags sought to point out the genuine evils of the Soviet state. Their foes began to draw parallels between the Armenian Revolutionary Federation and the rising fascist movement of Europe. Both, they said, were fanatical; both were terroristic; both were obsessed with anti-Communism. This alleged similarity was reiterated during World War II, when the best-selling book *Under Cover* accused some Dashnags of Nazi sympathies. *Under Cover* was written by John Roy Carlson, pen name for Avedis Derounian, himself of Armenian background. Derounian was, and continues to be, one of the principal foes of the Dashnags and has spoken and written widely against them.

Hundreds of Dashnag youth served in the armed forces during World War II, and Dashnag loyalty could not be questioned. Yet, some of the older generation did suffer a severe emotional conflict. On the one hand, they hated Nazism and feared the consequences of "liberation" by the Germans. At the same time, the hope lingered that somehow the war might weaken the Soviet Union sufficiently to allow the emergence of a free Armenia. Among Dashnags in parts of Europe, there was some open collaboration with Hitler, especially after the Germans promised the Armenians an independent state under their protection.

But opposition to Russia was softened among American Armenians who, like other Americans, were influenced by the wartime emphasis upon Soviet-American friendship. Events in Armenia also played an influential role. In 1941 the government granted permission for the naming of a new Catholicos. Late in 1942 religious toleration was fully proclaimed and prayers for Soviet victory were inaugurated in all churches. In 1943 the Soviet Government and Echmiadzin agreed upon an amicable working relationship for the defense and welfare of the nation. In 1944 the church newspaper was revived. On June 22, 1945, a new Catholicos, Gevorg VI, was elected, after the post had been vacant for seven years, and in 1946 a new building for the use of the Holy See was erected on Stalin Avenue in the capital city of Erevan.

By the time the war had come to an end, most Armenians in the United States, including many Dashnags, were far less critical of Soviet Armenia than before. A number of new groups had been organized to encourage friendship with Soviet Armenia; among them were the American Committee for Cultural Relations with Soviet Armenia, the American Committee for Armenian Rights, and, most important, the Armenian National Council, headed by a Presbyterian minister, Charles A. Vertanes. In the immediate postwar period, the Armenian National Council led a campaign to bring pressure against Turkey to return the land taken from Armenia in 1921. In 1948, thousands of Protestant clergy signed a petition urging the American Government to "place the cause of the Armenians before the United Nations Assembly." [6] Anti-Turkish sentiment helped rally fierce opposition among many Armenian Americans to the Truman Doctrine for its aid to Turkey and Greece.

Another popular issue was repatriation. In 1947 a group of 152 sailed for Armenia amid enthusiasm even of some Dashnags. The head of the American church, Bishop Tiran Nersoyan, sent them off with the words: "I know you will live a happy and full life because I visited and saw Armenia recently." [7] A few were returning to help in the building of a Communist state, certain that injustice and misery had all but disappeared. More knew that life in Armenia would be difficult, but they felt joy at returning from exile to a homeland now free from Turkish rule. Some wanted simply to die where they had been born. By the time a second group of 162 left in January 1949, however, repatriation had become more controversial and the Dashnags accused the church leadership of collaborating with Communist agents in sending the repatriates to Soviet slavery.

With the coming of the cold war, the Dashnags took the offensive. In spite of their early socialist professions, many had become so preoccupied with hatred of the Soviet Union that they found themselves allied with the extreme Right Wing. Their contention was precise: Armenians who were sympathetic to the government of Soviet Armenia and to the Catholicos in Echmiadzin were "playing the Communist game." They were traitors to both their native land and their adopted country. Dashnags were particularly interested in discrediting the Ramgavars, who in their publications, *Baikar* and the *Mirror-Spectator,* viewed Soviet Armenia with more tolerance.

The Armenian Progressive League was the only faction to describe conditions in Soviet Armenia with uncritical enthusiasm. Through its newspaper it hailed the rise of Mikoyan, an Armenian, within the Soviet political hierarchy; endorsed all major aspects of Soviet foreign policy; promoted the Progressive Party not only in 1948, but also in 1952; and co-operated with the Communist peace campaign. *Lraper* and the *Armenian Tribune* (later combined with *Lraper* and called the *Armenian Herald*) published material by such Protestant ministers as William Howard Melish and Harry F. Ward, devoted considerable attention to the Dean of Canterbury, and came to the support of Willard Uphaus and his activities in the American Peace Crusade. A 1955 article attacking May 28th as "The Traitorous Anniversary of a Non-Existent Republic" summed up effectively the attitude of the Armenian Progressive League:

Dashnaks, those murderers of the Armenian people, and allies of Hitler, have no right to speak in the name of Armenia or the Armenian people. They are abominable traitors to their long suffering people. They are the stooges of Turks: the murderers of our people. May 28, 1918 should be a day of mourning, because it brought with it only new miseries, shame and death. The real day for celebration for all Armenians is November 29, 1920, when our country found its glorious freedom from exploitation and oppression, and entered into an era of triumphant achievements in the living standards and cultural life of our creative people, with the assistance of the great Russian people, dedicated to peace, justice, equality, and brotherhood.[8]

CILICIA VERSUS ECHMIADZIN

It became increasingly clear that the Catholicos, Gevorg VI, was being used by the Communists, particularly in their postwar peace campaign. In 1952 he attended the Moscow Conference in Defense of Peace. There he asked for action against Americans in Korea:

I have in mind the atrocities, which under the flag of the United Nations Organization, are being committed by the American armed forces in Korea and which demand from all humanity the most urgent and energetic efforts in order at all costs to check the use of the bacteriological weapon and save mankind from future unimaginable horrors, and put an end to the war in Korea.[9]

The Dashnags seized upon his words to prove that Gevorg VI was at best Stalin's prisoner but more likely his willing agent. The Ramgavar *Mirror-Spectator* repudiated Gevorg's sentiments. Gevorg was not free to express his honest opinions, some Ramgavars said. Others pointed out that he had been subjected to such a barrage of Communist propaganda that he could not possibly know truth from falsehood. They emphasized that he had specifically asked Armenians in other lands to be loyal to their respective governments. Finally, they said, Gevorg VI, whatever his political expressions, had labored industriously to preserve the prestige and the property of the church in Echmiadzin amid hostile forces.

Gevorg VI died on May 8, 1954. In October 1955, Vasgen I was elected his successor. The Dashnags again charged Soviet intrigue. Vasgen was little known among Armenians, they said, and would "never have ascended to the throne of the Catholicate if the Soviet had not insisted on his candidacy." [10] They further insisted that the delegates to Echmiadzin were almost all from the Soviet Union and were faced with no alternative—an accusation denied by Americans who attended the conclave. Vasgen, who was born in Romania, had been a bishop there since 1951. He was described in the Moscow newspaper *Pravda* as "one of the active leaders in the peace movement in Romania." [11] In 1954 the Star of the Republic Order of the Romanian People's Republic was awarded to him.

The controversy broke out with renewed fury in 1956 with the election of a Catholicos to rule the Holy See of Cilicia, which has jurisdiction over Armenians in Lebanon, Syria, and Cyprus. There had been some tension between the two sees in earlier years. Some claimed that the Holy See of Cilicia was technically equal with the Holy See of Echmiadzin, though in practice this was obviously not true. The Catholicate had left Echmiadzin in 405 A.D. and wandered from place to place, usually because of persecution, until it arrived in the city of Sis in the area known as Cilicia, now part of Turkey. In 1441, it returned to Echmiadzin, but another Holy See was established in Cilicia under another Catholicos. Because of Turkish pressure, this second Holy See fled to Antelias, near Beirut in Lebanon, where it exists today.

It seemed evident that the Dashnags would control the conference to elect the new Catholicos of Cilicia, and in a last-minute effort to head off their victory, Vasgen I dramatically flew to Antelias to plead for a delay. He called for church unity and emphasized the freedom now enjoyed by the church in its homeland. When his mission failed, he refused to stay for the election and left amid the weeping of 10,000 Armenian faithful at the airport, some shouting out, "Do not abandon us!" [12]

The election was held as scheduled on February 20, 1956, with gendarmes with rifles and machine guns on guard. Women hostile to the Dashnags occupied the church of the Holy See in a futile effort to prevent the election. Of the fifty delegates present, thirty-two voted for Bishop Zareh Payaslian of Aleppo and he was proclaimed Zareh I, Catholicos of the Holy Armenian National Apostolic Church See of Antelias, Lebanon.

The election and later consecration of Zareh had an immediate impact. He was not recognized by the supporters of Echmiadzin, who alleged irregularities in the naming of delegates. They also said that the choice of Zareh was contrary to the will of the people and the consecration did not meet the canonical requirements. Vasgen I called a meeting of bishops in Cairo, Egypt, the next month and proposed an agreement: Zareh would be declared legally elected if, among other things, he would recognize the supremacy of Echmiadzin and exercise no administrative powers beyond Lebanon, Syria, and Cyprus. The terms were promptly rejected.

The news of Zareh's election was greeted joyfully by the American

Dashnags. Since 1933, their parishes had operated independently of Echmiadzin, but without the ecclesiastical apparatus necessary to perpetuate a separate church organization. Their most urgent need was for bishops who would ordain clergy sympathetic to their cause. At the 1957 National Convention of the Armenian National Apostolic Church of America—the name of the affiliated Dashnag parishes—they officially petitioned Zareh to "admit our diocese into the hierarchial framework of the Catholicate of Cilicia." [13] Zareh cabled back a welcome. In October 1957, Zareh sent an emissary to America; he traveled among the churches, visited Vice-President Nixon and Secretary of State Dulles, called upon several Protestant dignitaries and upon the Lebanese and Syrian embassies. Two months later, Vasgen I issued an encyclical which refused to recognize the autonomy of the Zareh-led churches and warned Armenians to beware of efforts to "harass and distress Holy Echmiadzin."

Since 1957, both competing groups have been consolidating their positions in the United States. The Dashnags have contributed heavily to the financial support of the Cilician Catholicate; they have attempted to organize new congregations and strengthen their Armenian Youth Federation; they have continued to argue the charge that the Ramgavars and their allies are in league with the Communists. Archbishop Khoren Paroyian, prelate of the Dashnag diocese, spends six months of each year in America and six months in Lebanon, where he also heads the Armenian Church. While figures vary, about twenty-two American parishes are under his jurisdiction.

The diocese loyal to Echmiadzin, which represents the majority of the Armenian faithful in America, has established several new parishes, constructed a diocesan house in New York City, and made plans for a cathedral and cultural center there. It has launched an attractive English-language monthly newspaper, *The Armenian Church,* and joined the National Council of Churches—arousing the Dashnags to send a deluge of telegrams and other protests to the National Council. The presiding prelate of the Armenian Church of North America, the official name of the group, is Archbishop Sion Manoogian. There are forty-one churches under his jurisdiction; California, with ten churches, is organized as a separate diocese under Bishop Papken Vavarjabedian. In June 1960, Vasgen I visited many of these churches in the United States, where he was greeted enthusiastically.

Three conclusions may be drawn from the available evidence.

First, the Armenian Church has become an important political battlefield. Propagandists interested more in politics than in religion have tried to exploit the church.

The Catholicos of Echmiadzin himself, willingly or reluctantly, has been useful to the Soviet regime. This was especially true of Gevorg VI. Even more ironic, Communist sympathizers in the United States and abroad have come forth as champions of the faith. Thus, the Armenian Progressive League, which showed little concern when the Holy See in Echmiadzin was suffering severe persecution under the Communists, now becomes a pious defender of the mother church.

The Ramgavars present a different picture. As a group, they are genuinely devoted to the church; yet a few among them are motivated in their defense of Echmiadzin as much by their hatred of the Dashnags as by their religious fervor.

The Dashnags are a curious study in historical reversals. Some of their revolutionary forefathers boasted of their atheism and saw the deep religious faith of the Armenian people as detrimental to the struggle for freedom in a socialist state. Modern-day Dashnags generally have dropped both their atheism and their socialism.[14] They have clustered around their parishes in America often not because of religious piety, but because the church has been the heart of the Armenian community.

This is not to imply that members of these political factions are necessarily hypocrites. It is not as simple as that. The church is the cultural and nationalistic center for most Armenians abroad. It is inevitable, therefore, that each group fears that loss of the church to its enemies will gravely weaken its own position.

Second, the ways in which the rival political groups have characterized one another have been grossly unfair.

The Dashnags have been called "fascists," "terrorists," "murderers," "atheists," and "Marxists." They were guilty at times of fanatical terrorism, and a few hoped that a Nazi victory would "liberate" Armenia, but as a group they have made real contributions to the development and perpetuation of Armenian culture, scholarship, and national aspirations. Today, the Dashnags have little ideology any more. They are bound together by the common hatred for the Communist regime in Armenia.

Dashnag attacks upon their opponents are perhaps even more irresponsible. They lump together the "Ramgavar-Hunchag-'Progressive' clique" as pro-Communists and traitors. The small group of Progressives openly profess their Communist sympathies. The Hunchags are no longer of any importance. To level such charges at the American Ramgavars is unjust. Most are anti-Communist; they remain loyal to Echmiadzin for emotional and canonical reasons only. They are, in general, moderate, less militant and fanatical than the Dashnags, and more traditional.

Yet, as with the Dashnags, intense nationalism at times has led some Ramgavars astray. When glowing accounts come from their homeland, a number of Ramgavars believe them because they want to. Some support the Communist government as the lesser evil—the only real alternative, they feel, to Turkish rule and new massacres. The Dashnag goal of a totally independent Armenia is accepted by the Ramgavars as desirable, but at the present they regard it only as a nostalgic escape from reality. Unfortunately, the Dashnag–Ramgavar schism has succeeded in warping the true facts about Soviet Armenia. Whereas the Dashnags see a Soviet Armenia that wallows in misery and oppression, some Ramgavars see only a rainbow. The truth doubtless lies somewhere between.

There is a third conclusion, perhaps more significant than either of these two. To those involved in the controversy, whatever their views, the issues are real and urgent. Each group loves its native land and wants to help it. Objectively, it is possible to sympathize with both the Dashnags and with the Ramgavars. But the split within the Armenian community in the United States has been disastrous. It has perpetuated a bitterness and disharmony that has poisoned much of the creativity and vitality of the gifted Armenian people. To most Americans, including many Armenian Americans, the fierce struggle seems a bizarre relic of the Old World quite out of place in the New.

CONCLUSION · COMMUNISM AND THE CHURCHES

In early 1960 the United States Air Force released a training manual that contained this accusation: ". . . there appears to be overwhelming evidence of Communist antireligious activity in the United States through the infiltration of fellow-travelers into churches and educational institutions."[1] It specifically charged that thirty of the ninety-five persons who translated the Revised Standard Version of the Bible, sponsored by the National Council of Churches, were "affiliated with pro-Communist fronts, projects, and publications." James W. Wine, Associate General Secretary of the National Council, protested immediately to the Secretary of Defense, Thomas S. Gates, Jr., that the manual was "an example of irresponsibility at its worst." Within a few days Gates had apologized, and Dudley C. Sharp, Secretary of the Air Force, ordered the manual withdrawn.[2]

Despite the Air Force's prompt action, a sharp nationwide debate ensued. A host of Protestant church bodies, backed by the major Jewish religious groups, condemned the manual. Hundreds of newspapers voiced disgust, among them the New York *Times,* which warned that "something is wrong in our defense organization when this kind of venomous nonsense can be put out at Government expense."[3] The New York *Herald Tribune* also spoke bluntly: "We think the Air Force has the duty to make known which one of its birdbrains is writing its manuals these days."[4] *Time*'s news story on the subject began with these words: "When it comes to writing man-

uals, the U.S. Air Force is very good at flying airplanes and setting
off missiles." [5] Many critics linked the controversial publication to
other "helpful instructions" in some of the Air Force's 500-odd manuals: how to set a table, how to hold a hammer, how bachelors could
get dates, and even how to estimate the number of drinks consumed
at cocktail parties.[6]

Others welcomed the debate as a new opportunity to sow seeds of
distrust of America's Protestant church leadership. Carl McIntire and
Edgar C. Bundy, for example, wrote and spoke widely on the "Com-
munists" in the churches and called for a "complete investigation."
Night after night, radio commentator Fulton Lewis, Jr., urged his
Protestant listeners to insist that their local parishes repudiate the
National Council of Churches. On the floor of Congress, Donald L.
Jackson of California, probably still brooding over his humiliation
at the hands of Bishop Oxnam in 1953, arose to defend the manual.
Francis E. Walter, chairman of the Un-American Activities Committee, supported it also. But many more in Congress sided with the
churches. Among them was Senator John F. Kennedy, who called the
manual "shocking" and an "unwarranted slur on the Protestant ministry in general and the National Council of Churches in particular." [7]

The manual's discussion of the churches displayed such astounding
incompetence that to analyze it line by line would be to give an inane
document too much serious consideration. Eleven paragraphs—cov-
ering two of the manual's twenty-four pages—were included under
the heading, "Communism and Religion." In the first paragraph appeared the initial assertion of wide Communist influence in the
churches. The next five paragraphs tried to cast doubt upon the loyalty of the translators of the Revised Standard Version of the Bible.
Among these translators were most of the leading Biblical scholars
of the nation; some of them had at times voiced healthy independent
political views, but none of them, the manual's flamboyant charge to
the contrary, had ever been pro-Communist. Two paragraphs of the
manual then proceeded to quote the noted missionary E. Stanley
Jones out of context so as to distort his actual views on Communism
and the Soviet Union. Another paragraph falsely described Harry F.
Ward as "long a recognized leader in the National Council of
Churches" (Ward has never served the National Council in any capacity whatsoever) The two final paragraphs listed the books of

Louis F. Budenz and quoted a sensational charge of Communist infiltration of the churches made by Herbert Philbrick before a meeting of the Daughters of the American Revolution. Another section of the manual, discussing the persecution of religion in Communist China and North Korea, included a flagrant attack upon the distinguished Presbyterian leader John A. Mackay.

How had such distorted material found its way into the manual to begin with? Gradually the full story unfolded. Its principal author turned out to be Homer H. Hyde, a civilian and an active member of a Baptist church in Texas. In collecting material for the manual, he had apparently first approached his own minister, who recommended that he contact Billy James Hargis, an evangelist in Tulsa, Oklahoma, and head of The Christian Crusade. Hargis sent him two pamphlets he had written—*The National Council of Churches Indicts Itself on 50 Counts of Treason to God and Country!* and *Apostate Clergymen Battle for God-Hating Communist China.* Hyde made no attempt to check any of the extreme charges in the pamphlets, but simply put some of them into the manual. He depended greatly upon yet another pamphlet, *30 of the 95 Men Who Gave Us the Revised Standard Version of the Bible.* This one had been prepared and distributed by the Circuit Riders, Inc., an equally unreliable group, which had originally focused its attention upon Methodists, and later had branched out to attack clergy of other denominations as well.

The controversy over the Air Force manual tended to underscore the main fallacy in the argument of those who raise the alarming cry of "Communism in the Churches!" These critics have never investigated the facts. They seem to be incapable of distinguishing between different political positions—between liberalism, pacifism, socialism, and Communism; between religious social concern and international conspiracy. They are not seriously interested in understanding the complexities of history, any more than they are in grasping those of ideology. The Communist label has become to them merely a convenient and indiscriminate weapon for use against church leadership. Some exploit the issue for prestige, some for money, still others out of envy. They are effective only among the gullible and the uninformed; unfortunately, however, some decent, sincere churchmen are still easily aroused by tall tales of Communist intrigue among the clergy.

It may be wise at this point to be even more precise to avoid the possibility of any misunderstanding. The notion that America's churches and religious leaders are significantly influenced by Communists or Communist sympathizers is absurd. Nearly every Protestant denomination has had to face such charges, and the National Council of Churches has been a favorite target of the accusers since its creation in 1950. It is true that some Protestants will disagree with one or another of the policy pronouncements of the General Board of the National Council—such as its resolutions of 1952 and 1957 encouraging desegregation or its resolution of 1954 endorsing technical assistance to underdeveloped nations or its resolution of 1956 urging the release of all Japanese war criminals still held in prison. A free and vigorous exchange of ideas and opinions within the churches is healthy—and certainly neither the National Council of Churches nor the policy-making bodies of the various denominations are above intelligent and constructive criticism. But to give serious consideration to the charge that such policy pronouncements are pro-Communist, or even to hint that a single outstanding Protestant leader in the United States today is a Communist sympathizer, is to close one's eyes to the obvious truth. Indeed, to some, the National Council of Churches and the major Protestant denominations seem far too cautious and conservative. To the Communists, of course, they are incurably "reactionary."

This book has attempted to present the main facts on the relation of the Communist movement to the American churches, though, to be sure, space has not permitted a discussion of every relevant episode.[8] Some of the risks involved in undertaking this study were emphasized in the introduction. Four general conclusions are summarized here.

1) The Communist Party in America never did undertake a full-scale campaign to infiltrate the churches. In the twenties and early thirties, the churches were considered part and parcel of the capitalist system; they could be infiltrated, the Communists thought, with no more likelihood of success than could the American Legion or the National Association of Manufacturers. The Communists did not abandon their ideological antagonism toward religion, but in later years they assumed a new attitude of benevolence toward the

churches. Nevertheless, no plans to capture organized religion—like the plans to capture organized labor—were ever drawn up in Communist Party circles.

2) Only a small number of clergymen over the past forty years ever joined the Communist Party, possibly as few as fifty, perhaps as many as two hundred. There is no credible evidence that such men as Harry F. Ward and William B. Spofford, Sr.—enamored with the Soviet Union for more than a quarter-century and often accused of party membership—became Communists. The party did not always encourage friendly clergymen to join; they could be valuable when they could honestly deny party membership. Far more important, the Wards and Spoffords thought of themselves not as Communists at all, but as loyal followers of Jesus and the prophets. They hoped to influence the churches, and especially the Protestant churches, toward what they believed to be a more Christian position.

Of the small group of clergymen who did join the party, the evidence suggests that the majority may have been Negroes. Many factors would account for this. From its earliest history, the American Communist Party gave special attention to Negroes, and by the early thirties it had learned that it was both possible and desirable to recruit among the thousands of Negro ministers. They were wooed by the party because as clergymen, in a community where religion was important, they were viewed by the Communists as useful. In scattered instances Communists won pastors by careful infiltration into their churches. In more cases, they reached them by the skillful manipulation of the race issue or by the use of flattery. Overnight the Communist press would transform an unsung pastor of a small congregation into "a brilliant leader of the Negro people."

Most of the few Negro ministers who joined the Communist Party knew nothing about Marx and little more about the Soviet Union. They were Communists in affiliation only, seldom abandoning their traditional religious beliefs and practices. The Communists on the one hand romanticized these ministers, and on the other showed evidence of condescension toward them. Negro comrades were allowed to cling to unsophisticated religious forms, and there were instances in which Negro ministers delivered prayers at Communist meetings. Despite these and other concessions, however, Negroes generally were a bitter disappointment to the Communists, for they failed to respond with any enthusiasm to the party's recruitment drives.[9] Few Negroes who actually joined, including the handful of ministers, remained members for very long.

3) The main device used by the Communists among churchmen was the front group, discussed in greater detail in Chapter 11. The front was designed to lure non-Communists into Communist-oriented organizations. Sometimes these organizations were run by the party, either directly or through key officers; in other instances, as in the American League for Peace and Democracy, the Communists allowed dependable nonparty people a considerable measure of freedom.

Why have the names of several thousand clergymen appeared on front-group literature over the past three decades? Many, of course, were tricked by clever Communist strategy. The names of most fronts seemed innocent enough, with their use of highly cherished words like "peace" and "democracy." Their declared purposes were admirable. The letterheads that invited participation usually carried the names of distinguished fellow clergy. Not much was asked—seldom more than the "privilege of adding your name to a list of prominent sponsors." It all seemed honorable, above board, even righteous. The McCarthy era had not yet left its impress; in any case, ministers did not have the time, the resources, nor the inclination to keep dossiers on "non-Communist" and "Communist" individuals and groups seeking their help. Most objectives for which these individuals and groups claimed to be fighting—peace, racial equality, higher wages, public housing, better schools, and others—had a broad and legitimate appeal.

Indeed, the success of many front groups was helped by the fact that they seemed to be more vigorous in promoting worthy goals than the churches. There were official and unofficial church social-action agencies, to be sure, but they did not have the spark, flexibility, funds, and support available to the principal fronts. Had the churches been more zealous in their social concern, Communists would have had less success in appealing to those clergymen who desired to give expression to their deep humanitarian impulses. This is not necessarily an indictment of the churches. Many eminent religious spokesmen— Reinhold Niebuhr, G. Bromley Oxnam, Kirby Page, Stephen S. Wise, and others—were striving to strengthen the social consciousness in the churches. But ministers were not able to compete with Communists in this realm. They had to put their many-sided spiritual and parish responsibilities before any "extracurricular" activities. In contrast, the Communists were well-disciplined and single-minded; their energies were not generally as diffused; their supreme loyalty was to the party and its program.

What can be said about the ministers who were not tricked by Communist fronts, but who supported them anyway? A few of these clergymen were genuinely pro-Communist, but the overwhelming majority were not. Their involvement can only be understood if an honest effort is made to reconstruct the atmosphere and circumstances of the past.

The period of the thirties is illustrative. Many ministers, inspired by the social gospel, were hoping for a better social order. The Depression had made them wary of unfettered capitalism. Meanwhile, in Europe and the Far East, fascism and militarism were on the rampage. The Western allies, especially England and France, protested, but signed the Munich agreement with Hitler. Many Americans still were isolationists. Only the Soviet Union, whose government was now recognized by the United States, seemed to some observers to be genuinely interested in peace, and yet firm in its opposition to fascism. In such a situation as this, it is not surprising that many liberals and even some pacifists—though later revealed as mistaken—were impressed by Russia and open to Communist blandishments. Added to these considerations was a widespread fear of the power and the role of the Roman Catholic Church in both international and domestic affairs. This hostility toward the Vatican and the Roman Catholic hierarchy reached its peak, especially among liberals, at the time of the Spanish Civil War, but it has been a factor at all times.

Less tangible and more personal factors also influenced some to support front groups. Many clergymen abhorred the popular stereotype of the pious, other-worldly minister, and their eagerness to associate with radicals of all camps stemmed in part from a rebellion against this stereotype. Others felt that the churches were too conservative, too respectable, too homogeneous, too aloof from the "masses"; they welcomed the opportunity to rub shoulders with the persons of diverse political, religious, and economic backgrounds who were active in the fronts. Some clergymen found satisfaction and even a sense of accomplishment in having their name on imposing letterheads. In a number of cases they felt almost compelled to lend their name when an old friend—or a distinguished colleague—asked them to. There were cases in which men were following in the footsteps of a parent; others were rebelling against their homes; some were influenced by their wives. The cultural climate was another factor; for a few years in the decade of the thirties and in the years immediately after World War II, pro-Communism was part of what appeared to be the sophisticated and liberal milieu. In order "to belong" it was necessary to praise what seemed to be the social progress and vitality of Russia and to belittle what many considered the stale capitalist *status quo* of the United States. Those who sought to counter this trend were deemed naïve; they were confronted by an impressive array of "facts," for Communists were notoriously well-schooled.

An additional word should be added regarding the small group of persistent fellow travelers among the clergy who have worked with the Communists over the years and have willingly been used by the Communists as camouflage. Included among these ministers are some whose professional lives have suffered considerably because they have stood by their political convictions—men like William Howard Melish, Jack R. McMichael, and Dryden L. Phelps. Some always have been forthright and honest in espousing their views. Others at times have used dubious methods. In some cases they have shown an irresponsibility in handling the facts. In other instances, a number of these clergymen approved of, and actively co-operated with, carefully deceptive Communist strategies. At times some have exploited the friendship and humanitarianism of fellow clergymen and lured them into groups and activities secretly organized by Communists and geared to Communist objectives. The efforts of these few Communist sympathizers among the clergy have severely injured the cause of social action in the churches.

4) Today Communist influence within the American churches is near the zero mark. The Communists and their sympathizers have consistently lost ground among clergymen since World War II. They reached their zenith during two periods: from 1936 to 1939, at the height of the united-front movement; and from 1943 to 1946, during the war and during the immediate postwar afterglow. The first period came to an abrupt end with the announcement of the Hitler-Stalin pact. The second period closed more gradually under the gathering

momentum of the cold war and a growing awareness of the true nature and objectives of Soviet Communism.

In 1956 the Communist movement in the United States reached the lowest ebb in its history. The Khrushchev speech against Stalin, the acknowledgments of Soviet anti-Semitism, and the Hungarian revolt cut party membership from an estimated 20,000 in late 1955 to 3,000 in late 1957. John Gates, editor of the *Daily Worker,* left the party. Howard Fast, Max Gordon, Doxey Wilkerson, Joseph Clark, and thousands of greater and lesser stature were driven out by their disappointment and by a sense that they had somehow been betrayed. The impact was obvious among the small group of pro-Soviet sympathizers in or near the churches. Harry F. Ward, their principal "spiritual father," was disturbed by the "terrible violations" of Soviet justice under Stalin. William Howard Melish, Jack R. McMichael, and Stephen H. Fritchman specifically expressed their disapproval of Soviet repression in Hungary.

By the late fifties, the situation appeared confused. The lessons of the Twentieth Congress and the mass defections from party ranks— combined with a thaw in the cold war—had created a state of instability on the Communist Left. The "party line" was not as precise as before. The party could not exercise the rigid discipline of earlier years. It did not have adequate support or funds to operate its former many-sided front apparatus. Only an occasional picket, petition, and public-protest meeting served as a reminder of the elaborate American Communist Party strategy of the previous four decades.

The situation among the few consistent fellow travelers among the clergy became equally confused. Their ardent admiration for the Russia of Stalin had met a bitter fate; doubtless they found it painful, in some cases impossible, to concede the hollowness of the illusions of earlier years. They now are wiser, less dogmatic, more reluctant to trust unwaveringly in the Soviet Union. Still, their enthusiasm for the U.S.S.R., while diminished, has remained high. They are confident that Khrushchev has corrected the errors made under Stalin, that Russia is leading the forces of world progress, and that the United States is no less controlled by Wall Street than in years past.

These, then, are the four main conclusions of *Communism and the Churches*. This study has not attempted to deal with many complex problems related to the issue of Communism and religion in

American life. What are the ways in which Communism may be said to be a religion? Certainly, Communism has a faith, a sacred literature, a concept of a "Kingdom of God," of a devil and saints, of a chosen people. How should Christians and Jews respond to individual Communists—with hostility or pity or missionary zeal? How has the Judeo-Christian tradition influenced Communism—and vice versa? How has Marxism affected the trends of modern theology in the recent past and at the present time? [10]

Nor has this study attempted to give specific answers to intricate questions implicit in the facts presented. What steps should a church take to guard against Communist influence? What attitudes should a denomination take toward any Communist sympathizers in its midst? What course of action would be most wise if a minister is discovered to be a member of the Communist Party? Do such matters pose different problems in different denominations whose church governments vary from local autonomy to centralized administration? These questions involve delicate ethical considerations. In general, each case must be judged individually and in the light of surrounding circumstances.

There are a number of other complex problems that merit a special word.

One such problem has been characterized by the *Christian Century* as the "dupe-potential" still latent among Americans. This has two main facets, but one common denominator—an alarming failure to understand the vast chasm that has divided genuine democrats from Communists and Communist sympathizers. Millions of Americans do not yet appreciate the basic differences between the intelligent, independent thinking of the Oxnams and the Mackays, on the one hand, over and against the consistent pro-Soviet views of the Wards and the Spoffords on the other. This confusion has led, throughout the years, to two serious perils. First, it has enabled professional malcontents to spread distrust of church leadership—a distrust that is far more widespread across America than is sometimes recognized. Second, part of the success of Communist fronts in times past may be traced to the fact that thousands of people, among them some well-meaning clergymen, have continued to cling to the fiction that all imputations of "pro-Communism" are equally false. Ignorance or naïveté on both extremes—among those who see Communists everywhere and among those who contend that anti-Communism rests wholly upon a myth—succeeds only in injuring the cause of religion in America.

Another problem involves civil liberties. The United States has a rich tradition of nonconformity and has nourished a wide variety of bizarre religious cults and unorthodox political movements. Americans must never mistake dissent for conspiracy, nor be fearful of different, even revolutionary, ideas, nor attempt to stifle freedom of debate, however objectionable some opinions may be. Illustrative of the complexities of this matter is the recent case of Willard Uphaus, a Methodist layman, who was jailed by the State of New Hampshire in 1959. Uphaus entered the pro-Soviet periphery in the fifties and provided a platform for some persons with similar views at a summer camp he directed. That his ideas may be open to legitimate criticism is obvious. Nevertheless, his imprisonment for refusal to reveal the names of the guests at his summer camp has been one of the shameful episodes in recent years. It threatens the freedom of speech and the freedom of association by punishing one who has been charged with little more than encouraging both of them. Of course, just as the right of dissent must be zealously preserved, so also must be the right to criticize the dissenters.

A third danger is that forces far more influential in the churches than Communism will continuously exploit the Communist issue to delay social advance. The current urgent integration efforts provide the most significant example of this. Those who oppose integration are a thousand times more numerous in American churches than are Communists or Communist sympathizers. Yet, as they are forced to retreat year after year, some will become more and more reckless in their attempts to depict their antagonists as Communists. Intelligent citizens will refuse to be misled by such false accusations.

What are the prospects for the future with regard to Communism and the churches? It is possible that the course of events will revitalize the American Communist Party. A depression could quickly recreate a militant Communist movement. Serious American bungling or poor judgment in international affairs might have the same effect. A few among the young, normally rebellious and untutored in the political lessons of the past years, may find Communist utopianism appealing—as some of their parents and grandparents did before them. But at the present time the churches are faced with the more serious and pressing problems of apathy and complacency and a disquieting lack of social zeal. It is ironic that with all the deceit and arrogance and rigidity and slavishness of the Communist Party, it helped to bring to the American scene an exciting and contagious, though indeed devious, passion for justice. At the same time, however, the Communists—in a curious *de facto* alliance with extremist elements of the Right Wing—have dealt a severe blow to legitimate social concern and protest in the United States. The nation desperately needs clergy and laymen who, from *democratic* motives and by *democratic* means, will strive to convert the prophetic ideals of their Judeo-Christian heritage into reality.

BIBLIOGRAPHICAL ESSAY · NOTES · INDEX

BIBLIOGRAPHICAL ESSAY

No study has ever been undertaken on the relation of the Communist movement to the churches of America. Now that I have attempted it, I can better understand why not. The first difficulty, of course, is posed by the problem of fairness; a conscientious writer in the field is constantly aware of the risk that somehow, through oversight or misinformation, some injustice, however slight, may be done. This problem is accentuated by the obstacles which I faced in the years of research preliminary to this study. I came to understand more fully that truth is often elusive, that it sometimes seems to have many sides, and that honest people may re-create situations and recall facts in different and contradictory ways.

There are no trustworthy secondary works on the subject of the Communist movement and the American churches. I found much useful information in the daily press and particularly in such New York City newspapers as the New York *Times,* the New York *Herald Tribune,* and the New York *World-Telegram and Sun.* A number of important articles also appeared in current magazines and other periodicals. There were ten other major sources of information.

1) COMMUNIST PUBLICATIONS. The most productive single written source on Communism and the churches proved to be the *Daily Worker.* I read most issues from 1924 to 1941 and for such other periods as seemed necessary. It was surprising to find a number of frank accounts of contact with churches and churchmen: *e.g.,* how Donald L. West rode a motorcycle to New York City in 1934 to join the Communist Party; how members of the Young Communist League used a synagogue club as a front in 1935; and how a number of Negro ministers were recruited into the Communist Party and the Communist Political Association during World War II. Through the news stories and editorials in the *Daily*

Worker, it was also possible to trace the shifts in the party position on religion.

There were a number of discussions of religion and the churches in other publications either published by the Communist Party or openly Communist in their orientation, including *The Communist, Political Affairs, Party Organizer, New Masses,* and *Mainstream.* Some front-group periodicals occasionally carried relevant articles: *China Today, Spotlight on the Far East, Fight, Jewish Life, Champion of Youth, Young Communist Builder, Soviet Russia Today, New World Review,* and others.

2) RELIGIOUS PERIODICALS. Most important religious periodicals— ranging all the way from the fundamentalist *Moody Monthly* to the Unitarian *Christian Register*—were surveyed, at least to discover their editorial reactions to such abrupt shifts in the Communist position as occurred at the time of the Hitler-Stalin pact in 1939 and when Germany attacked Russia in 1941. Some Protestant periodicals are examined in the text itself, especially the *Social Questions Bulletin, The Protestant, The Witness,* and *The Churchman.* Others, like *The Christian Century, The World Tomorrow, Zions Herald,* and *Radical Religion,* gave generous coverage to social and political action within the churches.

The most informative Roman Catholic periodicals were *America, The Commonweal, The Catholic Worker,* and the Brooklyn *Tablet.* Useful information on Communist infiltration of trade unions with predominately Roman Catholic membership was found in publications of the Association of Catholic Trade Unionists and of the trade unions themselves.

Research in the area of American Eastern Orthodoxy and of the Armenian Apostolic Church was complicated by the language barrier. I was fortunate in having the assistance of Dmitry Grigorieff in my research on the Russian Orthodox Church. He translated various documents and articles published in the Russian language. The Armenians have published voluminous material in both Armenian and English. There are several pamphlets on the controversy among Romanian Orthodox printed in English, but apparently only one English-language pamphlet, *Albanian Exposé,* on the dispute over Bishop Fan S. Noli. Some of these materials, however, are propagandistic in tenor and of questionable reliability.

3) GOVERNMENT PUBLICATIONS. Fortunately, the American Government has not often intervened in the affairs of the churches. Of the relevant hearings held by the Un-American Activities Committee, the 1939 testimony of Earl Browder and the 1953 testimonies of Bishop G. Bromley Oxnam and Jack R. McMichael were of greatest interest. A few other printed hearings focused attention upon such diverse matters as alleged Communist efforts to infiltrate the First Unitarian Church of San

Diego and recruitment of Negro ministers into the party in the State of Washington. Such publications of the Un-American Activities Committee as *100 Things You Should Know About Communism and Religion* and *Review of the Methodist Federation for Social Action* showed incompetence and are in part inaccurate. Nevertheless, I want to thank Robert H. Michel, formerly administrative assistant to Chairman Harold H. Velde (and elected to succeed Velde), for the many courtesies he extended to me.

Some of the verbatim transcripts of hearings before the Subversive Activities Control Board were useful. They have not been published and I found it necessary to examine them in Washington, D.C.

4) BOOKS. The published writings of Harry F. Ward, Jerome Davis, Hewlett Johnson, and others discussed in the study were, of course, fundamental. A few other books, such as those of Sherwood Eddy and Bishop G. Bromley Oxnam's *I Protest,* proved useful. Several attacks upon Protestant church leadership have been published, such as Edgar C. Bundy's *Collectivism in the Churches* (1958) and Carl McIntire's *Servants of Apostasy* (1955), but they are irresponsible. Incidentally, this study has not discussed the Right Wing extremists at great length because they were the main subject of my book *Apostles of Discord* (Boston: Beacon Press, 1953).

Some distinguished scholars have summarized various aspects of Protestant social concern in the twentieth century. Three among the many that were particularly instructive to me were: Robert Moats Miller, *American Protestantism and Social Issues, 1919-1939* (Chapel Hill: University of North Carolina Press, 1958); Paul A. Carter, *The Decline and Revival of the Social Gospel: Social and Political Liberalism in American Protestant Churches, 1920-1940* (Ithaca: Cornell University Press, 1956); J. Neal Hughley, *Trends in Protestant Social Idealism* (New York: King's Crown Press, 1948).

5) LIBRARIES AND SPECIAL COLLECTIONS. The libraries utilized most frequently were: the Library of Congress, the New York Public Library, the Union Theological Seminary Library, and the Library of Tamiment Institute in New York City. The Swarthmore Peace Collection, Swarthmore College, Swarthmore, Pa., has considerable material on Communist peace activities. The Schomburg Collection in Harlem specializes in literature on the American Negro.

Loyd F. Worley, President of the Methodist Federation for Social Action, graciously made available the files of the Federation since World War II, which were stored in the cellar in his home in Hartford, Connecticut. John Mecartney was willing to part with his admirable collection of letters and other material on the Federation. Newspaper morgues are reservoirs of news clippings and many were visited across the country.

Frederick Woltman of the New York *World-Telegram and Sun* generously gave me access to his personal files.

6) PERSONAL INTERVIEWS. An effort was made to interview most living persons discussed in any controversial way within the book. To ac-
complish this, it was necessary to visit such cities as Boston, Hartford,
New Haven, Detroit, Chicago, San Francisco, Los Angeles, San Diego,
and Washington, D.C. I spent many hours talking with Earl Browder and
A. J. Muste in New York. Among others interviewed who play a major
role in the story which the study tells were the following: Melvin Arnold,
John Roy Carlson, Henry Hitt Crane, Jerome Davis, Clarence Duffy,
Solomon Freeman, Israel Goldstein, Donald L. Harrington, Kenneth
DeP. Hughes, Owen A. Knox, Joseph Kornfeder, John Miles, Glicherie
Moraru, Reinhold Niebuhr, Fan S. Noli, G. M. Panarity, Herbert A. Phil-
brick, Adam Clayton Powell, Jr., Herman F. Reissig, Lewis G. Reynolds,
Norman Thomas, Irwin St. John Tucker, Willard Uphaus, Mary Van
Kleeck, and Eliot White.

I shall not attempt to mention everyone interviewed. Some requested
anonymity. Below is a list of seventy-five, chosen somewhat at random,
which will indicate an effort to hear all points of view:

Paul B. Anderson, Ralph M. Arkush, Roger Baldwin, M. Searle Bates,
A. A. Bedikian, Hillman Bishop, Shelton Hale Bishop, Dickran H.
Boyajian, Dwight J. Bradley, Mampre Calfayan, Matthew A. Callender,
Varoslav Chyz, Frank Crane, Frank R. Crosswaith, Gloster Current,
Malcolm G. Dade, Reuben Darbinian, Hubert T. Delany, Peter Drosdoff,
Phillips Packer Elliott, Paul E. Fekula, George Florovsky, Margaret For-
syth, Roscoe T. Foust, F. M. Galdau, George Grabbe, Stanley Gue,
William Lloyd Imes, Muriel Jacobson, Philip Jaffe, John Paul Jones,
Howard Kester, Kourken Koudoulian, Alexander Kukulevsky, John H.
Lathrop, and Lim P. Lee.

Also, Robert Lee, Edwin C. Lewis, David N. Licorish, Paul Louie,
Clarence Manning, Mary K. Matossian, Glenn A. McClain, Dorothy
McConnell, Edward McHale, Clyde R. Miller, Norman B. Nash, Beglar
Navassardin, Kenneth Neigh, Ed Nestigen, Bedros Norehad, Harriet I.
Pickens, Frank Price, Paul Reid, Lewis G. Reynolds, B. C. Robeson,
James H. Robinson, Eleanor Roosevelt, Alexander Schmemann, Paul
Schneirla, George Schuyler, Charles M. Sherover, Herman S. Sidener,
Jesse Stitt, Paul Sturtevant, John M. Swomley, James H. Tashjian, Henry
Tom, David Toong, Vahan C. Vahan, Pierre Van Paassen. George A.
Warmer, Jr., Edward N. West, M. Moran Weston, Winifred Wygal.

7) CORRESPONDENCE. Correspondence was carried on with several hundred clergy and laymen on questions arising in connection with the research. Perhaps the names of some of those focused upon in the study
should be mentioned: F. Hastings Smyth, Donald L. West, J. Spencer

Kennard, Jr., Tucker P. Smith, Warren H. McKenna, Viorel Trifa, and Adam Philippovsky. Typifying scores of clergymen and laymen who contributed extremely valuable material or insights were these: Gross W. Alexander, Franklin H. Littell, Bradford Young, Edward L. Peet, Jack A. Sessions, Ralph McGill, John A. Mackay, W. A. Visser t'Hooft.

Three surveys involving over 150 ministers and rabbis were made. Their purpose was to obtain reasons why clergy supported front groups of different kinds at various times. The results are covered briefly in the text. The proportion of responses was high and the answers were often significant. I regret that space did not allow a fuller discussion of these surveys.

A letter to the editor was sent to religious periodicals and to many daily newspapers in 1955 requesting readers to send "documented evidence of actual Communist attempts to infiltrate the churches or make use of clergymen" and "examples of false and irresponsible charges of Communist influence on religion in America." The letter was widely printed and about eighty responses were received. In only a few cases, however, was the information reliable and useful.

8) EPHEMERAL MATERIALS. As important as any materials were small pamphlets, leaflets, brochures, tracts, and clippings—sometimes discovered accidentally in unexpected places. These sources created problems in the footnotes. In many cases, dates were missing or page numbers were gone. There were even times when useful clippings would be found without their source, date, or page.

9) PERSONAL EXPERIENCES. I was able to be present at some episodes described in the study, among them: the Oxnam and McMichael hearings; the funeral of Ed Strong; the turbulent annual event of the National Council of American-Soviet Friendship in November 1956; the Progressive Party Convention of 1948; the morning service at Church of the Holy Trinity in Brooklyn on January 15, 1956, and the service of installation of Herman S. Sidener on March 5, 1956; a Dashnag anniversary meeting; the Evanston Assembly of 1954; services at St. Nicholas Cathedral in New York City when Metropolitan Nikolai and again when Archbishop Boris officiated; and many "peace" meetings, protest rallies, forums, lectures, and other functions of the Communist Party or of front groups.

10) INACCESSIBLE RESOURCES. A number of persons did not co-operate with this study. Some apparently chose not to respond to letters; *e.g.,* Louis F. Budenz, Benjamin Gitlow, Jack R. McMichael, and Claude Williams. Others equivocated or demanded impossible terms—such as, "first repudiate the Fund for the Republic!" A few replies did not waste words. I wrote J. B. Matthews on June 30, 1955, requesting the opportunity of interviewing him. His letter of reply of July 11, 1955, read in full as follows: "No, thanks."

An organization known as the Religious Freedom Committee recommended to its members in 1955 that they refuse to co-operate with me on the grounds that my inquiry would be conducted on the basis of "guilt by association" and that this study would have a repressive effect upon the free exercise of religion. Clinton Rossiter and I met with three leaders of the Religious Freedom Committee—William Howard Melish, Lee H. Ball, and Miss Janice Roberts—to discuss the objectives of this study, but the impasse remained. Melish, Harry F. Ward, Guy Emery Shipler, Martin Hall, and Lee H. Ball were among those who refused to talk with me. The Religious Freedom Committee and several of its members seem to have inspired protests to the Fund for the Republic urging that it withdraw its support of my study. The Fund has at no time interfered with my freedom of research.

NOTES

CHAPTER ONE: RED STAR IN THE EAST

1. Ray H. Abrams, *Preachers Present Arms* (New York: Round Table Press, Inc., 1933), p. 57.
2. *Ibid.*, p. 50.
3. *Ibid.*, p. 58.
4. *Ibid.*, p. 57.
5. William Warren Sweet, *The Story of Religion in America* (New York: Harper & Brothers, 1950), p. 401.
6. *The Living Church*, June 16, 1917, p. 212.
7. *Ibid.*, Dec. 22, 1919, p. 541.
8. *Ibid.*, May 24, 1919.
9. *Federal Council Bulletin*, July 1919, p. 126.
10. *The Christian Century*, Jan. 30, 1919, p. 4.
11. *Ibid.*, Feb. 6, 1919, p. 4.
12. *Ibid.*, Feb. 6, 1919, p. 14.
13. *Ibid.*, Feb. 6, 1919, p. 15.
14. *The World Tomorrow*, April 1918, p. 76.
15. *Ibid.*, June 1918, p. 155.
16. *Ibid.*, Feb. 1919, p. 37.
17. *Ibid.*, Feb. 1919, p. 38.
18. *Ibid.*, March 1919, p. 79.
19. *Ibid.*, Jan. 1920, p. 3.
20. William Montgomery Brown, *My Heresy* (New York: John Day, 1926), p. 21.
21. *Ibid.*, pp. 51-52.
22. *Ibid.*, p. 66.
23. *Ibid.*, p. 67.
24. William Montgomery Brown, *My Heresy*, No. VII, April 1932, p. 27. Using the same title as his book of 1926, Brown published pamphlets from time to time.
25. William Montgomery Brown, *Communism and Christianism* (Bradford Brown Educational Co., Inc., 1920), p. 86.
26. *Ibid.*, p. 25.
27. *Ibid.*, p. 68.
28. *Ibid.*, p. 16.
29. *Ibid.*, p. 30.
30. Brown, *My Heresy*, 1926, p. 74.
31. *Idem.*
32. *Ibid.*, p. 76.
33. *The Witness*, June 14, 1924, p. 4.
34. *Idem.*
35. Edward Bushnell, *The Narrow Bed*, 1925 (a pamphlet), p. 1.
36. *Daily Worker*, Jan. 17, 1925, p. 4.
37. *Ibid.*, Dec. 29, 1925, p. 5.
38. *Ibid.*, April 2, 1931, p. 4.
39. *Ibid.*, Sept. 4, 1935, p. 2.
40. *Ibid.*, July 6, 1935, p. 1.
41. *Ibid.*, Nov. 2, 1935, p. 1.
42. Brown, *My Heresy*, 1926, p. 27.
43. *Daily Worker*, March 27, 1944, p. 6.

CHAPTER TWO: RELIGION, AN "OPIUM OF THE PEOPLE"

1. *Daily Worker,* April 1, 1927, p. 6.
2. *The Worker,* Jan. 12, 1924, p. 6.
3. *Daily Worker,* Oct. 4, 1927, p. 6.
4. *Ibid.,* Oct. 4, 1928, p. 6.
5. *Ibid.,* Jan. 12, 1924, p. 6.
6. *Ibid.,* July 23, 1924, p. 6. See also June 29, 1925, p. 3.
7. *Ibid.,* Feb. 18, 1925, p. 5. See also Jan. 22, 1925, p. 1.
8. *Ibid.,* May 29, 1925, p. 5.
9. *Ibid.,* April 7, 1927, p. 5.
10. Bennett Stevens, *The Church and the Workers* (New York: International Pamphlets, 1932), p. 10. This pamphlet was No. 15 of a series prepared under the direction of the Labor Research Association.
11. *Ibid.,* p. 11.
12. *Daily Worker,* Oct. 1, 1928, p. 1.
13. *Ibid.,* Oct. 25, 1930, p. 6.
14. *Ibid.,* Feb. 13, 1924, p. 6.
15. *Ibid.,* Oct. 22, 1924, p. 6.
16. From the column "With Young Workers" of the Young Workers League, in *The Worker Magazine,* May 27, 1924, p. 4.
17. *Daily Worker,* April 21, 1927, p. 6.
18. *Ibid.,* Nov. 30, 1925, p. 3.
19. *Ibid.,* May 8, 1925, p. 2.
20. *Ibid.,* July 2, 1931, p. 4.
21. *Ibid.,* March 20, 1924, p. 6.
22. *Ibid.,* May 8, 1925, p. 2.
23. *Ibid.,* Oct. 10, 1924, p. 2.
24. *Ibid.,* Sept. 4, 1924, p. 3.
25. *Ibid.,* April 6, 1927, p. 6.
26. *Ibid.,* Dec. 19, 1925, p. 5.
27. *Ibid.,* Aug. 30, 1924, p. 2.
28. Jay Lovestone, "The 1928 Elections," *The Communist,* Dec. 1928, p 745.
29. *Daily Worker,* April 21, 1927, p. 1.
30. *Ibid.,* May 26, 1928, pp. 4-7.
31. *Ibid.,* Sept. 4, 1924, p. 3.
32. *Ibid.,* Nov. 5, 1926, p. 3.
33. *Ibid.,* Nov. 2, 1927, p. 6.
34. *Ibid.,* June 1, 1928, p. 6.
35. *Ibid.,* May 30, 1928, p. 6.
36. *Ibid.,* June 1, 1928, p. 6.
37. *Ibid.,* July 24, 1924, p. 6.
38. *Ibid.,* April 4, 1924, p. 6.
39. *Ibid.,* Sept. 28, 1927, p. 1.
40. *Ibid.,* Oct. 28, 1924, p. 6.
41. *Ibid.,* Oct. 23, 1925, p. 6.
42. *Ibid.,* June 2, 1928, p. 8.
43. *Ibid.,* Nov. 28, 1928, p. 1.
44. *Ibid.,* June 7, 1928, p. 4.
45. *Ibid.,* July 31, 1926, p. 1.
46. *Ibid.,* March 4, 1924, p. 4.
47. *Ibid.,* Feb. 23, 1924, p. 4.
48. *Ibid.,* April 1, 1927, p. 6.
49. *Ibid.,* Aug. 20, 1926, p. 2.
50. *Ibid.,* June 20, 1925 (Magazine).
51. *The Worker,* March 3, 1923, p. 4.
52. *Ibid.,* Feb. 10, 1923, p. 6.
53. *Ibid.,* March 31, 1923, p. 4.

54. *Daily Worker*, Nov. 30, 1927, p. 4.
55. *Ibid.*, June 20, 1925 (Magazine).
56. *Ibid.*, Aug. 26, 1924, p. 1.
57. See *ibid.*, Nov. 11, 1924, p. 4, and Sept. 18, 1924, p. 1.
58. *The Worker*, April 22, 1922, p. 3.
59. *The Toiler*, Feb. 6, 1920, p. 3.
60. *Idem.*
61. Don Ryan, "Aimee and the Elders," *New Masses*, Dec. 1926, pp. 21-22.
62. *Daily Worker*, Oct. 3, 1927, p. 2.
63. *Ibid.*, Oct. 2, 1924, p. 6.
64. *Ibid.*, Sept. 11, 1925, p. 3.
65. *Ibid.*, Oct. 4, 1927, p. 6.
66. *Ibid.*, April 2, 1927 (Magazine).
67. *Ibid.*, May 7, 1927, p. 6 (Magazine).
68. *Ibid.*, April 7, 1927, p. 5.
69. *Ibid.*, Feb. 28, 1925 (Magazine).
70. *Ibid.*, March 10, 1925, p. 5.
71. *Ibid.*, April 20, 1931, p. 4.
72. *Ibid.*, May 23, 1924, p. 4.
73. *Ibid.*, Oct. 9, 1925, p. 5.
74. *Ibid.*, May 20, 1931, p. 2.
75. *Ibid.*, Sept. 25, 1931, p. 2.
76. *New Masses*, Oct. 1931, p. 31.

CHAPTER THREE: THE COMMUNISTS DISCOVER THE CHURCHES

1. B. D. Amis, review of *The Rural Negro*, *The Communist*, Feb. 1931, p. 187.
2. *Daily Worker*, Feb. 1, 1924, p. 6.
3. *Ibid.*, Nov. 28, 1925, p. 3 (Magazine).
4. *The Communist*, Jan. 1930, p. 54.
5. *Daily Worker*, March 9, 1929, p. 2.
6. *Ibid.*, Nov. 3, 1930, p. 1.
7. *Ibid.*, Dec. 29, 1930, p. 2.
8. *The World Tomorrow*, Feb. 1932, p. 38.
9. K. E., "Overcoming Sectarianism," *Party Organizer*, May-June 1933, p. 17.
10. *Daily Worker*, Dec. 9, 1933, p. 6.
11. *Ibid.*, April 30, 1931, p. 2.
12. *Ibid.*, Feb. 17, 1932, p. 2.
13. *Ibid.*, April 16, 1935, p. 4.
14. See *The Communist*, Feb. 1935, p. 169.
15. *The Communist*, Feb. 1935, p. 169.
16. *Daily Worker*, Sept. 30, 1932, p. 4.
17. *The Spoken Word*, Dec. 22, 1934, p. 4.
18. Quoted in *The Communist*, Feb. 1935, p. 171.
19. James W. Ford, "The United Front in the Field of Negro Work," *The Communist*, Feb. 1935, p. 172.
20. *Daily Worker*, April 9, 1935, p. 3.
21. *Ibid.*, April 25, 1935, p. 6.
22. *Ibid.*, May 10, 1935, p. 5.
23. *Communist International*, May 5, 1935, p. 503.
24. *The Spoken Word*, Nov. 2, 1935, p. 12.
25. *Ibid.*, Jan. 14, 1936, p. 9.
26. *Daily Worker*, Feb. 11, 1936, p. 6.
27. *Ibid.*, Dec. 26, 1925, p. 1 (Magazine).
28. *Ibid.*, Jan. 1, 1932, p. 2.
29. Earl Browder, *Religion and Communism* (New York: Workers Library, 1935).
30. *Daily Worker*, Feb. 26, 1935, p. 4.
31. *Ibid.*, April 6, 1935, p. 6.

32. *Ibid.,* Jan. 22, 1935, p. 5.
33. *Ibid.,* June 15, 1935, p. 7.
34. *Ibid.,* Aug. 12, 1935, p. 5.
35. *Ibid.,* Nov. 25, 1937, p. 3.
36. *Ibid.,* Oct. 28, 1935, p. 6.
37. *Ibid.,* Jan. 3, 1936, p. 5.
38. *Ibid.,* July 16, 1936, p. 8.
39. *Ibid.,* Sept. 4, 1936, p. 8.
40. *The Worker,* Jan. 10, 1937, p. 9.
41. Investigation of Un-American Propaganda Activities in the United States, Hearings before a Special Committee on Un-American Activities, House of Representatives, 76th Congress, 1st Session on H. Res. 282, Vol. 7, Sept. 6, 1939, beginning p. 4456.
42. The "Holy Rollers," of course, are not a religious sect. The expression is used to indicate religious groups, usually small in membership and influence, whose services for worship are characterized by shouting, physical movements, and in some instances even rolling on the church floor—hence the expression.
43. James W. Ford, *The Negro and the Democratic Front* (New York: International Publishers, 1938), p. 75.
44. *Idem.*
45. *Ibid.,* p. 83.
46. *Daily Worker,* June 23, 1936, p. 6.
47. *Party Organizer,* April 1938, p. 13.
48. *Ibid.,* April 1938, pp. 21-22.

CHAPTER FOUR: THE IMAGE OF RUSSIA IN THE THIRTIES: PRO AND CON

1. A further breakdown of the poll by denominations provides some interesting comparisons. The following material is excerpted from *The World Tomorrow,* May 30, 1934, in which answers were tabulated to the question: "Which economic system appears to you to be less antagonistic to and more consistent with the ideals and methods of Jesus and the noblest of the Hebrew Prophets?" Some clergymen did not answer; others preferred a different economic system from those alternatives listed.

	Capitalism	Drastically reformed capitalism	Socialism	Communism	Fascism
Methodist Episcopal	171	2,696	1,845	22	14
Presbyterian	171	1,601	509	5	9
Baptist	122	1,113	452	8	9
Congregational	76	866	582	30	11
Lutheran	142	954	192	4	25
Seminary Students	31	523	715	30	7
Protestant Episcopal	72	682	320	4	19
Disciples of Christ	45	451	285	4	1
Evangelical	26	380	235	1	11
Church of the Brethren	28	257	136	1	1
Reformed	14	235	143	2	2
Unitarian and Universalist	13	143	110	5	0
United Brethren	21	138	51	0	0
Jewish Rabbis	4	87	84	4	0
Miscellaneous	99	565	220	3	2
Total	1,035	10,691	5,879	123	111

2. These opinions were contained in a confidential memorandum published by The American Foundation, May 25, 1933.
3. *Christian Standard,* Nov. 25, 1933, p. 11.
4. *Moody Monthly,* Dec. 1933, p. 208.
5. *The Living Church,* Nov. 11, 1933, p. 42.
6. Confidential memorandum published by The American Foundation, May 25, 1933.
7. *America,* March 25, 1933, p. 121.
8. *The Witness,* April 12, 1924, p. 7.
9. Sherwood Eddy, *The Challenge of Russia* (New York: Farrar and Rinehart, 1931), p. 20.
10. Sherwood Eddy, *Russia Today* (New York: Farrar and Rinehart, 1934), p. 67.
11. *The Christian Century,* Feb. 7, 1934, pp. 189-90.
12. Eddy, *Russia Today,* p. x.
13. *Ibid.,* p. 33.
14. Sherwood Eddy, *Eighty Adventurous Years* (New York: Harper and Brothers, 1955), p. 143.
15. *Ibid.,* pp. 143-44.
16. *Daily Worker,* July 25, 1935, p. 6.
17. *Ibid.,* Feb. 15, 1936, p. 3.
18. William I. Hull, *Friends Intelligencer,* Tenth Month 19, 1935, p. 657.
19. *The Christian Century,* Dec. 11, 1935, p. 1594.
20. *The Presbyterian,* May 14, 1936, p. 1.
21. *The Christian Century,* Feb. 20, 1935, p. 244.
22. *Ibid.,* Dec. 6, 1933, pp. 1526-27.
23. Bishop Logan H. Roots in *The Witness,* May 19, 1938, p. 7.
24. *China Today,* Jan. 1938, p. 235.
25. *The Living Church,* March 16, 1938, p. 343. See also *The Churchman,* Aug. 1938, pp. 11-12.
26. It is interesting that the *Churchman* of May 1938 carried an article attempting to refute the Japanese claim of saving China from Communism. The article, entitled "Is China Fighting for Communism?" was written by Kimber H. K. Den, an Episcopal clergyman in Nanchang and president of The Chinese Mission to Lepers. "It is rather strange that Japan should make such a claim of fighting Communism in China," Den wrote, "by launching a ruthless attack against the regime of General Chiang Kai-shek, who has been fighting against Communism for years." The article lauds the loyalty of the Communists to the war effort and quotes Chou En-lai, then a Communist delegate to the National government, on the need for united action against Japan.
27. *The Christian Century,* June 24, 1936, p. 897.
28. *The Presbyterian,* July 9, 1936, p. 1.
29. *Daily Worker,* June 20, 1936, p. 2.
30. *Christian Evangelist,* Oct. 31, 1935, p. 1418.
31. *The Christian Century,* June 13, 1934, pp. 788-89.
32. *Ibid.,* March 18, 1936, p. 248.
33. *Ibid.,* Aug. 19, 1953, pp. 936-37.
34. *Ibid.,* April 10, 1935, p. 474.
35. *Radical Religion,* Spring 1937, p. 1.
36. *Ibid.,* Summer 1938, p. 3.
37. *The Christian Century,* June 23, 1937, p. 797.
38. *The Friend,* Ninth Month 24, 1936, p. 114.
39. *Christian Advocate,* June 24, 1937, p. 588.
40. Arthur Burd McCormick, "The World As I See It," *The Presbyterian,* March 10, 1938, p. 5. McCormick's column also appeared in other religious journals.
41. *Christian Standard,* Aug. 29, 1936, p. 2.
42. *Zions Herald,* June 16, 1937, p. 747.
43. *Daily Worker,* Feb. 9, 1937, p. 2; *Soviet Russia Today,* March 1937, pp. 14-15.
44. *The Witness,* March 31, 1938, p. 6.
45. *Ibid.,* Sept. 2, 1937, p. 5.

46. *Daily Worker,* Feb. 12, 1937, p. 2; *Soviet Russia Today,* March 1937, pp. 14-15.
47. See *The Protestant Digest* of April 1939, pp. 53-58, for Davis' article "Why Not Be Fair to the Soviet Union?"

CHAPTER FIVE: THE STRATEGY OF THE UNITED FRONT

1. *Daily Worker,* Dec. 1, 1933, p. 3.
2. The American Committee for Struggle Against War published a full report on the 1932 Congress in Amsterdam entitled *The World Congress Against War.*
3. *Daily Worker,* Oct. 2, 1933. By the following day, however, Browder had yielded to socialist and liberal demands and a Lovestoneite was named to the executive body of the League.
4. *The Christian Century,* Nov. 1, 1933, p. 1365.
5. *The World Tomorrow,* Oct. 12, 1933, p. 571.
6. *The Christian Century,* Feb. 14, 1934, p. 218.
7. *Ibid.,* Dec. 12, 1934, p. 1598.
8. *Ibid.,* Jan. 8, 1936, p. 48.
9. *The Presbyterian,* Jan. 30, 1936, p. 4.
10. *Christian Advocate,* Oct. 17, 1935, p. 924.
11. *The World Tomorrow,* Sept. 14, 1932, p. 260.
12. *Ibid.,* Oct. 26, 1933, p. 588.
13. *Ibid.,* May 1931 and May 10, 1934. Ten to 15 per cent of the total voting did not reply to the questions.
14. The discussion at the F.O.R. meeting was reported in *The Christian Century,* Nov. 1, 1933, pp. 1383-85.
15. *The World Tomorrow,* Jan. 4, 1934, pp. 9-11.
16. *The Christian Century,* Jan. 3, 1934, pp. 17-19. The lengthy quotation is from p. 19.
17. *The World Tomorrow,* March 1, 1934, p. 100.
18. *The Christian Century,* March 7, 1934, p. 339.
19. *Ibid.,* Dec. 18, 1935, p. 1622.
20. *The Social Service Bulletin,* Dec. 15, 1932, pp. 3-4.
21. *Daily Worker,* Oct. 2, 1934, p. 3.
22. *Party Organizer,* Sept. 1935, p. 14.
23. From the *Proceedings* of the Second Congress (1934) published by the American League, p. 15.
24. Interview with Herman F. Reissig, Sept. 27, 1956.
25. From the *Proceedings* of the Third Congress (1936) published by the American League, p. 43.
26. *Amplifier,* monthly newsletter of the American League, Aug. 15, 1935, p. 2.
27. These figures were compiled from the *Proceedings* of the five congresses published separately by the American League.
28. The author made contact with all persons mentioned here except Waldo McNutt, whose present political views cannot therefore be assessed.
29. Quoted in *Moody Monthly,* Dec. 1936, p. 193.
30. *The Witness,* Mar. 5, 1936, p. 9.
31. *The Churchman,* March 1, 1936, p. 28.
32. *Christian Advocate,* Oct. 17, 1935, p. 925.
33. Thomas F. Neblett, "Youth Movements in the United States," *Annals of the American Academy of Political and Social Science,* Nov. 1937, p. 146.
34. Quoted in Robert Moats Miller, *American Protestantism and Social Issues* (Chapel Hill: The University of North Carolina Press, 1958), p. 68.
35. *Idem.*
36. Resolutions of the Eighth Convention of the Communist Party were published in *The Communist,* May 1934.
37. *The World Tomorrow,* May 1931 and May 10, 1934.
38. James A. Wechsler, *The Age of Suspicion* (New York: Random House, 1953), p. 70.

39. *Daily Worker*, Sept. 28, 1935.
40. *The Communist*, July 1935, p. 613.
41. *Daily Worker*, Sept. 2, 1935.
42. "Organizing a Local Committee of the American Youth Congress," *Young Communist Builder*, Aug. 1935, pp. 8-9.
43. The story of this effort to infiltrate a Negro church youth group, including the quotations, was told in the *Daily Worker* of Aug. 13, 1935, p. 6. Such attempts were made in several churches. Dr. William Lloyd Imes, for many years a distinguished civic leader in Harlem and pastor of St. James Presbyterian Church there from 1925 to 1943, recalls how in the mid-thirties half a dozen Communists sought to infiltrate the Six O'Clock Group, one of his parish's youth organizations. The Communists were popular, worked hard, and were ready to sacrifice for the building of the club. Most of them, he recalls, were white. Imes and his wife became increasingly disturbed as the club moved further and further away from its Christian emphasis. Finally, Mrs. Imes, the club's adviser, told its members that the organization was religious and that those from the outside would not be allowed to change its orientation. Soon after, the Communists disappeared. This story was related when Imes was interviewed on Aug. 5, 1956.
44. The convention was held from April 29 to May 5, 1936, and the proceedings and resolutions were published.
45. Letter from Franklin H. Littell, Jan. 15, 1957.
46. Published proceedings of the Fifth American Youth Congress, p. 46.
47. *Daily Worker*, Mar. 14, 1936, p. 2.
48. The writer attended the Strong funeral on April 13, 1957, held in the Concord Baptist Church in Brooklyn. The interesting blend of religion and politics was typified in the spirituals and gospel songs sung by Paul Robeson. A year later, Gardner C. Taylor, the church's minister, was elected president of the Protestant Council of the City of New York and was named by Mayor Robert F. Wagner to serve on the city's Board of Education. Because of his participation in the Strong funeral, Walter Winchell, J. B. Matthews, and others began a campaign to discredit Taylor. Actually, of course, the distinguished Brooklyn minister was only performing what he saw as his duty as a pastor. At the time of such a family tragedy as the death of Strong, still only a young man and the father of four children (ages 15, 10, 7, 3), it would be a callous clergyman indeed who would not be willing to respond to the request for a church funeral.
49. *The Communist*, June 1940, p. 552.

CHAPTER SIX: THE CHURCHES AND THE SPANISH CIVIL WAR

1. *The Worker*, March 20, 1938.
2. *Daily Worker* of March 1, 1938, p. 4, reported the following results of a nationwide poll conducted by the American Institute of Public Opinion: pro-Loyalist, 36 per cent; pro-Franco, 12 per cent; no opinion or no preference, 52 per cent.
3. *Daily Worker*, Sept. 16, 1936, p. 8.
4. *Ibid.*, Jan. 24, 1937, p. 16.
5. *Ibid.*, Sept. 4, 1937, p. 8.
6. *Ibid.*, April 29, 1937, p. 6.
7. *The Worker*, Jan. 24, 1937, p. 16.
8. *Daily Worker*, Oct. 26, 1936, p. 4.
9. *Ibid.*, June 8, 1937, p. 2.
10. *Ibid.*, May 24, 1937, p. 8.
11. *Congressional Record*, March 10, 1938, A959.
12. These figures were taken from *The United States and the Spanish Civil War* by F. Jay Taylor (New York: Bookman Associates, 1956), p. 161. Taylor, in turn, took the data from an unpublished Ph.D. dissertation by Hugh Jones Parry, "The Spanish Civil War," University of Southern California, 1949, p. 373.
13. *The Nation*, Dec. 18, 1937, pp. 683-85.

14. *America,* Jan. 15, 1938.
15. *The Christian Century,* Oct. 14, 1936, p. 1366.
16. *The Churchman,* June 15, 1939, p. 8.
17. *Daily Worker,* Dec. 3, 1936, p. 2.
18. It was also in 1940 that Reissig broke with all Communist-front activities. He was serving at the time as chairman of the American Committee for Protection of Foreign Born. At its national meeting, he joined with others in introducing a resolution attacking both fascism and Communism. It was shouted down. This convinced him that the Communists had packed the meeting and that the Communist pretensions of a genuine "united front" were false. Reissig resolved never to support Communist-front activities again.
19. *Radical Religion,* Autumn 1937, p. 8.
20. *Daily Worker,* Oct. 5, 1937, p. 7.
21. The New York *Times,* Oct. 14, 1937.
22. *Daily Worker,* Oct. 20, 1937, p. 2.
23. *The Witness,* Nov. 19, 1936, p. 7.
24. *The Christian Century,* Sept. 22, 1937, p. 1165.
25. *The Presbyterian,* Aug. 6, 1936, p. 5.
26. *The Living Church,* March 30, 1938, p. 391.
27. *The Christian Century,* Dec. 30, 1936, p. 1742.
28. *Ibid.,* Jan. 27, 1937, p. 105.

CHAPTER SEVEN: THE "OUTSTRETCHED HAND" TO ROMAN CATHOLICS

1. *Daily Worker,* Nov. 22, 1937, p. 6.
2. *Ibid.,* Dec. 28, 1937, p. 4. This article was headlined: "Pope Counsels French Catholics to Accept Communist 'Outstretched Hand' in Struggles."
3. *Ibid.,* Dec. 29, 1937, p. 6.
4. Earl Browder, *A Message to Catholics,* a pamphlet published by the Workers Library, New York, in June 1938. The statement of the party's national committee served as the introduction to the pamphlet.
5. *Ibid.,* p. 5.
6. *Ibid.,* p. 8.
7. *Ibid.,* p. 12.
8. *Ibid.,* p. 15.
9. *Party Organizer,* Aug. 1938, pp. 30-32.
10. The New York *Times,* Aug. 25, 1938.
11. *America,* Oct. 26, 1918.
12. *Catholic News,* Oct. 5, 1918.
13. *Ibid.,* March 26, 1921.
14. Quoted in *America,* March 8, 1924, p. 510.
15. *Daily Worker,* Dec. 20, 1924, p. 4.
16. *Ibid.,* April 4, 1924, p. 6.
17. Max Bedacht, *The Menace of Opportunism* (Chicago, 1926). Quoted in *The American Communist Party* by Irving Howe and Lewis Coser (Boston: Beacon Press, 1947).
18. *Daily Worker,* May 16, 1924, p. 6.
19. *Ibid.,* Aug. 14, 1926, p. 6.
20. *Ibid.,* Aug. 6, 1926, p. 6.
21. *Ibid.,* Aug. 9, 1926, p. 1.
22. *Ibid.,* Aug. 6, 1926, p. 6.
23. *Ibid.,* Nov. 4, 1926, p. 6.
24. *Ibid.,* March 4, 1932, p. 4.
25. *Ibid.,* Sept. 26, 1930, p. 1.
26. *The Communist,* March 1930, p. 197.
27. *Daily Worker,* May 19, 1932, p. 3.
28. *Ibid.,* March 24, 1930, p. 1.
29. *Ibid.,* Feb. 27, 1930, p. 1.

30. *Ibid.*, March 6, 1930, p. 2.
31. *Ibid.*, May 19, 1932, p. 3.
32. *Interracial Review*, June 1933, p. 117.
33. *The Catholic Worker*, Nov. 1933, p. 1.
34. *Daily Worker*, Oct. 19, 1936, p. 1.
35. *Ibid.*, May 11, 1936, p. 8.
36. *Ibid.*, July 2, 1936, p. 8.
37. *Ibid.*, Aug. 17, 1934, p. 5.
38. *Ibid.*, Feb. 24, 1937, p. 6.
39. *Ibid.*, May 17, 1935, p. 5.
40. *Ibid.*, July 9, 1937, p. 2.
41. *Party Organizer*, May 1938, p. 16.
42. *America*, Sept. 7, 1935, p. 525.
43. *Daily Worker*, Nov. 18, 1935, p. 2.
44. *Ibid.*, Nov. 12, 1936, p. 6.
45. *The Catholic Worker*, July-Aug. 1949, p. 2.
46. Earl Browder, *Religion and Communism* (New York: Workers Library, 1939), p. 11.
47. *The New Republic*, Dec. 15, 1937, p. 164.
48. William Martin Canning is discussed in *The Communists and the Schools* by Robert W. Iversen (New York: Harcourt, Brace, 1959), pp. 213, 216-17.
49. *Labor Leader*, May 5, 1941.
50. *Ibid.*, April 7, 1941.
51. *Crown Heights Comment*, Feb. 5, 1946.
52. Brooklyn *Tablet*, Dec. 6, 1947.
53. James J. Matles, *The Members Run This Union*, UE Publication 94, 1947, p. 37.
54. *UE News*, Feb. 23, 1946.
55. Matles, *op. cit.*, p. 37.
56. *UE News*, Oct. 3, 1949.
57. Quoted in *Labor Leader*, Sept. 30, 1950.
58. *Daily Worker*, March 17, 1937, p. 3.
59. *Ibid.*, May 14, 1940.
60. *Ibid.*, Feb. 12, 1940.
61. *Ibid.*, Feb. 23, 1940.
62. *Ibid.*, March 3, 1940.
63. *Ibid.*, March 4, 1940.
64. *The Communist*, March 1940, p. 231.

CHAPTER EIGHT: INTERVENTION TO ISOLATION—AND BACK AGAIN

1. *Daily Worker*, Aug. 27, 1939, p. 1.
2. *Ibid.*, p. 2.
3. From a statement of the national executive board entitled "The Task of the American League for Peace and Democracy in the Present War Situation."
4. New York *Herald Tribune*, Oct. 29, 1939.
5. The New York *Times*, Oct. 23, 1939. This was confirmed in a telephone conversation with Dr. Bowman in March 1960.
6. The New York *Times*, Feb. 2, 1940.
7. *Idem.*
8. Eleanor Roosevelt, *This I Remember* (New York: Harper, 1949), p. 200.
9. Franklin D. Roosevelt, "Address to the American Youth Congress," in *Public Papers and Addresses of Franklin D. Roosevelt* (New York: Macmillan, 1941), Vol. IX.
10. Ralph J. Bunche, *The Programs, Ideologies, Tactics and Achievements of Negro Betterment and Interracial Organizations*, a research memorandum, part of the Carnegie-Myrdal study entitled *The Negro in America*, Vol. II, p. 366.
11. See *Christian Advocate*, Sept. 7, 1939, p. 853; *Advance*, Dec. 1939, p. 531; *Zions Herald*, Sept. 13, 1939, p. 886; *Christian Standard*, Sept. 2, 1939, p. 3.

12. *The Presbyterian,* Sept. 7, 1939, p. 5; *Watchman-Examiner,* Oct. 12, 1939, p. 1119.
13. *The Christian Century,* Aug. 30, 1939, p. 1035.
14. *The Presbyterian Tribune,* Sept. 14, 1939, p. 9.
15. *The Christian Century,* Oct. 25, 1939, pp. 1298-99.
16. *The Messenger,* Jan. 18, 1940, p. 4.
17. *Fellowship,* Feb. 1940, p. 21.
18. *Radical Religion,* Spring 1940, pp. 9-10.
19. *The Lutheran,* Dec. 13, 1939, p. 14.
20. John Haynes Holmes, "Why We Liberals Went Wrong on the Russian Revolu-tion," Series 1939-40, No. VIII, published by Community Church in New York City.
21. *Ibid.,* p. 1.
22. *Ibid.,* p. 8.
23. *Ibid.,* p. 9.
24. *Ibid.,* p. 14.
25. *Ibid.,* p. 17.
26. The Chicago *Daily News,* Sept. 3, 1940.
27. *Daily Worker,* Sept. 2, 1940, p. 1.
28. "What is APM?"—a leaflet published by the American Peace Mobilization, 1133 Broadway, New York City. Some of the newsletters and other material portraying the final days of the American Peace Mobilization are in the Swarthmore Peace Collection, Swarthmore College, Swarthmore, Pa.
29. Copies of the *Facts for Peace* are located in the Swarthmore Peace Collection, Swarthmore College.
30. *Fellowship,* April 1940, p. 59.
31. A letter and accompanying form were sent in January 1956 to forty-five ministers whose names had been listed by the American Peace Mobilization as officers or sponsors. Many others, of course, could not be located; some had died. Most of those contacted replied. Some were willing to have their names used; others stated their preference that their answer be anonymous. We have followed their wishes in reporting the responses below. One, Lee H. Ball, refused to participate. Replies were not received from a few, including Jack R. McMichael and Donald L. West.
32. Testifying in 1949 before the Seditious Activities Investigation Commission, State of Illinois, Thompson stated: "I am not a Communist. I have never been a Com-munist. I have a profound philosophical criticism for Communism, and I have expressed that on many occasions." (*Investigation of University of Chicago and Roosevelt College.*) Attempts to correspond with Thompson have met with no response.
33. For example, a letter signed by Thompson and Howard Lee was sent to leaders in the Southern Conference for Human Welfare on March 14, 1941, boosting the American People's Meeting in New York on April 5-6, 1941. Thompson and Lee "as individuals" urged participation in the meeting, but the letter was written on S.C.H.W. stationery.
34. One of Thompson's addresses was published by *New Masses,* Feb. 11, 1941, pp. 7-8.
35. Among the books of poetry of Donald L. West are *Crab Grass, Between the Plow Handles, Toil and Hunger, Clods of Southern Earth,* and *The Road Is Rocky.*
36. *Daily Worker,* June 11, 1934, p. 1.
37. A few copies of *The Country Parson* from that period were located in the Swarthmore Peace Collection, Swarthmore College.
38. West's response was included in a confidential memo sent out July 17, 1941, dis-cussing reactions to the new A.P.M. policy.
39. West came into the forefront again during late 1955 and early 1956 when he co-operated with the Church of God of the Union Assembly and became editor of the sect's newspaper, *The Southerner.* A group of workers were fired from their jobs in textile mills in Dalton, Ga., because of their membership in the group. West was ousted from the sect in early 1956 by the Rev. C. T. Pratt, its principal leader, when West refused to testify regarding his past or present Communist

affiliations. The case was given considerable publicity in various newspapers; see, for example, the *Daily Worker* of Feb. 12, 1956, p. 7, in which West is defended against Pratt.

40. F. Hastings Smyth, *Manhood into God* (New York: Round Table Press, 1940), p. 86.
41. *Ibid.*, p. 459.
42. Letter of Smyth to the author, Jan. 30, 1956.
43. Letter of Smyth to the author, Aug. 18, 1957.
44. Detroit *News*, Oct. 24, 1941.
45. Interview with Owen A. Knox in Detroit, Dec. 12, 1956.
46. *The Communist*, Sept. 1942, p. 688.
47. *The Witness*, Oct. 31, 1935, p. 5.
48. *New Masses*, Dec. 25, 1945, p. 7.
49. *The Social Service Bulletin*, Feb. 15, 1933, p. 4.
50. Hewlett Johnson, *The Soviet Power* (New York: International Publishers, 1940), p. 334.
51. *Ibid.*, p. 335.
52. *Ibid.*, p. 336.
53. *Ibid.*, p. 338.
54. *Daily Worker*, March 29, 1941.

CHAPTER NINE: THE ERA OF GOOD WILL

1. Some pacifists, such as Muste, warned of postwar Soviet expansionism. See, for example, *Fellowship* of July, 1944.
2. *Daily Worker*, Feb. 14, 1944.
3. See *Daily Worker* of Jan. 26, 1944, Feb. 13, 1944, March 4, 1944.
4. *Daily Worker*, Jan. 29, 1944, p. 1.
5. *Ibid.*, Feb. 25, 1944, p. 3.
6. *Ibid.*, April 7, 1944, p. 1.
7. *Ibid.*, April 30, 1944, p. 7.
8. *Ibid.*, Aug. 19, 1943, p. 3.
9. *Ibid.*, Aug. 29, 1943, p. 7.
10. The New York *Times*, March 24, 1931.
11. *Daily Worker*, Aug. 29, 1943, p. 7.
12. Letter of Eliot White to the author, Oct. 10, 1955.
13. *Daily Worker*, Aug. 29, 1943, p. 7.
14. Letter of White to the author, Oct. 10, 1955.
15. *Daily Worker*, Feb. 6, 1944, p. 4.
16. *Ibid.*, June 4, 1944, p. 7.
17. *Ibid.*, Jan. 9, 1944, p. 4.
18. Interview with Eliot White in Arlington, Mass., Sept. 20, 1956. The other quotations of the paragraph are from the same interview.
19. *Daily Worker*, Oct. 28, 1941.
20. *Ibid.*, Jan. 12, 1944.
21. Adam Clayton Powell, *Marching Blacks* (New York: Dial Press, 1945), p. 68.
22. Interview with Solomon Freeman in Brooklyn, July 16, 1956.
23. *The Worker*, Jan. 2, 1944, p. 5 (Magazine).
24. *Ibid.*, May 7, 1944.
25. Detroit *News*, May 9, 1944.
26. *Ibid.*, May 13, 1944.
27. *Daily Worker*, May 17, 1944, p. 1.

CHAPTER TEN: THE CHURCHES AND THE COLD WAR

1. Louie D. Newton, *An American Churchman in the Soviet Union*, published by the American-Russian Institute in New York City (no date), p. 38.
2. *Life*, Dec. 15, 1947, p. 26.

3. For an interesting account of Davis' dismissal from Yale and his leadership in the American Federation of Teachers, see Iversen, *op. cit.*, especially pp. 166-69.
4. The New York *Times* followed the Davis libel suit closely. See issues of May 18, 1943, p. 27; May 20, 1943, pp. 27, 46; May 25, 1943, p. 24; May 28, 1943, p. 13 C; June 2, 1943, p. 3; June 3, 1943, p. 23; June 4, 1943, p. 9; June 8, 1943, p. 23; June 9, 1943, p. 230; and June 10, 1943, p. 23 C. The *Christian Advocate* of May 22, 1952 carried Davis' five main criticisms of Communism and the Soviet Union.
5. Jerome Davis, *Behind Soviet Power* (New York: Reader's Press, 1946), p. 12.
6. From Poling's undated syndicated column entitled "Americans All."
7. *Saturday Evening Post*, April 24, 1954, p. 67.
8. The accompanying letter, dated May 29, 1947, was signed by Bishop G. Bromley Oxnam, who was president of the Division of Foreign Missions, and R. S. Diffendorfer, executive secretary of the Division.
9. *Classmate*, July 20, 1947, p. 15.
10. *Ibid.*, June 8, 1947, p. 7.
11. Information on the clergymen who returned to Yugoslavia is not easy to verify from reliable sources. One, Nikola Drenovac, apparently entered the United States on July 7, 1938, as an immigrant. He was ousted from the Serbian Orthodox Church by the strongly anti-Communist presiding bishop in America, Dionisije Milojevich. For a time, Drenovac claimed to be heading a new "progressive" church, then became editor of *Slobodna Rech,* and was active in the American Slav Congress. He returned to Yugoslavia on Oct. 19, 1947.

    A second priest, Voyeslav Gachinovich, played a leading role in the American Slav Congress and served as secretary of the American Serbian Committee for Relief of War Orphans in Yugoslavia. He was pastor for a while of an independent Serbian Orthodox congregation in Pittsburgh. In 1948 he suddenly returned to Yugoslavia. He had entered the United States in 1939.

    Strahinja Maletich, a third clergyman, was executive secretary of the United Committee of South Slavic Americans and a member of the national committee of the American Slav Congress. According to the testimony of Matthew Cvetic, undercover agent for the F.B.I., Maletich was recalled to Yugoslavia. Maletich had entered the United States with Drenovac in 1938 and left with him in 1947. Cvetic charged that Drenovac and Gachinovich were both Communist Party members, while Maletich was an agent of the Yugoslav secret police. It has not been possible to confirm this Cvetic testimony. The relevant testimony was given on March 14, 1950, and June 22, 1950, before the Un-American Activities Committee.
12. *The Churchman*, Jan. 1, 1947, p. 19.
13. *Zions Herald*, Sept. 3, 1947, p. 847.
14. New York *World Telegram*, Aug. 27, 1947.
15. Release of the National Conference of Christians and Jews dated Aug. 26, 1947.
16. New York *Herald Tribune*, Sept. 11, 1947.
17. Such pro-Tito sentiment has persisted rather widely among some clergymen who have taken a dim view of the Soviet Union. Sherwood Eddy, for example, wrote an article for *The Churchman* of Jan. 1, 1953, in which he said: "I have seen no other country pass through such a complete revolution to the founding of such a democratic Republic, except Czechoslovakia, which Stalin now has dragged back into the vortex of his totalitarian police state. I believe in Tito's honest effort to achieve an eventual democracy, and in the guilt of Cardinal Stepinac, to whom high schools in America are now being dedicated."
18. *The Churchman*, Feb. 15, 1946, p. 7.
19. *Ibid.*, Jan. 1, 1949, p. 24.
20. *Daily Worker*, Nov. 28, 1948.
21. There are at least two helpful doctoral theses on missionary reaction to political developments in China during recent years. "American Protestant Missions and Communist China, 1946-1950" was written by David J. Galligan at Rutgers University in 1952. "Protestant Missions in Communist China," by Creighton Lacy, was done at the Graduate School of Yale University in 1953.

22. Reprinted in *The Churchman,* April 1, 1948, pp. 24-26. The date of the original article was not indicated.
23. Liu Liang-Mo, "Christianity in China Enters a New Era," *China Monthly Review,* June 1951.
24. Letter from Dryden L. Phelps to A. E. Fridell, Dec. 15, 1947. Quoted in Galligan, *op. cit.,* p. 43.
25. *Soviet Russia Today,* Nov. 1950, p. 23.
26. The comments of Phelps and the statement of the Board were included in a Board release dated Jan. 22, 1952.
27. See J. Spencer Kennard, "The Lesson of Korea," *The Churchman,* Nov. 1, 1955.
28. *The Witness,* Jan. 16, 1958, p. 15. In reporting on Ting's earlier consecration, W. B. Spofford, Sr., showed a curious callousness toward an old friend. For several years *The Witness* and the Church League for Industrial Democracy raised funds for Kimber Den, whom Spofford had regarded as a "progressive" clergyman worthy of his support. Den became bishop of Chekiang before Ting, but he was imprisoned in Feb. 1952, according to a report of a bishop carried in *The Witness* of Apr. 26, 1926 (p. 4), "and since then none of his family or friends have had the slightest inkling of his whereabouts. . . . The fact that a new bishop has now been elected and consecrated would seem to imply that definite word has been received of the death of Bishop Den, or of his permanent disability." Spofford reacted to this news with peculiar nonchalance: "His successor, the Rev. K. H. Ting so the Church in China seems to be carrying on its own program of revitalization without waiting for help from the Protestant Episcopal Church in the USA or—more important—without waiting for the 'collapse' of their own government which, I suspect, they neither expect nor desire, whatever the difficulties they have to face" (p. 6). The inconsistency of Spofford in decrying imprisonment of Communists in the United States and yet minimizing imprisonment of church leaders in Eastern Europe and abandoning his friend in China is appalling. Warren McKenna reported after his trip to China in 1957 (see Chapter 12) that Den had been released from prison.
29. V. J. Jerome, "The Vatican War on Peace," *Political Affairs,* April 1946, p. 313.
30. An article in *Political Affairs* of March 1950 suggests that Browder's opposition to the anti-Catholic line was one factor in his expulsion. Browder was ousted as head of the party in 1945, but not expelled from membership until Feb. 1946.
31. V. J. Jerome, "A World 'Christian Front,'" *New Masses,* Nov. 26, 1946. The article was reprinted as a pamphlet and distributed by *New Masses.* See also *Political Affairs* of Aug. 1947, p. 730, for an attempt to link John Foster Dulles and the Federal Council of Churches to the Taft-Hartley Act.
32. *Daily Worker,* Nov. 10, 1947.
33. *Ibid.,* Nov. 18, 1947, and Jan. 5, 1948.
34. *Ibid.,* June 9, 1948.
35. *Ibid.,* Feb. 17, 1949.
36. *Ibid.,* April 17, 1949.
37. *Ibid.,* June 25, 1950.
38. *Ibid.,* Nov. 17, 1948.
39. *Ibid.,* June 1, 1950.
40. William Z. Foster, *The Twilight of World Capitalism* (New York: International Publishers, 1949), p. 158.
41. *Ibid.,* p. 87.
42. *Ibid.,* p. 88.
43. *Ibid.,* pp. 93-94.

CHAPTER ELEVEN: COMMUNIST FRONTS AND THE CLERGY

1. John W. Darr, Jr., a graduate of Harvard (1941) and Union Theological Seminary (1944), was ordained into the ministry of social action by the Congregational Church in 1944. He spent two years in the infantry and then devoted much of his time from 1947 to 1950 to political activities. His main emphasis

following the war was upon the United Christian Council for Democracy. His zeal may be measured by listing some of his organizational ties during those early postwar years. He was a national vice-chairman of the Young Progressives of America; a vice-chairman of the American Labor Party and a candidate for State Assembly on the A.L.P. ticket in 1948; chairman of the board of directors of the American Committee for Protection of Foreign Born; a member of the board of directors of the National Council of American-Soviet Friendship; a member of the board of directors of the Committee for a Democratic Far Eastern Policy; a sponsor of the National Non-Partisan Committee to Defend the Rights of the 12 Communist Leaders; a sponsor of the May Day parades of 1947 and 1948; and a sponsor of the Civil Rights Congress. His role in the Communist peace campaign is discussed briefly in Chapter 12.

2. Richard Morford attended Union Theological Seminary in New York City during the height of the Depression, directed a Presbyterian settlement house in Albany, then became executive secretary of the United Christian Council for Democracy, a federation of six Protestant social-action agencies. Three of its participating groups became inactive during World War II and a fourth, the Unitarian Fellowship for Social Justice, voted to withdraw later. Only the Church League for Industrial Democracy and the Methodist Federation for Social Action remained. Hence, the U.C.C.D. devolved into an ineffective letterhead group moving within the Communist orbit. In 1945 Morford began his full-time work with the National Council of American-Soviet Friendship. John W. Darr, Jr., took over the U.C.C.D., which gradually withered away.

3. One graduate of Union Theological Seminary, Arnold Johnson, went to prison under the Smith Act. After he completed his seminary work in 1932, Johnson immediately moved into the political arena, first associating with the Ohio Unemployed League, later with the Communist Party. He now serves on the national committee of the party.

4. The text of the petition, as well as the names of its signers, was released by Edward D. McGowan, then of Epworth Methodist Church in Bronx, N. Y. It was dated Jan. 13, 1953.

5. The New York *Times,* Dec. 21, 1955.

6. The most important petition among clergymen was launched by three Protestant ministers, Jesse Stitt, Bernard M. Loomis, and James Luther Adams—all sharply critical of Soviet Communism. Among other non-Communist petitions was one released to the press by A. J. Muste. There is a considerable body of literature on the Rosenberg case, including several books, many pamphlets, and various publications of the Un-American Activities Committee.

7. *We Charge Genocide* was edited by William L. Patterson. Among those listed as serving on the staff in charge of preparation were Howard Fast, Stetson Kennedy, and Elizabeth Lawson.

8. *We Charge Genocide,* p. 23.

9. *Ibid.,* p. 27.

10. Hearing before the Subversive Activities Control Board on the American Committee for Protection of Foreign Born, Jan. 26, 1956, Docket 109-53, Frank J. McCabe of Washington, D. C., official reporter, p. 5846.

11. Detroit *News,* Nov. 6, 1941.

12. Hearings of the Un-American Activities Committee, "Communism in the Detroit Area—Part I," p. 2823 (Feb. 27, 1952).

13. *Michigan Chronicle,* March 8, 1952, p. 24.

14. Hearings of the Un-American Activities Committee, "Investigation of Communist Activities in the Pacific Northwest Area—Part 2 (Seattle)," p. 6120-2. Mrs. Bartle actually identified three ministers but did not identify the race of the third.

15. *Ibid.,* Part 5, pp. 6329-34.

16. *Daily Worker,* Aug. 29, 1948.

17. *Ibid.,* March 25, 1949.

18. *Ibid.,* Nov. 2, 1949.

19. The remarks of Edward D. McGowan were circulated in a leaflet by the National Committee to Defend Negro Leadership.
20. *Daily Worker,* Feb. 22, 1948.
21. Yergan's statement that he was not a member of the Communist Party was made on May 13, 1952, and may be found in Part 13 of the Committee's hearings on the Institute of Pacific Relations, p. 4598. Since Yergan appeared willingly to assist the Committee, it is unlikely that he was not telling the truth. His statement, therefore, casts doubt upon the testimonies of at least eight informants who earlier had "identified" Yergan as a party member. These eight included Benjamin Gitlow, Manning Johnson, and Louis Budenz. While in the Communist orbit, however, Yergan had been associated in some way with at least fifty front groups and held high offices in several of them.
22. The writer was present at the press conference in 1948, when as a student at Swarthmore College, he attended the Republican, Democratic, Progressive, and Socialist conventions that year. A considerable amount of the information included in this section on the Progressive Party was collected at that time.

CHAPTER TWELVE: THE COMMUNIST PEACE CAMPAIGN

1. *Political Affairs,* Jan. 1945, p. 63.
2. Letter of John M. Swomley, Jr., of Dec. 30, 1947. Later, in 1954, Swomley wrote an excellent pamphlet entitled *The Peace Offensive and the Cold War,* published by the National Council Against Conscription.
3. *The Churchman,* June 1, 1950, p. 27. See also April 1, 1951.
4. From literature of the World Peace Council and the American Peace Crusade in the Swarthmore Peace Collection, Swarthmore College.
5. From the Swarthmore Peace Collection, Swarthmore College.
6. *The Churchman,* Nov. 1, 1950, p. 21.
7. See *The Witness,* Oct. 5, 1950, p. 20; Oct. 23, 1950, p. 21; April 19, 1951, p. 20.
8. From the Swarthmore Peace Collection, Swarthmore College.
9. See *Information Service,* Sept. 23, 1950; also *The Churchman,* Aug. 1950, p. 21.
10. The New York *Times,* Aug. 3, 1950.
11. *Social Questions Bulletin,* Nov. 1950, p. 36.
12. *The Protestant,* July-Aug.-Sept. 1952, p. 12.
13. In its issue of July 27, 1950, *The Witness* carried a headline "World and Federal Councils Endorse Korean War." Two paragraphs summarized their actions; seven paragraphs in the same story told in detail how the pacifist Fellowship of Reconciliation and two front organizations—the Peace Information Center and the Committee for a Democratic Far Eastern Policy—had stated their opposition to United Nations military action in Korea. It was obvious where the editor, William B. Spofford, Sr., stood.
14. *The Witness,* Sept. 7, 1950, p. 15.
15. *The Churchman,* Sept. 15, 1950, pp. 18-19.
16. In 1956, a study of seventy ministers listed as signers of the Stockholm Peace Appeal was made by the author. Space does not permit an adequate summation of the findings, but the ministers quoted here participated in the survey and their answers are taken from replies to a letter of Aug. 13, 1956.
17. *Daily Worker,* March 16, 1951.
18. *The Witness,* Oct. 25, 1951, p. 4. The *Daily Worker* of Oct. 8, 1951, estimated that 9,000 attended; *The Living Church* of Oct. 28, 1951, estimated 5,000.
19. *Daily Worker,* Oct. 8, 1951, p. 3.
20. Confidential letter from a leader in the American Friends Service Committee to Uphaus, Oct. 23, 1951.
21. Jessica Smith, *The American People Want Peace* (New York: S.R.T. Publications, 1955), p. 21.
22. *Ibid.,* p. 22.
23. Mrs. Buckner was subpoenaed by the Un-American Activities Committee in 1956 and appeared on June 19 of that year. She was questioned with regard

to Save Our Sons, of which she was secretary-treasurer. She pleaded the Fifth Amendment in response to most queries, including one asking her if she had been a member of the Argo Branch of the Communist Party in Argo, Ill. See the hearings of June 18-19, 1956, entitled "Investigation of Communist Propaganda Among Prisoners of War in Korea (Save Our Sons)," pp. 5147-50.

24. The list of Negro signers was in the *Daily Worker* of Aug. 25, 1950. The prayer vigil was held on June 23, 1951, and was announced in an undated memo of the Negro People's Committee for Peace and Freedom.

25. *Daily Worker,* Aug. 17, 1950.

26. The executive committee of the Fellowship of Reconciliation authorized a memorandum dated May 1, 1950, stating its views on the Mid-Century Conference for Peace. In June a report on the Conference written by Herman Will, Jr., was also distributed among religious pacifist leaders. Another interesting document of the period was a statement on "The Peace Movements and United Fronts," adopted by the executive committee of F.O.R. in July 1950.

27. The text of Uphaus' Warsaw address was found in the files of the Methodist Federation for Social Action in Hartford, Connecticut, in the basement of the parsonage of Loyd F. Worley, who kindly made them available to the author.

28. *The Witness,* Jan. 29, 1953, p. 13.

29. There is much published material on the Uphaus case. Uphaus presented his own view in *Zions Herald* of Jan. 1960. He was defended in an article by Kermit Eby in *The Christian Century* of April 13, 1960, pp. 442-43. The New York *Times* of April 21, 1960, editorialized on behalf of his release from jail. Wyman presented his case against Uphaus in his report dated Jan. 5, 1955, and published under the title *Subversive Activities in New Hampshire.* It is interesting to note that Wyman expressed special appreciation to extreme and careless observers for "providing voluminous documented information and exhibits. . . ." They include: J. B. Matthews; M. J. Lowman of the Circuit Riders of Cincinnati; Clarence Lohman of the Committee for the Preservation of Methodism; George Washington Robnett of the Church League of America; and Walter S. Steele, editor of the *National Republic.*

30. *The Witness,* June 26, 1952.

31. Boston *Globe,* Sept. 29, 1950.

32. *Our Common Concern,* No. 1, a periodical launched in 1950 by Warren H. McKenna and Robert Muir.

33. *Ibid.*

34. *The Churchman,* Sept. 1, 1950.

35. Hearings before the Un-American Activities Committee, "Investigation of the Unauthorized Use of United States Passports—Part 4," pp. 4598-622 (June 14, 1956).

36. Address (mimeographed) given at the Maple Leaf Gardens on May 11, 1952.

37. *China Monthly Review,* June 1952, p. 546.

38. *The Protestant,* April-May-June 1952, p. 1.

39. *The Witness,* Aug. 21, 1952.

40. Clarence Duffy, *Peace on Earth* (Staten Island, N. Y., 1952), p. 7.

41. Moulton's testimony before the Subversive Activities Control Board was on March 13, 1956, in Salt Lake City, Utah. The hearings on the American Committee for Protection of Foreign Born were recorded by Frank J. McCabe, official reporter, of Washington, D. C. The quotation is from p. 7068.

42. *Ibid.,* p. 7069.

43. *Ibid.,* p. 7064.

44. *Ibid.,* p. 7066.

CHAPTER THIRTEEN: PATRIOTS, EX-COMMUNISTS, AND CONGRESSMEN

1. *Christian Beacon,* Sept. 6, 1945, p. 8. Additional information on the McIntire group and other factions of Protestantism's extreme Right Wing may be found in my earlier book, *Apostles of Discord* (Boston: Beacon Press, 1953).

2. Donald Grey Barnhouse, *Scandal in Korea* (Philadelphia: The Evangelical Foundation, 1960), p. 27.
3. This error was caught in later editions of *100 Things You Should Know About Communism and Religion.* The reply to No. 81 was changed to read: "Yes. For instance, a minister was discharged as editor of an official church publication for permitting communistic propaganda to appear in this publication."
4. The Committee also changed the latter part of this reply to read simply: "Also, church youth groups."
5. The New York *Times,* March 11, 1953, p. 12.
6. *Congressional Record,* March 17, 1953, p. 2102.
7. Washington *Post,* April 5, 1953.
8. The New York *Times,* May 2, 1953, p. 17.
9. Carl McIntire, *Bishop Oxnam, Prophet of Marx* (Collingswood, N. J.: Christian Beacon Press, 1953), p. 3.
10. Hearings before the Committee on Un-American Activities, "Investigation of Communist Activities in the New York City Area—Part 6," p. 2053 (July 7, 1953).
11. *Ibid.,* p. 2054.
12. *Ibid.,* p. 2055.
13. *Ibid.,* p. 2053.
14. Los Angeles *Times,* March 16, 1955, Pt. II, p. 10.
15. *Subversion in Racial Unrest.* Public Hearings of the State of Louisiana Joint Legislative Committee, Part 1, p. 125 (March 8, 1957).
16. "Investigation of Communist Activities in the New York City Area Part 6," *op. cit.,* p. 2218.
17. *Ibid.,* p. 2231.
18. *Ibid.,* p. 2279.
19. *Subversion in Racial Unrest, op. cit.,* p. 204.
20. *Ibid.,* p. 201.
21. Stephen S. Wise was never a fellow traveler. He often denounced Communism and was, in turn, bitterly attacked by the Communists. On Feb. 2, 1927, for example, the *Daily Worker* described him as under the spell of the "harlot press of the capitalists." During the time of the Hitler-Stalin pact, he was lampooned as a warmonger. Before his death in 1949, he sought to uproot divisive pro-Communist elements within the American Jewish Congress. To present the full picture, however, it should be noted that during a few years—notably during the height of united-front activities in the thirties and during World War II—he, like many others, did lend his name to several front groups and showed a degree of enthusiasm for the U.S.S.R. The Gitlow testimony can be found in the source listed in note 10.
22. *Congress Weekly,* Oct. 19, 1953, p. 6.
23. See Herbert A. Philbrick, *I Led Three Lives* (New York: McGraw-Hill, 1952), p. 269.
24. Philbrick is quoted against Senator McCarthy in *McCarthy: The Man, the Senator, the "Ism"* by Jack Anderson and Ronald W. May (Boston: Beacon Press, 1952), pp. 244-45.
25. Hearings before the Un-American Activities Committee in Boston, "Exposé of Communist Activities in the State of Massachusetts" (based on the testimony of Herbert A. Philbrick), p. 1292 (July 23, 1951).
26. Philbrick said that he knew of the existence of a ministers' cell because it "came up in the course of one of our fund-raising drives, and in our cell meeting we were discussing the sources of—we had to raise $3,500 from our pro-group section of 70 to 80 people, which was quite a large sum for that small number, and that posed the problem as to just how we were to go about it, and it was said at that time that we can't expect very much from our 7 to 8 ministers" (p. 2015). When this reply is analyzed, and then the names of the ministers he named are examined, a serious problem arises. When $3,500 is split evenly seventy ways, each person would be responsible for $50—which men like Fritchman, Fletcher, and Lothrop certainly could have contributed.

Assuming that there was a ministers' cell in the Boston area (a big assumption), it might be reasonable to conjecture on the basis of other evidence in this study that it may have been composed of Negro clergy. The Communists had a small nucleus among Boston's Negro population, including at least one of its prominent leaders. It was among a few Negro ministers of small congregations that the Communists seemed to have their greatest success in actually recruiting members.

27. "Investigation of Communist Activities in the New York City Area—Part 5," *op. cit.*, p. 2010.
28. *Ibid.*, p. 2016.
29. Efforts to locate Anthony de Lucca (the spelling given by Philbrick) have failed. In an interview on Feb. 1, 1957, Philbrick indicated that Anthony de Lucca was a Baptist. The Baptists do not have a minister serving by that name at the present time.
30. "Investigation of Communist Activities in the New York City Area—Part 5," *op. cit.*, p. 2017.
31. From the "Statement of Purpose" of the Community Church of Boston.
32. Letter of Donald Lothrop, Sept. 23, 1952.
33. Boston *Globe*, Sept. 13, 1953. This statement of Lothrop's hints at his belief that Philbrick may have been a genuine member of the Communist Party, who, when he decided to quit, sought to protect himself by becoming an informant for the F.B.I.
34. Donald G. Lothrop, *I Read It in the Papers*, p. 16, a pamphlet giving Lothrop's interpretation of, and reply to, the Philbrick charges against him. It was published by the Community Church of Boston.
35. *Ibid.*, p. 10.
36. *Ibid.*, p. 13.
37. *Ibid.*, p. 23.
38. "Investigation of Communist Activities in the New York City Area—Part 5," *op. cit.*, p. 2018.
39. Boston *Globe*, Sept. 13, 1953.
40. Quoted in *The Churchman*, Nov. 15, 1953, p. 14.
41. From a brief undated statement by Bishop Nash released by his office in Boston.
42. New York *Herald Tribune*, Nov. 14, 1954, Section II, p. 2.
43. *Zions Herald*, Nov. 24, 1954, p. 2. A letter from John M. Swomley, Jr., appeared in the New York *Herald Tribune* on Dec. 5, 1954. Swomley left the F.O.R. on July 1, 1960, to join the faculty of the National Methodist Theological Seminary in Kansas City, Mo.
44. New York *Herald Tribune*, March 13, 1955.
45. *Ibid.*, April 28, 1959.
46. The New York *Times*, July 10, 1953.
47. *Daily Worker*, Feb. 27, 1953.
48. See J. B. Matthews and R. E. Shallcross, *Partners in Plunder* (New York: Covici Friede, 1935), pp. 329-42.
49. *Daily Worker*, Oct. 16, 1935, p. 3.
50. From the minutes of the National Bureau of the American League Against War and Fascism, Oct. 7, 1935 (in the Swarthmore Peace Collection, Swarthmore College).
51. Pike was quoted in an undated release from the Cathedral of St. John the Divine which gave the substance of his remarks over WABC on July 16, 1953.
52. Several brief interpretations of the life of J. B. Matthews have been published. One of the best was written by Paul Hutchinson in *The Christian Century* of July 29, 1953.

CHAPTER FOURTEEN: THE CHURCHES TAKE THE OFFENSIVE

1. Hearings before the Un-American Activities Committee, "Testimony of Bishop G. Bromley Oxnam," p. 3587 (July 21, 1953).

2. *Ibid.,* p. 3586.
3. *Ibid.,* p. 3592.
4. G. Bromley Oxnam, *I Protest* (New York: Harper, 1954), p. 27.
5. "Testimony of Bishop G. Bromley Oxnam," *op. cit.,* p. 3701.
6. *Ibid.,* p. 3621.
7. *The Methodist Challenge,* May 1950, p. 4.
8. "Testimony of Bishop G. Bromley Oxnam," *op. cit.,* p. 3710.
9. *Ibid.,* p. 2712.
10. *Ibid.,* p. 3725.
11. Ward wrote to the New York *Times* on July 24, 1953, from the Canadian back-woods in Ontario (the letter appeared on July 31): "Such testimony is completely false. I am not and never have been a member of any political party." *The Churchman* of Oct. 1, 1953, reported that Ward sent a letter to Chairman Velde on Sept. 12, 1953, which stated in part: "I repeat, I am not and never have been a member of any political party. . . . This means plainly that I am not and never have been a member of the Communist Party either openly or secretly. . . . This statement I am willing to support under oath before any properly constituted tribunal. . . . This also means that none of my activities have ever been directed by the Communist Party." In addition to the testimony of Manning Johnson and Leonard Patterson regarding Ward, there was also testimony before the Un-American Activities Committee on July 7, 1953, by Benjamin Gitlow that Ward (and McMichael) were members of the Communist Party. He, too, like Johnson and Patterson, offered no corroborating evidence to support his charge.
12. *The Protestant,* June-July 1941.
13. "Testimony of Bishop G. Bromley Oxnam," *op. cit.,* p. 3602.
14. *Ibid.,* p. 3801.
15. The New York *Times,* July 23, 1953.
16. These three newspapers were quoted in the brochure "In Freedom's Defense," published by Methodist Information shortly after the Oxnam hearing.
17. Quoted in the *Christian Advocate,* Aug. 6, 1953, p. 11.
18. Brooklyn *Tablet,* Aug. 15, 1953.
19. *One,* Sept. 1953, p. 9.
20. *The Progressive,* Oct. 1953, p. 20.
21. "Testimony of Bishop G. Bromley Oxnam," *op. cit.,* p. 3727.
22. Moulder and Doyle were quoted in the Washington *Post,* July 21, 1953.
23. *Zions Herald,* March 3, 1954.
24. See *American Mercury,* May 1953.
25. From a statement by John A. Mackay, "Concerning a Smear Campaign," dated Jan. 6, 1950, pp. 4-5.
26. Letter to the New York *Times* published on July 12, 1953.
27. Letter to Presbyterians, p. 2. This letter appeared in many forms, including that of a separate leaflet.
28. *Presbyterian Life,* Nov. 28, 1953, p. 18.
29. *Idem.*
30. Edward A. Dowey, Jr., wrote an excellent article on "Poling and the Presbyterian Letter" in *Christianity and Crisis,* Oct. 4, 1954. He demonstrated how inaccurate the implications of the Poling statement were.
31. Letter from Herbert A. Philbrick to Edgar C. Bundy, June 10, 1954.
32. *Time,* Nov. 23, 1953, p. 89.
33. *Zions Herald,* Dec. 16, 1953, p. 1.
34. The New York *Times,* May 27, 1954.
35. New York *Post,* April 12, 1954, p. 30.
36. *The Churchman,* Sept. 15, 1948.
37. *Ibid.,* March 1, 1949, p. 19; see also March 15, 1949, p. 26.
38. *Ibid.,* Oct. 1, 1951, p. 11.
39. Chicago *Tribune,* March 10, 1954.
40. The New York *Times,* July 18, 1954.
41. *The New Leader,* July 26, 1954, p. 21.

42. Chicago *Tribune,* July 23, 1954. This same Bentley, incidentally, was the most seriously wounded of five representatives who were shot at random by Puerto Rican nationalists who entered the House in March 1954. His subcommittee was known as the Subcommittee on Communist Take-Over and Occupation of Hungary and was part of the Kersten Select Committee on Communist Aggression.

43. *Eternity,* Sept. 1954, p. 7. Matthew Spinka has written an interesting discussion of Hromadka under the title "Church in Communist Society: A Study of J. L. Hromadka's Theological Politics." It was published in the Hartford Seminary Foundation *Bulletin,* No. 17, June 1954.

44. The New York *Times,* July 21, 1954.

45. Chicago *News,* Aug. 23, 1954.

46. *Michigan Christian Advocate,* Sept. 9, 1954.

47. Washington *Post,* Jan. 16, 1955. *The Hungarian Church Press* of June 1, 1957, tells of attempts to oust Peter and Bereczky—and their "vindication" after the revolution.

48. Arnold T. Ohrn, general secretary of the Baptist World Alliance, told of his experiences in Russia in the *Watchman-Examiner,* Sept. 29, 1955. *Ebony* of Nov. 1955 carried an illustrated story on the trip of J. H. Jackson, president of the National Baptist Convention, Inc.

49. *Time,* March 26, 1956, p. 52.

50. *Presbyterian Life,* April 28, 1956, p. 8. *The U.S. News and World Report* of April 8, 1956, carried the text of a statement issued by the delegation entitled, "Our Mission—Understanding in a Time of Tension." The same issue also published the proceedings of a press conference held upon their return.

51. The New York *Times,* June 9, 1956.

52. *Ibid.,* June 7, 1956.

53. *The Witness,* June 28, 1956, p. 4.

54. *Idem.*

55. The New York *Times,* July 6, 1956.

56. *Ibid.,* Nov. 26, 1956.

57. *The Witness,* Jan. 17, 1957, p. 16.

58. There were accusations from pro-Communist sources that the World Council of Churches helped to incite the Hungarian revolution. The *New Christian,* formerly the *Protestant* (discussed in Chapter 15), took this point of view. The editor, Kenneth Leslie, writing in the issue of March-April 1958, gave a word of advice to the Hungarian churches. "The New Christian has never tried to interfere with the life of the Hungarian churches. We have tried, however, to inform the church people of Hungary about the nature and function of the World Council of Churches. This organization is a paper organization foisted upon the churches by one of the greatest cartel powers in the world, the Rockefeller Dynasty. Its function is to prepare in the Protestant churches the seed-bed of middle-class morality, the moral basis for world war against socialism. . . . When Protestant churches in the socialist countries dallied with the World Council they must have been extremely naïve to think that the World Council would hold itself aloof from power politics. The very fact that Dulles, the Rockefeller lawyer, the anti-Soviet hessian, became the spokesman for World Council policy should have been enough, and certainly today should be enough to open their eyes." Leslie then urged the Hungarian churches to withdraw from the World Council. "For the World Council betrayed peace in Korea, and after that betrayal any church that remained in the World Council shared in that betrayal. Today the World Council stands convicted by its own testimony of the crime of aiding and abetting a Hapsburg counter-revolution in Hungary. . . . Come out from among them!" (pp. 6-7).

CHAPTER FIFTEEN: IN THE NAME OF RELIGION

1. *100 Things You Should Know About Communism and Religion* (released originally by the Committee on Un-American Activities in 1948), revised edition, May 14, 1951, p. 43.

2. *Ibid.,* p. 44.
3. Cedric Belfrage, *A Faith to Free the People* (New York: Dryden Press, 1944), p. 126.
4. *Ibid.,* p. 134.
5. *Radical Religion,* Winter 1935-1936, p. 42.
6. Belfrage, *op. cit.,* pp. 192-204.
7. *Ibid.,* p. 141.
8. The quotation is found on the first page of the document entitled "Complete Proceedings, Trial of Claude C. Williams, By the Executive Council, Southern Tenant Farmers Union, September 16 and 17, 1938."
9. *Religion: Barrier or Bridge to a People's World,* a "handbook for progressive leaders" published by the People's Institute in 1947, p. 62.
10. *Ibid.,* p. 5.
11. *Ibid.,* p. 11.
12. *Ibid.,* p. 63.
13. *Ibid.,* p. 58.
14. *Ibid.,* p. 61.
15. *Ibid.,* p. 46.
16. *Daily Worker,* March 8, 1959.
17. *The Churchman,* Jan. 15, 1949.
18. *Ibid.,* Oct. 1, 1950.
19. Proceedings had and testimony taken in The Presbyterian Church, U.S.A., versus Rev. Claude Williams, at Detroit, Jan. 4, 12, 13, 1954.
20. *Ibid.,* p. 176.
21. *National Guardian,* March 22, 1954, p. 2.
22. *Michigan Christian Advocate,* Dec. 9, 1954, p. 10 (Religious News Service).
23. Belfrage, *op. cit.,* p. 238.
24. *Religion: Barrier or Bridge to a People's World,* pp. 20-1.
25. Proceedings of 1954 church trial, p. 245.
26. *Ibid.,* p. 326.
27. *Protestant Digest,* Oct. 1939, p. 3.
28. *The Protestant,* June-July 1941, p. 24.
29. *Ibid.,* Oct.-Nov. 1941, p. 77.
30. *Ibid.,* Dec.-Jan. 1942, p. 2.
31. *Ibid.,* June-July 1942, p. 4.
32. *Ibid.,* Jan. 1945, p. 12.
33. *Ibid.,* Nov. 1943, p. 47.
34. *Ibid.,* March 1944, p. 3.
35. *Ibid.,* Oct.-Nov. 1942, p. 57.
36. *Ibid.,* Aug.-Sept. 1943, p. 7.
37. *Ibid.,* Oct.-Nov. 1942, p. 57.
38. *Ibid.,* Feb. 1945, p. 3.
39. *Ibid.,* June-July 1946, p. 7.
40. *Ibid.,* Jan.-Feb. 1948, p. 15.
41. *Ibid.,* June-July, 1947, p. 7.
42. *Ibid.,* Oct. 1945, p. 8.
43. *Ibid.,* Jan.-Feb. 1948, p. 16.
44. *Ibid.,* p. 8.
45. This group was led by Pierre van Paassen, a contributing editor, and included James M. Freeman, managing editor, and three associate editors—Ben Richardson, Gerald Richardson, and Joseph Brainin. Apparently political differences were not the main issue. While several of these may be viewed as critics of Communism in more recent years, Joseph Brainin continued to be very active within the Communist orbit and in 1952-53 served as chairman of the National Committee to Secure Justice in the Rosenberg Case.
46. *The Protestant,* Jan. 1949, p. 20.
47. *One,* Nov. 1954, p. 7.
48. *New Christian,* March 1955, p. 2.
49. *Idem.*

50. *The Protestant,* Summer 1950, p. 19. When this special issue, entitled "Common Sense About Korea," appeared, several clergy withdrew, among them Adam Clayton Powell, Jr., and Lee H. Ball.
51. *One,* Aug. 1954, p. 5.
52. *One,* May 1954, p. 8.
53. Most of the clergymen responded. Some agreed to allow the use of their names; others preferred anonymity. The author sought to follow their wishes in each case.
54. *The Protestant,* Dec.-Jan. 1947, p. 4.
55. *Ibid.,* Dec. 1943, p. 1.
56. *Ibid.,* Oct. 1945, pp. 18-19.
57. The statements of the Jewish agencies on *The Protestant* were collected in a memorandum distributed by the National Community Relations Advisory Council, Sept. 21, 1947.
58. In the fifties, Leslie concluded that Zionism and Israel had become puppets of "anti-Soviet money imperialism" and had sold themselves "to the service of the Napalm Knights of the new world aggression." (*The Protestant,* Vol. IX, No. 4, p. 2.) At the time of Israeli-Egyptian hostilities in 1956 he made sharper attacks upon Israel. See *New Christian,* March-April 1956, p. 11; Jan.-Feb. 1957, p. 1.

CHAPTER SIXTEEN: THE METHODIST CONTROVERSY

1. *100 Things You Should Know About Communism and Religion,* reply to question #92.
2. *Review of the Methodist Federation for Social Action,* Feb. 15, 1952 (original release date). This document makes a pretense of coming to no conclusion but of simply providing factual background on the Federation.
3. *Handbook for Americans,* April 23, 1956, p. 91. Curiously, the House Committee on Un-American Activities, in its *Guide to Subversive Organizations and Publications* (revised edition, Jan. 2, 1957), uses the Senate Subcommittee's indictment of the Federation rather than its own description.
4. The five churchmen were Worth M. Tippy, then a pastor in Cleveland; E. Robb Waring of the *Western Christian Advocate;* Frank Mason North of the New York City Society; Bishop Herbert Welch; and Ward, then a pastor in the stockyards district of Chicago.
5. *The Social Service Bulletin,* Sept. 1918, p. 1.
6. Upon his return, Ward wrote *In Place of Profit* (New York: Charles Scribner's Sons, 1933).
7. *Daily Worker,* Sept. 14, 1932, p. 1; also Nov. 6, 1932, p. 2.
8. *The Social Service Bulletin,* May 15, 1932, p. 4.
9. *Epworth Herald,* March 3, 1934.
10. *Social Questions Bulletin,* May 1934, p. 1. The *Bulletin* from January through June 1934 focused upon discrediting the New Deal. (The name was changed in Oct. 1933.)
11. *Ibid.,* Nov. 1934, p. 4.
12. Quoted in the *Social Questions Bulletin,* May 1936, p. 2.
13. John Milton Huber, Jr., "A History of the Methodist Federation for Social Action," unpublished doctoral dissertation at Boston University Graduate School, 1949, p. 218. The Huber study is the best study of the Federation to date, although it was written too early to include the Federation's later demise.
14. *Social Questions Bulletin,* Nov. 1939, p. 3.
15. *Ibid.,* Dec. 1939, p. 4.
16. Harry F. Ward, *Democracy and Social Change* (New York: Modern Age Books, 1940), p. 259.
17. *New Masses,* Nov. 11, 1941, p. 10.
18. *Social Questions Bulletin,* Oct. 1941, p. 1.
19. Harry F. Ward, *The Soviet Spirit* (New York: International Publishers, 1944).
20. *Social Questions Bulletin,* April 1944, p. 4.
21. Letter of Jack R. McMichael to John M. Swomley, Jr., March 6, 1945. Among others who expressed serious doubts about the wisdom of selecting McMichael

were Franklin H. Littell and Owen M. Geer. As an illustration of the unreliability of Gitlow's 1953 testimony (see Chapter 13), he sought to leave the impression that Littell, an astute anti-Communist, was in the pro-Communist camp.

22. *Social Questions Bulletin,* Dec. 1946, pp. 132-33.
23. *Ibid.,* April 1947, p. 53. Alson J. Smith was serving as editor.
24. *Idem.*
25. New York *World-Telegram,* Dec. 26, 1947.
26. *Social Questions Bulletin,* Feb.-March 1948, p. 2.
27. The New York *Times,* March 21, 1948.
28. *The Facts,* p. 16. *The Facts* was a pamphlet published by the New York *World-Telegram* which included the articles and editorials from the newspaper and then sought to reply to the Federation and McMichael's rebuttals.
29. Letter of Clyde R. Miller to the delegates, April 5, 1948.
30. The letter from Smith and that from McMichael are in the Federation files in Hartford, Conn.
31. Letter of McMichael, Feb. 11, 1949.
32. Letter of Owen Geer to McMichael, March 22, 1949.
33. Oxnam's article was distributed as a pamphlet. The quotation is from p. 8.
34. W. W. Reid, "On a Wide Circuit," Feb. 20, 1950.
35. The Bishops' resolution, "On Stanley High's Article 'Methodism's Pink Fringe,'" was distributed as a leaflet.
36. *Social Questions Bulletin,* Oct. 1950, p. 32.
37. From brochure distributed by the Circuit Riders, Inc. The Board of Social and Economic Relations of The Methodist Church has sponsored an examination of material distributed by the Circuit Riders regarding Methodist ministers. The study, made by J. Philip Wogaman, was scheduled for publication as a pamphlet in late summer or early fall of 1960.
38. Letter of John M. Mecartney to the editor of the *Social Questions Bulletin,* Dec. 26, 1948.
39. Mecartney's principal colleague in this effort was Hiel Bollinger, secretary of the Methodist Student Movement, and the document was called the "Mecartney–Bollinger" document by many. Others who signed included Owen M. Geer, Franklin H. Littell, Caxton Doggett, Chester H. Kingsbury, and Charles H. Schofield.
40. The organizations listed by Mecartney were as follows: American Continental Congress for Peace (1949); American Peace Mobilization; American Youth Congress; Bill of Rights Conference (1949); Citizens Committee to Free Earl Browder; Civil Rights Congress; Committee for a Democratic Far Eastern Policy; Conference on China and the Far East (1946); International Workers Order; May Day Parade (1947); National Committee to Defeat the Mundt Bill; National Committee to Win the Peace; National Conference on American Policy in China; National Federation for Constitutional Liberties; Schappes Defense Committee.
41. The reply of Albert E. Barnett was dated June 5, 1950. The quotation is from its first page.
42. *Zions Herald,* May 16, 1951, p. 467.
43. Dean Muelder had written an analysis on this McMichael article, entitled "Truth and the Social Zealot" in *Zions Herald,* May 16, 1951, p. 467.
44. Chicago *Tribune,* Sept. 2, 1951.
45. *Christian Advocate,* Sept. 28, 1950, p. 1171.
46. The New York *Times,* May 6, 1952.
47. Quoted in the *Social Questions Bulletin,* June 1952, p. 28.
48. *Idem.*
49. *Idem.*
50. *Social Questions Bulletin,* May 1952, pp. 20-22.
51. Letter of Albert E. Barnett to McMichael, March 18, 1952.
52. Letter of Barnett to McMichael, Jan. 10, 1953.
53. Letter of Barnett to McMichael, Sept. 4—year not certain, but probably 1952.
54. Letter of Albert E. Barnett to Edgar A. Love, Feb. 27, 1953.
55. Letter of Georgia Harkness to McMichael, May 15, 1953.

56. Hearings before the Un-American Activities Committee, "Testimony of Bishop G. Bromley Oxnam," pp. 3746, 3736 (July 21, 1953).
57. *Ibid.*, pp. 3749-50.
58. *Christian Advocate,* Aug. 13, 1953, p. 970.
59. Undated letter of Loyd F. Worley, president; Lee H. Ball, vice-president and interim secretary; Clarence T. R. Nelson, vice-president; Edward L. Peet, vice-president.
60. Hearings before the Un-American Activities Committee, "Testimony of Jack R. McMichael," p. 2648 (July 30-31, 1953).
61. *Ibid.,* p. 2669.
62. *Ibid.,* p. 2661.
63. *Ibid.,* p. 2805.
64. *Ibid.*
65. *Ibid.,* p. 2806.
66. *Ibid.,* p. 2704.
67. *Social Questions Bulletin,* June 1953, p. 4.
68. "Testimony of Jack R. McMichael," *op. cit.,* p. 2696.
69. *Ibid.,* p. 2762.
70. *Ibid.,* pp. 2806-07.
71. New York *Post,* July 31, 1953.
72. "Testimony of Jack R. McMichael," *op. cit.,* p. 2649.
73. *Ibid.,* p. 2773.
74. *Ibid.,* p. 2845.
75. *Ibid.,* p. 2627.
76. *Ibid.,* p. 2826. Earlier in the hearing (p. 2647) McMichael had testified that as chairman of the American Youth Congress in July 1941 he had led a fight for a resolution against an American Expeditionary Force, "which resolution obviously was opposed by the young Communists present, and which resolution was adopted and was part of the policy of the American Youth Congress." This was immediately after the invasion of the U.S.S.R.
77. Letter of Henry Hitt Crane to Loyd F. Worley, Dec. 11, 1953.
78. Letter of Worley to the author, Oct. 19, 1956.
79. *Social Questions Bulletin,* Jan. 1948, p. 4.
80. *Ibid.,* Dec. 1952, p. 39.
81. *Ibid.,* Feb. 1953, p. 5.
82. *Ibid.,* Dec. 1952, p. 39.
83. *Ibid.,* Feb. 1951, p. 6.
84. *Ibid.,* Nov. 1952, p. 36.
85. A letter from Arthur Kahn to McMichael dated March 26, 1952, indicated that the "business man who offered to donate 1000 books is no longer sure he will be able to keep his bargain."
86. *Social Questions Bulletin,* Dec. 1954, p. 34.
87. Among the books in which the Khrushchev speech on the "Cult of the Individual" may be found is the useful compilation of documents edited by The Russian Institute of Columbia University entitled *The Anti-Stalin Campaign and International Communism* (New York: Columbia University Press, 1956).
88. *The Churchman,* April 15, 1953, p. 16.
89. *Social Questions Bulletin,* May 1956, p. 20.
90. *Ibid.,* Nov. 1956, p. 29.
91. *Ibid.,* p. 30.
92. *Ibid.,* p. 31.
93. *New World Review,* Nov. 1956, p. 92.
94. *Social Questions Bulletin,* Summer 1957, p. 23.

CHAPTER SEVENTEEN: THE *Witness* AND THE *Churchman*

1. *The Witness,* Nov. 16, 1933, p. 10.
2. *Ibid.,* Sept. 2, 1937, p. 5.

3. *Ibid.*, March 31, 1938, p. 5.
4. *Ibid.*, Sept. 16, 1937, p. 4.
5. *Ibid.*, p. 6.
6. *The Living Church*, Sept. 21, 1938, p. 253.
7. *The Witness*, Sept. 22, 1938, p. 4.
8. Proceedings before the Subversive Activities Control Board, Herbert Brownell, Jr., Attorney General of the United States, Petitioner v. National Council of American-Soviet Friendship, Inc., Respondent, Vol. VI, p. 3102 (July 9, 1954).
9. *The Witness*, Sept. 7, 1939, p. 5.
10. *Ibid.*, Sept. 23, 1939.
11. *Ibid.*, Sept. 4, 1941, pp. 4-5.
12. *Ibid.*, Jan. 15, 1942, p. 11.
13. *Ibid.*, Aug. 6, 1942, p. 3.
14. *Ibid.*, April 20, 1944.
15. *Ibid.*, March 15, 1945, p. 8.
16. *Ibid.*, June 7, 1945, p. 9.
17. *Ibid.*, Nov. 29, 1945, p. 10.
18. *Ibid.*, Oct. 17, 1946, p. 8.
19. *Ibid.*, March 20, 1947, p. 7.
20. *Ibid.*, March 2, 1950, p. 9.
21. *Ibid.*, May 5, 1949.
22. *Ibid.*, April 19, 1956, p. 9.
23. *Idem.*
24. *Ibid.*, Dec. 29, 1955, p. 7.
25. *Ibid.*, March 24, 1949, p. 15
26. *Ibid.*, Feb. 9, 1950, p. 21.
27. *Ibid.*, Feb. 10, 1955, pp. 3-4.
28. *Ibid.*, March 23, 1950, p. 16.
29. *Ibid.*, May 23, 1946, p. 10.
30. *Ibid.*, Feb. 13, 1947, pp. 8-10. See also March 6, 1947, pp. 9-11.
31. Quoted in *The Witness*, Feb. 16, 1950, p. 18.
32. See *The Witness*, Feb. 16, 1950, p. 19; April 13, 1950, p. 21; Sept. 21, 1950, p. 13.
33. *The Witness*, May 3, 1956
34. *Ibid.*, Aug. 4, 1949, p. 8.
35. *Ibid.*, March 23, 1939, p. 8.
36. *Ibid.*, Jan. 24, 1946, p. 10.
37. *Ibid.*, March 20, 1952.
38. Quoted in *Episcopal Churchnews*, March 29, 1953, p. 14.
39. *The Witness*, June 9, 1955, p. 7.
40. *Ibid.*, March 29, 1951, p. 3.
41. *Episcopal Churchnews*, March 29, 1953, pp. 14-15. The 1960 *Episcopal Church Annual* notes that there was no president of the League at the time of its publication. The officers were listed as follows: vice-presidents, Hubert T. Delany, Joseph F. Fletcher, Kenneth DeP. Hughes, and Mary Van Kleeck; treasurer, Arthur H. Fawcett; secretary, Elizabeth P. Frazier. Spofford was listed as chairman of the executive committee, on which Forbes served.
42. *The New Leader*, April 16, 1949.
43. Letter of Guy Emery Shipler to Leon M. Birkhead, Feb. 3, 1949.
44. *The Churchman*, Nov. 15, 1939.
45. *Ibid.*, March 15, 1941, p. 8.
46. *Ibid.*, Sept. 1, 1949, p. 6.
47. Abba Eban stated that his country did not want to involve itself in domestic controversies. Bishop G. Bromley Oxnam then agreed to present a citation to Israel to Rabbi Israel Goldstein, former president of the Zionist Organization of America, who said he would give it to the proper Israeli authorities. Shipler traced his difficulties to an organized effort to make Protestantism appear synonymous with Communism in the public mind.
48. *The Churchman*, Oct. 1, 1947, p. 6.
49. *Ibid.*, Nov. 15, 1947, p. 23.

50. *Ibid.*, May 1, 1948, p. 19.
51. *Ibid.*, Feb. 15, 1950, p. 28.
52. *Ibid.*, May 1, 1953, p. 23.
53. *Ibid.*, July 1955, p. 50.
54. *Ibid.*, May 1, 1955, p. 9.
55. *Ibid.*, June 1955, pp. 10-11.
56. *Ibid.*, July 1955, p. 9.
57. *Ibid.*, p. 10.

CHAPTER EIGHTEEN: THE MELISH CASE

1. *The Worker*, March 19, 1944; July 2, 1944; Nov. 19, 1944.
2. This third article, published on Nov. 19, 1944, was reprinted from *The Churchman*.
3. *Daily Worker*, Jan. 9, 1944.
4. *The Worker*, April 1, 1945, 8 M.
5. See *Daily Worker*, Nov. 3, 1944, p. 7; see also *New Masses*, Feb. 20, 1945, p. 2. Melish accused the A.L.P. "right wing," which withdrew, of "applying dictatorial standards to party membership." (*The Worker*, Nov. 19, 1944.) It should be borne in mind, of course, that most persons affiliated with the A.L.P. were non-Communists.
6. *Soviet Russia Today*, June 1944.
7. *New Masses*, Feb. 20, 1945, p. 2.
8. William Howard Melish, *Strength for Struggle* (Brooklyn: The Bromwell Press, 1953), p. 159. The address of the Bromwell Press was given as 157 Montague Street, Brooklyn, which is also the address of the church. Among his other writings which Melish lists in *The Clerical Directory of the Protestant Episcopal Church in the U.S. of A.* (1959) are the two pamphlets *The Story of a Congregation* and *The Melish Case: Challenge to the Church*, both of which deal with the church's controversy.
9. *Ibid.*, p. 158.
10. The New York *Times*, Jan. 9, 1956.
11. *Ibid.*, Jan. 11, 1956.
12. Interview with Lewis G. Reynolds.
13. New York *World-Telegram and Sun*, Jan. 9, 1956.
14. The events of Jan. 15, 1956, were reported in great detail in all New York daily newspapers and even across the world. The author attended the service.
15. New York *World-Telegram and Sun*, Jan. 16, 1956.
16. The installation service was also covered widely. The author attended.
17. New York *World-Telegram and Sun*, March 5, 1956.
18. *Amsterdam News*, March 31, 1956.
19. The New York *Times*, April 30, 1956.
20. Melish's address, later mimeographed, was entitled "A Call for Patience, Self-Discipline and the Taking of a Long View," Nov. 13, 1956. The quotation is from p. 5. The address was published in the *New World Review*.
21. *Ibid.*, p. 6.
22. The New York *Times*, Nov. 17, 1956.
23. New York *Herald Tribune*, Nov. 18, 1956.
24. Quoted in the New York *Herald Tribune*, July 8, 1957.
25. Quoted in the New York *Herald Tribune*, July 22, 1957.
26. *Congressional Record*, May 12, 1950, p. 6971.
27. Proceedings before the Subversive Activities Control Board, Herbert Brownell, Jr., Attorney General of the United States, Petitioner, v. National Council of American-Soviet Friendship, Inc., Respondent, pp. 2230-31 (June 9, 1954).
28. *Ibid.*, p. 3118.
29. *Ibid.*, pp. 2173-74.
30. *Ibid.*, pp. 2718-19.
31. *Ibid.*, p. 2670.
32. *Ibid.*, p. 2886.

33. *Ibid.,* p. 2895.
34. *Ibid.,* p. 3165.
35. *Ibid.,* p. 2791.
36. *Ibid.,* p. 2793.
37. *Ibid.,* p. 2800.
38. *Idem.*
39. *Ibid.,* pp. 2805-06.
40. *Ibid.,* p. 2815.
41. The possibility of further controversy over actual possession of the premises of the Church of the Holy Trinity was evident when, on May 19, 1960, two pro-Melish vestrymen, E. DeWitt Ramel and Phillips Brooks, sent an ominous telegram to Bishop DeWolfe. The telegram said in part: "Since the church was closed down by you, there was no authority in the Convention to declare it extinct for our failure to maintain the services. Please be advised that any attempt on the part of yourself and the other Trustees of the Diocese to take possession and administer the property of the Church of the Holy Trinity will constitute a trespass. We give you this notice in performance of our duty to the parishioners who elected us and who still exist as the congregation of the Church of the Holy Trinity." The full telegram was published by *The Churchman* of July 1960, p. 15.

CHAPTER NINETEEN: THE BATTLE OF BEACON HILL

1. *The Christian Register,* Feb. 1944, p. 62. The review was written by Lewis O. Hartman.
2. *The Christian Register,* Nov. 1944, p. 414.
3. Howard Selsam, *What Is Philosophy?* (New York: International Publishers, 1938).
4. *The Christian Register,* July 1945, p. 255.
5. *Ibid.,* April 1946, pp. 158-59. This was an editorial entitled "Kagawa Is Our Concern."
6. *Ibid.,* Aug. 1946, p. 350.
7. *Ibid.,* Oct. 1946. The N.A.A.C.P. is an excellent organization, but would hardly serve as a good public-relations firm for the State of Georgia. The National Council of American-Soviet Friendship, in contrast, had shown itself ecstatic over everything Soviet.
8. *Ibid.,* Dec. 1945, p. 466.
9. *Ibid.,* March 1946, p. 108.
10. *Ibid.,* May 1946, p. 203.
11. *Ibid.,* Jan. 1946, p. 3.
12. The letters of both John Haynes Holmes and William B. Spofford, Sr., appeared in *The Christian Register* of Feb. 1946, pp. 63-64.
13. *The Christian Register,* Oct. 1946, p. 381.
14. The written protest of Melvin Arnold was dated Sept. 18, 1946.
15. This analysis of the *Register* content was dated Nov. 8, 1946.
16. Arnold's statement of policy for the division of publications was made in a document entitled "An informal guide in the selection of authors and editorial contributors." The final draft was dated Feb. 7, 1947.
17. *The Christian Register,* May 1947, p. 181.
18. *The Churchman,* June 15, 1947.
19. Boston *Globe,* May 22, 1947.
20. *The Churchman,* June 15, 1947, pp. 8-9.
21. *The Witness,* May 22, 1947, pp. 11-12.
22. *Zions Herald,* May 28, 1947.
23. *Christian Leader,* June 7, 1947.
24. *Letter to Unitarians,* dated July 1, 1947, p. 2. This pamphlet contained considerable useful background material presented from a pro-Fritchman viewpoint.
25. "A Report on the Christian Register, 1945-46," Friends of Democracy, Oct. 1947.
26. *The Christian Register,* Sept. 1945, p. 347.

27. See Philbrick's testimony before the Un-American Activities Committee, *op. cit.*, p. 2012. Philbrick made this charge in other hearings and in his writings.
28. "The World Federation of Democratic Youth," a report to American Unitarian Youth from the A.U.Y. Council, prepared by the Coordination Committee, Charles Eddis, chairman, 1948.
29. *The Christian Register*, Dec. 1946, Section 2, p. 508.
30. *Ibid.*, p. 505.
31. Matthews' testimony is quoted in the interesting report of the Un-American Activities Committee *The Erica Wallach Story*, March 21, 1958, p. 57. This report was prepared with the co-operation of Mrs. Erica Wallach, the foster daughter of Field and his wife, who disappeared behind the Iron Curtain, states that she was imprisoned by the Communists, then released. The testimony of Mrs. Wallach adds still another mystery to the many surrounding the story of the Fields.
32. See Hede Massing, *This Deception* (New York: Duell, Sloan and Pearce, 1951), especially pp. 163-80.
33. The New York *Times*, Dec. 26, 1956.
34. *Ibid.*, June 27, 1957.
35. Kurt Singer suggests this in his chapter entitled "Noel Field—'Double Spy'?" in his book *The Men in the Trojan Horse* (Boston: Beacon Press, 1953).
36. "Testimony of Bishop G. Bromley Oxnam," *op. cit.*, p. 3790.
37. Hearings before the Committee on Un-American Activities, "Testimony of Stephen H. Fritchman" (Sept. 12, 1951). Fritchman denounced the Committee at the time of the hearing as "seeking to invade the intimate confidence of the confessional."
38. The reliability of the testimony of Benjamin Gitlow before the Un-American Activities Committee on July 7, 1953, was discussed in Chapter 13. Gitlow was very specific in his references to Hall. He stated (p. 2130): "Martin Hall is also known by the name of Herman Jacobs. He is a Communist of long standing, a well-known figure in the Communist Party of Germany. He has sponsored Communist-front movements in the country which gave him asylum and citizenship. He was vice-president of the German-American League for Culture, a Communist organization. He was also editor of the German Communist newspaper published in the United States, *Volksecho*. He was a contributor to the monthly magazine of the Communist Party, the *New Masses*. He contributed numerous articles to the official publication of the Communist International, International Press Correspondence, in 1935, 1936 and 1937. None but accredited Communist Party leaders wrote for International Press Correspondence. In order to get his United States citizenship he had to swear falsely and deny that he was a Communist, that he entertained Communist beliefs, and was affiliated with Communist organizations." In an effort to discover the truth on this matter, the author on two occasions wrote Hall, sending a copy of Gitlow's testimony and asking for his analysis. Hall did not reply. When the author was in Los Angeles in August 1956, he reached Hall personally by telephone and asked for the opportunity of talking with him. Hall refused. Gitlow's testimony is uncorroborated.
39. Stephen H. Fritchman, "What Will People Say?" a sermon delivered at the First Unitarian Church of Los Angeles, June 27, 1954.
40. Steinmetz had an interesting and complicated background. According to the San Diego *Union*, he joined the faculty of California State College in 1930 and as early as 1936 was the center of considerable controversy. That year, for example, the American Federation of Labor expelled him from its executive committee— although Steinmetz claimed that he was absolved of all the charges against him. In 1948 he was a candidate for Congress on the Independent Progressive Party ticket, until he withdrew in favor of the Democrat. In October 1950, he signed the state loyalty oath under protest, but this did not satisfy his critics. The state legislature passed a bill designed to oust him from his faculty position—a bill vetoed by Governor Earl Warren. In April 1953, Steinmetz refused to answer questions regarding his political affiliations before the Un-American Activities Committee, pleading the Fifth, and also the First, Fourth, Sixth, Ninth, and Tenth Amendments. Then, in 1954, he was dismissed by the State Board of Education.

In July 1955, he appeared before the House committee again and swore that he had not been a member of the Communist Party after 1939. He refused to say whether or not he had been a member before.

41. See the Hearings before the Un-American Activities Committee, "Investigation of Communist Activities in the San Diego, Calif., Area" (July 5-6, 1955). There was considerable testimony at these hearings regarding the Community Unitarian Fellowship. Mrs. Anita Bell Schneider, a former Communist Party member who served as an undercover agent for the F.B.I., testified that the Communists deliberately infiltrated the Unitarian Church and, when Samsom resisted, they decided upon the schism that resulted in the creation of the Community Unitarian Fellowship. This was emphatically denied by leaders of the Fellowship. The hearings also include the testimonies of Steinmetz and of Stanley Gue, who served for a time as lay minister for the Fellowship and then withdrew in protest.

42. Stephen H. Fritchman, "The Devil Theory of Russia Must Go," a sermon delivered at the First Unitarian Church of Los Angeles, Feb. 16, 1958.

43. Fritchman, "The Need of Living Two Lives," a typewritten copy of a sermon sent to the author by Fritchman shortly after it was delivered on Nov. 25, 1956.

44. Fritchman, "The Pulpit Perilous," *Mainstream*, Sept. 1956, pp. 32-42.

45. Fritchman, "Is It Utopian to Advocate Socialism?" *Toward a Socialist America*, Helen Alfred, ed. (New York: Peace Publications, 1958), p. 28.

46. Fritchman, "An American in Stockholm," a sermon delivered at the First Unitarian Church of Los Angeles, May 31, 1959.

47. The New York *Times*, Aug. 7, 1960.

CHAPTER TWENTY: CONFLICT WITHIN EASTERN ORTHODOXY

1. From the archives of the Russian Orthodox Church of North America in the Library of Congress (translated by Dmitry Grigorieff).

2. *Novy Mir*, March 15, 1917 (translated by Dmitry Grigorieff).

3. *Russky Golos*, Sept. 19, 1917 (translated by Dmitry Grigorieff).

4. William Chauncey Emhardt, *Religion in Soviet Russia* (Milwaukee: Morehouse, 1929), p. 90.

5. The New York *Times*, Nov. 9, 1923.

6. The resolutions from the 1924 *sobor* were introduced as an exhibit of Platon in the legal struggle for control of St. Nicholas Cathedral. There are two or more different translations.

7. *The Witness*, July 7, 1923, p. 2. The National Council of the Protestant Episcopal Church adopted a resolution supporting Platon in 1926; it was quoted in *The Eastern Church in the Western World*, written by William Chauncey Emhardt in co-operation with Thomas Burgess and Robert Frederick Lau (Milwaukee: Morehouse, 1928), p. 101.

8. Emhardt, *Religion in Soviet Russia*, op. cit., p. 197.

9. Matthew Spinka, *The Church in Soviet Russia* (New York: Oxford Univ., 1956), p. 25.

10. Quoted in Emhardt, *Religion in Soviet Russia*, op. cit., p. 255.

11. *Daily Worker*, April 3, 1933.

12. Resolution unanimously adopted at the annual convention of the Federated Russian Orthodox Clubs at Detroit, Mich., Sept. 24, 1933, "Petitioning His Excellency Franklin D. Roosevelt, President: the Senate and House of Representatives of the United States of America on the Relationship Between the United States of America and the Union of Socialist Soviet Republics."

13. Metropolitan Sergius based his actions largely upon the decree allegedly issued by Patriarch Tikhon—the controversial Ukase No. 28 of Jan. 16, 1924. The Holy Synod officially condemned Platon on Aug. 16, 1933.

14. *Russky Golos*, July 30, 1933 (translated by Dmitry Grigorieff).

15. Reported in *Rossia*, a Russian-language daily of New York, July 13, 1941 (translated by Dmitry Grigorieff).

16. *Daily Worker*, May 22, 1944.

17. *The Christian Register,* Oct. 1943, p. 348.
18. *Russian American Orthodox Messenger,* 1943, No. 10.
19. *Russkaya pravoslavnaya tserkov v Amerike,* Jordanville, N. Y., 1955, p. 110 (translated by Dmitry Grigorieff).
20. From the "Minutes" of the plenum of the American Russian Fraternal Society, Oct. 6-7, 1945.
21. From the "Minutes," A.R.F.S., *op. cit.*
22. From the "Minutes," A.R.F.S., *op. cit.*
23. *One Church,* 1947, No. 3.
24. *Russian American Orthodox Messenger,* 1947, No. 11.
25. *The Witness,* April 21, 1949, p. 19.
26. *Ibid.,* March 30, 1950, p. 19.
27. *The Churchman,* June 1, 1950, p. 27.
28. *Translation of Extracts from Articles Published in Journal of The Moscow Patriarchate* (a pamphlet with no notations as to publisher or date), p. 13.
29. *Ibid.,* p. 11.
30. *Ibid.,* p. 24.
31. *Ibid.,* p. 51.
32. St. Nicholas Cathedral v. John Kedroff and Benjamin Fedchenkoff, 276 App. Div. 344. Van Voorhis gave the dissenting opinion.
33. 276 App. Div. 320.
34. 276 App. Div. 322.
35. *One Church,* March-April, 1956, p. 73.
36. Thomas J. Halford, "The Archbishop Boris Case," *The Churchman,* Jan. 15, 1956.
37. *The Christian Century,* Jan. 15, 1956.
38. The New York *Times,* Dec. 10, 1955.
39. See footnote 11 of Chapter 10 for reference to the Serbian Orthodox Church. A word should be added here regarding the Syrian Antiochian Orthodox Archdiocese of New York and North America, which has eighty-eight parishes and an estimated 100,000-200,000 American adherents of Syrian and Lebanese descent. The Patriarchate of Antioch, with its center at Damascus, maintained close spiritual and financial ties with the Russian Orthodox Church during the centuries of czarist reign. These ties continued after the Bolshevik revolution, and money still is channeled from Russia for the support of some Orthodox parishes in Syria and Lebanon. Patriarch Alexander III of Antioch (succeeded in 1959 by Theodosius VI) was extremely pro-Russian and on several occasions expressed his support of the Soviet Union and against the United States. The *Journal* of the Russian Patriarchate of Sept. 1951, for example, quoted Alexander's remarks as reported in *Izvestia* of Aug. 25, 1951. He had said in part: "I am sincerely glad that the Antioch Orthodox Church is also taking an active part in this great and holy cause [of peace], as war is the infringement of the fundamentals of Christian morality, calamity and a burden for simple people in the name of the enrichment of those few who own factories for the manufacture of the weapons of war, in the name of the attempt of the USA to achieve world domination." Alexander was criticized sharply among Americans under his spiritual jurisdiction, and despite the Patriarchate's close Russian ties, there is no evidence that Communist or Soviet sympathies have played any significant role in Syrian Antiochian Orthodox circles in the United States.
40. *Translation of Extracts from Articles Published in Journal of The Moscow Patriarchate,* p. 8.
41. *Ibid.,* pp. 113-14.
42. *Ibid.,* p. 117.
43. Two of the principal pieces of literature have been the *Official Statement* of the Romanian Orthodox Missionary Episcopate in America, a 28-page pamphlet dated June 10, 1952, and published in Jackson, Mich., by the Moldovan-Moraru group, and a 50-page mimeographed document, *Communistic Attempts to Gain Control Over American Church Organizations,* published by the public-relations office of the Romanian Orthodox Episcopate of America, now led by Bishop Viorel D. Trifa.

44. The charges against Trifa are published in the *Official Statement* cited above. Trifa's reply was contained in a letter to the author dated June 23, 1958.
45. *Communistic Attempts to Gain Control Over American Church Organizations* (see note 43), p. 24.
46. *Ibid.*, p. 25.
47. *Ibid.*, p. 21.
48. Among persons interviewed with regard to the Albanian Orthodox Church were Glenn A. McClain, author of *Albanian Exposé;* Stephen Peters; Bishop Fan S. Noli; G. M. Panarity; and Clarence A. Manning. The Albanian community has been served by such newspapers as *Shquiperia, Dielli,* and *Liria. Liria* has continued to favor the Communist regime in Albania and in other ways has given aid to the Soviet position in world affairs.

CHAPTER TWENTY-ONE: THE ARMENIAN SCHISM

1. Monophysitism teaches that Christ has only a single composite nature, not two distinct natures (divine and human). The doctrine was condemned as heresy by the Council of Chalcedon in 451 A.D. The contention has been that Monophysitism stressed the divinity of Jesus at the expense of his humanity. Monophysitism is professed by the Coptic and Jacobite churches, as well as by the Church of Armenia.
2. *Armenian Mirror,* Sept. 22, 1933.
3. *Hairenik Weekly,* Aug. 24, 1934.
4. *Daily Worker,* Dec. 28, 1933, p. 6.
5. *Ibid.,* Sept. 28, 1935, p. 4. The *Daily Worker* published the lengthy agreement between the Communists and the Hunchags, which included joint support of Soviet Armenia and united hostility toward the Dashnags.
6. *The Churchman,* July 1, 1948, p. 24.
7. *Armenian Tribune,* Nov. 8, 1947.
8. *Laper,* May 24, 1955, p. 4 (English-language section).
9. *Conference in Defense of Peace of All Churches and Religious Associations in the U.S.S.R.,* held in the Troitse-Sergiyeva Monastery, Zagorsk, on May 9-12, 1952, published by the Moscow Patriarchate, p. 128.
10. *Armenian Review,* Summer 1956, p. 4.
11. Quoted in *Laper,* Oct. 22, 1955, p. 4.
12. The *New York Times,* Feb. 21, 1956.
13. *Hairenik Weekly,* Oct. 17, 1957.
14. The Armenian Revolutionary Federation is still a member of the Second Socialist International and officially it remains a socialist party.

CONCLUSION: COMMUNISM AND THE CHURCHES

1. The manual was entitled *Air Force Center Training Manual* 45-0050, Increment V, Volume 7. It was published specifically "for use by Reservists participating in the Continental Air Command Air Reserve Center Training Program and enrolled in the Reserve Noncommissioned Officers Course 45-0050."
2. In March 1960, the National Council of Churches prepared an extensive compilation of material on the controversy under the title *The Churches and the Air Force Manual.* Included in it were copies of the correspondence between Wine and Gates. Gates wrote on Feb. 17, 1960: "I am very glad you came direct to us and can only express my very deep regret over the entire incident. I assure you that the unfortunate contents of the manual in no way reflect the attitude of the Air Force or the Department of Defense toward the National Council of Churches." Dudley C. Sharp wrote on Feb. 18 that the manual had been withdrawn "and action is being taken to prevent recurrence of the issuance of such material."

3. The New York *Times*, Feb. 19, 1960.
4. New York *Herald Tribune*, Feb. 18, 1960.
5. *Time*, Feb. 29, 1960, p. 22.
6. *Life* discussed some of the Air Force manuals in an article "Mania for Manuals," March 7, 1960, pp. 79-82.
7. New York *Herald Tribune*, April 18, 1960.
8. Among the various interesting episodes not discussed in this book are the hearings involving two Presbyterian ministers, John A. Hutchison and Joseph S. Nowak, accused before the House Committee on Un-American Activities in March 1954 of co-operating with the Communist Party in Baltimore in the mid-thirties. The testimonies of Hutchison, Nowak, Leonard Patterson, Earl C. Reno, a Communist from 1931-42, and a Sam Swerdloff were published in three parts in 1954 under the heading, "Investigation of Communist Activities in the Baltimore Area." The testimonies and corroborating information indicate that neither Nowak nor Hutchison were Communists in Baltimore; that Nowak was a member of the Communist Party for a few months in 1946, a decade later, in Chicago; and that Hutchison was never a member of the party but, as he testified, regarded Communism "as an altogether evil thing which free men must resist at all costs, and furthermore, a thing which derives its demonic and evil quality from the fact that it is held as a religious faith."
9. Two interesting and helpful books on the Negroes and the American Communist Party are: Wilson Record, *The Negro and the Communist Party* (Chapel Hill: University of North Carolina Press, 1951), and William A. Nolan, *Communism Versus the Negro* (Chicago: Henry Regnery, 1951).
10. A number of books deal with the question of how Christians should view Communism. Perhaps the best discussion is contained in the brief book by John C. Bennett, now almost a classic in the field, entitled *Christianity and Communism* (New York: Association Press, 1948). It was completely revised and published again in 1960 under the title *Christianity and Communism Today*. Two other excellent books are Charles C. West, *Communism and the Theologians* (Philadelphia: Westminster Press, 1958), and William Hordern, *Christianity, Communism and History* (Nashville: Abingdon, 1954).

INDEX